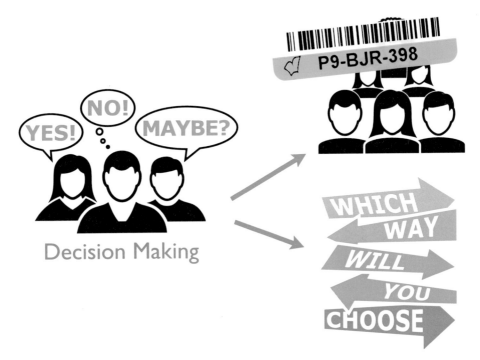

- **Decision making simulations** – place your students in the role of a key decision-maker where they are asked to make a series of decisions. The simulation will change and branch based on the decisions students make, providing a variation of scenario paths. Upon completion of each simulation, students receive a grade, as well as a detailed report of the choices they made during the simulation and the associated consequences of those decisions.

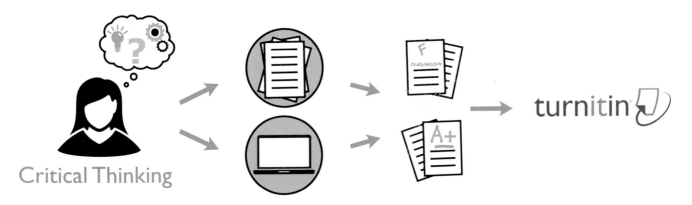

- **Writing Space** – better writers make great learners—who perform better in their courses. Providing a single location to develop and assess concept mastery and critical thinking, the Writing Space offers automatic graded, assisted graded and create your own writing assignments; allowing you to exchange personalized feedback with students quickly and easily.

  Writing Space can also check students' work for improper citation or plagiarism by comparing it against the world's most accurate text comparison database available from **Turnitin**.

http://www.pearsonmylabandmastering.com

PEARSON

Strategic Management Model

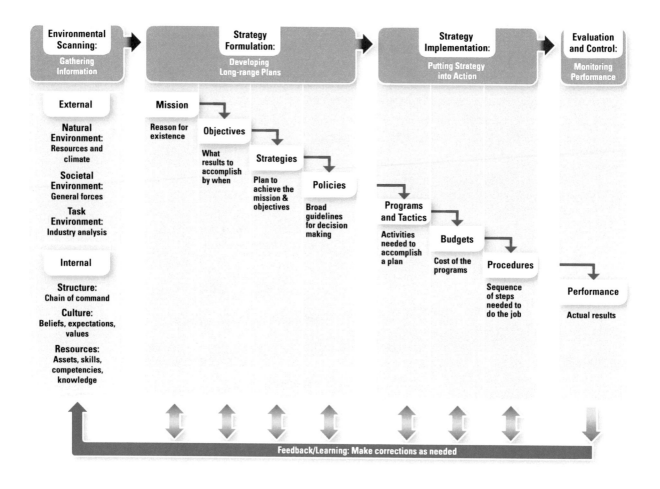

Concepts in
Strategic
Management
and Business
Policy

GLOBALIZATION, INNOVATION, AND SUSTAINABILITY

Thomas L. Wheelen
Formerly with University of Virginia,
Trinity College, Dublin, Ireland

J. David Hunger
Iowa State University,
St. John's University

Alan N. Hoffman
Bentley University

Charles E. Bamford
University of Notre Dame

PEARSON

Boston   Columbus   Indianapolis   New York   San Francisco   Upper Saddle River
Amsterdam   Cape Town   Dubai   London   Madrid   Milan   Munich   Paris   Montreal   Toronto
Delhi   Mexico City   São Paulo   Sydney   Hong Kong   Seoul   Singapore   Taipei   Tokyo

Editor in Chief: Stephanie Wall
Acquisitions Editor: Daniel Tylman
Program Management Lead: Ashley Santora
Program Manager: Sarah Holle
Editorial Assistant: Bernard Ollila
Director of Marketing: Maggie Moylan
Marketing Manager: Erin Gardner
Marketing Assistant: Gianni Sandri
Project Management Lead: Judy Leale
Project Manager: Karalyn Holland
Procurement Specialist: Michelle Klein
Creative Director: Blair Brown
Central Design Manager: Jayne Conte
Cover Designer: Bruce Kenselaar

Cover Image: © JaySi / Shutterstock
VP, Director of Digital Strategy & Assessment: Paul Gentile
Digital Editor: Brian Surette
Digital Development Manager: Robin Lazrus
MyLab Project Manager: Joan Waxman
Digital Project Manager: Alana Coles
Media Project Manager: Lisa Rinaldi
Full-Service Project Management: S4Carlisle Publishing Services
Composition: S4Carlisle Publishing Services
Printer/Binder: RR Donnelley/Harrisonburg
Cover Printer: RR Donnelley/Harrisonburg
Text Font: 10/12 Times LT Std

Credits and acknowledgments borrowed from other sources and reproduced, with permission, in this textbook appear on the appropriate page within text. Additional photo/image credits: Sustainability issue, LehaKok/Shutterstock; Innovation issue, ssuaphotos/Shutterstock; Global issue, Rob Wilson/Shutterstock; Strategy highlight, Triff/Shutterstock; Chapter opener globe, Nelson Marques/Shutterstock.

Many of the designations by manufacturers and sellers to distinguish their products are claimed as trademarks. Where those designations appear in this book, and the publisher was aware of a trademark claim, the designations have been printed in initial caps or all caps.

Library of Congress Cataloging-in-Publication Data
Wheelen, Thomas L.
   Concepts in Strategic management and business policy: Globalization, Innovation, and Sustainability/ Thomas L. Wheelen, Formerly with University of Virginia Trinity College, Dublin, Ireland, J. David Hunger, Iowa State University St. John's University; Alan N. Hoffman, Bentley University; Charles Bamford, University of Notre Dame.—Fourteenth edition.
      pages cm
   ISBN-13: 978-0-13-312612-9
   ISBN-10: 0-13-312612-9
   1. Strategic planning. 2. Strategic planning—Case studies. 3. Sustainability. I. Hunger, J. David, II. Title.
   HD30.28.W43 2015
   658.4'012—dc23
                                                                                   2013047454

10 9 8 7 6 5

ISBN 10:   0-13-312612-9
ISBN 13: 978-0-13-312612-9

Brief Contents

Contents

Dedicated to

SPECIAL DEDICATION TO TOM WHEELEN

Tom originated this book in the late 1970s and with his friend David Hunger brought the first edition to fruition in 1982. What a ride it has been! After battling bone cancer, Tom died in Saint Petersburg, Florida, on December 24, 2011. It was Tom's idea from the very beginning to include the latest research and useful material written in such a way that the typical student could read and understand the book without outside assistance. That has been a key reason for the success of the book through its many editions. Tom's last months were spent working with the two new co-authors to map out the direction for the 14th edition. We thank you, Tom, and bid you a fond farewell! This 14th edition is for you.

J. David Hunger
Alan N. Hoffman
Charles E. Bamford

This is a special dedication to Thomas L. Wheelen, co-author, father, and best friend, May 30, 1935 – December 24, 2011. This is the 14th edition of SMBP the creation you and Mr. Hunger started due to your friendship at the McIntire School of Commerce at UVA with that adjoining door! It is not very often that two co-authors become the best of friends, but you both did. That was a very special gift that Tom treasured until the end. We are so glad you were able to meet as the dynamic foursome to discuss the 14th edition of SMBP! The new addition of co-authors Alan Hoffman and Chuck Bamford gave you and Mr. Hunger the ability to relax and smell the roses. We have come full circle with you being back at UVA! You were an amazing friend, visionary, teacher, and leader! Thank you for pushing us to be who we are today! You were very blessed to have two children as your best friends! You will never know how much you are missed!

Dad – chailleann againn go mbainfidh tú agus grá agat. Tá do Spiorad na hÉireann le linn i gcónaí!

GNPD KEW and RDW

Betty, Kari and Jeff, Maddie and Megan, Suzi and Nick, Summer and Kacey, Lori, Merry, Dylan, and newborn Edan. Also to Wolfie (arf!).

David Hunger

To Will Hoffman, the greatest son in the world. . . . and to our saint Wendy Appel. In memory of my good friend, Tom Wheelen, via con dios. Thank you, Tom and David.

Alan Hoffman

To Yvonne, for your support, advice, encouragement, love, and confidence. To David and Tom, for your confidence, council, and mental energy in the revision of this remarkable text.

Chuck Bamford

Preface

Welcome to the 14th edition of Concepts in *Strategic Management and Business Policy*! All of the chapters have been updated.

This edition revamps the theme that runs throughout all 12 chapters. We utilize a three-legged approach consisting of ***globalization, innovation, and sustainability***. These three strategic issues comprise the cornerstone that all organizations must build upon to push their businesses forward. Each chapter incorporates specific vignettes about these three themes. We continue to be the most comprehensive and practical strategy book on the market, with chapters ranging from corporate governance and social responsibility to competitive strategy, functional strategy, and strategic alliances.

FEATURES NEW TO THIS 14TH EDITION

For the first time in 30 years, the 14th edition has added two new authors to the text. Alan Hoffman, a major contributor to the 13th edition, is a former textbook author and world-renowned author of strategy business cases, and Chuck Bamford, who was a student of Tom Wheelen and David Hunger back in 1980 at the University of Virginia (McIntire School of Commerce), has authored four other textbooks. They join J. David Hunger and bring a fresh perspective to this extraordinarily well-researched and practically crafted text. In that vein, this edition of the text has:

- Vignettes on Sustainability (which is widely defined as Business Sustainability), Globalization (which we view as an expectation of business), and Innovation (which is the single most important element in achieving competitive advantage) appear in every chapter of the text.
- Every example, chapter opening, and story has been updated. This includes chapter opening vignettes examining companies such as: Five Guys, RIM (BlackBerry), HP's Board of Directors, Tata Motors, Costco, and Pfizer among many others.
- Resource-based analysis (Chapter 5) has been added to the toolbox of students' understanding of competitive advantage.
- Extensive additions have been made to the text on strategy research.
- Current consulting practices have been added to the topics of strategy formulation and strategy implementation.

HOW THIS BOOK IS DIFFERENT FROM OTHER STRATEGY TEXTBOOKS

This book contains a **Strategic Management Model** that runs through the first 11 chapters and is made operational through the **Strategic Audit**, a complete case analysis methodology. The Strategic Audit provides a professional framework for case analysis in terms of external and internal factors and takes the student through the generation of strategic alternatives and implementation programs.

To help the student synthesize the many factors in a complex strategy case, we developed three useful techniques:

- **The External Factor Analysis (EFAS) Table in Chapter 4**
  This reduces the external opportunities and threats to the 8 to 10 most important external factors facing management.

- **The Internal Factor Analysis (IFAS) Table in Chapter 5**
  This reduces the internal strengths and weaknesses to the 8 to 10 most important internal factors facing management.
- **The Strategic Factor Analysis Summary (SFAS) Matrix in Chapter 6**
  This condenses the 16 to 20 factors generated in the EFAS and IFAS tables into the 8 to 10 most important (strategic) factors facing the company. These strategic factors become the basis for generating alternatives and act as a recommendation for the company's future direction.

Suggestions for case analysis are provided in **Appendix 12.B (end of Chapter 12)** and contain step-by-step procedures on how to use a strategic audit in analyzing a case. This appendix includes an example of a student-written strategic audit. Thousands of students around the world have applied this methodology to case analysis with great success.

FEATURES

This edition contains many of the same features and content that helped make previous editions successful. Some of the features include the following:

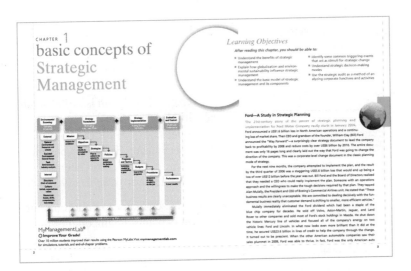

- A **strategic management model** runs throughout the first 11 chapters as a unifying concept. (Explained in *Chapter 1*)

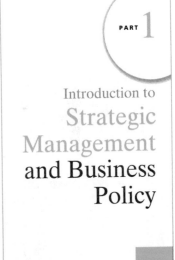

- The **strategic audit**, a way to operationalize the strategic decision-making process, serves as a checklist in case analysis. (*Chapter 1*)

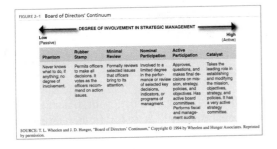

FIGURE 2–1 Board of Directors' Continuum

SOURCE: T. L. Wheelen and J. D. Hunger, "Board of Directors' Continuum," Copyright © 1994 by Wheelen and Hunger Associates. Reprinted by permission.

- **Corporate governance** is examined in terms of the roles, responsibilities, and interactions of top management and the board of directors and includes the impact of the Sarbanes–Oxley Act. (*Chapter 2*)

FIGURE 3–1
Responsibilities
of Business

SOURCE: Suggested by Archie Carroll in A. B. Carroll, "A Three Dimensional Conceptual Model of Corporate Performance," Academy of Management Review (October 1979), pp. 497–505; A. B. Carroll, "Managing Ethically with Global Stakeholders: A Present and Future Challenge," Academy of Management Executive (May 2004), pp. 114–120; and A. B. Carroll, "The Pyramid of Corporate Social Responsibility: Toward the Moral Management of Organizational Stakeholders," Business Horizons (July–August 1991), pp. 39–48.

- **Social responsibility and managerial ethics** are examined in detail in terms of how they affect strategic decision making. They include the process of stakeholder analysis and the concept of social capital. (***Chapter 3***)

- Equal emphasis is placed on **environmental scanning** of the societal environment as well as on the task environment. Topics include forecasting and Miles and Snow's typology in addition to competitive intelligence techniques and Porter's industry analysis. (***Chapter 4***)

- **Core and distinctive competencies** are examined within the framework of the resource-based view of the firm. (***Chapter 5***)

- **Organizational analysis** includes material on business models, supply chain management, and corporate reputation. (***Chapter 5***)

- Internal and external strategic factors are emphasized through the use of specially designed **EFAS**, **IFAS**, and **SFAS tables**. (***Chapters 4, 5, and 6***)

- **Functional strategies** are examined in light of **outsourcing**. (***Chapter 8***)

- Two chapters deal with issues in **strategy implementation**, such as organizational and job design, as well as strategy-manager fit, action planning, corporate culture, and international strategic alliances. (***Chapters 9 and 10***)

- A separate chapter on **evaluation and control** explains the importance of measurement and incentives to organizational performance. (***Chapter 11***)

- **Suggestions for in-depth case analysis** provide a complete listing of financial ratios, recommendations for oral and written analysis, and ideas for further research. (***Chapter 12***)

■ The **strategic audit worksheet** is based on the time-tested strategic audit and is designed to help students organize and structure daily case preparation in a brief period of time. The worksheet works exceedingly well for checking the level of daily student case preparation—especially for open class discussions of cases. (*Chapter 12*)

End of Chapter SUMMARY

Every day, about 17 truckloads of used diesel engines and other parts are dumped at a receiving facility at Caterpillar's remanufacturing plant in Corinth, Mississippi. The filthy iron engines are then broken down by two workers, who manually hammer and drill for half a day until they have taken every bolt off the engine and put each component into its own bin. The engines are then cleaned and remade at half of the cost of a new engine and sold for a tidy profit. This system works at Caterpillar because, as a general rule, 70% of the cost to build something new is in the materials and 30% is in the labor. Remanufacturing simply starts the manufacturing process over again with materials that are essentially free and which already contain most of the energy costs needed to make them. The would-be discards become fodder for the next product, eliminating waste, and cutting costs. Caterpillar's management was so impressed by the remanufacturing operation that they made the business a separate division in 2005. The unit earned more than US$1 billion in sales in 2005 and in 2012 employed more than 8500 workers in 16 countries.

■ An **experiential exercise** focusing on the material covered in each chapter helps the reader apply strategic concepts to an actual situation.

■ A list of **key terms** and the pages in which they are discussed let the reader keep track of important concepts as they are introduced in each chapter.

KEY TERMS

budget (p. 251)
cellular/modular organization (p. 263)
geographic-area structure (p. 269)
job design (p. 265)
matrix of change (p. xx)
matrix structure (p. 260)
multinational corporation (MNC) (p. 266)

network structure (p. 262)
organizational life cycle (p. 258)
procedure (p. 252)
product-group structure (p. 269)
program (p. 248)
reengineering(p. 263)
Six Sigma (p. 264)

stages of corporate development (p. 255)
stages of international development (p. 267)
strategy implementation (p. 246)
structure follows strategy (p. 253)
synergy (p. 252)
virtual organization (p. 262)

■ **Learning objectives** begin each chapter.
■ **Timely, well-researched, and class-tested cases** deal with interesting companies and industries. Many of the cases are about well-known, publicly held corporations—ideal subjects for further research by students wishing to "update" the cases.

Both the text and the cases have been class-tested in strategy courses and revised based on feedback from students and instructors. The first 11 chapters are organized around a strategic management model that begins each chapter and provides a structure for both content and case analysis. We emphasize those concepts that have proven to be most useful in understanding strategic decision making and in conducting case analysis. Our goal was to make the text as comprehensive as possible without getting bogged down in any one area. Extensive endnote references are provided for those who wish to learn more about any particular topic. All cases are about actual organizations. The firms range in size from large, established multinationals to small, entrepreneurial ventures, and cover a broad variety of issues. As an aid to case analysis, we propose the strategic audit as an analytical technique.

SUPPLEMENTS

Instructor Resource Center

At **www.pearsonhighered.com/irc**, instructors can access teaching resources available with this text in a downloadable, digital format. Registration is simple and gives you immediate access to new titles and editions. Please contact your Pearson sales representative for your access code. As a registered faculty member, you can download resource files and receive immediate access and instructions for installing course management content on your campus server. In case you ever need assistance, our dedicated technical support team is ready to assist instructors with questions about the media supplements that accompany this text. Visit **http://247.pearsoned.com** for answers to frequently asked questions and toll-free user support phone numbers. The Instructor Resource Center provides the following electronic resources.

Concepts Instructor's Manual

To aid in discussing the 12 strategy chapters, the *Concepts Instructor's Manual* includes:

- **Suggestions for Teaching Strategic Management:** These include various teaching methods and suggested course syllabi.
- **Chapter Notes:** These include summaries of each chapter, suggested answers to discussion questions, and suggestions for using end-of-chapter cases/exercises and part-ending cases, plus additional discussion questions (with answers) and lecture modules.

PowerPoint Slides

PowerPoint slides, provided in a comprehensive package of text outlines and figures corresponding to the text, are designed to aid the educator and supplement in-class lectures.

Test Item File

The Test Item File contains over 1200 questions, including multiple-choice, true/false, and essay questions. Each question is followed by the correct answer, AACSB category, and difficulty rating.

TestGen

TestGen software is preloaded with all of the *Test Item File* questions. It allows instructors to manually or randomly view test questions, and to add, delete, or modify test-bank questions as needed to create multiple tests.

VIDEO LIBRARY

Videos illustrating the most important subject topics are available in two formats:

- DVD – available for in classroom use by instructors, includes videos mapped to Pearson textbooks.
- MyLab – available for instructors and students, provides round the clock instant access to videos and corresponding assessment and simulations for Pearson textbooks.

    Contact your local Pearson representative to request access to either format.

CourseSmart eTextbooks Online

CourseSmart eTextbooks were developed for students looking to save the cost on required or recommended textbooks. Students simply select their eText by title or author and purchase immediate access to the content for the duration of the course using any major credit card. With a CourseSmart eText, students can search for specific keywords or page numbers, take notes online, print out reading assignments that incorporate lecture notes, and bookmark important passages for later review. For more information or to purchase a CourseSmart eTextbook, visit **www.coursesmart.com**

Acknowledgments

We would like to thank the many people at Pearson who helped make this edition possible. We are especially grateful to our senior project manager, Karalyn Holland, who managed to keep everything on an even keel. We also would like to thank Stephanie Wall, Sarah Holle, Norine Strang, Judy Leale, Estelle Simpson, Michael Joyce, Michael McGee, Bernard Ollila, Erin Gardner, and Brooks Hill-Whilton and everyone at Pearson who guided the book through the production and marketing processes. Special thanks to Dave Ostrow at Pearson for his hard work in the trenches.

We are very thankful to Paul D. Maxwell, *St. Thomas University, Miami, FL*; Terry J. Schindler, *University of Indianapolis*; Anne Walsh, *La Salle University*; Angelo Camillo, *Woodbury University*; Jeannine L Scherenberg, *Rockford College*; William Reisel, *St. John's University*; Ronaldo Parente, *Florida International University*; Roxana Wright, *Plymouth State University*; J. Barry Dickinson, *Holy Family University*; Theodore E Davis, *Jr., PhD, SUNY College at Buffalo*; Manzoor Chowdhury, *Lincoln University*; David Olson, *California State University at Bakersfield*; and Janis Dietz, *University of La Verne* for their constructive criticism of the 14th edition.

We are especially thankful to the many students who tried out the cases we chose to include in this book. Their comments helped us find any flaws in the cases before the book went to the printer.

We also offer a big thanks to the many case authors who have provided us with excellent cases for the 14th edition of this book. We consider many of these case authors to be our friends. A special thanks to you!! The adage is true: The path to greatness is through others.

Alan Hoffman would like to thank the following colleagues for their valuable insight, support, and feedback during the writing process: Janet Forte, Kathy Connolly, Robert Frisch, Barbara Gottfried, Bonnie Kornman, Gail Goldman, Janyce Lee, Raj Sisodia, Ken Kornman, Donna Gallo, Jeff Shuman, Linda Edelman, Anna Forte, Emily Murphy, Tatiana Manolova, Michael Montalbano, Goli Eshghi, Marie Rock, Deb Kennedy, Linda Bee, Alex Zampieron, Alyssa Goldman, Jill Brown, Natalia Gold, Jayne Pollack, Aileen Cordette, Andrea Harding, Martha Bailey, Lew Sudarsky, Ed Ottensmeyer, Tim Stearns, Gloria Larson, Christopher Forte, Sam Vitali, Michael Page, Chip Wiggins, Vicki Lafarge, Dorothy Feldmann, Duncan Spelman, Josh Senn, Gary Cordette, Bob Cronin, Joe Goldman, Ed Harding, Anne Nelson, Tao Yue, Dianne Bevelander, Rick Vitali, Catherine Usoff, Beverley Earle, and William Wiggins. Special thanks to Joyce Vincelette, Kathryn Wheelen, Patricia Ryan, Jim Schwartz and Pamela Goldberg.

Lastly, to the many strategy instructors and students who have relayed to us their thoughts about teaching the strategy course: We have tried to respond to your problems and concerns as best we could by providing a comprehensive yet usable text coupled with recent and complex cases. To you, the people who work hard in the strategy trenches, we acknowledge our debt. This book is yours.

T. L. W.
Saint Petersburg, Florida

J. D. H.
St. Joseph, Minnesota

A. N. H.
Waltham, Massachusetts

C. E. B.
Charlotte, North Carolina

About the Authors

THOMAS L. WHEELEN, *May 30, 1935 – December 24, 2011.* DBA, MBA, BS Cum Laude (George Washington University, Babson College, and Boston College, respectively), College, MBA (1961); Boston College, BS cum laude (1957). Teaching Experience: Visiting Professor— *Trinity College—University of Dublin* (Fall 1999); *University of South Florida*—Professor of Strategic Management (1983–2008); University of Virginia - *McIntire School of Commerce*; Ralph A. Beeton Professor of Free Enterprise (1981–1985); Professor (1974–1981); Associate Professor (1971–1974); and Assistant Professor (1968–1971); Visiting Professor—*University of Arizona* (1979–1980 and *Northeastern University* (Summer 1975, 1977, and 1979). **Academic, Industry and Military Experience:** *University of Virginia College of Continuing Education:* (1) Coordinator for Business Education (1978–1983, 1971–1976)—approved all undergraduate courses offered at seven Regional Centers and approved faculty; (2) Liaison Faculty and Consultant to the National Academy of the FBI Academy (1972–1983) and; (3) developed, sold, and conducted over 200 seminars for local, state, and national governments, and companies for the McIntire School of Commerce and Continuing Education. *General Electric Company* - various management positions (1961–1965); *U.S. Navy Supply Corps* (SC)—Lt. (SC) USNR—assistant supply officer aboard nuclear support tender (1957–1960). **Publications:** (1) *Monograph, An Assessment of Undergraduate Business Education in the United States* (with J. D. Hunger), 1980; (2) *Books: **60 books published**; **14 books translated into eight languages** (Arabic, Bahasa-Indonesian, Chinese, Chinese Simplified, Greek, Italian, Japanese, Portuguese, and Thai)*; (3) *Books*—co-author with J. D. Hunger—five active books: *Strategic Management and Business Policy*, 10th edition (2006); *Cases in Strategic Management and Business Policy*, 10th edition (2006); *Concepts in Strategic Management and Business Policy*, 10th edition (2006); *Strategic Management and Business Policy*, 10th edition; *International Edition* (2006); and *Essentials of Strategic Management*, 3rd edition (2003); (4) *Co-editor: Developments in Information Systems* (1974) and *Collective Bargaining in the Public Sector* (1977); and (5) *Co-developer of software*—STrategic Financial ANalyzer (ST. FAN) (1993, 1990, 1989—different versions); (6) *Articles*—authored over 40 articles that have appeared in such journals as the *Journal of Management, Business Quarterly, Personnel Journal, SAM Advanced Management Journal, Journal of Retailing, International Journal of Management,* and the *Handbook of Business Strategy*; (6) *Cases*—have about 280 cases appearing in over 83 text and case books, as well as the *Business Case Journal, Journal of Management Case Studies, International Journal of Case Studies and Research,* and the *Case Research Journal.* **Awards:** (1) *Fellow* elected by the *Society for Advancement of Management* in 2002; (2) *Fellow* elected by the *North American Case Research Association* in 2000; (3) *Fellow* elected by the *Text and Academic Authors Association* in 2000; (4) the 1999 Phil Carroll Advancement of Management Award in Strategic Management from the Society for Advancement of Management; (5) 1999 McGuffey Award for *Excellence and Longevity for Strategic Management and Business Policy*, 6th edition, from the Text and Academic Authors Association; (6) 1996/97 Teaching Incentive Program Award for teaching undergraduate strategic management; (7) Fulbright, 1996–1997, to Ireland but had to turn it down; (8) Endowed Chair, Ralph A. Beeton Professor, at University of Virginia (1981–1985); (9) a Sesquicentennial Associateship research grant from the Center for Advanced Studies at the University of Virginia, 1979–1980; (10) Small Business Administration (Small Business Institute), supervised undergraduate team that won District, Regional III, and Honorable Mention Awards; and (11) awards for two articles. **Associations:** Dr. Wheelen served on the Board of Directors of the Adhia Mutual Fund, the Society for Advancement of Management, and on the Editorial Board and as Associate Editor of *SAM Advanced Management Journal.* He served on the Board of Directors of Lazer Surgical Software Inc. and the Southern Management Association, and on the Editorial Boards of the *Journal of Management* and *Journal of Management Case Studies,* the *Journal of Retail Banking,* the *Case Research Journal,* and *the Business Case Journal.* He was Vice President of *Strategic Management* for the *Society for the Advancement of Management,* and President of the *North American Case Research Association.* Dr. Wheelen was a member of the *Academy of Management, Beta Gamma Sigma,* the *Southern Management Association,* the *North American Case Research Association,* the *Society for Advancement of Management,* the *Society for Case Research,* the *Strategic Management Association,* and the *World Association for Case Method Research and Application.* He has been listed in *Who's Who in Finance and Industry, Who's Who in the South and Southwest,* and *Who's Who in American Education.*

J. DAVID HUNGER, Ph.D. (Ohio State University), is currently Strategic Management Scholar in Residence at Saint John's University in Minnesota. He is also Professor Emeritus at Iowa State University where he taught for 23 years. He previously taught at George Mason University, the University of Virginia, and Baldwin-Wallace College. He worked in brand management at Procter & Gamble Company, as a selling supervisor at Lazarus Department Store, and served as a Captain in U.S. Army Military Intelligence. He has been active as a consultant and trainer to business corporations, as well as to state and federal government agencies. He has written numerous articles and cases that have appeared in the *Academy of Management Journal, International Journal of Management, Human Resource Management, Journal of Business Strategies, Case Research Journal, Business Case Journal, Handbook of Business Strategy, Journal of Management Case Studies, Annual Advances in Business Cases, Journal of Retail Banking, SAM Advanced Management Journal,* and *Journal of Management,* among others. Dr. Hunger is a member of the Academy of Management, the North American Case Research Association, the Society for Case Research, the North American Management Society, the Textbook and Academic Authors Association, and the Strategic Management Society. He is past-President of the North American Case Research Association, the Society for Case Research, and the Iowa State University Press Board of Directors. He also served as a Vice President of the U.S. Association for Small Business and Entrepreneurship. He was Academic Director of the Pappajohn Center for Entrepreneurship at Iowa State University. He has served on the editorial review boards of *SAM Advanced Management Journal, the Journal of Business Strategies,* and *Journal of Business Research.* He has served on the board of directors of the North American Case Research Association, the Society for Case Research, the Iowa State University Press, and the North American Management Society. He is co-author with Thomas L. Wheelen of *Strategic Management and Business Policy* and *Essentials of Strategic Management* plus *Concepts in Strategic Management and Business Policy* and *Cases in Strategic Management and Business Policy,* as well as *Strategic Management Cases* (PIC: Preferred Individualized Cases), and a monograph assessing undergraduate business education in the United States. The 8th edition of *Strategic Management and Business Policy* received the McGuffey Award for Excellence and Longevity in 1999 from the Text and Academic Authors Association. Dr. Hunger received the Best Case Award given by the McGraw-Hill Publishing Company and the Society for Case Research in 1991 for outstanding case development. He is listed in various versions of *Who's Who,* including *Who's Who in the United States* and *Who's Who in the World.* He was also recognized in 1999 by the Iowa State University College of Business with its Innovation in Teaching Award and was elected a Fellow of the Teaching and Academic Authors Association and of the North American Case Research Association.

ALAN N. HOFFMAN, MBA, DBA (Indiana University), is Professor of Strategic Management at Bentley University in Waltham, Massachusetts. He is the former Director of the MBA Program at Bentley University. He served as the course coordinator and Visiting Professor of Strategic Management for the Global Strategy course in the OneMBA Program at the Rotterdam School of Management at Erasmus University, Rotterdam, The Netherlands. He is also the owner of Dr. Alan N. Hoffman Investment Management, founded in 1995. His major areas of interest include strategic management, global competition, investment strategy, design thinking, and technology. Professor Hoffman is coauthor of *The Strategic Management Casebook and Skill Builder* textbook (with Hugh O'Neill). His academic publications have appeared in the *Academy of Management Journal*, *Human Relations*, the *Journal of Business Ethics*, the *Journal of Business Research*, and *Business Horizons*. He has authored more than 30 strategic management cases, including The Boston YWCA, Ryka Inc., Liz Claiborne, Ben & Jerry's, Cisco Systems, Sun Microsystems, Palm Inc., Handspring, eBay, AOL/Time Warner, McAfee, Apple Computer, TiVo Inc., Wynn Resorts, TomTom, Blue Nile, GE, Amazon, Netflix, Delta Airlines, A123, Tesla Motors, and Whole Foods Market. He is the recipient of the 2004 Bentley University Teaching Innovation Award for his course: "The Organizational Life Cycle—The Boston Beer Company Brewers of Samuel Adams Lager Beer." He teaches strategic management in many executive programs and also teaches business to artists at The Massachusetts College of Art and Design.

CHARLES E. BAMFORD, Ph.D. (University of Tennessee), MBA (Virginia Tech), and BS (University of Virginia). He is an adjunct professor at the University of Notre Dame, where he has been awarded the EMBA Professor of the Year Award three times. Chuck worked in industry for 12 years prior to pursuing his Ph.D. His last position was as the Manager of Business Analysis (Mergers & Acquisitions, Dispositions, and Business Consulting) for Dominion Bankshares Corporation (now Wells Fargo). For the past 20 years, Chuck has been an active consultant as the Founder of Bamford Associates, LLC. He has worked with thousands of managers in the development of implementable strategic plans and an entrepreneurial orientation to growth.

His research has been published in the *Strategic Management Journal*, *Journal of Business Venturing*, *Entrepreneurship Theory & Practice*, *Journal of Business Research*, *Journal of Business Strategies*, *Journal of Technology Transfer*, and *Journal of Small Business Management,* among others. Chuck has co-authored four textbooks and is the author of the fiction novel *Some Things Are Never Forgiven* (Penguin Press).

He has taught courses in strategy and entrepreneurship at the undergraduate, graduate, and executive levels. His teaching experience includes courses taught at universities in Scotland, Hungary, and the Czech Republic. He was a Professor and held the Dennis Thompson Chair of Entrepreneurship at Queens University of Charlotte and previously held positions as an Associate Professor at Texas Christian University and at the University of Richmond. He has taught Executive MBA courses at The University of Notre Dame, Texas Christian University, Tulane University, and at Queens University of Charlotte.

Chuck has won 18 individual teaching excellence awards during his career, including 9 Executive MBA Professor of the Year Awards. He is also a Noble Foundation Fellow in Teaching Excellence.

PART 1

Introduction to Strategic Management and Business Policy

CHAPTER 1

basic concepts of Strategic Management

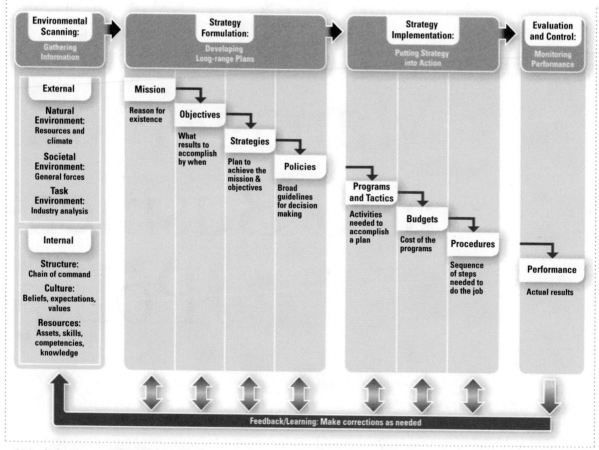

MyManagementLab®

⭐ Improve Your Grade!

Over 10 million students improved their results using the Pearson MyLabs. Visit **mymanagementlab.com** for simulations, tutorials, and end-of-chapter problems.

Learning Objectives

After reading this chapter, you should be able to:

- Understand the benefits of strategic management
- Explain how globalization and environmental sustainability influence strategic management
- Understand the basic model of strategic management and its components

- Identify some common triggering events that act as stimuli for strategic change
- Understand strategic decision-making modes
- Use the strategic audit as a method of analyzing corporate functions and activities

Ford—A Study in Strategic Planning

The 21st-century story of the power of strategic planning and implementation for Ford Motor Company really starts in January 2006. Ford announced a US$1.6 billion loss in North American operations and a continuing loss of market share. Then CEO and grandson of the founder, William Clay (Bill) Ford announced the "Way Forward"—a surprisingly clear strategy document to lead the company back to profitability by 2008 and reduce costs by over US$6 billion by 2010. The entire document was only 16 pages long and clearly laid out the way that Ford was going to change the direction of the company. This was a corporate-level change document in the classic planning mode of strategy.

For the next nine months, the company attempted to implement the plan, and the result by the third quarter of 2006 was a staggering US$5.6 billion loss that would end up being a loss of over US$12 billion before the year was out. Bill Ford and the Board of Directors realized that they needed a CEO who could really implement the plan. Someone with an operations approach and the willingness to make the tough decisions required by that plan. They tapped Alan Mulally, the President and CEO of Boeing's Commercial Airlines unit. He stated that "These business results are clearly unacceptable. We are committed to dealing decisively with the fundamental business reality that customer demand is shifting to smaller, more efficient vehicles."

Mulally immediately eliminated the Ford dividend which had been a staple of the blue chip company for decades. He sold off Volvo, Aston-Martin, Jaguar, and Land Rover to other companies and sold most of Ford's stock holdings in Mazda. He shut down the historic Mercury line of vehicles and focused all of the company's energy on two vehicle lines: Ford and Lincoln. In what now looks even more brilliant than it did at the time, he secured US$23.6 billion in lines of credit to help the company through the change. It turned out to be prescient. When the other American automobile companies saw their sales plummet in 2009, Ford was able to thrive. In fact, Ford was the only American auto company that didn't require a government bailout. If not for the bailout moneys from the U.S. government, Ford may well have become the only American automaker that remained.

The results speak for themselves. In early 2012, Ford announced that for the calendar year of 2011 it earned US$20.2 billion in net income and US$8.8 billion in pre-tax profit, which was the third year in a row it reported an increase in annual profits. Ford has moved into the solid #2 spot for worldwide sales of vehicles and has reduced its total debt position to less than US$13 billion. Mulally credits the results to a companywide focus on a strategy that matters to customers.

SOURCES: R. Jones, "'Way Forward' for Ford Looking Long and Hard," MSNBC (2011), http://www .msnbc.msn.com/id/10988134/ns/business-autos/t/way-forward-ford-looking-long-hard/; "Ford Hits Another Big Pothole," *BusinessWeek* (October 23, 2006), http://www.businessweek.com/ stories/2006-10-23/ford-hits-another-big-potholebusinessweek-business-news-stock-market-and-financial-advice; http://media.ford.com/article_display.cfm?article_id=24203/; N. Vardy, "Ford: An All American Success Story," *MSN Money* (December 14, 2011), http://money.msn.com/top-stocks/post.aspx?post=f7a06d6b-9b5f-48fd-ac35-0a1d0747a582; http://topics.nytimes.com/top/news/ business/companies/ford_motor_company/index.html; http://media.ford.com/article_display.cfm?article_ id=35878.

The Study of Strategic Management

Strategic management is a set of managerial decisions and actions that help determine the long-term performance of an organization. It includes environmental scanning (both external and internal), strategy formulation (strategic or long-range planning), strategy implementation, and evaluation and control. Originally called *business policy*, strategic management has advanced substantially with the concentrated efforts of researchers and practitioners. Today we recognize both a science and an art to the application of strategic management techniques.

PHASES OF STRATEGIC MANAGEMENT

Many of the concepts and techniques that deal with strategic management have been developed and used successfully by business corporations as large as General Electric and as small as the newest startup. Over time, business practitioners and academic researchers have expanded and refined these concepts. Initially, strategic management was of most use to large corporations operating in multiple industries. Increasing risks of error, costly mistakes, and even economic ruin are causing today's professional managers in all organizations to take strategic management seriously in order to keep their companies competitive in an increasingly volatile environment.

As managers attempt to better deal with their changing world, a firm generally evolves through the following four **phases of strategic management:**[1]

Phase 1—Basic financial planning: Managers initiate serious planning when they are requested to propose the following year's budget. Projects are proposed on the basis of very little analysis, with most information coming from within the firm. The sales force usually provides the small amount of environmental information. Such simplistic operational planning only pretends to be strategic management, yet it is quite time consuming. Normal company activities are often suspended for weeks while managers try to cram ideas into the proposed budget. The time horizon is usually one year.

Phase 2—Forecast-based planning: As annual budgets become less useful at stimulating long-term planning, managers attempt to propose five-year plans. At this point, they consider projects that may take more than one year. In addition to internal information, managers gather any available environmental data—usually on an ad hoc basis—and extrapolate current trends five years into the future. This phase is also time consuming, often involving a full month or more of managerial activity to make sure all the proposed budgets fit together. The process gets very political as managers compete for larger shares of limited funds. Seemingly endless meetings take place to evaluate proposals and justify assumptions. The time horizon is usually three to five years.

Phase 3—Externally oriented (strategic) planning: Frustrated with highly political yet ineffectual five-year plans, top management takes control of the planning process by initiating strategic planning. The company seeks to increase its responsiveness to changing markets and competition by thinking strategically. Planning is taken out of the hands of lower-level managers and concentrated in a planning staff whose task is to develop strategic plans for the corporation. Consultants often provide the sophisticated and innovative techniques that the planning staff uses to gather information and forecast future trends. Organizations start competitive intelligence units. Upper-level managers meet once a year at a resort "retreat" led by key members of the planning staff to evaluate and update the current strategic plan. Such top-down planning emphasizes formal strategy formulation and leaves the implementation issues to lower-management levels. Top management typically develops five-year plans with help from consultants but minimal input from lower levels.

Phase 4—Strategic management: Realizing that even the best strategic plans are worthless without the input and commitment of lower-level managers, top management forms planning groups of managers and key employees at many levels, from various departments and workgroups. They develop and integrate a series of strategic plans aimed at achieving the company's primary objectives. Strategic plans at this point detail the implementation, evaluation, and control issues. Rather than attempting to perfectly forecast the future, the plans emphasize probable scenarios and contingency strategies. The sophisticated annual five-year strategic plan is replaced with strategic thinking at all levels of the organization throughout the year. Strategic information, previously available only centrally to top management, is available virtually to people throughout the organization. Instead of a large centralized planning staff, internal and external planning consultants are available to help guide group strategy discussions. Although top management may still initiate the strategic planning process, the resulting strategies may come from anywhere in the organization. Planning is typically interactive across levels and is no longer strictly top down. People at all levels are now involved.

General Electric, one of the pioneers of strategic planning, led the transition from strategic planning to strategic management during the 1980s.[2] By the 1990s, most other corporations around the world had also begun the conversion to strategic management.

BENEFITS OF STRATEGIC MANAGEMENT

Strategic management emphasizes long-term performance. Many companies can manage short-term bursts of high performance, but only a few can sustain it over a longer period of time. For example, of the original *Fortune 500* companies listed in 1955, only 6 of the Top 25 in that original list are still in the Top 25 as of 2012 and 10 of the original companies are no longer in business. To be successful in the long-run, companies must not only be able to *execute* current activities to satisfy an existing market, but they must also *adapt* those activities to satisfy new and changing markets.[3]

Research reveals that organizations that engage in strategic management generally outperform those that do not.[4] The attainment of an appropriate match, or "fit," between an organization's environment and its strategy, structure, and processes has positive effects on the organization's performance.[5] Strategic planning becomes increasingly important as the environment becomes more unstable.[6] For example, studies of the impact of deregulation on the U.S. railroad and trucking industries found that companies that changed their strategies and structures as their environment changed outperformed companies that did not change.[7]

A survey of nearly 50 corporations in a variety of countries and industries found the three most highly rated benefits of strategic management to be:

- A clearer sense of strategic vision for the firm.
- A sharper focus on what is strategically important.
- An improved understanding of a rapidly changing environment.[8]

A survey by McKinsey & Company of 800 executives found that formal strategic planning processes improved overall satisfaction with strategy development.[9] To be effective, however, strategic management need not always be a formal process. It can begin with a few simple questions:

1. Where is the organization now? (Not where do we hope it is!)
2. If no changes are made, where will the organization be in one year? Two years? Five years? Ten years? Are the answers acceptable?
3. If the answers are not acceptable, what specific actions should management undertake? What are the risks and payoffs involved?

Although Bain & Company's *2011 Management Tools and Trends* survey of 1,230 global executives revealed that benchmarking had replaced strategic planning as the perennial number one tool used by businesses, this was most likely a reaction to the global slowdown of the past few years. Strategic planning was listed as second and was said to be particularly effective at identifying new opportunities for growth and in ensuring that all managers have the same goals.[10] Other highly ranked strategic management tools were mission and vision statements, core competencies, change management programs and balanced scorecards.[11] A study by Joyce, Nohria, and Roberson of 200 firms in 50 subindustries found that devising and maintaining an engaged, focused strategy was the first of four essential management practices that best differentiated between successful and unsuccessful companies.[12] Based on these and other studies, it can be concluded that strategic management is crucial for long-term organizational success.

Research into the planning practices of companies in the oil industry concludes that the real value of modern strategic planning is more in the *strategic thinking* and *organizational learning* that is part of a future-oriented planning process than in any resulting written strategic plan.[13] Small companies, in particular, may plan informally and irregularly. Nevertheless, studies of small- and medium-sized businesses reveal that the greater the level of planning intensity, as measured by the presence of a formal strategic plan, the greater the level of financial performance, especially when measured in terms of sales increases.[14]

Planning the strategy of large, multidivisional corporations can be complex and time consuming. It often takes slightly more than a year for a large company to move from situation assessment to a final decision agreement. For example, strategic plans in the global oil industry tend to cover 4 to 5 years. The planning horizon for oil exploration is even longer—up to 15 years.[15] Because of the relatively large number of people affected by a strategic decision in a large firm, a formalized, more sophisticated system is needed to ensure that strategic planning leads to successful performance. Otherwise, top management becomes isolated from developments in the business units, and lower-level managers lose sight of the corporate mission and objectives.

Globalization, Innovation, and Sustainability: Challenges to Strategic Management

Not too long ago, a business corporation could be successful by focusing only on making and selling goods and services within its national boundaries. International considerations were minimal. Profits earned from exporting products to foreign lands were considered frosting on the cake, but not really essential to corporate success. During the 1960s, for example, most U.S. companies organized themselves around a number of product divisions that made and sold goods only in the United States. All manufacturing and sales outside the United States were typically managed through one international division. An international assignment was usually considered a message that the person was no longer promotable and should be looking for another job.

For a very long time, many established companies viewed innovation as the domain of the new entrant. The efficiencies that came with size were considered to be the competitive advantage of the large organization. That view has been soundly defeated during the past 30 years. The ability to create unique value and grow an organization organically requires innovation skills. A strategic management approach suggests that if an organization stands still, it will be run over by the competition. What was extraordinary last year is the standard expectation of customers this year. We have watched many large corporations succumb to the lack of innovation in their organization. Sears was the dominant retailer in the United States for more 70 years. Today, it is struggling to find an approach that will give it a competitive advantage. IBM was a company that dominated mainframe computing and was fortunate enough to find a visionary CEO when the mainframe market was crushed by the advent of the PC. That CEO (Louis V. Gerstner, Jr.) transformed the organization with innovation that was cultural, structural, and painful for the company employees. Innovation is rarely easy and it is almost never painless. Nonetheless, it is a core element of successful strategic management.

Similarly, until the later part of the 20th century, a business firm could be very successful without considering sustainable business practices. Companies dumped their waste products in nearby streams or lakes and freely polluted the air with smoke containing noxious gases. Responding to complaints, governments eventually passed laws restricting the freedom to pollute the environment. Lawsuits forced companies to stop old practices. Nevertheless, until the dawn of the 21st century, most executives considered pollution abatement measures to be a cost of business that should be either minimized or avoided. Rather than clean up a polluting manufacturing site, they often closed the plant and moved manufacturing offshore to a developing nation with fewer environmental restrictions. Similarly, the issues of recycling and refurbishing, as well as a company's responsibility to both the local inhabitants and the environment where it operated, were not considered appropriate business approaches, because it was felt these concerns did not help maximize shareholder value. In those days, the word *sustainability* was used to describe competitive advantage, not the environment.

Today, the term used to describe a business's sustainability is the **triple bottom line.** This phrase was first used by John Elkington in 1994 to suggest that companies prepare three different bottom lines in their annual report.[16]

1. Traditional Profit/Loss
2. People Account – The social responsibility of the organization
3. Planet Account – The environmental responsibility of the organization

This triple bottom line has become increasingly important to business today. Companies seek LEED certification for their buildings and mold a reputation for being a business that is friendly to the world. LEED (Leadership in Energy and Environmental Design) certification is available for all structures and includes a number of levels depending upon the efforts made to have a building be self-sustaining or to have as little impact (the smallest footprint) on the environment as possible.[17]

IMPACT OF GLOBALIZATION

Today, everything has changed. **Globalization,** the integrated internationalization of markets and corporations, has changed the way modern corporations do business. As Thomas Friedman points out in *The World Is Flat*, jobs, knowledge, and capital are now able to move across borders with far greater speed and far less friction than was possible only a few years ago.[18]

For example, the interconnected nature of the global financial community meant that the mortgage lending problems of U.S. banks led to a global financial crisis that started in 2008 and impacted economies for years. The worldwide availability of the Internet and supply-chain logistical improvements, such as containerized shipping, mean that companies can now locate anywhere and work with multiple partners to serve any market. For companies seeking a low-cost approach, the internationalization of business has been a new avenue for competitive advantage. Nike and Reebok manufacture their athletic shoes in various countries throughout Asia for sale on every continent. Many other companies in North America and Western Europe are outsourcing their manufacturing, software development, or customer service to companies in China, Eastern Europe, or India. English language proficiency, lower wages in India, and large pools of talented software programmers now enable IBM to employ an estimated 100,000 people in its global delivery centers in Bangalore, Delhi, or Kolkata to serve the needs of clients in Atlanta, Munich, or Melbourne.[19] Instead of using one international division to manage everything outside the home country, large corporations are now using matrix structures in which product units are interwoven with country or regional units. Today, international assignments are considered key for anyone interested in reaching top management.

As more industries become global, strategic management is becoming an increasingly important way to keep track of international developments and position a company for long-term competitive advantage. For example, General Electric moved a major research and development lab for its medical systems division from Japan to China in order to learn more about developing new products for developing economies. Microsoft's largest research center outside Redmond, Washington, is in Beijing.

The formation of regional trade associations and agreements, such as the European Union, NAFTA, Mercosur, Andean Community, CAFTA, and ASEAN, is changing how international business is being conducted. See the **Global Issue** feature to learn how regional trade associations are forcing corporations to establish a manufacturing presence wherever they wish to market goods or else face significant tariffs. These associations have led to the increasing harmonization of standards so that products can more easily be sold and moved across national boundaries. International considerations have led to the strategic alliance between British Airways and American Airlines and to the acquisition of the Anheuser-Busch Companies by the Belgium company InBev, creating AB InBev, among others.

IMPACT OF INNOVATION

Innovation, as the term is used in business, is meant to describe new products, services, methods and organizational approaches that allow the business to achieve extraordinary returns. Innovation has become such an important part of business that *Bloomberg Business-week* has a weekly section of articles on the topic. A 2012 survey of more than 160 CEOs in the United States administered by consulting group PWC found that CEOs expected the following areas of change in their innovation portfolios:[20]

- New Business Models—56%
- New Products/Services—72%
- Significant Changes to Existing Products/Services—57%
- Cost Reductions for Existing Processes—6%

Innovation is the machine that generates business opportunities in the market; however, it is the implementation of potential innovations that truly drives businesses to be remarkable. While there is a value in being a first mover, there is also a tremendous value in being a second

GLOBAL issue

REGIONAL TRADE ASSOCIATIONS REPLACE NATIONAL TRADE BARRIERS

Formed as the European Economic Community in 1957, the **European Union (EU)** is the most significant trade association in the world. The goal of the EU is the complete economic integration of its 27 member countries so that goods made in one part of Europe can move freely without ever stopping for a customs inspection. The EU includes Austria, Belgium, Bulgaria, Cyprus, the Czech Republic, Denmark, Estonia, Finland, France, Germany, Greece, Hungary, Ireland, Italy, Latvia, Lithuania, Luxembourg, Malta, the Netherlands, Poland, Portugal, Romania, Slovakia, Slovenia, Spain, Sweden, and the United Kingdom. Croatia is an acceding country and Macedonia, Iceland, Montenegro, Serbia, and Turkey are candidate countries in the process of applying. The EU is less than half the size of the United States of America, but has 50% more people. One currency, the euro, is being used throughout the region (with the exception of the United Kingdom) as members integrate their monetary systems. The steady elimination of barriers to free trade is providing the impetus for a series of mergers, acquisitions, and joint ventures among business corporations. The requirement of at least 60% local content to avoid tariffs has forced many U.S. and Asian companies to abandon exporting in favor of having a strong local presence in Europe.

Canada, the United States, and Mexico are affiliated economically under the **North American Free Trade Agreement (NAFTA).** The goal of NAFTA is improved trade among the three member countries rather than complete economic integration. Launched in 1994, the agreement required all three members to remove all tariffs among themselves over 15 years, but they were allowed to have their own tariff arrangements with nonmember countries. Cars and trucks must have 62.5% North American content to qualify for duty-free status. Transportation restrictions and other regulations have been being significantly reduced. A number of Asian and European corporations, such as Sweden's Electrolux, have built manufacturing facilities in Mexico to take advantage of the country's lower wages and easy access to the entire North American region.

or third mover with the right implementation. PC tablets had been developed and even sold almost two decades before the iPad stormed the market. Many people forget that Apple released the Newton tablet back in 1992.[21] Not only was the timing not right, but the product was not promoted in a way that consumers felt a compelling need to buy one. Many elements have to come together for an innovation to bring long-term success to a company.

IMPACT OF SUSTAINABILITY

Sustainability refers to the use of business practices to manage the triple bottom line as was discussed earlier. That triple bottom line involves (1) the management of traditional profit/loss; (2) the management of the company's social responsibility; and (3) the management of its environmental responsibility.

The company has a relatively obvious long-term responsibility to the shareholders of the organization. That means that the company has to be able to thrive despite changes in the industry, society, and the physical environment. This is the focus of much of this textbook and the focus of strategy in business.

The company that pursues a sustainable approach to business has a responsibility to its employees, its customers, and the community in which it operates. Companies that have embraced sustainable practices have seen dramatic increases in risk mitigation and innovation, and an overall feeling of corporate social responsibility. A 2010 research study out of the University of Notre Dame found that employees at companies who focused on business sustainability report higher levels of engagement, high-quality connections, and more creative involvement.[22] In fact, a Gallop research study found that these engaged organizations had 3.9 times the earnings per share (EPS) growth rates when compared to organizations with lower engagement in the same industry.[23]

The company also has a responsibility to treat the environment well. This is usually defined as trying to achieve (or approach) zero impact on the environment. Recycling, increased use of renewable resources, reduction of waste, and refitting buildings to reduce their impact on the environment, among many other techniques, are included in this element of the triple bottom line. The most recognized worldwide standard for environmental efficiency is the ISO 14001 designation. It is not a set of standards, but a framework of activities aimed at effective environmental management.[24]

South American countries are also working to harmonize their trading relationships with each other and to form trade associations. The establishment of the **Mercosur** (**Mercosul** in Portuguese) free-trade area among Argentina, Brazil, Uruguay, and Venezuela means that a manufacturing presence within these countries is becoming essential to avoid tariffs for non-member countries. Paraguay was an original member but is currently suspended following the hasty impeachment of its President Fernando Lugo. The **Andean Community** (Comunidad Andina de Naciones) is a free-trade alliance composed of Columbia, Ecuador, Peru, and Bolivia. On May 23, 2008, the **Union of South American Nations** was formed to unite the two existing free-trade areas with a secretariat in Ecuador and a parliament in Bolivia. It consists of 12 South American countries.

In 2004, the five Central American countries of El Salvador, Guatemala, Honduras, Nicaragua, and Costa Rica, plus the United States, signed the **Central American Free Trade Agreement (CAFTA).** The Dominican Republic joined soon thereafter. Previously, Central American textile manufacturers had to pay import duties of 18%–28% to sell their clothes in the United States unless they bought their raw material from U.S. companies. Under CAFTA, members can buy raw material from anywhere, and their exports are duty free. In addition, CAFTA eliminated import duties on 80% of U.S. goods exported to the region, with ther-emaining tariffs being phased out over 10 years.

The **Association of Southeast Asian Nations (ASEAN)**—composed of Brunei Darussalam, Cambodia, Indonesia, Laos, Malaysia, Myanmar, Philippines, Singapore, Thailand, and Vietnam—is in the process of linking its members into a borderless economic zone by 2020. Tariffs had been significantly reduced among member countries by 2008 and a new agreement is expected by early 2013. Increasingly referred to as ASEAN+3, ASEAN now includes China, Japan, and South Korea in its annual summit meetings. The ASEAN nations negotiated linkage of the ASEAN Free Trade Area (AFTA) with the existing free-trade area of Australia and New Zealand. With the EU extending eastward and NAFTA extending southward to someday connect with CAFTA and the Union of South American Nations, pressure is building on the independent Asian nations to join ASEAN.

Porter and Reinhardt warn that "in addition to understanding its emissions costs, every firm needs to evaluate its vulnerability to climate-related effects such as regional shifts in the availability of energy and water, the reliability of infrastructures and supply chains, and the prevalence of infectious diseases."[25] Swiss Re, the world's second-largest reinsurer, estimated that the overall economic costs of climate catastrophes related to climate change threatens to double to US$150 billion per year by 2014. The insurance industry's share of this loss would be US$30–$40 billion annually.[26]

Although global warming remains a controversial topic, the best argument in favor of working toward environmental sustainability is a variation of Pascal's Wager on the existence of God:

> The same goes for global warming. If you accept it as reality, adapting your strategy and practices, your plants will use less energy and emit fewer effluents. Your packaging will be more biodegradable, and your new products will be able to capture any markets created by severe weather effects. Yes, global warming might not be as damaging as some predict, and you might have invested more than you needed, but it's just as Pascal said: Given all the possible outcomes, the upside of being ready and prepared for a "fearsome event" surely beats the alternative.[27]

Theories of Organizational Adaptation

Globalization, innovation, and sustainability present real challenges to the strategic management of businesses. How can any one company keep track of all the changing technological, economic, political–legal, and sociocultural trends around the world in order to make the necessary adjustments? This is not an easy task. Various theories have been proposed to account for how organizations obtain fit with their environment and how these approaches have been used to varying degrees by researchers trying to understand firm performance. The theory of **population ecology** suggests that once an organization is successfully established in a particular environmental niche, it is unable to adapt to changing conditions. Inertia prevents the organization from changing in any significant manner. The company is thus replaced (is bought out or goes bankrupt) by other organizations more suited to the new environment. Although it is a popular theory in sociology, research fails to support the arguments of population ecology.[28] **Institution theory,** in contrast, proposes that organizations can and do adapt to changing conditions by imitating other successful organizations. To its credit, many examples can be found of companies that have adapted to changing circumstances by imitating an admired firm's strategies and management techniques.[29] The theory does not, however, explain how or by whom successful new strategies are developed in the first place. The **strategic choice perspective** goes one step further by proposing that not only do organizations adapt to a changing environment, but they also have the opportunity and power to reshape their environment. This perspective is supported by research indicating that the decisions of a firm's management have at least as great an impact on firm performance as overall industry factors.[30] Because of its emphasis on managers making rational strategic decisions, the strategic choice perspective is the dominant one taken in strategic management. Its argument that adaptation is a dynamic process fits with the view of **organizational learning theory,** which says that an organization adjusts defensively to a changing environment and uses knowledge offensively to improve the fit between itself and its environment. This perspective expands the strategic choice perspective to include people at all levels becoming involved in providing input into strategic decisions.[31]

In agreement with the concepts of organizational learning theory, an increasing number of companies are realizing that they must shift from a vertically organized, top-down type of organization to a more horizontally managed, interactive organization. They are attempting to adapt more quickly to changing conditions by becoming "learning organizations."

Creating a Learning Organization

Strategic management has now evolved to the point that its primary value is in helping an organization operate successfully in a dynamic, complex environment. To be competitive in dynamic environments, corporations are becoming less bureaucratic and more flexible. In stable environments such as those that existed in years past, a competitive strategy simply involved defining a competitive position and then defending it. As it takes less and less time for one product or technology to replace another, companies are finding that there is no such thing as a permanent competitive advantage. Many agree with Richard D'Aveni, who says in his book *Hypercompetition* that any sustainable competitive advantage lies not in doggedly following a centrally managed five-year plan but in stringing together a series of strategic short-term thrusts (as Apple does by cutting into the sales of its own offerings with periodic introductions of new products).[32] This means that corporations must develop *strategic flexibility*—the ability to shift from one dominant strategy to another.[33]

Strategic flexibility demands a long-term commitment to the development and nurturing of critical resources. It also demands that the company become a **learning organization**—an organization skilled at creating, acquiring, and transferring knowledge and at modifying its behavior to reflect new knowledge and insights. Organizational learning is a critical component of competitiveness in a dynamic environment. It is particularly important to innovation and new product development.[34] Siemens, a major electronics company, created a global knowledge-sharing network, called ShareNet, in order to quickly spread information technology throughout the firm. Based on its experience with ShareNet, Siemens established PeopleShareNet, a system that serves as a virtual expert marketplace for facilitating the creation of cross-cultural teams composed of members with specific knowledge and competencies.[35]

Learning organizations are skilled at four main activities:

- Solving problems systematically
- Experimenting with new approaches
- Learning from their own experiences and past history as well as from the experiences of others
- Transferring knowledge quickly and efficiently throughout the organization[36]

Business historian Alfred Chandler proposes that high-technology industries are defined by "paths of learning" in which organizational strengths derive from learned capabilities.[37] According to Chandler, companies spring from an individual entrepreneur's knowledge, which then evolves into organizational knowledge. This organizational knowledge is composed of three basic strengths: technical skills, mainly in research; functional knowledge, such as production and marketing; and managerial expertise. This knowledge leads to new businesses where the company can succeed and creates an entry barrier to new competitors. Chandler points out that once a corporation has built its learning base to the point where it has become a core company in its industry, entrepreneurial startups are rarely able to successfully enter. Thus, organizational knowledge becomes a competitive advantage that is difficult to understand and imitate.

Strategic management is essential for learning organizations to avoid stagnation through continuous self-examination and experimentation. People at all levels, not just top management, participate in strategic management—helping to scan the environment for critical information, suggesting changes to strategies and programs to take advantage of environmental shifts, and working with others to continuously improve work methods, procedures, and evaluation techniques. The Toyota production system is famous for empowering employees to improve. If an employee spots a problem on the line, he/she pulls the andon cord, which immediately starts a speedy diagnosis. The line continues if the problem can be solved within one minute. If not, the production line is shut down until the problem is solved. At Toyota, they learn from their mistakes as much as they learn from their successes. Improvements are sent to all factories worldwide.[38]

Organizations that are willing to experiment and are able to learn from their experiences are more successful than those that are not.[39] This was seen in a study of U.S. manufacturers of diagnostic imaging equipment, the most successful firms were those that improved products sold in the United States by incorporating some of what they had learned from their manufacturing and sales experiences in other nations. The less successful firms used the foreign operations primarily as sales outlets, not as important sources of technical knowledge.[40] Research also reveals that multidivisional corporations that establish ways to transfer knowledge across divisions are more innovative than other diversified corporations that do not.[41]

Basic Model of Strategic Management

Strategic management consists of four basic elements:

- Environmental scanning
- Strategy formulation
- Strategy implementation
- Evaluation and control

Figure 1–1 illustrates how these four elements interact; **Figure 1–2** expands each of these elements and serves as the model for this book. This model is both rational and prescriptive. It is a planning model that presents what a corporation *should* do in terms of the strategic management process, not what any particular firm may actually do. The rational planning model predicts that as environmental uncertainty increases, corporations that work more diligently to analyze and predict more accurately the changing situation in which they operate will outperform those that do not. Empirical research studies support this model.[42] The terms used in Figure 1–2 are explained in the following pages.

FIGURE 1–1
Basic Elements
of the Strategic
Management
Process

FIGURE 1–2   Strategic Management Model

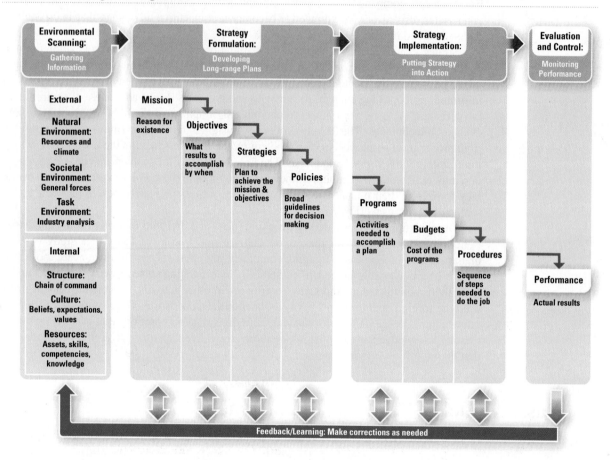

SOURCE: T. L. Wheelen, "Strategic Management Model," adapted from "Concepts of Management," presented to Society for Advancement of Management (SAM), International Meeting, Richmond, VA, 1981. Kathryn E. Wheelen solely owns all of (Dr.) Thomas L. Wheelen's copyright materials. Kathryn E. Wheelen requires written reprint permission for each book that this material is to be printed in. Copyright © 1981 by T. L. Wheelen and SAM. Copyright © 1982, 1985, 1988, and 2005 by T. L. Wheelen and J. D. Hunger. Revised 1989, 1995, 1998, 2000, 2005, 2009, and 2013. Reprinted by permission of the copyright holders.

ENVIRONMENTAL SCANNING

Environmental scanning is the monitoring, evaluating, and disseminating of information from the external and internal environments to key people within the corporation. Its purpose is to identify **strategic factors**—those external and internal elements that will assist in the analysis in deciding the strategic decisions of the corporation. The simplest way to conduct environmental scanning is through **SWOT analysis.** SWOT is an acronym

FIGURE 1–3   Environmental Variables

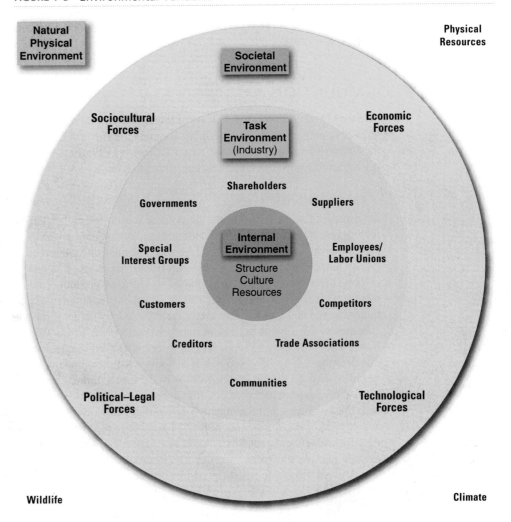

used to describe the particular **S**trengths, **W**eaknesses, **O**pportunities, and **T**hreats that are strategic factors for a specific company. The **external environment** consists of variables (**O**pportunities and **T**hreats) that are outside the organization and not typically within the short-run control of top management. These variables form the context within which the corporation exists. **Figure 1–3** depicts key environmental variables. They may be general forces and trends within the natural or societal environments or specific factors that operate within an organization's specific task environment—often called its *industry*. The analysis techniques available for the examination of these environmental variables are the focus of **Chapter 4.**

The **internal environment** of a corporation consists of variables (**S**trengths and **W**eaknesses) that are within the organization itself and are not usually within the short-run control of top management. These variables form the context in which work is done. They include the corporation's structure, culture, and resources. Key strengths form a set of core competencies that the corporation can use to gain competitive advantage. While strategic management is fundamentally concerned with strengths, weaknesses, opportunities, and threats, the methods to analyze each has developed substantially in the past two decades. No longer do we simply list the SWOT variables and have employees try to populate the quadrants. Each of the four is rich with processes and techniques that will allow for a robust and sophisticated understanding of the company. This will be examined in detail beginning with **Chapter 5** of the text.

STRATEGY FORMULATION

Strategy formulation is the process of investigation, analysis, and decision making that provides the company with the criteria for attaining a competitive advantage. It includes defining the competitive advantages of the business (Strategy), crafting the corporate mission, specifying achievable objectives, and setting policy guidelines.

Mission: Stating Purpose

An organization's **mission** is the purpose or reason for the organization's existence. It announces what the company is providing to society—either a service such as consulting or a product such as automobiles. A well-conceived mission statement defines the fundamental, unique purpose that sets a company apart from other firms of its type and identifies the scope or domain of the company's operations in terms of products (including services) offered. Research reveals that firms with mission statements containing explicit descriptions of customers served and technologies used have significantly higher growth than firms without such statements.[43] A mission statement may also include the firm's values and philosophy about how it does business and treats its employees; however, that is usually better kept as a separate document. It can put into words not only what the company is now but what it wants to become—management's strategic vision of the firm's future. The mission statement promotes a sense of shared expectations in employees and communicates a public image to important stakeholder groups in the company's task environment. Some people like to consider vision and mission as two different concepts: Mission describes what the organization is now; **vision** describes what the organization would like to become. We prefer to combine these ideas into a single mission statement.[44]

A classic example is that etched in bronze at Newport News Shipbuilding, unchanged since its founding in 1886:

> We shall build good ships here—at a profit if we can—at a loss if we must—but always good ships.[45]

A mission may be defined narrowly or broadly in scope. An example of a *broad* mission statement is that used by many corporations: "Serve the best interests of shareowners, customers, and employees." A broadly defined mission statement such as this keeps the company from restricting itself to one field or product line, but it fails to clearly identify either what it makes or which products/markets it plans to emphasize. Because this broad statement is so general, a *narrow* mission statement, such as the preceding example by Newport News Shipbuilding, is significantly more useful. A narrow mission very clearly states the organization's primary business and will limit the scope of the firm's activities in terms of the product or service offered, the technology used, and probably the market served.

Objectives: Listing Expected Results

Objectives are the end results of planned activity. They should be stated as *action verbs* and tell what is to be accomplished by when and quantified if possible. The achievement of corporate objectives should result in the fulfillment of a corporation's mission. In effect, this is what society gives back to the corporation when the corporation does a good job of fulfilling its mission. Coca-Cola has set the standard of a focused, international company. In their new Vision 2020 plan, they have laid out specific objectives including reducing the overall carbon footprint of their business operations by 15% by 2020, as compared to the 2007 baseline, and reducing the impact of their packaging by maximizing their use of renewable, reusable, and recyclable resources to recover the equivalent of 100% of their packaging. This type of focus has made Coca-Cola a perennial member of the Fortune 500, one of the Fortune 50 Most Admired Companies, one of Barron's Most Respected Companies in the World and a Diversity, Inc. Top 50 company. Over the past 10 years they have raised their dividend an average of 9.8% per year and the company's earnings per share have jumped 11.3% per year over the past 5 years.[46]

The term *goal* is often used interchangeably with the term objective. In this book, we prefer to differentiate the two terms. In contrast to an objective, we consider a *goal* as an open-ended statement of what one wants to accomplish, with no quantification of what is to be achieved and no time criteria for completion. For example, a simple statement of "increased profitability" is thus a goal, not an objective, because it does not state how much profit the firm wants to make the next year. A good objective should be action-oriented and begin with the word *to*. An example of an objective is "to increase the firm's profitability in 2014 by 10% over 2013."

Some of the areas in which a corporation might establish its goals and objectives are:

- Profitability (net profits)
- Efficiency (low costs, etc.)
- Growth (increase in total assets, sales, etc.)
- Shareholder wealth (dividends plus stock price appreciation)
- Utilization of resources (ROE or ROI)
- Reputation (being considered a "top" firm)
- Contributions to employees (employment security, wages, diversity)
- Contributions to society (taxes paid, participation in charities, providing a needed product or service)
- Market leadership (market share)
- Technological leadership (innovations, creativity)
- Survival (avoiding bankruptcy)
- Personal needs of top management (using the firm for personal purposes, such as providing jobs for relatives)

Strategy: Defining the Competitive Advantages

An organization must examine the external environment in order to determine who constitutes the perfect customer for the business as it exists today, who the most direct competitors are for that customer, what the company does that is necessary to compete and what the company does that truly sets it apart from its competitors. These elements can be rephrased into the strengths of the business, the understanding of its weaknesses relative to its competitors, what opportunities would be most prudent, and what threats might affect the business's primary competitive advantages.

A **strategy** of a corporation forms a comprehensive master approach that states how the corporation will achieve its mission and objectives. It maximizes competitive advantage and minimizes competitive disadvantage. Pfizer, the giant drug company has embraced the need for this type of approach. Faced with the rapid fall-off of its biggest blockbuster drugs (patents expiring), Pfizer was faced with the question of how to generate the R&D to create new drugs. Historically, the company had relied upon its cadre of scientists, but this changed in the past few years. Pfizer plans to have 50 drug development projects running with university research centers by 2015. They opened their first one in 2010. This is the crucial new ground from which they hope to replace such blockbusters as Lipitor, which expects to see sales drop by more than 80% (from US$12 billion in 2012) when the patent expired.[47]

The typical business firm usually considers three types of strategy: corporate, business, and functional.

1. **Corporate strategy** describes a company's overall direction in terms of its general attitude toward growth and the management of its various businesses and product lines. Corporate strategies typically fit within the three main categories of stability, growth, and retrenchment.

2. **Business strategy** usually occurs at the business unit or product level, and it emphasizes improvement of the competitive position of a corporation's products or services in the specific industry or market segment served by that business unit. Business strategies may fit within the two overall categories: *competitive* and *cooperative* strategies. For example, Staples, the U.S. office supply store chain, has used a competitive strategy to differentiate its retail stores from its competitors by adding services to its stores, such as copying, UPS shipping, and hiring mobile technicians who can fix computers and install networks. British Airways has followed a cooperative strategy by forming an alliance with American Airlines in order to provide global service. Cooperative strategy may thus be used to provide a competitive advantage. Intel, a manufacturer of computer microprocessors, uses its alliance (cooperative strategy) with Microsoft to differentiate itself (competitive strategy) from AMD, its primary competitor.

3. **Functional strategy** is the approach taken by a functional area to achieve corporate and business unit objectives and strategies by maximizing resource productivity. It is concerned with developing and nurturing a distinctive competence to provide a company or business unit with a competitive advantage. Examples of research and development (R&D) functional strategies are technological followership (imitation of the products of other companies) and technological leadership (pioneering an innovation). For years, Magic Chef had been a successful appliance maker by spending little on R&D but by quickly imitating the innovations of other competitors. This helped the company keep its costs lower than those of its competitors and consequently to compete with lower prices. In terms of marketing functional strategies, Procter & Gamble (P&G) is a master of marketing "pull"—the process of spending huge amounts on advertising in order to create customer demand. This supports P&G's competitive strategy of differentiating its products from those of its competitors.

Business firms use all three types of strategy simultaneously. A **hierarchy of strategy** is a grouping of strategy types by level in the organization. Hierarchy of strategy is a nesting of one strategy within another so that they complement and support one another. (See **Figure 1–4.**) Functional strategies support business strategies, which, in turn, support the corporate strategy(ies).

Policies: Setting Guidelines

A **policy** is a broad guideline for decision making that links the formulation of a strategy with its implementation. Companies use policies to make sure that employees throughout the firm make decisions and take actions that support the corporation's mission, objectives, and

FIGURE 1–4
Hierarchy of
Strategy

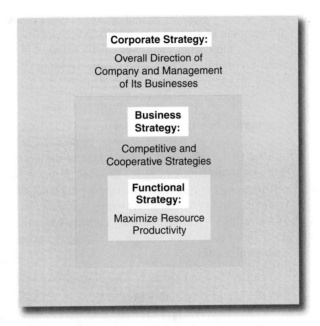

strategies. For example, when Cisco decided on a strategy of growth through acquisitions, it established a policy to consider only companies with no more than 75 employees, 75% of whom were engineers.[48] Consider the following company policies:

- **3M:** 3M says researchers should spend 15% of their time working on something other than their primary project. (This supports 3M's strong product development strategy.)

- **Google:** Google's health care plan includes their onsite medical staff. Any employee who feels ill at work can make an appointment with the doctor at the Googleplex. This supports the Google HRM functional strategy to support its employees.

- **General Electric:** GE must be number one or two wherever it competes. (This supports GE's objective to be number one in market capitalization.)

- **Starbucks:** All Starbucks employees are offered a Total Pay Package that includes a 401(k) savings plan, stock options, and an employee stock purchase plan. This goes a long way toward their goal of having every employee feel like a partner in the business.

- **Ryanair:** Ryanair charges for everything a passenger might want or need on a flight. The only thing you get with your ticket is the right to a seat on the plane (and that seat depends upon how fast you can run to the plane).

Policies such as these provide clear guidance to managers throughout the organization. (Strategy formulation is discussed in greater detail in **Chapters 6, 7**, and **8.**)

STRATEGY IMPLEMENTATION

Strategy implementation is a process by which strategies and policies are put into action through the development of programs, budgets, and procedures. This process might involve changes within the overall culture, structure, and/or management system of the entire organization. Except when such drastic corporatewide changes are needed, however, the implementation of strategy is typically conducted by middle- and lower-level managers, with review by top management. Sometimes referred to as *operational planning*, strategy implementation often involves day-to-day decisions in resource allocation.

Programs and Tactics: Defining Actions

A **program** or a **tactic** is a statement of the activities or steps needed to support a strategy. The terms are interchangeable. In practice, a program is a collection of tactics where a tactic is the individual action taken by the organization as an element of the effort to accomplish a plan. A program or tactic makes a strategy action-oriented. It may involve restructuring the corporation, changing the company's internal culture, or beginning a new research effort. For example, Boeing's strategy to regain industry leadership with its new 787 Dreamliner meant that the company had to increase its manufacturing efficiency in order to keep the price low. To significantly cut costs, management decided to implement a series of tactics:

- Outsource approximately 70% of manufacturing.
- Reduce final assembly time to three days (compared to 20 for its 737 plane) by having suppliers build completed plane sections.
- Use new, lightweight composite materials in place of aluminum to reduce inspection time.
- Resolve poor relations with labor unions caused by downsizing and outsourcing.

Another example is a set of programs or tactics used by automaker BMW to achieve its objective of increasing production efficiency by 5% each year: (a) shorten new model development time from 60 to 30 months, (b) reduce preproduction time from a year to no more than 5 months, and (c) build at least two vehicles in each plant so that production can shift among models depending upon demand.

Budgets: Costing Programs

A **budget** is a statement of a corporation's programs in terms of dollars. Used in planning and control, a budget lists the detailed cost of each program. Many corporations demand a certain percentage return on investment, often called a "hurdle rate," before management will approve a new program. This is done so that the new program has the potential to significantly add to the corporation's profit performance and thus build shareholder value. The budget thus not only serves as a detailed plan of the new strategy in action, it also specifies through pro forma financial statements the expected impact on the firm's financial future.

A company that has really invested in the future is Atlantic Gulf & Pacific Company (AG&P) based in the Philippines. The company makes modular units for large construction projects (e.g., power plants) and sees modular building to be the wave of the future as skilled labor costs go up. In the past year, it has expanded its facility from 450,000 square meters to over 1.5 million square meters in anticipation of future work flow. The CEO expects to invest another US$250 million into the business by the end of 2013.[49]

Procedures: Detailing Activities

Procedures, sometimes termed Standard Operating Procedures (SOP), are a system of sequential steps or techniques that describe in detail how a particular task or job is to be done. They typically detail the various activities that must be carried out in order to complete the corporation's program. For example, when the home improvement retailer Home Depot noted that sales were lagging because its stores were full of clogged aisles, long checkout times, and too few salespeople, management changed its procedures for restocking shelves and pricing the products. Instead of requiring its employees to do these activities at the same time they were working with customers, management moved these activities to when the stores were closed at night. Employees were then able to focus on increasing customer sales during the day. Both UPS and FedEx put such an emphasis on consistent, quality service that both companies have strict rules for employee behavior, ranging from how a driver dresses to how keys are held when approaching a customer's door. (Strategy implementation is discussed in more detail in **Chapters 9** and **10.**)

EVALUATION AND CONTROL

Evaluation and control is a process in which corporate activities and performance results are monitored so that actual performance can be compared with desired performance. Managers at all levels use the resulting information to take corrective action and resolve problems. Although evaluation and control is the final major element of strategic management, it can also pinpoint weaknesses in previously implemented strategic plans and thus stimulates the entire process to begin again.

Performance is the end result of activities.[50] It includes the actual outcomes of the strategic management process. The practice of strategic management is justified in terms of its ability to improve an organization's performance, typically measured in terms of profits and return on investment. For evaluation and control to be effective, managers must obtain clear, prompt, and unbiased information from the people below them in the corporation's hierarchy. Using this information, managers compare what is actually happening with what was originally planned in the formulation stage.

Starbucks had created a mystique around the enjoyment of coffee. Carefully designed stores and an experience that encouraged people to stay and chat had built Starbucks into a powerhouse. In 2000, Howard Schultz (Founder and CEO) stepped down from active management of the business. In 2005, Jim Donald took over as CEO and drove the company toward efficiency and diversification. The company went from an American success story to one with a 97% drop in net income and same store sales in the negative territory. Despite a well-known e-mail from Schultz to Donald in 2007 encouraging him to return to core elements of the business, things did not improve, and in January 2008 Schultz replaced Donald as CEO. In February 2008, all 7,100+ Starbucks in North America shut their doors for a three-hour video conference with Schultz so they could reset the Starbucks experience. The turnaround at Starbucks has been a remarkable story of regaining the cache they almost lost.[51]

The evaluation and control of performance completes the strategic management model. Based on performance results, management may need to make adjustments in its strategy formulation, in implementation, or in both. (Evaluation and control is discussed in more detail in **Chapter 11.**)

FEEDBACK/LEARNING PROCESS

Note that the strategic management model depicted in **Figure 1–2** includes a feedback/learning process. Arrows are drawn coming out of each part of the model and taking information to each of the previous parts of the model. As a firm or business unit develops strategies, programs, and the like, it often must go back to revise or correct decisions made earlier in the process.

For example, poor performance (as measured in evaluation and control) usually indicates that something has gone wrong with either strategy formulation or implementation. It could also mean that a key variable, such as a new competitor, was ignored during environmental scanning and assessment. In the case of Starbucks, the recession had hit and the mantra in the country had become, "save money, don't buy Starbucks." The business was built on an image as the comfortable place away from home, but had trended toward a fast-food operation. Schultz eliminated hot sandwiches which were filing the place with the smell of burnt cheese instead of coffee. Starbucks needed to reassess the environment and find a better way to profitably apply its core competencies.

Initiation of Strategy: Triggering Events

After much research, Henry Mintzberg discovered that strategy formulation is typically not a regular, continuous process: "It is most often an irregular, discontinuous process, proceeding in fits and starts. There are periods of stability in strategy development, but also there are periods of flux, of groping, of piecemeal change, and of global change."[52] This view of strategy formulation as an irregular process can be explained by the very human tendency to continue on a particular course of action until something goes wrong or a person is forced to question his or her actions. This period of strategic drift may result from inertia on the part of the organization, or it may reflect management's belief that the current strategy is still appropriate and needs only some fine-tuning.

Most large organizations tend to follow a particular strategic orientation for a period of years (often 15–20 years) before making a significant change in direction.[53] This phenomenon, called *punctuated equilibrium*, describes corporations as evolving through relatively long periods of stability (equilibrium periods) punctuated by relatively short bursts of fundamental change (revolutionary periods).[54] After this rather long period of fine-tuning an existing strategy, some sort of shock to the system is needed to motivate management to seriously reassess the corporation's situation.

A **triggering event** is something that acts as a stimulus for a change in strategy. Some possible triggering events are:[55]

- **New CEO:** By asking a series of embarrassing questions, a new CEO cuts through the veil of complacency and forces people to question the very reason for the corporation's existence.

- **External intervention:** A firm's bank suddenly refuses to approve a new loan or suddenly demands payment in full on an old one. A key customer complains about a serious product defect.

- **Threat of a change in ownership:** Another firm may initiate a takeover by buying a company's common stock.

- **Performance gap:** A *performance gap* exists when performance does not meet expectations. Sales and profits either are no longer increasing or may even be falling.

- **Strategic inflection point:** Coined by Andy Grove, past-CEO of Intel Corporation, a *strategic inflection point* is what happens to a business when a major change takes place due to the introduction of new technologies, a different regulatory environment, a change in customers' values, or a change in what customers prefer.[56]

Strategic Decision Making

The distinguishing characteristic of strategic management is its emphasis on strategic decision making. As organizations grow larger and more complex, with more uncertain environments, decisions become increasingly complicated and difficult to make. In agreement with the strategic choice perspective mentioned earlier, this book proposes a strategic decision-making framework that can help people make these decisions regardless of their level and function in the corporation.

WHAT MAKES A DECISION STRATEGIC

Unlike many other decisions, **strategic decisions** deal with the long-term future of an entire organization and have three characteristics:

1. **Rare:** Strategic decisions are unusual and typically have no precedent to follow.
2. **Consequential:** Strategic decisions commit substantial resources and demand a great deal of commitment from people at all levels.
3. **Directive:** Strategic decisions set precedents for lesser decisions and future actions throughout an organization.[57]

One example of a strategic decision with all of these characteristics was that made by Genentech, a biotechnology company that had been founded in 1976 to produce protein-based drugs from cloned genes. After building sales to US$9 billion and profits to US$2 billion in 2006, the company's sales growth slowed and its stock price dropped in 2007. The company's products were reaching maturity with few new ones in the pipeline. To regain revenue growth, management decided to target autoimmune diseases, such as multiple sclerosis, rheumatoid arthritis, lupus, and 80 other ailments for which there was no known lasting treatment. This was an enormous opportunity, but also a very large risk for the company. Existing drugs in this area either weren't effective for many patients or caused side effects that were worse than the disease. Competition from companies like Amgen and Novartis were already vying for leadership in this area. A number of Genentech's first attempts in the area had failed to do well against the competition.

The strategic decision to commit resources to this new area was based on a report from a British physician that Genentech's cancer drug Rituxan eased the agony of rheumatoid arthritis in five of his patients. CEO Arthur Levinson was so impressed with this report that he immediately informed Genentech's board of directors. He urged them to support a full research program for Rituxan in autoimmune disease. With the board's blessing, Levinson launched a program to study the drug as a treatment for rheumatoid arthritis, MS, and lupus. The company deployed a third of its 1,000 researchers to pursue new drugs to fight autoimmune diseases. In 2006, Rituxan was approved to treat rheumatoid arthritis and captured 10% of the market. By 2012, Rituxan had sales of more than US$3 billion. The research mandate was to consider ideas others might overlook. This has led to a series of FDA-approved drugs for breast cancer and vision loss. "There's this tremendous herd instinct out there," said Levinson. "That's a great opportunity, because often the crowd is wrong."[58]

MINTZBERG'S MODES OF STRATEGIC DECISION MAKING

Some strategic decisions are made in a flash by one person (often an entrepreneur or a powerful chief executive officer) who has a brilliant insight and is quickly able to convince others to adopt his or her idea. Other strategic decisions seem to develop out of a series of small incremental choices that over time push an organization more in one direction than another. According to Henry Mintzberg, the three most typical approaches, or modes, of strategic decision making are entrepreneurial, adaptive, and planning (a fourth mode, logical incrementalism, was added later by Quinn):[59]

- **Entrepreneurial mode:** Strategy is made by one powerful individual. The focus is on opportunities; problems are secondary. Strategy is guided by the founder's own vision of direction and is exemplified by large, bold decisions. The dominant goal is growth of the corporation. Amazon.com, founded by Jeff Bezos, is an example of this mode of strategic decision making. The company reflected Bezos' vision of using the Internet to market books and more. Although Amazon's clear growth strategy was certainly an advantage of the entrepreneurial mode, Bezos' eccentric management style made it difficult to retain senior executives.[60]

- **Adaptive mode:** Sometimes referred to as "muddling through," this decision-making mode is characterized by reactive solutions to existing problems, rather than a proactive search for new opportunities. Much bargaining goes on concerning priorities of objectives. Strategy is fragmented and is developed to move a corporation forward incrementally. This mode is typical of most universities, many large hospitals, a large number of governmental agencies, and a surprising number of large corporations. Encyclopædia Britannica Inc. operated successfully for many years in this mode, but it continued to rely on the door-to-door selling of its prestigious books long after dual-career couples made that marketing approach obsolete. Only after it was acquired in 1996 did the company change its door-to-door sales to television advertising and Internet marketing. The company now charges libraries and individual subscribers for complete access via its Web site and has apps for the iPad and iPhone that cost users US$70. In May 2012, the company stopped producing the bound set of encyclopedias that had been in print for over 244 years.[61]

- **Planning mode:** This decision-making mode involves the systematic gathering of appropriate information for situation analysis, the generation of feasible alternative strategies, and the rational selection of the most appropriate strategy. It includes both the proactive search for new opportunities and the reactive solution of existing problems. IBM under CEO Louis Gerstner is an example of the planning mode. When Gerstner accepted the position of CEO in 1993, he realized that IBM was in serious difficulty. Mainframe computers, the company's primary product line, were suffering a rapid decline both in sales and market share. One of Gerstner's first actions was to convene a two-day meeting on corporate strategy with senior executives. An in-depth analysis of IBM's product lines revealed that the only part of the company that was growing was services, but it was a relatively small segment and not very profitable. Rather than focusing on making and selling its own computer hardware, IBM made the strategic decision to invest in services that integrated information technology. IBM thus decided to provide a complete set of services from building systems to defining architecture to actually running and managing the computers for the customer—regardless of who made the products. Because it was no longer important that the company be completely vertically integrated, it sold off its DRAM, disk-drive, and laptop computer businesses and exited software application development. Since making this strategic decision in 1993, 80% of IBM's revenue growth has come from services. Most of this is chronicled in an outstanding business practices book written by Gerstner himself entitled "Who Says Elephants Can't Dance." It should be one of the top reads for anyone really interested in this topic.[62]

■ **Logical incrementalism:** A fourth decision-making mode can be viewed as a synthesis of the planning, adaptive, and, to a lesser extent, the entrepreneurial modes. In this mode, top management has a reasonably clear idea of the corporation's mission and objectives, but, in its development of strategies, it chooses to use "an interactive process in which the organization probes the future, experiments, and learns from a series of partial (incremental) commitments rather than through global formulations of total strategies."[63] Thus, although the mission and objectives are set, the strategy is allowed to emerge out of debate, discussion, and experimentation. This approach appears to be useful when the environment is changing rapidly and when it is important to build consensus and develop needed resources before committing an entire corporation to a specific strategy. In his analysis of the petroleum industry, Grant described strategic planning in this industry as "planned emergence." Corporate headquarters established the mission and objectives but allowed the business units to propose strategies to achieve them.[64]

STRATEGIC DECISION-MAKING PROCESS: AID TO BETTER DECISIONS

Good arguments can be made for using either the entrepreneurial or adaptive modes (or logical incrementalism) in certain situations.[65] This book proposes, however, that in most situations the planning mode, which includes the basic elements of the strategic management process, is a more rational and thus better way of making strategic decisions. Research indicates that the planning mode is not only more analytical and less political than are the other modes, but it is also more appropriate for dealing with complex, changing environments.[66] We therefore propose the following eight-step **strategic decision-making process** to improve the making of strategic decisions (see **Figure 1–5**):

1. **Evaluate current performance results** in terms of (a) return on investment, profitability, and so forth, and (b) the current mission, objectives, strategies, and policies.

2. **Review corporate governance**—that is, the performance of the firm's board of directors and top management.

3. **Scan and assess the external environment** to determine the strategic factors that pose **O**pportunities and **T**hreats.

4. **Scan and assess the internal corporate environment** to determine the strategic factors that are **S**trengths (especially core competencies) and **W**eaknesses.

5. **Analyze strategic factors** to (a) pinpoint problem areas and (b) review and revise the corporate mission and objectives, as necessary.

6. **Generate, evaluate, and select the best alternative strategy** in light of the analysis conducted in step 5.

7. **Implement selected strategies** via programs, budgets, and procedures.

8. **Evaluate implemented strategies** via feedback systems, and the control of activities to ensure their minimum deviation from plans.

This rational approach to strategic decision making has been used successfully by corporations such as Warner-Lambert, Target, General Electric, IBM, Avon Products, Bechtel Group Inc., and Taisei Corporation.

FIGURE 1–5
Strategic Decision-
Making Process

SOURCE: T. L. Wheelen and J. D. Hunger, "Strategic Decision-Making Process." Copyright © 1994 and 1977 by
Wheelen and Hunger Associates. Reprinted by permission.

The Strategic Audit: Aid to Strategic Decision Making

One effective means of putting the strategic decision-making process into action is through
a technique known as the strategic audit. A **strategic audit** provides a checklist of questions,
by area or issue, that enables a systematic analysis to be made of various corporate functions
and activities. (See **Appendix 1.A** at the end of this chapter.) Note that the numbered primary
headings in the audit are the same as the numbered blocks in the strategic decision-making
process in **Figure 1–5**. Beginning with an evaluation of current performance, the audit continues with environmental scanning, strategy formulation, and strategy implementation, and it
concludes with evaluation and control. A strategic audit is a type of management audit and is
extremely useful as a diagnostic tool to pinpoint corporatewide problem areas and to highlight
organizational strengths and weaknesses.[67] A strategic audit can help determine why a certain
area is creating problems for a corporation and help generate solutions to the problem.

A strategic audit is not an all-inclusive list, but it presents many of the critical questions
needed for a detailed strategic analysis of any business corporation. Some questions or even

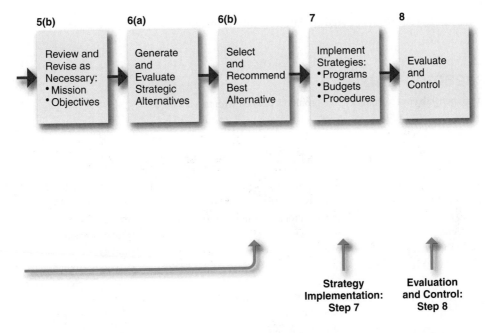

some areas might be inappropriate for a particular company; in other cases, the questions may be insufficient for a complete analysis. However, each question in a particular area of a strategic audit can be broken down into an additional series of subquestions. An analyst can develop these subquestions when they are needed for a complete strategic analysis of a company.

End of Chapter SUMMARY

Strategy scholars Donald Hambrick and James Fredrickson propose that a good strategy has five elements, providing answers to five questions:

1. Arenas: Where will we be active?
2. Vehicles: How will we get there?
3. Differentiators: How will we win in the marketplace?
4. Staging: What will be our speed and sequence of moves?
5. Economic logic: How will we obtain our returns?[68]

This chapter introduces you to a well-accepted model of strategic management (**Figure 1–2**) in which environmental scanning leads to strategy formulation, strategy implementation, and evaluation and control. It further shows how that model can be put into action through the strategic decision-making process (**Figure 1–5**) and a strategic audit (**Appendix 1.A**). As pointed out by Hambrick and Fredrickson, "strategy consists of an integrated set of choices."[69] The questions "Where will we be active?" and "How will we get there?" are dealt with by a company's mission, objectives, and corporate strategy. The question "How will we win in the marketplace?" is the concern of business strategy. The question "What will be our speed and sequence of moves?" is answered not only by business strategy and tactics but also by functional strategy and by implemented programs, budgets, and procedures. The question "How will we obtain our returns?" is the primary emphasis of the evaluation and control element of the strategic management model. Each of these questions and topics will be dealt with in greater detail in the chapters to come. Welcome to the study of strategic management!

MyManagementLab®

Go to **mymanagementlab.com** to complete the problems marked with this icon .

KEY TERMS

budget (p. 20)
business strategy (p. 18)
corporate strategy (p. 18)
environmental scanning (p. 14)
evaluation and control (p. 21)
external environment (p. 15)
functional strategy (p. 18)
globalization (p. 8)
hierarchy of strategy (p. 18)
innovation (p. 9)
institution theory (p. 11)
internal environment (p. 15)
learning organization (p. 12)

mission (p. 16)
objective (p. 16)
organizational learning theory (p. 12)
performance (p. 21)
phases of strategic
    management (p. 4)
policy (p. 18)
population ecology (p. 11)
procedure (p. 20)
program (p. 20)
strategic audit (p. 26)
strategic choice perspective (p. 11)
strategic decision (p. 23)

strategic decision-making
    process (p. 25)
strategic factor (p. 14)
strategic management (p. 4)
strategy (p. 17)
strategy formulation (p. 16)
strategy implementation (p. 19)
sustainability (p. 10)
SWOT analysis (p. 14)
tactic (p. 20)
triggering event (p. 22)
triple bottom line (p. 8)
vision (p. 16)

MyManagementLab®

Go to **mymanagmentlab.com** for Auto-graded writing questions as well as the following Assisted-graded writing questions:

1-1. How do the three elements of Globalization, Innovation and Sustainability impact your understanding of Strategy?

1-2. Organizational strategy can be divided roughly into two categories: a) formulation and b) implementation. While there is legitimate crossover between the two, how would you characterize the issues involved in each effort?

DISCUSSION QUESTIONS

⭐ 1-3. Why has strategic management become so important to today's corporations?

1-4. How does strategic management typically evolve in a corporation?

⭐ 1-5. What is a learning organization? Is this approach to strategic management better than the more traditional top-down approach in which strategic planning is primarily done by top management?

1-6. Why are strategic decisions different from other kinds of decisions?

⭐ 1-7. When is the planning mode of strategic decision making superior to the entrepreneurial and adaptive modes?

STRATEGIC PRACTICE EXERCISES

Most people in business on most days deal with company tactics and decisions at a level that is not strategic. However, every decision made by every employee in a company ultimately impacts the success of the strategy for that company. As pointed out by Malcolm Gladwell in his book *The Tipping Point*, it is the collection of thousands of decisions all aimed in relatively the same direction that can lead a company to the achievement of a strategy. How do you decide what type of decision is strategic?

1. Open today's issue of *The Wall Street Journal* and look for an article about new moves being made by a corporation. Specify those decisions that are strategic.

2. At what level is each of the decisions that you identified? Functional/Business/Corporate? Why do you believe this to be the case?

3. What is your assessment of these decisions? Will they be effective? Why? How have you decided this?

NOTES

1. F. W. Gluck, S. P. Kaufman, and A. S. Walleck, "The Four Phases of Strategic Management," *Journal of Business Strategy* (Winter 1982), pp. 9–21.

2. M. R. Vaghefi and A. B Huellmantel, "Strategic Leadership at General Electric," *Long Range Planning* (April 1998), pp. 280–294. For a detailed description of the evolution of strategic management at GE, see W. Ocasio and J. Joseph, "Rise and Fall—or Transformation?" *Long Range Planning* (June 2008), pp. 248–272.

3. E. D. Beinhocker, "The Adaptable Corporation," *McKinsey Quarterly* (2006, Number 2), pp. 77–87.

4. B. W. Wirtz, A. Mathieu, and O. Schilke, "Strategy in High-Velocity Environments," *Long Range Planning* (June 2007), pp. 295–313; L. F. Teagarden, Y. Sarason, J. S. Childers, and D. E. Hatfield, "The Engagement of Employees in the Strategy Process and Firm Performance: The Role of Strategic Goals and Environment," *Journal of Business Strategies* (Spring 2005), pp. 75–99; T. J. Andersen, "Strategic Planning, Autonomous Actions and Corporate Performance," *Long Range Planning* (April 2000), pp. 184–200; C. C. Miller and L. B. Cardinal, "Strategic Planning and Firm Performance: A Synthesis of More than Two Decades of Research," *Academy of Management Journal* (December 1994), pp. 1649–1665; P. Pekar Jr., and S. Abraham, "Is Strategic Management Living Up to Its Promise?" *Long Range Planning* (October 1995), pp. 32–44; W. E. Hopkins and S. A. Hopkins, "Strategic Planning—Financial Performance Relationship in Banks: A Causal Examination," *Strategic Management Journal* (September 1997), pp. 635–652.

5. E. J. Zajac, M. S. Kraatz, and R. F. Bresser, "Modeling the Dynamics of Strategic Fit: A Normative Approach to Strategic Change," *Strategic Management Journal* (April 2000), pp. 429–453; M. Peteraf and R. Reed, "Managerial Discretion and Internal Alignment Under Regulatory Constraints and Change," *Strategic Management Journal* (November 2007), pp. 1089–1112; C. S. Katsikeas, S. Samiee, and M. Theodosiou, "Strategy Fit and Performance Consequences of International Marketing Standardization," *Strategic Management Journal* (September 2006), pp. 867–890.

6. P. Brews and D. Purohit, "Strategic Planning in Unstable Environments," *Long Range Planning* (February 2007), pp. 64–83.

7. K. G. Smith and C. M. Grimm, "Environmental Variation, Strategic Change and Firm Performance: A Study of Railroad Deregulation," *Strategic Management Journal* (July–August 1987), pp. 363–376; J. A. Nickerson and B. S. Silverman, "Why Firms Want to Organize Efficiently and What Keeps Them from Doing So: Inappropriate Governance, Performance, and Adaptation in a Deregulated Industry," *Administrative Science Quarterly* (September 2003), pp. 433–465.

8. I. Wilson, "Strategic Planning Isn't Dead—It Changed," *Long Range Planning* (August 1994), p. 20.

9. R. Dye and O. Sibony, "How to Improve Strategic Planning," *McKinsey Quarterly* (2007, Number 3), pp. 40–48.

10. W. M. Becker and V. M. Freeman, "Going from Global Trends to Corporate Strategy," *McKinsey Quarterly* (2006, Number 2), pp. 17–27

11. D. Rigby and B. Bilodeau, *Management Tools and Trends 2007* (Bain & Company, 2007); D. Rigby and B. Bilodeau, *Management Tools and Trends 2011* (Bain & Company, 2011).

12. W. Joyce, "What Really Works: Building the 4+2 Organization," *Organizational Dynamics* (Vol. 34, Issue 2, 2005), pp. 118–129. See also W. Joyce, N. Nohria, and B. Roberson, *What Really Works: The 4+2 Formula for Sustained Business Success* (HarperBusiness, 2003).

13. R. M. Grant, "Strategic Planning in a Turbulent Environment: Evidence from the Oil Majors," *Strategic Management Journal* (June 2003), pp. 491–517.

14. M. J. Peel and J. Bridge, "How Planning and Capital Budgeting Improve SME Performance," *Long Range Planning* (December 1998), pp. 848–856; L. W. Rue and N. A. Ibrahim, "The Relationship Between Planning Sophistication and Performance in Small Businesses," *Journal of Small Business Management* (October 1998), pp. 24–32; J. C. Carland and J. W. Carland, "A Model of Entrepreneurial Planning and Its Effect on Performance," paper presented to Association for Small Business and Entrepreneurship (Houston, TX, 2003).

15. R. M. Grant, "Strategic Planning in a Turbulent Environment: Evidence from the Oil Majors," *Strategic Management Journal* (June 2003), pp. 491–517.

16. "Triple Bottom Line," *The Economist* (November 17, 2009), (www.economist.com/node/14301663).

17. www.usgbc.org/.

18. T. L. Friedman, *The World Is Flat* (NY: Farrar, Strauss & Giroux, 2005).

19. R. Cohen, "America Abroad," *The New York Times*, January 9, 2012, (www.nytimes.com/2012/01/10/opinion/america-abroad.html); A. K. Gupta, V. Govindarajan, and H. Wang, *The*

Quest for Global Dominance, 2nd ed. (San Francisco: Jossey-Bass, 2008).

20. "The CEO Agenda for Innovation," 2012, (www.pwc.com/us/en/issues/ceo-agenda-for-innovation-and-technology/index.jhtml).

21. http://www.ign.com/articles/2010/01/26/apples-first-tablet.

22. A. Glavas and S. Piderit. "How Does Doing Good Matter," *Journal of Corporate Citizenship*, Winter, 36 (2009), pp. 51–70.

23. R. Sylvan and K. Rainey, "2012 Workplace Trends Report: Workplaces that Promote Sustainabilty," (www.sodexousa.com/usen/roles/facilmgmt/workplaces_that_promote_sustainability.asp).

24. www.iso.org/iso/iso14000.

25. M. E. Porter and F. L. Reinhardt, "A Strategic Approach to Climate," *Harvard Business Review* (October 2007), p. 22.

26. "The Rising Costs of Global Warming," *Futurist* (November–December 2005), p. 13.

27. J. Welch and S. Welch, "The Global Warming Wager," *BusinessWeek* (February 26, 2007), p. 130.

28. J. A. C. Baum, "Organizational Ecology," in *Handbook of Organization Studies*, edited by S. R. Clegg, C. Handy, and W. Nord (London: Sage, 1996), pp. 77–114.

29. B. M. Staw and L. D. Epstein, "What Bandwagons Bring: Effects of Popular Management Techniques on Corporate Performance, Reputation, and CEO Pay," *Administrative Science Quarterly* (September 2000), pp. 523–556; M. B. Lieberman and S. Asaba, "Why Do Firms Imitate Each Other?" *Academy of Management Review* (April 2006), pp. 366–385.

30. T. W. Ruefli and R. R. Wiggins, "Industry, Corporate, and Segment Effects and Business Performance: A Non-Parametric Approach," *Strategic Management Journal* (September 2003), pp. 861–879; Y. E. Spanos, G. Zaralis, and S. Lioukas, "Strategy and Industry Effects on Profitability: Evidence from Greece," *Strategic Management Journal* (February 2004), pp. 139–165; E. H. Bowman and C. E. Helfat, "Does Corporate Strategy Matter?" *Strategic Management Journal* (January 2001), pp. 1–23; T. H. Brush, P. Bromiley, and M. Hendrickx, "The Relative Influence of Industry and Corporation on Business Segment Performance: An Alternative Estimate," *Strategic Management Journal* (June 1999), pp. 519–547; K. M. Gilley, B. A. Walters, and B. J. Olson, "Top Management Team Risk Taking Propensities and Firm Performance: Direct and Moderating Effects," *Journal of Business Strategies* (Fall 2002), pp. 95–114.

31. For more information on these theories, see A. Y. Lewin and H. W. Voloberda, "Prolegomena on Coevolution: A Framework for Research on Strategy and New Organizational Forms," *Organization Science* (October 1999), pp. 519–534, and H. Aldrich, *Organizations Evolving* (London: Sage, 1999), pp. 43–74.

32. R. A. D'Aveni, *Hypercompetition* (New York: The Free Press, 1994). Hypercompetition is discussed in more detail in Chapter 4.

33. R. S. M. Lau, "Strategic Flexibility: A New Reality for World-Class Manufacturing," *SAM Advanced Management Journal* (Spring 1996), pp. 11–15.

34. M. A. Hitt, B. W. Keats, and S. M. DeMarie, "Navigating in the New Competitive Landscape: Building Strategic Flexibility and Competitive Advantage in the 21st Century," *Academy of Management Executive* (November 1998), pp. 22–42.

35. S. C. Voelpel, M. Dous, and T. H. Davenport, "Five Steps to Creating a Global Knowledge-Sharing System: Siemens'

ShareNet," *Academy of Management Executive* (May 2005), pp. 9–23.

36. D. A. Garvin, "Building a Learning Organization," *Harvard Business Review* (July/August 1993), p. 80. See also P. M. Senge, *The Fifth Discipline: The Art and Practice of the Learning Organization* (New York: Doubleday, 1990).

37. A. D. Chandler, *Inventing the Electronic Century* (New York: The Free Press, 2001).

38. N. Collier, F. Fishwick, and S. W. Floyd, "Managerial Involvement and Perceptions of Strategy Process," *Long Range Planning* (February 2004), pp. 67–83; J. A. Parnell, S. Carraher, and K. Holt, "Participative Management's Influence on Effective Strategic Planning," *Journal of Business Strategies* (Fall 2002), pp. 161–179; M. Ketokivi and X. Castaner, "Strategic Planning as an Integrative Device," *Administrative Science Quarterly* (September 2004), pp. 337–365; Edmondson, A. 2011. "Strategies for Learning from Failure," *Harvard Business Review* (April 2011).

39. E. W. K. Tsang, "Internationalization as a Learning Process: Singapore MNCs in China," *Academy of Management Executive* (February 1999), pp. 91–101; J. M. Shaver, W. Mitchell, and B. Yeung, "The Effect of Own-Firm and Other Firm Experience on Foreign Direct Investment Survival in the U.S., 1987–92," *Strategic Management Journal* (November 1997), pp. 811–824; P. Kale and H. Singh, "Building Firm Capabilities through Learning: The Role of the Alliance Learning Process in Alliance Capability and Firm-Level Alliance Success," *Strategic Management Journal* (October 2007), pp. 981–1000; H. Barkema and M. Schijven, "How Do Firms Learn to Make Acquisitions? A Review of Past Research and an Agenda for the Future," *Journal of Management* (June 2008), pp. 594–634; D. D. Bergh and E. N-K Lim, "Learning How to Restructure: Absorptive Capacity and Improvisational Views of Restructuring Actions and Performance," *Strategic Management Journal* (June 2008), pp. 593–616.

40. W. Mitchell, J. M. Shaver, and B. Yeung, "Getting There in a Global Industry: Impacts on Performance of Changing International Presence," *Strategic Management Journal* (September 1992), pp. 419–432.

41. D. J. Miller, M. J. Fern, and L. B. Cardinal, "The Use of Knowledge for Technological Innovation Within Diversified Firms," *Academy of Management Journal* (April 2007), pp. 308–326.

42. R. Wiltbank, N. Dew, S. Read, and S. D. Sarasvathy, "What to Do Next? The Case for Non-Predictive Strategy," *Strategic Management Journal* (October 2006), pp. 981–998; J. A. Smith, "Strategies for Start-Ups," *Long Range Planning* (December 1998), pp. 857–872.

43. J. S. Sidhu, "Business-Domain Definition and Performance: An Empirical Study," *SAM Advanced Management Journal* (Autumn 2004), pp. 40–45.

44. See A. Campbell and S. Yeung, "Brief Case: Mission, Vision, and Strategic Intent," *Long Range Planning* (August 1991), pp. 145–147; S. Cummings and J. Davies, "Mission, Vision, Fusion," *Long Range Planning* (December 1994), pp. 147–150.

45. J. Cosco, "Down to the Sea in Ships," *Journal of Business Strategy* (November/December 1995), p. 48.

46. "Is PepsiCo a Better Dividend Stock than Coca-Cola?" *Seeking Alpha* (August 7, 2012), (www.seekingalpha.com/article/786211-is-pepsi-a-better-dividend-stock-than-coca-cola); www.thecoca-coalacompany.com.

47. D. Armstrong, "Pfizer Sees Harvard Collaboration as Spark for New Drugs," *Bloomberg Businessweek* (June 15, 2012), (www.bloomberg.com/news/2012-06-15/pfizer-sees-harvard-collaboration-as-spark-for-new-drugs.html).

48. K. M. Eisenhardt and D. N. Sull, "Strategy as Simple Rules," *Harvard Business Review* (January 2001), p. 110.

49. M. Wood, "Facebook Buys Instagram . . . But for What?" CBS News, April 10, 2012, (http://www.cbsnews.com/8301-205_162-57411761/facebook-buys-instagram-...but-for-what/); D. Dumlao. "American Entrepreneur Bets Big on PH," *Philippine Daily Inquirer* (August 11, 2012), (http://business.inquirer.net/76323/american-entrepreneur-bets-big-on-ph).

50. H. A. Simon, *Administrative Behavior*, 2nd edition (New York: The Free Press, 1957), p. 231.

51. "Starbucks to Close All U.S. Stores for Training," MSNBC (February 26, 2008), (www.msnbc.com/id/23351151/ns/business-us_business/t/starbucks-close-all-us-stores-trainign/#.uco_I2t5mk0); "Howard Schultz on How Starbucks Got Its Groove Back," careerbuilder.com (June 3, 2011), (http://thehiringsite.careerbuilder.com/2011/06/03/howard-schultz-on-how-starbucks-got-its-groove-back/); B. Stone. "Starbucks Profits Down Sharply on Restructuring Costs," *The New York Times* (November 10, 2008), (http://www.nytimes.com/2008/11/11/business/11sbux.html).

52. H. Mintzberg, "Planning on the Left Side and Managing on the Right," *Harvard Business Review* (July–August 1976), p. 56.

53. R. A. Burgelman and A. S. Grove, "Let Chaos Reign, Then Reign in Chaos—Repeatedly: Managing Strategic Dynamics for Corporate Longevity," *Strategic Management Journal* (October 2007), pp. 965–979.

54. E. Romanelli and M. L. Tushman, "Organizational Transformation as Punctuated Equilibrium: An Empirical Test," *Academy of Management Journal* (October 1994), pp. 1141–1166.

55. S. S. Gordon, W. H. Stewart, Jr., R. Sweo, and W. A. Luker, "Convergence versus Strategic Reorientation: The Antecedents of Fast-Paced Organizational Change," *Journal of Management* (Vol. 26, No. 5, 2000), pp. 911–945.

56. Speech to the 1998 Academy of Management, reported by S. M. Puffer, "Global Executive: Intel's Andrew Grove on Competitiveness," *Academy of Management Executive* (February 1999), pp. 15–24.

57. D. J. Hickson, R. J. Butler, D. Cray, G. R. Mallory, and D. C. Wilson, *Top Decisions: Strategic Decision Making in Organizations* (San Francisco: Jossey-Bass, 1986), pp. 26–42.

58. A. Weintraub, "Genentech's Gamble," *BusinessWeek* (December 17, 2007), pp. 44–48; http://www.fiercepharma.com/special-reports/top-10-best-selling-cancer-drugs/rituxan-3-billion; http://diabetes.webmd.com/news/20120814/new-drug-for-diabetes-related-vision-loss.

59. H. Mintzberg, "Strategy-Making in Three Modes," *California Management Review* (Winter 1973), pp. 44–53.

60. F. Vogelstein, "Mighty Amazon," *Fortune* (May 26, 2003), pp. 60–74.

61. Stern, J. 2012, "Encyclopedia Britannica Kills Its Print Edition," *ABC News* (March 13, 2012), (http://abcnews.go.com/blogs/technology/2012/03/encyclopaedia-britannica-kills-its-print-edition/).

62. L. V. Gerstner, *Who Says Elephants Can't Dance?* (New York: HarperCollins, 2002).

63. J. B. Quinn, *Strategies for Change: Logical Incrementalism* (Homewood, IL.: Irwin, 1980), p. 58.

64. R. M. Grant, "Strategic Planning in a Turbulent Environment: Evidence from the Oil Majors," *Strategic Management Journal* (June 2003), pp. 491–517.

65. G. Gavetti and J. W. Rivkin, "Seek Strategy the Right Way at the Right Time," *Harvard Business Review* (January 2008), pp. 22–23.

66. P. J. Brews and M. R. Hunt, "Learning to Plan and Planning to Learn: Resolving the Planning School/Learning School Debate," *Strategic Management Journal* (October 1999), pp. 889–913; I. Gold and A. M. A. Rasheed, "Rational Decision-Making and Firm Performance: The Moderating Role of the Environment," *Strategic Management Journal* (August 1997), pp. 583–591; R. L. Priem, A. M. A. Rasheed, and A. G. Kotulic, "Rationality in Strategic Decision Processes, Environmental Dynamism and Firm Performance," *Journal of Management*, Vol. 21, No. 5 (1995), pp. 913–929; J. W. Dean, Jr., and M. P. Sharfman, "Does Decision Process Matter? A Study of Strategic Decision-Making Effectiveness," *Academy of Management Journal* (April 1996), pp. 368–396.

67. T. L. Wheelen and J. D. Hunger, "Using the Strategic Audit," *SAM Advanced Management Journal* (Winter 1987), pp. 4–12; G. Donaldson, "A New Tool for Boards: The Strategic Audit," *Harvard Business Review* (July–August 1995), pp. 99–107.

68. D. C. Hambrick and J. W. Fredrickson, "Are You Sure You Have a Strategy?" *Academy of Management Executive* (November, 2001), pp. 48–59.

69. Hambrick and Fredrickson, p. 49.

1.A

Strategic Audit of a Corporation

I. Current Situation

A. Current Performance

How did the corporation perform in the past year overall in terms of return on investment, market share, and profitability?

B. Strategic Posture

What are the corporation's current mission, objectives, strategies, and policies?

1. Are they clearly stated, or are they merely implied from performance?
2. **Mission:** What business(es) is the corporation in? Why?
3. **Objectives:** What are the corporate, business, and functional objectives? Are they consistent with each other, with the mission, and with the internal and external environments?
4. **Strategies:** What strategy or mix of strategies is the corporation following? Are they consistent with each other, with the mission and objectives, and with the internal and external environments?
5. **Policies:** What are the corporation's policies? Are they consistent with each other, with the mission, objectives, and strategies, and with the internal and external environments?
6. Do the current mission, objectives, strategies, and policies reflect the corporation's international operations, whether global or multidomestic?

II. Corporate Governance

A. Board of Directors

1. Who is on the board? Are they internal (employees) or external members?
2. Do they own significant shares of stock?
3. Is the stock privately held or publicly traded? Are there different classes of stock with different voting rights?
4. What do the board members contribute to the corporation in terms of knowledge, skills, background, and connections? If the corporation has international operations, do board members have international experience? Are board members concerned with environmental sustainability?

SOURCE: T. L. Wheelen and J. D. Hunger, *Strategic Audit of a Corporation*, Copyright © 1982 and 2005 by Wheelen and Hunger Associates. Thomas L. Wheelen, "A Strategic Audit," paper presented to Society for Advancement of Management (SAM). Presented by J. D. Hunger and T. L. Wheelen in "The Strategic Audit: An Integrative Approach to Teaching Business Policy," *Academy of Management* (August 1983). Published in "Using the Strategic Audit," by T. L. Wheelen and J. D. Hunger in *SAM Advanced Management Journal* (Winter 1987), pp. 4–12. Reprinted by permission of the copyright holders. Revised 1988, 1994, 1997, 2000, 2002, 2004, 2005, 2009, and 2013.

5. How long have the board members served on the board?

6. What is their level of involvement in strategic management? Do they merely rubber-stamp top management's proposals or do they actively participate and suggest future directions? Do they evaluate management's proposals in terms of environmental sustainability?

B. Top Management

1. What person or group constitutes top management?

2. What are top management's chief characteristics in terms of knowledge, skills, background, and style? If the corporation has international operations, does top management have international experience? Are executives from acquired companies considered part of the top management team?

3. Has top management been responsible for the corporation's performance over the past few years? How many managers have been in their current position for less than three years? Were they promoted internally or externally hired?

4. Has top management established a systematic approach to strategic management?

5. What is top management's level of involvement in the strategic management process?

6. How well does top management interact with lower-level managers and with the board of directors?

7. Are strategic decisions made ethically in a socially responsible manner?

8. Are strategic decisions made in an environmentally sustainable manner?

9. Do top executives own significant amounts of stock in the corporation?

10. Is top management sufficiently skilled to cope with likely future challenges?

III. External Environment: Opportunities and Threats (SW**OT**)

A. Natural Physical Environment: Sustainability Issues

1. What forces from the natural physical environmental are currently affecting the corporation and the industries in which it competes? Which present current or future threats? Opportunities?
   a. Climate, including global temperature, sea level, and fresh water availability
   b. Weather-related events, such as severe storms, floods, and droughts
   c. Solar phenomena, such as sunspots and solar wind

2. Do these forces have different effects in other regions of the world?

B. Societal Environment

1. What general environmental forces are currently affecting both the corporation and the industries in which it competes? Which present current or future threats? Opportunities?
   a. Economic
   b. Technological
   c. Political–legal
   d. Sociocultural

2. Are these forces different in other regions of the world?

C. Task Environment

1. What forces drive industry competition? Are these forces the same globally or do they vary from country to country? Rate each force as **high**, **medium**, or **low**.
   a. Threat of new entrants

    b. Bargaining power of buyers
    c. Threat of substitute products or services
    d. Bargaining power of suppliers
    e. Rivalry among competing firms
    f. Relative power of unions, governments, special interest groups, etc.

2. What key factors in the immediate environment (that is, customers, competitors, suppliers, creditors, labor unions, governments, trade associations, interest groups, local communities, and shareholders) are currently affecting the corporation? Which are current or future threats? Opportunities?

D. Summary of External Factors (List in the EFAS Table 4–5, p. 121)

Which of these forces and factors are the most important to the corporation and to the industries in which it competes at the present time? Which will be important in the future?

IV. Internal Environment: Strengths and Weaknesses (**SW**OT)

A. Corporate Structure

1. How is the corporation structured at present?
    a. Is the decision-making authority centralized around one group or decentralized to many units?
    b. Is the corporation organized on the basis of functions, projects, geography, or some combination of these?
2. Is the structure clearly understood by everyone in the corporation?
3. Is the present structure consistent with current corporate objectives, strategies, policies, and programs, as well as with the firm's international operations?
4. In what ways does this structure compare with those of similar corporations?

B. Corporate Culture

1. Is there a well-defined or emerging culture composed of shared beliefs, expectations, and values?
2. Is the culture consistent with the current objectives, strategies, policies, and programs?
3. What is the culture's position on environmental sustainability?
4. What is the culture's position on other important issues facing the corporation (that is, on productivity, quality of performance, adaptability to changing conditions, and internationalization)?
5. Is the culture compatible with the employees' diversity of backgrounds?
6. Does the company take into consideration the values of the culture of each nation in which the firm operates?

C. Corporate Resources

1. **Marketing**
    a. What are the corporation's current marketing objectives, strategies, policies, and programs?
       i. Are they clearly stated or merely implied from performance and/or budgets?
       ii. Are they consistent with the corporation's mission, objectives, strategies, and policies and with internal and external environments?

b. How well is the corporation performing in terms of analysis of market position and marketing mix (that is, product, price, place, and promotion) in both domestic and international markets? How dependent is the corporation on a few customers? How big is its market? Where is it gaining or losing market share? What percentage of sales comes from developed versus developing regions? Where are current products in the product life cycle?
   i. What trends emerge from this analysis?
   ii. What impact have these trends had on past performance and how might these trends affect future performance?
   iii. Does this analysis support the corporation's past and pending strategic decisions?
   iv. Does marketing provide the company with a competitive advantage?
c. How well does the corporation's marketing performance compare with that of similar corporations?
d. Are marketing managers using accepted marketing concepts and techniques to evaluate and improve product performance? (Consider product life cycle, market segmentation, market research, and product portfolios.)
e. Does marketing adjust to the conditions in each country in which it operates?
f. Does marketing consider environmental sustainability when making decisions?
g. What is the role of the marketing manager in the strategic management process?

2. **Finance**
   a. What are the corporation's current financial objectives, strategies, and policies and programs?
      i. Are they clearly stated or merely implied from performance and/or budgets?
      ii. Are they consistent with the corporation's mission, objectives, strategies, and policies and with internal and external environments?
   b. How well is the corporation performing in terms of financial analysis? (Consider ratio analysis, common size statements, and capitalization structure.) How balanced, in terms of cash flow, is the company's portfolio of products and businesses? What are investor expectations in terms of share price?
      i. What trends emerge from this analysis?
      ii. Are there any significant differences when statements are calculated in constant versus reported dollars?
      iii. What impact have these trends had on past performance and how might these trends affect future performance?
      iv. Does this analysis support the corporation's past and pending strategic decisions?
      v. Does finance provide the company with a competitive advantage?
   c. How well does the corporation's financial performance compare with that of similar corporations?
   d. Are financial managers using accepted financial concepts and techniques to evaluate and improve current corporate and divisional performance? (Consider financial leverage, capital budgeting, ratio analysis, and managing foreign currencies.)
   e. Does finance adjust to the conditions in each country in which the company operates?
   f. Does finance cope with global financial issues?
   g. What is the role of the financial manager in the strategic management process?

3. **Research and Development (R&D)**
   a. What are the corporation's current R&D objectives, strategies, policies, and programs?
      i. Are they clearly stated or merely implied from performance or budgets?
      ii. Are they consistent with the corporation's mission, objectives, strategies and policies, and with internal and external environments?
      iii. What is the role of technology in corporate performance?

      iv. Is the mix of basic, applied, and engineering research appropriate given the corporate mission and strategies?

      v. Does R&D provide the company with a competitive advantage?

  b. What return is the corporation receiving from its investment in R&D?

  c. Is the corporation competent in technology transfer? Does it use concurrent engineering and cross-functional work teams in product and process design?

  d. What role does technological discontinuity play in the company's products?

  e. How well does the corporation's investment in R&D compare with the investments of similar corporations? How much R&D is being outsourced? Is the corporation using value-chain alliances appropriately for innovation and competitive advantage?

  f. Does R&D adjust to the conditions in each country in which the company operates?

  g. Does R&D consider environmental sustainability in product development and packaging?

  h. What is the role of the R&D manager in the strategic management process?

4. **Operations and Logistics**

  a. What are the corporation's current manufacturing/service objectives, strategies, policies, and programs?

    i. Are they clearly stated or merely implied from performance or budgets?

    ii. Are they consistent with the corporation's mission, objectives, strategies, and policies and with internal and external environments?

  b. What are the type and extent of operations capabilities of the corporation? How much is done domestically versus internationally? Is the amount of outsourcing appropriate to be competitive? Is purchasing being handled appropriately? Are suppliers and distributors operating in an environmentally sustainable manner? Which products have the highest and lowest profit margins?

    i. If the corporation is product-oriented, consider plant facilities, type of manufacturing system (continuous mass production, intermittent job shop, or flexible manufacturing), age and type of equipment, degree and role of automation and/or robots, plant capacities and utilization, productivity ratings, and availability and type of transportation.

    ii. If the corporation is service-oriented, consider service facilities (hospital, theater, or school buildings), type of operations systems (continuous service over time to the same clientele or intermittent service over time to varied clientele), age and type of supporting equipment, degree and role of automation and use of mass communication devices (diagnostic machinery, video machines), facility capacities and utilization rates, efficiency ratings of professional and service personnel, and availability and type of transportation to bring service staff and clientele together.

  c. Are manufacturing or service facilities vulnerable to natural disasters, local or national strikes, reduction or limitation of resources from suppliers, substantial cost increases of materials, or nationalization by governments?

  d. Is there an appropriate mix of people and machines (in manufacturing firms) or of support staff to professionals (in service firms)?

  e. How well does the corporation perform relative to the competition? Is it balancing inventory costs (warehousing) with logistical costs (just-in-time)? Consider costs per unit of labor, material, and overhead; downtime; inventory control management and scheduling of service staff; production ratings; facility utilization percentages; and number of clients successfully treated by category (if service firm) or percentage of orders shipped on time (if product firm).

    i. What trends emerge from this analysis?

    ii. What impact have these trends had on past performance and how might these trends affect future performance?

    iii. Does this analysis support the corporation's past and pending strategic decisions?

    iv. Does operations provide the company with a competitive advantage?

f. Are operations managers using appropriate concepts and techniques to evaluate and improve current performance? Consider cost systems, quality control and reliability systems, inventory control management, personnel scheduling, TQM, learning curves, safety programs, and engineering programs that can improve efficiency of manufacturing or of service.

g. Do operations adjust to the conditions in each country in which it has facilities?

h. Do operations consider environmental sustainability when making decisions?

i. What is the role of the operations manager in the strategic management process?

5. **Human Resources Management (HRM)**

a. What are the corporation's current HRM objectives, strategies, policies, and programs?

    i. Are they clearly stated or merely implied from performance and/or budgets?

    ii. Are they consistent with the corporation's mission, objectives, strategies, and policies and with internal and external environments?

b. How well is the corporation's HRM performing in terms of improving the fit between the individual employee and the job? Consider turnover, grievances, strikes, layoffs, employee training, and quality of work life.

    i. What trends emerge from this analysis?

    ii. What impact have these trends had on past performance and how might these trends affect future performance?

    iii. Does this analysis support the corporation's past and pending strategic decisions?

    iv. Does HRM provide the company with a competitive advantage?

c. How does this corporation's HRM performance compare with that of similar corporations?

d. Are HRM managers using appropriate concepts and techniques to evaluate and improve corporate performance? Consider the job analysis program, performance appraisal system, up-to-date job descriptions, training and development programs, attitude surveys, job design programs, quality of relationships with unions, and use of autonomous work teams.

e. How well is the company managing the diversity of its workforce? What is the company's record on human rights? Does the company monitor the human rights record of key suppliers and distributors?

f. Does HRM adjust to the conditions in each country in which the company operates? Does the company have a code of conduct for HRM for itself and key suppliers in developing nations? Are employees receiving international assignments to prepare them for managerial positions?

g. What is the role of outsourcing in HRM planning?

h. What is the role of the HRM manager in the strategic management process?

6. **Information Technology (IT)**

a. What are the corporation's current IT objectives, strategies, policies, and programs?

    i. Are they clearly stated or merely implied from performance and/or budgets?

    ii. Are they consistent with the corporation's mission, objectives, strategies, and policies and with internal and external environments?

b. How well is the corporation's IT performing in terms of providing a useful database, automating routine clerical operations, assisting managers in making routine decisions, and providing information necessary for strategic decisions?

    i. What trends emerge from this analysis?

    ii. What impact have these trends had on past performance and how might these trends affect future performance?

    iii. Does this analysis support the corporation's past and pending strategic decisions?

    iv. Does IT provide the company with a competitive advantage?

c. How does this corporation's IT performance and stage of development compare with that of similar corporations? Is it appropriately using the Internet, intranet, and extranets?

d. Are IT managers using appropriate concepts and techniques to evaluate and improve corporate performance? Do they know how to build and manage a complex database, establish Web sites with firewalls and virus protection, conduct system analyses, and implement interactive decision-support systems?

e. Does the company have a global IT and Internet presence? Does it have difficulty with getting data across national boundaries?

f. What is the role of the IT manager in the strategic management process?

D. Summary of Internal Factors
(List in the IFAS Table 5–2, p. 154)

Which of these factors are core competencies? Which, if any, are distinctive competencies? Which of these factors are the most important to the corporation and to the industries in which it competes at the present time? Which might be important in the future? Which functions or activities are candidates for outsourcing?

V. Analysis of Strategic Factors (SWOT)

A. Situational Analysis
(List in SFAS Matrix, Figure 6–1, pp. 166–167)

Of the external (EFAS) and internal (IFAS) factors listed in III.D and IV.D, which are the strategic (most important) factors that strongly affect the corporation's present and future performance?

B. Review of Mission and Objectives

1. Are the current mission and objectives appropriate in light of the key strategic factors and problems?

2. Should the mission and objectives be changed? If so, how?

3. If they are changed, what will be the effects on the firm?

VI. Strategic Alternatives and Recommended Strategy

A. Strategic Alternatives

1. Can the current or revised objectives be met through more careful implementation of those strategies presently in use (for example, fine-tuning the strategies)?

2. What are the major feasible alternative strategies available to the corporation? What are the pros and cons of each? Can corporate scenarios be developed and agreed on? (Alternatives must fit the natural physical environment, societal environment, industry, and corporation for the next three to five years.)

   a. Consider *stability*, *growth*, and *retrenchment* as corporate strategies.

   b. Consider *cost leadership* and *differentiation* as business strategies.

   c. Consider any functional strategic alternatives that might be needed for reinforcement of an important corporate or business strategic alternative.

B. Recommended Strategy

1. Specify which of the strategic alternatives you are recommending for the corporate, business, and functional levels of the corporation. Do you recommend different business or functional strategies for different units of the corporation?

2. Justify your recommendation in terms of its ability to resolve both long- and short-term problems and effectively deal with the strategic factors.

3. What policies should be developed or revised to guide effective implementation?

4. What is the impact of your recommended strategy on the company's core and distinctive competencies?

VII. Implementation

A. What Kinds of Programs or Tactics (for Example, Restructuring the Corporation or Instituting TQM) Should Be Developed to Implement the Recommended Strategy?

1. Who should develop these programs/tactics?

2. Who should be in charge of these programs/tactics?

B. Are the Programs/Tactics Financially Feasible? Can Pro Forma Budgets Be Developed and Agreed On? Are Priorities and Timetables Appropriate to Individual Programs/Tactics?

C. Will New Standard Operating Procedures Need to Be Developed?

VIII. Evaluation and Control

A. Is the Current Information System Capable of Providing Sufficient Feedback on Implementation Activities and Performance? Can It Measure Strategic Factors?

1. Can performance results be pinpointed by area, unit, project, or function?

2. Is the information timely?

3. Is the corporation using benchmarking to evaluate its functions and activities?

B. Are Adequate Control Measures in Place to Ensure Conformance with the Recommended Strategic Plan?

1. Are appropriate standards and measures being used?

2. Are reward systems capable of recognizing and rewarding good performance?

corporate
Governance

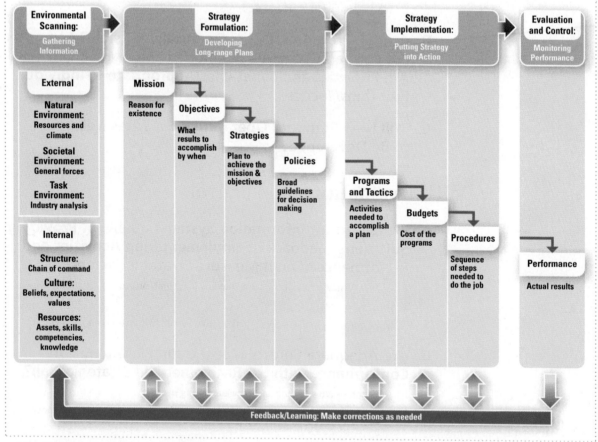

MyManagementLab®

⭐ Improve Your Grade!

Over 10 million students improved their results using the Pearson MyLabs. Visit **mymanagementlab.com** for simulations, tutorials, and end-of-chapter problems.

Learning Objectives

After reading this chapter, you should be able to:

- Describe the role and responsibilities of the board of directors in corporate governance
- Understand how the composition of a board can affect its operation
- Describe the impact of the Sarbanes–Oxley Act on corporate governance in the United States
- Discuss trends in corporate governance
- Explain how executive leadership is an important part of strategic management

Disarray with the HP Board of Directors

Sometimes an activist or even catalyst board does more harm than good. This has certainly been the case at Hewlett-Packard Company, the Palo Alto pioneer in technology.

Lewis Platt was only the fourth CEO in the history of the company, and like his predecessor (John A. Young), he was a long-time engineering employee of the company. Under his leadership, the company prospered as it had through most of its 50-year history up to that point. With the support of the board, he spun off the Medical Instruments division and made tentative moves toward the new information age, but was slow to recognize the importance of the Internet.

In 1999, along with the board of directors, he decided to look outside the company for the first time and try to hire a visible, passionate leader for the staid engineering-oriented firm. On July 19, 1999, HP announced that Carly Fiorina would be the new CEO, making her the first woman to head a DOW 30 company. Fiorina made her name at Lucent Technologies where she was President of a company that made a remarkable turnaround in the face of the huge changes in technology of the day.

Some of the same board members that hired her then turned against her in one of the most public proxy battles of our times when she announced a US$25 billion merger with Compaq Computer Company in September 2001. Walter Hewlett and Lewis Platt openly opposed the merger. The plan to move HP into an innovation machine in the Internet age was now moving to put most of its resources in a low-margin, shrinking PC manufacturing business. Wall Street hated the idea. HP stock lost 18% of its value on the day the merger was announced and many analysts in the industry thought this was a bad move. Fiorina forced the merger forward with the support of the majority of the board of directors.

On February 22, 2002, the HP Board of Directors sent a very public and stinging letter of criticism against Hewlett to all of its shareholders. Hewlett responded by taking out ads in major newspapers opposing the acquisition. In the end, the merger was approved, but by only a scant 3% majority.

The history of acquisitions is not a good one. Very few bring real value to the companies that are the acquirer. The bigger the acquisition, the more likely this is the case. Such was the fate of HP. By the end of 2004, the board was fed up with Carly Fiorina's inability to move the new, huge HP forward. The board began meeting in private without their high-profile CEO. On February 6, 2005, the board met with Fiorina at Chicago's O'Hare Hyatt Hotel and expressed their frustration with her leadership and her unwillingness to work with the board of directors on the future of the company. The next day they asked her to resign.

Believing that it was a failure of execution, the board moved to hire someone with strict operating credentials. The result was Mark Hurd, the 25-year veteran CEO at NCR Corporation. Hurd roared into the company, eliminating 15,000+ jobs, cutting R&D, and attempting to automate consulting services. A leak of information discussed at a board of directors strategy meeting in late 2005 led then–Board Chairman Patricia Dunn and CEO Mark Hurd to initiate an investigation of fellow board members. Using detectives who posed as reporters, they obtained phone records of those people on the board that they suspected, and the spying scandal exploded into the open.

Dunn was fired from her board seat in 2006 and *Newsweek* magazine put her on the cover with the title "The Boss Who Spied on Her Board." Mark Hurd escaped any serious repercussions from the scandal and announced a new, very strict code of conduct for the corporation.

By all accounts, Mark Hurd was successful at turning the company around and was listed as one of the best CEOs in 2009. However, another scandal broke, with Hurd being accused of sexual harassment with an HP marketing consultant. While the board found that he did not actually violate the company's sexual-harassment policies, they did find that he submitted inaccurate expense reports intended to conceal the relationship. He was forced to resign in August 2010 by a powerful but small group of directors.

In the wake of the Hurd resignation, there was a major board shakeup. Four directors involved in forcing the Hurd resignation resigned their board seats and five new board members were named. In November, 2010, the board named Leo Apotheker as the new CEO. He was the former head of Global Field Operations at SAP, and would remain the company's CEO for little more than 10 months.

Apotheker's move to push forward the HP TouchPad tablet was a commercial failure at the same time that HP phones were taking a beating in the market. In a stunning announcement in September 2011, he stated that HP would exit the PC business entirely. HP was the leader in PC sales both within the United States and globally. The outrage was immediate and overwhelming. The company reversed position two weeks later, but the board was appalled at his lack of leadership. After firing Apotheker, the board named one of its own members, former eBay CEO Meg Whitman to run the company.

One of the most important responsibilities that a board of directors has is to effectively recruit and work with management that will lead the business. The CEO revolving door at HP has cost the company more than US$83 million in severance pay for CEOs that the board no longer wants to run the company. *CNN Money* reported in 2012 that "Before Apotheker ever came to HP, the company was known for its fractious board. Individual directors would cycle in and out, yet somehow the group seemed constantly divided by personal rivalries, bickering, and leaks to the press."

SOURCES: Bandler, J. and Burke, D. "How Hewlett-Packard Lost Its Way," Accessed 5/30/13, www.tech .fortune.cnn.com/2012/05/08/500-hp-apotheker/; Lohr, S. "Lewis E. Platt, 64, Chief of Hewlett-Packard in 1990's Dies," nytimes.com, Accessed 5/30/13, www.nytimes.com/2005/09/10/technology/10platt .html; Stanford Graduate School of Business Case SM-130. "HP and Compaq Combined: In Search of Scale and Scope," Accessed 5/30/13, www.cendix.com/downloads/education/HP%20Compaq .pdf; Elgin, B. "The Inside Story of Carly's Ouster," Accessed 5/30/13, www.businessweek.com/ stories/2005-02-20/the-inside-story-of-carlys-ouster; Oracle.com, "Mark Hurd – President," Accessed, 5/30/13, www.oracle.com/us/corporate/press/executives/mark-hurd-170533.html; Gregory, S. "Corporate Scandals: Why HP had to Oust Mark Hurd," Accessed 5/30/13, www.time.com/time/business/ article/0,8599,2009617,00.html; Arnold, L. and Turner, N. "Patricia Dunn, HP Chairman Fired in Spying Scandal, Dies at 58," Accessed 5/30/13, www.businessweek.com/news/2011-12-05/patricia-dunn-hp-chairman-fired-in-spying-scandal-dies-at-58.html.

Role of the Board of Directors

A *corporation* is a mechanism established to allow different parties to contribute capital, expertise, and labor for their mutual benefit. The investor/shareholder participates in the profits (in the form of dividends and stock price increases) of the enterprise without taking responsibility for the operations. Management runs the company without being responsible for personally providing the funds. To make this possible, laws have been passed that give shareholders limited liability and, correspondingly, limited involvement in a corporation's activities. That involvement does include, however, the right to elect directors who have a legal duty to represent the shareholders and protect their interests. As representatives of the shareholders, directors have both the authority and the responsibility to establish basic corporate policies and to ensure that they are followed.[1]

The board of directors, therefore, has an obligation to approve all decisions that might affect the long-term performance of the corporation. This means that the corporation is fundamentally governed by the *board of directors* overseeing *top management*, with the concurrence of the *shareholder*. The term **corporate governance** refers to the relationship among these three groups in determining the direction and performance of the corporation.[2]

Over the past decade and a half, shareholders and various interest groups have seriously questioned the role of the board of directors in corporations. They are concerned that inside board members may use their position to feather their own nests and that outside board members often lack sufficient knowledge, involvement, and enthusiasm to do an adequate job of monitoring and providing guidance to top management. Instances of widespread corruption and questionable accounting practices at Enron, Global Crossing, WorldCom, Tyco, and Qwest, among others, seem to justify their concerns. The board at HP appeared to be incapable of deciding upon the direction of the business, moving CEOs in and out as its ideas changed.

The general public has not only become more aware and more critical of many boards' apparent lack of responsibility for corporate activities, it has begun to push government to demand accountability. As a result, the board as a rubber stamp of the CEO or as a bastion of the "old-boy" selection system is slowly being replaced by more active, more professional boards.

RESPONSIBILITIES OF THE BOARD

Laws and standards defining the responsibilities of boards of directors vary from country to country. For example, board members in Ontario, Canada, face more than 100 provincial and federal laws governing director liability. The United States, however, has no clear national standards or federal laws. Specific requirements of directors vary, depending on the state in which the corporate charter is issued. There is, nevertheless, a developing worldwide consensus concerning the major responsibilities of a board. An article by Spencer Stuart written by an international team of contributors suggested the following five **board of director responsibilities**:

1. Effective Board Leadership including the processes, makeup and output of the board
2. Strategy of the Organization
3. Risk vs. initiative and the overall risk profile of the organization
4. Succession planning for the board and top management team
5. Sustainability[3]

These results are in agreement with a survey by the National Association of Corporate Directors, in which U.S. CEOs reported that the four most important issues boards should address are corporate performance, CEO succession, strategic planning, and corporate governance.[4] Directors in the United States must make certain, in addition to the duties just listed, that the corporation is managed in accordance with the laws of the state in which it is incorporated. Because more than half of all publicly traded companies in the United States are incorporated in the state of Delaware, this state's laws and rulings have more impact than do those of any other state.[5] Directors must also ensure management's adherence to laws and regulations, such as those dealing with the issuance of securities, insider trading, and other conflict-of-interest situations. They must also be aware of the needs and demands of constituent groups so that they can achieve a judicious balance among the interests of these diverse groups while ensuring the continued functioning of the corporation.

In a legal sense, the board is required to direct the affairs of the corporation but not to manage them. It is charged by law to act with **due care**. If a director or the board as a whole fails to act with due care and, as a result, the corporation is in some way harmed, the careless director or directors can be held personally liable for the harm done. This is no small concern given that one survey of outside directors revealed that more than 40% had been named as part of lawsuits against corporations.[6] For example, board members of Equitable Life in Britain were sued for up to US$5.4 billion for their failure to question the CEO's reckless policies.[7] For this reason, corporations have found that they need directors' and officers' liability insurance in order to attract people to become members of boards of directors.

A 2011 global survey of directors by McKinsey & Company revealed the average amount of time boards spend on a given issue during their meetings. The top 5 are:[8]

- Strategy (development and analysis of strategies)—23%
- Execution (prioritizing programs and approving mergers and acquisitions)—22%
- Performance management (development of incentives and measuring performance)—18%
- Governance and compliance (nominations, compensation, audits)—14%
- Talent management—10%

Role of the Board in Strategic Management

How does a board of directors fulfill these many responsibilities? The *role of the board of directors in strategic management* is to carry out three basic tasks:

- **Monitor:** By acting through its committees, a board can keep abreast of developments inside and outside the corporation, bringing to management's attention developments it might have overlooked. A board should at the minimum carry out this task.

- **Evaluate and influence:** A board can examine management's proposals, decisions, and actions; agree or disagree with them; give advice and offer suggestions; and outline alternatives. More active boards perform this task in addition to monitoring.

- **Initiate and determine:** A board can delineate a corporation's mission and specify strategic options to its management. Only the most active boards take on this task in addition to the two previous ones.

Board of Directors' Continuum

A board of directors is involved in strategic management to the extent that it carries out the three tasks of monitoring, evaluating and influencing, and initiating and determining. The **board of directors' continuum** shown in **Figure 2–1** shows the possible degree of involvement (from low to high) in the strategic management process. Boards can range from phantom boards with no real involvement to catalyst boards with a very high degree of involvement.[9] Research suggests that active board involvement in strategic management is positively related to a corporation's financial performance and its credit rating.[10]

Highly involved boards tend to be very active. They take their tasks of monitoring, evaluating and influencing, and initiating and determining very seriously; they provide advice when necessary and keep management alert. As depicted in **Figure 2–1**, their heavy involvement in the strategic management process places them in the active participation or even catalyst positions. Although 74% of public corporations have periodic board meetings devoted primarily to the review of overall company strategy, the boards may not have had much influence in generating the plan itself.[11] The same 2011 global survey of directors by McKinsey & Company found that 44% of respondents reviewed and approved management's proposed strategy, 41% developed strategy with management, and 11% developed strategy, which management was then assigned to execute. Those boards reporting high influence typically shared a common

FIGURE 2–1   Board of Directors' Continuum

DEGREE OF INVOLVEMENT IN STRATEGIC MANAGEMENT

Low (Passive)					High (Active)
Phantom	**Rubber Stamp**	**Minimal Review**	**Nominal Participation**	**Active Participation**	**Catalyst**
Never knows what to do, if anything; no degree of involvement.	Permits officers to make all decisions. It votes as the officers recommend on action issues.	Formally reviews selected issues that officers bring to its attention.	Involved to a limited degree in the performance or review of selected key decisions, indicators, or programs of managment.	Approves, questions, and makes final decisions on mission, strategy, policies, and objectives. Has active board committees. Performs fiscal and management audits.	Takes the leading role in establishing and modifying the mission, objectives, strategy, and policies. It has a very active strategy committee.

SOURCE: T. L. Wheelen and J. D. Hunger, "Board of Directors' Continuum," Copyright © 1994 by Wheelen and Hunger Associates. Reprinted by permission.

plan for creating value and had healthy debate about what actions the company should take to create value. Together with top management, these high-influence boards considered global trends and future scenarios and developed plans. In contrast, those boards with low influence tended not to do any of these things.[12] Nevertheless, studies indicate that boards are becoming increasingly active.

These and other studies suggest that most large publicly owned corporations have boards that operate at some point between nominal and active participation. Some corporations with actively participating boards are Target, Medtronic, Best Western, Service Corporation International, Bank of Montreal, Mead Corporation, Rolm and Haas, Whirlpool, 3M, Apria Healthcare, General Electric, Pfizer, and Texas Instruments.[13] Target, a corporate governance leader, has a board that each year sets three top priorities, such as strategic direction, capital allocation, and succession planning. Each of these priority topics is placed at the top of the agenda for at least one meeting. Target's board also devotes one meeting a year to setting the strategic direction for each major operating division.[14]

As a board becomes less involved in the affairs of the corporation, it moves farther to the left on the continuum (see **Figure 2–1**). On the far left are passive phantom or rubber-stamp boards that typically never initiate or determine strategy unless a crisis occurs. In these situations, the CEO also serves as Chairman of the Board, personally nominates all directors, and works to keep board members under his or her control by giving them the "mushroom treatment"—throw manure on them and keep them in the dark!

Generally, the smaller the corporation, the less active is its board of directors in strategic management.[15] In an entrepreneurial venture, for example, the privately held corporation may be 100% owned by the founders—who also manage the company. In this case, there is no need for an active board to protect the interests of the owner-manager shareholders—the interests of the owners and the managers are identical. In this instance, a board is really unnecessary and only meets to satisfy legal requirements. If stock is sold to outsiders to finance growth, however, the board becomes more active. Key investors want seats on the board so they can oversee their investment. To the extent that they still control most of the stock, however, the founders dominate the board. Friends, family members, and key shareholders usually become members, but the board acts primarily as a rubber stamp for any proposals put forward by the owner-managers. In this type of company, the founder tends to be both CEO and Chairman of the Board and the board includes few people who are not affiliated with the firm or family.[16] This cozy relationship between the board and management should change, however, when the corporation goes public and stock is more widely dispersed. The founders, who are still acting as management, may sometimes make decisions that conflict with the needs of the other shareholders (especially if the founders own less than 50% of the common stock). In this instance, problems could occur if the board fails to become more active in terms of its roles and responsibilities. This situation can occur in large organizations as well. Even after the high profile IPO, Facebook was still more than 50% controlled by founder Mark Zuckerberg and he used his position to make significant strategic decisions without input from the board of directors. In 2012, just ahead of the IPO of Facebook, he bought Instagram for roughly US$1 billion and only then informed the board of his move. [17]

MEMBERS OF A BOARD OF DIRECTORS

The boards of most publicly owned corporations are composed of both inside and outside directors. **Inside directors** (sometimes called management directors) are typically officers or executives employed by the corporation. **Outside directors** (sometimes called non-management directors) may be executives of other firms but are not employees of the board's corporation. Although there is yet no clear evidence indicating that a high proportion of outsiders on a board results in improved financial performance,[18] there is a trend in

INNOVATION issue

JCPENNEY AND INNOVATION

Ron Johnson joined erstwhile retailer JCPenney in November 2011 with a mandate from the board of directors to shake up the organization. The board members were not interested in another decade of classic retailer wisdom, they wanted someone who would create a new JCPenney. They got exactly what they were looking for. The question is whether that bold move will allow the company to thrive or force it out of business.

Johnson was the architect behind the "cheap chic" approach at Target before he moved to Apple with the mandate to create "THE" store experience. He designed an Apple retail approach that is the envy of the retailer world and in the process created the world's most profitable stores. Johnson was personally recruited to take over JCPenney by Bill Ackman. His company (Pershing Square Capital Management) owns 18% of JCPenney.

Johnson's vision was to create a company that was not dependent upon sales coupons or continuous promotions for its survival. He joined a 110-year-old company that was running 590 different promotions a year that cost the company (in promotion costs alone) more than US$1 billion. Ninety-nine percent of those promotions were ignored by

their primary customer group. The real sales price for virtually every product in the store was substantially less than the list price on the shelf.

The fundamental strategic approach was sound. He was separating the company from its competitors and doing so with an approach that was rare in the retailing world, durable as long as the competitors didn't believe that approach would work, and might have been valuable for the company both from a cost containment approach as well as its potential to draw in new customers. The story was over almost before it began. Sales plummeted, profits evaporated and after 18 months on the job, Johnson was fired only to be replaced by the former CEO of the company. Perhaps Johnson's biggest failure was rollout. Rather than experimenting with the new concept to refine the effort, he demanded that it be put in place system-wide. He had the support of the board until his unwillingness to compromise or re-evaluate his strategy drove the board to act.

....

SOURCES: Berfield, S. and Maheshwari, S. 2012. "J.C. Penney vs. The Bargain Hunters," *Bloomberg Businessweek*, May 28 – June 3, 2012, pg. 21–22. Rooney, J. "JCPenney's New Strategy a Tough Sell on the Sales Floor," Forbes.com, Accessed 5/30/13, www.forbes.com/sites/jenniferrooney/2012/03/14/jc-penneys-new-strategy-a-tough-sell-on-the-sales-floor/

the United States to increase the number of outsiders on boards and to reduce the total size of the board.[19] The board of directors of a typical large U.S. corporation has an average of 10 directors, 2 of whom are insiders.[20]

Outsiders thus account for 80% of the board members in large U.S. corporations (approximately the same as in Canada). Boards in the UK typically have 5 inside and 5 outside directors, whereas in France boards usually consist of 3 insiders and 8 outsiders. Japanese boards, in contrast, contain 2 outsiders and 12 insiders.[21] The board of directors in a typical small U.S. corporation has 4 to 5 members, of whom only 1 or 2 are outsiders.[22] Research from large and small corporations reveals a negative relationship between board size and firm profitability.[23]

People who favor a high proportion of outsiders state that outside directors are less biased and more likely to evaluate management's performance objectively than are inside directors. This is the main reason why the U.S. Securities and Exchange Commission (SEC) in 2003 required that a majority of directors on the board be independent outsiders. The SEC also required that all listed companies staff their audit, compensation, and nominating/corporate governance committees entirely with independent, outside members. This view is in agreement with **agency theory**, which states that problems arise in corporations because the agents (top management) are not willing to bear responsibility for their decisions unless they own a substantial amount of stock in the corporation. The theory suggests that a majority of a board needs to be from outside the firm so that top management is prevented from acting selfishly to the detriment of the shareholders. For example, proponents of agency theory argue that managers in management-controlled firms (contrasted with owner-controlled firms in which the founder or family still own a significant amount of stock) select less risky strategies with quick payoffs in order to keep their jobs.[24] This view is supported by research revealing that manager controlled firms (with weak boards) are more likely to go into debt to diversify into unrelated markets (thus quickly boosting sales and assets to justify higher salaries for themselves). These actions result in poorer long-term performance than owner-controlled firms.[25] Boards with a larger proportion of outside directors tend to favor growth through international expansion and innovative venturing activities than do boards with a smaller proportion of outsiders.[26] Outsiders tend to be more objective and critical of corporate activities. For example, research reveals that the likelihood of a firm engaging in illegal behavior or being sued declines with the addition of outsiders on the board.[27] Research on family businesses has found that boards with a larger number of outsiders on the board tended to have better corporate governance and better performance than did boards with fewer outsiders.[28]

In contrast, those who prefer inside over outside directors contend that outside directors are less effective than are insiders because the outsiders are less likely to have the necessary interest, availability, or competency. **Stewardship theory** proposes that, because of their long tenure with the corporation, insiders (senior executives) tend to identify with the corporation and its success. Rather than use the firm for their own ends, these executives are thus most interested in guaranteeing the continued life and success of the corporation. (See the **Strategy Highlight** feature for a discussion of Agency Theory contrasted with Stewardship Theory.) Excluding all insiders but the CEO reduces the opportunity for outside directors to see potential successors in action or to obtain alternate points of view of management decisions. Outside directors may sometimes serve on so many boards that they spread their time and interest too thin to actively fulfill their responsibilities. The average board member of a U.S. Fortune 500 firm serves on three boards. Research indicates that firm performance decreases as the number of directorships held by the average board member increases.[29] Although only 40% of surveyed U.S. boards currently limit the number of directorships a board member may hold in other corporations, 60% limit the number of boards on which their CEO may be a member.[30]

Those who question the value of having more outside board members point out that the term *outsider* is too simplistic because some outsiders are not truly objective and should be considered more as insiders than as outsiders. For example, there can be:

1. **Affiliated directors**, who, though not really employed by the corporation, handle the legal or insurance work for the company or are important suppliers (and thus dependent on the current management for a key part of their business). These outsiders face a conflict of interest and are not likely to be objective. As a result of recent actions by the U.S. Congress, the Securities and Exchange Commission, the New York Stock Exchange, and NASDAQ, affiliated directors are being banned from U.S. corporate boardrooms. U.S. boards can no longer include representatives of major suppliers or customers or even professional organizations that might do business with the firm, even though these people could provide valuable knowledge and expertise.[31] The New York Stock Exchange decided in 2004 that anyone paid by the company during the previous three years could not be classified as an independent outside director.[32]

2. **Retired executive directors**, who used to work for the company, such as the past CEO who is partly responsible for much of the corporation's current strategy and who probably groomed the current CEO as his or her replacement. In the recent past, many boards of large firms kept the firm's recently retired CEO on the board for a year or two after retirement as a courtesy, especially if he or she had performed well as the CEO. It is almost certain, however, that this person will not be able to objectively evaluate the corporation's

STRATEGY highlight

AGENCY THEORY VERSUS STEWARDSHIP THEORY IN CORPORATE GOVERNANCE

Managers of large, modern publicly held corporations are typically not the owners. In fact, most of today's top managers own only nominal amounts of stock in the corporation they manage. The real owners (shareholders) elect boards of directors who hire managers as their agents to run the firm's day-to-day activities. Once hired, how trustworthy are these executives? Do they put themselves or the firm first? There are two significant schools of thought on this.

Agency Theory. As suggested in the classic study by Berle and Means, top managers are, in effect, "hired hands" who are very likely more interested in their personal welfare than that of the shareholders. For example, management might emphasize strategies, such as acquisitions, that increase the size of the firm (to become more powerful and to demand increased pay and benefits) or that diversify the firm into unrelated businesses (to reduce short-term risk and to allow them to put less effort into a core product line that may be facing difficulty) but that result in a reduction of dividends and/or stock price.

Agency theory is concerned with analyzing and resolving two problems that occur in relationships between principals (owners/shareholders) and their agents (top management):

1. *Conflict of interest* arises when the desires or objectives of the owners and the agents conflict. For example, attitudes toward risk may be quite different. Agents may shy away from riskier strategies in order to protect their jobs.

2. *Moral hazard* refers to the situation where it is difficult or expensive for the owners to verify what the agents are actually doing.

According to agency theory, the likelihood that these problems will occur increases when stock is widely held (that is, when no one shareholder owns more than a small percentage of the total common stock), when the board of directors is composed of people who know little of the company or who are personal friends of top management, and when a high percentage of board members are inside (management) directors.

To better align the interests of the agents with those of the owners and to increase the corporation's overall performance, agency theory suggests that top management

have a significant degree of ownership in the firm and/or have a strong financial stake in its long-term performance. In support of this argument, research indicates a positive relationship between corporate performance and the amount of stock owned by directors.

Stewardship Theory. In contrast, stewardship theory suggests that executives tend to be more motivated to act in the best interests of the corporation than in their own self-interests. Whereas agency theory focuses on extrinsic rewards that serve lower-level needs, such as pay and security, stewardship theory focuses on the higher-order needs, such as achievement and self-actualization. Stewardship theory argues that senior executives over time tend to view the corporation as an extension of themselves. Rather than use the firm for their own ends, these executives are most interested in guaranteeing the continued life and success of the corporation. The relationship between the board and top management is thus one of principal and steward, not principal and agent ("hired hand"). Stewardship theory notes that in a widely held corporation, the shareholder is free to sell his or her stock at any time. In fact, the average share of stock is held less than 10 months. A diversified investor or speculator may care little about risk at the company level—preferring management to assume extraordinary risk so long as the return is adequate. Because executives in a firm cannot easily leave their jobs when in difficulty, they are more interested in a merely satisfactory return and put heavy emphasis on the firm's continued survival. Thus, stewardship theory argues that in many instances top management may care more about a company's long-term success than do more short-term–oriented shareholders.

....

SOURCES: For more information about agency and stewardship theory, see A. A. Berle and G. C. Means, *The Modern Corporation and Private Property* (NY: Macmillan, 1936). Also see J. H. Davis, F. D. Schoorman, and L. Donaldson, "Toward a Stewardship Theory of Management," *Academy of Management Review* (January 1997), pp. 20–47; P. J. Lane, A. A. Cannella, Jr., and M. H. Lubatkin, "Agency Problems as Antecedents to Unrelated Mergers and Diversification: Amihud and Lev Reconsidered," *Strategic Management Journal* (June 1998), pp. 555–578; M. L. Hayward and D. C. Hambrick, "Explaining the Premiums Paid for Large Acquisitions: Evidence of CEO Hubris," *Administrative Science Quarterly* (March 1997), pp. 103–127; and C. M. Christensen and S. D. Anthony, "Put Investors in Their Place," *BusinessWeek* (May 28, 2007), p. 108.

performance. Because of the likelihood of a conflict of interest, only 30% of boards in the Americas and 28% in Europe now include the former CEO on their boards.[33]

3. **Family directors,** who are descendants of the founder and own significant blocks of stock (with personal agendas based on a family relationship with the current CEO). The Schlitz Brewing Company, for example, was unable to complete its turnaround strategy with a non-family CEO because family members serving on the board wanted their money out of the company, forcing it to be sold.[34]

The majority of outside directors are active or retired CEOs and COOs of other corporations. Others are major investors/shareholders, academicians, attorneys, consultants, former government officials, and bankers. Given that 66% of the outstanding stock in the largest U.S. and UK corporations is now owned by institutional investors, such as mutual funds and pension plans, these investors are taking an increasingly active role in board membership and activities.[35] For example, TIAA-CREF's Corporate Governance team monitors governance practices of the 4000 companies in which it invests its pension funds through its Corporate Assessment Program. If its analysis of a company reveals problems, TIAA-CREF first sends letters stating its concerns, followed up by visits, and it finally sponsors a shareholder resolution in opposition to management's actions.[36] Institutional investors are also powerful in many other countries. In Germany, bankers are represented on almost every board—primarily because they own large blocks of stock in German corporations. In Denmark, Sweden, Belgium, and Italy, however, investment companies assume this role. For example, the investment company Investor casts 42.5% of the Electrolux shareholder votes, thus guaranteeing itself positions on the Electrolux board.

Boards of directors have been working to increase the number of women and minorities serving on boards and well they should. A 2012 study of 2360 companies found that shares of companies with female board members outperformed comparable businesses with all-male boards by 26% worldwide over a six-year time period.[37] Korn/Ferry International reported that amongst the 100 largest companies listed in 2011 that 96% of boards of directors had at least one female director, while at the same time women made up only 16% of all directors.

This number was quite different when we look at the situation in some other countries. A 2011 study by Korn/Ferry examined the 100 largest companies in seven countries across the Pacific Rim (Australia, China, Hong Kong, India, Malaysia, Singapore, and New Zealand). They found female board representation to be:

- Australia—(11.2%)
- China—(8.1%)
- Hong Kong—(8.6%)
- India—(4.7%)
- Malaysia—(7.8%)
- Singapore—(6.4%)
- New Zealand—(7.5%)[38]

Korn/Ferry's survey also revealed that 78% of the U.S. boards had at least one ethnic minority in 2007 (African-American, 47%; Latino, 19%; Asian, 11%) as director compared to only 47% in 1995, comprising around 14% of total directors.[39] Among the top 200 S&P companies in the U.S., however, 84% have at least one African-American director.[40] The globalization of business is having an impact on board membership. According to the Spencer Stuart executive recruiting firm, 33% of U.S. boards had an international director.[41] Europe was the most "globalized" region of the world, with most companies reporting one or more non-national directors.[42] Although Asian and Latin American boards are still predominantly staffed by nationals, they are working to add more international directors.[43]

A 2011 study of the top 100 public firms in the U.S. found that 3.7% of the companies paid their directors more than US$150K as a cash retainer (not counting money paid for meeting attendance or other obligations). The same study found that the median cash retainer was between US$75K and US$100K (26.7%).[44] Directors serving on the boards of small companies usually received much less compensation (around US$10,000). One study found directors of a sample of large U.S. firms to hold, on average, 3% of their corporations' outstanding stock.[45]

The vast majority of inside directors are the chief executive officer and either the chief operating officer (if not also the CEO) or the chief financial officer. Presidents or vice presidents of key operating divisions or functional units sometimes serve on the board. Few, if any, inside directors receive any extra compensation for assuming this extra duty. Very rarely does a U.S. board include any lower-level operating employees.

Codetermination: Should Employees Serve on Boards?

Codetermination, the inclusion of a corporation's workers on its board, began only recently in the United States. Corporations such as Chrysler, Northwest Airlines, United Airlines (UAL), and Wheeling-Pittsburgh Steel added representatives from employee associations to their boards as part of union agreements or Employee Stock Ownership Plans (ESOPs). For example, United Airlines workers traded 15% in pay cuts for 55% of the company (through an ESOP) and 3 of the firm's 12 board seats. In this instance, workers represent themselves on the board not so much as employees but primarily as owners. At Chrysler, however, the United Auto Workers union obtained a temporary seat on the board as part of a union contract agreement in exchange for changes in work rules and reductions in benefits. This was at a time when Chrysler was facing bankruptcy in the late 1970s. In situations like this when a director represents an internal stakeholder, critics raise the issue of conflict of interest. Can a member of the board, who is privy to confidential managerial information, function, for example, as a union leader whose primary duty is to fight for the best benefits for his or her members? Although the movement to place employees on the boards of directors of U.S. companies shows little likelihood of increasing (except through employee stock ownership), the European experience reveals an increasing acceptance of worker participation (without ownership) on corporate boards.

Germany pioneered codetermination during the 1950s with a two-tiered system: (1) a supervisory board elected by shareholders and employees to approve or decide corporate strategy and policy and (2) a management board (composed primarily of top management) appointed by the supervisory board to manage the company's activities. Most other Western European countries have either passed similar codetermination legislation (as in Sweden, Denmark, Norway, and Austria) or use worker councils to work closely with management (as in Belgium, Luxembourg, France, Italy, Ireland, and the Netherlands).

Interlocking Directorates

CEOs often nominate chief executives (as well as board members) from other firms to membership on their own boards in order to create an interlocking directorate. A *direct* **interlocking directorate** occurs when two firms share a director or when an executive of one firm sits on the board of a second firm. An *indirect* interlock occurs when two corporations have directors who also serve on the board of a third firm, such as a bank.

Although the Clayton Act and the Banking Act of 1933 prohibit interlocking directorates by U.S. companies competing in the same industry, interlocking continues to occur in almost all corporations, especially large ones. Interlocking occurs because large firms have a large impact on other corporations and these other corporations, in turn, have some control over the firm's inputs and marketplace. For example, most large corporations in the United States, Japan, and Germany are interlocked either directly or indirectly with financial institutions.[46]

Eleven of the 15 largest U.S. corporations have at least two board members who sit together on another board. Twenty percent of the 1000 largest U.S. firms share at least one board member.[47]

Interlocking directorates are useful for gaining both inside information about an uncertain environment and objective expertise about potential strategies and tactics.[48] For example, Kleiner Perkins, a high-tech venture capital firm, not only has seats on the boards of the companies in which it invests, but it also has executives (which Kleiner Perkins hired) from one entrepreneurial venture who serve as directors on others. Kleiner Perkins refers to its network of interlocked firms as its *keiretsu*, a Japanese term for a set of companies with interlocking business relationships and share-holdings.[49] Family-owned corporations, however, are less likely to have interlocking directorates than are corporations with highly dispersed stock ownership, probably because family-owned corporations do not like to dilute their corporate control by adding outsiders to boardroom discussions.

There is some concern, however, when the chairs of separate corporations serve on each other's boards. Twenty-two such pairs of corporate chairs (who typically also served as their firm's CEO) existed in 2003. In one instance, the three chairmen of Anheuser-Busch, SBC Communications, and Emerson Electric served on all three of the boards. Typically, a CEO sits on only one board in addition to his or her own—down from two additional boards in previous years. Although such interlocks may provide valuable information, they are increasingly frowned upon because of the possibility of collusion.[50] Nevertheless, evidence indicates that well-interlocked corporations are better able to survive in a highly competitive environment.[51]

NOMINATION AND ELECTION OF BOARD MEMBERS

Traditionally, the CEO of a corporation decided whom to invite to board membership and merely asked the shareholders for approval in the annual proxy statement. All nominees were usually elected. There are some dangers, however, in allowing the CEO free rein in nominating directors. The CEO might select only board members who, in the CEO's opinion, will not disturb the company's policies and functioning. Given that the average length of service of a U.S. board member is three 3-year terms (but can range up to 20 years for some boards), CEO-friendly, passive boards are likely to result. This is especially likely given that only 7% of surveyed directors indicated that their company had term limits for board members. Nevertheless, 60% of U.S. boards and 58% of European boards have a mandatory retirement age—typically around 70.[52] Research reveals that boards rated as least effective by the Corporate Library, a corporate governance research firm, tend to have members serving longer (an average of 9.7 years) than boards rated as most effective (7.5 years).[53] Directors selected by the CEO often feel that they should go along with any proposal the CEO makes. Thus board members find themselves accountable to the very management they are charged to oversee. Because this is likely to happen, more boards are using a nominating committee to nominate new outside board members for the shareholders to elect. Ninety-seven percent of large U.S. corporations now use nominating committees to identify potential directors. This practice is less common in Europe where 60% of boards use nominating committees.[54]

Many corporations whose directors serve terms of more than one year divide the board into classes and stagger elections so that only a portion of the board stands for election each year. This is called a *staggered board*. Sixty-three percent of U.S. boards currently have staggered boards.[55] Arguments in favor of this practice are that it provides continuity by reducing the chance of an abrupt turnover in its membership and that it reduces the likelihood of electing people unfriendly to management (who might be interested in a hostile takeover) through cumulative voting. An argument against staggered boards is that they make it more difficult for concerned shareholders to curb a CEO's power—especially when that CEO is also Chairman of the board. An increasing number of shareholder resolutions to replace staggered boards with annual elections of all board members are currently being passed at annual meetings.

When nominating people for election to a board of directors, it is important that nominees have previous experience dealing with corporate issues. For example, research reveals that a firm makes better acquisition decisions when the firm's outside directors have had experience with such decisions.[56]

A survey of directors of U.S. corporations revealed the following criteria in a good director:

- Willing to challenge management when necessary—95%
- Special expertise important to the company—67%
- Available outside meetings to advise management—57%
- Expertise on global business issues—41%
- Understands the firm's key technologies and processes—39%
- Brings external contacts that are potentially valuable to the firm—33%
- Has detailed knowledge of the firm's industry—31%
- Has high visibility in his or her field—31%
- Is accomplished at representing the firm to stakeholders—18%[57]

ORGANIZATION OF THE BOARD

The size of a board in the United States is determined by the corporation's charter and its bylaws, in compliance with state laws. Although some states require a minimum number of board members, most corporations have quite a bit of discretion in determining board size. The average large, publicly held U.S. firm has 10 directors on its board. The average small, privately held company has 4 to 5 members. The average size of boards elsewhere is Japan, 14; Non-Japan Asia, 9; Germany, 16; UK, 10; and France, 11.[58]

Approximately 68% of the 100 largest U.S. company's top executives hold the dual designation of Chairman and CEO.[59] The combined Chair/CEO position is being increasingly criticized because of the potential for conflict of interest. The CEO is supposed to concentrate on strategy, planning, external relations, and responsibility to the board. The Chairman's responsibility is to ensure that the board and its committees perform their functions as stated in the board's charter. Further, the Chairman schedules board meetings and presides over the annual shareholders' meeting. Critics of having one person in the two offices ask how the board can properly oversee top management if the Chairman is also a part of top management. For this reason, the Chairman and CEO roles are separated by law in Germany, the Netherlands, South Africa, and Finland. A similar law has been considered in the United Kingdom and Australia. Although research is mixed regarding the impact of the combined Chair/CEO position on overall corporate financial performance, firm stock price and credit ratings both respond negatively to announcements of CEOs also assuming the Chairman position.[60] Research also shows that corporations with a combined Chair/CEO have a greater likelihood of fraudulent financial reporting when CEO stock options are not present.[61]

Many of those who prefer that the Chairman and CEO positions be combined agree that the outside directors should elect a **lead director**. This person is consulted by the Chair/CEO regarding board affairs and coordinates the annual evaluation of the CEO.[62] The lead director position is very popular in the United Kingdom, where it originated. Of those U.S. companies combining the Chairman and CEO positions, 96% had a lead director.[63] Korn/Ferry found that in 2003 72% of respondents thought a lead director was the right thing to do, while 85%

thought so in 2007. A lead director creates a balance in power when the CEO is also the Chair of the Board. The same survey showed that board members are spending 16 hours a month on board business and that 86% were either very satisfied or extremely satisfied with their role in the business. The lead director becomes increasingly important because 94% of U.S. boards in 2007 (compared to only 41% in 2002) held regular executive sessions without the CEO being present.[64] Nevertheless, there are many ways in which an unscrupulous Chair/CEO can guarantee a director's loyalty. Research indicates that an increase in board independence often results in higher levels of CEO ingratiation behavior aimed at persuading directors to support CEO proposals. Long-tenured directors who support the CEO may use social pressure to persuade a new board member to conform to the group. Directors are more likely to be recommended for membership on other boards if they "don't rock the boat" and engage in low levels of monitoring and control behavior.[65] Even in those situations when the board has a nominating committee composed only of outsiders, the committee often obtains the CEO's approval for each new board candidate.[66]

The most effective boards accomplish much of their work through committees. Although they do not usually have legal duties, most committees are granted full power to act with the authority of the board between board meetings. Typical standing committees (in order of prevalence) are the audit (100%), compensation (99%), nominating (97%), corporate governance (94%), stock options (84%), director compensation (52%), and executive (43%) committees.[67] The executive committee is usually composed of two inside and two outside directors located nearby who can meet between board meetings to attend to matters that must be settled quickly. This committee acts as an extension of the board and, consequently, may have almost unrestricted authority in certain areas.[68] Except for the executive, finance, and investment committees, board committees are now typically staffed only by outside directors. Although each board committee typically meets four to five times annually, the average audit committee met nine times during 2007.[69]

IMPACT OF THE SARBANES–OXLEY ACT ON U.S. CORPORATE GOVERNANCE

In response to the many corporate scandals uncovered since 2000, the U.S. Congress passed the **Sarbanes–Oxley Act** in June 2002. This act was designed to protect shareholders from the excesses and failed oversight that characterized criminal activities at Enron, Tyco, WorldCom, Adelphia Communications, Qwest, and Global Crossing, among other prominent firms. Several key elements of Sarbanes–Oxley were designed to formalize greater board independence and oversight. For example, the act requires that all directors serving on the audit committee be independent of the firm and receive no fees other than for services of the director. In addition, boards may no longer grant loans to corporate officers. The act has also established formal procedures for individuals (known as "whistleblowers") to report incidents of questionable accounting or auditing. Firms are prohibited from retaliating against anyone reporting wrongdoing. Both the CEO and CFO must certify the corporation's financial information. The act bans auditors from providing both external and internal audit services to the same company. It also requires that a firm identify whether it has a "financial expert" serving on the audit committee who is independent from management.

Although the cost to a large corporation of implementing the provisions of the law was US$8.5 million in 2004, the first year of compliance, the costs to a large firm fell to US$1–$5 million annually during the following years as accounting and information processes were refined and made more efficient.[70] Pitney Bowes, for example, saved more than US$500,000 in 2005 simply by consolidating four accounts receivable offices into one. Similar savings were realized at Cisco and Genentech.[71] An additional benefit of the increased disclosure requirements is more reliable corporate financial statements. Companies are now reporting numbers with fewer adjustments for unusual charges and write-offs, which in the past have been used to boost reported earnings.[72] The new rules have also made it more difficult for firms to post-date executive stock options. "This is an unintended consequence of disclosure," remarked Gregory Taxin, CEO of Glass, Lewis & Company, a stock research firm.[73] See the **Global Issue** feature to learn how board activism affects the managing of a global company.

Improving Governance

In implementing the Sarbanes–Oxley Act, the U.S. Securities and Exchange Commission (SEC) required in 2003 that a company disclose whether it has adopted a code of ethics that applies to the CEO and to the company's principal financial officer. Among other things, the SEC requires that the audit, nominating, and compensation committees be staffed entirely by outside directors. The New York Stock Exchange reinforced the mandates of Sarbanes–Oxley by requiring that companies have a nominating/governance committee composed entirely of independent outside directors. Similarly, NASDAQ rules require that nominations for new directors be made by either a nominating committee of independent outsiders or by a majority of independent outside directors.[74]

Partially in response to Sarbanes–Oxley, a survey of directors of Fortune 1000 U.S. companies by Mercer Delta Consulting and the University of Southern California revealed that 60% of directors were spending more time on board matters than before Sarbanes–Oxley, with 85% spending more time on their company's accounts, 83% more on governance practices, and 52% on monitoring financial performance.[75] Newly elected outside directors with financial management experience increased to 10% of all outside directors in 2003 from only 1% of outsiders in 1998.[76] Seventy-eight percent of Fortune 1000 U.S. boards in 2006 required that directors own stock in the corporation, compared to just 36% in Europe, and 26% in Asia.[77]

Evaluating Governance

To help investors evaluate a firm's corporate governance, a number of independent rating services, such as Standard & Poor's (S&P), Moody's, Morningstar, The Corporate Library, Institutional Shareholder Services (ISS), and Governance Metrics International (GMI), have established criteria for good governance. *Bloomberg Businessweek* annually publishes a list of the best and worst boards of U.S. corporations. Whereas rating service firms like S&P, Moody's, and The Corporate Library use a wide mix of research data and criteria to evaluate companies, ISS and GMI have been criticized because they primarily use public records to score firms, using simple checklists.[78] In contrast, the S&P Corporate Governance Scoring System researches four major issues:

- Ownership Structure and Influence
- Financial Stakeholder Rights and Relations
- Financial Transparency and Information Disclosure
- Board Structure and Processes

Although the S&P scoring system is proprietary and confidential, independent research using generally accepted measures of S&P's four issues revealed that moving from the poorest to the best-governed categories nearly doubled a firm's likelihood of receiving an investment-grade credit rating.[79]

Avoiding Governance Improvements

A number of corporations are concerned that various requirements to improve corporate governance will constrain top management's ability to effectively manage the company. For

GLOBAL issue

GLOBAL BUSINESS BOARD ACTIVISM AT YAHOO!

In the digital age in general and with Internet-based companies in particular, the impact of board activism now cuts across geographic boundaries like nothing has in the past. Yahoo grew to become the largest Internet search engine company in the world used by individuals in their own language.

Yahoo! was founded in a Stanford University campus trailer in early 1994 by Ph.D. candidates David Filo and Jerry Yang as a means for people to keep track of their favorite interests on the Internet. Yahoo! is an acronym for "Yet Another Hierarchical Officious Oracle." Young companies often see dramatic moves by the board of directors who are unaccustomed to the growth phases in a business. An activist board will hold management responsible for their actions and may take on the role of a catalyst board in some circumstances.

Yahoo! grew quickly before the Internet bubble nearly bankrupted the company. Terry Semel, a legendary Hollywood dealmaker who didn't even use e-mail, was hired to turn the company into a media giant. In the summer of 2002, Semel tried to buy Google for roughly US$3 billion (this was two years before Google went public). At the time, Google's revenue stood at a paltry US$240 million, while Yahoo!'s was in excess of US$800 million. Despite failures to purchase Google, Facebook, and YouTube, Yahoo! became an Internet search giant serving more than 345 million individuals a month. By 2005, Yahoo! was the number one global Internet brand. Forbes listed Semel's total compensation as US$230.6 million. His reign saw both the rise and fall of the company. The board grew increasingly dissatisfied. By 2007, the company was losing market share and repeated acquisitions had failed to produce any real bump in the stock price. The board moved to act in June 2007. Semel assumed the role of non-executive chairman and Jerry Yang became the CEO once again.

Things did not improve. There were regular calls for Yang's resignation as the company continued to flounder. At a time when tech companies were growing dramatically, Yahoo! continued its long, slow slide. Frustrated by his inability to strike deals with rivals Microsoft and Google, Yang and the board agreed that it was best for him to resign as CEO. His tenure lasted a scant 18 months.

Carol Bartz was hired in January 2009 to turn the company around and help it regain its stature. She was the former CEO of Autodesk and was viewed as a no-nonsense industry veteran. She instituted layoffs, reshuffled management, and turned over search operations to Microsoft in a deal that brought US$900 million to Yahoo!. However, shares remained effectively flat during her tenure

and market share continued to drop. The board became increasingly dissatisfied with her performance and acted suddenly in September 2011. Without a replacement in hand, she was notified via a phone call from the Chairman of the Board that she was fired.

After a lengthy search, Scott Thompson was hired as the CEO in January 2012. He had previously been the CEO of eBay's PayPal unit and had done what most experts believed was a very good job. Unfortunately, he listed a computer science degree from Stonehill College that he had not earned. He did graduate, but with an accounting degree. Activist shareholder group Third Point (who has a chair on the board and owns 5.8% of the company) released details about his resumé padding. The information was part of a proxy fight that led to a board shakeup in February of 2012. That shakeup saw most of the previous board members removed and a new group of members (approved of by Third Point) elected.

Thompson resigned and Ross Levinsohm, the former head of global media for the company, was named the interim CEO while the company did yet another search. That search ended in July 2012 when the company named Marissa Mayer as the new CEO. Mayer was a longtime Google executive who ran their search group.

The continuous changes at Yahoo! have served to damage the company's ability to perform. It is difficult to gain any momentum in an industry when the top management changes so often and with such dramatic flair. The board of directors has a responsibility to the shareholders. The question is: At what point have they failed to do their job?

. . . .

SOURCES: B. Stone. "Marissa Mayer Is Yahoo's New CEO," *Bloomberg Businessweek* (July 16, 2012), (www.businessweek.com/articles/2012-07-16/marissa-mayer-is the-new-yahoo-ceo); Yahoo! Website - http://pressroom.yahoo.net/pr/ycorp/overview.aspx; Damouni, N. "Yahoo CEO Search down to Leninsohn, Hulu CEO's Jason Kilar," Accessed 5/30/13, www.huffingtonpost.com/2012/07/05/yahoo-ceo-search-down-to-levinsohn-kilar_n_1652674.html; Temin, D. "Little Lies; Big Lies - Yahoo! CEO Scott Thompson's Revisionist History", Accessed 5/30/13; www.forbes.com/sites/daviatemin/2012/05/07/little-lies-big-lies-yahoo-ceo-scott-thomponson-revisionist-history.html; Pepitone, J. "Yahoo confirms CEO is out after resume scandal," Accessed 5/30/13. www.money.cnn.com/2012/05/13/technology/yahoo-ceo-out/index.html; Kopytoff, V. and Miller, C. "Yahoo Board Fires Chief Executive," Accessed 5/30/13 www.nytimes.com/2011/09/07/technology/carol-bartz-yahoos-chief-executive-is-fired.html; Carmody, T. "Co-Founder, Ex-CEO Jerry Yang Resigns From Yahoo's Board," Accessed 5/30/13, www.wired.com/business/2012/01/jerry-yang-resigns-yahoo/; Compensation - Terry S Semel, Accessed 5/30/13, www.forbes.com/static/pvp2005/LIRXC25.html; Vogelstein, F. "How Yahoo! Blew It," Accessed 5/30/13, www.wired.com/wired/archive/15.02/yahoo.html.

example, more U.S. public corporations have gone private in the years since the passage of Sarbanes–Oxley than before its passage. Other companies use multiple classes of stock to keep outsiders from having sufficient voting power to change the company. Insiders, usually the company's founders, get stock with extra votes, while others get second-class stock with fewer votes. For example, in 2012 Mark Zuckerberg, the CEO of Facebook, owned approximately 28% of the outstanding shares, but because of a two-class stock system, he controlled 57% of the voting shares.[80] A comprehensive analysis of firms completed in 2006 reported that approximately 6% of the companies had multiple classes of stock.[81]

Another approach to sidestepping new governance requirements is being used by corporations such as Google, Infrasource Services, Orbitz, and W&T Offshore. If a corporation in which an individual group or another company controls more than 50% of the voting shares decides to become a "controlled company," the firm is then exempt from requirements by the New York Stock Exchange and NASDAQ that a majority of the board and all members of key board committees be independent outsiders. It is easy to see that the minority shareholders have virtually no power in these situations.

TRENDS IN CORPORATE GOVERNANCE

The role of the board of directors in the strategic management of a corporation is likely to be more active in the future. Although neither the composition of boards nor the board leadership structure has been consistently linked to firm financial performance, better governance does lead to higher credit ratings and stock prices. A McKinsey survey reveals that investors are willing to pay 16% more for a corporation's stock if it is known to have good corporate governance. The investors explained that they would pay more because, in their opinion (1) good governance leads to better performance over time, (2) good governance reduces the risk of the company getting into trouble, and (3) governance is a major strategic issue.[82]

Some of today's trends in governance (particularly prevalent in the United States and the United Kingdom) that are likely to continue include the following:

- Boards are getting more involved not only in reviewing and evaluating company strategy but also in shaping it.

- Institutional investors, such as pension funds, mutual funds, and insurance companies, are becoming active on boards and are putting increasing pressure on top management to improve corporate performance. This trend is supported by a U.S. SEC requirement that a mutual fund must publicly disclose the proxy votes cast at company board meetings in its portfolio. This reduces the tendency for mutual funds to rubber-stamp management proposals.[83]

- Shareholders are demanding that directors and top managers own more than token amounts of stock in the corporation. Research indicates that boards with equity ownership use quantifiable, verifiable criteria (instead of vague, qualitative criteria) to evaluate the CEO.[84] When compensation committee members are significant shareholders, they tend to offer the CEO less salary but with a higher incentive component than do compensation committee members who own little to no stock.[85]

- Non-affiliated outside (non-management) directors are increasing their numbers and power in publicly held corporations as CEOs loosen their grip on boards. Outside members are taking charge of annual CEO evaluations.

- Women and minorities are being increasingly represented on boards.

- Boards are establishing mandatory retirement ages for board members—typically around age 70.

- Boards are evaluating not only their own overall performance, but also that of individual directors.

- Boards are getting smaller—partially because of the reduction in the number of insiders but also because boards desire new directors to have specialized knowledge and expertise instead of general experience.

- Boards continue to take more control of board functions by either splitting the combined Chair/CEO into two separate positions or establishing a lead outside director position.

- Boards are eliminating 1970s anti-takeover defenses that served to entrench current management. In just one year, for example, 66 boards repealed their staggered boards and 25 eliminated poison pills.[86]

- As corporations become more global, they are increasingly looking for board members with international experience.

- Instead of merely being able to vote for or against directors nominated by the board's nominating committee, shareholders may eventually be allowed to nominate board members. This was originally proposed by the U.S. Securities and Exchange Commission in 2004, but was not implemented. Supported by the AFL-CIO, a more open nominating process would enable shareholders to vote out directors who ignore shareholder interests.[87]

- Society, in the form of special interest groups, increasingly expects boards of directors to balance the economic goal of profitability with the social needs of society. Issues dealing with workforce diversity and environmental sustainability are now reaching the board level.

The Role of Top Management

The top management function is usually conducted by the CEO of the corporation in coordination with the COO (Chief Operating Officer) or president, executive vice president, and vice presidents of divisions and functional areas.[88] Even though strategic management involves everyone in the organization, the board of directors holds top management primarily responsible for the strategy and implementation of that strategy at the firm.[89]

RESPONSIBILITIES OF TOP MANAGEMENT

Top management responsibilities, especially those of the CEO, involve getting things accomplished through and with others in order to meet the corporate objectives. Top management's job is thus multidimensional and is oriented toward the welfare of the total organization. Specific top management tasks vary from firm to firm and are developed from an analysis of the mission, objectives, strategies, and key activities of the corporation. Tasks are typically divided among the members of the top management team. A diversity of skills can thus be very important. Research indicates that top management teams with a diversity of functional backgrounds, experiences, and length of time with the company tend to be significantly related to improvements in corporate market share and profitability.[90] In addition, highly diverse teams with some international experience tend to emphasize international growth strategies and strategic innovation, especially in uncertain environments, as a means to boost financial performance.[91] The CEO, with the support of the rest of the top management team, has two primary responsibilities when it comes to strategic management. The first is to provide

SUSTAINABILITY issue

CEO PAY AND CORPORATE PERFORMANCE

What leads a CEO to perform in the best interests of the shareholders? This has been a question for some time (see Strategy Highlight). Egregious pay for CEOs who don't perform has been a contention for many years. Leo Apotheker was paid over US$30 million dollars during his 11-month tenure at HP despite making strategic choices that cost the company hundreds of millions in sales and a share price that dropped almost in half. Financial research firm Obermatt did a study on CEO pay and company performance between 2008 and 2010. They calculated a "deserved pay" based upon earnings growth and shareholder return. They found that there is no correlation in the S&P 100 between CEO pay and company performance.

The 2011 median pay for the nation's 200 top-paid CEOs was US$14.5 million, according to a study conducted for *The New York Times*.

In 2010, the Dodd–Frank financial reform law was enacted, which requires companies to submit executive compensation packages for a nonbinding shareholder vote at least once every six years. The changes in the boardroom to the means and methods of executive compensation have been affected because of the potential for public embarrassment. While less than 2% of "say-on-pay" proposals were rejected in 2012, those rejections have led to more alignment in compensation packages throughout public corporations. In 2011, shareholders rejected CEO Vikram Pandit's (Citigroup) US$14.8 million pay package after the stock dropped over 40%, and in 2012 shareholders rejected Chiquita Brands CEO pay package by a 4-to-1 margin.

BusinessWeek reported that companies who suffered shareholder rejections of executive pay packages, as well as those that received yes votes, changed their compensation systems to align them with the interest of shareholders. By 2012, a *Wall Street Journal* analysis of the top 300 U.S. companies found that pay now generally tracked performance. Balancing the interests of the owners of a corporation with those who run the corporation is one of the most important issues in sustainable business practices.

....

SOURCES: *"Executive Pay and Performance,"* Accessed 5/30/13, www.economist.com/blogs/graphicdetail/2012/02/focus-O; Brady, D. "Say on Pay: Boards Listen When Shareholders Speak," Accessed 5/30/13, www.businessweek.com/articles/2012-06-07/say-on-pay-boards-listen-when-shareholders-speak.html; Popper, N. "C.E.O. Pay Is Rising Despite the Din," Accessed 5/30/13, www.nytimes.com/2012/06/17/business/executive-pay-still-climbing-despite-a-shareholder-din.html.

executive leadership and a vision for the firm. The second is to manage a strategic planning process. (See the **Sustainability Issue** feature for an example of how CEO pay is affecting the economic viability of corporations.)

Executive Leadership and Strategic Vision

Executive leadership is the directing of activities toward the accomplishment of corporate objectives. Executive leadership is important because it sets the tone for the entire corporation. A **strategic vision** is a description of what the company is capable of becoming. It is often communicated in the company's vision statement (as described in Chapter 1). People in an organization want to have a sense of direction, but only top management is in the position to specify and communicate their unique strategic vision to the general workforce. Top management's enthusiasm (or lack of it) about the corporation tends to be contagious. The importance of executive leadership is wonderfully illustrated by the quote in the United States Infantry Journal from 1948: "No man is a leader until his appointment is ratified in the minds and hearts of his men."[92]

Successful CEOs are noted for having a clear strategic vision, a strong passion for their company, and an ability to communicate with others. They are often perceived to be dynamic and charismatic leaders—which is especially important for high firm performance and investor confidence in uncertain environments.[93] They have many of the characteristics of **transformational leaders**—that is, leaders who provide change and movement in an organization by providing a vision for that change.[94] For instance, the positive attitude characterizing many well-known current and former leaders—such as Bill Gates at Microsoft, Anita Roddick at the Body Shop, Richard Branson at Virgin, Steve Jobs at Apple Computer, Meg Whitman at eBay and now HP, Howard Schultz at Starbucks, and Herb Kelleher at Southwest Airlines—energized their respective corporations at important times. These transformational leaders have been able to command respect and execute effective strategy formulation and implementation because they have exhibited three key characteristics:[95]

1. **The CEO articulates a strategic vision for the corporation:** The CEO envisions the company not as it currently is but as it can become. The new perspective that the CEO's vision brings gives renewed meaning to everyone's work and enables employees to see beyond the details of their own jobs to the functioning of the total corporation.[96] Louis Gerstner proposed a new vision for IBM when he proposed that the company change its business model from computer hardware to services: "If customers were going to look to an integrator to help them envision, design, and build end-to-end solutions, then the companies playing that role would exert tremendous influence over the full range of technology decisions—from architecture and applications to hardware and software choices."[97] In a survey of 1,500 senior executives from 20 different countries, when asked the most important behavioral trait a CEO must have, 98% responded that the CEO must convey "a strong sense of vision."[98]

2. **The CEO presents a role for others to identify with and to follow:** The leader empathizes with followers and sets an example in terms of behavior, dress, and actions. The CEO's attitudes and values concerning the corporation's purpose and activities are clear-cut and constantly communicated in words and deeds. For example, when design engineers at General Motors had problems with monitor resolution using the Windows operating system, Steve Ballmer, CEO of Microsoft, personally crawled under conference room tables to plug in PC monitors and diagnose the problem.[99] People need to know what to expect and have trust in their CEO. Research indicates that businesses in which the general manager has the trust of the employees have higher sales and profits with lower turnover than do businesses in which there is a lesser amount of trust.[100]

3. **The CEO communicates high performance standards and also shows confidence in the followers' abilities to meet these standards:** The leader empowers followers by raising their beliefs in their own capabilities. No leader ever improved performance by setting easily attainable goals that provided no challenge. Communicating high expectations to others can often lead to high performance.[101] The CEO must be willing to follow through by coaching people. As a result, employees view their work as very important and thus motivating.[102] Ivan Seidenberg, chief executive of Verizon Communications, was closely involved in deciding Verizon's strategic direction, and he showed his faith in his people by letting his key managers handle important projects and represent the company in public forums. "All of these people could be CEOs in their own right. They are warriors and they are on a mission," explained Seidenberg. Grateful for his faith in them, his managers were fiercely loyal both to him and the company.[103]

The negative side of confident executive leaders is that their very confidence may lead to *hubris*, in which their confidence blinds them to information that is contrary to a decided course of action. For example, overconfident CEOs tend to charge ahead with mergers and acquisitions even though they are aware that most acquisitions destroy shareholder value. Research by Tate and Malmendier found that "overconfident CEOs are more likely to conduct mergers than rational CEOs at any point in time. Overconfident CEOs view their company as undervalued by outside investors who are less optimistic about the prospects of the firm." Overconfident CEOs were most likely to make acquisitions when they could avoid selling new stock to finance them, and they were more likely to do deals that diversified their firm's lines of businesses.[104] Carly Fiorina used the power of her office and her considerable influence with a relatively weak board of directors to push through the Compaq Computer acquisition.

Managing the Strategic Planning Process

As business corporations adopt more of the characteristics of the learning organization, strategic planning initiatives can come from any part of an organization. A survey of 156 large corporations throughout the world revealed that, in two-thirds of the firms, strategies were first proposed in the business units and sent to headquarters for approval.[105] However, unless top management encourages and supports the planning process, it is unlikely to result in a strategy. In most corporations, top management must initiate and manage the strategic planning process. It may do so by first asking business units and functional areas to propose strategic plans for themselves, or it may begin by drafting an overall corporate plan within which the units can then build their own plans. Research suggests that bottom-up strategic planning may be most appropriate in multidivisional corporations operating in relatively stable environments but that top-down strategic planning may be most appropriate for firms operating in turbulent environments.[106] Other organizations engage in concurrent strategic planning in which all the organization's units draft plans for themselves after they have been provided with the organization's overall mission and objectives.

Regardless of the approach taken, the typical board of directors expects top management to manage the overall strategic planning process so that the plans of all the units and functional areas fit together into an overall corporate plan. Top management's job therefore includes the tasks of evaluating unit plans and providing feedback. To do this, it may require each unit to justify its proposed objectives, strategies, and programs in terms of how well they satisfy the organization's overall objectives in light of available resources. If a company is not organized into business units, top managers may work together as a team to do strategic planning. CEO Jeff Bezos tells how this is done at Amazon.com:

> We have a group called the S Team—S meaning "senior" [management]—that stays abreast of what the company is working on and delves into strategy issues. It meets for about four hours every Tuesday. Once or twice a year the S Team also gets together in a two-day meeting where different ideas are explored. Homework is assigned ahead of time. . . . Eventually we have to choose just a couple of things, if they're big, and make bets.[107]

In contrast to the seemingly continuous strategic planning being done at Amazon.com, most large corporations conduct the strategic planning process just once a year—often at offsite strategy workshops attended by senior executives.[108]

Many large organizations have a *strategic planning staff* charged with supporting both top management and the business units in the strategic planning process. This staff may prepare the background materials used in senior management's offsite strategy workshop. This planning staff typically consists of fewer than 10 people, headed by a senior executive with the title of Director of Corporate Development or Chief Strategy Officer. The staff's major responsibilities are to:

1. Identify and analyze companywide strategic issues, and suggest corporate strategic alternatives to top management.

2. Work as facilitators with business units to guide them through the strategic planning process.[109]

End of Chapter SUMMARY

Who determines a corporation's performance? According to the popular press, it is the Chief Executive Officer who seems to be personally responsible for a company's success or failure. When a company is in trouble, one of the first alternatives usually presented is to fire the CEO. That was certainly the case at the Walt Disney Company under Michael Eisner, as well as Hewlett-Packard under Carly Fiorina. Both CEOs were first viewed as transformational leaders who made needed strategic changes to their companies. Later both were perceived to be the primary reason for their company's poor performance and were fired by their boards. The truth is rarely this simple.

According to research by Margarethe Wiersema, firing the CEO rarely solves a corporation's problems. In a study of CEO turnover caused by dismissals and retirements in the 500 largest public U.S. companies, 71% of the departures were involuntary. In those firms in which the CEO was fired or asked to resign and replaced by another, Wiersema found *no* significant improvement in the company's operating earnings or stock price. She couldn't find a single measure suggesting that CEO dismissal had a positive effect on corporate performance! Wiersema placed the blame for the poor results squarely on the shoulders of the boards of directors. Boards typically lack an in-depth understanding of the business and consequently rely too heavily on executive search firms that know even less about the business. According to Wiersema, boards that successfully managed the executive succession process had three things in common:

- The board set the criteria for candidate selection based on the strategic needs of the company.
- The board set realistic performance expectations rather than demanding a quick fix to please the investment community.
- The board developed a deep understanding of the business and provided strong strategic oversight of top management, including thoughtful annual reviews of CEO performance.[110]

As noted at the beginning of this chapter, corporate governance involves not just the CEO or the board of directors. It involves the combined active participation of the board, top management, and shareholders. One positive result of the many corporate scandals occurring over the past decade is the increased interest in governance. Institutional investors are no longer content to be passive shareholders. Thanks to new regulations, boards of directors are taking their responsibilities more seriously and including more independent outsiders on key oversight committees. Top managers are beginning to understand the value of working with boards as partners, not just as adversaries or as people to be manipulated. Although there will always be passive shareholders, rubber-stamp boards, and dominating CEOs, the simple truth is that good corporate governance means better strategic management.

MyManagementLab®

Go to **mymanagementlab.com** to complete the problems marked with this icon .

KEY TERMS

affiliated director (p. 48)

agency theory (p. 47)

board of directors' continuum (p. 45)

board of director responsibilities (p. 44)

codetermination (p. 51)

corporate governance (p. 43)

due care (p. 44)

executive leadership (p. 59)

inside director (p. 46)

MyManagementLab®

Go to **mymanagementlab.com** for Auto-graded writing questions as well as the following Assisted-graded writing questions:

2-1. What are the roles and responsibilities of an effective and active Board of Directors?

2-2. What are the issues that suggest the need for oversight of a particular company's management team?

DISCUSSION QUESTIONS

2-3. When does a corporation need a board of directors?

✪ **2-4.** Who should and should not serve on a board of directors? What about environmentalists or union leaders?

✪ **2-5.** Should a CEO be allowed to serve on another company's board of directors? Why or why not?

2-6. What would the impact be if the only insider on a corporation's board were the CEO?

✪ **2-7.** Should all CEOs be transformational leaders? Would you like to work for a transformational leader?

STRATEGIC PRACTICE EXERCISE

A. Think of the **best manager** for whom you have ever worked. What was it about this person that made him or her such a good manager? Consider the following statements as they pertain to that person. Fill in the blank *in front of each statement* with one of the following values:

**STRONGLY AGREE = 5; AGREE = 4; NEUTRAL = 3;
DISAGREE = 2; STRONGLY DISAGREE = 1**

1. ___ I respect him/her personally, and want to act in a way that merits his/her respect and admiration.

2. ___ I respect her/his competence about things she/he is more experienced about than I.

3. ___ He/she can give special help to those who cooperate with him/her.

4. ___ He/she can apply pressure on those who cooperate with him/her.

5. ___ He/she has a legitimate right, considering his/her position, to expect that his/her suggestions will be carried out.

6. ___ I defer to his/her judgment in areas with which he/she is more familiar than I.

7. ___ He/she can make things difficult for me if I fail to follow his/her advice.

8. ___ Because of his/her job title and rank, I am obligated to follow his/her suggestions.

9. ___ I can personally benefit by cooperating with him/her.

10. ___ Following his/her advice results in better decisions.

11. ___ I cooperate with him/her because I have a high regard for him/her as an individual.

12. ___ He/she can penalize those who do not follow his/her suggestions.

13. ___ I feel I have to cooperate with him/her.

14. ___ I cooperate with him/her because I wish to be identified with him/her.

15. ___ Cooperating with him/her can positively affect my performance.

SOURCE: Questionnaire developed by J. D. Hunger from the article "Influence and Information: An Exploratory Investigation of the Boundary Role Person's Bases of Power" by Robert Spekman, *Academy of Management Journal*, March 1979. Copyright © 2004 by J. David Hunger.

B. Now think of the **worst manager** for whom you have ever worked. What was it about this person that made him or her such a poor manager? Please consider the statements earlier as they pertain to that person. Please place a number *after each statement*

with one of the values, from 5 = strongly agree to 1 = strongly disagree.

C. Add the values you marked for the best manager within each of the five categories of power below. Then, do the same for the values you marked for the worst manager.

BEST MANAGER

Reward	Coercive	Legitimate	Referent	Expert
3.	4.	5.	1.	2.
9.	7.	8.	11.	6.
15.	12.	13.	14.	10.
Total	Total	Total	Total	Total

WORST MANAGER

Reward	Coercive	Legitimate	Referent	Expert
3.	4.	5.	1.	2.
9.	7.	8.	11.	6.
15.	12.	13.	14.	10.
Total	Total	Total	Total	Total

D. Consider the differences between how you rated your best and your worst manager. How different are the two profiles? In many cases, the best manager's profile tends to be similar to that of transformational leaders in that the best manager tends to score highest on referent, followed by expert and reward, power—especially when compared to the worst manager's profile. The worst manager often scores highest on coercive and legitimate power, followed by reward power. The results of this survey may help you answer the fifth discussion question for this chapter.

NOTES

1. A. G. Monks and N. Minow, *Corporate Governance* (Cambridge, MA: Blackwell Business, 1995), pp. 8–32.
2. Ibid., p. 1.
3. C. Corsi, G. Dale, J. H. Daum, J. W. Mumm, and W. Schoppen, "5 Things Boards of Directors Should Be Thinking About," *Point of View*: A special issue focusing on today's board and CEO agenda (2010), Spencer Stuart. © 2010 Spencer Stuart. All rights reserved. For information about copying, distributing, and displaying this work, contact permissions@spencerstuart.com.
4. Reported by E. L. Biggs in "CEO Succession Planning: An Emerging Challenge for Boards of Directors," *Academy of Management Executive* (February 2004), pp. 105–107.
5. A. Borrus, "Less Laissez-Faire in Delaware?" *BusinessWeek* (March 22, 2004), pp. 80–82.
6. L. Light, "Why Outside Directors Have Nightmares," *BusinessWeek* (October 23, 1996), p. 6.
7. "Where's All the Fun Gone?" *The Economist* (March 20, 2004), p. 76.
8. A. Chen, J. Osofsky, and E. Stephenson, "Making the Board More Strategic: A McKinsey Global Survey," *McKinsey Quarterly* (March 2008), pp. 1–10.
9. Nadler proposes a similar five-step continuum for board involvement ranging from the least involved "passive board" to the most involved "operating board," plus a form for measuring board involvement in D. A. Nadler, "Building Better Boards," *Harvard Business Review* (May 2004), pp. 102–111.

10. H. Ashbaugh, D. W. Collins, and R. LaFond, "The Effects of Corporate Governance on Firms' Credit Ratings," unpublished paper (March, 2004); W. Q. Judge Jr., and C. P. Zeithaml, "Institutional and Strategic Choice Perspectives on Board Involvement in the Strategic Choice Process," *Academy of Management Journal* (October 1992), pp. 766–794; J. A. Pearce II, and S. A. Zahra, "Effective Power-Sharing Between the Board of Directors and the CEO," *Handbook of Business Strategy*, 1992/93 Yearbook (Boston: Warren, Gorham, and Lamont, 1992), pp. 1.1–1.16.
11. *Current Board Practices*, American Society of Corporate Secretaries, 2002 as reported by B. Atkins in "Directors Don't Deserve such a Punitive Policy," *Directors & Boards* (Summer 2002), p. 23.
12. A. Chen, J. Osofsky, and E. Stephenson, "Making the Board More Strategic: A McKinsey Global Survey," *McKinsey Quarterly* (March 2008), pp. 1–10.
13. D. A. Nadler, "Building Better Boards," *Harvard Business Review* (May 2004), pp. 102–111; L. Lavelle, "The Best and Worst Boards," *BusinessWeek* (October 7, 2002), pp. 104–114.
14. Nadler, p. 109.
15. M. K. Fiegener, "Determinants of Board Participation in the Strategic Decisions of Small Corporations," *Entrepreneurship Theory and Practice* (September 2005), pp. 627–650.
16. A. L. Ranft and H. M. O'Neill, "Board Composition and High-Flying Founders: Hints of Trouble to Come?" *Academy of Management Executive* (February 2001), pp. 126–138.

17. B. Stone, D. MacMilan, A. Vance, A. Satariano, and D. Bass, "How Zuck Hacked the Valley," *BusinessWeek* (May 21, 2012).

18. D. R. Dalton, M. A. Hitt, S. Trevis Certo, and C. M. Dalton, "The Fundamental Agency Problem and Its Mitigation," Chapter One in *Academy of Management Annals*, edited by J. F. Westfall and A. F. Brief (London: Rutledge, 2007); Y. Deutsch, "The Impact of Board Composition on Firms' Critical Decisions: A Meta-Analytic Review," *Journal of Management* (June 2005), pp. 424–444; D. F. Larcher, S. A. Richardson, and I. Tuna, "Does Corporate Governance Really Matter?" *Knowledge @ Wharton* (September 8–21, 2004); J. Merritt and L. Lavelle, "A Different Kind of Governance Guru," *BusinessWeek* (August 9, 2004), pp. 46–47; A. Dehaene, V. DeVuyst, and H. Ooghe, "Corporate Performance and Board Structure in Belgian Companies," *Long Range Planning* (June 2001), pp. 383–398; M. W. Peng, "Outside Directors and Firm Performance During Institutional Transitions," *Strategic Management Journal* (May 2004), pp. 453–471.

19. D. R. Dalton, M. A. Hitt, S. Trevis Certo, and C. M. Dalton, "The Fundamental Agency Problem and Its Mitigation," Chapter One in *Academy of Management Annals*, edited by J. F. Westfall and A. F. Brief (London: Rutledge, 2007).

20. *33rd Annual Board of Directors Study* (New York: Korn/Ferry International, 2007), p. 11.

21. *30th Annual Board of Directors Study* (New York: Korn/Ferry International, 2003).

22. M. K. Fiegerer, "Determinants of Board Participation in the Strategic Decisions of Small Corporations," *Entrepreneurship Theory and Practice* (September 2005), pp. 627–650; S. K. Lee and G. Filbeck, "Board Size and Firm Performance: Case of Small Firms," *Proceedings of the Academy of Accounting and Financial Studies* (2006), pp. 43–46; W. S. Schulze, M. H. Lubatkin, R. N. Dino, and A. K. Buchholtz, "Agency Relationships in Family Firms: Theory and Evidence," *Organization Science* (March–April, 2001), pp. 99–116.

23. S. K. Lee and G. Filbeck, "Board Size and Firm Performance: The Case of Small Firms," *Proceedings of the Academy of Accounting and Financial Studies* (2006), pp. 43–46.

24. J. J. Reur and R. Ragozzino, "Agency Hazards and Alliance Portfolios," *Strategic Management Journal* (January 2006), pp. 27–43.

25. M. Goranova, T. M. Alessandri, P. Brades, and R. Dharwadkar, "Managerial Ownership and Corporate Diversification: A Longitudinal View," *Strategic Management Journal* (March 2007), pp. 211–225; B. K. Boyd, S. Gove, and M. A. Hitt, "Consequences of Measurement Problems in Strategic Management Research: The Case of Amihud and Lev," *Strategic Management Journal* (April 2005), pp. 367–375; J. P. Katz and B. P. Niehoff, "How Owners Influence Strategy—A Comparison of Owner-Controlled and Manager-Controlled Firms," *Long Range Planning* (October 1998), pp. 755–761; M. Kroll, P. Wright, L. Toombs, and H. Leavell, "Form of Control: A Critical Determinant of Acquisition Performance and CEO Rewards," *Strategic Management Journal* (February 1997), pp. 85–96.

26. L. Tihanyi, R. A. Johnson, R. E. Hoskisson, and M. A. Hitt, "Institutional Ownership Differences and International Diversification: The Effects of Boards of Directors and Technological Opportunity," *Academy of Management Journal* (April 2003), pp. 195–211; A. E. Ellstrand, L. Tihanyi, and J. L. Johnson, "Board Structure and International Political Risk," *Academy of Management Journal* (August 2002), pp. 769–777; S. A. Zahra, D. O. Neubaum, and M. Huse, "Entrepreneurship in Medium-Size Companies: Exploring the Effects of Ownership and

Governance Systems," *Journal of Management* (Vol. 26, No. 5, 2000), pp. 947–976.

27. G. Kassinis and N. Vafeas, "Corporate Boards and Outside Stakeholders as Determinants of Environmental Litigation," *Strategic Management Journal* (May 2002), pp. 399–415; P. Dunn, "The Impact of Insider Power on Fraudulent Financial Reporting," *Journal of Management* (Vol. 30, No. 3, 2004), pp. 397–412.

28. R. C. Anderson and D. M. Reeb, "Board Composition: Balancing Family Influence in S&P 500 Firms," *Administrative Science Quarterly* (June 2004), pp. 209–237; W. S. Schulze, M. H. Lubatkin, R. N. Dino, and A. K. Buchholtz, "Agency Relationships in Family Firms: Theory and Evidence," *Organization Science* (March–April, 2001), pp. 99–116.

29. M. N. Young, A. K. Buchholtz, and D. Ahlstrom, "How Can Board Members Be Empowered If They Are Spread Too Thin?" *SAM Advanced Management Journal* (Autumn 2003), pp. 4–11.

30. *33rd Annual Board of Directors Study* (New York: Korn/Ferry International, 2007), p. 21.

31. C. M. Daily and D. R. Dalton, "The Endangered Director," *Journal of Business Strategy*, (Vol. 25, No. 3, 2004), pp. 8–9.

32. I. Sager, "The Boardroom: New Rules, New Loopholes," *BusinessWeek* (November 29, 2004), p. 13.

33. *34th Annual Board of Directors Study* (New York: Korn/Ferry International, 2008), pp. 25–32.

34. See S. Finkelstein, and D. C. Hambrick, *Strategic Leadership: Top Executives and Their Impact on Organizations* (St. Paul, MN: West, 1996), p. 213.

35. D. R. Dalton, M. A. Hitt, S. Trevis Certo, and C. M. Dalton, "The Fundamental Agency Problem and Its Mitigation," Chapter One in *Academy of Management Annals*, edited by J. F. Westfall and A. F. Brief (London: Rutledge, 2007).

36. "TIAA-CREF's Role in Corporate Governance," *Investment Forum* (June 2003), p. 13.

37. Credit Suisse Research Institutes (July 31, 2012), (www .credit-suisse.com/news/en/media_release.jsp).

38. M. Teen, "The Diversity Scorecard," (Korn/Ferry Institute, 2011).

39. *33rd Annual Board of Directors Study* (New York: Korn/Ferry International, 2007), p. 11; T. Neff and J. H. Daum, "The Empty Boardroom," *Strategy + Business* (Summer 2007), pp. 57–61.

40. R. O. Crockett, "The Rising Stock of Black Directors," *BusinessWeek* (February 27, 2006), p. 34.

41. J. Daum, "Portrait of Boards on the Cusp of Historic Change," *Directors & Boards* (Winter 2003), p. 56; J. Daum, "SSBI: Audit Committees Are Leading the Change," *Directors & Boards* (Winter 2004), p. 59.

42. *30th Annual Board of Directors Study* (New York: Korn/Ferry International, 2003) p. 38

43. *Globalizing the Board of Directors: Trends and Strategies* (New York: The Conference Board, 1999).

44. "The Korn/Ferry Market Cap 100 – 2011," p. 20.

45. R. W. Pouder and R. S. Cantrell, "Corporate Governance Reform: Influence on Shareholder Wealth," *Journal of Business Strategies* (Spring 1999), pp. 48–66.

46. M. L. Gerlach, "The Japanese Corporate Network: A Block-Model Analysis," *Administrative Science Quarterly* (March 1992), pp. 105–139.

47. W. E. Stead and J. G. Stead, *Sustainable Strategic Management* (Armonk, NY: M. E. Sharp, 2004), p. 47.

48. J. D. Westphal, M. L. Seidel, and K. J. Stewart, "Second-Order Imitation: Uncovering Latent Effects of Board Network Ties," *Administrative Science Quarterly* (December 2001),

pp. 717–747; M. A. Geletkanycz, B. K. Boyd, and S. Finkelstein, "The Strategic Value of CEO External Directorate Networks: Implications for CEO Compensation," *Strategic Management Journal* (September 2001), pp. 889–898; M. A. Carpenter and J. D. Westphal, "The Strategic Context of External Network Ties: Examining the Impact of Director Appointments on Board Involvement in Strategic Decision Making," *Academy of Management Journal* (August 2001), pp. 639–660.

49. M. Warner, "Inside the Silicon Valley Money Machine," *Fortune* (October 26, 1998), pp. 128–140.

50. D. Jones and B. Hansen, "Chairmen Still Doing Do-Si-Do," *USA Today* (November 5, 2003), p. 3B; J. H. Daum and T. J. Neff, "SSBI: Audit Committees Are Leading the Charge," *Directors & Boards* (Winter 2003), p. 59.

51. J. A. C. Baum and C. Oliver, "Institutional Linkages and Organizational Mortality," *Administrative Science Quarterly* (June 1991) pp. 187–218; J. P. Sheppard, "Strategy and Bankruptcy: An Exploration into Organizational Death," *Journal of Management* (Winter 1994), pp. 795–833.

52. *33rd Annual Board of Directors Study* (New York: Korn/Ferry International, 2007), p. 44, and *Directors' Compensation and Board Practices in 2003*, Research Report R-1339-03-RR (New York: Conference Board, 2003) Table 49, p. 38.

53. J. Canavan, B. Jones, and M. J. Potter, "Board Tenure: How Long Is Too Long?" *Boards & Directors* (Winter 2004), pp. 39–42.

54. *34th Annual Board of Directors Study* (New York: Korn/Ferry International, 2008), p. 18, and *30th Annual Board of Directors Study Supplement: Governance Trends of the Fortune 1000* (New York: Korn/Ferry International, 2004), p. 5.

55. D. F. Larcker and S. A. Richardson, "Does Governance Really Matter?" *Knowledge @ Wharton* (September 8–21, 2004).

56. M. L. McDonald, J. D. Westphal, and M. E. Graebner, "What Do they Know? The Effects of Outside Director Acquisition Experience on Firm Acquisition Experience," *Strategic Management Journal* (November 2008), pp. 1155–1177.

57. *26th Annual Board of Directors Study* (New York: Korn/Ferry International, 1999), p. 30.

58. *30th Annual Board of Directors Study* (New York: Korn/Ferry International, 2003), pp. 8, 31, 44.

59. D. R. Dalton, M. A. Hitt, S. Trevis Certo, and C. M. Dalton, "The Fundamental Agency Problem and Its Mitigation," Chapter One in *Academy of Management Annals*, edited by J. F. Westfall and A. F. Brief (London: Rutledge, 2007); P. Coombes and S. C-Y Wong, "Chairman and CEO—One Job or Two?" *McKinsey Quarterly* (2004, No. 2), pp. 43–47; "The Korn/Ferry Market Cap 100 – 2011."

60. A. Desai, M. Kroll, and P. Wright, "CEO Duality, Board Monitoring, and Acquisition Performance," *Journal of Business Strategies* (Fall 2003), pp. 147–156; D. Harris and C. E. Helfat, "CEO Duality, Succession, Capabilities and Agency Theory: Commentary and Research Agenda," *Strategic Management Journal* (September 1998), pp. 901–904; C. M. Daily and D. R. Dalton, "CEO and Board Chair Roles Held Jointly or Separately: Much Ado About Nothing," *Academy of Management Executive* (August 1997), pp. 11–20; D. L. Worrell, C. Nemec, and W. N. Davidson III, "One Hat Too Many: Key Executive Plurality and Shareholder Wealth," *Strategic Management Journal* (June 1997), pp. 499–507; J. W. Coles and W. S. Hesterly, "Independence of the Chairman and Board Composition: Firm Choices and Shareholder Value," *Journal of Management*, Vol. 26, No. 2 (2000), pp. 195–214; H. Ashbaugh, D. W. Collins, and R. LaFond, "The Effects of Corporate Governance on Firms' Credit Ratings," unpublished paper, March 2004.

61. J. P. O'Connor, R. I. Priem, J. E. Coombs, and K. M. Gilley, "Do CEO Stock Options Prevent or Promote Fraudulent Financial Reporting?" *Academy of Management Journal* (June 2006), pp. 483–500.

62. N. R. Augustine, "How Leading a Role for the Lead Director?" *Directors & Boards* (Winter 2004), pp. 20–23.

63. D. R. Dalton, M. A. Hitt, S. Trevis Certo, and C. M. Dalton, "The Fundamental Agency Problem and Its Mitigation," Chapter One in *Academy of Management Annals*, edited by J. F. Westfall and A. F. Brief (London: Rutledge, 2007).

64. *34th Annual Board of Directors Study* (New York: Korn/Ferry International, 2008), p. 19.

65. J. D. Westphal and I. Stern, "Flattery Will Get You Everywhere (Especially If You Are a Male Caucasian): How Ingratiation, Boardroom Behavior, and Demographic Minority Status Affect Additional Board Appointments at U.S. Companies," *Academy of Management Journal* (April 2007), pp. 267–288; J. D. Westphal, "Board Games: How CEOs Adapt to Increases in Structural Board Independence from Management," *Administrative Science Quarterly* (September 1998), pp. 511–537; J. D. Westphal and P. Khanna, "Keeping Directors in Line: Social Distancing as a Control Mechanism in the Corporate Elite," *Administrative Science Quarterly* (September 2003), pp. 361–398.

66. H. L. Tosi, W. Shen, and R. J. Gentry, "Why Outsiders on Boards Can't Solve the Corporate Governance Problem," *Organizational Dynamics* (Vol. 32, No. 2, 2003), pp. 180–192.

67. *33rd Annual Board of Directors Study* (New York: Korn/Ferry International, 2007), p. 12. Other committees are succession planning (39%), finance (30%), corporate responsibility (17%), and investment (15%).

68. Perhaps because of their potential to usurp the power of the board, executive committees are being used less often.

69. *34th Annual Board of Directors Study* (New York: Korn/Ferry International, 2008), p. 19.

70. "The Trial of Sarbanes–Oxley," *The Economist* (April 22, 2006), pp. 59–60; *33rd Annual Board of Directors Study* (New York: Korn/Ferry International, 2007), p. 14; S. Wagner and L. Dittmar, "The Unexpected Benefits of Sarbanes–Oxley," *Harvard Business Review* (April 2006), pp. 133–140.

71. A. Borrus, "Learning to Love Sarbanes–Oxley," *BusinessWeek* (November 21, 2005), pp. 126–128.

72. D. Henry, "Not Everyone Hates SarbOx," *BusinessWeek* (January 29, 2007), p. 37.

73. D. Henry, "A SarbOx Surprise," *BusinessWeek* (January 12, 2006), p. 38.

74. *30th Annual Board of Directors Study Supplement: Governance Trends of the Fortune 1000* (New York: Korn/Ferry International, 2004), p. 5.

75. "Where's All the Fun Gone?" *The Economist* (March 20, 2004), pp. 75–77.

76. Daum and Neff (2004), p. 58.

77. *33rd Annual Board of Directors Study* (New York: Korn/Ferry International, 2007), p. 7.

78. J. Sonnenfeld, "Good Governance and the Misleading Myths of Bad Metrics." *Academy of Management Executive* (February 2004), pp. 108–113.

79. H. Ashbaugh, D. W. Collins, and R. LaFond, "The Effects of Corporate Governance on Firms' Credit Ratings," unpublished paper (March 2002).

80. M. Hiltzik, "Facebook Shareholders Are Wedded to the Whims of Mark Zuckerberg," *The Los Angeles Times* (May 20, 2012), (www.articles.latimes.com/2012/may/20/business/la-fi-hiltzik-20120517).

81. P. A. Gompers, J. Ishii, and A. Metrick, "*Extreme Governance: An Analysis of Dual-Class Firms in the United States*," (2006), (www.hbs.edu/units/am/pdf/dual.pdf), pp. 1–48.

82. D. R. Dalton, C. M. Daily, A. E. Ellstrand, and J. L. Johnson, "Meta-Analytic Reviews of Board Composition, Leadership Structure, and Financial Performance," *Strategic Management Journal* (March 1998), pp. 269–290; G. Beaver, "Competitive Advantage and Corporate Governance—Shop Soiled and Needing Attention!" *Strategic Change* (September–October 1999), p. 330.

83. A. Borrus and L. Young, "Nothing Like a Little Exposure," *BusinessWeek* (September 13, 2004), p. 92.

84. P. Silva, "Do Motivation and Equity Ownership Matter in Board of Directors' Evaluation of CEO Performance?" *Journal of Management Issues* (Fall 2005), pp. 346–362.

85. L. He and M. J. Conyon, "The Role of Compensation Committees in CEO and Committee Compensation Decisions," paper presented to *Academy of Management* (Seattle, WA, 2003).

86. P. Coy, E. Thornton, M. Arndt, B. Grow, and A. Park, "Shake, Rattle, and Merge," *BusinessWeek* (January 10, 2005), pp. 32–35.

87. L. Lavelle, "A Fighting Chance for Boardroom Democracy," *BusinessWeek* (June 9, 2003), p. 50; L. Lavelle, "So That's Why Boards Are Waking Up," *BusinessWeek* (January 19, 2004), pp. 72–73.

88. For a detailed description of the COO's role, see N. Bennett and S. A. Miles, "Second in Command," *Harvard Business Review* (May 2006), pp. 71–78.

89. S. Finkelstein and D. C. Hambrick, *Strategic Leadership: Top Executives and Their Impact on Organizations* (St. Louis: West, 1996).

90. H. G. Barkema and O. Shvyrkov, "Does Top Management Team Diversity Promote or Hamper Foreign Expansion?" *Strategic Management Journal* (July 2007), pp. 663–680; D. C. Hambrick, T. S. Cho, and M-J Chen, "The Influence of Top Management Team Heterogeneity on Firms' Competitive Moves," *Administrative Science Quarterly* (December 1996), pp. 659–684.

91. P. Pitcher and A. D. Smith, "Top Management Heterogeneity: Personality, Power, and Proxies," *Organization Science* (January–February 2001), pp. 1–18; M. A. Carpenter and J. W. Fredrickson, "Top Management Teams, Global Strategic Posture, and the Moderating Role of Uncertainty," *Academy of Management Journal* (June 2001), pp. 533–545; M. A. Carpenter, "The Implications of Strategy and Social Context for the Relationship Between Top Management Team Heterogeneity and Firm Performance," *Strategic Management Journal* (March 2002), pp. 275–284; L. Tihanyi, A. E. Ellstrand, C. M. Daily, and D. R. Dalton, "Composition of the Top Management Team and Firm International Expansion," *Journal of Management* (Vol. 26, No. 6, 2000), pp. 1157–1177.

92. "One on One with Steve Reinemund," *BusinessWeek* (December 17, 2001), special advertising insert on leadership by Heidrick & Struggles, executive search firm.

93. D. A. Waldman, G. G. Ramirez, R. J. House, and P. Puranam, "Does Leadership Matter? CEO Leadership Attributes and Profitability Under Conditions of Perceived Environmental Uncertainty," *Academy of Management Journal* (February 2001), pp. 134–143; F. J. Flynn and B. M. Staw, "Lend Me Your Wallets: The Effect of Charismatic Leadership on External Support for an Organization," *Strategic Management Journal* (April 2004), pp. 309–330.

94. J. Burns, *Leadership* (New York: HarperCollins, 1978); B. Bass, "From Transactional to Transformational Leadership: Learning to Share the Vision," *Organizational Dynamics* (Vol. 18, 1990), pp. 19–31; W. Bennis and B. Nanus, *Leaders: Strategies for Taking Charge* (New York: HarperCollins, 1997).

95. Based on R. J. House, "A 1976 Theory of Charismatic Leadership," in J. G. Hunt and L. L. Larson (Eds.), *Leadership: The Cutting Edge* (Carbondale, IL: Southern Illinois University Press, 1976), pp. 189–207. Also see J. Choi, "A Motivational Theory of Charismatic Leadership: Envisioning, Empathy, and Empowerment," *Journal of Leadership and Organizational Studies* (Vol. 13, No. 1, 2006), pp. 24–43.

96. I. D. Colville and A. J. Murphy, "Leadership as the Enabler of Strategizing and Organizing," *Long Range Planning* (December 2006), pp. 663–677.

97. L. V. Gerstner Jr., *Who Says Elephants Can't Dance?* (New York: HarperCollins, 2002), p. 124.

98. M. Lipton, "Demystifying the Development of an Organizational Vision," *Sloan Management Review* (Summer 1996), p. 84.

99. S. Hahn, "Why High Tech Has to Stay Humble," *BusinessWeek* (January 19, 2004), pp. 76–77.

100. J. H. David, F. D. Schoorman, R. Mayer, and H. H. Tan, "The Trusted General Manager and Business Unit Performance: Empirical Evidence of a Competitive Advantage," *Strategic Management Journal* (May 2000), pp. 563–576.

101. D. B. McNatt and T. A. Judge, "Boundary Conditions of the Galatea Effect: A Field Experiment and Constructive Replication," *Academy of Management Journal* (August 2004), pp. 550–565.

102. R. F. Piccolo and J. A. Colquitt, "Transformational Leadership and Job Behaviors: The Mediating Role of Core Job Characteristics," *Academy of Management Journal* (April 2006), pp. 327–340; J. E. Bono and T. A. Judge, "Self-Concordance at Work: Toward Understanding the Motivational Effects of Transformational Leaders," *Academy of Management Journal* (October 2003), pp. 554–571.

103. T. Lowry, R. O. Crockett, and I. M. Kunii, "Verizon's Gutsy Bet," *BusinessWeek* (August 4, 2003), pp. 52–62.

104. G. Tate and U. Malmendier, "Who Makes Acquisitions? CEO Overconfidence and the Market's Reaction," summarized by *Knowledge @ Wharton* (February 25, 2004).

105. M. C. Mankins and R. Steele, "Stop Making Plans, Start Making Decisions," *Harvard Business Review* (January 2006), pp. 76–84.

106. T. R. Eisenmann and J. L. Bower, "The Entrepreneurial M Form: Strategic Integration in Global Media Firms," *Organization Science* (May–June 2000), pp. 348–355.

107. J. Kirby and T. A. Stewart, "The Institutional Yes," *Harvard Business Review* (October 2007), p. 76.

108. M. C. Mankins and R. Steele, "Stop Making Plans, Start Making Decisions," *Harvard Business Review* (January 2006), pp. 76–84; G. P. Hodgkinson, R. Whittington, G. Johnson, and M. Schwarz, "The Role of Strategy Workshops in Strategy Development Processes: Formality, Communication, Co-ordination and Inclusion," *Long Range Planning* (October 2006), pp. 479–496; B. Frisch and L. Chandler, "Off-Sites that Work," *Harvard Business Review* (June 2006), pp. 117–126.

109. For a description of the Chief Strategy Officer, see R. T. S. Breene, P. F. Nunes, and W. E. Shill, "The Chief Strategy Officer," *Harvard Business Review* (October 2007), pp. 84–93; R. Dye, "How Chief Strategy Officers Think about Their Role: A Roundtable," *McKinsey Quarterly* (May 2008), pp. 1–8.

110. M. Wiersema, "Holes at the Top: Why CEO Firings Backfire," *Harvard Business Review* (December 2002), pp. 70–77.

CHAPTER 3

social responsibility
and Ethics in
Strategic Management

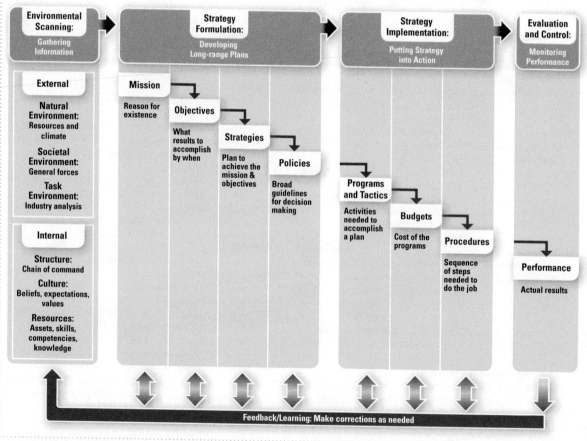

MyManagementLab®

⭐ **Improve Your Grade!**

Over 10 million students improved their results using the Pearson MyLabs. Visit **mymanagementlab.com**
for simulations, tutorials, and end-of-chapter problems.

Learning Objectives

After reading this chapter, you should be able to:

- Compare and contrast Friedman's traditional view with Carroll's contemporary view of social responsibility
- Understand the relationship between social responsibility and corporate performance
- Explain the concept of sustainability

- Conduct a stakeholder analysis
- Explain why people may act unethically
- Describe different views of ethics according to the utilitarian, individual rights, and justice approaches

Coca-Cola and Environmental Stewardship

Each year, *Fortune* magazine publishes its list of the most admired companies. Companies are rated in innovation, people management, use of corporate assets, social responsibility, quality of management, financial soundness, long-term investment, quality of products/services, and global competitiveness. When the 2012 list was announced, it was no surprise to see Coca-Cola in the top five. Coca-Cola has been a consistent member of this elite group for some time. They were cited for their environmental efforts, including water conservation and their PlantBottle Packaging Platform.

The PlantBottle is the only bottle in the market that is made partially with plants (30%), is commercially recyclable, and meets all the high-performance standards set by Coke. However, Coca-Cola's biggest impact has been in the use and reuse of water. Water is obviously critical to the operations of the company, but they have gone far beyond the classic business approach in creating their supply. By 2020, the company plans to return both to nature and the communities where it operates an amount of water equivalent to what is used in all of its beverages and their production. The company has written in a Water Stewardship code that applies to all 900 bottling plants worldwide. It is committed to watershed stewardship, and since 2005 has been involved with more than 300 community water partnership projects.

One such effort is with the United Nations Development Program in China. Coca-Cola has donated more than US$5 million to support the quality and quantity of high-quality drinking water in underserved rural areas. This work is outside the classic bounds of business and is being done far from the operating plants in China.

Coca-Cola has not always been on the front end of this issue, and some would argue that it should not be there now. In its 2002 annual filing, Coca-Cola did not even list water under its raw materials, but today it is listed as the main ingredient in its processes. It takes approximately 2.5 liters of water to produce 1 liter of its products. By 2002, the company was under worldwide pressure to improve its business practices. That year, the residents of Plachimada, a village in India, accused the company of sucking the wells dry and polluting the ground water. In 2004, the local government forced Coca-Cola to shut down their plant. The public relations impact around the world was substantial. The company announced that "if people are perceiving that we're using water at their expense, that's not a sustainable operation. . . and for us, having the goodwill in the community is an important thing." In response, the company spent US$10 million establishing a foundation to improve water in India, installed 320 rainwater harvesting systems, and was providing clean drinking water to more than 1000 schools in the country.

Did Coca-Cola over compensate for their business use of water? What is the proper role for a company? Are sustainable business practices part of a business's responsibilities?

SOURCES: Coca-Cola Stories, Accessed 5/30/13, www.thecoca-colacompany.com/citizenship/water_main.html; "World's Most Admired Companies," CNNmoney.com, Accessed 5/30/13, http://money.cnn.com/magazines/fortune/most-admired/2012/full_list; "Coca-Cola Helps Advance Water Sustainability Projects in the Pacific Region," May 12, 2011, Environmental Protection, (www.epoline.com/articles/2011/05/12/coca-cola-advances-water-sustainability-projects-in-pacific-region.aspx); Liu, L.W. 2008, "Water Pressure," Time, June 12, 2008 (www.time.com/time/magazine/article/0,9171,1814261,00.html);.

Social Responsibilities of Strategic Decision Makers

Should strategic decision makers be responsible only to shareholders, or do they have broader responsibilities? The concept of **social responsibility** proposes that a private corporation has responsibilities to society that extend beyond making a profit. Strategic decisions often affect more than just the corporation. A decision to retrench by closing some plants and discontinuing product lines, for example, affects not only the firm's workforce but also the communities where the plants are located and the customers with no other source for the discontinued product. Such situations raise questions about the appropriateness of certain missions, objectives, and strategies of business corporations. Managers must be able to deal with these conflicting interests in an ethical manner to formulate a viable strategic plan.

RESPONSIBILITIES OF A BUSINESS FIRM

What are the responsibilities of a business firm and how many of them must be fulfilled? Milton Friedman and Archie Carroll offer two contrasting views of the responsibilities of business firms to society.

Friedman's Traditional View of Business Responsibility

Urging a return to a laissez-faire worldwide economy with minimal government regulation, Milton Friedman argues against the concept of social responsibility as a function of business. A business person who acts "responsibly" by cutting the price of the firm's product to aid the poor, or by making expenditures to reduce pollution, or by hiring the hard-core unemployed, according to Friedman, is spending the shareholder's money for a general social interest. Even if the businessperson has shareholder permission or encouragement to do so, he or she is still acting from motives other than economic and may, in the long run, harm the very society the firm is trying to help. By taking on the burden of these social costs, the business becomes less efficient—either prices go up to pay for the increased costs or investment in new activities and research is postponed. These results negatively affect—perhaps fatally—the long-term efficiency of a business. Friedman thus referred to the social responsibility of business as a "fundamentally subversive doctrine" and stated that:

> There is one and only one social responsibility of business—to use its resources and engage in activities designed to increase its profits so long as it stays within the rules of the game, which is to say, engages in open and free competition without deception or fraud.[1]

Following Friedman's reasoning, the management of Coca-Cola was clearly guilty of misusing corporate assets and negatively affecting shareholder wealth. The millions spent in social services could have been invested in new product development or given back as dividends to the shareholders. Instead of Coca-Cola's management acting on its own, shareholders could have decided which charities to support.

Carroll's Four Responsibilities of Business

Friedman's contention that the primary goal of business is profit maximization is only one side of an ongoing debate regarding corporate social responsibility (CSR). According to William J. Byron, Distinguished Professor of Ethics at Georgetown University and past President of Catholic University of America, profits are merely a means to an end, not an end in itself. Just as a person needs food to survive and grow, so does a business corporation need profits to survive and grow. "Maximizing profits is like maximizing food." Thus, contends Byron, maximization of profits cannot be the primary obligation of business.[2]

As shown in **Figure 3–1**, Archie Carroll proposed that the managers of business organizations have four responsibilities: economic, legal, ethical, and discretionary.[3]

1. **Economic** responsibilities of a business organization's management are to produce goods and services of value to society so that the firm may repay its creditors and increase the wealth of its shareholders.

2. **Legal** responsibilities are defined by governments in laws that management is expected to obey. For example, U.S. business firms are required to hire and promote people based on their credentials rather than to discriminate on non-job-related characteristics such as race, gender, or religion.

3. **Ethical** responsibilities of an organization's management are to follow the generally held beliefs about behavior in a society. For example, society generally expects firms to work with the employees and the community in planning for layoffs, even though no law may require this. The affected people can get very upset if an organization's management fails to act according to generally prevailing ethical values.

4. **Discretionary** responsibilities are the purely voluntary obligations a corporation assumes. Examples are philanthropic contributions, training the hard-core unemployed, and providing day-care centers. The difference between ethical and discretionary responsibilities is that few people expect an organization to fulfill discretionary responsibilities, whereas many expect an organization to fulfill ethical ones.[4]

FIGURE 3–1
Responsibilities of Business

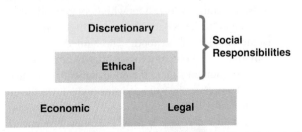

SOURCE: Suggested by Archie Carroll in A. B. Carroll, "A Three Dimensional Conceptual Model of Corporate Performance," Academy of Management Review (October 1979), pp. 497–505; A. B. Carroll, "Managing Ethically with Global Stakeholders: A Present and Future Challenge," Academy of Management Executive (May 2004), pp. 114–120; and A. B. Carroll, "The Pyramid of Corporate Social Responsibility: Toward the Moral Management of Organizational Stakeholders," Business Horizons (July–August 1991), pp. 39–48.

Carroll lists these four responsibilities *in order of priority*. A business firm must first make a profit to satisfy its economic responsibilities. To continue in existence, the firm must follow the laws, thus fulfilling its legal responsibilities. There is evidence that companies found guilty of violating laws have lower profits and sales growth after conviction.[5] On this point, Carroll and Friedman are in agreement. Carroll, however, goes further by arguing that business managers have responsibilities beyond economic and legal ones.

Having satisfied the two basic responsibilities, according to Carroll, a firm should look to fulfilling its social responsibilities. Social responsibility, therefore, includes both ethical and discretionary, but not economic and legal, responsibilities. A firm can fulfill its ethical responsibilities by taking actions that society tends to value but has not yet put into law. When ethical responsibilities are satisfied, a firm can focus on discretionary responsibilities— purely voluntary actions that society has not yet decided to expect from every company. For example, when Cisco Systems decided to dismiss 6000 full-time employees, it provided a novel severance package. Those employees who agreed to work for a local nonprofit organization for a year would receive one-third of their salaries plus benefits and stock options and be the first to be rehired. Nonprofits were delighted to hire such highly qualified people and Cisco was able to maintain its talent pool for when it could hire once again.[6]

As societal values evolve, the discretionary responsibilities of today may become the ethical responsibilities of tomorrow. For example, in 1990, 86% of people in the United States believed that obesity was caused by the individuals themselves, with only 14% blaming either corporate marketing or government guidelines. By 2003, however, only 54% blamed obesity on individuals and 46% put responsibility on corporate marketing and government guidelines. Thus, the offering of healthy, low-calorie food by food processors and restaurants is moving rapidly from being a discretionary to an ethical responsibility.[7] In recent years, school cafeterias across the United States have added fresh vegetables, removed soda machines, and in 2012, many school systems also moved to eliminate the much maligned *pink slime* from their beef product lines.

Carroll suggests that to the extent that business corporations fail to acknowledge discretionary or ethical responsibilities, society, through government, will act, making them legal responsibilities. Government may do this, moreover, without regard to an organization's economic responsibilities. As a result, the organization may have greater difficulty in earning a profit than it would have if it had voluntarily assumed some ethical and discretionary responsibilities.

Both Friedman and Carroll argue their positions based on the impact of socially responsible actions on a firm's profits. Friedman says that socially responsible actions hurt a firm's efficiency. Carroll proposes that a lack of social responsibility results in increased government regulations, which reduce a firm's efficiency because it must not only comply with the law, but must prove its compliance with regulators.

Friedman's position on social responsibility appears to be losing traction with business executives. For example, a 2006 survey of business executives across the world by McKinsey & Company revealed that only 16% felt that business should focus solely on providing the highest possible returns to investors while obeying all laws and regulations, contrasted with 84% who stated that business should generate high returns to investors but balance it with contributions to the broader public good.[8] The United National Global Compact was started in 2001 as an initiative for a company to voluntarily commit to aligning their operations with 10 principles covering human rights, the environment, labor and corruption among others. By 2012, over 6,800 companies in 140 countries had signed the compact. Those CEOs have agreed to report on their activities annually.[9]

Empirical research now indicates that socially responsible actions may have a positive effect on a firm's financial performance. Although a number of studies in the past have found no significant relationship,[10] an increasing number are finding a small, but positive relationship.[11]

A recent in-depth analysis by Margolis and Walsh of 127 studies found that "there is a positive association and very little evidence of a negative association between a company's social performance and its financial performance."[12] Another meta-analysis of 52 studies on social responsibility and performance reached this same conclusion.[13]

According to Porter and Kramer, "social and economic goals are not inherently conflicting, but integrally connected."[14] Being known as a socially responsible firm may provide a company with *social capital*, the goodwill of key stakeholders, that can be used for competitive advantage.[15] Target, for example, tries to attract socially concerned younger consumers by offering brands from companies that can boast ethical track records and community involvement.[16] A 2008 study conducted by Grant Thornton found that privately held businesses were forgoing the big publicity campaigns run by multinational companies and focusing their attention on CSR as a means for recruitment and retention of the best employees. In the same report, they found that 58% of these private companies had formally adopted transparent CSR policies as a means of influencing larger companies that may use their services/products.[17]

Being socially responsible does provide a firm with a more positive overall reputation.[18] A survey of more than 700 global companies by The Conference Board reported that 60% of the managers state that citizenship activities had led to (1) goodwill that opened doors in local communities and (2) an enhanced reputation with consumers.[19] Another survey of 140 U.S. firms revealed that being more socially responsible regarding environmental sustainability resulted not only in competitive advantages but also in cost savings.[20] For example, companies that take the lead in being environmentally friendly, such as by using recycled materials, preempt attacks from environmental groups and enhance their corporate image. Programs to reduce pollution, for example, can actually reduce waste and maximize resource productivity. One study that examined 70 ecological initiatives taken by 43 companies found the average payback period to be 18 months.[21] Other examples of benefits received from being socially responsible are:[22]

- Their environmental concerns may enable them to charge premium prices and gain brand loyalty (for example, Stoneyfield Yogurt, Whole Foods, and Ben & Jerry's Ice Cream).
- Their trustworthiness may help them generate enduring relationships with suppliers and distributors without requiring them to spend a lot of time and money policing contracts.
- They can attract outstanding employees who prefer working for a responsible firm (for example, Procter & Gamble and Starbucks).
- They are more likely to be welcomed into a foreign country (for example, Levi Strauss).
- They can utilize the goodwill of public officials for support in difficult times.
- They are more likely to attract capital infusions from investors who view reputable companies as desirable long-term investments. For example, mutual funds investing only in socially responsible companies more than doubled in size from 1995 to 2007 and outperformed the S&P 500 list of stocks.[23]

SUSTAINABILITY

As we pointed out in Chapter 1, sustainability includes much more than just ecological concerns and the natural environment. Crane and Matten point out that the concept of sustainability should be broadened to include economic and social as well as environmental concerns. They argue that it is sometimes impossible to address the sustainability of the natural environment without considering the social and economic aspects of relevant communities and their activities. For example, even though environmentalists may oppose road-building programs because of their effect on wildlife and conservation efforts, others point to the benefits to local communities of less traffic congestion and more jobs.[24] Dow Jones & Company, a leading provider of global business news and information, developed a sustainability index that considers not only environmental, but also economic and social factors. See the **Sustainability Issue** feature to learn how a global company is using environmental sustainability efforts to improve its bottom line.

The broader concept of sustainability has much in common with Carroll's list of business responsibilities presented earlier. In order for a business corporation to be sustainable—that is, to be successful over a long period of time—it must satisfy all of its economic, legal, ethical, and discretionary responsibilities. Sustainability thus involves many issues, concerns, and tradeoffs—leading us to an examination of corporate stakeholders.

CORPORATE STAKEHOLDERS

The concept that business must be socially responsible sounds appealing until we ask, "Responsible to whom?" A corporation's task environment includes a large number of groups with interest in a business organization's activities. These groups are referred to as **stakeholders** because they affect or are affected by the achievement of the firm's objectives.[25] Should a corporation be responsible only to some of these groups, or does business have an equal responsibility to all of them?

A survey of the U.S. general public by Penn Schoen Berland of Corporate Social Responsibility found that companies utilize a number of activities to appease their stakeholders and provide something back to a wide range of stakeholders. This included 33% who practiced recycling and energy savings approaches and 24% who donated to charities.[26] As scandal after scandal breaks in the press, support for corporate leaders plunges. A 2012 survey of

SUSTAINABILITY issue

MARKS & SPENCER LEADS THE WAY

There have been many moves over the past few years to increase the sustainability of business practices. The idea that waste is not a given in the operation of businesses has led to new ways of doing business that not only make a business a good citizen, but save a company a substantial amount of money. None has been more focused than Marks and Spencer Group (M&S), the enormous retailer of goods from clothing to food that is based in the UK. M&S announced in June 2012 that it had achieved its goal of going "carbon neutral."

A huge financial incentive exists in the UK to do so. There is a landfill tax of 64 pounds (roughly US$100) per ton, and that number is slated to increase by 8 pounds a year indefinitely because the country is rapidly running out of landfill space. M&S now recycles 89% of its food waste from its 511 UK stores. That waste goes to biogas facilities, and in the past 12 months has saved the company more than 105 million pounds.

The effort was started in 2007 with what the company called Plan A. Plan A was designed to transform the company into the carbon neutral firm it is today. The company's efforts in this area extend to everything in their operation. Over the past five years, they have worked with suppliers and cut food packaging by 20%, made hanger recycling the norm, and reduced food carrier bag use by 80%.

Management takes the whole business very seriously. Progress on Plan A is reviewed by a "how we do business" committee and reported annually. Furthermore, progress on Plan A constitutes 20% of the bonuses for the CEO and the directors of the company.

M&S is not done, however. In 2010, they started a new five-year plan aimed at making M&S the most sustainable major retailer in the world. Their efforts have been good for their business and good for society at large.

SOURCES: www.marksandspencer.com; "Finally, a Use for Sandwich Crusts," *BusinessWeek* (June 18, 2012); L. Thorpe, "Marks & Spencer – An Ambitious Commitment to Tackling Waste," *The Guardian* (2011), (http://www.guardian.co.uk/sustainable-business/marks-spencer-waste-recycling).

169 Chief Financial Officers at publicly traded companies in the U.S. found that 20% intentionally misrepresented their economic performance primarily to influence stock price.[27]

In any one strategic decision, the interests of one stakeholder group can conflict with those of another. For example, a business firm's decision to use only recycled materials in its manufacturing process may have a positive effect on environmental groups, but a negative effect on shareholder dividends. In another example, arguably the worst environmental disaster in the past decade occurred in the Gulf of Mexico when the Deepwater Horizon platform exploded, killing 11 workers and unleashing the worst oil spill in the nation's history. Much of the investigation since that explosion centered on a series of cost-saving approaches used by Trans Ocean (under contract to BP). On the one hand, shareholders were being rewarded with lower costs and higher profits. Had the rig not exploded, the focus would have remained on extracting the oil at the least possible cost. On the other hand, officials and the population along the gulf coast were decimated by the economic and environmental impact of a spill that was entirely preventable.[28] Which group's interests should have priority?

In order to answer this question, the corporation may need to craft an *enterprise strategy*—an overarching strategy that explicitly articulates the firm's ethical relationship with its stakeholders. This requires not only that management clearly state the firm's key ethical values, but also that it understands the firm's societal context, and undertakes stakeholder analysis to identify the concerns and abilities of each stakeholder.[29]

Stakeholder Analysis

Stakeholder analysis is the identification and evaluation of corporate stakeholders. This can be done in a three-step process.

The *first step* in stakeholder analysis is to identify primary stakeholders, those who have a *direct connection* with the corporation and who have sufficient bargaining power to *directly* affect corporate activities. Primary stakeholders include customers, employees, suppliers, shareholders, and creditors.

Unfortunately, determining exactly who constitutes the firm's customers and exactly what they want is difficult. This is particularly difficult when companies sell items for other companies (many retail organizations are simply flow-through operations for the products on their shelf, e.g., Wal-Mart, Target, etc.) or they sell items for which they have only limited influence. Coca-Cola Bottling Company Consolidated (CCBCC) is the largest independent bottler for Coca-Cola. While they are in direct contact with the retailers who display their products, most of those products are controlled by Coca-Cola in Atlanta, Georgia. Furthermore, these retailers while customers of CCBCC, are really just conduits for the consumer of the beverage. Marketing outwardly focuses on the end consumer of the beverage, while that same consumer probably has no idea that CCBCC has done all the work to ensure that the shelves are stocked. Coca-Cola in Atlanta may create a new flavor or drink brand (think Coconut Water) and pressure CCBCC to find a way to get those products accepted by the retailer who really only wants the product if it will outsell what was on the shelf before it arrived.

While difficult to determine at times, it is nonetheless important for businesses to determine who their stakeholders are and what they want. The corporation systematically monitors these stakeholders because they are important to a firm meeting its economic and legal responsibilities. Employees want a fair pay and fringe benefits. Customers want safe products and a value for price they pay. Shareholders want dividends and stock price appreciation. Suppliers want predictable orders and bills paid. Creditors want commitments to be met on time. In the normal course of affairs, the relationship between a firm and many of its primary stakeholders is regulated by written or verbal agreements and laws. Once a problem is identified, negotiation takes place based on costs and benefits to each party. (Government is not usually considered a primary stakeholder because laws apply to everyone in a particular category and usually cannot be negotiated.)

The *second step* in stakeholder analysis is to identify the *secondary stakeholders*—those who have only an *indirect* stake in the corporation but who are also affected by corporate activities. These usually include nongovernmental organizations (NGOs, such as Greenpeace), activists, local communities, trade associations, competitors, and governments. Because the corporation's relationship with each of these stakeholders is usually not covered by any written or verbal agreement, there is room for misunderstanding. As in the case of NGOs and activists, there actually may be no relationship until a problem develops—usually brought up by the stakeholder. In the normal course of events, these stakeholders do not affect the corporation's ability to meet its economic or legal responsibilities. Aside from competitors, these secondary stakeholders are not usually monitored by the corporation in any systematic fashion. As a result, relationships are usually based on a set of questionable assumptions about each other's needs and wants. Although these stakeholders may not directly affect a firm's short-term profitability, their actions could impact a corporation's reputation and thus its long-term performance.

The *third step* in stakeholder analysis is to estimate the effect on each stakeholder group from any particular strategic decision. Since the primary decision criteria used by management is generally economic, this is the point where secondary stakeholders may be ignored or discounted as unimportant. For a firm to fulfill its ethical or discretionary responsibilities, it must seriously consider the needs and wants of its secondary stakeholders in any strategic decision. For example, how much will specific stakeholder groups lose or gain? What other alternatives do they have to replace what may be lost?

Stakeholder Input

Once stakeholder impacts have been identified, managers should decide whether stakeholder input should be invited into the discussion of the strategic alternatives. A group is more likely to accept or even help implement a decision if it has some input into which alternative is chosen and how it is to be implemented. In the case of the huge BP oil spill, the company committed more than US$20 billion to the restoration of the gulf coast and the reimbursement of lost earnings to businesses affected by the spill. While there are still outstanding lawsuits and many claim to not have been made whole, the main effort by BP has been made without any legal requirement.

Given the wide range of interests and concerns present in any organization's task environment, one or more groups, at any one time, probably will be dissatisfied with an organization's activities—even if management is trying to be socially responsible. A company may have some stakeholders of which it is only marginally aware and in some cases does not seem interested in appeasing. For example, when Chick-fil-A announced their support for a ban on gay marriage, a firestorm of protests erupted. The mayors of Chicago and Boston opposed moves by Chick-fil-A to add stores in their area, The Jim Henson Company pulled their Muppet toys from the kids meals and gay-rights groups called for a boycott. On the other hand, the company found a quick and vocal group of supporters. Radio talk show host and former Presidential candidate, Mike Huckabee called for a "Chick-fil-A Appreciation Day."[30]

Therefore, before making a strategic decision, strategic managers should consider how each alternative will affect various stakeholder groups. What seems at first to be the best decision because it appears to be the most profitable may actually result in the worst set of consequences to the corporation. One example of a company that does its best to consider its responsibilities to its primary and secondary stakeholders when making strategic decisions is Johnson & Johnson. See the **Strategy Highlight** feature for the J & J Credo.

STRATEGY highlight

JOHNSON & JOHNSON CREDO

We believe our first responsibility is to the doctors, nurses, and patients, to mothers and fathers and all others who use our products and services. In meeting their needs everything we do must be of high quality. We must constantly strive to reduce our costs in order to maintain reasonable prices. Customers' orders must be serviced promptly and accurately. Our suppliers and distributors must have an opportunity to make a fair profit.

We are responsible to our employees, the men and women who work with us throughout the world. Everyone must be considered as an individual. We must respect their dignity and recognize their merit. They must have a sense of security in their jobs. Compensation must be fair and adequate, and working conditions clean, orderly, and safe. We must be mindful of ways to help our employees fulfill their family responsibilities. Employees must feel free to make suggestions and complaints. There must be equal opportunity for employment, development, and advancement for those qualified. We must provide competent management, and their actions must be just and ethical.

We are responsible to the communities where we live and work and to the world community as well. We must be good citizens—support good works and charities and bear our fair share of taxes. We must encourage civic improvements and better health and education. We must maintain in good order the property we are privileged to use, protecting the environment and natural resources.

Our final responsibility is to our stockholders. Business must make a sound profit. We must experiment with new ideas. Research must be carried on, innovative programs developed, and mistakes paid for. New equipment must be purchased, new facilities provided, and new products launched. Reserves must be created for adverse times. When we operate according to these principles, the stockholders should realize a fair return.

....

Ethical Decision Making

Some people joke that there is no such thing as "business ethics." They call it an oxymoron—a concept that combines opposite or contradictory ideas. Unfortunately, there is some truth to this sarcastic comment. The 2011 (released in 2012) survey by the Ethics Resource Center of more than 4600 employees found that 45% of employees surveyed said that they had witnessed misconduct at work, but only 65% reported it.[31] The most commonly reported types of misconduct were misuse of company time (33%), abusive behavior (21%), lying to employees (20%), and violating company Internet use policies (16%). However, there were other more egregious observed behaviors including stealing (12%), falsifying time reports or hours worked (12%), and environmental violation (7%).[32] In a survey from 1996 to 2005 of top managers at 2270 firms, researchers found that 29.2% of the firms analyzed had backdated or otherwise manipulated stock option grants to take advantage of favorable share-price movements.[33]

The Financial Crimes Enforcement Network found that mortgage fraud cases jumped by over 88% from 2010 to 2011 to just over 29,500. The most common type of mortgage fraud are debt-elimination scams, falsifying information on loan applications and identity theft.[34] In one instance, Allison Bice, office manager at Leonard Fazio's RE/MAX A-1 Best Realtors in Urbandale, Iowa, admitted that she submitted fake invoices and copies of checks drawn on a closed account as part of a scheme to obtain more money from Homecoming Financial, a mortgage company that had hired Fazio's agency to resell foreclosed homes.

A study of more than 5000 graduate students at 32 colleges and universities in the United States and Canada revealed that 56% of business students and 47% of non-business students admitted to cheating at least once during the past year. Cheating was more likely when a student's peers also cheated.[35] In another example, 6000 people paid US$30 to enter a VIP section on ScoreTop.com's Web site to obtain access to actual test questions posted by those who had recently taken the Graduate Management Admission Test (GMAT). In response, the Graduate Management Admission Council promised to cancel the scores of anyone who posted "live" questions to the site or knowingly read them.[36] Given this lack of ethical behavior among students, it is easy to understand why some could run into trouble if they obtained a job at a corporation having an unethical culture, such as Enron, World-Com, or Tyco.

SOME REASONS FOR UNETHICAL BEHAVIOR

Why are many business people perceived to be acting unethically? It may be that the involved people are not even aware that they are doing something questionable. There is no worldwide standard of conduct for business people. This is especially important given the global nature of business activities. Cultural norms and values vary between countries and even between different geographic regions and ethnic groups within a country. For example, what is considered in one country to be a bribe to expedite service is sometimes considered in another country to be normal business practice. Some of these differences may derive from whether a country's governance system is *rule-based* or *relationship-based*. Relationship-based countries tend to be less transparent and have a higher degree of corruption than do rule-based countries.[37] See the **Global Issue** feature for an explanation of country governance systems and how they may affect business practices

Another possible reason for what is often perceived to be unethical behavior lies in differences in values between business people and key stakeholders. Some businesspeople may believe profit maximization is the key goal of their firm, whereas concerned interest groups may have other priorities, such as the hiring of minorities and women or the safety of their neighborhoods. Of the six values measured by the Allport-Vernon-Lindzey Study of Values test (aesthetic, economic, political, religious, social, and theoretical), both U.S. and UK executives consistently score highest on economic and political values and lowest on social and religious ones. This is similar to the value profile of managers from Japan, Korea, India, and Australia, as well as those of U.S. business school students. U.S. Protestant ministers, in contrast, score highest on religious and social values and very low on economic values.[38]

This difference in values can make it difficult for one group of people to understand another's actions. For example, Michael Bloomberg, mayor of New York City has pushed through regulations that changed the type of oil that fast-food companies could use in their fryers, mandated calorie listings for all eating establishments, and in 2012 pushed through a plan that prohibited food-service establishments from selling sodas and similarly sweet drinks in sizes larger than 16 oz. "*Let the buyer beware*" is a traditional saying by free-market proponents who argue that customers in a free market democracy have the right to choose how they spend their money and live their lives. Social progressives contend that business people working in tobacco, alcoholic beverages, gambling, and maybe now the soft drink industries are acting unethically by making and advertising products with potentially dangerous and expensive side effects, such as cancer, alcoholism, obesity, and addiction. People working in these industries could respond by asking whether it is ethical for people who don't smoke, drink, or gamble to reject another person's right to do so.

GLOBAL issue

HOW RULE-BASED AND RELATIONSHIP-BASED GOVERNANCE SYSTEMS AFFECT ETHICAL BEHAVIOR

The developed nations of the world operate under governance systems quite different from those used by developing nations. Developed nations and the business firms within them follow well-recognized rules in their dealings and financial reporting. To the extent that a country's rules force business corporations to publicly disclose in-depth information about the company to potential shareholders and others, that country's financial and legal system is said to be *transparent*. Transparency helps simplify transactions and reduces the temptation to behave illegally or unethically. Finland, the United Kingdom, Hong Kong, the United States, and Australia have very transparent business climates. The Kurtzman Group, a consulting firm, developed an *opacity index* that measures the risks associated with unclear legal systems, regulations, economic policies, corporate governance standards, and corruption in 48 countries. The countries with the most opaque/least transparent ratings are Indonesia, Venezuela, China, Nigeria, India, Egypt, and Russia.

Developing nations tend to have *relationship-based governance*. Transactions are based on personal and implicit agreements, not on formal contracts enforceable by a court. Information about a business is largely local and private—thus, it cannot be easily verified by a third party. In contrast, *rule-based governance* relies on publicly verifiable information—the type of information that is typically not available in a developing country. The rule-based system has an infrastructure, based on accounting, auditing, ratings systems, legal cases, and codes, to provide and monitor this information. If present in a developing nation, the infrastructure is not very sophisticated. This is why investing in a developing country is very risky. The relationship-based system in a developing

nation is inherently nontransparent due to the local and non-verifiable nature of its information. A business person needs to develop and nurture a wide network of personal relationships. *What* you know is less important than *who* you know.

The investment in time and money needed to build the necessary relationships to conduct business in a developing nation creates a high entry barrier for any newcomers to an industry. Thus, key industries in developing nations tend to be controlled by a small number of companies, usually privately owned, family-controlled conglomerates. Because public information is unreliable and insufficient for decisions, strategic decisions may depend more on a CEO playing golf with the prime minister than with questionable market share data. In a relationship-based system, the culture of the country (and the founder's family) strongly affects corporate culture and business ethics. What is "fair" depends on whether one is a family member, a close friend, a neighbor, or a stranger. Because behavior tends to be less controlled by laws and agreed-upon standards than by tradition, businesspeople from a rule-based developed nation perceive the relationship-based system in a developing nation to be less ethical and more corrupt. According to Larry Smeltzer, ethics professor at Arizona State University: "The lack of openness and predictable business standards drives companies away. Why would you want to do business in, say Libya, where you don't know the rules?"

....

SOURCES: S. Li, S. H. Park, and S. Li, "The Great Leap Forward: The Transition from Relation-Based Governance to Rule-Based Governance," *Organizational Dynamics* (Vol. 33, No. 1, 2003), pp. 63–78; M. Davids, "Global Standards, Local Problems," *Journal of Business Strategy* (January/February 1999), pp. 38–43; "The Opacity Index," *The Economist* (September 18, 2004), p. 106.

Seventy percent of executives representing 111 diverse national and multinational corporations reported that they bend the rules to attain their objectives.[39] The three most common reasons given were:

- Organizational performance required it—74%
- Rules were ambiguous or out of date—70%
- Pressure from others and everyone does it—47%

The financial community's emphasis on short-term earnings performance is a significant pressure for executives to "manage" quarterly earnings. For example, a company achieving its forecasted quarterly earnings figure signals the investment community that its strategy and operations are proceeding as planned. Failing to meet its targeted objective signals that the company is in trouble—thus causing the stock price to fall and shareholders to become worried. Research by Degeorge and Patel involving more than 100,000 quarterly earnings reports revealed that a preponderance (82%) of reported earnings *exactly* matched analysts' expectations or exceeded them by 1%. The disparity between the number of earnings reports that missed estimates by a penny and the number that exceeded them by a penny suggests that executives who risked falling short of forecasts "borrowed" earnings from future quarters.[40]

In explaining why executives and accountants at Enron engaged in unethical and illegal actions, former Enron Vice-President Sherron Watkins used the *"frogs in boiling water"* analogy. If, for example, one were to toss a frog into a pan of boiling water, according to the folk tale, the frog would quickly jump out. It might be burned, but the frog would survive. However, if one put a frog in a pan of cold water and turned up the heat very slowly, the frog would not sense the increasing heat until it was too lethargic to jump out and would be boiled.

Moral Relativism

Some people justify their seemingly unethical positions by arguing that there is no one absolute code of ethics and that morality is relative. Simply put, **moral relativism** claims that morality is relative to some personal, social, or cultural standard and that there is no method for deciding whether one decision is better than another.

At one time or another, most managers have probably used one of the four types of moral relativism—naïve, role, social group, or cultural—to justify questionable behavior.[41]

Naïve relativism: Based on the belief that all moral decisions are deeply personal and that individuals have the right to run their own lives, adherents of moral relativism argue that each person should be allowed to interpret situations and act on his or her own moral values. This is not so much a belief as it is an excuse for not having a belief or is a common excuse for not taking action when observing others lying or cheating.

Role relativism: Based on the belief that social roles carry with them certain obligations to that role, adherents of role relativism argue that a manager in charge of a work unit must put aside his or her personal beliefs and do instead what the role requires—that is, act in the best interests of the unit. Blindly following orders was a common excuse provided by Nazi war criminals after World War II.

Social group relativism: Based on a belief that morality is simply a matter of following the norms of an individual's peer group, social group relativism argues that a decision is considered legitimate if it is common practice, regardless of other considerations ("everyone's doing it"). A real danger in embracing this view is that the person may incorrectly believe that a certain action is commonly accepted practice in an industry when it is not.

Cultural relativism: Based on the belief that morality is relative to a particular culture, society, or community, adherents of cultural relativism argue that people should understand the practices of other societies, but not judge them. This view not only suggests that one should not criticize another culture's norms and customs, but also that it is acceptable to personally follow these norms and customs ("When in Rome, do as the Romans do.").

Although each of these arguments have some element that may be understandable, moral relativism could enable a person to justify almost any sort of decision or action, so long as it is not declared illegal.

Kohlberg's Levels of Moral Development

Another reason why some business people might be seen as unethical is that they may have no well-developed personal sense of ethics. A person's ethical behavior is affected by his or her level of moral development, certain personality variables, and such situational factors as the job itself, the supervisor, and the organizational culture.[42] Kohlberg proposes that a person progresses through three **levels of moral development**.[43] Similar in some ways to Maslow's hierarchy of needs, in Kohlberg's system, the individual moves from total self-centeredness to a concern for universal values. Kohlberg's three levels are as follows:

1. **The preconventional level:** This level is characterized by a concern for self. Small children and others who have not progressed beyond this stage evaluate behaviors on the basis of personal interest—avoiding punishment or quid pro quo.

2. **The conventional level:** This level is characterized by considerations of society's laws and norms. Actions are justified by an external code of conduct.

3. **The principled level:** This level is characterized by a person's adherence to an internal moral code. An individual at this level looks beyond norms or laws to find universal values or principles. See the Innovation Issue to see how someone turned a pressing world need into a viable business.

Kohlberg places most people in the conventional level, with fewer than 20% of U.S. adults in the principled level of development.[44] Research appears to support Kohlberg's concept. For example, one study found that individuals higher in cognitive moral development, lower in Machiavellianism, with a more internal locus of control, a less-relativistic moral philosophy, and higher job satisfaction are less likely to plan and enact unethical choices.[45]

INNOVATION issue

TURNING A NEED INTO A BUSINESS TO SOLVE THE NEED

Tying an innovative idea to a social problem and turning it into a viable business is no small feat. Putting those three concepts together was exactly what David Auerbach accomplished. After returning from a two-year fellowship in China's Hunan province, he and several of his MIT classmates put their heads together to solve a horrifying problem that he encountered. He found that vast rural stretches of the Chinese provinces had no adequate sanitation. Pit latrines that spread disease and made life miserable were more the norm than he realized.

Today, 2.6 billion people on the earth have no access to adequate sanitation. The resulting disease and pollution cause more than 1.7 million deaths and the loss of some US$84 billion in worker time each year. A particularly poor area of the world is Kenya, where some 8 million people lack any access to adequate sanitation.

The key was to turn this issue into something more than a charity. Charities come and go with the interest level of donors. If Auerbach and his team could figure out how to make it into a business, then the potential for vastly improving the lives of millions might be possible. With that, he and his classmates put together a business plan and won the 2009 business plan competition at MIT. Armed with their prize money and US$20,000 from the Eleos Foundation (a nonprofit that makes venture capital investments in social businesses), they set off to start a company in Kenya.

Today that company is Sanergy (http://saner.gy). They build prefab concrete toilets and sell them to local entrepreneurs for US$500. Those entrepreneurs charge "customers" roughly 5 cents per use. The units are well stocked with toilet paper, soap, and water. The waste is collected by the company at the end of each day and is processed and sold as fertilizer. By July 2012, they had 30 franchises and 50 toilets serving more than 2000 residents. The team is now looking at pitching the toilets to landlords as a means for them to charge a bit more in rent but provide better sanitation to their tenants.

There are no easy answers in addressing some of these almost intractable problems, but a consistent theme of success is turning a "good" into a business that thrives for local residents.

....
SOURCES: "Getting to Sanitation for All: Always Be Closing," (July 9, 2012), (http://saner.gy/2012/07/09/getting-to-sanitation-for-all-always-be-closing); P. Clark, "Innovator Cleaning Up," *BusinessWeek* (October 17, 2011).

ENCOURAGING ETHICAL BEHAVIOR

Following Carroll's work, if business people do not act ethically, government will be forced to pass laws regulating their actions—and usually increasing their costs. For self-interest, if for no other reason, managers should be more ethical in their decision making. One way to do that is by developing codes of ethics. Another is by providing guidelines for ethical behavior.

Codes of Ethics

A **code of ethics** specifies how an organization expects its employees to behave while on the job. Developing a code of ethics can be a useful way to promote ethical behavior, especially for people who are operating at Kohlberg's conventional level of moral development. Such codes are currently being used by more than half of U.S. business corporations. A code of ethics (1) clarifies company expectations of employee conduct in various situations and (2) makes clear that the company expects its people to recognize the ethical dimensions in decisions and actions.[46]

Various studies indicate that an increasing number of companies are developing codes of ethics and implementing ethics training workshops and seminars. However, research also indicates that when faced with a question of ethics, managers tend to ignore codes of ethics and try to solve dilemmas on their own.[47] To combat this tendency, the management of a company that wants to improve its employees' ethical behavior should not only develop a comprehensive code of ethics but also communicate the code in its training programs, in its performance appraisal system, policies and procedures, and through its own actions.[48] It may even include key values in its values and mission statements. According to a 2011 survey conducted by the National Business Ethics Survey (NBES), the strength of ethics cultures declined dramatically in 2011 with 42% of respondents finding that their corporate ethics culture was either weak or weak leaning. This was an increase from the 2009 survey that found only 35% in the same situation. Specific findings of interest were:

- 90% of employees who observed corporate misconduct rated their cultures as Weak.
- 34% of employees felt that their supervisor did not display ethical behavior.
- 34% said their management watches them more closely.[49]

In addition, U.S. corporations have attempted to support **whistle-blowers**, those employees who report illegal or unethical behavior on the part of others. The U.S. False Claims Act gives whistle-blowers 15% to 30% of any damages recovered in cases where the government is defrauded. Even though the Sarbanes–Oxley Act forbids firms from retaliating against anyone reporting wrongdoing, 22% of employees who reported misconduct in one study said they experienced retaliation, which was up from 15% in 2009 and 12% in 2007.[50]

Corporations appear to benefit from well-conceived and implemented ethics programs. For example, companies with strong ethical cultures and enforced codes of conduct have fewer unethical choices available to employees—thus fewer temptations.[51] A study by the Open Compliance and Ethics Group found that no company with an ethics program in place for 10 years or more experienced "reputational damage" in the last five years.[52] Some of the companies identified in surveys as having strong moral cultures are Canon, Hewlett-Packard, Johnson & Johnson, Levi Strauss, Medtronic, Motorola, Newman's Own, Patagonia, S. C. Johnson, Shorebank, Smucker, and Sony.[53]

A corporation's management should consider establishing and enforcing a code of ethical behavior not only for itself, but also for those companies with which it does business—especially if it outsources its manufacturing to a company in another country. Apple is one of the most profitable and powerful companies in the world. Much of their product manufacturing is outsourced to Chinese factories that have a reputation for harsh working conditions.

Apple has a supplier code of conduct and a relatively vigorous auditing effort. Despite those efforts, *The New York Times* reported in 2012 that some of the suppliers audited by Apple had violated at least one aspect of the code every year since 2007. Critics have pointed out that for a variety of reasons Apple is relatively lax in its enforcement of the code. *The New York Times* reported that Apple conducted 312 audits over a three-year time period finding more than half the companies in violation and 70 core violations. Yet, despite all the evidence, Apple has terminated only 15 contracts over the past 5 years.[54]

Recent surveys of over one hundred companies in the Global 2000 uncovered that 64% have some code of conduct that regulates supplier conduct, but only 40% require suppliers to actually take any action with respect to the code, such as disseminating it to employees, offering training, certifying compliance, or even reading or acknowledging receipt of the code.[55]

It is important to note that having a code of ethics for suppliers does not prevent harm to a corporation's reputation if one of its offshore suppliers is able to conceal abuses. Numerous Chinese factories, for example, keep double sets of books to fool auditors and distribute scripts for employees to recite if they are questioned. Consultants have found new business helping Chinese companies evade audits.[56]

Guidelines for Ethical Behavior

Ethics is defined as the consensually accepted standards of behavior for an occupation, a trade, or a profession. **Morality**, in contrast, constitutes one's rules of personal behavior based on religious or philosophical grounds. **Law** refers to formal codes that permit or forbid certain behaviors and may or may not enforce ethics or morality.[57] Given these definitions, how do we arrive at a comprehensive statement of ethics to use in making decisions in a specific occupation, trade, or profession? A starting point for such a code of ethics is to consider the three basic approaches to ethical behavior:[58]

1. **Utilitarian approach:** The **utilitarian approach** proposes that actions and plans should be judged by their consequences. People should therefore behave in a way that will produce the greatest benefit to society and produce the least harm or the lowest cost. A problem with this approach is the difficulty in recognizing all the benefits and costs of any particular decision. Research reveals that only the stakeholders who have the most *power* (ability to affect the company), *legitimacy* (legal or moral claim on company resources), and *urgency* (demand for immediate attention) are given priority by CEOs.[59] It is therefore likely that only the most obvious stakeholders will be considered, while others are ignored.

2. **Individual rights approach:** The **individual rights approach** proposes that human beings have certain fundamental rights that should be respected in all decisions. A particular decision or behavior should be avoided if it interferes with the rights of others. A problem with this approach is in defining "fundamental rights." The U.S. Constitution includes a Bill of Rights that may or may not be accepted throughout the world. The approach can also encourage selfish behavior when a person defines a personal need or want as a "right."

3. **Justice approach:** The **justice approach** proposes that decision makers be equitable, fair, and impartial in the distribution of costs and benefits to individuals and groups. It follows the principles of *distributive justice* (people who are similar on relevant dimensions such as job seniority should be treated in the same way) and *fairness* (liberty should be equal for all persons). The justice approach can also include the concepts of *retributive justice* (punishment should be proportional to the offense) and *compensatory justice* (wrongs should be compensated in proportion to the offense). Affirmative action issues such as reverse discrimination are examples of conflicts between distributive and compensatory justice.

Cavanagh proposes that we solve ethical problems by asking the following three questions regarding an act or a decision:

1. **Utility:** Does it optimize the satisfactions of all stakeholders?
2. **Rights:** Does it respect the rights of the individuals involved?
3. **Justice:** Is it consistent with the canons of justice?[60]

For example, what if a company allows one vice-president to fly first class to Europe, but not others? Using the utility criterion, this action increases the company's costs and thus does not optimize benefits for shareholders or customers. Using the rights approach, the VP allowed to fly first class might argue that he or she is owed this type of reward for the extra strain that an international trip puts on personal relationships or work performance. Using the justice criterion, unless everyone at the VP level is allowed to fly first class, the privilege is not justifiable.

Another approach to resolving ethical dilemmas is by applying the logic of the philosopher Immanuel Kant. Kant presents two principles (called **categorical imperatives**) to guide our actions:

1. A person's action is ethical only if that person is willing for that same action to be taken by everyone who is in a similar situation. This is the same as the Golden Rule: Treat others as you would like them to treat you. For example, staying at upscale hotels while on the trip to Europe is only ethical if the same opportunity is available to others in the company at the same level.

2. A person should never treat another human being simply as a means but always as an end. This means that an action is morally wrong for a person if that person uses others merely as a means for advancing his or her own interests. To be moral, the act should not restrict other people's actions so they are disadvantaged in some way.[61]

End of Chapter SUMMARY

In his book *Defining Moments*, Joseph Badaracco states that most ethics problems deal with "right versus right" problems in which neither choice is wrong. These are what he calls "dirty hands problems" in which a person has to deal with very specific situations that are covered only vaguely in corporate credos or mission statements. For example, many mission statements endorse fairness but fail to define the term. At the personal level, *fairness* could mean playing by the rules of the game, following basic morality, treating everyone alike and not playing favorites, treating others as you would want to be treated, being sensitive to individual needs, providing equal opportunity for everyone, or creating a level playing field for the disadvantaged. According to Badaracco, codes of ethics are not always helpful because they tend to emphasize problems of misconduct and wrongdoing, not a choice between two acceptable alternatives, such as keeping an inefficient plant operating for the good of the community or closing the plant and relocating to a more efficient location to lower costs.[62]

This chapter provides a framework for evaluating the social responsibilities of a business. Following Carroll, it proposes that a manager should consider not only the economic and legal responsibilities of the business but also its ethical and discretionary responsibilities. It also provides a method for making ethical choices, whether they are right versus right or some combination of right and wrong. It is important to consider Cavanaugh's questions about using the utilitarian, individual rights, and justice approaches, plus Kant's categorical imperatives, when making a strategic decision. In general, a corporation should try to move from Kohlberg's conventional development to a principled level of ethical development. If nothing else, the frameworks should contribute to well-reasoned strategic decisions that a person can defend when interviewed by hostile media or questioned in a court room.

MyManagementLab®

Go to **mymanagementlab.com** to complete the problems marked with this icon ⭐.

KEY TERMS

categorical imperatives (p. 84)

code of ethics (p. 82)

ethics (p. 83)

individual rights approach (p. 83)

justice approach (p. 83)

law (p. 83)

levels of moral development (p. 81)

morality (p. 83)

moral relativism (p. 80)

social responsibility (p. 70)

stakeholder analysis (p. 75)

stakeholders (p. 74)

utilitarian approach (p. 83)

whistle-blowers (p. 82)

MyManagementLab®

Go to **mymanagmentlab.com** for Auto-graded writing questions as well as the following Assisted-graded writing questions:

3-1. How has moral relativism led to criminal activities by some employees in companies?

3-2. How does a company ensure that its code of ethics is integrated into the daily decision-making process of the company and is not just a symbolic trophy or plaque hanging on the wall?

DISCUSSION QUESTIONS

3-3. What is the relationship between corporate governance and social responsibility?

⭐ **3-4.** What is your opinion of Apple having a code of conduct for its suppliers? What would Milton Friedman say? Contrast his view with Archie Carroll's view.

⭐ **3-5.** Does a company have to act selflessly to be considered socially responsible? For example, when building a new plant, a corporation voluntarily invested in additional equipment that enabled it to reduce its pollution emissions beyond any current laws. Knowing that it would be very expensive for its competitors to do the same, the firm lobbied the government to make pollution regulations more restrictive on the entire industry. Is this company socially responsible? Were its managers acting ethically?

3-6. Are people living in a relationship-based governance system likely to be unethical in business dealings?

⭐ **3-7.** Given that people rarely use a company's code of ethics to guide their decision making, what good are the codes?

STRATEGIC PRACTICE EXERCISE

It was certainly not the first time it had happened to the new social gaming company, but it was more of a worry this time. It was taking a lot longer to release the first version of the game being designed than had ever been anticipated. The firm had raised money four times already, but this round was more of an issue. The company probably needed an additional US$25 million, and more and more it was looking like the sales projections were far too optimistic.

The original idea for the game had morphed quite a bit and now was slated to use Facebook as its platform. The problem had occurred during the almost three years it had taken to bring the product to market. Two other games had been released that had taken the wind out of the new offering.

Knowing this, the company had quietly begun work on a new gaming platform. The problem was that it would take another 18 months before it has any marketability, and investors were unlikely to provide the type of valuations the company needed to keep afloat. The key to raising the funds needed was to keep talking about the existing game and getting it released into the market.

Private company valuations and market potential is difficult under the best circumstances. They are not required to provide audited financials, the risk of failure is quite high, and sales projections are at best a guess. They do not exist in the marketplace, so there is no history from which to judge their performance. In addition, competitor reactions to their entry is unknown.

All of this is hard enough for investors, let alone the issue of management trying to hide known issues. The management of the business is convinced that they can be a big player in the market with their newer product, however to get there they need the finances that may only be available if they act as if the product closer to release will be THE ONE. What should the manager do? Why do you believe so? What are the ethical implications of your decision?

NOTES

1. M. Friedman, "The Social Responsibility of Business Is to Increase Its Profits," *The New York Times Magazine* (September 13, 1970), pp. 30, 126–127; M. Friedman, *Capitalism and Freedom* (Chicago: University of Chicago Press, 1963), p. 133.

2. W. J. Byron, *Old Ethical Principles for the New Corporate Culture*, presentation to the College of Business, Iowa State University, Ames, Iowa (March 31, 2003).

3. A. B. Carroll, "A Three-Dimensional Conceptual Model of Corporate Performance," *Academy of Management Review* (October 1979), pp. 497–505. This model of business responsibilities was reaffirmed in A. B. Carroll, "Managing Ethically with Global Stakeholders: A Present and Future Challenge," *Academy of Management Executive* (May 2004), pp. 114–120.

4. Carroll refers to discretionary responsibilities as philanthropic responsibilities in A. B. Carroll, "The Pyramid of Corporate Social Responsibility: Toward the Moral Management of Organizational Stakeholders," *Business Horizons* (July–August 1991), pp. 39–48.

5. M. S. Baucus and D. A. Baucus, "Paying the Piper: An Empirical Examination of Longer-Term Financial Consequences of Illegal Corporate Behavior," *Academy of Management Journal* (February 1997), pp. 129–151.

6. J. Oleck, "Pink Slips with a Silver Lining," *BusinessWeek* (June 4, 2001), p. 14.

7. S. M. J. Bonini, L. T. Mendonca, and J. M. Oppenheim, "When Social Issues Become Strategic," *McKinsey Quarterly* (2006, Number 2), pp. 20–31.

8. "The McKinsey Global Survey of Business Executives: Business and Society," *McKinsey Quarterly*, Web edition (March 31, 2006).

9. "Corporate Social Responsibility Now a Staple at Davos," *CNBC* (January 22, 2012), (www.cnbc.com/id/45856248/corporate_social_responsibility_now_a_staple_at_Davos).

10. A. McWilliams and D. Siegel, "Corporate Social Responsibility and Financial Performance: Correlation or Misspecification?" *Strategic Management Journal* (May 2000), pp. 603–609; P. Rechner and K. Roth, "Social Responsibility and Financial Performance: A Structural Equation Methodology," *International Journal of Management* (December 1990), pp. 382–391; K. E. Aupperle, A. B. Carroll, and J. D. Hatfield, "An Empirical Examination of the Relationship Between Corporate Social Responsibility and Profitability," *Academy of Management Journal* (June 1985), p. 459.

11. M. M. Arthur, "Share Price Reactions to Work-Family Initiatives: An Institutional Perspective," *Academy of Management Journal* (April 2003), pp. 497–505; S. A. Waddock and S. B. Graves, "The Corporate Social Performance—Financial Performance Link," *Strategic Management Journal* (April 1997), pp. 303–319; M. V. Russo and P. A. Fouts, "Resource Based Perspective on Corporate Environmental Performance and Profitability" *Academy of Management Journal* (July 1997), pp. 534–559; H. Meyer, "The Greening of Corporate America," *Journal of Business Strategy* (January/February 2000), pp. 38–43.

12. J. D. Margolis and J. P. Walsh, "Misery Loves Companies: Re-thinking Social Initiatives by Business," *Administrative Science Quarterly* (June 2003), pp. 268–305.

13. M. F. L. Orlitzky, F. L. Schmidt, and S. L. Rynes, "Corporate Social and Financial Performance: A Meta Analysis," *Organization Studies* (Vol. 24, 2003), pp. 403–441.

14. M. Porter and M. R. Kramer, "The Competitive Advantage of Corporate Philanthropy," *Harvard Business Review* (December 2002), p. 59.

15. P. S. Adler and S. W. Kwon, "Social Capital: Prospects for a New Concept," *Academy of Management Journal* (January 2002), pp. 17–40. Also called "moral capital" in P. C. Godfrey, "The Relationship Between Corporate Philanthropy and Shareholder Wealth: A Risk Management Perspective," *Academy of Management Review* (October 2005), pp. 777–799.

16. L. Gard, "We're Good Guys, Buy from Us," *BusinessWeek* (November 22, 2004), pp. 72–74.

17. G. Thornton, "Corporate Social Responsibility – A Necessity Not a Choice for Privately Held Businesses," (2008), (www.internationalbusinessreport.com/2008/corporate-social-responsibility.asp).

18. C. J. Fombrun, "Corporate Reputation as an Economic Asset," in M. A. Hitt, E. R. Freeman, and J. S. Harrison (Eds.), *The Blackwell Handbook of Strategic Management* (Oxford: Blackwell Publishers, 2001), pp. 289–310.

19. S. A. Muirhead, C. J. Bennett, R. E. Berenbeim, A. Kao, and D. J. Vidal, *Corporate Citizenship in the New Century* (New York: The Conference Board, 2002), p. 6.

20. *2002 Sustainability Survey Report*, PriceWaterhouseCoopers, reported in "Corporate America's Social Conscience," Special Advertising Section, *Fortune* (May 26, 2003), pp. 149–157.

21. C. L. Harman and E. R. Stafford, "Green Alliances: Building New Business with Environmental Groups" *Long Range Planning* (April 1997), pp. 184–196.

22. D. B. Turner and D. W. Greening, "Corporate Social Performance and Organizational Attractiveness to Prospective Employees," *Academy of Management Journal* (July 1997), pp. 658–672; S. Preece, C. Fleisher, and J. Toccacelli, "Building a Reputation Along the Value Chain at Levi Strauss," *Long Range Planning* (December 1995), pp. 88–98; J. B. Barney and M. H. Hansen, "Trustworthiness as a Source of Competitive Advantage," *Strategic Management Journal* (Special Winter Issue, 1994), pp. 175–190: R. V. Aguilera, D. E. Rupp, C. A. Williams, and J. Ganapathi, "Putting the S Back in Corporate Social Responsibility: A Multilevel Theory of Social Change in Organizations," *Academy of Management Review* (July 2007), pp. 836–863; S. Bonini and S. Chenevert, "The State of Corporate Philanthropy: A McKinsey Global Survey," *McKinsey Quarterly*, Web edition (March 1, 2008); P. Kotler and N. Lee (Eds.), *Corporate Social Responsibility: Doing the Most Good for Your Company and Your Cause* (Hoboken, NJ: Wiley, 2005).

23. "Numbers: Do-Good Investments Are Holding Up Better," *BusinessWeek* (July 14 and 21, 2008), p. 15.

24. A. Crane and D. Matten, *Business Ethics: A European Perspective* (Oxford: Oxford University Press, 2004), p. 22.

25. R. E. Freeman and D. R. Gilbert, *Corporate Strategy and the Search for Ethics* (Upper Saddle River, NJ: Prentice Hall, 1988), p. 6.

26. "CSR Branding Survey 2010," (www.slideshare.net/bmglobalnews/csr-branding-survey-2010-final).

27. M. Boesler, "Study: 20% of Companies Lie on Earnings Reports, Top Reason Is to Boost Stock Price," *Business Insider* (July 25, 2012), (www.businessinsider.com/study-20-of-companies-lie-earnings-stock-prices-2012-7).

28. "BP expert defends controversial cost saving decision before blast," ProjectNola.com (July 22, 2010), (http://projectnola.com/the-news/news/42-fox-8/98578-bp-expert-defends-controversial-cost-saving-decision-before-blast).

29. W. E. Stead and J. G. Stead, *Sustainable Strategic Management* (Armonk, NY: M. E. Sharpe, 2004), p. 41.

30. B. Barrow, "Chick-fil-A Sandwiches at Center of Latest Political Storm," *The Charlotte Observer* (July 27, 2012), pg. A1.

31. M. Oxley and P. Harned, "2011 National Business Ethics Survey," (2012), pp. 1–62.

32. Ibid.

33. "Dates from Hell," *The Economist* (July 22, 2006), pp. 59–60.

34. B. O'Connell, "Mortgage Fraud Cases Climbing," NuWire Investor (2011), www.nuwireinvestor.com/articles/mortgage-fraud-cases-climbing-57871.aspx.

35. D. L. McCabe, K. D. Butterfield, and L. K. Trevino, "Academic Dishonesty in Graduate Business Programs: Prevalence, Causes, and Proposed Action," *Academy of Management Learning & Education* (September 2006), pp. 294–305.

36. L. Lavelle, "The GMAT Cheat Sheet," *BusinessWeek* (July 14 and 21, 2008), p. 34.

37. S. Li, S. H. Park, and S. Li, "The Great Leap Forward: The Transition from Relation-Based Governance to Rule-Based Governance," *Organizational Dynamics* (Vol. 33, No. 1, 2004), pp. 63–78; M. Davids, "Global Standards, Local Problems," *Journal of Business Strategy* (January/February 1999), pp. 38–43; "The Opacity Index," *The Economist* (September 18, 2004), p. 106.

38. K. Kumar, "Ethical Orientation of Future American Executives: What the Value Profiles of Business School Students Portend," *SAM Advanced Management Journal* (Autumn 1995), pp. 32–36, 47; M. Gable and P. Arlow, "A Comparative Examination of the Value Orientations of British and American Executives," *International Journal of Management* (September 1986), pp. 97–106; W. D. Guth and R. Tagiuri, "Personal Values and Corporate Strategy," *Harvard Business Review* (September–October 1965), pp. 126–127; G. W. England, "Managers and Their Value Systems: A Five Country Comparative Study," *Columbia Journal of World Business* (Summer 1978), p. 35.

39. J. F. Veiga, T. D. Golden, and K. Dechant, "Why Managers Bend Company Rules," *Academy of Management Executive* (May 2004), pp. 84–91.

40. H. Collingwood, "The Earnings Game," *Harvard Business Review* (June 2001), pp. 65–74; J. Fox, "Can We Trust Them Now?" *Fortune* (March 3, 2003), pp. 97–99.

41. R. E. Freeman and D. R. Gilbert, Jr., *Corporate Strategy and the Search for Ethics* (Englewood Cliffs, NJ: Prentice Hall, 1988), pp. 24–41.

42. L. K. Trevino, "Ethical Decision Making in Organizations: A Person-Situation Interactionist Model," *Academy of Management Review* (July 1986), pp. 601–617.

43. L. Kohlberg, "Moral Stage and Moralization: The Cognitive-Development Approach," in T. Lickona (Ed.), *Moral Development and Behavior* (New York: Holt, Rinehart & Winston, 1976).

44. L. K. Trevino, "Ethical Decision Making in Organizations: A Person-Situation Interactionist Model," *Academy of Management Review* (July 1986), p. 606; L. K. Trevino, G. R. Weaver, and S. J. Reynolds, "Behavioral Ethics in Organizations: A Review," *Journal of Management* (December 2006), pp. 951–990.

45. J. K. Gephart, D. A. Harrison, and L. K. Trevino, "The Who, When, and Where of Unethical Choices: Meta-Analytic Answers to Fundamental Ethics Questions." Paper presented to the *Academy of Management* annual meeting, Philadelphia, PA (2007).

46. J. Keogh (Ed.), *Corporate Ethics: A Prime Business Asset* (New York: The Business Roundtable, 1988), p. 5.

47. G. F. Kohut, and S. E. Corriher, "The Relationship of Age, Gender, Experience and Awareness of Written Ethics Policies to Business Decision Making," *SAM Advanced Management Journal* (Winter 1994), pp. 32–39; J. C. Lere and B. R. Gaumitz, "The Impact of Codes of Ethics on Decision Making: Some Insights from Information Economics," *Journal of Business Ethics* (Vol. 48, 2003), pp. 365–379.

48. W. I. Sauser, "Business Ethics: Back to Basics," *Management in Practice* (2005, No. 2), pp. 2–3; J. M. Stevens, H. K. Steensma, D. A. Harrison, and P. L. Cochran, "Symbolic or Substantive Document? The Influence of Ethics Codes on Financial Executives' Decisions," *Strategic Management Journal* (February 2005), pp. 181–195.

49. M. Oxley and P. Harned, "2011 National Business Ethics Survey," (2012), pp. 1–62.

50. Ibid.

51. J. K. Gephart, D. A. Harrison, and L. K. Trevino, "The Who, When, and Where of Unethical Choices: Meta-Analytic Answers to Fundamental Ethics Questions." Paper presented to the *Academy of Management* annual meeting, Philadelphia, PA (2007).

52. "A 'How Am I Doing?' Guide for Ethics Czars," *Business Ethics* (Fall 2005), p. 11.

53. S. P. Feldman, "Moral Business Cultures: The Keys to Creating and Maintaining Them," *Organizational Dynamics* (Vol. 36, No. 2, 2007), pp. 156–170. Also see the "World's Most Ethical Companies," published annually by Ethisphere at http://ethisphere.com.

54. "In China, Human Costs Are Built into an iPad," *The New York Times* (January 25, 2012), (www.nytimes.com/2012/01/26/business/ieconomy-apples-ipad-and-the-human-costs-for-workers-in-china.html).

55. M. Levin, "Building an Ethical Supply Chain," *Sarbanes-Oxley Compliance Journal* (April 3, 2008).

56. A. Bernstein, S. Holmes, and X. Ji, "Secrets, Lies, and Sweatshops," *BusinessWeek* (November 27, 2006), pp. 50–58.

57. T. J. Von der Embse, and R. A. Wagley, "Managerial Ethics: Hard Decisions on Soft Criteria," *SAM Advanced Management Journal* (Winter 1988), p. 6.

58. G. F. Cavanagh, *American Business Values*, 3rd ed. (Upper Saddle River, NJ: Prentice Hall, 1990), pp. 186–199.

59. B. R. Agle, R. K. Mitchell, and J. A. Sonnenfeld, "Who Matters Most to CEOs? An Investigation of Stakeholder Attributes and Salience, Corporate Performance, and CEO Values," *Academy of Management Journal* (October 1999), pp. 507–525.

60. G. F. Cavanagh, *American Business Values*, 3rd ed. (Upper Saddle River, NJ: Prentice Hall, 1990), pp. 195–196.

61. I. Kant, "The Foundations of the Metaphysic of Morals," in *Ethical Theory: Classical and Contemporary Readings*, 2nd ed., by L. P. Pojman (Belmont, CA: Wadsworth Publishing, 1995), pp. 255–279.

62. J. L. Badaracco Jr., *Defining Moments* (Boston: Harvard Business School Press, 1997).

PART 2

Scanning the
Environment

environmental scanning and Industry Analysis

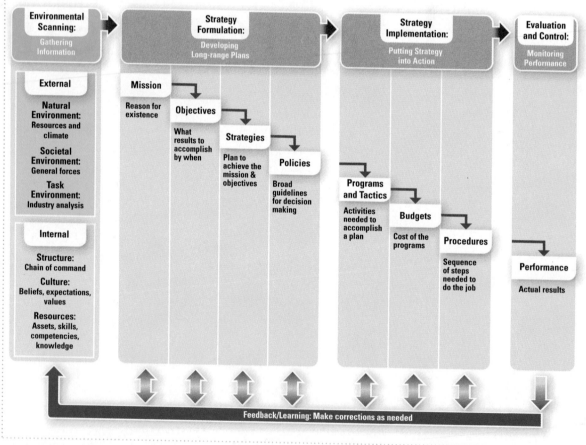

MyManagementLab®
⭐ Improve Your Grade!

Over 10 million students improved their results using the Pearson MyLabs. Visit **mymanagementlab.com** for simulations, tutorials, and end-of-chapter problems.

Learning Objectives

After reading this chapter, you should be able to:

- Recognize aspects of an organization's environment that can influence its long-term decisions
- Identify the aspects of an organization's environment that are most strategically important
- Conduct an industry analysis to understand the competitive forces that influence the intensity of rivalry within an industry
- Understand how industry maturity affects industry competitive forces
- Categorize international industries based on their pressures for coordination and local responsiveness

- Construct strategic group maps to assess the competitive positions of firms in an industry
- Identify key success factors and develop an industry matrix
- Use publicly available information to conduct competitive intelligence
- Know how to develop an industry scenario
- Be able to construct an EFAS Table that summarizes external environmental factors

No More Oil

Depending upon whom you listen to, the world will either run out of oil within 50 years or there will be oil for much longer because of new oil extraction techniques and undiscovered reserves. Both approaches suggest significant price increases to keep using oil as we do; however, the view you take for your business is likely to cause significantly different decisions.

According to a study by HSBC (the second largest bank in the world), at our current worldwide consumption rate (that does not include growth), the world is likely to have little or no oil left in 50 years. Enormous oil price increases will no doubt cause a significant drop in consumption and the associated extension of oil's availability. However, a change away from oil as a primary input to business will impact every economic enterprise on the earth. These changes are generally being ignored by the vast majority of businesses, and yet it's one area where proper planning can make a difference.

On the other side of this debate is an argument that there are many means with which to attain energy in a useable form. This includes oil sands, deep-water drilling, new oil extraction techniques like horizontal drilling, fracking, synthetic oils, and coal liquefaction to name a few. This supply/demand approach suggests that as price and demand rises, so will the means by which businesses satisfy those needs.

What might this mean for the economies of the world and the speed with which this event will arrive? What companies are working on alternative approaches to the use of oil? It is incumbent upon business leaders to think about the future and prepare their organizations for changes in the environment—be it the natural environment, competitive environment, political environment, technological environment, or social environment.

SOURCES: J. C. Rudolf, "Less than 50 Years of Oil Left, HSBC Warns," *The New York Times* (March 30, 2011), (http://green.blogs.nytimes.com/2011/01/20/less-than-50-years-of-oil-left-hsbc-warns/); C. Krauss, "There Will Be Fuel," *The New York Times* (November 16, 2010), (http://www.nytimes.com/2010/11/17/business/energy-environment/17fuel.html).

A changing environment can help as well as hurt a company. Many pioneering companies have gone out of business because of their failure to adapt to environmental change or, even worse, because of their failure to create change. For example, Baldwin Locomotive, the major manufacturer of steam locomotives, was very slow in making the switch to diesel locomotives. General Electric and General Motors soon dominated the diesel locomotive business and Baldwin went out of business. The dominant manufacturers of vacuum tubes failed to make the change to transistors and consequently lost this market. Eastman Kodak, the pioneer and market leader of chemical-based film photography, has been in a long decline as it struggles to find its place in the post-film world. Failure to adapt is, however, only one side of the coin. The aforementioned oil example shows how a changing environment usually creates new opportunities at the same time it destroys old ones. The lesson is simple: To be successful over time, an organization needs to be in tune with its external environment. There must be a strategic fit between what the environment wants and what the corporation has to offer, as well as between what the corporation needs and what the environment can provide.

Current predictions are that the environment for all organizations will become even more uncertain with every passing year. What is **environmental uncertainty**? It is the *degree of complexity* plus the *degree of change* that exists in an organization's external environment. As more and more markets become global, the number of factors a company must consider in any decision increases in size and difficulty. With new technologies being discovered every year, markets change and products must change with them.

On the one hand, environmental uncertainty is a threat to strategic managers because it hampers their ability to develop long-range plans and to make strategic decisions to keep the corporation in equilibrium with its external environment. On the other hand, environmental uncertainty is an opportunity because it creates a new playing field in which creativity and innovation can play a major part in strategic decisions.

Environmental Scanning

Before managers can begin strategy formulation, they must understand the context of the environment in which it competes. It is virtually impossible for a company to design a strategy without a deep understanding of the external environment. Once management has framed the aspects of the environment that impact the business, they are in a position to determine the firm's competitive advantages. **Environmental scanning** is an overarching term encompassing the monitoring, evaluation, and dissemination of information relevant to the organizational development of strategy. A corporation uses this tool to avoid strategic surprise and to ensure its long-term health. Research has found a positive relationship between environmental scanning and profits.[1] A 2011 study by McKinsey & Company found that executives ranked Macrolevel trends as the most important input to be considered when developing corporate strategy.[2]

IDENTIFYING EXTERNAL ENVIRONMENTAL VARIABLES

In undertaking environmental scanning, strategic managers must first be aware of the many variables within a corporation's natural, societal, and task environments (see **Figure 1–3**). The **natural environment** includes physical resources, wildlife, and climate that are an inherent part of existence on Earth. These factors form an ecological system of interrelated life. The **societal environment** is mankind's social system that includes general forces that do not directly touch on the short-run activities of the organization, but that can influence its long-term decisions. These factors affect multiple industries and are as follows:

- **Economic forces** that regulate the exchange of materials, money, energy, and information.
- **Technological forces** that generate problem-solving inventions.
- **Political–legal forces** that allocate power and provide constraining and protecting laws and regulations.
- **Sociocultural forces** that regulate the values, mores, and customs of society.

The **task environment** includes those elements or groups that directly affect a corporation and, in turn, are affected by it. These are governments, local communities, suppliers, competitors, customers, creditors, employees/labor unions, special-interest groups, and trade associations. A corporation's task environment is typically focused on the industry within which the firm operates. **Industry analysis** (popularized by Michael Porter) refers to an in-depth examination of key factors within a corporation's task environment. The natural, societal, and task environments must be monitored to examine the strategic factors that have a strong impact on corporate success or failure. Significant changes in the natural environment tend to impact the societal environment of the business (resource availability and costs), and finally the task environment because it impacts the growth or decline of whole industries.

Scanning the Natural Environment

The natural environment includes physical resources, wildlife, and climate that are an inherent part of existence on Earth. Until the 20th century, the natural environment was generally perceived by business people to be a given—something to exploit, not conserve. It was viewed as a free resource, something to be taken or fought over, like arable land, diamond mines, deep water harbors, or fresh water. Once they were controlled by a person or entity, these resources were considered assets and thus valued as part of the general economic system—a resource to be bought, sold, or sometimes shared. Side effects, such as pollution, were considered to be *externalities*, costs not included in a business firm's accounting system, but felt by others. Eventually these externalities were identified by governments, which passed regulations to force business corporations to deal with the side effects of their activities.

The concept of sustainability argues that a firm's ability to continuously renew itself for long-term success and survival is dependent not only upon the greater economic and social system of which it is a part, but also upon the natural ecosystem in which the firm is embedded.[3] For more information on innovative approaches to this issue, see the **Sustainability Issue** feature.

A business must scan the natural environment for factors that might previously have been taken for granted, such as the availability of fresh water and clean air. Global warming means that aspects of the natural environment, such as sea level, weather, and climate, are becoming increasingly uncertain and difficult to predict. Management must therefore scan not only the natural environment for possible strategic factors, but also include in its strategic decision-making processes the impact of its activities upon the natural environment. In a world concerned with climate change, a company could measure and reduce its *carbon footprint*—the amount of greenhouse gases it is emitting into the air. Research reveals that scanning the market for environmental issues is positively related to firm performance because it helps management identify opportunities to fulfill future market demand based upon environmentally friendly products or processes.[4] See the Sustainability Issue feature to learn how the high-end car companies saw an opportunity in green cars.

SUSTAINABILITY issue

GREEN SUPERCARS

The move to greener cars has finally reached ultra-high-end car companies, including Porsche, Ferrari, and Bentley. The push to get car manufacturing companies to increase gas mileage and reduce emissions has come from a combination of regulations, purchasing patterns, and pressure from environmental groups. Although some form of hybrid vehicle technology has been around since the beginning of the automobile, the Toyota Prius, introduced to the Japanese market in 1997, quickly became the standard of economy in the industry.

Higher-end car makers have been making hybrid vehicles for some time, even though the price of these vehicles has kept their sales relatively modest. BMW offers the 750i, four-door sedan for US$101,000, while the equivalent Mercedes sedan (S400) goes for roughly US$92,000. Despite this, ultra-luxury car makers waited until the 2013 model year to release their hybrid models.

Ferrari announced the F70, which has two electric motors along with a 12-cylinder gasoline engine that cuts fuel consumption by more than 40%. The price tag is something to see, however. The vehicle will most likely be priced above US$850,000. Porsche already has hybrid versions of its Cayenne SUV and Panamera four-door cars, clocking in at US$70,000 and US$96,000, respectively. However, they are also gearing up for a new 918 Spyder sports coupe to be released for the 2014 model year, which will cost more than US$950,000. Even venerable Bentley is planning a plug-in hybrid version of its SUV that will come with a price tag of around US$250,000.

All of these vehicles require battery packs that weigh in excess of 1000 pounds and must be disposed of when the vehicle is no longer useful. The increase in sustainability from an environmental approach on one end triggers an environmental issue at the other end of the product's useful life. So what is the right answer for these companies? And what about the environment?

....

SOURCES: http://www.hybridcars.com/history/history-of-hybrid-vehicles.html; T. Ebhardt, "Supercar Makers Seek a Different Shade of Green," *BusinessWeek* (May 28, 2012), (www.businessweek.com).

Scanning the Societal Environment: STEEP Analysis

The number of possible strategic factors in the societal environment is very high. The number becomes enormous when we realize that, generally speaking, each country in the world can be represented by its own unique set of societal forces—some of which are very similar to those of neighboring countries and some of which are very different.

For example, even though Korea and China share Asia's Pacific Rim area with Thailand, Taiwan, and Hong Kong (sharing many similar cultural values), they have very different views about the role of business in society. It is generally believed in Korea and China (and to a lesser extent in Japan) that the role of business is primarily to contribute to national development. However, in Hong Kong, Taiwan, and Thailand (and to a lesser extent in the Philippines, Indonesia, Singapore, and Malaysia), the role of business is primarily to make profits for the shareholders.[5] Such differences may translate into different trade regulations and varying difficulty in the *repatriation of profits* (the transfer of profits from a foreign subsidiary to a corporation's headquarters) from one group of Pacific Rim countries to another.

STEEP Analysis: Monitoring Trends in the Societal and Natural Environments. As shown in **Table 4–1,** large corporations categorize the natural and societal environments in any one geographic region into five areas and focus their scanning in each area on trends that have corporatewide relevance. For ease of remembering the approach, this scanning can be called **STEEP Analysis,** the scanning of Sociocultural, Technological, Economic, Ecological, and Political–legal environmental forces.[6] (It may also be called *PESTEL Analysis* for Political, Economic, Sociocultural, Technological, Ecological, and Legal forces.) Obviously, trends in any one area may be very important to firms in one industry but of lesser importance to firms in other industries.

Demographic trends are part of the *sociocultural* aspect of the societal environment. Even though the world's population has grown from 3.71 billion people in 1970 to 7.03 billion in

TABLE 4–1	Some Important Variables in the Societal Environment			
Sociocultural	**Technological**	**Economic**	**Ecological**	**Political–Legal**
Lifestyle changes	Total government spending for R&D	GDP trends	Environmental protection laws	Antitrust regulations
Career expectations	Total industry spending for R&D	Interest rates	Global warming impacts	Environmental protection laws
Consumer activism		Money supply		Global warming legislation
Rate of family formation	Focus of technological efforts	Inflation rates	Non-governmental organizations	Immigration laws
Growth rate of population	Patent protection	Unemployment levels	Pollution impacts	Tax laws
Age distribution of population	New products	Wage/price controls	Reuse	Special incentives
Regional shifts in population	New developments in technology transfer from lab to marketplace	Devaluation/ revaluation	Triple bottom line	Foreign trade regulations
Life expectancies		Energy alternatives	Recycling	Attitudes toward foreign companies
Birthrates	Productivity improvements through automation	Energy availability and cost		Laws on hiring and promotion
Pension plans		Disposable and discretionary income		
Health care	Internet availability	Currency markets		Stability of government
Level of education	Telecommunication infrastructure	Global financial system		Outsourcing regulation
Living wage	Computer hacking activity			Foreign "sweatshops"
Unionization				

2012 and is expected to increase to 8.72 billion by 2040, not all regions will grow equally. Most of the growth will be in the developing nations. It is predicted that the population of the developed nations will fall from 14% of the total world population in 2000 to only 10% in 2050.[7] Around 75% of the world will live in a city by 2050, compared to little more than half in 2008.[8] Developing nations will continue to have more young than old people, but it will be the reverse in the industrialized nations. For example, the demographic bulge in the U.S. population caused by the baby boom after WWII continues to affect market demand in many industries. This group of 77 million people now in their 50s and 60s is the largest age group in all developed countries, especially in Europe. (See **Table 4–2.**) Although the median age in the United States will rise from 35 in 2000 to 40 by 2050, it will increase from 40 to 47 during the same time period in Germany, and it will increase to up to 50 in Italy as soon as 2025.[9] By 2050, one in three Italians will be over 65, nearly double the number in 2005.[10] With its low birthrate, Japan's population is expected to fall from 127.6 million in 2004 to around 100 million by 2050.[11] China's stringent birth control policy is predicted to cause the ratio of workers to retirees to fall from 20 to 1 during the early 1980s to 2.5 to one by 2020.[12] Companies with an eye on the future can find many opportunities to offer products and services to the growing number of "woofies" (well-off old folks)—defined as people over 50 with money to spend.[13] These people are very likely to purchase recreational vehicles (RVs), take ocean cruises, and enjoy leisure sports, in addition to needing financial services and health care. Anticipating the needs of seniors for prescription drugs is one reason Walgreens opened 261 new stores in 2011![14]

To attract older customers, retailers will need to place seats in their larger stores so aging shoppers can rest. Washrooms will need to be more handicap-accessible. Signs will need to be larger. Restaurants will need to raise the level of lighting so people can read their menus. Home appliances will require simpler and larger controls. Automobiles will need larger door openings and more comfortable seats. Zimmer Holdings, an innovative manufacturer

TABLE 4–2		Generation	Born	Age in 2010	% of Total Adult Population
Current U.S. Generations	Current U.S. Generations	WWII / Silent Generation	1936–1945	65–74	16%
		Baby Boomers	1946–1964	46–64	34%
		Generation X	1965–1976	43–45	19%
		Millennials	1977–1992	18–33	30%

SOURCES: Developed from K. Zickuhr, "Generations 2010," Pew Research Center (December 16, 2010), (www.pewinternet.org/reports/2010/generations-2010.aspx).

of artificial joints, is looking forward to its market growing rapidly over the next 20 years. According to J. Raymond Elliot, Chair and CEO of Zimmer, "It's simple math. Our best years are still in front of us."[15]

Eight current sociocultural trends are transforming North America and the rest of the world:

1. **Increasing environmental awareness:** Recycling and conservation are becoming more than slogans. Busch Gardens, for example, has eliminated the use of disposable Styrofoam trays in favor of washing and reusing plastic trays.

2. **Growing health consciousness:** Concerns about personal health fuel the trend toward physical fitness and healthier living. There has been a general move across the planet to attack obesity. The U.S. Centers for Disease Control and Prevention cites that more than two-thirds of American adults and one-third of American youth are now obese or overweight. A number of states have enacted provisions to encourage grocery stores to open in so-called "food deserts" where the population has virtually no access to fresh foods.[16] In 2012, Chile decided to ban toys that are included in various fast-food meals aimed at children in order to increase the fight against childhood obesity.[17]

3. **Expanding seniors market:** As their numbers increase, people over age 55 will become an even more important market. Already some companies are segmenting the senior population into Young Matures, Older Matures, and the Elderly—each having a different set of attitudes and interests. Both mature segments, for example, are good markets for the health care and tourism industries; whereas, the elderly are the key market for long-term care facilities. The desire for companionship by people whose children are grown is causing the pet care industry to grow by more than 5% annually in the United States. In 2012, for example, 72.9 million households in the United States spent US$52 billion on their pets. That was up from just above US$41 billion just five years ago.[18]

4. **Impact of Millennials:** Born between 1977 and 1992 to the baby boomers and Generation Xers, this cohort is almost as large as the baby boom generation. In 1957, the peak year of the postwar boom, 4.3 million babies were born. In 1990, there were 4.2 million births in Millennials peak year. By 2000, they were overcrowding elementary and high schools and entering college in numbers not seen since the baby boomers. Now in its 20s and 30s, this cohort is expected to have a strong impact on future products and services.

5. **Declining mass market:** Niche markets are defining the marketers' environment. People want products and services that are adapted more to their personal needs. For example, Estée Lauder's "All Skin" and Maybelline's "Shades of You" lines of cosmetic products are specifically made for African-American women. "Mass customization"—the making and marketing of products tailored to a person's requirements is replacing the mass production and marketing of the same product in some markets. The past 10 years have seen a real fracturing of the chocolate market with the advent of craft chocolate making

and flavored chocolates. These products command significantly higher margins and have become a force in the retailing environment. By 2010, 43% of chocolate sales occurred in nontraditional channels.[19]

6. **Changing pace and location of life:** Instant communication via e-mail, cell phones, and overnight mail enhances efficiency, but it also puts more pressure on people. Merging the personal or tablet computer with the communication and entertainment industries through telephone lines, satellite dishes, and Internet connections increases consumers' choices and allows workers to telecommute from anywhere.

7. **Changing household composition:** Single-person households, especially those of single women with children, could soon become the most common household type in the United States. According to the U.S. Census, married-couple households slipped from nearly 80% in the 1950s to 48% of all households by 2010.[20] By 2007, for the first time in U.S. history, more than half the adult female population were single.[21] Those women are also having more children. As of 2012, 41% of all births in the United States were to unmarried women.[22] A typical family household is no longer the same as it was once portrayed in *Happy Days* in the 1970s or *The Cosby Show* in the 1980s.

8. **Increasing diversity of workforce and markets:** Between now and 2050, minorities will account for nearly 90% of population growth in the United States. Over time, group percentages of the total U.S. population are expected to change as follows: Non- Hispanic Whites—from 90% in 1950 to 74% in 1995 to 53% by 2050; Hispanic Whites—from 9% in 1995 to 22% in 2050; Blacks—from 13% in 1995 to 15% in 2050; Asians—from 4% in 1995 to 9% in 2050; American Indians—1%, with slight increase.[23]

Heavy immigration from developing to developed nations is increasing the number of minorities in all developed countries and forcing an acceptance of the value of diversity in races, religions, and lifestyles. For example, 24% of the Swiss population was born elsewhere.[24] Traditional minority groups are increasing their numbers in the workforce and are being identified as desirable target markets. Coca-Cola, Nestlé, and Pepsi have targeted African-American and Latino communities for the sale of bottled water after a study by the department of pediatrics at the Medical College of Wisconsin in 2011 found that African-American and Latino families were three times more likely to give their children bottled water as compared to white families.[25]

Changes in the *technological* part of the societal environment can also have a great impact on multiple industries. Improvements in computer microprocessors have not only led to the widespread use of personal computers but also to better automobile engine performance in terms of power and fuel economy through the use of microprocessors to monitor fuel injection. Digital technology allows movies and music to be available instantly over the Internet or through cable service, but it has also meant falling fortunes for movie rental shops such as Blockbuster and CD stores like Tower Records. Advances in nanotechnology are enabling companies to manufacture extremely small devices that are very energy efficient. Developing biotechnology, including gene manipulation techniques, is already providing new approaches to dealing with disease and agriculture. Researchers at George Washington University have identified a number of technological breakthroughs that are already having a significant impact on many industries:

- **Portable information devices and electronic networking:** Combining the computing power of the personal computer, the networking of the Internet, the images of television, and the convenience of the telephone, tablets and Smartphones will soon be used by a majority of the population of industrialized nations to make phone calls, stay connected in business and personal relationships, and transmit documents and other data. Homes, autos, and offices are rapidly being connected (via wires and wirelessly) into intelligent networks that interact with one another. This trend is being accelerated by the development of *cloud computing*, in which a person can access their data anywhere through a Web connection.[26] This is being dramatically improved by companies like Microsoft who are releasing *cloud* versions of their Office package available for rent.[27] The traditional stand-alone desktop computer will someday join the manual typewriter as a historical curiosity.

- **Alternative energy sources:** The use of wind, geothermal, hydroelectric, solar, biomass, and other alternative energy sources should increase considerably. Over the past two decades, the cost of manufacturing and installing a photovoltaic solar-power system has decreased by 20% with every doubling of installed capacity.[28]

- **Precision farming:** The computerized management of crops to suit variations in land characteristics will make farming more efficient and sustainable. Farm equipment dealers such as Case and John Deere now add this equipment to tractors for an additional US$6,000 or so. It enables farmers to reduce costs, increase yields, and decrease environmental impact. The old system of small, low-tech farming is becoming less viable as large corporate farms increase crop yields on limited farmland for a growing population.

- **Virtual personal assistants:** Very smart computer programs that monitor e-mail, faxes, and phone calls will be able to take over routine tasks, such as writing a letter, retrieving a file, making a phone call, or screening requests. Acting like a secretary, a person's virtual assistant could substitute for a person at meetings or in dealing with routine actions.

- **Genetically altered organisms:** A convergence of biotechnology and agriculture is creating a new field of life sciences. Plant seeds can be genetically modified to produce more needed vitamins or to be less attractive to pests and more able to survive. Animals (including people) could be similarly modified for desirable characteristics and to eliminate genetic disabilities and diseases.

- **Smart, mobile robots:** Robot development has been limited by a lack of sensory devices and sophisticated artificial intelligence systems. Improvements in these areas mean that robots will be created to perform more sophisticated factory work, run errands, do household chores, and assist the disabled.[29]

Trends in the *economic* part of the societal environment can have an obvious impact on business activity. For example, an increase in interest rates means fewer sales of major home appliances. Why? A rising interest rate tends to be reflected in higher mortgage rates. Because higher mortgage rates increase the cost of buying a house, the demand for new and used houses tends to fall. Because most major home appliances are sold when people change houses, a reduction in house sales soon translates into a decline in sales of refrigerators, stoves, and dishwashers and reduced profits for everyone in the appliance industry. Changes in the price of oil have a similar impact upon multiple industries, from packaging and automobiles to hospitality and shipping.

The rapid economic development of Brazil, Russia, India, and China (often called the *BRIC* countries) is having a major impact on the rest of the world. By 2007, China had become the world's second-largest economy according to the World Bank. With India graduating more English-speaking scientists, engineers, and technicians than all other nations combined, it has become the primary location for the outsourcing of services, computer software, and telecommunications.[30] Eastern Europe has become a major manufacturing supplier to the European Union countries. According to the International Monetary Fund, emerging markets make up less than one-third of total world gross domestic product (GDP), but account for more than half of GDP growth.[31]

Trends in the *ecological* part of the environment have been accelerating at a pace that is difficult to stay up with. This element is focused upon the natural environment and its consideration/impacts upon the operation of a business. The effects of climate change on companies can be grouped into six categories of risks: regulatory, supply chain, product and technology, litigation, reputational, and physical.[32]

1. **Regulatory Risk:** Companies in much of the world are already subject to the *Kyoto Protocol,* which requires the developed countries (and thus the companies operating within them) to reduce carbon dioxide and other greenhouse gases by an average of 6% from 1990 levels by 2012. The European Union has an emissions trading program that allows companies that emit greenhouse gases beyond a certain point to buy additional allowances from other companies whose emissions are lower than that allowed. Companies can also earn credits toward their emissions by investing in emissions abatement projects outside their own firms. Although the United States withdrew from the Kyoto Protocol, various regional, state, and local government policies affect company activities in the United States. For example, seven Northeastern states, six Western states, and four Canadian provinces have adopted proposals to cap carbon emissions and establish carbon-trading programs.

2. **Supply Chain Risk:** Suppliers will be increasingly vulnerable to government regulations—leading to higher component and energy costs as they pass along increasing carbon-related costs to their customers. Global supply chains will be at risk from an increasing intensity of major storms and flooding. Higher sea levels resulting from the melting of polar ice will create problems for seaports. China, where much of the world's manufacturing is currently being outsourced, is becoming concerned with environmental degradation. Twelve Chinese ministries produced a report on global warming foreseeing a 5%–10% reduction in agricultural output by 2030; more droughts, floods, typhoons, and sandstorms; and a 40% increase in population threatened by plague.[33]

   The increasing scarcity of fossil-based fuel is already boosting transportation costs significantly. For example, Tesla Motors, the maker of an electric-powered sports car, transferred assembly of battery packs from Thailand to California because Thailand's low wages were more than offset by the costs of shipping thousand-pound battery packs across the Pacific Ocean.[34]

3. **Product and Technology Risk:** Environmental sustainability can be a prerequisite to profitable growth. Sixty percent of U.S. respondents to an Environics study stated that knowing a company is mindful of its impact on the environment and society makes them more likely to buy their products and services.[35] Carbon-friendly products using new technologies are becoming increasingly popular with consumers. Those automobile companies, for example, that were quick to introduce hybrid or alternative energy cars gained a competitive advantage.

4. **Litigation Risk:** Companies that generate significant carbon emissions face the threat of lawsuits similar to those in the tobacco, pharmaceutical, and building supplies (e.g., asbestos) industries. For example, oil and gas companies were sued for greenhouse gas emissions in the federal district court of Mississippi, based on the assertion that these companies contributed to the severity of Hurricane Katrina.

5. **Reputational Risk:** A company's impact on the environment can affect its overall reputation. The Carbon Trust, a consulting group, found that in some sectors the value of a company's brand could be at risk because of negative perceptions related to climate change. In contrast, a company with a good record of environmental sustainability may create a competitive advantage in terms of attracting and keeping loyal consumers, employees, and investors. For example, Wal-Mart's pursuit of environmental sustainability as a core business strategy has helped soften its negative reputation as a low-wage, low-benefit employer. By setting objectives for its retail stores of reducing greenhouse

gases by 20%, reducing solid waste by 25%, increasing truck fleet efficiency by 25%, and using 100% renewable energy, it is also forcing its suppliers to become more environmentally sustainable.[36] Tools have recently been developed to measure sustainability on a variety of factors. For example, the SAM (Sustainable Asset Management) Group of Zurich, Switzerland, has been assessing and documenting the sustainability performance of over 1000 corporations annually since 1999. SAM lists the top 15% of firms in its *Sustainability Yearbook* and classifies them into gold, silver, and bronze categories.[37]

BusinessWeek published its first list of the world's 100 most sustainable corporations January 29, 2007. The *Dow Jones Sustainability Indexes* and the *KLD Broad Market Social Index*, which evaluate companies on a range of environmental, social, and governance criteria are used for investment decisions.[38] Financial services firms, such as Goldman Sachs, Bank of America, JPMorgan Chase, and Citigroup have adopted guidelines for lending and asset management aimed at promoting clean-energy alternatives.[39]

6. **Physical Risk:** The direct risk posed by climate change includes the physical effects of droughts, floods, storms, and rising sea levels. Average Arctic temperatures have risen four to five degrees Fahrenheit (two to three degrees Celsius) in the past 50 years, leading to melting glaciers and sea levels rising one inch per decade.[40] Industries most likely to be affected are insurance, agriculture, fishing, forestry, real estate, and tourism. Physical risk can also affect other industries, such as oil and gas, through higher insurance premiums paid on facilities in vulnerable areas. Coca-Cola, for example, studies the linkages between climate change and water availability in terms of how this will affect the location of its new bottling plants. The warming of the Tibetan plateau has led to a thawing of the permafrost—thereby threatening the newly-completed railway line between China and Tibet.[41]

Trends in the *political–legal* part of the societal environment have a significant impact not only on the level of competition within an industry but also on which strategies might be successful.[42] For example, periods of strict enforcement of U.S. antitrust laws directly affect corporate growth strategy. As large companies find it more difficult to acquire another firm in the same or a related industry, they are typically driven to diversify into unrelated industries.[43] High levels of taxation and constraining labor laws in Western European countries stimulate companies to alter their competitive strategies or find better locations elsewhere. It is because Germany has some of the highest labor and tax costs in Europe that German companies have been forced to compete at the top end of the market with high-quality products or else move their manufacturing to lower-cost countries.[44] Government bureaucracy can create regulations that make it almost impossible for a business firm to operate profitably in some countries. The World Bank's 2012 report on red tape around the world found amazing examples of government bureaucracy, including: 1) A company in the Congo with a profit margin of 20% or more faces a tax bill of 340% of profits; 2) obtaining a construction permit in Russia requires 51 steps; 3) enforcing a contract through the courts takes 150 days in Singapore and 1,420 in India; 4) while winding up an insolvent firm, creditors in Japan can recover 92.7 cents on the dollar, those in Chad get nothing.[45]

The US$66 trillion global economy operates through a set of rules established by the World Trade Organization (WTO). Composed of 155 member nations and 29 observer nations, the WTO is a forum for governments to negotiate trade agreements and settle trade disputes. Originally founded in 1947 as the General Agreement on Tariffs and Trade (GATT), the WTO was created in 1995 to extend the ground rules for international commerce. The system's purpose is to encourage free trade among nations with the least undesirable side effects. Among its principles is trade without discrimination. This is exemplified by its *most-favored nation* clause, which states that a country cannot grant a trading partner lower customs duties without granting them to all other WTO member nations. Another principle is that of lowering trade barriers gradually though negotiation. It implements this principle through a series of rounds of trade negotiations. As a result of these negotiations, industrial countries' tariff rates on industrial goods had fallen steadily to less than 4% by the mid-1990s. The WTO is currently negotiating its latest round of negotiations, called the Doha Round. The WTO is also in favor of fair competition, predictability of member markets, and the encouragement of economic development and reform. As a result of many negotiations, developed nations have started to allow duty-free and quota-free imports from almost all products from the least-developed countries.[46]

International Societal Considerations. Each country or group of countries in which a company operates presents a unique societal environment with a different set of sociocultural, technological, economic, ecological, and political-legal variables for the company to face. International societal environments vary so widely that a corporation's internal environment and strategic management process must be very flexible. Cultural trends in Germany, for example, have resulted in the inclusion of worker representatives in corporate strategic planning. Because Islamic law (*sharia*) forbids interest (*riba*), loans of capital in Islamic countries must be arranged on the basis of profit-sharing instead of interest rates.[47]

Differences in societal environments strongly affect the ways in which a **multinational corporation (MNC)**, a company with significant assets and activities in multiple countries, conducts its marketing, financial, manufacturing, and other functional activities. For example, Europe's lower labor productivity, due to a shorter work week and restrictions on the ability to lay off unproductive workers, forces European-based MNCs to expand operations in countries where labor is cheaper and productivity is higher.[48] Moving manufacturing to a lower-cost location, such as China, was a successful strategy during the 1990s, but a country's labor costs rise as it develops economically. For example, China required all firms in January 2008 to consult employees on material work-related issues, enabling the country to achieve its stated objective of having trade unions in all of China's non-state-owned enterprises. By September 2008, the All-China Federation of Trade Unions had signed with 80% of the largest foreign companies.[49] See the **Global Issues** feature to see how demand for SUVs has exploded in China.

To account for the many differences among societal environments from one country to another, consider **Table 4–3.** It includes a list of economic, technological, political–legal, and sociocultural variables for any particular country or region. For example, an important economic variable for any firm investing in a foreign country is currency convertibility. Without convertibility, a company cannot convert its money. Almost all nations allow for some method of currency conversion. As of 2012, only the Cuban national peso and the North Korean won are nonconvertible. In terms of sociocultural variables, many Asian cultures (especially China) are less concerned with a Western version of human rights than are European and North American cultures. Some Asians actually contend that U.S. companies are trying to impose Western human rights requirements on them in an attempt to make Asian products less competitive by raising their costs.[50]

Before planning its strategy for a particular international location, a company must scan that country's environment(s) for its similarities and differences with the company's home country. Focusing only on developed nations may cause a corporation to miss important market opportunities. Although those nations may not have developed to the point that they have significant demand for a broad spectrum of products, they may very likely be on the threshold of rapid growth in the demand for specific products. Using the concept of entering where the competition is not, this may be an opportunity for a company to enter this market—before competition is established. The key is to be able to identify the *trigger point* when demand for a particular product or service is ready to boom.

Creating a Scanning System. Although the Internet has opened up a tremendous volume of information, scanning and making sense of that data is one of the important skills in an effective manager.

TABLE 4–3   Some Important Variables in *International* Societal Environments

Sociocultural	Technological	Economic	Ecological	Political–Legal
Customs, norms, values	Regulations on technology transfer	Economic development	Non-governmental groups	Form of government
Language	Energy availability/ cost	Per capita income	Passion for environmental causes	Political ideology
Demographics	Natural resource availability	Climate	Infrastructure to handle recycling	Tax laws
Life expectancies		GDP trends		Stability of government
Social institutions	Transportation network	Monetary and fiscal policies		Government attitude toward foreign companies
Status symbols	Skill level of workforce	Unemployment levels		
Lifestyle		Currency convertibility		Regulations on foreign ownership of assets
Religious beliefs	Patent-trademark protection	Wage levels		Strength of opposition groups
Attitudes toward foreigners		Nature of competition		
Literacy level	Internet availability	Membership in regional economic associations—e.g., EU, NAFTA, ASEAN		Trade regulations
Human rights	Telecommunication infrastructure			Protectionist sentiment
Environmentalism				
"Sweatshops"	Computer hacking technology	Membership in World Trade Organization (WTO)		Foreign policies
Pension plans	New energy sources			Terrorist activity
Health care		Outsourcing capability		Legal system
Slavery		Global financial system		Global warming laws
				Immigration laws

GLOBAL issue

SUVs POWER ON IN CHINA

U.S. and European automakers are looking to China for most of their growth potential in the next two decades. The Chinese middle class is expected to grow to between 600 million and 800 million consumers in the next 10 to 15 years. That is a market that is equivalent to the ENTIRE population of the Unites States AND every country in the European Union combined.

This growing middle class in China (it stood at less than 300 million in 2012) has spurred a huge demand for sport utility vehicles (SUVs). Ford, BMW, Mercedes-Benz, and Porsche are all selling SUVs at a significant clip. The total SUV market in China is predicted to grow by more than 100% in the next three years. BMW reported that they sold more than 20,000 SUVs in the first quarter of 2012. That was a 92% increase over the same quarter a year earlier.

Growing prosperity is leading to this push by consumers. *BusinessWeek* reported seeing the same trend in China that has been seen in the United States, with women in particular being drawn to the flexibility of the SUV. A Ford spokesperson said that "For Tiger Moms—and other moms—SUVs offer great appeal as the whole family can be transported safely and in style." The sharp increase in demand has drawn in the ultra-high-end car companies as well. Maserati and Lamborghini have both announced new SUVs for the Chinese market starting in 2013 and 2014, respectively.

BMW has approached the market with products that they sell around the world, including the BMW X5. This is an example of a global organization. On the other hand, Mercedes-Benz is producing a Chinese-built GLK SUV that is tailored to the market. This is an example of a multi-domestic organization. Figuring out how to address global markets is a key strategic area for any management team.

....

SOURCES: "China's Soccer Moms Want SUVs, Too," *Bloomberg BusinessWeek* (May 7, 2012), (www.businessweek.com/articles/2012-05-03/chinas-soccer-moms-want-suvs-too); Eurostat news release, "EU27 population 502.5 million at 1 January 2011". Accessed 5/30/13, http://epp.eurostat.ec.europa.eu/cache/ITY_PUBLIC/3-28072011-AP/EN/3-28072011-AP-EN.PDF).

FIGURE 4–1
Scanning External
Environment

It is a daunting task for even a large corporation with many resources. To deal with this problem, in 2002 IBM created a tool called *WebFountain* to help the company analyze the vast amounts of environmental data available on the internet. WebFountain is an advanced information discovery system designed to help extract trends, detect patterns, and find relationships within vast amounts of raw data. For example, IBM sought to learn whether there was a trend toward more positive discussions about e-business. Within a week, the company had data that experts within the company used to replace their hunches with valid conclusions.

Scanning the Task Environment

As shown in **Figure 4–1**, a corporation's scanning of the environment includes analyses of all the relevant elements in the task environment. These analyses take the form of individual reports written by various people in different parts of the firm. At Procter & Gamble (P&G), for example, people from each of the brand management teams work with key people from the sales and market research departments to research and write a "competitive activity report" each quarter on each of the product categories in which P&G competes. People in purchasing also write similar reports concerning new developments in the industries that supply P&G. These and other reports are then summarized and transmitted up the corporate hierarchy for top management to use in strategic decision making. If a new development is reported regarding a particular product category, top management may then send memos asking people throughout the organization to watch for and report on developments in related product areas. The many reports resulting from these scanning efforts, when boiled down to their essentials, act as a detailed list of external strategic factors.

IDENTIFYING EXTERNAL STRATEGIC FACTORS

The origin of competitive advantage lies in the ability to identify and respond to environmental change well in advance of competition.[51] Although this seems obvious, why are some companies better able to adapt than others? One reason is because of differences in the ability of managers to recognize and understand external strategic issues and factors. Booz & Company found that companies that are most successful at avoiding surprises had a well-defined system that integrated planning, budgeting, and business reviews.[52]

No firm can successfully monitor all external factors. Choices must be made regarding which factors are important and which are not. Even though managers agree that strategic importance determines what variables are consistently tracked, they sometimes miss or choose to ignore crucial new developments.[53] Personal values and functional experiences of a corporation's managers, as well as the success of current strategies, are likely to bias both their perception of what is important to monitor in the external environment and their interpretations of what they perceive.[54]

This willingness to reject unfamiliar as well as negative information is called *strategic myopia*.[55] If a firm needs to change its strategy, it might not be gathering the appropriate external information to change strategies successfully. For example, when Daniel Hesse became CEO of Sprint Nextel in December 2007, he assumed that improving customer service would be one of his biggest challenges. He quickly discovered that none of the current Sprint Nextel executives were even thinking about the topic. "We weren't talking about the customer when I first joined," said Hesse. "Now this is the No. 1 priority of the company."[56]

Hesse insists that "great customer service costs less—when we were last in the industry, we were spending twice as much." By 2012, Sprint had closed down 29 call centers and was answering calls faster than ever. The second quarter of 2012 saw Sprint receiving the fewest calls ever from customers.[57]

Industry Analysis: Analyzing the Task Environment

An **industry** is a group of firms that produces a similar product or service, such as soft drinks or financial services. An examination of the important stakeholder groups, like suppliers and customers, in a particular corporation's task environment is a part of industry analysis.

PORTER'S APPROACH TO INDUSTRY ANALYSIS

Michael Porter, an authority on competitive strategy, contends that a corporation is most concerned with the intensity of competition within its industry. The level of this intensity is determined by basic competitive forces, as depicted in **Figure 4–2**. "The collective strength of these forces," he contends, "determines the ultimate profit potential in the industry, where profit potential is measured in terms of long-run return on invested capital."[58] In carefully scanning its industry, a corporation must assess the importance to its success of each of six forces: threat of new entrants, rivalry among existing firms, threat of substitute products or services, bargaining power of buyers, bargaining power of suppliers, and relative power of other stakeholders.[59] The stronger each of these forces are, the more limited companies are in their ability to raise prices and earn greater profits. Although Porter mentions only five forces, a sixth—other stakeholders—is added here to reflect the power that governments, local communities, and other groups from the task environment wield over industry activities.

Using the model in **Figure 4–2**, a high force can be regarded as a threat because it is likely to reduce profits. A low force, in contrast, can be viewed as an opportunity because it may allow the company to earn greater profits. In the short run, these forces act as constraints on a company's activities. In the long run, however, it may be possible for a company, through its choice of strategy, to change the strength of one or more of the forces to the company's advantage. For example, Dell's early use of the Internet to market its computers was an effective way to negate the bargaining power of distributors in the PC industry.

FIGURE 4–2
Forces Driving
Industry
Competition

A strategist can analyze any industry by rating each competitive force as high, medium, or low in strength. For example, the global athletic shoe industry could be rated as follows: rivalry is high (Nike, Reebok, New Balance, Converse, and Adidas are strong competitors worldwide), threat of potential entrants is high (the industry has seen clothing firms such as UnderArmour and Fila as well as specialty shoe brands like the wildly popular Vibram Five Fingers shoes), threat of substitutes is low (other shoes don't provide support for sports activities), bargaining power of suppliers is medium but rising (suppliers in Asian countries are increasing in size and ability), bargaining power of buyers is medium but increasing (prices are falling as the low-priced shoe market has grown to be half of the U.S.-branded athletic shoe market), and threat of other stakeholders is medium to high (government regulations and human rights concerns are growing). Based on current trends in each of these competitive forces, the industry's level of competitive intensity will continue to be high—meaning that sales increases and profit margins should continue to be modest for the industry as a whole.[60]

Threat of New Entrants

New entrants to an industry typically bring to it new capacity, a desire to gain market share, and potentially substantial resources. They are, therefore, threats to an established corporation. The threat of entry depends on the presence of entry barriers and the reaction that can be expected from existing competitors. An **entry barrier** is an obstruction that makes it difficult for a company to enter an industry. For example, no new, full-line domestic automobile companies have been successfully established in the United States since the 1930s because of the high capital requirements to build production facilities and to develop a dealer distribution network. Some of the possible barriers to entry are:

- **Economies of scale:** Scale economies in the production and sale of microprocessors, for example, gave Intel a significant cost advantage over any new rival.

- **Product differentiation:** Corporations such as Procter & Gamble and General Mills, which manufacture products such as Tide and Cheerios, create high entry barriers through their high levels of advertising and promotion.

- **Capital requirements:** The need to invest huge financial resources in manufacturing facilities in order to produce large commercial airplanes creates a significant barrier to entry to any competitor for Boeing and Airbus.

- **Switching costs:** Once a software program such as Excel or Word becomes established in an office, office managers are very reluctant to switch to a new program because of the high training costs.

- **Access to distribution channels:** Smaller new firms often have difficulty obtaining supermarket shelf space for their goods because large retailers charge for space on their shelves and give priority to the established firms who can pay for the advertising needed to generate high customer demand.

- **Cost disadvantages independent of size:** Once a new product earns sufficient market share to be accepted as the *standard* for that type of product, the maker has a key advantage. Microsoft's development of the first widely adopted operating system (MS-DOS) for the IBM-type personal computer gave it a significant competitive advantage over potential competitors. Its introduction of Windows helped to cement that advantage so that the Microsoft operating system is now on more than 90% of personal computers worldwide.

- **Government policy:** Governments can limit entry into an industry through licensing requirements by restricting access to raw materials, such as oil-drilling sites in protected areas.

Rivalry among Existing Firms

In most industries, corporations are mutually dependent. A competitive move by one firm can be expected to have a noticeable effect on its competitors and thus may cause retaliation. For example, the successful entry by companies such as Samsung, Amazon and unsuccessful entries by HP and RIM into a Tablet industry previously dominated by Apple changed the level of competitive activity to such an extent that each new product change was quickly followed by similar moves from other tablet makers. The same is true of prices in the United States airline industry. According to Porter, intense rivalry is related to the presence of several factors, including:

- **Number of competitors:** When competitors are few and roughly equal in size, such as in the auto and major home appliance industries, they watch each other carefully to make sure they match any move by another firm with an equal countermove.

- **Rate of industry growth:** Any slowing in passenger traffic tends to set off price wars in the airline industry because the only path to growth is to take sales away from a competitor.

- **Product or service characteristics:** A product can be very unique, with many qualities differentiating it from others of its kind, or it may be a *commodity*, a product whose characteristics are the same, regardless of who sells it. For example, most people choose a gas station based on location and pricing because they view gasoline as a commodity.

- **Amount of fixed costs:** Because airlines must fly their planes on a schedule, regardless of the number of paying passengers for any one flight, some offer cheap standby fares whenever a plane has empty seats.

- **Capacity:** If the only way a manufacturer can increase capacity is in a large increment by building a new plant (as in the paper industry), it will run that new plant at full capacity to keep its unit costs as low as possible—thus producing so much that the selling price falls throughout the industry.

■ **Height of exit barriers: Exit barriers** keep a company from leaving an industry. The brewing industry, for example, has a low percentage of companies that voluntarily leave the industry because breweries are specialized assets with few uses except for making beer.

■ **Diversity of rivals:** Rivals that have very different ideas of how to compete are likely to cross paths often and unknowingly challenge each other's position. This happens frequently in the retail clothing industry when a number of retailers open outlets in the same location—thus taking sales away from each other. This is also likely to happen in some countries or regions when multinational corporations compete in an increasingly global economy.

Threat of Substitute Products or Services

A **substitute product** is a product that appears to be different but can satisfy the same need as another product. For example, texting is a substitute for e-mail, Nutrasweet is a substitute for sugar, the Internet is a substitute for video stores, and bottled water is a substitute for a cola. According to Porter, "Substitutes limit the potential returns of an industry by placing a ceiling on the prices firms in the industry can profitably charge."[61] To the extent that switching costs are low, substitutes may have a strong effect on an industry. Tea can be considered a substitute for coffee. If the price of coffee goes up high enough, coffee drinkers will slowly begin switching to tea. The price of tea thus puts a price ceiling on the price of coffee. Sometimes a difficult task, the identification of possible substitute products or services means searching for products or services that can perform the same function, even though they have a different appearance and may not appear to be easily substitutable.

The Bargaining Power of Buyers

Buyers affect an industry through their ability to force down prices, bargain for higher quality or more services, and play competitors against each other. A buyer or a group of buyers is powerful if some of the following factors hold true:

■ A buyer purchases a large proportion of the seller's product or service (for example, oil filters purchased by a major automaker).

■ A buyer has the potential to integrate backward by producing the product itself (for example, a newspaper chain could make its own paper).

■ Alternative suppliers are plentiful because the product is standard or undifferentiated (for example, motorists can choose among many gas stations).

■ Changing suppliers costs very little (for example, office supplies are easy to find).

■ The purchased product represents a high percentage of a buyer's costs, thus providing an incentive to shop around for a lower price (for example, gasoline purchased for resale by convenience stores makes up half their total costs).

■ A buyer earns low profits and is thus very sensitive to costs and service differences (for example, grocery stores have very small margins).

■ The purchased product is unimportant to the final quality or price of a buyer's products or services and thus can be easily substituted without affecting the final product adversely (for example, electric wire bought for use in lamps).

The Bargaining Power of Suppliers

Suppliers can affect an industry through their ability to raise prices or reduce the quality of purchased goods and services. A supplier or supplier group is powerful if some of the following factors apply:

■ The supplier industry is dominated by a few companies, but it sells to many (for example, the petroleum industry).

- Its product or service is unique and/or it has built up switching costs (for example, word processing software).

- Substitutes are not readily available (for example, electricity).

- Suppliers are able to integrate forward and compete directly with their present customers for example, a microprocessor producer such as Intel can make PCs).

- A purchasing industry buys only a small portion of the supplier group's goods and services and is thus unimportant to the supplier (for example, sales of lawn mower tires are less important to the tire industry than are sales of auto tires).

The Relative Power of Other Stakeholders

A sixth force should be added to Porter's list to include a variety of stakeholder groups from the task environment. Some of these groups are governments (if not explicitly included elsewhere), local communities, creditors (if not included with suppliers), trade associations, special-interest groups, unions (if not included with suppliers), shareholders, and complementors. According to Andy Grove, Chairman and past CEO of Intel, a **complementor** is a company (e.g., Microsoft) or an industry whose product works well with a firm's (e.g., Intel's) product and without which the product would lose much of its value.[62] An example of complementary industries is the tire and automobile industries. Key international stakeholders who determine many of the international trade regulations and standards are the World Trade Organization, the European Union, NAFTA, ASEAN, and Mercosur.

The importance of these stakeholders varies by industry. For example, environmental groups in Maine, Michigan, Oregon, and Iowa successfully fought to pass bills outlawing disposable bottles and cans, and thus deposits for most drink containers are now required. This effectively raised costs across the board, with the most impact on the marginal producers who could not internally absorb all these costs. The traditionally strong power of national unions in the United States' auto and railroad industries has effectively raised costs throughout these industries but is of little importance in computer software.

INDUSTRY EVOLUTION

Over time, most industries evolve through a series of stages from growth through maturity to eventual decline. The strength of each of the six forces mentioned earlier varies according to the stage of industry evolution. The industry life cycle is useful for explaining and predicting trends among the six forces that drive industry competition. For example, when an industry is new, people often buy the product, regardless of price, because it uniquely fulfills an existing need. This usually occurs in a **fragmented industry**—where no firm has large market share, and each firm serves only a small piece of the total market in competition with others (for example, cleaning services).[63] As new competitors enter the industry, prices drop as a result of competition. Companies use the experience curve (discussed in Chapter 5) and economies of scale to reduce costs faster than the competition. Companies integrate to reduce costs even further by acquiring their suppliers and distributors. Competitors try to differentiate their products from one another's in order to avoid the fierce price competition common to a maturing industry.

By the time an industry enters maturity, products tend to become more like commodities. This is now a **consolidated industry**—dominated by a few large firms, each of which struggles to differentiate its products from those of the competition. As buyers become more sophisticated over time, purchasing decisions are based on better information. Price becomes a dominant concern, given a minimum level of quality and features, and profit margins decline. The automobile, petroleum, and major home appliance industries are examples of mature,

INNOVATION issue

TAKING STOCK OF AN OBSESSION

It is worth periodically taking stock of innovations to understand their profound impact upon consumers, competitors, and perhaps in this case, every business operation in the world. The Apple iPhone was released to great fanfare on June 29, 2007 and by mid-2012 more than 217 million had been sold. Cisco Systems estimates that by 2016 there will be more mobile devices than people in the world. In his book *iDisorder: Understanding Our Obsession with Technology and Overcoming Its Hold on Us*, psychologist Larry Rosen observes that "the iPhone has changed everything about how we relate to technology, for both good and bad."

The iPhone led the way to using a touchscreen for every aspect of the phone's use. The Apple focus on simplicity in design and functionality changed the way that phones would look and be used. The laptop computer was the state-of-the-art mobile business platform when the iPhone was released. More and more people not only realized that they could use their phone to keep up with e-mails, make calls, and check Web pages, but more importantly, they were exposed to the App for the first time.

The app (a staple of the iPhone's capability) provides people with a means to achieve a result with a minimum of additional effort. Besides playing games, the business application apps have become a time-saver and confidence builder for people throughout the world. By 2012, there were more than half a million apps in the iTunes App Store. Apps run the gamut from games that probably waste productive time, to translators that quickly help international travelers, to digital books that allow one to take any book with them wherever they go, to programs that allow one to access all their files wherever they may be.

Mobile access is accelerating with the introduction of the iPad tablet, along with the many look-alike tablets and Smartphones. Where will this all go? What will business communication look like in 10 years? No one predicted that a phone would become our computer.

SOURCES: P. Burrows, "The First Five Years of Mass Obsession," *Bloomberg BusinessWeek* (June 25, 2012), www.apple.com/iphone/built-in-apps/app-store.html.

---

consolidated industries, each controlled by a few large competitors. In the case of the United States' major home appliance industry, the industry changed from being a fragmented industry (pure competition) composed of hundreds of appliance manufacturers in the industry's early years to a consolidated industry (mature oligopoly) composed of three companies controlling over 90% of U.S. appliance sales. A similar consolidation is occurring now in European major home appliances.

As an industry moves through maturity toward possible decline, its products' growth rate of sales slows and may even begin to decrease. To the extent that exit barriers are low, firms begin converting their facilities to alternate uses or sell them to other firms. The industry tends to consolidate around fewer but larger competitors. The tobacco industry is an example of an industry currently in decline.

CATEGORIZING INTERNATIONAL INDUSTRIES

According to Porter, worldwide industries vary on a continuum from multidomestic to global (see **Figure 4–3**).[64] **Multidomestic industries** are specific to each country or group of countries. This type of international industry is a collection of essentially domestic industries, such as retailing and insurance. The activities in a subsidiary of a multinational corporation (MNC) in this type of industry are essentially independent of the activities of the MNC's subsidiaries in other countries. Within each country, it has a manufacturing facility to produce goods for sale within that country. The MNC is thus able to tailor its products or services to the very specific needs of consumers in a particular country or group of countries having similar societal environments.

FIGURE 4–3
Continuum of
International
Industries

Multidomestic ◀──────────────────────────────▶ **Global**

Industry in which companies tailor
their products to the specific needs
of consumers in a particular country.
• Retailing
• Insurance
• Banking

Industry in which companies manufacture
and sell the same products, with only minor
adjustments made for individual countries
around the world.
• Automobiles
• Tires
• Television sets

Global industries, in contrast, operate worldwide, with MNCs making only small adjustments for country-specific circumstances. In a global industry an MNC's activities in one country are not significantly affected by its activities in other countries. MNCs in global industries produce products or services in various locations throughout the world and sell them, making only minor adjustments for specific country requirements. Examples of global industries are commercial aircraft, television sets, semiconductors, copiers, automobiles, watches, and tires. The largest industrial corporations in the world in terms of sales revenue are, for the most part, MNCs operating in global industries.

The factors that tend to determine whether an industry will be primarily multidomestic or primarily global are:

1. *Pressure for coordination* within the MNCs operating in that industry
2. *Pressure for local responsiveness* on the part of individual country markets

To the extent that the pressure for coordination is strong and the pressure for local responsiveness is weak for MNCs within a particular industry, that industry will tend to become global. In contrast, when the pressure for local responsiveness is strong and the pressure for coordination is weak for multinational corporations in an industry, that industry will tend to be multidomestic. Between these two extremes lie a number of industries with varying characteristics of both multidomestic and global industries. These are **regional industries**, in which MNCs primarily coordinate their activities within regions, such as the Americas or Asia.[65] The major home appliance industry is a current example of a regional industry becoming a global industry. Japanese appliance makers, for example, are major competitors in Asia, but only minor players in Europe or America. The dynamic tension between the pressure for coordination and the pressure for local responsiveness is contained in the phrase, "*Think globally but act locally.*"

INTERNATIONAL RISK ASSESSMENT

Some firms develop elaborate information networks and computerized systems to evaluate and rank investment risks. Small companies may hire outside consultants, such as Boston's Arthur D. Little Inc., to provide political-risk assessments. Among the many systems that exist to assess political and economic risks are the Business Environment Risk Index, the Economist Intelligence Unit, and Frost and Sullivan's World Political Risk Forecasts. The Economist Intelligence Unit, for example, provides a constant flow of analysis and forecasts on more than 200 countries and eight key industries. Regardless of the source of data, a firm must develop its own method of assessing risk. It must decide on its most important risk factors and then assign weights to each.

STRATEGIC GROUPS

A **strategic group** is a set of business units or firms that "pursue similar strategies with similar resources."[66] Categorizing firms in any one industry into a set of strategic groups is very useful as a way of better understanding the competitive environment.[67] Research shows that some strategic groups in the same industry are more profitable than others.[68] Because a corporation's structure and culture tend to reflect the kinds of strategies it follows, companies or business units belonging to a particular strategic group within the same industry tend to be strong rivals and tend to be more similar to each other than to competitors in other strategic groups within the same industry.[69]

For example, although McDonald's and Olive Garden are a part of the same industry, the restaurant industry, they have different missions, objectives, and strategies, and thus they belong to different strategic groups. They generally have very little in common and pay little attention to each other when planning competitive actions. Burger King and Wendy's, however, have a great deal in common with McDonald's in terms of their similar strategy of producing a high volume of low-priced meals targeted for sale to the average family. Consequently, they are strong rivals and are organized to operate similarly.

Strategic groups in a particular industry can be mapped by plotting the market positions of industry competitors on a two-dimensional graph, using two strategic variables as the vertical and horizontal axes (**Figure 4–4**):

1. Select two broad characteristics, such as price and menu, that differentiate the companies in an industry from one another.

2. Plot the firms, using these two characteristics as the dimensions.

3. Draw a circle around those companies that are closest to one another as one strategic group, varying the size of the circle in proportion to the group's share of total industry sales. (You could also name each strategic group in the restaurant industry with an identifying title, such as quick fast food or buffet-style service.)

FIGURE 4–4
Mapping Strategic Groups in the U.S. Restaurant Chain Industry

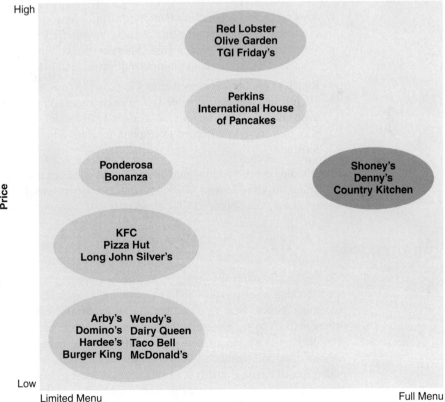

Other dimensions, such as quality, service, location, or degree of vertical integration, could also be used in additional graphs of the restaurant industry to gain a better understanding of how the various firms in the industry compete. Keep in mind, however, that the two dimensions should not be highly correlated; otherwise, the circles on the map will simply lie along the diagonal, providing very little new information other than the obvious.

STRATEGIC TYPES

In analyzing the level of competitive intensity within a particular industry or strategic group, it is useful to characterize the various competitors for predictive purposes. A **strategic type** is a category of firms based on a common strategic orientation and a combination of structure, culture, and processes consistent with that strategy. According to Miles and Snow, competing firms within a single industry can be categorized into one of four basic types on the basis of their general strategic orientation.[70] This distinction helps explain why companies facing similar situations behave differently and why they continue to do so over long periods of time.[71] These general types have the following characteristics:

- **Defenders** are companies with a limited product line that *focus on improving the efficiency of their existing operations*. This cost orientation makes them unlikely to innovate in new areas. With its emphasis on efficiency, Lincoln Electric is an example of a defender.

- **Prospectors** are companies with fairly broad product lines that *focus on product innovation and market opportunities*. This sales orientation makes them somewhat inefficient. They tend to emphasize creativity over efficiency. Frito Lay's emphasis on new product development makes it an example of a prospector.

- **Analyzers** are corporations that *operate in at least two different product-market areas*, one stable and one variable. In the stable areas, efficiency is emphasized. In the variable areas, innovation is emphasized. Multidivisional firms, such as BASF and Procter & Gamble, which operate in multiple industries, tend to be analyzers.

- **Reactors** are corporations that *lack a consistent strategy-structure-culture relationship*. Their (often ineffective) responses to environmental pressures tend to be piecemeal strategic changes. Most major U.S. airlines have recently tended to be reactors—given the way they have been forced to respond to more nimble airlines such as Southwest and JetBlue.

Dividing the competition into these four categories enables the strategic manager not only to monitor the effectiveness of certain strategic orientations, but also to develop scenarios of future industry developments (discussed later in this chapter).

HYPERCOMPETITION

Most industries today are facing an ever-increasing level of environmental uncertainty. They are becoming more complex and more dynamic. Industries that used to be multidomestic are becoming global. New flexible, aggressive, innovative competitors are moving into established markets to rapidly erode the advantages of large previously dominant firms. Distribution channels vary from country to country and are being altered daily through the use of sophisticated information systems. Closer relationships with suppliers are being forged to reduce costs, increase quality, and gain access to new technology. Companies learn to quickly imitate the successful strategies of market leaders, and it becomes harder to sustain any competitive advantage for very long. Consequently, the level of competitive intensity is increasing in most industries.

Richard D'Aveni contends that as this type of environmental turbulence reaches more industries, competition becomes **hypercompetition**. According to D'Aveni:

> *In hypercompetition the frequency, boldness, and aggressiveness of dynamic movement by the players accelerates to create a condition of constant disequilibrium and change. Market stability is threatened by short product life cycles, short product design cycles, new technologies, frequent entry by unexpected outsiders, repositioning by incumbents, and tactical redefinitions of market boundaries as diverse industries merge. In other words, environments escalate toward higher and higher levels of uncertainty, dynamism, heterogeneity of the players and hostility.*[72]

In hypercompetitive industries such as information technology, competitive advantage comes from an up-to-date knowledge of environmental trends and competitive activity, coupled with a willingness to risk a current advantage for a possible new advantage. Companies must be willing to *cannibalize* their own products (that is, replace popular products before competitors do so) in order to sustain their competitive advantage. (Hypercompetition is discussed in more detail in Chapter 6.)

USING KEY SUCCESS FACTORS TO CREATE AN INDUSTRY MATRIX

Within any industry, there are usually certain variables—key success factors—that a company's management must understand in order to be successful. **Key success factors** are variables that can significantly affect the overall competitive positions of companies within any particular industry. They typically vary from industry to industry and are crucial to determining a company's ability to succeed within that industry. They are usually determined by the economic and technological characteristics of the industry and by the competitive weapons on which the firms in the industry have built their strategies.[73] For example, in the major home appliance industry, a firm must achieve low costs, typically by building large manufacturing facilities dedicated to making multiple versions of one type of appliance, such as washing machines. Because 60% of major home appliances in the United States are sold through "power retailers" such as Sears and Best Buy, a firm must have a strong presence in the mass merchandiser distribution channel. It must offer a full line of appliances and provide a just-in-time delivery system to keep store inventory and ordering costs to a minimum. Because the consumer expects reliability and durability in an appliance, a firm must have excellent process R&D. Any appliance manufacturer that is unable to deal successfully with these key success factors will not survive long in the U.S. market.

An **industry matrix** summarizes the key success factors within a particular industry. As shown in **Table 4–4**, the matrix gives a weight for each factor based on how important that factor is for success within the industry. The matrix also specifies how well various competitors in the industry are responding to each factor. To generate an industry matrix

TABLE 4–4	Industry Matrix				
Key Success Factors	Weight	Company A Rating	Company A Weighted Score	Company B Rating	Company B Weighted Score
1	2	3	4	5	6
Total	1.00		___		___

SOURCE: T. L. Wheelen and J. D. Hunger, *Industry Matrix*. Copyright © 1997, 2001, and 2005 by Wheelen & Hunger Associates. Reprinted with permission.

using two industry competitors (called A and B), complete the following steps for the industry being analyzed:

1. In **Column 1** (*Key Success Factors*), list the 8 to 10 factors that appear to determine success in the industry.

2. In **Column 2** (*Weight*), assign a weight to each factor, from **1.0** (*Most Important*) to **0.0** (*Not Important*) based on that factor's probable impact on the overall industry's current and future success. (**All weights must sum to 1.0 regardless of the number of strategic factors.**)

3. In **Column 3** (*Company A Rating*), examine a particular company within the industry— for example, Company A. Assign a rating to each factor from **5** (*Outstanding*) to **1** (*Poor*) based on Company A's current response to that particular factor. Each rating is a judgment regarding how well that company is specifically dealing with each key success factor.

4. In **Column 4** (*Company A Weighted Score*) multiply the weight in **Column 2** for each factor by its rating in **Column 3** to obtain that factor's weighted score for Company A.

5. In **Column 5** (*Company B Rating*) examine a second company within the industry—in this case, Company B. Assign a rating to each key success factor from **5.0** (*Outstanding*) to **1.0** (*Poor*), based on Company B's current response to each particular factor.

6. In **Column 6** (*Company B Weighted Score*) multiply the weight in **Column 2** for each factor times its rating in **Column 5** to obtain that factor's weighted score for Company B.

7. Finally, add the weighted scores for all the factors in **Columns 4** and **6** to determine the total weighted scores for companies A and B. **The total weighted score indicates how well each company is responding to current and expected key success factors in the industry's environment.** Check to ensure that the total weighted score truly reflects the company's current performance in terms of profitability and market share. (An average company should have a total weighted score of 3.)

The industry matrix can be expanded to include all the major competitors within an industry through the addition of two additional columns for each additional competitor.

Competitive Intelligence

Most external environmental scanning is done on an informal and individual basis. Information is obtained from a variety of sources—suppliers, customers, industry publications, employees, industry experts, industry conferences, and the Internet.[74] For example, scientists and engineers working in a firm's R&D lab can learn about new products and competitors' ideas at professional meetings; someone from the purchasing department, speaking with supplier- representatives' personnel, may also uncover valuable bits of information about a competitor. A study of product innovation found that 77% of all product innovations in scientific instruments and 67% in semiconductors and printed circuit boards were initiated by the customer in the form of inquiries and complaints.[75] In these industries, the sales force and service departments must be especially vigilant.

A recent survey of global executives by McKinsey & Company found that the single factor contributing most to the increasing competitive intensity in their industries was the improved capabilities of competitors.[76] Yet, without competitive intelligence, companies run the risk of flying blind in the marketplace. According to work by Ryall, firms can have competitive advantages simply because their rivals have erroneous beliefs about them.[77] This is why competitive intelligence has become an important part of environmental scanning in most companies.

Competitive intelligence is a formal program of gathering information on a company's competitors. Often called *business intelligence*, it is one of the fastest growing fields within strategic management. Research indicates that there is a strong association between corporate performance and competitive intelligence activities.[78] According to a 2011 survey of competitive intelligence by the Global Intelligence Alliance, nearly 70% of North American companies plan to increase their budgets for competitive intelligence. 94% felt that they had benefited from their competitive intelligence efforts, while 42% of those companies without a competitive intelligence program intend to start one within the year.[79]

In about a third of the firms, the competitive/business intelligence function is housed in its own unit, with the remainder being housed within marketing, strategic planning, information services, business development (merger and acquisitions), product development, or other units.[80] Competitive Intelligence software maker GoodData estimated the size of the total spent on competitive intelligence activities was more than US$25 Billion in 2012.[81] At General Mills, for example, all employees have been trained to recognize and tap sources of competitive information. Janitors no longer simply place orders with suppliers of cleaning materials; they also ask about relevant practices at competing firms!

SOURCES OF COMPETITIVE INTELLIGENCE

Most corporations use outside organizations to provide them with environmental data. Firms such as A. C. Nielsen Co. provide subscribers with bimonthly data on brand share, retail prices, percentages of stores stocking an item, and percentages of stock-out stores. Strategists can use this data to spot regional and national trends as well as to assess market share. Information on market conditions, government regulations, industry competitors, and new products can be bought from "information brokers" such as Market Research.com (Findex), Lexis-Nexis (company and country analyses), and Finsbury Data Services. Company and industry profiles are generally available from the Hoover's Web site at www.hoovers.com. Many business corporations have established their own in-house libraries and computerized information systems to deal with the growing mass of available information.

The Internet has changed the way strategists engage in environmental scanning. It provides the quickest means to obtain data on almost any subject. Although the scope and quality of Internet information is increasing geometrically, it is also littered with "noise," misinformation, and utter nonsense. Unlike the library, the Internet lacks the tight bibliographic control standards that exist in the print world. There is no ISBN or Dewey Decimal System to identify, search, and retrieve a document. Many Web documents lack the name of the author and the date of publication. A Web page providing useful information may be accessible on the Web one day and gone the next. Unhappy ex-employees, far-out environmentalists, and prank-prone hackers create "blog" Web sites to attack and discredit an otherwise reputable corporation. Rumors with no basis in fact are spread via chat rooms and personal Web sites. This creates a serious problem for researchers. How can one evaluate the information found on the Internet? For a way to evaluate intelligence information, see the **Strategy Highlight** on the next page.

Some companies choose to use industrial espionage or other intelligence-gathering techniques to get their information straight from their competitors. According to a survey by the American Society for Industrial Security, PricewaterhouseCoopers, and the United States

Chamber of Commerce, Fortune 1000 companies lost an estimated US$59 billion in one year alone due to the theft of trade secrets.[82] By using current or former competitors' employees and private contractors, some firms attempt to steal trade secrets, technology, business plans, and pricing strategies. For example, Avon Products hired private investigators to retrieve from a public dumpster documents (some of them shredded) that Mary Kay Corporation had thrown away. Oracle Corporation also hired detectives to obtain the trash of a think tank that had defended the pricing practices of its rival Microsoft. Studies reveal that 32% of the trash typically found next to copy machines contains confidential company data, in addition to personal data (29%) and gossip (39%).[83] Even P&G, which defends itself like a fortress from information leaks, is vulnerable. A competitor was able to learn the precise launch date of a concentrated laundry detergent in Europe when one of its people visited the factory where machinery was being made. Simply asking a few questions about what a certain machine did, whom it was for, and when it would be delivered was all that was necessary.

Some of the firms providing investigatory services are Altegrity Inc. with 11,000 employees in 30 countries, Fairfax, Security Outsourcing Solutions, Trident Group, and Diligence Inc.[84]

Trident, for example, specializes in helping American companies enter the Russian market and is a U.S.-based corporate intelligence firm founded and managed by former veterans of Russian intelligence services, like the KGB.[85]

STRATEGY highlight

EVALUATING COMPETITIVE INTELLIGENCE

A basic rule in intelligence gathering is that before a piece of information can be in any report or briefing, it must first be evaluated in two ways. *First*, the source of the information should be judged in terms of its truthfulness and reliability. How trustworthy is the source? How well can a researcher rely upon it for truthful and correct information? One approach is to rank the reliability of the source on a scale from A (extremely reliable), B (reliable), C (unknown reliability), D (probably unreliable), to E (very questionable reliability). The reliability of a source can be judged on the basis of the author's credentials, the organization sponsoring the information, and past performance, among other factors. *Second*, the information or data should be judged in terms of its likelihood of being correct. The correctness of the data may be ranked on a scale from 1 (correct), 2 (probably correct), 3 (unknown), 4 (doubtful), to 5 (extremely doubtful). The correctness of a piece of data or information can be judged on the basis of its agreement with other bits of separately obtained information or with a general trend supported by previous data. For every piece of information found on the Internet, for example, list not only the URL of the Web page, but also the evaluation of the information from A1 (good stuff) to E5 (bad doodoo). Information found through library research in sources such as Moody's Industrials, Standard & Poor's, or Value Line can generally be evaluated as having a reliability of A. The correctness of the data can still range anywhere from 1 to 5, but in most instances is likely to be either 1 or 2, but probably no worse than 3 or 4. Web sites are quite different.

Web sites, such as those sponsored by the U.S. Securities and Exchange Commission (www.sec.gov), *The Economist* (www.economist.com), or Hoovers Online (www.hoovers.com) are extremely reliable. Company-sponsored Web sites are generally reliable, but are not the place to go for trade secrets, strategic plans, or proprietary information. For one thing, many firms think of their Web sites primarily in terms of marketing and provide little data aside from product descriptions and distributors. Other companies provide their latest financial statements and links to other useful Web sites. Nevertheless, some companies in very competitive industries may install software on their Web site to ascertain a visitor's Web address. Visitors from a competitor's domain name are thus screened before they are allowed to access certain Web sites. They may not be allowed beyond the product information page or they may be sent to a bogus Web site containing misinformation. Cisco Systems, for example, uses its Web site to send visitors coming in from other high-tech firm web sites to a special Web page asking if they would like to apply for a job at Cisco!

To combat the increasing theft of company secrets, the U.S. government passed the Economic Espionage Act in 1996. The law makes it illegal (with fines up to US$5 million and 10 years in jail) to steal any material that a business has taken "reasonable efforts" to keep secret and that derives its value from not being known.[86] The Society of Competitive Intelligence Professionals (www.scip.org) urges strategists to stay within the law and to act ethically when searching for information. The society states that illegal activities are foolish because the vast majority of worthwhile competitive intelligence is available publicly via annual reports, Web sites, and libraries. Unfortunately, a number of firms hire "kites," consultants with questionable reputations, who do what is necessary to get information when the selected methods do not meet SPIC ethical standards or are illegal. This allows the company that initiated the action to deny that it did anything wrong.[87]

MONITORING COMPETITORS FOR STRATEGIC PLANNING

The primary activity of a competitive intelligence unit is to monitor **competitors**—organizations that offer same, similar, or substitutable products or services in the business area in which a particular company operates. To understand a competitor, it is important to answer the following 10 questions:

1. Why do your competitors exist? Do they exist to make profits or just to support another unit?

2. Where do they add customer value—higher quality, lower price, excellent credit terms, or better service?

3. Which of your customers are the competitors most interested in? Are they cherry-picking your best customers, picking the ones you don't want, or going after all of them?

4. What is their cost base and liquidity? How much cash do they have? How do they get their supplies?

5. Are they less exposed with their suppliers than your firm? Are their suppliers better than yours?

6. What do they intend to do in the future? Do they have a strategic plan to target your market segments? How committed are they to growth? Are there any succession issues?

7. How will their activity affect your strategies? Should you adjust your plans and operations?

8. How much better than your competitor do you need to be in order to win customers? Do either of you have a competitive advantage in the marketplace?

9. Will new competitors or new ways of doing things appear over the next few years? Who is a potential new entrant?

10. If you were a customer, would you choose your product over those offered by your competitors? What irritates your current customers? What competitors solve these particular customer complaints?[88]

To answer these and other questions, competitive intelligence professionals utilize a number of analytical techniques. In addition to the previously discussed industry forces analysis, and strategic group analysis, some of these techniques are Porter's four-corner exercise, Treacy and Wiersema's value disciplines, Gilad's blind spot analysis, and war gaming.[89] Done right, competitive intelligence is a key input to strategic planning.

Forecasting

Environmental scanning provides reasonably hard data on the present situation and current trends, but intuition and luck are needed to accurately predict whether these trends will continue. The resulting forecasts are, however, usually based on a set of assumptions that may or may not be valid.

DANGER OF ASSUMPTIONS

Faulty underlying assumptions are the most frequent cause of forecasting errors. Nevertheless, many managers who formulate and implement strategic plans rarely consider that their success is based on a series of basic assumptions. Many strategic plans are simply based on projections of the current situation. For example, few people in 2007 expected the price of oil (light, sweet crude, also called West Texas intermediate) to rise above US$80 per barrel and were extremely surprised to see the price approach US$150 by July 2008, especially since the price had been around US$20 per barrel in 2002. U.S. auto companies in particular had continued to design and manufacture large cars, pick-up trucks, and SUVs under the assumption of gasoline being available for around US$2.00 a gallon. Market demand for these types of cars collapsed when the price of gasoline passed US$3.00 to reach US$4.00 a gallon in July 2008. While the price of gas modified some by 2012, at US$112 a barrel and retail gas prices in the mid US$3 range, the car makers are trying to move to vehicles with increasing efficiency. In another example, many banks made a number of questionable mortgages based on the assumption that housing prices would continue to rise as they had in the past. When housing prices began to fall in late 2006, these "sub-prime" mortgages were almost worthless—causing the banking crisis that gripped the nation for the next three plus years. The lesson here: Assumptions can be dangerous to your business's health!

USEFUL FORECASTING TECHNIQUES

Various techniques are used to forecast future situations. They do not tell the future; they merely state what can be, not what will be. As such, they can be used to form a set of reasonable assumptions about the future. Each technique has its proponents and its critics. A study of nearly 500 of the world's largest corporations revealed trend extrapolation to be the most widely practiced form of forecasting—over 70% use this technique either occasionally or frequently.[90] Simply stated, *extrapolation* is the extension of present trends into the future. It rests on the assumption that the world is reasonably consistent and changes slowly in the short run. Time-series methods are approaches of this type. They attempt to carry a series of historical events forward into the future. The basic problem with extrapolation is that a historical trend is based on a series of patterns or relationships among so many different variables that a change in any one can drastically alter the future direction of the trend. As a rule of thumb, the further back into the past you can find relevant data supporting the trend, the more confidence you can have in the prediction.

Brainstorming, expert opinion, and statistical modeling are also very popular forecasting techniques. *Brainstorming* is a non-quantitative approach that simply requires the presence of people with some knowledge of the situation in order to concept out the future. The basic ground rule is to propose ideas without first mentally screening them. No criticism is allowed. "Wild" ideas are encouraged. Ideas should build on previous ideas until a consensus is reached.[91] This is a good technique to use with operating managers who have more faith in "gut feel" than in more quantitative number-crunching techniques. *Expert opinion* is a non-quantitative technique in which experts in a particular area attempt to forecast likely developments. This type of forecast is based on the ability of a knowledgeable person(s) to construct probable future developments based on the interaction of key variables. One application, developed by the RAND Corporation, is the *Delphi Technique*, in which separated experts independently assess the likelihoods of specified events. These assessments are combined and sent back to each expert for fine-tuning until agreement is reached. These assessments are most useful if they are shaped into several possible scenarios that allow decision makers to more fully understand their implication.[92] *Statistical modeling* is a quantitative technique that attempts to discover causal or at least explanatory factors that link two or more time series together. Examples of statistical modeling are regression analysis and other econometric methods. Although very useful in the grasping of historic trends, statistical modeling, such as trend extrapolation, is based on historical data. As the patterns of relationships change, the accuracy of the forecast deteriorates.

Prediction markets is a recent forecasting technique enabled by easy access to the Internet. As emphasized by James Surowiecki in *The Wisdom of Crowds*, the conclusions of large groups can often be better than those of experts because such groups can aggregate a large amount of dispersed wisdom.[93] Prediction markets are small-scale electronic markets, frequently open to any employee, that tie payoffs to measurable future events, such as sales data for a computer workstation, the number of bugs in an application, or product usage patterns. These markets yield prices on prediction contracts—prices that can be interpreted as market-aggregated forecasts.[94] Companies including Microsoft, Google, and Eli Lilly have asked their employees to participate in prediction markets by betting on whether products will sell, when new offices will open, and whether profits will be high in the next quarter. Early predictions have been exceedingly accurate.[95] Intrade.com offers a free Web site in which people can buy or sell various predictions in a manner similar to buying or selling common stock. On August 17, 2012, for example, Intrade.com listed the bidding price for democratic presidential candidate Barack Obama as US$5.62 compared to US$4.26 for Mitt Romney. Thus far, prediction markets have not been documented for long-term forecasting, so its value in strategic planning has not yet been established. Other forecasting techniques, such as *cross-impact analysis (CIA)* and *trend-impact analysis (TIA)*, have not established themselves successfully as regularly employed tools.[96]

Scenario writing is the most widely used forecasting technique after trend extrapolation. Originated by Royal Dutch Shell, *scenarios* are focused descriptions of different likely futures presented in a narrative fashion. A scenario thus may be merely a written description of some future state, in terms of key variables and issues, or it may be generated in combination with other forecasting techniques. Often called scenario planning, this technique has been successfully used by 3M, Levi-Strauss, General Electric, United Distillers, Electrolux, British Airways, and Pacific Gas and Electricity, among others.[97] According to Mike Eskew, Chairman and CEO of United Parcel Service, UPS uses scenario writing to envision what its customers might need 5 to 10 years in the future.[98]

An **industry scenario** is a forecasted description of a particular industry's likely future. Such a scenario is developed by analyzing the probable impact of future societal forces on key groups in a particular industry. The process may operate as follows:[99]

1. Examine possible shifts in the natural environment and in societal variables globally.
2. Identify uncertainties in each of the six forces of the task environment (that is, potential entrants, competitors, likely substitutes, buyers, suppliers, and other key stakeholders).
3. Make a range of plausible assumptions about future trends.

4. Combine assumptions about individual trends into internally consistent scenarios.

5. Analyze the industry situation that would prevail under each scenario.

6. Determine the sources of competitive advantage under each scenario.

7. Predict competitors' behavior under each scenario.

8. Select the scenarios that are either most likely to occur or most likely to have a strong impact on the future of the company. Use these scenarios as assumptions in strategy formulation.

The Strategic Audit: A Checklist for Environmental Scanning

One way of scanning the environment to identify opportunities and threats is by using the Strategic Audit found in **Appendix 1.A** at the end of Chapter 1. The audit provides a checklist of questions by area of concern. For example, Part III of the audit examines the natural, societal, and task environments. It looks at the societal environment in terms of economic, technological, political–legal, and sociocultural forces. It also considers the task environment (industry) in terms of the threat of new entrants, the bargaining power of buyers and suppliers, the threat of substitute products, rivalry among existing firms, and the relative power of other stakeholders.

Synthesis of External Factors—EFAS

After strategic managers have scanned the natural, societal, and task environments and identified a number of likely external factors for their particular corporation, they may want to refine their analysis of these factors by using a form such as that given in **Table 4–5.** Using an **EFAS (External Factors Analysis Summary) Table** is one way to organize the external factors into the generally accepted categories of opportunities and threats, as well as to analyze how well a particular company's management (rating) is responding to these specific factors in light of the perceived importance (weight) of these factors to the company. To generate an EFAS Table for the company being analyzed, complete the following steps:

1. In **Column 1** (*External Factors*), list the 8 to 10 most important opportunities and threats facing the company.

2. In **Column 2** (*Weight*), assign a weight to each factor from **1.0** (*Most Important*) to **0.0** (*Not Important*) based on that factor's probable impact on a particular company's current strategic position. The higher the weight, the more important is this factor to the current and future success of the company. (**All weights must sum to 1.0 regardless of the number of factors.**)

3. In **Column 3** (*Rating*), assign a rating to each factor from **5.0** (*Outstanding*) to **1.0** (*Poor*) based on that particular company's specific response to that particular factor. Each rating is a judgment regarding how well the company is currently dealing with each specific external factor.

TABLE 4–5	External Factor Analysis Summary (EFAS Table): Maytag as Example				
External Factors	**Weight**	**Rating**	**Weighted Score**	**Comments**	
1	2	3	4	5	
Opportunities					
▪ Economic integration of European Community	.20	4.1	.82	Acquisition of Hoover	
▪ Demographics favor quality appliances	.10	5.0	.50	Maytag quality	
▪ Economic development of Asia	.05	1.0	.05	Low Maytag presence	
▪ Opening of Eastern Europe	.05	2.0	.10	Will take time	
▪ Trend to "Super Stores"	.10	1.8	.18	Maytag weak in this channel	
Threats					
▪ Increasing government regulations	.10	4.3	.43	Well positioned	
▪ Strong U.S. competition	.10	4.0	.40	Well positioned	
▪ Whirlpool and Electrolux strong globally	.15	3.0	.45	Hoover weak globally	
▪ New product advances	.05	1.2	.06	Questionable	
▪ Japanese appliance companies	.10	1.6	.16	Only Asian presence in Australia	
Total Scores	1.00		3.15		

NOTES:

1. List opportunities and threats (8–10) in Column 1.
2. Weight each factor from 1.0 (Most Important) to 0.0 (Not Important) in Column 2 based on that factor's probable impact on the company's strategic position. **The total weights must sum to 1.00.**
3. Rate each factor from 5.0 (Outstanding) to 1.0 (Poor) in Column 3 based on the company's response to that factor.
4. Multiply each factor's weight times its rating to obtain each factor's weighted score in Column 4.
5. Use Column 5 (comments) for the rationale used for each factor.
6. Add the individual weighted scores to obtain the total weighted score for the company in Column 4. This tells how well the company is responding to the factors in its external environment.

SOURCE: Thomas L. Wheelen. Copyright © 1982, 1985, 1987, 1988, 1989, 1990, 1991, 1998, and every year after that. Kathryn E. Wheelen solely owns all of (Dr.) Thomas L. Wheelen's copyright materials. Kathryn E. Wheelen requires written reprint permission for each book that this material is to be printed in. Thomas L. Wheelen and J. David Hunger, copyright © 1991–first year "External Factor Analysis Summary" (EFAS) appeared in this text (4th ed.). Reprinted by permission of the copyright holders.

4. In **Column 4** (*Weighted Score*), multiply the weight in **Column 2** for each factor times its rating in **Column 3** to obtain that factor's weighted score.

5. In **Column 5** (*Comments*), note why a particular factor was selected and how its weight and rating were estimated.

6. Finally, add the weighted scores for all the external factors in **Column 4** to determine the total weighted score for that particular company. The **total weighted** score indicates how well a particular company is responding to current and expected factors in its external environment. The score can be used to compare that firm to other firms in the industry. Check to ensure that the total weighted score truly reflects the company's current performance in terms of profitability and market share. **The total weighted score for an average firm in an industry is always 3.0.**

As an example of this procedure, **Table 4–5** includes a number of external factors for Maytag Corporation with corresponding weights, ratings, and weighted scores provided. This table is appropriate for 1995, long before Maytag was acquired by Whirlpool. Note that Maytag's total weight was 3.15, meaning that the corporation was slightly above average in the major home appliance industry at that time.

End of Chapter SUMMARY

Wayne Gretzky was one of the most famous people ever to play professional ice hockey. He wasn't very fast. His shot was fairly weak. He was usually last in his team in strength training. He tended to operate in the back of his opponent's goal, anticipating where his team members would be long before they got there and fed them passes so unsuspected that he would often surprise his own team members. In an interview with *Time* magazine, Gretzky stated that the key to winning is skating not to where the puck is but to where it is going to be. "People talk about skating, puck handling and shooting, but the whole sport is angles and caroms, forgetting the straight direction the puck is going, calculating where it will be diverted, factoring in all the interruptions," explained Gretzky.[100]

Environmental scanning involves monitoring, collecting, and evaluating information in order to understand the current trends in the natural, societal, and task environments. The information is then used to forecast whether these trends will continue or whether others will take their place. How will developments in the natural environment affect the world? What kind of developments can we expect in the societal environment to affect our industry? What will an industry look like in 10 to 20 years? Who will be the key competitors? Who is likely to fall by the wayside? We use this information to make certain assumptions about the future—assumptions that are then used in strategic planning. In many ways, success in the business world is like ice hockey: The key to winning is not to assume that your industry will continue as it is now but to assume that the industry will change and to make sure your company will be in position to take advantage of those changes.

MyManagementLab®

Go to **mymanagementlab.com** to complete the problems marked with this icon .

KEY TERMS

competitive intelligence (p. 115)
competitors (p. 117)
complementor (p. 108)
consolidated industry (p. 108)
EFAS Table (p. 120)
entry barrier (p. 105)
environmental scanning (p. 92)
environmental uncertainty (p. 92)
exit barrier (p. 107)
fragmented industry (p. 108)

global industry (p. 110)
hypercompetition (p. 113)
industry (p. 104)
industry analysis (p. 93)
industry matrix (p. 113)
industry scenario (p. 119)
key success factor (p. 113)
multidomestic industry (p. 109)
multinational corporation (MNC) (p. 101)

natural environment (p. 92)
new entrant (p. 105)
regional industries (p. 110)
societal environment (p. 93)
STEEP analysis (p. 94)
strategic group (p. 110)
strategic type (p. 112)
substitute product (p. 107)
task environment (p. 93)

MyManagementLab®

Go to **mymanagementlab.com** for Auto-graded writing questions as well as the following Assisted-graded writing questions:

4-1. How does STEEP analysis aid in the development of the strategy of a company?
4-2. The effects of climate change on companies can be grouped into six categories of risks. Use any two of these to explain the impact upon the resort hotel industry?

DISCUSSION QUESTIONS

4-3. Discuss how a development in a corporation's natural and societal environments can affect the corporation through its task environment.

4-4. How would you determine the level of competitive intensity in an industry?

4-5. Is Pepsi Cola a substitute for Coca-Cola?

4-6. How can a decision maker identify strategic factors in a corporation's external international environment?

4-7. Compare and contrast trend extrapolation with the writing of scenarios as forecasting techniques.

STRATEGIC PRACTICE EXERCISE

How far should people in a business firm go in gathering competitive intelligence? Where do you draw the line?

Take a look at each of the following approaches that a person might use to gather information about competitors. Which do you believe are techniques that you might use? Why?

1. ___ Using a "clipping agency" to scour the popular press for information on competitors ___

- Being a customer to competitors
- Creating a phony company to act as a potential customer
- Reverse engineering competitors' products
- Hiring consultants who have worked for competitors
- Asking suppliers about your competitors
- Hiring companies to collect and examine competitors' garbage

- Changing the interview process for a new position when a candidate is from a direct competitor.
- Taking public tours of competitors' facilities
- Using social media to cause competitors harm
- Using trade shows and conferences to learn more about competitors
- Hiring key employees from competitors
- What other approaches came to your mind as you considered the above? Add those ideas and evaluate the approach.

2. Go to the Web site of the Society for Competitive Intelligence Professionals (www.scip.org). What does SCIP say about these approaches?

NOTES

1. J. B. Thomas, S. M. Clark, and D. A. Gioia, "Strategic Sense-making and Organizational Performance: Linkages Among Scanning, Interpretation, Action, Outcomes," *Academy of Management Journal* (April 1993), pp. 239–270; J. A. Smith, "Strategies for Start-Ups," *Long Range Planning* (December 1998), pp. 857–872.
2. M. Birshan, R. Dye, and S. Hall, "Creating More Value with Corporate Strategy: McKinsey Global Survey Results," (2011), (www.mckinseyquarterly.com/surveys/creating_more_value_with_corporate_strategy_McKinsey_Global_Survey_results_2733).
3. W. E. Stead and J. G. Stead, *Sustainable Strategic Management* (Armonk, NY: M. E. Sharpe, 2004), p. 6.
4. F. Montabon, R. Sroufe, and R. Narasimhan, "An Examination of Corporate Reporting, Environmental Management Practices and Firm Performance," *Journal of Operations Management* (August 2007), pp. 998–1014.
5. P. Lasserre and J. Probert, "Competing on the Pacific Rim: High Risks and High Returns," *Long Range Planning* (April 1994), pp. 12–35.
6. J. J. McGonagle, "Mapping and Anticipating the Competitive Landscape," *Competitive Intelligence Magazine* (March–April 2007), p. 49.
7. M. J. Cetron and O. Davies, "Trends Now Shaping the Future," *The Futurist* (March–April 2005), pp. 28–29; M. Cetron and O. Davies, "Trends Shaping Tomorrow's World," *The Futurist* (March–April 2008), pp. 35–52.
8. "Trend: Urbane Urban Portraits," *BusinessWeek* (April 28, 2008), p. 57.
9. "Old Europe," *The Economist* (October 2, 2004), pp. 49–50.
10. M. J. Cetron and O. Davies, "Trends Now Shaping the Future," *The Futurist* (March–April 2005), p. 30.
11. "The Incredible Shrinking Country," *The Economist* (November 13, 2004), pp. 45–46.
12. D. Levin, "Tradition Under Stress," *AARP Bulletin* (July–August 2008), pp. 16–18.
13. J. Wyatt, "Playing the Woofie Card," *Fortune* (February 6, 1995), pp. 130–132.
14. www.news.walgreens.com/article_display.cfm?article_id=831.
15. M. Arndt, "Zimmer: Growing Older Gracefully," *BusinessWeek* (June 9, 2003), pp. 82–84.
16. "Healthy Eating" Public Health Law Center—William Mitchell College of Law (2012), (www.publichealthlawcenter.org/topics/healthy-eating).
17. "Chile Bans Toys in Fast Food to Attack Child Obesity," *Fox News Latino* (August 2, 2012), (www.latino.foxnews.com/latino/lifestyle/2012/08/02/chile-bans-toys-in-fast-food-to-attack-child-obesity)
18. H. Yen, "Empty Nesters Push Growth of Pet Health Care Businesses," *The* (Ames, IA) *Tribune* (September 27, 2003), p. C8; "Industry Statistics and Trends—2012," American Pet Products Association, (www.americanpetproducts.org/press_industrytrends.asp); "Pampering Your Pet," *St. Cloud (MN) Times* (September 8, 2007), p. 3A.
19. "Chocolate Candy Market in the U.S.: Trends and Opportunities in Premium, Gourmet and Mass Market Products," *Packaged Facts* (www.packagedfacts.com/chocolate-2505082).

20. S. Tavernise, "Married Couples Are No Longer a Majority, Census Finds," *The New York Times*, May 26, 2011, (www.nytimes.com/2011/05/26/us/26marry.html).

21. "The Power of One," *Entrepreneur* (June 2007), p. 28.

22. "Unmarried Childbearing," Centers for Disease Control and Prevention, 2012, (www.cdc.gov/nchs/fastats/unmarry.html).

23. N. Irvin, II, "The Arrival of the Thrivals," *The Futurist* (March–April 2004), pp. 16–23.

24. "The Trouble with Migrants," *The Economist* (November 24, 2007), pp. 56–57.

25. G. Cheeseman, "Bottled Water Marketing Campaigns Target Minorities," (November 29, 2011), (www.triplepundit.com/2011/11/bottled-water-brands-target-minorities/).

26. E. Knorr and G. Gruman, "What Cloud Computing Really Means," *InfoWorld* (2012), (www.infoworld.com/d/cloud-computing/what-cloud-computing-really-means-031).

27. K. Boehret, "Is Hotmail Hotter Now than It's Outlook.com?" *The Wall Street Journal* (August 1, 2012), (http://online.wsj.com/article/SB10000872396390444226904577756113154505
2576.html?KEYWORDS=microsoft+and+cloud)

28. P. Lorenz, D. Pinner, and T. Seitz, "The Economics of Solar Power," *McKinsey Quarterly* (June 2008), p. 2.

29. W. E. Halal, "The Top 10 Emerging Technologies," *Special Report* (World Future Society, 2000).

30. M. J. Cetron, "Economics: Prospects for the 'Dragon' and the 'Tiger,'" *Futurist* (July–August 2004), pp. 10–11; "A Less Fiery Dragon," *The Economist* (December 1, 2007), p. 92.

31. "Investing Without Borders: A Different Approach to Global Investing," *T. Rowe Price Report* (Fall 2007), p. 1.

32. J. Lash and F. Wellington, "Competitive Advantage on a Warming Planet," *Harvard Business Review* (March 2007), pp. 95–102.

33. "Melting Asia," *The Economist* (June 7, 2008), pp. 29–32.

34. P. Engardia, "Can the U.S. Bring Jobs Back from China?" *BusinessWeek* (June 30, 2008), pp. 39–43.

35. D. Rigby, "Growth through Sustainability," Presentation to the 2008 Annual Meeting of the Consumer Industries Governors, World Economic Forum (January 24, 2008).

36. J. Carey and L. Woellert, "Global Warming: Here Comes the Lawyers," *BusinessWeek* (October 30, 2006), pp. 34–36.

37. C. Laszlo, *Sustainable Value: How the World's Leading Companies Are Doing Well by Doing Good* (Stanford: Stanford University Press, 2008), pp. 89–99.

38. R. Ringger and S. A. DiPizza, *Sustainability Yearbook 2008* (PricewaterhouseCoopers, 2008).

39. L. T. Mendonca and J. Oppenheim, "Investing in Sustainability: An Interview with Al Gore and David Blood," *McKinsey Quarterly* (May 2007).

40. A. J. Hoffman, *Getting Ahead of the Curve: Corporate Strategies that Address Climate Change* (Ann Arbor: University of Michigan, 2006), p. 2.

41. J. K. Bourne, Jr., "Signs of Change," *National Geographic* (Special report on Changing Climate, 2008), pp. 7–21.

42. F. Dobbin and T. J. Dowd, "How Policy Shapes Competition: Early Railroad Foundings in Massachusetts," *Administrative Science Quarterly* (September 1997), pp. 501–529.

43. A. Shleifer and R. W. Viskny, "Takeovers in the 1960s and the 1980s: Evidence and Implications," in R. P. Rumelt, D. E. Schendel, and D. J. Teece (Eds.), *Fundamental Issues in Strategy: A Research Agenda* (Boston: Harvard Business School Press, 1994), pp. 403–418.

44. "The Problem with Solid Engineering," *The Economist* (May 20, 2006), pp. 71–73.

45. "Doing Business," *The Economist* (October 22, 2011), (www.economist.com/node/21533395).

46. Web site, *World Trade Organization*, www.wto.org (accessed August 3, 2012).

47. "Islamic Finance: West Meets East," *The Economist* (October 25, 2003), p. 69.

48. "Giants Forced to Dance," *The Economist* (May 26, 2007), pp. 67–68.

49. "Membership Required," *The Economist* (August 2, 2008), p. 66.

50. J. Naisbitt, *Megatrends Asia* (New York: Simon & Schuster, 1996), p. 79.

51. I. M. Cockburn, R. M. Henderson, and S. Stern, "Untangling the Origins of Competitive Advantage," *Strategic Management Journal* (October–November, 2000), Special Issue, pp. 1123–1145.

52. J. Kerins and C. McNeese, "No Surprises: Creating an Effective "Early Warning" System, (October 2008), (www.booz.com/media/uploads/no_surprises.pdf).

53. H. Wissema, "Driving through Red Lights," *Long Range Planning* (October 2002), pp. 521–539; B. K. Boyd and J. Fulk, "Executive Scanning and Perceived Uncertainty: A Multidimensional Model," *Journal of Management* (Vol. 22, No. 1, 1996), pp. 1–21.

54. P. G. Audia, E. A. Locke, and K. G. Smith, "The Paradox of Success: An Archival and a Laboratory Study of Strategic Persistence Following Radical Environmental Change," *Academy of Management Journal* (October 2000), pp. 837–853; M. L. McDonald and J. D. Westphal, "Getting By with the Advice of Their Friends: CEOs Advice Networks and Firms' Strategic Responses to Poor Performance," *Administrative Science Quarterly* (March 2003), pp. 1–32; R. A. Bettis and C. K. Prahalad, "The Dominant Logic: Retrospective and Extension," *Strategic Management Journal* (January 1995), pp. 5–14; J. M. Stofford and C. W. F. Baden-Fuller, "Creating Corporate Entrepreneurship," *Strategic Management Journal* (September 1994), pp. 521–536; J. M. Beyer, P. Chattopadhyay, E. George, W. H. Glick, and D. Pugliese, "The Selective Perception of Managers Revisited," *Academy of Management Journal* (June 1997), pp. 716–737.

55. H. I. Ansoff, "Strategic Management in a Historical Perspective," in *International Review of Strategic Management* (Vol. 2, No. 1, 1991), D. E. Hussey (Ed.), (Chichester, England: Wiley, 1991), p. 61.

56. S. E. Ante, "Sprint's Wake-Up Call," *BusinessWeek* (March 3, 2008), p. 54.

57. I. Fried, "Sprint CEO Hesse: Good Customer Service Costs Less," *All Things D* (August 7, 2012), (www.allthingsd.com/20120807/sprint-ceo-hesse-good-customer-service-costs-less).

58. M. E. Porter, *Competitive Strategy* (New York: The Free Press, 1980), p. 3.

59. This summary of the forces driving competitive strategy is taken from Porter, *Competitive Strategy*, pp. 7–29.

60. M. McCarthy, "Rivals Scramble to Topple Nike's Sneaker Supremacy," *USA Today* (April 3, 2003), pp. B1–B2; S. Holmes, "Changing the Game on Nike," *BusinessWeek* (January 22, 2007), p. 80.

61. Porter, *Competitive Strategy*, p. 23.

62. A. S. Grove, "Surviving a 10x Force," *Strategy & Leadership* (January/February 1997), pp. 35–37.

63. A fragmented industry is defined as one whose market share for the leading four firms is equal to or less than 40% of total industry sales. See M. J. Dollinger, "The Evolution of Collective Strategies in Fragmented Industries," *Academy of Management Review* (April 1990), pp. 266–285.

64. M. E. Porter, "Changing Patterns of International Competition," *California Management Review* (Winter 1986), pp. 9–40.

65. A. M. Rugman, *The Regional Multinationals: MNEs and Global Strategic Management* (Cambridge: Cambridge University Press, 2005).

66. K. J. Hatten and M. L. Hatten, "Strategic Groups, Asymmetrical Mobility Barriers, and Contestability," *Strategic Management Journal* (July–August 1987), p. 329.

67. J. C. Short, D. J. Ketchen Jr., T. B. Palmer, and G. T. M. Hult, "Firm, Strategic Group, and Industry Influences on Performance," *Strategic Management Journal* (February 2007), pp. 147–167; J. D. Osborne, C. I. Stubbart, and A. Ramaprasad, "Strategic Groups and Competitive Enactment: A Study of Dynamic Relationships Between Mental Models and Performance," *Strategic Management Journal* (May 2001), pp. 435–454; A. Fiegenbaum and H. Thomas, "Strategic Groups as Reference Groups: Theory, Modeling and Empirical Examination of Industry and Competitive Strategy," *Strategic Management Journal* (September 1995), pp. 461–476; H. R. Greve, "Managerial Cognition and the Mimities Adoption of Market Positions: What You See Is What You Do," *Strategic Management Journal* (October 1998), pp. 967–988.

68. G. Leask and D. Parker, "Strategic Groups, Competitive Groups and Performance Within the U.K. Pharmaceutical Industry: Improving Our Understanding of the Competitive Process," *Strategic Management Journal* (July 2007), pp. 723–745.

69. C. C. Pegels, Y. I. Song, and B. Yang, "Management Heterogeneity, Competitive Interaction Groups, and Firm Performance," *Strategic Management Journal* (September 2000), pp. 911–923; W. S. Desarbo and R. Grewal, "Hybrid Strategic Groups," *Strategic Management Journal* (March 2008), pp. 293–317.

70. R. E. Miles and C. C. Snow, *Organizational Strategy, Structure, and Process* (New York: McGraw-Hill, 1978). See also D. J. Ketchen Jr., "An Interview with Raymond E. Miles and Charles C. Snow," *Academy of Management Executive* (November 2003), pp. 97–104.

71. B. Kabanoff and S. Brown, "Knowledge Structures of Prospectors, Analyzers, and Defenders: Content, Structure, Stability, and Performance," *Strategic Management Journal* (February 2008), pp. 149–171.

72. R. A. D'Aveni, *Hypercompetition* (New York: The Free Press, 1994), pp. xiii–xiv.

73. C. W. Hofer and D. Schendel, *Strategy Formulation: Analytical Concepts* (St. Paul, MN: West Publishing Co., 1978), p. 77.

74. "Information Overload," *Journal of Business Strategy* (January–February 1998), p. 4.

75. E. Von Hipple, *Sources of Innovation* (New York: Oxford University Press, 1988), p. 4.

76. "An Executive Takes on the Top Business Trends: A McKinsey Global Survey," *McKinsey Quarterly* (April 2006).

77. M. D. Ryall, "Subjective Rationality, Self-Confirming Equilibrium, and Corporate Strategy," *Management Science* (Vol. 49, 2003), pp. 936–949.

78. C. H. Wee and M. L. Leow, "Competitive Business Intelligence in Singapore," *Journal of Strategic Marketing* (Vol. 2, 1994), pp. 112–139.

79. Miller, G. 2011. "Online Retailers will spend more $$$ on competitive intelligence in 2012," Upstream Commerce (November 19, 2011), (www.upstreamcommerce.com/blog/2011/11/19/north-american-companies-spend-bit-on-competitive-intelligence-2012).

80. D. Fehringer, B. Hohhof, and T. Johnson, "State of the Art: Competitive Intelligence," Research Report of the *Competitive Intelligence Foundation* (2006), p. 6.

81. A. Andreescu, "GoodData Delivers Record-Breaking Second Quarter 2012," (August 6, 2012), (www.gooddata.com/blog/gooddata-delivers-record-breaking-second-quarter-2012).

82. E. Iwata, "More U.S. Trade Secrets Walk Out Door with Foreign Spies," *USA Today* (February 13, 2003), pp. B1, B2.

83. "Twenty-nine Percent Spy on Co-Workers," *USA Today* (August 19, 2003), p. B1.

84. M. Orey, "Corporate Snoops," *BusinessWeek* (October 9, 2006), pp. 46–49; E. Javers, "Spies, Lies, & KPMG," *BusinessWeek* (February 26, 2007), pp. 86–88; "Altegrity to Acquire Kroll, the World's Leading Risk Consulting Firm," from Marsh & McLennan, *Business Wire* (www.businesswire.com/news/home/20100607005989/en/altegrity-acquire-kroll-world-leading-risk-consulting)

85. E. Javers, "I Spy—For Capitalism," *BusinessWeek* (August 13, 2007), pp. 54–56.

86. B. Flora, "Ethical Business Intelligence in NOT Mission Impossible," *Strategy & Leadership* (January/February 1998), pp. 40–41.

87. A. L. Penenberg and M. Berry, *Spooked: Espionage in Corporate America* (Cambridge, MA: Perseus Publishing, 2000).

88. T. Kendrick and J. Blackmore, "Ten Things You Really Need to Know About Competitors," *Competitive Intelligence Magazine* (September–October 2001), pp. 12–15.

89. For the percentage of CI professionals using each analytical technique, see A. Badr, E. Madden, and S. Wright, "The Contributions of CI to the Strategic Decision Making Process: Empirical Study of the European Pharmaceutical Industry," *Journal of Competitive Intelligence and Management* (Vol. 3, No. 4, 2006), pp. 15–35; and D. Fehringer, B. Hohhof, and T. Johnson, "State of the Art: Competitive Intelligence," Research Report of the *Competitive Intelligence Foundation* (2006).

90. H. E. Klein and R. E. Linneman, "Environmental Assessment: An International Study of Corporate Practices," *Journal of Business Strategy* (Summer 1984), p. 72.

91. A. F. Osborn, *Applied Imagination* (NY: Scribner, 1957); R. C. Litchfield, "Brainstorming Reconsidered: A Goal-Based View," *Academy of Management Review* (July 2008), pp. 649–668; R. I. Sutton, "The Truth About Brainstorming," *Inside Innovation*, insert to *BusinessWeek* (September 26, 2006), pp. 17–21.

92. R. S. Duboff, "The Wisdom of Expert Crowds," *Harvard Business Review* (September 2007), p. 28.

93. J. Surowiecki, *The Wisdom of Crowds* (NY: Doubleday, 2004).

94. R. Dye, "The Promise of Prediction Markets: A Roundtable," *McKinsey Quarterly* (April 2008), pp. 83–93.

95. C. R. Sunstein, "When Crowds Aren't Wise," *Harvard Business Review* (September 2006), pp. 20–21.

96. See L. E. Schlange and U. Juttner, "Helping Managers to Identify the Key Strategic Issues," *Long Range Planning* (October 1997), pp. 777–786, for an explanation and application of the cross-impact matrix.

97. G. Ringland, *Scenario Planning: Managing for the Future* (Chichester, England: Wiley, 1998); N. C. Georgantzas and W. Acar, *Scenario-Driven Planning: Learning to Manage Strategic Uncertainty* (Westport, CN: Quorum Books, 1995); L. Fahey and R. M. Randall (Eds.), *Learning from the Future: Competitive Foresight Scenarios* (New York: John Wiley & Sons, 1998).

98. M. Eskew, "Stick with Your Vision," *Harvard Business Review* (July–August 2007), pp. 56–57. This process of scenario development is adapted from M. E. Porter, *Competitive Advantage* (New York: The Free Press, 1985), pp. 448–470.

99. This process of scenario development is adapted from M. E. Porter, *Competitive Advantage* (New York: The Free Press, 1985), pp. 448–470.

100. H. C. Sashittal and A. R. Jassawalla, "Learning from Wayne Gretzky," *Organizational Dynamics* (Spring 2002), pp. 341–355.

internal scanning: Organizational Analysis

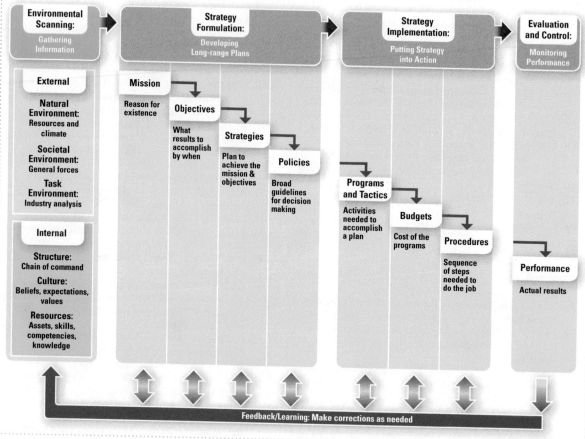

Learning Objectives

After reading this chapter, you should be able to:

- Apply the resource-based view of the firm to determine core and distinctive competencies
- Use the VRIO framework and the value chain to assess an organization's competitive advantage and how it can be sustained
- Understand a company's business model and how it could be imitated

- Assess a company's corporate culture and how it might affect a proposed strategy
- Scan functional resources to determine their fit with a firm's strategy
- Construct an IFAS Table that summarizes internal factors

The Nano Tries to Change the Auto Industry

Tata Motors introduced the world to the Nano at the Indian Auto Show in New Delhi back in 2008. Called the *People's Car*, the new auto was developed to sell for US$2500 in India. Even though many manufacturers were hoping to introduce cheap small cars into India and other developing nations, Tata Motors seemed to have significant advantages that other companies lacked. India's low labor costs meant that Tata could engineer a new model for 20% of the US$350 million it would cost in developed nations. A factory worker in Mumbai earned just US$1.20 per hour, less than autoworkers earned in China. The car was kept very simple. The company would save about US$900 per car by skipping equipment that the United States, Europe, and Japan required for emissions control. The engineers questioned everything about car design, putting the engine in the rear and the gas tank up front, and using fiber and plastic instead of steel. The People's Car did not have features like antilock brakes, air bags, or support beams to protect passengers in case of a crash. The dashboard contained just a speedometer, fuel gauge, and oil light. It lacked a radio, reclining seats, or power steering. It came with a small 650 cc engine that generated only 70 horsepower, but obtained 50 to 60 miles per gallon. The car's suspension system used old technology that was cheap and resulted in a rougher ride than in more expensive cars.

The vehicle was a smash success at its introduction. Tata used a lottery to choose the first 100,000 customers from more than 206,000 initial orders for the car. Then the fires started. Five cars caught fire in a short period in 2009 and sales plummeted. There was a reworking of some parts and the company extended the warranty to cover the first 60,000 miles; however, the standard line from the company was that there were no significant issues with the car other than a minor part that was defective.

The company built a plant capable of producing 20,000 Nano cars a month, but by July 2012 they sold only 5485. That was a 68% increase over a year earlier. The company sells approximately 75,000 Nanos a year. Although Tata Motors had intended to initially sell the people's car in India and then offer it in other developing markets, management has really retrenched and the Nano looks to be based in India for a long time to come.

SOURCES: S. Philip, "Chairman Tata Seeks to Salvage World's Cheapest Nano Car," *Bloomberg* (August 21, 2012), (www.bloomberg.com/news/2012-08-21/chairman-tata-seeks-to-salvage-world-s-cheapest-nan-car-html); A. K. Mishra, "Tata's Nano:Fire!" *Forbes* (May 21, 2010), (www.forbes.com/2010/05/20/forbes-india-wheels-of-fire-tata-motors.html); D. Welch and N. Lakshman, "My Other Car Is a Tata," *Business Week* (January 14, 2008), pp. 33–34.

A Resource-Based Approach to Organizational Analysis

Scanning and analyzing the external environment for opportunities and threats is necessary for the firm to be able to understand its competitive environment and its place in that environment; however, it is not enough to provide an organization with a competitive advantage. Once this external examination has been completed, the attention must turn to look within the corporation itself to identify *internal strategic factors*—critical *strengths and weaknesses* that are likely to determine whether a firm will be able to take advantage of opportunities while avoiding threats. This internal scanning, often referred to as **organizational analysis**, is concerned with identifying, developing, and taking advantage of an organization's resources and competencies.

CORE AND DISTINCTIVE COMPETENCIES

Resources are an organization's assets and are thus the basic building blocks of the organization. They include *tangible assets* (such as its plant, equipment, finances, and location), *human assets* (the number of employees, their skills, and motivation), and *intangible assets* (such as its technology [patents and copyrights], culture, and reputation).[1] **Capabilities** refer to a corporation's ability to exploit its resources. They consist of business processes and routines that manage the interaction among resources to turn inputs into outputs. For example, a company's marketing capability can be based on the interaction among its marketing specialists, distribution channels, and salespeople. A capability is functionally based and is resident in a particular function. Thus, there are marketing capabilities, manufacturing capabilities, and human resource management capabilities. When these capabilities are constantly being changed and reconfigured to make them more adaptive to an uncertain environment, they are called *dynamic capabilities*.[2] A **competency** is a cross-functional integration and coordination of capabilities. For example, a competency in new product development in one division of a corporation may be the consequence of integrating information systems capabilities, marketing capabilities, R&D capabilities, and production capabilities within the division. A **core competency** is a collection of competencies that crosses divisional boundaries, is widespread within the corporation, and is something that the corporation can do exceedingly well. Thus, new product development is a core competency if it goes beyond one division.[3] For example, a core competency of Avon Products is its expertise in door-to-door selling. FedEx has a core competency in its application of information technology to all its operations. A company must continually reinvest in a core competency or risk its becoming a *core rigidity* or *deficiency*—that is, a strength that over time matures and may become a weakness.[4] Although it is typically not an asset in the accounting sense, a core competency is a very valuable resource—it does not "wear out" with use. In general, the more core competencies are used, the more refined they get, and the more valuable they become. When core competencies are superior to those of the competition, they are called **distinctive competencies**. For example, General Electric is well known for its distinctive competency in management development. Its executives are sought out by other companies hiring top managers.[5]

Barney, in his **VRIO framework** of analysis, proposes four questions to evaluate a firm's competencies:

1. **Value:** Does it provide customer value and competitive advantage?
2. **Rareness:** Do no other competitors possess it?
3. **Imitability:** Is it costly for others to imitate?
4. **Organization:** Is the firm organized to exploit the resource?

If the answer to each of these questions is *yes* for a particular competency, it is considered to be a strength and thus a distinctive competence.[6] This should give the company a competitive advantage and lead to higher performance.[7]

It is important to evaluate the importance of a company's resources, capabilities, and competencies to ascertain whether they are internal strategic factors—that is, particular strengths and weaknesses that will help determine the future of the company. This can be done by comparing measures of these factors with measures of (1) the company's past performance, (2) the company's key competitors, and (3) the industry as a whole. To the extent that a resource (such as a firm's cash situation), capability, or competency is significantly different from the firm's own past resource, its key competitors', or the industry average, that resource is likely to be a strategic factor and should be considered in strategic decisions.

Even though a distinctive competency is certainly considered to be a corporation's key strength, a key strength may not always be a distinctive competency. As competitors attempt to imitate another company's competency (especially during hypercompetition), what was once a distinctive competency becomes a minimum requirement to compete in the industry.[8] Even though the competency may still be a core competency and thus a strength, it is no longer unique. Apple is well known for their functional design ability. The iPod, iPad, and mostly the iPhone are examples of their distinctive competency. As other phone manufacturers (in particular) imitated Apple's designs and released ever more stylish phones, we would say that this continued to be a key strength (that is, a core competency) of Apple, but it was less and less a distinctive competency.

USING RESOURCES TO GAIN COMPETITIVE ADVANTAGE

Proposing that a company's sustained competitive advantage is primarily determined by its resource endowments, Grant proposes a five-step, resource-based approach to strategy analysis.

1. Identify and classify the firm's resources in terms of strengths and weaknesses.
2. Combine the firm's strengths into specific capabilities and core competencies.
3. Appraise the profit potential of these capabilities and competencies in terms of their potential for sustainable competitive advantage and the ability to harvest the profits resulting from their use. Are there any distinctive competencies?
4. Select the strategy that best exploits the firm's capabilities and competencies relative to external opportunities.
5. Identify resource gaps and invest in upgrading weaknesses.[9]

Where do these competencies come from? A corporation can gain access to a distinctive competency in four ways:

- It may be an asset endowment, such as a key patent, coming from the founding of the company. Such was the case with Xerox, which grew on the basis of its original copying patent.

- It may be acquired from someone else. Disney bought Pixar in order to reestablish itself in the animated movie market.

- It may be shared with another business unit or alliance partner. LG has taken its electronics and production expertise into appliances with astonishing success in the market.

- It may be carefully built and accumulated over time within the company. For example, Honda carefully extended its expertise in small motor manufacturing from motorcycles to autos, boat engines, generators, and lawnmowers.[10]

There is some evidence that the best corporations prefer organic internal growth over acquisitions. One study of large global companies identified firms that outperformed their peers on both revenue growth and profitability over a decade. These excellent performers generated value from knowledge-intensive intangibles, such as copyrights, trade secrets, or strong brands, not from acquisitions.[11]

The desire to build or upgrade a core competency is one reason entrepreneurial and other fast-growing firms often tend to locate close to their competitors. They form *clusters*— geographic concentrations of interconnected companies and industries. Examples in the United States are computer technology in Silicon Valley in northern California; biotechnology in the Research Triangle area of North Carolina; financial services in New York City; clean energy in Colorado; and electric car batteries in Michigan.[12] According to Michael Porter, clusters provide access to employees, suppliers, specialized information, and complementary products.[13] Being close to one's competitors makes it easier to measure and compare performance against rivals. Capabilities may thus be formed externally through a firm's network resources. An example is the presence of many venture capitalists located in Silicon Valley who provide financial support and assistance to high-tech startup firms in the region. Employees from competitive firms in these clusters often socialize. As a result, companies learn from each other while competing with each other. Interestingly, research reveals that companies with strong core competencies have little to gain from locating in a cluster with other firms and therefore do not do so. In contrast, firms with the weakest technologies, human resources, training programs, suppliers, and distributors are strongly motivated to cluster. They have little to lose and a lot to gain from locating close to their competitors.[14]

DETERMINING THE SUSTAINABILITY OF AN ADVANTAGE

Just because a firm is able to use its resources, capabilities, and competencies to develop a competitive advantage does not mean it will be able to sustain it. Two characteristics determine the sustainability of a firm's distinctive competency(ies): durability and imitability.

Durability is the rate at which a firm's underlying resources, capabilities, or core competencies depreciate in value or become obsolete. New technology can make a company's core competency obsolete or irrelevant. However, more often we simply see that, over time, any core competency that is not continually updated and reinforced is likely to depreciate to the mean expectation in the industry and therefore cease to exist as an advantage. Sears was the dominant player in the department store industry for decades. It was not undone by a new technology, but by complacency. The management at Sears simply assumed that people would continue to shop at Sears even in the face of competitors who were catering to the new demographics in the market. Those seismic changes included the move toward designer clothes at Macy's and Target on the higher end, while on the low end Wal-Mart's explosive growth ate into sales, as well as the wave of discount tire-only retailers, and the move by Best Buy to sell appliances.

Imitability is the rate at which a firm's underlying resources, capabilities, or core competencies can be duplicated by others. To the extent that a firm's distinctive competency gives it competitive advantage in the marketplace, competitors will do what they can to learn and imitate that set of skills and capabilities. Competitors' efforts may range from *reverse engineering* (which involves taking apart a competitor's product in order to find out how it works), to hiring employees from the competitor, to outright patent infringement. A core competency can be easily imitated to the extent that it is transparent, transferable, and replicable.

- **Transparency** is the speed with which other firms can understand the relationship of resources and capabilities supporting a successful firm's strategy. Gillette has always supported its dominance in the marketing of razors with excellent R&D. A competitor could never understand how the Fusion razor was produced simply by taking one apart. Gillette's razor designs are very difficult to copy, partly because the manufacturing equipment needed to produce it is so expensive and complicated.

- **Transferability** is the ability of competitors to gather the resources and capabilities necessary to support a competitive challenge. For example, it may be very difficult for a winemaker to duplicate a French winery's key resources of land and climate, especially if the imitator is located in Iowa.

- **Replicability** is the ability of competitors to use duplicated resources and capabilities to imitate the other firm's success. For example, even though many companies have tried to imitate Procter & Gamble's success with brand management by hiring brand managers away from P&G, they have often failed to duplicate P&G's success. The competitors failed to identify less visible P&G coordination mechanisms or to realize that P&G's brand management style conflicted with the competitor's own corporate culture.

It is relatively easy to learn and imitate another company's core competency or capability if it comes from **explicit knowledge**—that is, knowledge that can be easily articulated and communicated. This is the type of knowledge that competitive intelligence activities can quickly identify and communicate. **Tacit knowledge**, in contrast, is knowledge that is *not* easily communicated because it is deeply rooted in employee experience or in a corporation's culture.[15] Tacit knowledge is more valuable and more likely to lead to a sustainable competitive advantage than is explicit knowledge because it is much harder for competitors to imitate.[16] The knowledge may be complex and combined with other types of knowledge in an unclear fashion in such a way that even management cannot clearly explain the competency.[17] Tacit knowledge is thus subject to a paradox. For a corporation to be successful and grow, its tacit knowledge must be clearly identified and codified if the knowledge is to be spread throughout the firm. Once tacit knowledge is identified and written down, however, it is easily imitable by competitors.[18] This forces companies to establish complex security systems to safeguard their key knowledge.

An organization's resources and capabilities can be placed on a continuum to the extent they are durable and can't be imitated (that is, aren't transparent, transferable, or replicable) by another firm. At one extreme are resources which are sustainable because they are shielded by patents, geography, strong brand names, or tacit knowledge. These resources and capabilities are distinctive competencies because they provide a sustainable competitive advantage. Gillette's razor technology is a good example of a product built around slow-cycle resources. The other extreme includes resources which face the highest imitation pressures because they are based on a concept or technology that can be easily duplicated, such as streaming movies. To the extent that a company has fast-cycle resources, the primary way it can compete successfully is through increased speed from lab to marketplace. Otherwise, it has no real sustainable competitive advantage.

With its low-cost position and innovative marketing strategy, Tata Motors appeared to have a competitive advantage in making and selling its new People's Car at the lowest price in the industry. Is a low-cost approach sustainable? In terms of durability, the car's lack of safety or emissions equipment could be a disadvantage when India and other developing nations begin to require such technology. Given that most developing nations also have low labor costs, Tata's low wages could be easily imitated—probably fairly quickly. In fact, Renault and Nissan had already formed an alliance in 2008 with Indian motorcycle maker Bajaj Auto to launch a US$3000 car in India in 2009.[19] That car never made it off the drawing board. By late 2011, Bajaj announced that it was reassessing the whole project because they felt the low-cost car was "unviable."[20] Overall, the sustainability of Tata Motors' potential competitive advantage seemed fairly low, given the fast-cycle nature of its resources.

Business Models

When analyzing a company, it is helpful to learn what sort of business model it is following. A **business model** is a company's method for making money in the current business environment. It includes the key structural and operational characteristics of a firm—how it earns revenue and makes a profit. A business model is usually composed of five elements:

- Who it serves
- What it provides
- How it makes money
- How it differentiates and sustains competitive advantage
- How it provides its product/service[21]

The simplest business model is to provide a good or service that can be sold such that revenues exceed costs and all expenses. Other models can be much more complicated. Some of the many possible business models are:

- **Customer solutions model:** IBM uses this model to make money not by selling IBM products, but by selling its expertise to improve its customers' operations. This is a consulting model.

- **Profit pyramid model:** General Motors offers a full line of automobiles in order to close out any niches where a competitor might find a position. The key is to get customers to buy in at the low-priced, low-margin entry point (Chevrolet Aveo – MSRP US$10235) and move them up to high-priced, high-margin products (Cadillac and Buick) where the company makes its money.

- **Multicomponent system/installed base model:** Gillette invented this classic model to sell razors at break-even pricing in order to make money on higher-margin razor blades. HP does the same with printers and printer cartridges. The product is thus a system, not just one product, with one component providing most of the profits.

- **Advertising model:** Similar to the multicomponent system/installed base model, this model offers its basic product free in order to make money on advertising. Originating in the newspaper industry, this model is used heavily in commercial radio and television. Internet-based firms, such as Google and Facebook, offer free services to users in order to expose them to the advertising that pays the bills.

- **Switchboard model:** In this model, a firm acts as an intermediary to connect multiple sellers to multiple buyers. Financial planners juggle a wide range of products for sale to multiple customers with different needs. This model has been successfully used by eBay and Amazon.com.

- **Time model:** Product R&D and speed are the keys to success in the time model. Being the first to market with a new innovation allows a pioneer like Google to earn extraordinary returns. By the time the rest of the industry catches up, Google has moved on to a newer, more innovative approach to keep people coming back.

- **Efficiency model:** In this model, a company waits until a product becomes standardized and then enters the market with a low-priced, low-margin product that appeals to the mass market. This model is used by Wal-Mart, KIA Motors, and Vanguard.

- **Blockbuster model:** In some industries, such as pharmaceuticals and motion picture studios, profitability is driven by a few key products. The focus is on high investment in a few products with high potential payoffs—especially if they can be protected by patents.

- **Profit multiplier model:** The idea of this model is to develop a concept that may or may not make money on its own but, through synergy, can spin off many profitable products. Walt Disney invented this concept by using cartoon characters to develop high-margin theme parks, merchandise, and licensing opportunities.

- **Entrepreneurial model:** In this model, a company offers specialized products/services to market niches that are too small to be worthwhile to large competitors but have the potential to grow quickly. Small, local brew pubs have been very successful in a mature industry dominated by AB InBev and MillerCoors. This model has often been used by small high-tech firms that develop innovative prototypes in order to sell off the companies (without ever selling a product) to Microsoft or DuPont.

- **De Facto industry standard model:** In this model, a company offers products free or at a very low price in order to saturate the market and become the industry standard. Once users are locked in, the company offers higher-margin products using this standard. Zynga uses this model with its famous Farmville game, and TurboTax makes its most basic program free.

In order to understand how some of these business models work, it is important to learn where on the value chain the company makes its money. Although a company might offer a large number of products and services, one product line might contribute most of the profits. At Hewlett-Packard, the printer and imaging division represents more than 20% of the company's revenues, with operating margins that exceed 15% compared to the PC division's 6% margins. However, the printer division's revenue is down 12% from 2008 as more people share pictures and documents in the cloud.[22]

Value-Chain Analysis

A **value chain** is a linked set of value-creating activities that begin with basic raw materials coming from suppliers, moving on to a series of value-added activities involved in producing and marketing a product or service, and ending with distributors getting the final goods into the hands of the ultimate consumer. Value-chain analysis works for every type of business regardless of whether they provide a service or manufacture a product. See **Figure 5–1** for an example of a typical value chain for a manufactured product. The focus of value-chain analysis is to examine the corporation in the context of the overall chain of value-creating activities, of which the firm may be only a small part.

FIGURE 5–1
Typical Value
Chain for a Manu-
factured Product

Very few corporations have a product's entire value chain in-house. Ford Motor Company did when it was managed by its founder, Henry Ford. During the 1920s and 1930s, the company owned its own iron mines, ore-carrying ships, and a small rail line to bring ore to its mile-long River Rouge plant in Detroit. Visitors to the plant would walk along an elevated walkway, where they could watch iron ore being dumped from the rail cars into huge furnaces. The resulting steel was poured and rolled out onto a moving belt to be fabricated into auto frames and parts while the visitors watched in awe. As visitors walked along the walkway, they observed an automobile being built piece by piece. Reaching the end of the moving line, the finished automobile was driven out of the plant into a vast adjoining parking lot. Ford trucks would then load the cars for delivery to dealers. Interestingly, Ford dealers had almost no power in the value-chain of the company. Dealerships were awarded by the company and taken away if a dealer was at all disloyal. Dealers received new vehicles not necessarily because they needed those particular models, but because Ford Motor chose those vehicles for sale at that dealership. Ford Motor Company at that time was completely vertically integrated—that is, it controlled (usually by ownership) every stage of the value chain, from the iron mines to the retailers.

INDUSTRY VALUE-CHAIN ANALYSIS

The value chains of most industries can be split into two segments, *upstream* and *downstream*. In the petroleum industry, for example, *upstream* refers to oil exploration, drilling, and moving the crude oil to the refinery, and *downstream* refers to refining the oil plus transporting and marketing gasoline and refined oil to distributors and gas station retailers. Even though most large oil companies are completely integrated, they often vary in the amount of expertise they have at each part of the value chain. Amoco, for example, had strong expertise downstream in marketing and retailing. British Petroleum, in contrast, was more dominant in upstream activities like exploration. That's one reason the two companies merged to form BP Amoco in 1998. The company has since changed its name to simply BP.[23]

An industry can be analyzed in terms of the profit margin available at any point along the value chain. For example, the U.S. auto industry's revenues and profits are divided among many value-chain activities, including manufacturing, new and used car sales, gasoline retailing, insurance, after-sales service and parts, and lease financing. From a revenue standpoint, auto manufacturers dominate the industry, accounting for almost 60% of total industry revenues. Profits, however, are a different matter. The various North American automakers have gone from earning most of their profit from leasing, insurance, and financing operations just a few years ago, to a resurgence of the manufacturing part of the value chain as the driver of profits. After undergoing a painful few years from 2008–2010, the automakers have emerged again as manufacturing-driven organizations. In 2012, the once bankrupt General Motors reported profits of US$7.6 Billion and Ford Motor Company which took no bailout from the government, reported profits of US$8.8 Billion.[24]

In analyzing the complete value chain of a product, note that even if a firm operates up and down the entire industry chain, it usually has an area of expertise where its primary activities lie. A company's *center of gravity* is the part of the chain where the company's greatest expertise and capabilities lie—its core competencies. According to Galbraith, a company's center of gravity is usually the point at which the company started. After a firm successfully establishes itself at this point by obtaining a competitive advantage, one of its first strategic moves is to move forward or backward along the value chain in order to reduce costs, guarantee access to key raw materials, or to guarantee distribution.[25] This process, called *vertical integration*, is discussed in more detail in **Chapter 7**.

In the paper industry, for example, Weyerhauser's center of gravity is in the raw materials and primary manufacturing parts of the value chain shown in **Figure 5–2**. Weyerhauser's expertise is in lumbering and pulp mills, which is where the company started. It integrated forward by using its wood pulp to make paper and boxes, but its greatest capability still lay in getting the greatest return from its lumbering activities. In contrast, P&G is primarily a consumer products company that also owned timberland and operated pulp mills. Its expertise is in the fabrication and distribution parts of the **Figure 5–2** value chain. P&G purchased these assets to guarantee access to the large quantities of wood pulp it needed to expand its disposable diaper, toilet tissue, and napkin products. P&G's strongest capabilities have always been in the downstream activities of product development, marketing, and brand management. It has never been as efficient in upstream paper activities as Weyerhauser. It had no real distinctive competency on that part of the value chain. When paper supplies became more plentiful (and competition got rougher), P&G gladly sold its land and mills to focus more on the part of the value chain where it could provide the greatest value at the lowest cost—creating and marketing innovative consumer products. As was the case with P&G's experience in the paper industry, it may make sense for a company to outsource any weak areas it may control internally on the industry value chain.

CORPORATE VALUE-CHAIN ANALYSIS

Each corporation has its own internal value chain of activities. See **Figure 5–2** for an example of a corporate value chain. Porter proposes that a manufacturing firm's *primary activities* usually begin with inbound logistics (raw materials handling and warehousing), go through an operations process in which a product is manufactured, and continue on to outbound logistics (warehousing and distribution), to marketing and sales, and finally to service (installation, repair, and sale of parts). Several *support activities*, such as procurement (purchasing),

FIGURE 5–2
A Corporation's
Value Chain

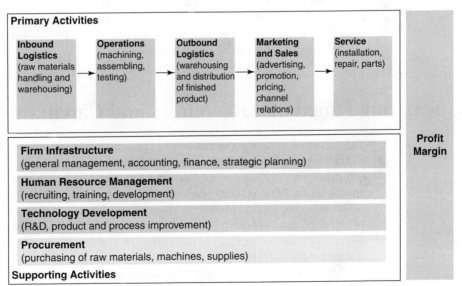

SOURCE: Based on The Free Press, a division of Simon & Schuster, from *Competitive Advantage: Creating and Sustaining Superior Performance* by Michael E. Porter. Copyright © 1985, 1998 by The Free Press. All rights reserved.

technology development (R&D), human resource management, and firm infrastructure (accounting, finance, strategic planning), ensure that the primary value-chain activities operate effectively and efficiently. Each of a company's product lines has its own distinctive value chain. Because most corporations make several different products or services, an internal analysis of the firm involves analyzing a series of different value chains.

The systematic examination of individual value activities can lead to a better understanding of a corporation's strengths and weaknesses. According to Porter, "Differences among competitor value chains are a key source of competitive advantage."[26] Corporate value-chain analysis involves the following three steps:

1. **Examine each product line's value chain in terms of the various activities involved in producing that product or service:** Which activities can be considered strengths (core competencies) or weaknesses (core deficiencies)? Do any of the strengths provide competitive advantage and can they thus be labeled distinctive competencies?

2. **Examine the "linkages" within each product line's value chain:** *Linkages* are the connections between the way one value activity (for example, marketing) is performed and the cost of performance of another activity (for example, quality control). In seeking ways for a corporation to gain competitive advantage in the marketplace, the same function can be performed in different ways with different results. For example, quality inspection of 100% of output by the workers themselves instead of the usual 10% by quality control inspectors might increase production costs, but that increase could be offset by the savings obtained from reducing the number of repair people needed to fix defective products and increasing the amount of salespeople's time devoted to selling instead of exchanging already-sold but defective products. It could also be used by the overall company as a differentiator when compared to competitors and allow the company to charge more.

3. **Examine the potential synergies among the value chains of different product lines or business units:** Each value element, such as advertising or manufacturing, has an inherent economy of scale in which activities are conducted at their lowest possible cost per unit of output. If a particular product is not being produced at a high enough level to reach economies of scale in distribution, another product could be used to share the same distribution channel. This is an example of **economies of scope**, which result when the value chains of two separate products or services share activities, such as the same marketing channels or manufacturing facilities. The cost of joint production of multiple products can be lower than the cost of separate production.

Scanning Functional Resources and Capabilities

The simplest way to begin an analysis of a corporation's value chain is by carefully examining its traditional functional areas for potential strengths and weaknesses. Functional resources and capabilities include not only the financial, physical, and human assets in each area but also the ability of the people in each area to formulate and implement the necessary functional objectives, strategies, and policies. These resources and capabilities include the knowledge of analytical concepts and procedural techniques common to each area, as well as the ability of the people in each area to use them effectively. If used properly, these resources and capabilities serve as strengths to carry out value-added activities and support strategic decisions. In addition to the usual business functions of marketing, finance, R&D, operations, human resources, and information systems/technology, we also discuss structure and culture as key parts of a business corporation's value chain.

BASIC ORGANIZATIONAL STRUCTURES

Although there is an almost infinite variety of structural forms, certain basic types predominate in modern complex organizations. **Figure 5–3** illustrates three basic **organizational structures**. The conglomerate structure is a variant of divisional structure and is thus not depicted as a fourth structure. Generally speaking, each structure tends to support some corporate strategies better than others:

- **Simple structure** has no functional or product categories and is appropriate for a small, entrepreneur-dominated company with one or two product lines that operates in a reasonably small, easily identifiable market niche. Employees tend to be generalists and jacks-of-all-trades. In terms of stages of development (to be discussed in **Chapter 9**), this is a Stage I company.

- **Functional structure** is appropriate for a medium-sized firm with several product lines in one industry. Employees tend to be specialists in the business functions that are important to that industry, such as manufacturing, marketing, finance, and human resources. In terms of stages of development (discussed in **Chapter 9**), this is a Stage II company.

- **Divisional structure** is appropriate for a large corporation with many product lines in several related industries. Employees tend to be functional specialists organized according to product/market distinctions. The Clorox Company is made up of five big divisions: (1) Cleaning (i.e., Clorox, 409, and Tilex); (2) Household (i.e., Glad, Kingsford and Fresh

FIGURE 5–3 Basic Organizational Structures

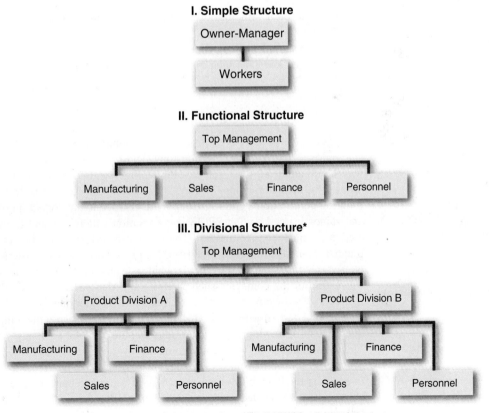

*Strategic Business Units and the conglomerate structure are variants of the divisional structure.

Step); (3) Lifestyle (i.e., Brita and Burt's Bees); (4) Professional (Commercial Solutions); and (5) International (i.e., Chux and Poett).[27] Management attempts to find some synergy among divisional activities through the use of committees and horizontal linkages. In terms of stages of development (to be discussed in **Chapter 9**), this is a Stage III company.

- **Strategic business units (SBUs)** are a modification of the divisional structure. Strategic business units are divisions or groups of divisions composed of independent product-market segments that are given primary responsibility and authority for the management of their own functional areas. *An SBU may be of any size or level, but it must have (1) a unique mission, (2) identifiable competitors, (3) an external market focus, and (4) control of its business functions.*[28] The idea is to decentralize on the basis of strategic elements rather than on the basis of size, product characteristics, or span of control and to create horizontal linkages among units previously kept separate. For example, rather than organize products on the basis of packaging technology like frozen foods, canned foods, and bagged foods, General Foods organized its products into SBUs on the basis of consumer-oriented menu segments: breakfast food, beverage, main meal, dessert, and pet foods. In terms of stages of development (to be discussed in **Chapter 9**), this is also a Stage III company.

- **Conglomerate structure** is appropriate for a large corporation with many product lines in several unrelated industries. A variant of the divisional structure, the conglomerate structure (sometimes called a holding company) is typically an assemblage of legally independent firms (subsidiaries) operating under one corporate umbrella but controlled through the subsidiaries' boards of directors. The unrelated nature of the subsidiaries prevents any attempt at gaining synergy among them. In terms of stages of development (discussed in **Chapter 9**), this is also a Stage III company.

If the current basic structure of a corporation does not easily support a strategy under consideration, top management must decide whether the proposed strategy is feasible or whether the structure should be changed to a more complicated structure such as a matrix or network. (Other structural designs such as the matrix and network are discussed in **Chapter 9.**)

CORPORATE CULTURE: THE COMPANY WAY

There is an oft-told story of a person new to a company asking an experienced co-worker what an employee should do when a customer calls. The old-timer responded: "There are three ways to do any job—the right way, the wrong way, and the company way. Around here, we always do things the company way." In most organizations, the "company way" is derived from the corporation's culture. **Corporate culture** is the collection of beliefs, expectations, and values learned and shared by a corporation's members and transmitted from one generation of employees to another. The corporate culture generally reflects the values of the founder(s) and the mission of the firm.[29] It gives a company a sense of identity: "This is who we are. This is what we do. This is what we stand for." The culture includes the dominant orientation of the company, such as R&D at 3M, shared responsibility at Nucor, customer service at Nordstrom, innovation at Google, or product quality at BMW. It often includes a number of informal work rules (forming the "company way") that employees follow without question. These work practices over time become part of a company's unquestioned tradition. The culture, therefore, reflects the company's values.

Corporate culture has two distinct attributes, intensity and integration.[30] *Cultural intensity* is the degree to which members of a unit accept the norms, values, or other cultural content associated with the unit. This shows the culture's depth. Organizations with strong norms promoting a particular value, such as quality at BMW, have intensive cultures, whereas new firms (or those in transition) have weaker, less intensive cultures. Employees in an intensive culture tend to exhibit consistent behavior—that is, they tend to act similarly over time. *Cultural integration* is the extent to which units throughout an organization share a common culture. This is the culture's breadth. Organizations with a pervasive dominant culture may be hierarchically controlled and power-oriented, such as a military unit, and have highly integrated cultures. All employees tend to hold the same cultural values and norms. In contrast, a company that is structured into diverse units by functions or divisions usually exhibits some strong subcultures (for example, R&D versus manufacturing) and a less integrated corporate culture.

Corporate culture fulfills several important functions in an organization:

1. Conveys a sense of identity for employees.
2. Helps generate employee commitment to something greater than themselves.
3. Adds to the stability of the organization as a social system.
4. Serves as a frame of reference for employees to use to make sense of organizational activities and to use as a guide for appropriate behavior.[31]

Corporate culture shapes the behavior of people in a corporation, thus affecting corporate performance. For example, corporate cultures that emphasize the socialization of new employees have less employee turnover, leading to lower costs.[32] Because corporate cultures have a powerful influence on the behavior of people at all levels, they can strongly affect a corporation's ability to shift its strategic direction. A strong culture should not only promote survival, but it should also create the basis for a superior competitive position by increasing motivation and facilitating coordination and control.[33] For example, a culture emphasizing constant renewal may help a company adapt to a changing, hypercompetitive environment.[34] To the extent that a corporation's distinctive competence is embedded in an organization's culture, it will be a form of tacit knowledge and very difficult for a competitor to imitate. The **Global Issue** feature shows the differences between ABB Asea Brown Boveri AG and Panasonic Corporation in terms of how they manage their corporate cultures in a global industry.

A change in mission, objectives, strategies, or policies is not likely to be successful if it is in opposition to the accepted culture of a firm. Foot-dragging and even sabotage may result, as employees fight to resist a radical change in corporate philosophy. As with structure, if an organization's culture is compatible with a new strategy, it is an internal strength. On the other hand, if the corporate culture is not compatible with the proposed strategy, it is a serious weakness. Circuit City ceased operations in January 2009 after a disastrous set of moves by then CEO Philip Schoonover. The history of Circuit City and its competitive advantage for years had been built around a level of expertise simply not available at other big box stores like Best Buy. However, in a move to save money, Schoonover fired 3400 of Circuit City's most experienced employees and replaced them with low-wage, low-level clerks. Analysts blasted the move for the devastating loss of morale and associated decline in customer service. The misalignment with the organization's culture spelled doom for the organization.[35]

Corporate culture is also important when considering an acquisition. The merging of two dissimilar cultures, if not handled wisely, can create some serious internal conflicts. Procter & Gamble's management knew, for example, that their 2005 acquisition of Gillette might create some cultural problems. Even though both companies were strong consumer goods marketers, they each had a fundamental difference that led to many, subtle differences between the cultures: Gillette sold its razors, toothbrushes, and batteries to men; whereas, P&G sold its health and beauty aids to women. Art Lafley, P&G's CEO, admitted a year after the merger that it would take an additional year to 15 months to align the two companies.[36]

GLOBAL issue

MANAGING CORPORATE CULTURE FOR GLOBAL COMPETITIVE ADVANTAGE: ABB VS. PANASONIC

Zurich-based ABB Asea Brown Boveri AG is a world-builder of power plants and electrical equipment with industrial factories in 140 countries. By establishing one set of multicultural values throughout its global operations, ABB's management believes that the company will gain an advantage over its rivals Siemens AG of Germany, France's Alcatel-Alsthom NV, and the U.S.'s General Electric Company. ABB is a company with no geographic base. Instead, it has many "home" markets where it can draw on expertise from around the globe. ABB created a set of 500 global managers who could adapt to local cultures while executing ABB's global strategies. These people are multilingual and move around each of ABB's 5000 profit centers in 140 countries. Their assignment is to cut costs, improve efficiency, and integrate local businesses with the ABB worldview.

Few multinational corporations are as successful as ABB in getting global strategies to work with local operations. In agreement with the resource-based view of the firm, the past Chairman of ABB, Percy Barnevik stated, "Our strength comes from pulling together. . . . If you can make this work real well, then you get a competitive edge out of the organization which is very, very difficult to copy."

Contrast ABB's globally oriented corporate culture with the more parochial culture of Panasonic Corporation of Japan. Panasonic is the third-largest electrical company in the world. Konosuke Matsushita founded the company in 1918. His management philosophy led to the company's success but became institutionalized in the corporate culture—a culture that was more focused on Japanese values than on cross-cultural globalization. As a result, Panasonic corporate culture does not adapt well to local conditions. Not only is Panasonic's top management *exclusively* Japanese, its subsidiary managers are *overwhelmingly* Japanese. The company's distrust of non-Japanese managers in the United States and some European countries results in a "rice-paper ceiling" that prevents non-Japanese people from being promoted into Panasonic subsidiaries' top management. Foreign employees are often confused by the corporate philosophy that has not been adapted to suit local realities. Panasonic's corporate culture perpetuates a cross-cultural divide that separates the Japanese from the non-Japanese managers, leaving the non-Japanese managers feeling frustrated and undervalued. This divide prevents the flow of knowledge and experience from regional operations to the headquarters and may hinder Panasonic's ability to compete globally.

. . . .

SOURCES: Summarized from J. Guyon, "ABB Fuses Units with One Set of Values," *The Wall Street Journal* (October 2, 1996), p. A15, and N. Holden, "Why Globalizing with a Conservative Corporate Culture Inhibits Localization of Management: The Telling Case of Matsushita Electric," *International Journal of Cross Cultural Management* (Vol. 1, No. 1, 2001), pp. 53–72.

STRATEGIC MARKETING ISSUES

The marketing manager is a company's primary link to the customer and the competition. The manager, therefore, must be especially concerned with the market position and marketing mix of the firm as well as with the overall reputation of the company and its brands.

Market Position and Segmentation

Market position deals with the question, "Who are our customers?" It refers to the selection of specific areas for marketing concentration and can be expressed in terms of market, product, and geographic locations. Through market research, corporations are able to practice *market segmentation* with various products or services so that managers can discover what niches to seek, which new types of products to develop, and how to ensure that a company's many products do not directly compete with one another.

Marketing Mix

Marketing mix refers to the particular combination of key variables under a corporation's control that can be used to affect demand and to gain competitive advantage. These variables

TABLE 5–1	Product	Place	Promotion	Price
Marketing Mix Variables	Quality Features Options Style Brand name Packaging Sizes Services Warranties Returns	Channels Coverage Locations Inventory Transport	Advertising Personal selling Sales promotion Publicity	List price Discounts Allowances Payment periods Credit items

SOURCE: Philip Kotler, *Marketing Management*, 11th edition © 2003, p. 16. Reprinted by Pearson Education Inc., Upper Saddle River, NJ.

are product, place, promotion, and price. Within each of these four variables are several sub-variables, listed in **Table 5–1**, that should be analyzed in terms of their effects on divisional and corporate performance.

Product Life Cycle

As depicted in **Figure 5–4**, the **product life cycle** is a graph showing time plotted against the sales of a product as it moves from introduction through growth and maturity to decline. This concept is used by marketing managers to discuss the marketing mix of a particular product or group of products in terms of where it might exist in the life cycle. From a strategic management perspective, this concept is of little value because the real position of any product can only be ascertained in hindsight. Strategy is about making decisions in real-time for the future of the business. The Innovation Issue feature shows how a company can use the conventional wisdom of the product life cycle to its advantage against leading-edge competitors.

FIGURE 5–4
Product Life Cycle

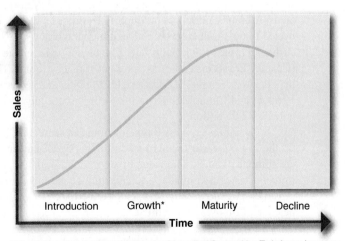

* The right end of the Growth stage is often called Competitive Turbulence because of price and distribution competition that shakes out the weaker competitors. For further information, see C. R. Wasson, *Dynamic Competitive Strategy and Product Life Cycles*. 3rd ed. (Austin, TX: Austin Press, 1978).

INNOVATION issue

DOCOMO MOVES AGAINST THE GRAIN

Years ago, DoCoMo (Japan's largest cell phone service provider in Japan) chose not to be a part of the iPhone phenomenon. The expense of the iPhone to the company was key in this decision. Sometimes innovation is needed because of strategic decisions. In this case, the iPhone has come to symbolize what constitutes "hip," so the company went on a search for opportunities in the market where they had core strengths that were not being addressed.

The fastest-growing demographic in Japan is the elderly. People age 65 and older make up 23% of the population and their needs are substantially different than the younger set. This is especially true in the cell phone market, where the latest iPhone helped push the percentage of adults age 20–29 with a Smartphone in Japan to over 51%. That compares to less than 6% of people age 65 or older who own a Smartphone.

The small screen and apps designed for the latest desires of the younger set simply don't appeal to an audience with weaker eyesight and a focus on more practical applications. DoCoMo seized on this apparent opportunity and went to work to create a must-have Smartphone experience for those over 60.

Today, the company is offering phones with larger keys, apps that are easier to understand and use, a new voice-recognition software that allows its customers to send e-mails, and is holding training sessions around the country to teach older customers how to use a Smartphone. By March of 2012, they had run more than 1100 such sessions. In each of these areas, they are separating themselves from the competition, which is far more interested in being seen as the most cutting-edge in the industry. While other competitors battle it out for the younger set, DoCoMo has captured the imagination of the older set. People over the age of 60 now account for more than 24% of the company's business, and DoCoMo's goal is to stay in the lead with the elderly market by anticipating their desires and providing innovative solutions that in some cases are more retro than cutting-edge.

....

SOURCES: R. Martin, "DoCoMo Shuns iPhone, Pushes Android Options," *The Japan Times* (May 23, 2012), (http://www.japantimes.co.jp/text/nc20120523ga.html); M. Yasu and S. Ozasa, "DoCoMo Savors an Older Vintage," *Bloomberg Businessweek* (July 2, 2012), (http://www.businessweek.com/articles/2012-06-28/docomo-looks-for-growth-among-japans-elderly).

Brand and Corporate Reputation

A **brand** is a name given to a company's product which embodies all of the characteristics of that item in the mind of the consumer. Over time and with effective advertising and execution, a brand connotes various characteristics in the consumers' minds. For example, Disney stands for family entertainment. Carnival has the "fun ships." BMW means high-performance autos. A brand can thus be an important corporate resource. If done well, a brand name is connected to the product to such an extent that a brand may stand for an entire product category, such as Kleenex for facial tissue. The objective is for the customer to ask for the brand name (Coke or Pepsi) instead of the product category (cola). The world's 10 most valuable brands in 2012 were Apple, IBM, Google, McDonald's, Microsoft, Coca-Cola, Marlboro, AT&T, Verizon, and China Mobile, in that order. According to *Forbes*, the value of the Apple brand is US$182.95 billion.[37]

A *corporate brand* is a type of brand in which the company's name serves as the brand. Of the top 10 world brands listed previously, all but one (Marlboro is part of Altria Group) are company names. The value of a corporate brand is that it typically stands for consumers' impressions of a company and can thus be extended onto products not currently offered—regardless of the company's actual expertise. For example, Caterpillar, a manufacturer of heavy earth-moving equipment, used consumer associations with the Caterpillar brand (*rugged, masculine, construction-related*) to market work boots. While this type of move may not be strategically advisable, consumer impressions of a brand can at least suggest new product categories to enter even though a company may have no competencies in making or marketing that type of product or service.[38]

A **corporate reputation** is a widely held perception of a company by the general public. It consists of two attributes: (1) stakeholders' perceptions of a corporation's ability to produce quality goods and (2) a corporation's prominence in the minds of stakeholders.[39] A good corporate reputation can be a strategic resource. It can serve in marketing as both a signal and an entry barrier. It contributes to its goods having a price premium.[40] Reputation is especially important when the quality of a company's product or service is not directly observable and can be learned only through experience. For example, retail stores are willing to stock a new product from P&G or Coca-Cola because they know that both companies market only good-quality products that are highly advertised. Like tacit knowledge, reputation tends to be long-lasting and hard for others to duplicate—thus providing a potential sustainable competitive advantage.[41] It might also have a significant impact on a firm's stock price.[42] Research reveals a positive relationship between corporate reputation and financial performance.[43]

STRATEGIC FINANCIAL ISSUES

A financial manager must ascertain the best sources of funds, uses of funds, and the control of funds. All strategic issues have financial implications. Cash must be raised from internal or external (local and global) sources and allocated for different uses. The flow of funds in the operations of an organization must be monitored. To the extent that a corporation is involved in international activities, currency fluctuations must be dealt with to ensure that profits aren't wiped out by the rise or fall of the dollar versus the yen, euro, or other currencies. Benefits in the form of returns, repayments, or products and services must be given to the sources of outside financing. All these tasks must be handled in a way that complements and supports overall corporate strategy. A firm's capital structure (amounts of debt and equity) can influence its strategic choices. Corporations with increased debt tend to be more risk-averse and less willing to invest in R&D.[44]

Financial Leverage

The mix of externally generated short-term and long-term funds in relation to the amount and timing of internally generated funds should be appropriate to the corporate objectives, strategies, and policies. The concept of **financial leverage** (the ratio of total debt to total assets) is helpful in describing how debt is used to increase the earnings available to common shareholders. When the company finances its activities by sales of bonds or notes instead of through stock, the earnings per share are boosted: the interest paid on the debt reduces taxable income, but fewer shareholders share the profits than if the company had sold more stock to finance its activities. The debt, however, does raise the firm's break-even point above what it would have been if the firm had financed from internally generated funds only. High leverage may therefore be perceived as a corporate strength in times of prosperity and ever-increasing sales, or as a weakness in times of a recession and falling sales. This is because leverage acts to magnify the effect on earnings per share of an increase or decrease in dollar sales. Research indicates that greater leverage has a positive impact on performance for firms in stable environments, but a negative impact for firms in dynamic environments.[45]

Capital Budgeting

Capital budgeting is the analyzing and ranking of possible investments in fixed assets such as land, buildings, and equipment in terms of the additional outlays and additional receipts that will result from each investment. A good finance department will be able to prepare such capital budgets and to rank them on the basis of some accepted criteria or *hurdle rate* (for example, years to pay back investment, rate of return, or time to break-even point) for the purpose of strategic decision making. Most firms have more than one hurdle rate and vary it as a function of the type of project being considered. Projects with high strategic significance, such as entering new markets or defending market share, will often have lower hurdle rates.[46]

STRATEGIC RESEARCH AND DEVELOPMENT (R&D) ISSUES

The R&D manager is responsible for suggesting and implementing a company's technological strategy in light of its corporate objectives and policies. The manager's job, therefore, involves (1) choosing among alternative new technologies to use within the corporation, (2) developing methods of embodying the new technology in new products and processes, and (3) deploying resources so that the new technology can be successfully implemented.

R&D Intensity, Technological Competence, and Technology Transfer

The company must make available the resources necessary for effective research and development. A company's **R&D intensity** (its spending on R&D as a percentage of sales revenue) is a principal means of gaining market share in global competition. The amount spent on R&D often varies by industry. For example, the U.S. computer software industry traditionally spends 13.5% of its sales dollar for R&D, whereas the paper and forest products industry spends only 1.0%.[47] A good rule of thumb for R&D spending is that a corporation should spend at a "normal" rate for that particular industry unless its strategic plan calls for unusual expenditures.

Simply spending money on R&D or new projects does not mean, however, that the money will produce useful results. Apple is one of the most profitable companies in the world and yet they ranked #18 on the 2012 S&P 500 in terms of R&D spending The top 5 on the list of companies that invest in R&D were Microsoft (US$9.4B), Pfizer (US$8.4B), Intel (US$8.4B), Merck (US$8.3B) and J&J (US$7.5B).[48]

A company's R&D unit should be evaluated for **technological competence** in both the development and the use of innovative technology. Not only should the corporation make a consistent research effort (as measured by reasonably constant corporate expenditures that result in usable innovations), it should also be proficient in managing research personnel and integrating their innovations into its day-to-day operations. A company should also be proficient in **technology transfer**, the process of taking a new technology from the laboratory to the marketplace. Aerospace parts maker Rockwell Collins, for example, is a master of developing new technology, such as the "heads-up display" (transparent screens in an airplane cockpit that tell pilots speed, altitude, and direction), for the military and then using it in products built for the civilian market.[49]

R&D Mix

Basic R&D is conducted by scientists in well-equipped laboratories where the focus is on theoretical problem areas. The best indicators of a company's capability in this area are its patents and research publications. *Product R&D* concentrates on marketing and is concerned with product or product-packaging improvements. The best measurements of ability in this area are the number of successful new products introduced and the percentage of total sales and profits coming from products introduced within the past five years. *Engineering (or process) R&D* is concerned with engineering, concentrating on quality control, and the development of design specifications and improved production equipment. A company's capability in this area can be measured by consistent reductions in unit manufacturing costs and by the number of product defects.

Most corporations will have a mix of basic, product, and process R&D, which varies by industry, company, and product line. The balance of these types of research is known as the

R&D mix and should be appropriate to the strategy being considered and to each product's life cycle. For example, it is generally accepted that product R&D normally dominates the early stages of a product's life cycle (when the product's optimal form and features are still being debated), whereas process R&D becomes especially important in the later stages (when the product's design is solidified and the emphasis is on reducing costs and improving quality).

Impact of Technological Discontinuity on Strategy

The R&D manager must determine when to abandon present technology and when to develop or adopt new technology. Richard Foster of McKinsey and Company states that the displacement of one technology by another (**technological discontinuity**) is a frequent and strategically important phenomenon. Such a discontinuity occurs when a new technology cannot simply be used to enhance the current technology, but actually substitutes for that technology to yield better performance. For each technology within a given field or industry, according to Foster, the plotting of product performance against research effort/expenditures on a graph results in an S-shaped curve.

Information technology is still on the steep upward slope of its S-curve in which relatively small increments in R&D effort result in significant improvement in performance. This is an example of *Moore's Law* (which is really a rule of thumb and not a scientific law), which states that the number of transistors that can be fit on a computer chip (microprocessors) will double (in other words, computing power will double) every 18 months.[50] The presence of a technological discontinuity in the world's steel industry during the 1960s explains why the large capital expenditures by U.S. steel companies failed to keep them competitive with the Japanese firms that adopted the new technologies. As Foster points out, "History has shown that as one technology nears the end of its S-curve, competitive leadership in a market generally changes hands."[51]

Christensen explains in *The Innovator's Dilemma* why this transition occurs when a "disruptive technology" enters an industry. In a study of computer disk drive manufacturers, he explains that established market leaders are typically reluctant to move in a timely manner to a new technology. This reluctance to switch technologies (even when the firm is aware of the new technology and may have even invented it!) is because the resource allocation process in most companies gives priority to those projects (typically based on the old technology) with the greatest likelihood of generating a good return on investment—those projects appealing to the firm's current customers (whose products are also based on the characteristics of the old technology). For example, in the 1980s a disk drive manufacturer's customers (PC manufacturers) wanted a better (faster) 5¼″ drive with greater capacity. These PC makers were not interested in the new 3½″ drives based on the new technology because (at that time) the smaller drives were slower and had less capacity. Smaller size was irrelevant since these companies primarily made desktop personal computers, which were designed to hold large drives.

The new technology is generally riskier and of little appeal to the current customers of established firms. Products derived from the new technology are more expensive and do not meet the customers' requirements—requirements based on the old technology. New entrepreneurial firms are typically more interested in the new technology because it is one way to appeal to a developing market niche in a market currently dominated by established companies. Even though the new technology may be more expensive to develop, it offers performance improvements in areas that are attractive to this small niche, but of no consequence to the customers of the established competitors.

This was the case with the entrepreneurial manufacturers of 3½″ disk drives. These smaller drives appealed to the PC makers who were trying to increase their small PC market share by offering laptop computers. Size and weight were more important to these customers than were capacity and speed. By the time the new technology was developed to the point that the 3½″ drive matched and even surpassed the 5¼″ drive in terms of speed and capacity (in addition to size and weight), it was too late for the established 5¼″ disk drive firms to switch to the new technology. Once their customers begin demanding smaller products using the new technology, the established firms were unable to respond quickly and lost their leadership position in the industry. They were able to remain in the industry (with a much reduced market share) only if they were able to utilize the new technology to be competitive in the new product line.[52]

The same phenomenon can be seen in many product categories ranging from flat-panel display screens to railroad locomotives to digital photography to musical recordings. For example, George Heilmeier created the first practical liquid-crystal display (LCD) in 1964 at RCA Labs. RCA unveiled the new display in 1968 with much fanfare about LCDs being the future of TV sets, but then refused to fund further development of the new technology. In contrast, Japanese television and computer manufacturers invested in long-term development of LCDs. Today, Japanese, Korean, and Taiwanese companies dominate the US$34 billion LCD business, and RCA no longer makes televisions. Interestingly, Heilmeier received the Kyoto Prize in 2005 for his LCD invention.[53]

STRATEGIC OPERATIONS ISSUES

The primary task of the operations (manufacturing or service) manager is to develop and operate a system that will produce the required number of products or services, with a certain quality, at a given cost, within an allotted time. Many of the key concepts and techniques popularly used in manufacturing can be applied to service businesses.

In very general terms, manufacturing can be intermittent or continuous. In *intermittent systems* (job shops), the item is normally processed sequentially, but the work and sequence of the process vary. An example is an auto body repair shop. At each location, the tasks determine the details of processing and the time required for them. These job shops can be very labor-intensive. For example, a job shop usually has little automated machinery and thus a small amount of fixed costs. It has a fairly low break-even point, but its variable cost line (composed of wages and the costs of special parts) has a relatively steep slope. Because most of the costs associated with the product are variable (many employees earn piece-rate wages), a job shop's variable costs are higher than those of automated firms. Its advantage over other firms is that it can operate at low levels and still be profitable. After a job shop's sales reach break-even, however, the huge variable costs as a percentage of total costs keep the profit per unit at a relatively low level. In terms of strategy, this firm should look for a niche in the marketplace for which it can produce and sell a reasonably small quantity of custom-made goods.

In contrast, *continuous systems* are those laid out as lines on which products can be continuously assembled or processed. An example is an automobile assembly line. A firm using continuous systems invests heavily in fixed investments such as automated processes and highly sophisticated machinery. Its labor force, relatively small but highly skilled, earns salaries rather than piece-rate wages. Consequently, this firm has a high amount of fixed costs. It also has a relatively high break-even point, but its variable cost line rises slowly. This is an example of **operating leverage**, the impact of a specific change in sales volume on net operating income. The advantage of high operating leverage is that once the firm reaches break-even, its profits rise faster than do those of less automated firms having lower operating leverage. Continuous systems reap benefits from economies of scale. In terms of strategy, this firm needs to find a high-demand niche in the marketplace for which it can produce and sell a large quantity of goods. However, a firm with high operating leverage is likely to suffer huge losses during a recession. During an economic downturn, the firm with less automation and thus less leverage is more likely to survive comfortably because a drop in sales primarily affects variable costs. It is often easier to lay off labor than to sell off specialized plants and machines.

Experience Curve

A conceptual framework that many large corporations have used successfully is the experience curve (originally called the learning curve). The **experience curve** suggests that unit production costs decline by some fixed percentage (commonly 20%–30%) each time the total accumulated volume of production in units doubles. The actual percentage varies by industry and is based on many variables: the amount of time it takes a person to learn a new task, scale economies, product and process improvements, and lower raw materials cost, among others. For example, in an industry with an 85% experience curve, a corporation might expect a 15% reduction in unit costs for every doubling of volume. The total costs per unit can be expected to drop from US$100 when the total production is 10 units, to US$85 (US$100 × 85%) when production increases to 20 units, and to US$72.25 (US$85 × 85%) when it reaches 40 units. Achieving these results often means investing in R&D and fixed assets; higher fixed costs and less flexibility thus result. Nevertheless, the manufacturing strategy is one of building capacity ahead of demand in order to achieve the lower unit costs that develop from the experience curve. On the basis of some future point on the experience curve, the corporation should price the product or service very low to preempt competition and increase market demand. The resulting high number of units sold and high market share should result in high profits, based on the low unit costs.

Management commonly uses the experience curve in estimating the production costs of (1) a product never before made with the present techniques and processes or (2) current products produced by newly introduced techniques or processes. The concept was first applied in the airframe industry and can be applied in the service industry as well. For example, a cleaning company can reduce its costs per employee by having its workers use the same equipment and techniques to clean many adjacent offices in one office building rather than just cleaning a few offices in multiple buildings. Although many firms have used experience curves extensively, an unquestioning acceptance of the industry norm (such as 80% for the airframe industry or 70% for integrated circuits) is very risky. The experience curve of the industry as a whole might not hold true for a particular company for a variety of reasons.[54]

Flexible Manufacturing for Mass Customization

The use of large, continuous, mass-production facilities to take advantage of experience-curve economies has recently been criticized. The use of **C**omputer-**A**ssisted **D**esign and **C**omputer-**A**ssisted **M**anufacturing (CAD/CAM) and robot technology means that learning times are shorter and products can be economically manufactured in small, customized batches in a process called *mass customization*—the low-cost production of individually customized goods and services.[55] Economies of scope (in which common parts of the manufacturing activities of various products are combined to gain economies even though small numbers of each product are made) replace **economies of scale** (in which unit costs are reduced by making large numbers of the same product) in flexible manufacturing. *Flexible manufacturing* permits the low-volume output of custom-tailored products at relatively low unit costs through economies of scope. It is thus possible to have the cost advantages of continuous systems with the customer-oriented advantages of intermittent systems. The automaker Hyundai/Kia is designing all of its manufacturing facilities so that any assembly line can build any car in the fleet with minimal change. They are automating plants so that robots are able to handle parts regardless of the model being produced. Previously, robots were capable of only handling parts for only one model line at a time.[56]

STRATEGIC HUMAN RESOURCE (HRM) ISSUES

The primary task of the manager of human resources is to improve the match between individuals and jobs. Research indicates that companies with good HRM practices have higher profits and a better survival rate than do firms without these practices.[57] A good HRM department should know how to use attitude surveys and other feedback devices to assess employees' satisfaction with their jobs and with the corporation as a whole. HRM managers should also use job analysis to obtain job description information about what each job needs to accomplish in terms of quality and quantity. Up-to-date job descriptions are essential not only for proper employee selection, appraisal, training, and development for wage and salary administration, and for labor negotiations, but also for summarizing the corporatewide human resources in terms of employee-skill categories. Just as a company must know the number, type, and quality of its manufacturing facilities, it must also know the kinds of people it employs and the skills they possess. The best strategies are meaningless if employees do not have the skills to carry them out or if jobs cannot be designed to accommodate the available workers. IBM, Procter & Gamble, and Hewlett-Packard, for example, use employee profiles to ensure that they have the best mix of talents to implement their planned strategies. Because project managers at IBM are now able to scan the company's databases to identify employee capabilities and availability, the average time needed to assemble a team has declined 20% for a savings of US$500 million overall.[58]

Increasing Use of Teams

Management is beginning to realize that it must be more flexible in its utilization of employees in order for human resources to be classified as a strength. Human resource managers, therefore, need to be knowledgeable about work options such as part-time work, job sharing, flex-time, extended leaves, and contract work, and especially about the proper use of teams. Over two- thirds of large U.S. companies are successfully using *autonomous (self-managing) work teams* in which a group of people work together without a supervisor to plan, coordinate, and evaluate their own work.[59] Connecticut Spring & Stamping is using self-directed work teams to achieve the dual goals of 100% on-time delivery and 100% quality. Since installing the work teams, the company has gone from what it referred to as a "very low on-time delivery performance" to an on-time delivery rate of 96%.[60]

As a way to move a product more quickly through its development stage, companies like Harley-Davidson, KPMG, Wendy's, LinkedIn, and Pfizer are using *cross-functional work teams*. Instead of developing products/services in a series of steps, companies are tearing down the traditional walls separating the departments so that people from each discipline can get involved in projects early on. In a process called *concurrent engineering*, the once-isolated specialists now work side by side and compare notes constantly in an effort to design cost-effective products with features customers want. Taking this approach enabled Chrysler Corporation to reduce its product development cycle from 60 to 36 months.[61] For such cross-functional work teams to be successful, the groups must receive training and coaching. Otherwise, poorly implemented teams may worsen morale, create divisiveness, and raise the level of cynicism among workers.[62]

Virtual teams are groups of geographically and/or organizationally dispersed co-workers that are assembled using a combination of telecommunications and information technologies to accomplish an organizational task.[63] A study conducted in 2012 found that 46% of organizations polled used virtual teams and that multinational companies were twice as likely (66%) to use virtual teams as compared to those having U.S.-based operations (28%).[64] According to the Gartner Group, more than 60% of professional employees now work in virtual teams.[65] Internet, intranet, and extranet systems are combining with other new technologies, such as desktop videoconferencing and collaborative software, to create a new workplace in which teams of workers are no longer restrained by geography, time, or organizational boundaries. This technology allows about 12% of the U.S. workforce, who have no permanent office at their companies, to do team projects over the Internet and report to a manager thousands of miles away. While the definition of telecommuting varies somewhat, the U.S. government reported that in 2012 approximately 24% of the workforce did at least part of their job from home. They define telecommuting as employees who work regularly, but not exclusively at home.[66]

As more companies outsource some of the activities previously conducted internally, the traditional organizational structure is being replaced by a series of virtual teams, which rarely, if ever, meet face to face. Such teams may be established as temporary groups to accomplish a specific task or may be more permanent to address continuing issues such as strategic planning. Membership on these teams is often fluid, depending upon the task to be accomplished. They may include not only employees from different functions within a company, but also members of various stakeholder groups, such as suppliers, customers, and law or consulting firms. The use of virtual teams to replace traditional face-to-face work groups is being driven by five trends:

1. Flatter organizational structures with increasing cross-functional coordination need
2. Turbulent environments requiring more interorganizational cooperation
3. Increasing employee autonomy and participation in decision making
4. Higher knowledge requirements derived from a greater emphasis on service
5. Increasing globalization of trade and corporate activity[67]

Union Relations and Temporary/Part-Time Workers

If the corporation is unionized, a good human resource manager should be able to work closely with the union. Even though union membership had dropped to only 11.8% of the U.S. workforce by 2011 compared to 20.1% in 1983, it still included 14.8 million people. Nevertheless, only 6.9% of private sector employees belonged to a union (compared to 37% of public sector employees).[68] To save jobs, U.S. unions are increasingly willing to support new strategic initiatives and employee involvement programs. For example, United Steel Workers hired Ron Bloom, an investment banker, to propose a strategic plan to make Goodyear Tire & Rubber globally competitive in a way that would preserve as many jobs as possible. In their landmark 2003 contract, the union gave up US$1.15 billion in wage and benefit concessions over three years in return for a promise by Goodyear's top management to invest in 12 of its 14 U.S. factories, to limit imports from its factories in Brazil and Asia, and to maintain 85% of its 19,000-person workforce. The company also agreed to aggressively restructure the firm's US$5 billion debt. According to Bloom, "We told Goodyear, 'We'll make you profitable, but you're going to adopt this strategy.'. . . We think the company should be a patient, long-term builder of value for the employees and shareholders." In their most recent contract, the U.S. tire maker expects to save some US$500+ million over four years and invest US$600 million in unionized plants.[69]

Outside the United States, the average proportion of unionized workers among major industrialized nations is around 50%. European unions tend to be militant, politically oriented, and much less interested in working with management to increase efficiency. Nationwide strikes can occur quickly. In contrast, Japanese unions are typically tied to individual companies and are usually supportive of management. These differences among countries have significant implications for the management of multinational corporations.

To increase flexibility, avoid layoffs, and reduce labor costs, corporations are using more temporary (also known as contingent) workers. Over 90% of U.S. and European firms use temporary workers in some capacity; 43% use them in professional and technical functions.[70] Approximately 23% of the U.S. workforce are part-time workers. The percentage is even higher in Japan, where 26% of workers are part-time, and in the Netherlands, where 36% of all employees work part-time.[71] Labor unions are concerned that companies use temps to avoid hiring costlier unionized workers.

Quality of Work Life and Human Diversity

Human resource departments have found that to reduce employee dissatisfaction and unionization efforts (or, conversely, to improve employee satisfaction and existing union relations), they must consider the *quality of work life* in the design of jobs. Partially a reaction to the traditionally heavy emphasis on technical and economic factors in job design, quality of work life emphasizes improving the human dimension of work. The knowledgeable human resource manager, therefore, should be able to improve the corporation's quality of work life by (1) introducing participative problem solving, (2) restructuring work, (3) introducing innovative reward systems, and (4) improving the work environment. It is hoped that these improvements will lead to a more participative corporate culture and thus higher productivity and quality products. Ford Motor Company, for example, rebuilt and modernized its famous River Rouge plant using flexible equipment and new processes. Employees work in teams and use Internet-connected PCs on the shop floor to share their concerns instantly with suppliers or product engineers. Workstations were redesigned to make them more ergonomic and reduce repetitive-strain injuries. "If you feel good while you're working, I think quality and productivity will increase, and Ford thinks that too, otherwise they wouldn't do this," observed Jerry Sullivan, president of United Auto Workers Local 600.[72]

Companies are also discovering that by redesigning their plants and offices for improved energy efficiency, they can receive a side effect of improving their employees' quality of work life—that is, raising labor productivity. See the **Sustainability Issue** feature to learn how improved environmental sustainability programs have changed the Olympic Games.

Human diversity refers to the mix in the workplace of people from different races, cultures, and backgrounds. Realizing that the demographics are changing toward an increasing percentage

SUSTAINABILITY issue

THE OLYMPIC GAMES—SOCHI 2014 AND RIO 2016

Prior to the 2012 Olympic Games in London, there had never been a plan in place for any sustainability standards for the event sector. The 2012 London Olympic Committee decided to not only make sustainability a cornerstone of that Olympics, but also to establish standards for future Olympics and other major events.

Rather than dictating a set of specific targets or checklists, the committee established a method for organizers to work with the local community, suppliers, and participants to identify the key impact areas of the event and a means to mitigate the negative impacts, measure progress, make improvements, and report those results. The committee worked with representatives from over 30 countries including the hosts for the 2014 and 2016 games. There were five areas of focus for the group: (1) Climate Change; (2) Waste; (3) Bio-diversity; (4) Inclusion; and (5) Healthy Living.

The results were stunning. Not only did the committee succeed in codifying the new standards (now referred to as ISO 20121), they also used the standards to design and run the games. Here are two of many examples of their success:

1. An industrial dump had existed in East London for over 100 years. The site was famous with the locals as an eyesore and a dangerous place. The committee took this on as one of their sustainability projects by cleaning the entire area up, putting many of the new sports venues on the site and creating what is now one of Europe's largest urban parks. The area has been transformed and eventually will see thousands of new homes in the heart of London.

2. The "Food Vision" program aimed to mitigate the impact of having to serve more than 14 million meals across 40 different venues during the 17 days of the Olympics. It required suppliers to use local sources as much as possible, and certify that food met a number of food-related standards including Fairtrade, Marine Stewardship Council Certified Fish, and Farm Assured Red Tractor. Sponsor companies such as McDonald's, Coca-Cola, and Cadbury voluntarily applied the standards to all of their meals.

While there is no way to have a zero-impact event with something the size of the Olympic games, the work done for the 2012 Olympics will change the way that all organizations plan for large events.

....

SOURCES: "London 2012 – Helping Set Sustainability Standards," *The Guardian* (August 10, 2012), (http://www.guardian.co.uk/sustainable-business/blog/london-2012-helping-set-sustainability-standards); http://www.london2012.com/about-us/publications/publication=london-2012-sustainability-plan-summary/; http://ukinjapan.fco.gov.uk/en/visiting-the-uk/london-2012-olympics/sustainability/.

of minorities and women in the U.S. workforce, companies are now concerned with hiring and promoting people without regard to ethnic background. Research does indicate that an increase in racial diversity leads to an increase in firm performance.[73] In a survey of 131 leading European companies, 67.2% stated that a diverse workforce can provide competitive advantage.[74] A manager from Nestlé stated: "To deliver products that meet the needs of individual consumers, we need people who respect other cultures, embrace diversity, and never discriminate on any basis."[75] Good human resource managers should be working to ensure that people are treated fairly on the job and not harassed by prejudiced co-workers or managers. Otherwise, they may find themselves subject to lawsuits. Coca-Cola Company, for example, agreed to pay US$192.5 million because of discrimination against African-American salaried employees in pay, promotions, and evaluations from 1995 and 2000. According to then Chairman and CEO Douglas Daft, "Sometimes things happen in an unintentional manner. And I've made it clear that can't happen anymore."[76]

An organization's human resources may be a key to achieving a sustainable competitive advantage. Advances in technology are copied almost immediately by competitors around the world. People, however, are not as willing to move to other companies in other countries. This means that the only long-term resource advantage remaining to corporations operating in the industrialized nations may lie in the area of skilled human resources.[77] Research does reveal that competitive strategies are more successfully executed in those companies with a high level of commitment to their employees than in those firms with less commitment.[78]

STRATEGIC INFORMATION SYSTEMS/TECHNOLOGY ISSUES

The primary task of the manager of information systems/technology is to design and manage the flow of information in an organization in ways that improve productivity and decision making. Information must be collected, stored, and synthesized in such a manner that it will answer important operating and strategic questions. A corporation's information system can be a strength or a weakness in multiple areas of strategic management. It can not only aid in environmental scanning and in controlling a company's many activities, it can also be used as a strategic weapon in gaining competitive advantage.

Impact on Performance

Information systems/technology offers four main contributions to corporate performance. *First,* (beginning in the 1970s with mainframe computers) it is used to automate existing back-office processes, such as payroll, human resource records, accounts payable and receivable, and to establish huge databases. *Second,* (beginning in the 1980s) it is used to automate individual tasks, such as keeping track of clients and expenses, through the use of personal computers with word processing and spreadsheet software. Corporate databases are accessed to provide sufficient data to analyze the data and create what-if scenarios. These first two contributions tend to focus on reducing costs. *Third,* (beginning in the 1990s) it is used to enhance key business functions, such as marketing and operations. This third contribution focuses on productivity improvements. The system provides customer support and help in distribution and logistics. For example, In an early effort on the Internet, FedEx found that by allowing customers to directly access its package-tracking database via the Web instead of their having to ask a human operator, the company saved up to US$2 million annually.[79] Business processes are analyzed to increase efficiency and productivity via reengineering. Enterprise resource planning (ERP) application software, such as SAP, PeopleSoft, Oracle, Baan, and J.D. Edwards (discussed further in **Chapter 10**), is used to integrate worldwide business activities so that employees need to enter information only once and that information is available to all corporate systems (including accounting) around the world. *Fourth*, (beginning in 2000) it is used to develop competitive advantage. For example, American Hospital Supply (AHS), a leading manufacturer and distributor of a broad line of products for doctors, laboratories, and hospitals, developed an order entry distribution system that directly linked the majority of its customers to AHS computers. The system was successful because it simplified ordering processes for customers, reduced costs for both AHS and the customer, and allowed AHS to provide pricing incentives to the customer. As a result, customer loyalty was high and AHS's share of the market became large.

A current trend in corporate information systems/technology is the increasing use of the Internet for marketing, intranets for internal communication, and extranets for logistics and distribution. An *intranet* is an information network within an organization that also has access to the external worldwide Internet. Intranets typically begin as ways to provide employees with company information such as lists of product prices, fringe benefits, and company policies. They are then converted into extranets for supply chain management. An *extranet* is an information network within an organization that is available to key suppliers and customers. The key issue in building an extranet is the creation of "fire walls" to block extranet users from accessing the firm's or other users' confidential data. Once this is accomplished, companies can allow employees, customers, and suppliers to access information and conduct business on the Internet in a completely automated manner. By connecting these groups, companies hope to obtain a competitive advantage by reducing the time needed to design and bring new products to market, slashing inventories, customizing manufacturing, and entering new markets.[80]

A recent development in information systems/technology is Web 2.0. *Web 2.0* refers to the use of wikis, blogs, RSS (Really Simple Syndication), social networks (e.g., LinkedIn and Facebook), podcasts, and mash-ups through company Web sites to forge tighter links with customers and suppliers and to engage employees more successfully. A 2010 survey by McKinsey revealed the percentage of companies using individual Web 2.0 technologies now exceeded 67% with the top uses being social networking (40%), and blogs (38%). The most heavily used tool is Web services, software that makes it easier to exchange information and conduct transactions. Satisfied users of these information technologies report that they are using these tools to interact with their customers, suppliers, and outside experts in product development efforts known as *co-creation*. For example, LEGO invited customers to suggest new models interactively and then financially rewarded the people whose ideas proved marketable.[81]

Supply Chain Management

The expansion of the marketing-oriented Internet into intranets and extranets is making significant contributions to organizational performance through supply chain management. **Supply chain management** is the forming of networks for sourcing raw materials, manufacturing products or creating services, storing and distributing the goods, and delivering them to customers and consumers.[82] Research indicates that supplier network resources have a significant impact on firm performance.[83] A survey of global executives revealed that their interest in supply chains was first to reduce costs, and then to improve customer service and get new products to market faster.[84] More than 85% of senior executives stated that improving their firm's supply-chain performance was a top priority. Companies like Wal-Mart, Dell, and Toyota, who are known to be exemplars in supply-chain management, spend only 4% of their revenues on supply-chain costs compared to 10% by the average firm.[85]

Industry leaders are integrating modern information systems into their corporate value chains to harmonize companywide efforts and to achieve competitive advantage. For example, Heineken beer distributors input actual depletion figures and replenishment orders to the Netherlands brewer through their linked Web pages. This interactive planning system generates time-phased orders based on actual usage rather than on projected demand. Distributors are then able to modify plans based on local conditions or changes in marketing. Heineken uses these modifications to adjust brewing and supply schedules. As a result of this system, lead times have been reduced from the traditional 10–12 weeks to 4–6 weeks. This time savings is especially useful in an industry competing on product freshness. In another example, Procter & Gamble participates in an information network to move the company's line of consumer products through Wal-Mart's many stores. *Radio-frequency identification (RFID)* tags containing product information are used to track goods through inventory and distribution channels. As part of the network with Wal-Mart, P&G knows by cash register and by store what products have passed through the system every hour of each day. The network is linked by satellite communications on a real-time basis. With actual point-of-sale information, products are replenished to meet current demand and minimize stockouts while maintaining exceptionally low inventories.[86]

The Strategic Audit: A Checklist for Organizational Analysis

One way of conducting an organizational analysis to ascertain a company's strengths and weaknesses is by using the Strategic Audit found in **Appendix 1.A** at the end of **Chapter 1**. The audit provides a checklist of questions by area of concern. For example, Part IV of the audit examines corporate structure, culture, and resources. It looks at organizational resources and capabilities in terms of the functional areas of marketing, finance, R&D, operations, human resources, and information systems, among others.

Synthesis of Internal Factors

After strategists have scanned the internal organizational environment and identified factors for their particular corporation, they may want to summarize their analysis of these factors using a form such as that given in **Table 5–2**. This **IFAS (Internal Factor Analysis Summary) Table** is one way to organize the internal factors into the generally accepted categories of strengths and weaknesses as well as to analyze how well a particular company's management is responding to these specific factors in light of the perceived importance of these factors to the company. Use the VRIO framework (**V**alue, **R**areness, **I**mitability, and **O**rganization) to assess the importance of each of the factors that might be considered strengths. Except for its internal orientation, this IFAS Table is built the same way as the EFAS Table described in **Chapter 4** (in **Table 4–5**). To use the IFAS Table, complete the following steps:

1. In **Column 1** (*Internal Factors*), list the 8 to 10 most important strengths and weaknesses facing the company.
2. In **Column 2** (*Weight*), assign a weight to each factor from **1.0** (*Most Important*) to **0.0** (*Not Important*) based on that factor's probable impact on a particular company's current strategic position. The higher the weight, the more important is this factor to the current and future success of the company. **All weights must sum to 1.0 regardless of the number of factors.**
3. In **Column 3** (*Rating*), assign a rating to each factor from **5.0** (*Outstanding*) to **1.0** (*Poor*) based on management's specific response to that particular factor. Each rating is a judgment regarding how well the company's management is currently dealing with each specific internal factor.

TABLE 5–2   Internal Factor Analysis Summary (IFAS Table): Maytag as Example

Internal Factors	Weight	Rating	Weighted Score	Comments
1	2	3	4	5
Strengths				
▪ Quality Maytag culture	.15	5.0	.75	Quality key to success
▪ Experienced top management	.05	4.2	.21	Know appliances
▪ Vertical integration	.10	3.9	.39	Dedicated factories
▪ Employer relations	.05	3.0	.15	Good, but deteriorating
▪ Hoover's international orientation	.15	2.8	.42	Hoover name in cleaners
Weaknesses				
▪ Process-oriented R&D	.05	2.2	.11	Slow on new products
▪ Distribution channels	.05	2.0	.10	Superstores replacing small dealers
▪ Financial position	.15	2.0	.30	High debt load
▪ Global positioning	.20	2.1	.42	Hoover weak outside the United Kingdom and Australia
▪ Manufacturing facilities	.05	4.0	.20	Investing now
Total Scores	1.00		3.05	

NOTES:

1. List strengths and weaknesses (8–10) in Column 1.
2. Weight each factor from **1.0** (Most Important) to **0.0** (Not Important) in Column 2 based on that factor's probable impact on the company's strategic position. **The total weights must sum to 1.00.**
3. Rate each factor from **5.0** (Outstanding) to **1.0** (Poor) in Column 3 based on the company's response to that factor.
4. Multiply each factor's weight times its rating to obtain each factor's weighted score in Column 4.
5. Use Column 5 (comments) for the rationale used for each factor.
6. Add the individual weighted scores to obtain the total weighted score for the company in Column 4. This tells how well the company is responding to the factors in its internal environment.

SOURCE: Thomas L. Wheelen, copyright © 1982, 1985, 1987, 1988, 1989, 1990, 1991, 1995, and every year after that. Kathryn E. Wheelen solely owns all of (Dr.) Thomas L. Wheelen's copyright materials. Kathryn E. Wheelen requires written reprint permission for each book that this material is to be printed in. Thomas L. Wheelen and J. David Hunger, copyright © 1991—first year "Internal Factor Analysis Summary" (IFAS) appeared in this text (4th ed.) Reprinted by permission of the copyright holders.

4. In **Column 4** (*Weighted Score*), multiply the weight in **Column 2** for each factor times its rating in **Column 3** to obtain that factor's weighted score.

5. In **Column 5** (*Comments*), note why a particular factor was selected and/or how its weight and rating were estimated.

6. Finally, add the weighted scores for all the internal factors in **Column 4** to determine the total weighted score for that particular company. The **total weighted score** indicates how well a particular company is responding to current and expected factors in its internal environment. The score can be used to compare that firm to other firms in its industry. Check to ensure that the total weighted score truly reflects the company's current performance in terms of profitability and market share. **The total weighted score for an average firm in an industry is always 3.0.**

As an example of this procedure, **Table 5–2** includes a number of internal factors for Maytag Corporation in 1995 (before Maytag was acquired by Whirlpool) with corresponding weights, ratings, and weighted scores provided. Note that Maytag's total weighted score is 3.05, meaning that the corporation is about average compared to the strengths and weaknesses of others in the major home appliance industry.

End of Chapter SUMMARY

Every day, about 17 truckloads of used diesel engines and other parts are dumped at a receiving facility at Caterpillar's remanufacturing plant in Corinth, Mississippi. The filthy iron engines are then broken down by two workers, who manually hammer and drill for half a day until they have taken every bolt off the engine and put each component into its own bin. The engines are then cleaned and remade at half of the cost of a new engine and sold for a tidy profit. This system works at Caterpillar because, as a general rule, 70% of the cost to build something new is in the materials and 30% is in the labor. Remanufacturing simply starts the manufacturing process over again with materials that are essentially free and which already contain most of the energy costs needed to make them. The would-be discards become fodder for the next product, eliminating waste, and cutting costs. Caterpillar's management was so impressed by the remanufacturing operation that they made the business a separate division in 2005. The unit earned more than US$1 billion in sales in 2005 and in 2012 employed more than 8500 workers in 16 countries.

Caterpillar's remanufacturing unit was successful not only because of its capability of wringing productivity out of materials and labor, but also because it designed its products for reuse. Before they are built new, remanufactured products must be designed for disassembly. In order to achieve this, Caterpillar asks its designers to check a "Reman" box on Caterpillar's product development checklist. The company also needs to know where its products are being used in order to take them back—known as the art of *reverse logistics*. This is achieved by Caterpillar's excellent relationship with its dealers throughout the world, as well as through financial incentives. For example, when a customer orders a crankshaft, that customer is offered a remanufactured one for half the cost of a new one—assuming the customer turns in the old crankshaft to Caterpillar. The products also should be built for performance with little regard for changing fashion. Since diesel engines change little from year to year, a remanufactured engine is very similar to a new engine and might perform even better.

Monitoring the external environment is only one part of environmental scanning. Strategists also need to scan a corporation's internal environment to identify its resources, capabilities, and competencies. What are its strengths and weaknesses? At Caterpillar, management clearly noted that the environment was changing in a way to make its remanufactured product more desirable. It took advantage of its strengths in manufacturing and distribution to offer a recycling service for its current customers and a low-cost alternative product for those who could not afford a new Caterpillar engine. It also happened to be an environmentally friendly, sustainable business model. Caterpillar's management felt that remanufacturing thus provided them with a strategic advantage over competitors who don't remanufacture. This is an example of a company using its capabilities in key functional areas to expand its business by moving into a new profitable position on its value chain.[87]

MyManagementLab®

Go to **mymanagementlab.com** to complete the problems marked with this icon ⭐.

KEY TERMS

brand (p. 142)

business model (p. 132)

capabilities (p. 128)

capital budgeting (p. 143)

competency (p. 128)

conglomerate structure (p. 138)

core competencies (p. 128)

corporate culture (p. 138)

corporate reputation (p. 143)

distinctive competencies (p. 129)
divisional structure (p. 137)
durability (p. 130)
economies of scale (p. 147)
economies of scope (p. 136)
experience curve (p. 147)
explicit knowledge (p. 131)
financial leverage (p. 143)
functional structure (p. 137)
IFAS Table (p. 153)
imitability (p. 131)

marketing mix (p. 140)
operating leverage (p. 146)
organizational analysis (p. 128)
organizational structures (p. 137)
product life cycle (p. 141)
R&D intensity (p. 144)
R&D mix (p. 145)
replicability (p. 131)
resource (p. 128)
simple structure (p. 137)
strategic business units (SBUs) (p. 138)

supply chain management (p. 152)
tacit knowledge (p. 131)
technological competence (p. 144)
technological discontinuity (p. 145)
technology transfer (p. 144)
transferability (p. 131)
transparency (p. 131)
value chain (p. 133)
virtual teams (p. 148)
VRIO framework (p. 129)

MyManagementLab®

Go to **mymanagmentlab.com** for Auto-graded writing questions as well as the following Assisted-graded writing questions:

5-1. How does the Resource-Based View of the Firm provide a superior means of evaluating a company's competitive advantage?

5-2. Explain how using an IFAS table impacts the understanding of a company's internal resources and capabilities?

DISCUSSION QUESTIONS

5-3. What is the relevance of the resource-based view of the firm to strategic management in a global environment?

5-4. How can value-chain analy sis help identify a company's strengths and weaknesses?

✪ **5-5.** In what ways can a corporation's structure and culture be internal strengths or weaknesses?

✪ **5-6.** What are the pros and cons of management's using the experience curve to determine strategy?

✪ **5-7.** How might a firm's management decide whether it should continue to invest in current known technology or in new, but untested technology? What factors might encourage or discourage such a shift?

STRATEGIC PRACTICE EXERCISES

Today, the primary means of information collection is through the Internet. Try the following exercise.

1. Form into teams of around three to five people. Select a well-known publicly owned company to research. Inform the instructor of your choice.

2. Assign each person a separate task. One task might be to find the latest financial statements. Another would be to learn as much as possible about its top management and board of directors. Another might be to identify its business model. Another might be to identify its key competitors.

3. Conduct research on the company *using the Internet only.*

4. Meet with your team members to discuss what you have found. What are the company's opportunities, threats, strengths, and weaknesses? Go back to the Internet for more information, if needed.

5. Prepare a three- to five-page typed report of the company. The report should include the following:
   a. Does the firm have any core competencies? Are any of these distinctive (better than the competition) competencies? Does the firm have any competitive advantage? Provide an analysis using EFAS and IFAS Tables.
   b. What is the likely future of this firm if it continues on its current path?
   c. Would you buy stock in this company? Assume that your team has US$25,000 to invest. Allocate the money among the four to five primary competitors in this industry. List the companies, the number of shares purchased of each, the cost of each share as of a given date, and the total cost for each purchase assuming a typical commission used by an Internet broker, such as E-Trade or Scottrade.

NOTES

1. R. M. Grant, *Contemporary Strategy Analysis*, 6th edition (Malden, MA: Blackwell Publishing, 2008), pp. 130–131.
2. G. Schreyogg and M. Kliesch-Eberl, "How Dynamic Can Organizational Capabilities Be? Towards a Dual-Process Model of Capability Dynamization," *Strategic Management Journal* (September 2007), pp. 913–933.
3. M. Javidan, "Core Competence: What Does It Mean in Practice?" *Long Range Planning* (February 1998), pp. 60–71.
4. M. A. Hitt, B. W. Keats, and S. M. DeMarie, "Navigating in the New Competitive Landscape: Building Strategic Flexibility and Competitive Advantage in the 21st Century," *Academy of Management Executive* (November 1998), pp. 22–42; C. E. Helfat and M. A. Peteraf, "The Dynamic Resources-Based View: Capability Life Cycles," *Strategic Management Journal* (October 2003), pp. 997–1010.
5. D. Brady and K. Capell, "GE Breaks the Mold to Spur Innovation," *BusinessWeek* (April 26, 2004), pp. 88–89.
6. J. B. Barney, *Gaining and Sustaining Competitive Advantage*, 2nd ed. (Upper Saddle River, NJ: Prentice Hall, 2002), pp. 159–172. Barney's VRIO questions are very similar to those proposed by G. Hamel and S. K. Prahalad in their book, *Competing for the Future* (Boston: Harvard Business School Press, 1994) on pages 202–207 in which they state that to be distinctive, a competency must (a) provide customer value, (b) be competitor unique, and (c) be extendable to develop new products and/or markets.
7. S. L. Newbert, "Value, Rareness, Competitive Advantage, and Performance: A Conceptual-Level Empirical Investigation of the Resource-Based View of the Firm," *Strategic Management Journal* (July 2008), pp. 745–768.
8. Barney, p. 161.
9. R. M. Grant, "The Resource-Based Theory of Competitive Advantage: Implications for Strategy Formulation," *California Management Review* (Spring 1991), pp. 114–135.
10. P. J. Verdin, and P. J. Williamson, "Core Competencies, Competitive Advantage and Market Analysis: Forging the Links," in G. Hamel and A. Heene (Eds.), *Competence-Based Competition* (New York: John Wiley and Sons, 1994), pp. 83–84; S. K. Ethiraj, P. Kale, M. S. Krishnan, and J. V. Singh, "Where Do Capabilities Come From and How Do They Matter? A Study in the Software Services Industry," *Strategic Management Journal* (January 2005), pp. 701–719.
11. J. Devan, M. B. Klusas, and T. W. Ruefli, "The Elusive Goal of Corporate Outperformance," *McKinsey Quarterly Online* (April 2007).
12. Davidson, P. 2011. "To Get Jobs, Areas Develop Industry Hubs in Emerging Fields," *USA Today* (June 7, 2011).
13. M. E. Porter, "Clusters and the New Economics of Competition," *Harvard Business Review* (November–December 1998), pp. 77–90.
14. J. M. Shaver and F. Flyer, "Agglomeration Economies, Firm Heterogeneity, and Foreign Direct Investment in the United States," *Strategic Management Journal* (December 2000), pp. 1175–1193; W. Chung and A. Kalnins, "Agglomeration Effects and Performance: A Test of the Texas Lodging Industry," *Strategic Management Journal* (October 2001), pp. 969–988.
15. M. Polanyi, *The Tacit Dimension* (London: Routledge & Kegan Paul, 1966).
16. S. K. McEvily and B. Chakravarthy, "The Persistence of Knowledge-Based Advantage: An Empirical Test for Product Performance and Technological Knowledge," *Strategic Management Journal* (April 2002), pp. 285–305.
17. P. E. Bierly III, "Development of a Generic Knowledge Strategy Typology," *Journal of Business Strategies* (Spring 1999), p. 3.
18. R. W. Coff, D. C. Coff, and R. Eastvold, "The Knowledge-Leveraging Paradox: How to Achieve Scale Without Making Knowledge Imitable," *Academy of Management Review* (April 2006), pp. 452–465.
19. D. Welch and N. Lakshman "My Other Car Is a Tata," *Business Week* (January 14, 2008), p. 33.
20. P. Doval, "Renault, Nissan Tight-Lipped on Bajaj's Views on Low-Cost Car," *The Times of India* (July 16, 2011), (Articles.timesofindia.indiatimes.com/2011-07-16/delhi/29781096_1_low-cost-car-bajaj-auto-renault-and-nissan).
21. S. Abraham, "Experiencing Strategic Conversations about the Central Forces of Our Time," *Strategy & Leadership* (Vol. 31, No. 2, 2003), pp. 61–62.
22. K. Kelleher, "HP's Printer Problem," *CNNMoney* (March 29, 2012), (www.tech.fortune.cnn.com/2012/03/29/hps-printer-problem/); P. Burrows, "Ever Wonder Why Ink Costs So Much?" *Business Week* (November 14, 2005), pp. 42–44.
23. http://www.bp.com/sectiongenericarticle.do?categoryId=9014445&contentId=7027526.
24. http://corporate.ford.com/our-company/investors/investor-quarterly-results/quarterly-results-detail/pr-ford-posts-2011-pretax-operating-35878?releaseId=1244755137166;http://articles.latimes.com/2012/feb/16/business/la-fi-mo-general-motors-profits-20120215.
25. J. R. Galbraith, "Strategy and Organization Planning," in H. Mintzberg and J. B. Quinn (Eds.), *The Strategy Process: Concepts, Contexts, and Cases*, 2nd ed. (Englewood Cliffs, N.J.: Prentice Hall, 1991), pp. 315–324.
26. M. Porter, *Competitive Advantage: Creating and Sustaining Superior Performance* (New York: The Free Press, 1985), p. 36.
27. www.thecloroxcompany.com/products/our-brands/.
28. M. Leontiades, "A Diagnostic Framework for Planning," *Strategic Management Journal* (January–March 1983), p. 14.
29. E. H. Schein, *The Corporate Culture Survival Guide* (San Francisco: Jossey-Bass, 1999), p. 12; L. C. Harris and E. Ogbonna, "The Strategic Legacy of Company Founders," *Long Range Planning* (June 1999), pp. 333–343.
30. D. M. Rousseau, "Assessing Organizational Culture: The Case for Multiple Methods," in B. Schneider (Ed.), *Organizational Climate and Culture* (San Francisco: Jossey-Bass, 1990), pp. 153–192.
31. L. Smircich, "Concepts of Culture and Organizational Analysis," *Administrative Science Quarterly* (September 1983), pp. 345–346; D. Ravasi and M. Schultz, "Responding to Organizational Identity Threats: Exploring the Role of Organizational Culture," *Academy of Management Journal* (June 2006), pp. 433–458.
32. D. G. Allen, "Do Organizational Socialization Tactics Influence Newcomer Embeddedness and Turnover?" *Journal of Management* (April 2006), pp. 237–256.
33. J. B. Sorensen, "The Strength of Corporate Culture and the Reliability of Firm Performance," *Administrative Science Quarterly*

(March 2002), pp. 70–91; R. E. Smerek and D. R. Denison, "Social Capital in Organizations: Understanding the Link to Firm Performance," presentation to the *Academy of Management* (Philadelphia, 2007).

34. K. E. Aupperle, "Spontaneous Organizational Reconfiguration: A Historical Example Based on Xenophon's Anabasis," *Organization Science* (July–August 1996), pp. 445–460.

35. P. Gogoi, "Circuit City: Due for a Change?" *Bloomberg Businessweek* (February 29, 2008), (www.businessweek.com/stories/2008-02-29/circuit-city-due-for-a-change-businessweek-business-news-stock-market-and-financial-advice; E. Gruenwedel, "Circuit City Ceases Operations," *HomeMedia Magazine* (January 16, 2009), (http://www.homemediamagazine.com/news/circuit-city-ceases-operations-14346).

36. "Face Value: A Post-Modern Proctoid," *The Economist* (April 15, 2006), p. 68.

37. E. Savitz, "Apple Tops Ranking of World's Most Valuable Brands," *Forbes* (May 22, 2012), (www.forbes.com/sites/ericsavitz/2012/05/22/apple-tops-ranking-of-worlds-most-valuable-brands/ Kiley).

38. R. T. Wilcox, "The Hidden Potential of Powerful Brands," *Batten Briefings* (Summer 2003), pp. 1, 4–5.

39. V. P. Rindova, I. O. Williamson, A. P. Petkova, and J. M. Sever, "Being Good or Being Known: An Empirical Examination of the Dimensions, Antecedents, and Consequences of Organizational Reputation," *Academy of Management Journal* (December 2005), pp. 1033–1049.

40. Ibid.

41. C. Fombrun and C. Van Riel, "The Reputational Landscape," *Corporate Reputation Review* (Vol. 1, Nos. 1&2, 1997), pp. 5–13.

42. P. Engardio and M. Arndt, "What Price Reputation?" *BusinessWeek* (July 9 and 16, 2007), pp. 70–79.

43. P. W. Roberts and G. R. Dowling, "Corporate Reputation and Sustained Financial Performance," *Strategic Management Journal* (December 2002), pp. 1077–1093; J. Shamsie, "The Context of Dominance: An Industry-Driven Framework for Exploiting Reputation," *Strategic Management Journal* (March 2003), pp. 199–215; M. D. Michalisin, D. M. Kline, and R. D. Smith, "Intangible Strategic Assets and Firm Performance: A Multi-Industry Study of the Resource-Based View," *Journal of Business Strategies* (Fall 2000), pp. 91–117; S. S. Standifird, "Reputation and E-Commerce: eBay Auctions and the Asymmetrical Impact of Positive and Negative Ratings," *Journal of Management* (Vol. 27, No. 3, 2001), pp. 279–295.

44. R. L. Simerly and M. Li, "Environmental Dynamism, Capital Structure and Performance: A Theoretical Integration and an Empirical Test," *Strategic Management Journal* (January 2000), pp. 31–49.

45. R. L. Simerly and M. Li, "Environmental Dynamism, Capital Structure and Performance: A Theoretical Integration and an Empirical Test," *Strategic Management Journal* (January 2000), pp. 31–49; A. Heisz and S. LaRochelle-Cote, "Corporate Financial Leverage in Canadian Manufacturing: Consequences for Employment and Inventories," *Canadian Journal of Administrative Science* (June 2004), pp. 111–128.

46. J. M. Poterba and L. H. Summers, "A CEO Survey of U.S. Companies' Time Horizons and Hurdle Rates," *Sloan Management Review* (Fall 1995), pp. 43–53.

47. "R&D Scoreboard," *BusinessWeek* (June 27, 1994), pp. 81–103.

48. M. Krantz, "Microsoft, Intel, Google Outspend Apple on R&D," *USA Today* (March 21, 2012), (www.usatoday.com/money/perfi/columnist/krantz/story/2012-02-20/apple-marketing-research-and-development-spending/53673126/1).

49. C. Palmeri, "Swords to Plowshares—And Back Again," *BusinessWeek* (February 11, 2008), p. 66.

50. G. E. Moore, "Cramming More Components onto Integrated Circuits," *Electronics* (38(8), April 19, 1965); D. J. Yang, "Leaving Moore's Law in the Dust," *U.S. News & World Report* (July 10, 2000), pp. 37–38; R. Fishburne and M. Malone, "Laying Down the Laws: Gordon Moore and Bob Metcalfe in Conversation," *Forbes ASAP* (February 21, 2000), pp. 97–100.

51. P. Pascarella, "Are You Investing in the Wrong Technology?" *Industry Week* (July 25, 1983), p. 38

52. C. M. Christensen, *The Innovator's Dilemma* (Boston: Harvard Business School Press, 1997).

53. O. Port, "Flat-Panel Pioneer," *BusinessWeek* (December 12, 2005), p. 22. This phenomenon has also been discussed in terms of paradigm shifts in which a new development makes the old game obsolete—See Joel A. Barker, *Future Edge* (New York: William Morrow and Company, 1992).

54. For examples of experience curves for various products, see M. Gottfredson, S. Schaubert, and H. Saenz, "The New Leader's Guide to Diagnosing the Business," *Harvard Business Review* (February 2008), pp. 63–73.

55. B. J. Pine, *Mass Customization: The New Frontier in Business Competition* (Boston: Harvard Business School Press, 1993).

56. J. Buckley, "Korea's Flexible Carmakers," *AMS* (May/June 2009), pp. 18–29.

57. S. L Rynes, K. G. Brown, and A. E. Colbert, "Seven Common Misconceptions about Human Resource Practices: Research Findings Versus Practitioner Belief," *Academy of Management Executive* (August 2002), pp. 92–103; R. S. Schuler and S. E. Jackson, "A Quarter-Century Review of Human Resource Management in the U.S.: The Growth in Importance of the International Perspective," in R. S. Schuler and S. E. Jackson (Eds.), *Strategic Human Resource Management*, 2nd ed. (Malden, MA: Blackwell Publishing, 2007), pp. 214–240; M. Guthridge and A. B. Komm, "Why Multinationals Struggle to Manage Talent," *McKinsey Quarterly* (May 2008), pp. 1–5.

58. J. McGregor and S. Hamm, "Managing the Global Workforce," *BusinessWeek* (January 28, 2008), pp. 34–48; D. A. Ready and J. A. Conger, "Make Your Company a Talent Factory," *Harvard Business Review* (June 2007), pp. 68–77.

59. E. E. Lawler, S. A. Mohrman, and G. E. Ledford, Jr., *Creating High Performance Organizations* (San Francisco: Jossey-Bass, 1995), p. 29.

60. "Building Perfection: Self-Directed Work Teams Deliver on Quality," *QualityDigest* (February 1, 2012), (www.qualtydigest.com/inside/quality-insider-article/connecticut-company-uses-self-directed-work-teams-improve-time.html).

61. R. Sanchez, "Strategic Flexibility in Product Competition," *Strategic Management Journal* (Summer 1995), p. 147.

62. A. R. Jassawalla and H. C. Sashittal, "Building Collaborative Cross-Functional New Product Teams," *Academy of Management Executive* (August 1999), pp. 50–63.

63. A. M. Townsend, S. M. DeMarie, and A. R. Hendrickson, "Virtual Teams' Technology and the Workplace of the Future," *Academy of Management Executive* (August 1998), pp. 17–29.

64. S. A. Furst, M. Reeves, B. Rosen, and R. S. Blackburn, "Managing the Life Cycle of Virtual Teams," *Academy of Management Executive* (May 2004), pp. 6–20; L. L. Martins,

L. L. Gilson, and M. T. Maynard, "Virtual Teams: What Do We Know and Where Do We Go From Here?" *Journal of Management* (Vol. 30, No. 6, 2004), pp. 805–835; T. Minton-Eversole, "Virtual Teams Used Most by Global Organizations, Survey Says," *SHRM* (July 19, 2012), (www.shrm.org/hrdisciplines/orgempdev/articles/pages/virtualteamsusedmostbyglobalorganizations,survesays.aspx).

65. C. B. Gibson and J. L. Gibbs, "Unpacking the Concept of Virtuality: The Effects of Geographic Dispersion, Electronic Dependence, Dynamic Structure, and National Diversity on Team Innovation," *Administrative Science Quarterly* (September 2006), pp. 451–495.

66. M. C. Noonan and J. L. Glass, "The Hard Truth about Telecommuting," *Monthly Labor Review* (June 2012), (www.bls.gov/opbu/mir/2012/06/art3full.pdf).

67. Townsend, DeMarie, and Hendrickson, p. 18.

68. "Economic News Release," *Bureau of Labor Statistics*, U.S. Department of Labor (January 27, 2012).

69. D. Welsh, "What Goodyear Got from Its Union," *BusinessWeek* (October 20, 2003), pp. 148–149; "Update 1 – Goodyear Union Contract Saves $215 Mln over 4-Yrs," *Reuters* (September 29, 2009), (www.reuters.com/articles/2009/09/29/goodyear-idUSN2915419220090929).

70. S. F. Matusik and C. W. L. Hill, "The Utilization of Contingent Work, Knowledge Creation, and Competitive Advantage," *Academy of Management Executive* (October 1998), pp. 680–697; W. Mayrhofer and C. Brewster, "European Human Resource Management: Researching Developments Over Time," in *Strategic Human Resource Management*, 2nd ed. (Malden, MA: Blackwell Publishing, 2007), pp. 241–269.

71. "Part-Time Work," *The Economist* (June 24, 2006), p. 112, (www.statistica.com/statistics/192342/unadjusted-monthly-number-of-part-time-employees-in-the-us/).

72. J. Muller, "A Ford Redesign," *BusinessWeek* (November 13, 2000), Special Report.

73. O. C. Richard, B. P. S. Murthi, and K. Ismail, "The Impact of Racial Diversity on Intermediate and Long-Term Performance: The Moderating Role of Environmental Context," *Strategic Management Journal* (December 2007), pp. 1213–1233; G. Colvin, "The 50 Best Companies for Asians, Blacks, and Hispanics," *Fortune* (July 19, 1999), pp. 53–58.

74. V. Singh and S. Point, "Strategic Responses by European Companies to the Diversity Challenge: An Online Comparison," *Long Range Planning* (August 2004), pp. 295–318.

75. Singh and Point, p. 310.

76. J. Bachman, "Coke to Pay $192.5 Million to Settle Lawsuit," *The (Ames, IA) Tribune* (November 20, 2000), p. D4.

77. O. Gottschalg and M. Zollo, "Interest Alignment and Competitive Advantage," *Academy of Management Review* (April 2007), pp. 418–437.

78. J. Lee and D. Miller, "People Matter: Commitment to Employees, Strategy, and Performance in Korean Firms," *Strategic Management Journal* (June 1999), pp. 579–593.

79. A. Cortese, "Here Comes the Intranet," *BusinessWeek* (February 26, 1996), p. 76.

80. D. Bartholomew, "Blue-Collar Computing," *Information Week* (June 19, 1995), pp. 34–43.

81. J. Bughin, J. Manyika, A. Miller, and M. Cjhui, "Building the Web 2.0 Enterprise," *McKinsey Quarterly Online* (December 2010); J. Bughin and M. Chui, "The Rise of the Networked Enterprise: Web 2.0 Finds Its Payday," *McKinsey Quarterly Online* (December 2010), pp. 1–4.

82. C. C. Poirier, *Advanced Supply Chain Management* (San Francisco: Berrett-Koehler Publishers, 1999), p. 2.

83. J. H. Dyer and N. W. Hatch, "Relation-Specific Capabilities and Barriers to Knowledge Transfers: Creating Advantage through Network Relationships," *Strategic Management Journal* (August 2006), pp. 701–719.

84. D. Paulonis and S. Norton, "Managing Global Supply Chains," *McKinsey Quarterly Online* (August 2008).

85. M. Cook and R. Hagey, "Why Companies Flunk Supply-Chain 101: Only 33 Percent Correctly Measure Supply-Chain Performance; Few Use the Right Incentives," *Journal of Business Strategy* (Vol. 24, No. 4, 2003), pp. 35–42.

86. C. C. Poirer, pp. 3–5. For further information on RFID technology, see F. Taghaboni-Dutta and B. Velthouse, "RFID Technology is Revolutionary: Who Should Be Involved in This Game of Tag?" *Academy of Management Perspectives* (November 2006), pp. 65–78.

87. M. Arndt, "Everything Old Is New Again," *BusinessWeek* (September 25, 2006), pp. 64–70, (www.cat.com/).

PART 3

Strategy
Formulation

strategy formulation: situation analysis and Business Strategy

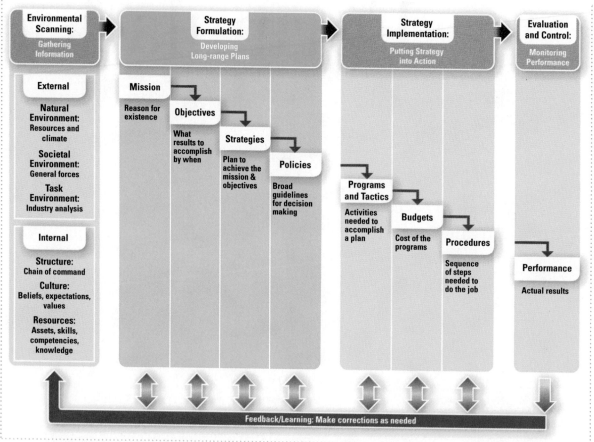

Environmental Scanning: Gathering Information	Strategy Formulation: Developing Long-range Plans	Strategy Implementation: Putting Strategy into Action	Evaluation and Control: Monitoring Performance

External

Natural Environment: Resources and climate

Societal Environment: General forces

Task Environment: Industry analysis

Internal

Structure: Chain of command

Culture: Beliefs, expectations, values

Resources: Assets, skills, competencies, knowledge

Mission
Reason for existence

Objectives
What results to accomplish by when

Strategies
Plan to achieve the mission & objectives

Policies
Broad guidelines for decision making

Programs and Tactics
Activities needed to accomplish a plan

Budgets
Cost of the programs

Procedures
Sequence of steps needed to do the job

Performance
Actual results

Feedback/Learning: Make corrections as needed

MyManagementLab®

⭐ **Improve Your Grade!**

Over 10 million students improved their results using the Pearson MyLabs. Visit **mymanagementlab.com** for simulations, tutorials, and end-of-chapter problems.

Learning Objectives

After reading this chapter, you should be able to:

- Organize environmental and organizational information using a SWOT approach and the SFAS matrix
- Understand the competitive and cooperative strategies available to corporations
- List the competitive tactics that would accompany competitive strategies
- Identify the basic types of strategic alliances

Target Makes a Strategic Move

Target started with a store in Roseville, Minnesota, in 1962 and for most of the next 50 years it followed families out to the suburbs with a cheap chic approach. Today, it boasts more than 1700 stores in the United States. The big-box stores carry everything from the latest Michael Graves teapot to groceries. Filling up the family minivan has served the company well. However, by 2012 the company realized that its growth days were ending. Had it not been for its wildly successful credit card that offered 5% off purchases and Target's robust sales in groceries, the company sales would have been virtually flat in 2011.

Monitoring the movement of young professionals back into city centers in Chicago, Seattle, Charlotte, Los Angeles, and San Francisco has spurred Target to try and differentiate itself in a whole new way. The company has created a new store concept called CITY Target. The stores are two-thirds the size of traditional Target stores and aim to cater to the needs of people in the city.

Gone will be 24 packs of toilet paper, replaced by 4 packs. The store eliminates lawn furniture and carries more air mattresses. It features a fresh foods section designed to pull people into the store more often. All of this is counter to the business model that is so successful outside of the city and represents a fairly risky strategic move.

The company plans to open 10 CITY locations by the end of 2013 and then evaluate their success. Other big-box retailers have tried to move into city locations, but their appeal has fallen flat with customers who walk home or take public transportation. Target's first store will be on State Street in the LOOP area of Chicago, just a block from Macy's and across the street from Forever 21.

Combining a low-cost strategy with a differentiation strategy is one of the more difficult approaches in business. This and other means of trying to achieve a sustainable competitive advantage will be discussed in this chapter.

SOURCES: http://sites.target.com/site/en/company/page.jsp?contentId=WCMP04-031761; M. Townsend, "Target's City Ambitions," *Bloomberg Businessweek* (June 4, 2012), (http://www.businessweek.com/articles/2012-05-31/targets-city-ambitions).

Situational Analysis: SWOT Approach

Strategy formulation, often referred to as strategic planning or long-range planning, is concerned with developing a corporation's mission, objectives, strategies, and policies. It begins with situation analysis: the process of finding a strategic fit between external opportunities and internal strengths while working around external threats and internal weaknesses. As shown in the Strategic Decision-Making Process in **Figure 1–5**, step 5(a) is analyzing strategic factors in light of the current situation using a SWOT approach. **SWOT** is an acronym used to describe the particular **S**trengths, **W**eaknesses, **O**pportunities, and **T**hreats that are potential strategic factors for a specific company. A SWOT approach should not only result in the identification of a corporation's distinctive competencies—the particular capabilities and resources that a firm possesses and the superior way in which they are used—but also in the identification of opportunities that the firm is not currently able to take advantage of due to a lack of appropriate resources.

It can be said that the essence of strategy is opportunity divided by capacity.[1] An opportunity by itself has no real value unless a company has the capacity (i.e., resources) to take advantage of that opportunity. By itself, a distinctive competency in a key resource or capability is no guarantee of competitive advantage. Weaknesses in other resource areas can prevent a strategy from being successful. SWOT can thus be used to take a broader view of strategy through the formula $SA = O/(S-W)$—that is, (Strategic Alternative equals Opportunity divided by Strengths minus Weaknesses). This reflects an important issue strategic managers face: Should we invest more in our strengths to make them even stronger (a distinctive competence) or should we invest in our weaknesses to at least make them competitive?

SWOT, by itself, is just a start to a strategic analysis. Some of the primary criticisms of SWOT are:

- It is simply the opinions of those filling out the boxes
- Virtually everything that is a strength is also a weakness
- Virtually everything that is an opportunity is also a threat
- Adding layers of effort does not improve the validity of the list
- It uses a single point in time approach
- There is no tie to the view from the customer
- There is no validated evaluation approach

Originally developed in the 1970s, SWOT was one of the original approaches as the field moved from business policy (looking at examples and inferring long-range plans) to strategy. In the intervening years, many techniques have developed that provide strategists with a keener insight into the elements of SWOT. However, as strategists, we need to understand our strengths, calculate the impact of weaknesses (whether they are real or perceived), take advantage of opportunities that match our strengths and minimize the impact of outside threats to the success of the organization. Thus, SWOT as a means of conceptualizing the organization is quite effective.

GENERATING A STRATEGIC FACTORS ANALYSIS SUMMARY (SFAS) MATRIX

The EFAS and IFAS Tables plus the SFAS Matrix have been developed to deal with the criticisms of SWOT analysis. When used together, they are a powerful analytical set of tools for strategic analysis. The **SFAS (Strategic Factors Analysis Summary) Matrix** summarizes an organization's strategic factors by combining the external factors from the EFAS Table with the internal factors from the IFAS Table. The EFAS and IFAS examples given of Maytag Corporation (as it was in 1995) in **Table 4–5** and **Table 5–2** list a total of 20 internal and external factors. These are too many factors for most people to use in strategy formulation. The SFAS Matrix requires a strategic decision maker to condense these strengths, weaknesses, opportunities, and threats into fewer than 10 strategic factors. This is done by reviewing and revising the weight given each factor. The revised weights reflect the priority of each factor as a determinant of the company's future success. The highest-weighted EFAS and IFAS factors should appear in the SFAS Matrix.

As shown in **Figure 6–1**, you can create an SFAS Matrix by following these steps:

1. In **Column 1** *(Strategic Factors)*, list the most important EFAS and IFAS items. After each factor, indicate whether it is a Strength **(S)**, Weakness **(W)**, an Opportunity **(O)**, or a Threat **(T)**.

2. In **Column 2** *(Weight)*, assign weights for all of the internal and external strategic factors. As with the EFAS and IFAS Tables presented earlier, the **weight column must total 1.00**. This means that the weights calculated earlier for EFAS and IFAS will probably have to be adjusted.

3. In **Column 3** *(Rating)* assign a rating of how the company's management is responding to each of the strategic factors. These ratings will probably (but not always) be the same as those listed in the EFAS and IFAS Tables.

4. In **Column 4** *(Weighted Score)* multiply the weight in **Column 2** for each factor by its rating in **Column 3** to obtain the factor's rated score.

5. In **Column 5** *(Duration)*, depicted in **Figure 6–1**, indicate **short-term** (less than one year), **intermediate-term** (one to three years), or **long-term** (three years and beyond).

6. In **Column 6** *(Comments)*, repeat or revise your comments for each strategic factor from the previous EFAS and IFAS Tables. **The total weighted score for the average firm in an industry is always 3.0**.

The resulting SFAS Matrix is a listing of the firm's external and internal strategic factors in one table. The example given in **Figure 6–1** is for Maytag Corporation in 1995, before the firm sold its European and Australian operations and it was acquired by Whirlpool. The SFAS Matrix includes only the most important factors gathered from environmental scanning, and thus provides information that is essential for strategy formulation. The use of EFAS and IFAS Tables together with the SFAS Matrix deals with some of the criticisms of SWOT analysis. For example, the use of the SFAS Matrix reduces the list of factors to a manageable number, puts weights on each factor, and allows one factor to be listed as both a strength and a weakness (or as an opportunity and a threat).

FINDING A PROPITIOUS NICHE

One desired outcome of analyzing strategic factors is identifying a niche where an organization can use its core competencies to take advantage of a particular market opportunity. A niche is a need in the marketplace that is currently unsatisfied. The goal is to find a **propitious niche**—an extremely favorable niche—that is so well suited to the firm's internal and external environment that other corporations are not likely to challenge or dislodge it.[2] A niche is propitious to the extent that it currently is just large enough for one firm to satisfy its demand. After a firm has found and filled that niche, it is not worth a potential competitor's time or money to also go after the same niche.

FIGURE 6–1   Strategic Factor Analysis Summary (SFAS) Matrix

Internal Strategic Factors	Weight	Rating	Weighted Score	Comments
	1	2	3	4	5
Strengths				
S1 Quality Maytag culture	.15	5.0	.75	Quality key to success
S2 Experienced top management	.05	4.2	.21	Know appliances
S3 Vertical integration	.10	3.9	.39	Dedicated factories
S4 Employee relations	.05	3.0	.15	Good, but deteriorating
S5 Hoover's international orientation	.15	2.8	.42	Hoover name in cleaners
Weaknesses				
W1 Process-oriented R&D	.05	2.2	.11	Slow on new products
W2 Distribution channels	.05	2.0	.10	Superstores replacing small dealers
W3 Financial position	.15	2.0	.30	High debt load
W4 Global positioning	.20	2.1	.42	Hoover weak outside the United Kingdom and Australia
W5 Manufacturing facilities	.05	4.0	.20	Investing now
Total Scores	1.00		3.05	

External Strategic Factors	Weight	Rating	Weighted Score	Comments
	1	2	3	4	5
Opportunities				
O1 Economic integration of European Community	.20	4.1	.82	Acquisition of Hoover
O2 Demographics favor quality appliances	.10	5.0	.50	Maytag quality
O3 Economic development of Asia	.05	1.0	.05	Low Maytag presence
O4 Opening of Eastern Europe	.05	2.0	.10	Will take time
O5 Trend to "Super Stores"	.10	1.8	.18	Maytag weak in this channel
Threats				
T1 Increasing government regulations	.10	4.3	.43	Well positioned
T2 Strong U.S. competition	.10	4.0	.40	Well positioned
T3 Whirlpool and Electrolux strong globally	.15	3.0	.45	Hoover weak globally
T4 New product advances	.05	1.2	.06	Questionable
T5 Japanese appliance companies	.10	1.6	.16	Only Asian presence is Australia
Total Scores	1.00		3.15	

*The most important external and internal factors are identified in the EFAS and IFAS Tables as shown here by shading these factors.

	1	2	3	4	Duration 5			6
Strategic Factors (Select the most important opportunities/threats from EFAS, Table 4–5 and the most important strengths and weaknesses from IFAS, Table 5–2)	Weight	Rating	Weighted Score	S H O R T	I N T E R M E D I A T E	L O N G	Comments
S1 Quality Maytag culture (S)	.10	5.0	.50			X	Quality key to success
S5 Hoover's international orientation (S)	.10	2.8	.28	X	X		Name recognition
W3 Financial position (W)	.10	2.0	.20	X	X		High debt
W4 Global positioning (W)	.15	2.2	.33		X	X	Only in N.A., U.K., and Australia
O1 Economic integration of European Community (O)	.10	4.1	.41			X	Acquisition of Hoover
O2 Demographics favor quality (O)	.10	5.0	.50		X		Maytag quality
O5 Trend to super stores (O + T)	.10	1.8	.18	X			Weak in this channel
T3 Whirlpool and Electrolux (T)	.15	3.0	.45	X			Dominate industry
T5 Japanese appliance companies (T)	.10	1.6	.16			X	Asian presence
Total Scores	1.00		3.01				

NOTES:
1. List each of the most important factors developed in your IFAS and EFAS Tables in Column 1.
2. Weight each factor from **1.0** (Most Important) to **0.0** (Not Important) in Column 2 based on that factor's probable impact on the company's strategic position. **The total weights must sum to 1.00.**
3. Rate each factor from **5.0** (Outstanding) to **1.0** (Poor) in Column 3 based on the company's response to that factor.
4. Multiply each factor's weight times its rating to obtain each factor's weighted score in Column 4.
5. For the duration in Column 5, check the appropriate column (short term—less than 1 year; intermediate—1 to 3 years; long term—over 3 years).
6. Use Column 6 (comments) for rationale used for each factor.

Finding such a niche or sweet spot is not easy. A firm's management must continually look for a *strategic window*—that is, a unique market opportunity that is available only for a particular time. The first firm through a strategic window can occupy a propitious niche and discourage competition (if the firm has the required internal strengths). One company that successfully found a propitious niche was Frank J. Zamboni & Company, the manufacturer of the machines that smooth the ice at ice skating rinks. Frank Zamboni invented the unique tractor-like machine in 1949 and no one has found a substitute for what it does. Before the machine was invented, people had to clean and scrape the ice by hand to prepare the surface for skating. Now hockey fans look forward to intermissions just to watch "the Zamboni" slowly drive up and down the ice rink, turning rough, scraped ice into a smooth mirror surface—almost like magic. So long as Zamboni's company was able to produce the machines in the quantity and quality desired, at a reasonable price, it was not worth another company's while to go after Frank Zamboni & Company's propitious niche.

As a niche grows, so can a company within that niche—by increasing its operations' capacity or through alliances with larger firms. The key is to identify a market opportunity in which the first firm to reach that market segment can obtain and keep dominant market share. For example, Church & Dwight was the first company in the United States to successfully market sodium bicarbonate for use in cooking. Its Arm & Hammer brand baking soda is still found in 95% of all U.S. households. The propitious niche concept is crucial to the software industry. Small initial demand in emerging markets allows new entrepreneurial ventures to go after niches too small to be noticed by established companies. When Microsoft developed its first disk operating system (DOS) in 1980 for IBM's personal computers, for example, the demand for such open systems software was very small—a small niche for a then very small Microsoft. The company was able to fill that niche and to successfully grow with it.

Niches can also change—sometimes faster than a firm can adapt to that change. A company's management may discover in their situation analysis that they need to invest heavily in the firm's capabilities to keep them competitively strong in a changing niche. South African Breweries (SAB), for example, took this approach when management realized that the only way to keep competitors out of its market was to continuously invest in increased productivity and infrastructure in order to keep its prices very low.

Review of Mission and Objectives

A reexamination of an organization's current mission and objectives must be made before alternative strategies can be generated and evaluated. Even when formulating strategy, decision makers tend to concentrate on the alternatives—the action possibilities—rather than on a mission to be fulfilled and objectives to be achieved. This tendency is so attractive because it is much easier to deal with alternative courses of action that exist right here and now than to really think about what you want to accomplish in the future. The end result is that we often choose strategies that set our objectives for us rather than having our choices incorporate clear objectives and a mission statement.

Problems in performance can derive from an inappropriate statement of mission, which may be too narrow or too broad. If the mission does not provide a **common thread** (a unifying theme) for a corporation's businesses, managers may be unclear about where the company is heading. Objectives and strategies might be in conflict with each other. Divisions might be competing against one another rather than against outside competition—to the detriment of the corporation as a whole.

A company's objectives can also be inappropriately stated. They can either focus too much on short-term operational goals or be so general that they provide little real guidance. There may be a gap between planned and achieved objectives. When such a gap occurs, either the strategies have to be changed to improve performance or the objectives need to be adjusted downward to be more realistic. Consequently, objectives should be constantly reviewed to ensure their usefulness. This is what happened at Boeing when management decided to change its primary objective from being the largest in the industry to being the most profitable. This had a significant effect on its strategies and policies. Following its new objective, the company canceled its policy of competing with Airbus on price and abandoned its commitment to maintaining a manufacturing capacity that could produce more than half a peak year's demand for airplanes.[3]

Business Strategies

Business strategy focuses on improving the competitive position of a company's or business unit's products or services within the specific industry or market segment that the company or business unit serves. Business strategy is extremely important because research shows that business unit effects have double the impact on overall company performance than do either corporate or industry effects.[4] Business strategy can be competitive (battling against all competitors for advantage) and/or cooperative (working with one or more companies to gain advantage against other competitors). Just as corporate strategy asks what industry(ies) the company should be in, business strategy asks how the company or its units should compete or cooperate in each industry.

PORTER'S COMPETITIVE STRATEGIES

Competitive strategy raises the following questions:

- Should we compete on the basis of lower cost (and thus price), or should we differentiate our products or services on some basis other than cost, such as quality or service?

- Should we compete head to head with our major competitors for the biggest but most sought-after share of the market, or should we focus on a niche in which we can satisfy a less sought-after but also profitable segment of the market?

Michael Porter proposed three "generic" competitive strategies for outperforming other corporations in a particular industry: overall cost leadership, differentiation, and focus.[5] These strategies are called generic because they can be pursued by any type or size of business firm, even by not-for-profit organizations:

- **Cost leadership** is the ability of a company or a business unit to design, produce, and market a comparable product more efficiently than its competitors.

- **Differentiation** is the ability of a company to provide unique and superior value to the buyer in terms of product quality, special features, or after-sale service.

- **Focus** is the ability of a company to provide unique and superior value to a particular buyer group, segment of the market line, or geographic market.

Porter proposed that a firm's competitive advantage in an industry is determined by its **competitive scope**—that is, the breadth of the company's or business unit's target market. Simply put, a company or business unit can choose a broad target (that is, aim at the middle of the mass market) or a narrow target (that is, aim at a market niche). Combining these two types of target markets with the three competitive strategies results in the four variations of generic strategies. When the lower-cost and differentiation strategies have a broad mass-market target, they are simply called *cost leadership* and *differentiation*. When they are focused on a market niche (narrow target), however, they are called *cost focus* and *differentiation focus*. Research does indicate that established firms pursuing broad-scope strategies outperform firms following narrow-scope strategies in terms of ROA (Return on Assets). Even though research has found that new entrepreneurial firms increase their chance of survival if they follow a narrow-scope strategy, it has unfortunately also found that new firms that take the risk and pursue a broad-scope strategy will significantly outperform those that follow a narrow-scope strategy regardless of the size and breadth of their initial resources.[6]

Cost leadership is a lower-cost competitive strategy that aims at the broad mass market and requires "aggressive construction of efficient-scale facilities, vigorous pursuit of cost reductions from experience, tight cost and overhead control, avoidance of marginal customer accounts, and cost minimization in areas like R&D, service, sales force, advertising, and so on."[7] Because of its lower costs, the cost leader is able to charge a lower price for its products than its competitors and still make a satisfactory profit. Although it may not necessarily have the lowest costs in the industry, it has lower costs than its competitors. Some companies successfully following this strategy are Wal-Mart (discount retailing), Taco Bell (fast-food restaurants), HP (computers), Enterprise (rental cars), Aldi (grocery stores), Southwest Airlines, and Timex (watches). Having a lower-cost position also gives a company or business unit a defense against rivals. Its lower costs allow it to continue to earn profits during times of heavy competition. Its high market share means that it will have high bargaining power relative to its suppliers (because it buys in large quantities). Its low price will also serve as a barrier to entry because few new entrants will be able to match the leader's cost advantage. As a result, cost leaders are likely to earn above-average returns on investment.

Differentiation is aimed at the broad mass market and involves the creation of a product or service that is perceived throughout its industry as unique. The company or business unit may then charge a premium for its product. This specialty can be associated with design or brand image, technology, features, a dealer network, or customer service. Differentiation is a viable strategy for earning above-average returns in a specific business because the resulting brand loyalty lowers customers' sensitivity to price. Increased costs can usually be passed on to the buyers. Buyer loyalty also serves as an entry barrier; new firms must develop their own distinctive competence to differentiate their products in some way in order to compete successfully. Examples of companies that successfully use a **differentiation strategy** are Walt Disney Company (entertainment), BMW (automobiles), Apple (computers, tablets, and cell phones), and Five Guys (fast food). Research does suggest that a differentiation strategy is more likely to generate higher profits than does a **lower-cost strategy** because differentiation creates a better entry barrier. A low-cost strategy is more likely, however, to generate increases in market share.[8] For an example of how two companies approach generic strategies, see the **Global Issue** feature on Nike versus New Balance.

Cost focus is a low-cost competitive strategy that focuses on a particular buyer group or geographic market and attempts to serve only this niche, to the exclusion of others. In using cost focus, the company or business unit seeks a cost advantage in its target segment. A good example of this strategy is Potlach Corporation, a manufacturer of toilet tissue. Rather than compete directly against Procter & Gamble's Charmin, Potlach makes the house brands for Albertson's, Safeway, Jewel, and many other grocery store chains. It matches the quality of the well-known brands, but keeps costs low by eliminating advertising and promotion expenses. As a result, Spokane-based Potlach makes 92% of the private-label bathroom tissue and one-third of all bathroom tissue sold in Western U.S. grocery stores. The phenomenal growth of store brand purchases is a testament to the power of a cost focus as a means to sell at lower prices. A 2012 study by Accenture found that annual sales of store brands had increased 40% over the past decade. A total of 64% of U.S. shoppers said that store brands comprised 50% of their groceries. The same study asked why people purchased store brands. They found that 66% of shoppers bought store brands because they were cheaper, and 87% said they would buy brand-name products but only if they were the same price as the store brand.[9]

Differentiation focus, like cost focus, concentrates on a particular buyer group, product line segment, or geographic market. This is the strategy successfully followed by Midamar Corporation (distributor of halal foods), Morgan Motor Car Company (a manufacturer of classic British sports cars), Nickelodeon (a cable channel for children), OrphageniX (pharmaceuticals), and local ethnic grocery stores. In using differentiation focus, a company or business unit seeks differentiation in a targeted market segment. This strategy is valued by those who

GLOBAL issue

THE NIKE SHOE STRATEGY VS. THE NEW BALANCE SHOE STRATEGY

Nike (based in Beaverton, Oregon) and New Balance (based in Boston, Massachusetts) are direct competitors in the shoe industry. While both companies concentrate on athletic shoes, they also carry a wide variety of shoes, from sandals to boots. Both companies continually push out new models to appeal to the sports enthusiast while maintaining a line of athletic shoes that spans the entire market. New Balance has shoes that range from US$19 to their latest creation, the Minimus, that is priced around $100, all the way up to their New Balance 2040, which runs $275.

However, the battlefield is really played out using unique generic strategies. Nike produces virtually all of its shoes in Indonesia, China, and Vietnam. The focus is on strict cost controls and the ability to bring a shoe into the U.S. market cheaper than their competitors. New Balance produces a majority of its shoes (though not all) in the United States (primarily in Maine). New Balance claims that the approach allows it the ability to react faster to demand from U.S. stores and thus help those stores maintain a lower inventory. The company also believes that their U.S. workers maintain better quality control than workers abroad.

This strategy difference is being put to the test with the latest free-trade effort currently in negotiations. The Trans-Pacific Partnership Free Trade agreement aims to open up markets by reducing or eliminating tariffs. Currently, there is a 20% tariff on imported athletic shoes, and New Balance argues that this tariff is necessary to keep production in the United States. Nike (and for that matter virtually every other athletic shoe maker) argues that this is a restriction of trade and favors one company over the desires of an entire industry. Nike would be able to take full advantage of their cost advantage if the trade tariffs were removed, while New Balance would have to find more compelling competitive advantages if it wanted to keep production in the United States. The tariffs provide an artificial leveling of the cost advantage approach.

SOURCES: K. Miller, "Congress Members, New Balance Workers Fight to Save Shoe Tariffs," *Morning Sentinel* (July 19, 2012). (http://www.onlinesentinel.com/news/mainers-in-congress-workers-fight-to-save-shoe-tariffs_2012-07-18.html); http://www.newbalance.com/men/new-and-popular/17000,default,sc.html; Global Exchange, "Nike FAQ's" Accessed 6/1/13, http://www.globalexchange.org/sweatfree/nike/faq; E. Martin, "New Balance Wants its Tariffs. Nike Doesn't," *Bloomberg Businessweek* (May 7, 2012), (http://www.businessweek.com/articles/2012-05-03/new-balance-wants-its-tariffs-dot-nike-doesnt).

believe that a company or a unit that focuses its efforts is better able to serve the special needs of a narrow strategic target more effectively than can its competition. For example, OrphageniX is a small biotech pharmaceutical company that avoids head-to-head competition with big companies like AstraZenica and Merck by developing drug therapies for "orphan" diseases. That is, diseases that are rare and often life threatening but do not have effective treatment options—for instance, diseases such as sickle cell anemia and spinal muscular atrophy that big drug makers are overlooking.[10]

Risks in Competitive Strategies

No one competitive strategy is guaranteed to achieve success, and some companies that have successfully implemented one of Porter's competitive strategies have found that they could not sustain the strategy. Each of the generic strategies has risks. For example, a company following a differentiation strategy must ensure that the higher price it charges for its higher quality is not too far above the price of the competition, otherwise customers will not see the extra quality as worth the extra cost. For years, Deere & Company was the leader in farm machinery until low-cost competitors from India and other developing countries began making low-priced products. Deere responded by building high-tech flexible manufacturing plants using mass-customization to cut its manufacturing costs and using innovation to create differentiated products which, although higher-priced, reduced customers' labor and fuel expenses.[11]

Issues in Competitive Strategies

Porter argues that to be successful, a company or business unit must achieve one of the previously mentioned generic competitive strategies. Otherwise, the company or business unit is *stuck in the middle* of the competitive marketplace with no competitive advantage and is doomed to below-average performance. A classic example of a company that found itself stuck in the middle was K-Mart. The company spent a lot of money trying to imitate both Wal-Mart's low-cost strategy and Target's quality differentiation strategy. The result was a bankruptcy filing and its continuation today as a floundering company with poor performance and no clear strategy. Although some studies do support Porter's argument that companies tend to sort themselves into either lower cost or differentiation strategies and that successful companies emphasize only one strategy,[12] other research suggests that some combination of the two competitive strategies may also be successful.[13]

The Toyota and Honda auto companies are often presented as examples of successful firms able to achieve both of these generic competitive strategies. Thanks to advances in technology, a company may be able to design quality into a product or service in such a way that it can achieve both high quality and lower costs thus achieving a higher market share.[14] Although Porter agrees that it is possible for a company or a business unit to achieve low cost and differentiation simultaneously, he continues to argue that this state is often temporary.[15] Porter does admit, however, that many different kinds of potentially profitable competitive strategies exist. Although there is generally room for only one company to successfully pursue the mass- market cost leadership strategy (because it is so often tied to maintaining a dominant market share), there is room for an almost unlimited number of differentiation and focus strategies (depending on the range of possible desirable features and the number of identifiable market niches).

Most entrepreneurial ventures follow focus strategies. The successful ones differentiate their product or service from those of others by focusing on customer wants in a segment of the market, thereby achieving a dominant share of that part of the market. Adopting guerrilla warfare tactics, these companies often go after opportunities in market niches too small to justify retaliation from the market leaders.

Industry Structure and Competitive Strategy

Although each of Porter's generic competitive strategies may be used in any industry, certain strategies are more likely to succeed depending upon the type of industry. In a **fragmented industry**, for example, where many small- and medium-sized local companies compete for relatively small shares of the total market, focus strategies will likely predominate. Fragmented industries are typical for products in the early stages of their life cycles. If few economies are to be gained through size, no large firms will emerge and entry barriers will be low—allowing a stream of new entrants into the industry. Sandwich shops, veterinary care, used-car lots, dry cleaners, and nail salons are examples. Even though P.F. Chang's and the Panda Restaurant Group have firmly established themselves as chains in the United States, local family-owned restaurants still comprise 86% of Asian casual dining restaurants.[16]

If a company is able to overcome the limitations of a fragmented market, however, it can reap the benefits of a broadly targeted cost-leadership or differentiation strategy. Until Pizza Hut was able to use advertising to differentiate itself from local competitors, the pizza fast-food business was a fragmented industry composed primarily of locally owned pizza parlors, each with its own distinctive product and service offering. Subsequently, Domino's used the cost-leadership strategy to achieve the number 2 U.S. national market share.

As an industry matures, fragmentation is overcome, and the industry tends to become a **consolidated industry** dominated by a few large companies. Although many industries start out being fragmented, battles for market share and creative attempts to overcome local or niche market boundaries often increase the market share of a few companies. After product standards become established for minimum quality and features, competition shifts to a greater emphasis on cost and service. Slower growth, overcapacity, and knowledgeable buyers combine to put a premium on a firm's ability to achieve cost leadership or differentiation along the dimensions most desired by the market. R&D shifts from product to process improvements. Overall product quality improves, and costs are reduced significantly.

The *strategic rollup* was developed in the mid-1990s as an efficient way to quickly consolidate a fragmented industry. With the aid of money from venture capitalists and private equity firms, a single company acquires hundreds of owner-operated small businesses. The resulting large firm creates economies of scale by building regional or national brands, applies best practices across all aspects of marketing and operations, and hires more sophisticated managers than the small businesses could previously afford. Rollups differ from conventional mergers and acquisitions in three ways: (1) they involve large numbers of firms, (2) the acquired firms are typically owner operated, and (3) the objective is not to gain incremental advantage, but to reinvent an entire industry.[18] Rollups are currently under way in the anti-freeze (waste glycol) recycling industry led by GlyEco Inc. and legendary rollup artist John Lorenz, and in the shredding and record storage industry led by Business Records Management and Cornerstone Records Management. Cornerstone has completed 24 acquisitions in the past four years as it attempts to consolidate this very local and fragmented industry.[19]

Once consolidated, an industry will become one in which cost leadership and differentiation tend to be combined to various degrees, even though one competitive strategy may be primarily emphasized. A firm can no longer gain and keep high market share simply through low price. The buyers are more sophisticated and demand a certain minimum level of quality for price paid. Colgate Palmolive Company, a leader in soap, toothpaste, and toothbrushes used the U.S. obsession for whiter teeth to create Colgate Optic White toothpaste (at a premium price) helping increase the company's overall market share in toothpaste to almost 37% and helping the company grow organic sales by an astonishing 6.5% in 2012.[20] The same is true for firms emphasizing high quality. Either the quality must be high enough and valued by the customer enough to justify the higher price, or the price must be dropped (through lowering costs) to compete effectively with the lower-priced products. Apple has consistently chosen to increase the capabilities of their products instead of dropping the price. Even though tablets are now available in a wide variety of sizes, capabilities, and price points, Apple has chosen to maintain their premium price and add features. They allow no discounting and no sales of their products. Consolidation is taking place worldwide in the banking, airline, cell phone, and home appliance industries. For an example of a how a company can challenge what is still a fragmented industry and change the way the whole industry operates, see the Innovation Issue feature on CHEGG.

Hypercompetition and Competitive Advantage Sustainability

Some firms are able to sustain their competitive advantage for many years,[21] but most find that competitive advantage erodes over time. In his book *Hypercompetition*, D'Aveni proposes that it is becoming increasingly difficult to sustain a competitive advantage for very long. "Market stability is threatened by short product life cycles, short product design cycles, new technologies, frequent entry by unexpected outsiders, repositioning by incumbents, and tactical redefinitions of market boundaries as diverse industries merge."[22] Consequently, a company or business unit must constantly work to improve its competitive advantage. It is not enough to be just the lowest-cost competitor. Through continuous improvement programs, competitors are usually working to lower their costs as well. Firms must find new ways not only to reduce costs further but also to add value to the product or service being provided.

INNOVATION issue

CHEGG AND COLLEGE TEXTBOOKS

Innovation in strategy sometimes means being able to gain advantage in an industry that refuses to acknowledge a change in customer behavior. One market that has remained mired in the past has been that of college textbooks. The business model dates back a long time and most colleges and universities used (or still use) the on-campus bookstore as a cash generator. Textbooks are chosen by professors, not students, to fit the mindset the professor wants for that particular class. Once chosen, the professors post the required material to their syllabus and let the bookstore know what they have chosen.

For many decades, students lined up to buy their books and pay whatever the bookstore charged (usually an amount that was staggering). The advent of the Internet and some very creative companies have changed the entire industry, upending both the bookstores and the publishers' means for generating income. Beyond the obvious avenue of used textbook sales, there were innovative companies taking advantage of the stagnation in the industry.

In 2007, CHEGG launched its online rental site for textbooks. Rather than paying hundreds of dollars for an "Introduction to Biology" textbook, you could rent it from CHEGG for as much as 80% off the cover price. CHEGG quickly became known as the Netflix of textbooks and their bright orange boxes became a staple at campuses throughout the United States. The company had sales of over US$200 million by 2012. However, not all was well at the company. Book rentals started to level off long before CHEGG hit any type of market saturation.

The winds had started changing again with the move to digital books, digital rentals, and a number of companies who were reimagining an industry where the textbook was not the center of the learning environment. CHEGG chose to move as well, but it moved in a different direction. The company saw the college experience as the new center for their business model and moved with it, spending US$50 million and buying up six companies in an effort to become the hub of the college student experience, offering discounts on dorm room decorations, homework help, professor recommendations, digital books, and connecting the whole operation to Facebook. CHEGG's rental book market acts as the core of its business, while CHUBB.com is used as a focused networking site for college students.

....

SOURCES: http://www.chegg.com/; A. Levy, "A College Hub. Togas Not Included," *Bloomberg Businessweek* (June 4, 2012), (http://www.businessweek.com/articles/2012-05-31/chegg-a-college-hub-dot-togas-not-included).

The same is true of a firm or unit that is following a differentiation strategy. Maytag Corporation, for example, was successful for many years by offering the most reliable brand in North American major home appliances. It was able to charge the highest prices for Maytag brand washing machines. When other competitors improved the quality of their products, however, it became increasingly difficult for customers to justify Maytag's significantly higher price. Consequently, Maytag Corporation was forced not only to add new features to its products but also to reduce costs through improved manufacturing processes so that its prices were no longer out of line with those of the competition. D'Aveni's theory of hypercompetition is supported by developing research on the importance of building *dynamic capabilities* to better cope with uncertain environments (discussed previously in Chapter 5 in the resource-based view of the firm).

D'Aveni contends that when industries become hypercompetitive, they tend to go through escalating stages of competition. Firms initially compete on cost and quality, until an abundance of high-quality, low-priced goods result. This occurred in the U.S. major home appliance industry up through 1980. In a second stage of competition, the competitors move into untapped markets. Others usually imitate these moves until their actions become too risky or expensive. This epitomized the major home appliance industry during the 1980s and 1990s, as strong U.S. and European firms like Whirlpool, Electrolux, and Bosch-Siemens established a presence in both Europe and the Americas and then moved into Asia. Strong Asian firms like LG and Haier likewise entered Europe and the Americas in the late 1990s.

According to D'Aveni, firms then raise entry barriers to limit competitors. Economies of scale, distribution agreements, and strategic alliances made it all but impossible for a new firm to enter the major home appliance industry by the end of the 20th century. After the established players have entered and consolidated all new markets, the next stage is for the remaining firms to attack and destroy the strongholds of other firms. Maytag's inability to hold onto its North American stronghold led to its acquisition by Whirlpool in 2006. Eventually, according to D'Aveni, the remaining large global competitors can work their way to a situation of perfect competition in which no one has any advantage and profits are minimal.

Before hypercompetition, strategic initiatives provided competitive advantage for many years, perhaps for decades. Except for a few stable industries, this is no longer the case. According to D'Aveni, as industries become hypercompetitive, there is no such thing as a sustainable competitive advantage. Successful strategic initiatives in this type of industry typically last only months to a few years. According to D'Aveni, the only way a firm in this kind of dynamic industry can sustain any competitive advantage is through a continuous series of multiple short-term initiatives aimed at replacing a firm's current successful products with the next generation of products before the competitors can do so. Consumer product companies like Procter & Gamble, Kraft, and Kimberly Clark are taking this approach in the hypercompetitive household products industry.

Hypercompetition views competition, in effect, as a distinct series of ocean waves on what used to be a fairly calm stretch of water. As industry competition becomes more intense, the waves grow higher and require more dexterity to handle. Although a strategy is still needed to sail from point A to point B, more turbulent water means that a craft must continually adjust course to suit each new large wave. One danger of D'Aveni's concept of hypercompetition, however, is that it may lead to an overemphasis on short-term tactics (discussed in the next section) over long-term strategy. Too much of an orientation on the individual waves of hyper-competition could cause a company to focus too much on short-term temporary advantage and not enough on achieving its long-term objectives through building sustainable competitive advantage. Nevertheless, research supports D'Aveni's argument that sustained competitive advantage is increasingly a matter not of a single advantage maintained over time, but more a matter of sequencing advantages over time.[23]

For an example of a how a company can achieve sustainable competitive advantages in a hypercompetitive market, see the **Sustainability Issue** feature about ESPN.

COOPERATIVE STRATEGIES

A company uses competitive strategies to gain competitive advantage within an industry by battling against other firms. These are not, however, the only business strategy options available to a company or business unit for competing successfully within an industry. A company can also use **cooperative strategies** to gain competitive advantage within an industry by working with other firms. The two general types of cooperative strategies are collusion and strategic alliances.

Collusion

Collusion is the active cooperation of firms within an industry to reduce output and raise prices in order to get around the normal economic law of supply and demand. Collusion may be explicit, in which case firms cooperate through direct communication and negotiation, or tacit, in which case firms cooperate indirectly through an informal system of signals. Explicit collusion is illegal in most countries and in a number of regional trade associations, such as the European Union. For example, Archer Daniels Midland (ADM), the large U.S. agricultural products firm, conspired with its competitors to limit the sales volume and raise the price of the food additive lysine. Executives from three Japanese and South Korean lysine

SUSTAINABILITY issue

STRATEGIC SUSTAINABILITY—ESPN

A sustainable strategy has many components. This is especially true in the hyper-competitive sports entertainment industry. Around the world, there is an almost maniacal love of sports, sports teams, sports superstars, and sports trivia. While this phenomenon is nothing new, technology advances have raised this "want" to an instant gratification level.

This was not always the way it was. Way back in the 1970s, we watched sports when the three networks deemed that we were to watch sports. We watched only the teams that they chose and it was rare to see any sports that were not considered to be mainstream. When you think about the staggering number of sporting events that occur every day around the world, it was amazing how few were shown on television.

All that changed with the founding of ESPN (Entertainment and Sports Programming Network) in 1979 in Bristol, Connecticut. Aired with little content, a show called *Sports Center*, and a lot of Australian Rules Football, the company sought out an approach in a field that had been dominated by the major league sports teams. The new ESPN moved to 24-hour broadcasting on September 1, 1980. ESPN quickly realized that a sustainable competitive advantage required contracts. All the analysis in the world would not make up for the fact that fans were watching other channels. The top management at ESPN also realized that it would not just be about keeping viewers tied to a single television channel as the industry standard was at the time.

The company opened up new television channels, created a radio station broadcast for stations across the country, moved aggressively into the Internet, and is the leader in mobile broadcasting of sports. Today, ESPN is the undisputed king of Sports broadcasting. Its projected 2013 revenues of over US$9 billion put it on a par with traditional media powerhouse CBS. ESPN charges cable companies US$5.13 per month/per subscriber in an industry where the average is US$.20/month/subscriber. The company has bet its sustainability in this market on its contracts with the NFL (through 2021), MLB (2021), NBA (2016), NASCAR (2013), and Wimbledon (2023), as well as a series of exclusive or partially shared contracts with major colleges and conferences. It caters to the sports enthusiast by providing that customer with the access and information they desire in the manner they desire it. The company then takes each successful platform to advertisers and monetizes the platform. ESPN is unconcerned about cannibalizing platforms because they seek to continually reinvent the company. John Skipper (ESPN President) believes that the company's dominance comes from a competitive approach that he calls "build, build, build."

SOURCES: K. T. Greenfeld, "ESPN Is Running Up the Score," *Bloomberg Businessweek* (September 3, 2012), pp. 58–64; http://frontrow.espn.go.com/category/espn-history/; http://a.espncdn.com/espninc/pressreleases/chronology.html; Hawkins, S. "Big 12 reaches $2.6B deal with ESPN, Fox Sports," Accessed 6/1/13, http://www.boston.comsports/colleges/2012/09/07/big-reaches-deal-with-espn-fox-sports/MbkpeOW4xEyX78F3FfHPcl/story.html.

manufacturers admitted meeting in hotels in major cities throughout the world to form a "lysine trade association." The three companies were fined more than US$20 million by the U.S. federal government.[24] Professional sports is big business and a fascinating collusion lawsuit was filed in May 2012 (*Reggie White, et al. v. NFL*) against the National Football League. The players contended they lost US$1 billion because of a secret salary cap for the 2010 season. As stipulated by collectively bargained language, such damages, if proved, would be automatically trebled to US$3 billion.[25]

Collusion can also be tacit, in which case there is no direct communication among competing firms. According to Barney, tacit collusion in an industry is most likely to be successful if (1) there are a small number of identifiable competitors, (2) costs are similar among firms, (3) one firm tends to act as the price leader, (4) there is a common industry culture that accepts cooperation, (5) sales are characterized by a high frequency of small orders, (6) large inventories and order backlogs are normal ways of dealing with fluctuations in demand, and (7) there are high entry barriers to keep out new competitors.[26]

Even tacit collusion can, however, be illegal. For example, when General Electric wanted to ease price competition in the steam turbine industry, it widely advertised its prices and publicly committed not to sell below those prices. Customers were even told that if GE reduced turbine prices in the future, it would give customers a refund equal to the price reduction. GE's message was not lost on Westinghouse, the major competitor in steam turbines. Both prices and profit margins remained stable for the next 10 years in this industry. The U.S. Department of Justice then sued both firms for engaging in "conscious parallelism" (following each other's lead to reduce the level of competition) in order to reduce competition.

Strategic Alliances

A **strategic alliance** is a long-term cooperative arrangement between two or more independent firms or business units that engage in business activities for mutual economic gain.[27] Alliances between companies or business units have become a fact of life in modern business. Each of the top 500 global business firms now averages 60 major alliances.[28] Some alliances are very short term, only lasting long enough for one partner to establish a beachhead in a new market. Over time, conflicts over objectives and control often develop among the partners. For these and other reasons, around half of all alliances (including international alliances) perform unsatisfactorily.[29] Others are more long-lasting and may even be preludes to full mergers between companies.

Many alliances do increase profitability of the members and have a positive effect on firm value.[30] A study by Cooper & Lybrand found that firms involved in strategic alliances had 11% higher revenue and a 20% higher growth rate than did companies not involved in alliances.[31]

Forming and managing strategic alliances is a capability that is learned over time. Research reveals that the more experience a firm has with strategic alliances, the more likely that its alliances will be successful.[32] (There is some evidence, however, that too much partnering experience with the same partners generates diminishing returns over time and leads to reduced performance.)[33] Consequently, leading firms are making investments in building and developing their partnering capabilities.[34]

Companies or business units may form a strategic alliance for a number of reasons, including:

1. **To obtain or learn new capabilities:** In May 2012, Hallmark formed an alliance with Shutterfly that put more than 1000 exclusive Hallmark-designed customizable cards on Shutterfly's new personalized greeting card site, Treat.com, as well as the core Shutterfly site.[35] Alliances are especially useful if the desired knowledge or capability is based on tacit knowledge or on new poorly understood technology.[36] A study found that firms with strategic alliances had more modern manufacturing technologies than did firms without alliances.[37]

2. **To obtain access to specific markets:** Rather than buy a foreign company or build breweries of its own in other countries, AB InBev chose to license the right to brew and market Budweiser to other brewers, such as Labatt in Canada, Modelo in Mexico, and Kirin in Japan. As another example, U.S. defense contractors and aircraft manufacturers selling to foreign governments are typically required by these governments to spend a percentage of the contract/purchase value, either by purchasing parts or obtaining sub-contractors, in that country. This is often achieved by forming value-chain alliances with foreign companies either as parts suppliers or as sub-contractors.[38] In a survey by the *Economist Intelligence Unit*, 59% of executives stated that their primary reason for engaging in alliances was the need for fast and low-cost expansion into new markets.[39]

3. **To reduce financial risk:** Alliances take less financial resources than do acquisitions or going it alone and are easier to exit if necessary.[40] For example, because the costs of developing new large jet airplanes were becoming too high for any one manufacturer, Aerospatiale of France, British Aerospace, Construcciones Aeronáuticas of Spain, and Daimler-Benz Aerospace of Germany formed a joint consortium called Airbus Industrie

to design and build such planes. Using alliances with suppliers is a popular means of outsourcing an expensive activity.

4. **To reduce political risk:** Forming alliances with local partners is a good way to overcome deficiencies in resources and capabilities when expanding into international markets.[41] To gain access to China while ensuring a positive relationship with the often restrictive Chinese government, Maytag Corporation formed a joint venture with the Chinese appliance maker, RSD.

Cooperative arrangements between companies and business units fall along a continuum from weak and distant to strong and close. (See **Figure 6–2**.) The types of alliances range from mutual service consortia to joint ventures and licensing arrangements to value-chain partnerships.[42]

Mutual Service Consortia. A **mutual service consortium** is a partnership of similar companies in similar industries that pool their resources to gain a benefit that is too expensive to develop alone, such as access to advanced technology. For example, IBM established a research alliance with Sony Electronics and Toshiba to build its next generation of computer chips. The result was the "cell" chip, a microprocessor running at 256 gigaflops—around 10 times the performance of the fastest chips currently used in desktop computers. Referred to as a "supercomputer on a chip," cell chips were to be used by Sony in its PlayStation 3, by Toshiba in its high-definition televisions, and by IBM in its super computers.[43] The mutual service consortia is a fairly weak and distant alliance—appropriate for partners that wish to work together but not share their core competencies. There is very little interaction or communication among the partners.

Joint Venture. A **joint venture** is a "cooperative business activity, formed by two or more separate organizations for strategic purposes, that creates an independent business entity and allocates ownership, operational responsibilities, and financial risks and rewards to each member, while preserving their separate identity/autonomy."[44] Along with licensing arrangements, joint ventures lie at the midpoint of the continuum and are formed to pursue an opportunity that needs a capability from two or more companies or business units, such as the technology of one and the distribution channels of another.

Joint ventures are the most popular form of strategic alliance. They often occur because the companies involved do not want to or cannot legally merge permanently. Joint ventures provide a way to temporarily combine the different strengths of partners to achieve an outcome of value to all. For example, Proctor & Gamble formed a joint venture with Clorox to produce food-storage wraps. P&G brought its cling-film technology and 20 full-time employees to the venture, while Clorox contributed its bags, containers, and wraps business.[45]

Extremely popular in international undertakings because of financial and political–legal constraints, forming joint ventures is a convenient way for corporations to work together without losing their independence. Between 30% and 55% of international joint ventures include three or more partners.[46] The disadvantages of joint ventures include loss of control, lower profits, probability of conflicts with partners, and the likely transfer of technological advantage to the partner. Joint ventures are often meant to be temporary, especially by some companies that may view them as a way to rectify a competitive weakness until they can achieve long-term dominance in the partnership. Partially for this reason, joint ventures have a high failure rate. Research indicates, however, that joint ventures tend to be more successful when both partners have equal ownership in the venture and are mutually dependent on each other for results.[47]

Licensing Arrangements. A **licensing arrangement** is an agreement in which the licensing firm grants rights to another firm in another country or market to produce and/or sell a product. The licensee pays compensation to the licensing firm in return for technical expertise. Licensing is an especially useful strategy if the trademark or brand name is well known but the MNC does not have sufficient funds to finance its entering the country directly. For example, Yum! Brands successfully used franchising and licensing to establish its KFC, Pizza Hut, Taco Bell, Long John Silver's, and A&W restaurants throughout the world. By 2012, Yum! Brands had used that strategy to open more than 3700 restaurants in China and had plans to open 700 more by year's end.[48] This strategy also becomes important if the country makes entry via investment either difficult or impossible. The danger always exists, however, that the licensee might develop its competence to the point that it becomes a competitor to the licensing firm. Therefore, a company should never license its distinctive competence, even for some short-run advantage.

Value-Chain Partnerships. A **value-chain partnership** is a strong and close alliance in which one company or unit forms a long-term arrangement with a key supplier or distributor for mutual advantage. For example, P&G, the maker of Folgers and Millstone coffee, worked with coffee appliance makers Mr. Coffee, Krups, and Hamilton Beach to use technology licensed from Black & Decker to market a pressurized, single-serve coffee-making system called Home Cafe. This was an attempt to reverse declining at-home coffee consumption at a time when coffeehouse sales were rising.[49]

To improve the quality of parts it purchases, companies in the U.S. auto industry, for example, have decided to work more closely with fewer suppliers and to involve them more in product design decisions. Activities that had previously been done internally by an automaker are being outsourced to suppliers specializing in those activities. The benefits of such relationships do not just accrue to the purchasing firm. Research suggests that suppliers that engage in long-term relationships are more profitable than suppliers with multiple short-term contracts.[50]

All forms of strategic alliances involve uncertainty. Many issues need to be dealt with when an alliance is initially formed, and others, which emerge later. Many problems revolve around the fact that a firm's alliance partners may also be its competitors, either immediately or in the future. According to Professor Peter Lorange, one thorny issue in any strategic alliance is how to cooperate without giving away the company or business unit's core competence: "Particularly when advanced technology is involved, it can be difficult for partners in an alliance to cooperate and openly share strategic know-how, but it is mandatory if the joint venture is to succeed."[51] It is therefore important that a company or business unit that is interested in joining or forming a strategic alliance consider the strategic alliance success factors listed in **Table 6–1**.

TABLE 6–1	
Strategic Alliance Success Factors	■ Have a clear strategic purpose. Integrate the alliance with each partner's strategy. Ensure that mutual value is created for all partners. ■ Find a fitting partner with compatible goals and complementary capabilities. ■ Identify likely partnering risks and deal with them when the alliance is formed. ■ Allocate tasks and responsibilities so that each partner can specialize in what it does best. ■ Create incentives for cooperation to minimize differences in corporate culture or organization fit. ■ Minimize conflicts among the partners by clarifying objectives and avoiding direct competition in the marketplace. ■ In an international alliance, ensure that those managing it have comprehensive cross-cultural knowledge. ■ Exchange human resources to maintain communication and trust. Don't allow individual egos to dominate. ■ Operate with long-term time horizons. The expectation of future gains can minimize short-term conflicts. ■ Develop multiple joint projects so that any failures are counterbalanced by successes. ■ Agree on a monitoring process. Share information to build trust and keep projects on target. Monitor customer responses and service complaints. ■ Be flexible in terms of willingness to renegotiate the relationship in terms of environmental changes and new opportunities. ■ Agree on an exit strategy for when the partners' objectives are achieved or the alliance is judged a failure.

SOURCES: Compiled from B. Gomes-Casseres, "Do You Really Have an Alliance Strategy?" *Strategy & Leadership* (September/October 1998), pp. 6–11; L. Segil, "Strategic Alliances for the 21st Century," *Strategy & Leadership* (September/October 1998), pp. 12–16; and A. C. Inkpen and K-Q Li, "Joint Venture Formation: Planning and Knowledge Gathering for Success," *Organizational Dynamics* (Spring 1999), pp. 33–47. Inkpen and Li provide a checklist of 17 questions on p. 46.

End of Chapter SUMMARY

Once environmental scanning is completed, situational analysis calls for the integration of this information. Using a SWOT approach is one of the more popular methods for examining external and internal information. We recommend using the SFAS Matrix as one way to identify a corporation's strategic factors.

Business strategy is composed of both competitive and cooperative strategy. As the external environment becomes more uncertain, an increasing number of corporations are choosing to simultaneously compete *and* cooperate with their competitors. These firms may cooperate to obtain efficiency in some areas, while each firm simultaneously tries to differentiate itself for competitive purposes. Raymond Noorda, Novell's founder and former CEO, coined the term *co-opetition* to describe such simultaneous competition and cooperation among firms.[52] One example is the collaboration between competitors DHL and UPS in the express delivery market. DHL's American delivery business was losing money and UPS' costly airfreight network had excess capacity. Under the terms of a 10-year agreement signed back in 2008, UPS carries DHL packages in its American airfreight network for a fee. The agreement covers only air freight, leaving both firms free to compete in the rest of the express parcel business.[53] A careful balancing act, co-opetition involves the careful management of alliance partners so that each partner obtains sufficient benefits to keep the alliance together. A long-term view is crucial. An unintended transfer of knowledge could be enough to provide one partner a significant competitive advantage over the others.[54] Unless that company forebears from using that knowledge against its partners, the alliance will be doomed.

MyManagementLab®

Go to **mymanagementlab.com** to complete the problems marked with this icon ⭐.

KEY TERMS

business strategy (p. 169)
collusion (p. 175)
common thread (p. 168)
competitive scope (p. 169)
competitive strategy (p. 175)
consolidated industry (p. 172)
cooperative strategy (p. 175)
cost focus (p. 170)
cost leadership (p. 169)

differentiation (p. 169)
differentiation focus (p. 170)
differentiation strategy (p. 170)
fragmented industry (p. 172)
joint venture (p. 178)
licensing arrangement (p. 179)
lower cost strategy (p. 170)
mutual service consortium (p. 178)
propitious niche (p. 165)

SFAS (Strategic Factors Analysis
   Summary) Matrix (p. 164)
strategic alliance (p. 177)
strategy formulation (p. 164)
SWOT (p. 164)
tactics (p. 175)
value-chain partnership (p. 179)

MyManagementLab®

Go to **mymanagementlab**.com for Auto-graded writing questions as well as the following Assisted-graded writing questions:

6-1. How does a hypercompetitive environment change the strategic approach for a company?

6-2. Explain how our understanding of the three generic strategic approaches available to companies can be used to direct the efforts of all employees at those companies.

DISCUSSION QUESTIONS

6-3. What industry forces might cause a propitious niche to appear or disappear?

⭐ **6-4.** What does a business have to consider when trying to follow a cost leadership strategy and a differentiation strategy simultaneously? Can you name a company doing this?

⭐ **6-5.** How can a company achieve a sustainable competitive advantage when its industry becomes hypercompetitive?

⭐ **6-6.** Why are many strategic alliances temporary?

STRATEGIC PRACTICE EXERCISE

Select an industry to analyze. Identify companies for each of Porter's four competitive strategies. How many different kinds of differentiation strategies can you find?

INDUSTRY: _____

Cost Leadership: _____

Differentiation: _____

Cost Focus: _____

Differentiation Focus: _____

NOTES

1. T. Brown, "The Essence of Strategy," *Management Review* (April 1997), pp. 8–13.

2. W. H. Newman, "Shaping the Master Strategy of Your Firm," *California Management Review* (Vol. 9, No. 3, 1967), pp. 77–88.

3. D. J. Collis and M. G. Rukstad, "Can You Say What Your Strategy Is?" *Harvard Business Review* (April 2008), pp.86.

4. V. F. Misangyi, H. Elms, T. Greckhamer, and J. A Lepine, "A New Perspective on a Fundamental Debate: A Multi-level Approach to Industry, Corporate, and Business Unit Effects," *Strategic Management Journal* (June 2006), pp. 571–590.

5. M. E. Porter, *Competitive Strategy* (New York: The Free Press, 1980), pp. 34–41 as revised in M. E. Porter, *The Competitive Advantage of Nations* (New York: The Free Press, 1990), pp. 37–40.

6. J. O. DeCastro and J. J. Chrisman, "Narrow-Scope Strategies and Firm Performance: An Empirical Investigation," *Journal of Business Strategies* (Spring 1998), pp. 1–16; T. M. Stearns, N. M. Carter, P. D. Reynolds, and M. L. Williams, "New Firm Survival: Industry, Strategy, and Location," *Journal of Business Venturing* (January 1995), pp. 23–42; C. E. Bamford, T. J. Dean, and P. P. McDougall, "Reconsidering the Niche Prescription for New Ventures: A Study of Initial Strategy and Growth," *Advances in Entrepreneurship: Firm Emergence and Growth* (Vol. 11, 2009). pp. 9–39.

7. Porter, *Competitive Strategy*, p. 35.

8. R. E. Caves, and P. Ghemawat, "Identifying Mobility Barriers," *Strategic Management Journal* (January 1992), pp. 1–12.

9. "Private Label Brands Winning the Retail Sales Game," *Food Product Design* (July 27, 2012), (http://www.foodproductdesign.com/news/2012/07/private-label-brands-winning-the-retail-sales-gam.aspx).

10. "Company Targets 'Orphan Drugs,'" *St. Cloud (MN) Times* (May 9, 2007), p. 2A, http://www.orphagenix.com/Home/research-technology-1.

11. M. Arndt, "Deere's Revolution on Wheels," *BusinessWeek* (July 2, 2007), pp. 78–79.

12. S. Thornhill and R. E. White, "Strategic Purity: A Multi-Industry Evaluation of Pure vs. Hybrid Business Strategies," *Strategic Management Journal* (May 2007), pp. 553–561; M. Delmas, M. V. Russo, and M. J. Montes-Sancho, "Deregulation and Environmental Differentiation in the Electric Utility Industry," *Strategic Management Journal* (February 2007), pp. 189–209.

13. C. Campbell-Hunt, "What Have We Learned About Generic Competitive Strategy? A Meta Analysis," *Strategic Management Journal* (February 2000), pp. 127–154.

14. M. Kroll, P. Wright, and R. A. Heiens, "The Contribution of Product Quality to Competitive Advantage: Impacts on Systematic Variance and Unexplained Variance in Returns," *Strategic Management Journal* (April 1999), pp. 375–384.

15. R. M. Hodgetts, "A Conversation with Michael E. Porter: A 'Significant Extension' Toward Operational Improvement and Positioning," *Organizational Dynamics* (Summer 1999), pp. 24–33.

16. M. Morrison, "Table Set for Fast Casual Asian Invasion," *Advertising Age* (May 16, 2011), (http://adage.com/article/news/table-set-fast-casual-asian-invasion/227577/); D. Banerjee and L. Patton, "P.F. Chang's to Be Bought by Centerbridge for $1 Billion," *Bloomberg Businessweek* (May 1, 2012), (http://www.businessweek.com/news/2012-05-01/p-dot-f-dot-chang-s-is-bought-by-centerbridge-for-1-dot-1-billion).

17. Pizza Industry Report 2011, (http://www.franchisedirect.com/foodfranchises/pizzafranchises/pizzaindustryreport2011productdiversitymarketleadersbusinessmodels2/80/294).

18. P. F. Kocourek, S. Y. Chung, and M. G. McKenna, "Strategic Rollups: Overhauling the Multi-Merger Machine," *Strategy + Business* (2nd Quarter 2000), pp. 45–53.

19. J. A. Tannenbaum, "Acquisitive Companies Set Out to 'Roll Up' Fragmented Industries," *The Wall Street Journal* (March 3, 1997), pp. A1, A6; 2007 Form 10-K and Quarterly Report (July 2008); VCA Antech Inc. "A Best Idea", "Legendary Roll-Up Virtuoso John Lorenz Inks Acquisition #7 in just over Four Months," *SmallCap Network* (June 14, 2012), (http://www.smallcapnetwork.com/A-Best-Idea-Legendary-roll-up-virtuoso-John-Lorenz-inks-acquisition-7-in-just-over-four-months/s/via/8996/article/view/p/mid/1/id/43/); "BRM Acquires Paper Exchange," *Shred Nations* (August 31, 2012), (http://www.shrednations.com/news/category/acquisition/).

20. "Colgate Announces First Quarter Results," (April 26, 2012), (http://finance.yahoo.com/news/colgate-announces-1st-quarter-results-110000350.html).

21. J. C. Bou and A. Satorra, "The Persistence of Abnormal Returns at Industry and Firm Levels: Evidence from Spain," *Strategic Management Journal* (July 2007), pp. 707–722.

22. R. A. D'Aveni, *Hypercompetition* (New York: The Free Press, 1994), pp. xiii–xiv.

23. R. R. Wiggins and T. W. Ruefli, "Schumpeter's Ghost: Is Hypercompetition Making the Best of Times Shorter?" *Strategic Management Journal* (October 2005), pp. 887–911.

24. T. M. Burton, "Archer-Daniels Faces a Potential Blow as Three Firms Admit Price-Fixing Plot," *The Wall Street Journal* (August 28, 1996), pp. A3, A6; R. Henkoff, "The ADM Tale Gets Even Stranger," *Fortune* (May 13, 1996), pp. 113–120.

25. M. McCann, "Proving that NFL Teams Agreed to a Secret Salary Cap Will Not Be Easy," *Sports Illustrated* (May 24, 2012), (http://sportsillustrated.cnn.com/2012/writers/michael_mccann/05/23/nfl/index.html).

26. Much of the content on cooperative strategies was summarized from J. B. Barney, *Gaining and Sustaining Competitive Advantage* (Reading, MA: Addison-Wesley, 1997), pp. 255–278.

27. A. C. Inkpen and E. W. K. Tsang, "Learning and Strategic Alliances," *Academy of Management Annals* (Vol. 1, December 2007), J. F. Walsh and A. F. Brief (Eds.), pp. 479–511.

28. R. D. Ireland, M. A. Hitt, and D. Vaidyanath, "Alliance Management as a Source of Competitive Advantage," *Journal of Management* (Vol. 28, No. 3, 2002), pp. 413–446.

29. S. H. Park and G. R. Ungson, "Interfirm Rivalry and Managerial Complexity: A Conceptual Framework of Alliance Failure," *Organization Science* (January–February 2001), pp. 37–53.; D. C. Hambrick, J. Li, K. Xin, and A. S. Tsui, "Compositional Gaps and Downward Spirals in International Joint Venture Management Groups," *Strategic Management Journal* (November 2001), pp. 1033–1053; T. K. Das and B. S. Teng, "Instabilities of Strategic Alliances: An Internal Tensions Perspective," *Organization Science* (January–February 2000),

pp. 77–101; J. F. Hennart, D. J. Kim, and M. Zeng, "The Impact of Joint Venture Status on the Longevity of Japanese Stakes in U.S. Manufacturing Affiliates," *Organization Science* (May–June 1998), pp. 382–395.

30. N. K. Park, J. M. Mezias, and J. Song, "A Resource-Based View of Strategic Alliances and Firm Value in the Electronic Marketplace," *Journal of Management* (Vol. 30, No. 1, 2004), pp. 7–27; T. Khanna and J. W. Rivkin, "Estimating the Performance Effects of Business Groups in Emerging Markets," *Strategic Management Journal* (January 2001), pp. 45–74; G. Garai, "Leveraging the Rewards of Strategic Alliances," *Journal of Business Strategy* (March–April 1999), pp. 40–43.

31. L. Segil, "Strategic Alliances for the 21st Century," *Strategy & Leadership* (September/October 1998), pp. 12–16.

32. R. C. Sampson, "Experience Effects and Collaborative Returns in R&D Alliances," *Strategic Management Journal* (November 2005), pp. 1009–1031; J. Draulans, A-P de Man, and H. W. Volberda, "Building Alliance Capability: Management Techniques for Superior Alliance Performance," *Long Range Planning* (April 2003), pp. 151–166; P. Kale, J. H. Dyer, and H. Singh, "Alliance Capability, Stock Market Response, and Long-Term Alliance Success: The Role of the Alliance Function," *Strategic Management Journal* (August 2002), pp. 747–767.

33. H. Hoang and F. T. Rothaermel, "The Effect of General and Partner-Specific Alliance Experience on Joint R&D Project Performance," *Academy of Management Journal* (April 2005), pp. 332–345; A. Goerzen, "Alliance Networks and Firm Performance: The Impact of Repeated Partnerships," *Strategic Management Journal* (May 2007), pp. 487–509.

34. A. MacCormack and T. Forbath, "Learning the Fine Art of Global Collaboration," *Harvard Business Review* (January 2008), pp. 24–26.

35. "Hallmark Announces Strategic Alliance with Shutterfly," *PR Newswire* (June 20, 2012), (http://www.prnewswire.com/news-releases/hallmark-announces-strategic-alliance-with-shutterfly-159781365.html).

36. H. Bapuji and M. Crossan, "Knowledge Types and Knowledge Management Strategies," in M. Gibbert and T. Durand (Eds.) *Strategic Networks: Learning to Compete* (Malden, MA: Blackwell Publishing, 2007), pp. 8–25; F. T. Rothaermel and W. Boeker, "Old Technology Meets New Technology: Complementarities, Similarities, and Alliance Formation," *Strategic Management Journal* (January 2008), pp. 47–77.

37. M. M. Bear, "How Japanese Partners Help U.S. Manufacturers to Raise Productivity," *Long Range Planning* (December 1998), pp. 919–926.

38. According to M. J. Thome of Rockwell Collins in a June 26, 2008, e-mail, these are called "international offsets."

39. P. Anslinger and J. Jenk, "Creating Successful Alliances," *Journal of Business Strategy* (Vol. 25, No. 2, 2004), p. 18.

40. X. Yin and M. Shanley, "Industry Determinants of the 'Merger Versus Alliance' Decision," *Academy of Management Review* (April 2008), pp. 473–491.

41. J. W. Lu and P. W. Beamish, "The Internationalization and Performance of SMEs," *Strategic Management Journal* (June–July 2001), pp. 565–586.

42. R. M. Kanter, "Collaborative Advantage: The Art of Alliances," *Harvard Business Review* (July–August 1994), pp. 96–108.

43. "The Cell of the New Machine," *The Economist* (February 12, 2005), pp. 77–78.

44. R. P. Lynch, *The Practical Guide to Joint Ventures and Corporate Alliances* (New York: John Wiley and Sons, 1989), p. 7.

45. "Will She, Won't She?" *The Economist* (August 11, 2007), pp. 61–63.

46. Y Gong, O Shenkar, Y. Luo, and M-K Nyaw, "Do Multiple Parents Help or Hinder International Joint Venture Performance? The Mediating Roles of Contract Completeness and Partner Cooperation," *Strategic Management Journal* (October 2007), pp. 1021–1034.

47. L. L. Blodgett, "Factors in the Instability of International Joint Ventures: An Event History Analysis," *Strategic Management Journal* (September 1992), pp. 475–481; J. Bleeke and D. Ernst, "The Way to Win in Cross-Border Alliances," *Harvard Business Review* (November–December 1991), pp. 127–135; J. M. Geringer, "Partner Selection Criteria for Developed Country Joint Ventures," in H. W. Lane and J. J. DiStephano (Eds.), *International Management Behavior*, 2nd ed. (Boston: PWS-Kent, 1992), pp. 206–216.

48. Schreiner, B. 2012, "YUM Brands Posts Rare Profit Setback in China," *USA Today* (July 18, 2012), (http://www.usatoday.com/money/companies/earnings/story/2012-07-18/yum-brands-earnings/56321222/1).

49. B. Horovitz, "New Coffee Maker May Jolt Industry," *USA Today* (February 18, 2004), pp. 1E–2E.

50. K. Z. Andrews, "Manufacturer/Supplier Relationships: The Supplier Payoff," *Harvard Business Review* (September–October 1995), pp. 14–15.

51. P. Lorange, "Black-Box Protection of Your Core Competencies in Strategic Alliances," in P. W. Beamish and J. P. Killing (Eds.), *Cooperative Strategies: European Perspectives* (San Francisco: The New Lexington Press, 1997), pp. 59–99.

52. E. P. Gee, "Co-opetition: The New Market Milieu," *Journal of Healthcare Management* (Vol. 45, 2000), pp. 359–363.

53. "Make Love—and War," *The Economist* (August 9, 2008), pp. 57–58.

54. D. J. Ketchen Jr., C. C. Snow, and V. L. Hoover, "Research on Competitive Dynamics: Recent Accomplishments and Future Challenges," *Journal of Management* (Vol. 30, No. 6, 2004), pp. 779–804.

CHAPTER 7

strategy formulation:
Corporate Strategy

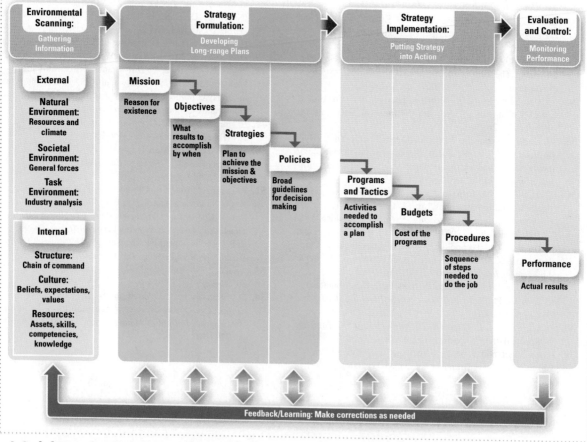

Environmental Scanning:	Strategy Formulation:	Strategy Implementation:	Evaluation and Control:
Gathering Information	Developing Long-range Plans	Putting Strategy into Action	Monitoring Performance

External

Natural Environment: Resources and climate

Societal Environment: General forces

Task Environment: Industry analysis

Internal

Structure: Chain of command

Culture: Beliefs, expectations, values

Resources: Assets, skills, competencies, knowledge

Mission — Reason for existence

Objectives — What results to accomplish by when

Strategies — Plan to achieve the mission & objectives

Policies — Broad guidelines for decision making

Programs and Tactics — Activities needed to accomplish a plan

Budgets — Cost of the programs

Procedures — Sequence of steps needed to do the job

Performance — Actual results

Feedback/Learning: Make corrections as needed

MyManagementLab®

⭐ **Improve Your Grade!**

Over 10 million students improved their results using the Pearson MyLabs. Visit **mymanagementlab.com** for simulations, tutorials, and end-of-chapter problems.

Learning Objectives

After reading this chapter, you should be able to:

- Understand the three aspects of corporate strategy
- Apply the directional strategies of growth, stability, and retrenchment
- Understand the differences between vertical and horizontal growth as well as concentric and conglomerate diversification

- Identify strategic options to enter a foreign country
- Apply portfolio analysis to guide decisions in companies with multiple products and businesses
- Develop a parenting strategy for a multiple-business corporation

How Does a Company Grow if Its Primary Business Is Maturing?

Pfizer Remakes the Company

Pfizer, Inc. was founded in 1849 by Charles Pfizer and Charles Erhart. The company was the breakthrough leader in the development of the means for producing Penicillin on a large scale. In fact, most of the Penicillin carried by troops on D-Day in 1944 was made by Pfizer. The company became a major research lab for the development of drugs. In 1972, Pfizer increased funding of research and development from 5% of sales (an astounding figure in any industry) to 20% of sales. The company viewed its mission as discovering and developing innovative pharmaceuticals. By 2011, the company had sales of US$67.4 billion but had also absorbed several very large acquisitions from 1999–2009, including Wyeth, Warner-Lambert, and Pharmacia. A number of blockbuster drugs had or were coming off patent protection and new ones were becoming increasingly difficult to find. Most of the diseases that still lacked effective treatment, such as Alzheimer's, were more complicated.

By 2012, new drug successes were becoming increasingly difficult to find. The company poured US$2.8 billion into an inhalable insulin (Exubera) and a cholesterol-reducing replacement for Lipitor (Torcetrapib), but both failed to take hold in the market. History has shown that only 16% of drugs under development ever get regulatory approval.

In a bold move, Pfizer's CEO, Ian Read, made the decision in 2012 to consolidate around five areas: cardiovascular diseases, cancer, neuroscience, vaccines, and inflammation/immunology. Redirecting resources in the company, Pfizer closed the famed Sandwich, England, research campus (the birthplace of Viagra) laying off more than 2000 employees because its focus was on areas not included in the new direction of the company. It then divested its animal health and infant nutrition businesses. It also cut more than 3000 research jobs at its flagship New London, Connecticut, campus.

All of the cuts were being plowed back into one of the five areas the company will focus on in the future. This type of corporate repositioning is a hallmark of portfolio management and the techniques described in this chapter.

SOURCES: "Pfizer Embarks on an Overdue Crash Diet," *Bloomberg Businessweek* (March 12, 2012), pp. 24–25; http://www.pfizer.com/about/history/history.jsp; http://www.pfizer.com/about/history/1951_1999.jsp.

Corporate Strategy

The vignette about Pfizer illustrates the importance of corporate strategy to a firm's survival and success. Corporate strategy addresses three key issues facing the corporation as a whole:

1. The firm's overall orientation toward growth, stability, or retrenchment (**directional strategy**)
2. The industries or markets in which the firm competes through its products and business units (**portfolio analysis**)
3. The manner in which management coordinates activities and transfers resources and cultivates capabilities among product lines and business units (**parenting strategy**)

Corporate strategy is primarily about the choice of direction for a firm as a whole and the management of its business or product portfolio.[1] This is true whether the firm is a small company or a large multinational corporation (MNC). In a large multiple-business company, in particular, corporate strategy is concerned with managing various product lines and business units for maximum value. In this instance, corporate headquarters must play the role of the organizational "parent," in that it must deal with various product and business unit "children." Even though each product line or business unit has its own competitive or cooperative strategy that it uses to obtain its own competitive advantage in the marketplace, the corporation must coordinate these different business strategies so that the corporation as a whole succeeds as a "family."[2]

Corporate strategy, therefore, includes decisions regarding the flow of financial and other resources to and from a company's product lines and business units. Through a series of coordinating devices, a company transfers skills and capabilities developed in one unit to other units that need such resources. In this way, it attempts to obtain synergy among numerous product lines and business units so that the corporate whole is greater than the sum of its individual business unit parts.[3] All corporations, from the smallest company offering one product in only one industry to the largest conglomerate operating in many industries with many products, must at one time or another consider one or more of these issues.

To deal with each of the key issues, this chapter is organized into three parts that examine corporate strategy in terms of *directional strategy* (orientation toward growth), *portfolio analysis* (coordination of cash flow among units), and *corporate parenting* (the building of corporate synergies through resource sharing and development).[4]

Directional Strategy

Just as every product or business unit must follow a business strategy to improve its competitive position, every corporation must decide its orientation toward growth by asking the following three questions:

1. Should we expand, cut back, or continue our operations unchanged?

2. Should we concentrate our activities within our current industry, or should we diversify into other industries?

3. If we want to grow and expand nationally and/or globally, should we do so through internal development or through external acquisitions, mergers, or strategic alliances?

A corporation's **directional strategy** is composed of three general orientations (sometimes called *grand strategies*):

- **Growth strategies** expand the company's activities.
- **Stability strategies** make no change to the company's current activities.
- **Retrenchment strategies** reduce the company's level of activities.

Having chosen the general orientation (such as growth), a company's managers can select from several more specific corporate strategies such as concentration within one product line/industry or diversification into other products/industries. (See **Figure 7–1**.) These strategies are useful both to corporations operating in only one industry with one product line and to those operating in many industries with many product lines.

GROWTH STRATEGIES

By far, the most widely pursued corporate directional strategies are those designed to achieve growth in sales, assets, profits, or some combination of these. Companies that do business in expanding industries must grow to survive. Continuing growth means increasing sales and a chance to take advantage of the experience curve to reduce the per-unit cost of products sold, thereby increasing profits. This cost reduction becomes extremely important if a corporation's industry is growing quickly or consolidating and if competitors are engaging in price wars in attempts to increase their shares of the market. Firms that have not reached "critical mass" (that is, gained the necessary economy of large-scale production) face large losses unless they can find and fill a small, but profitable, niche where higher prices can be offset by special product or service features. That is why Oracle has been on the acquisition trail for the past seven years. In that time period, Oracle acquired 85 businesses in a wide variety of areas. Although still growing, the software industry is maturing around a handful of large firms. According to CEO Larry Ellison, Oracle needed to double or even triple in size by buying smaller and weaker rivals if it wants to compete with SAP and Microsoft.[5] Growth is a popular strategy because larger businesses tend to survive longer than smaller companies due to the greater availability of financial resources, organizational routines, and external ties.[6]

A corporation can grow internally by expanding its operations both globally and domestically, or it can grow externally through mergers, acquisitions, and strategic alliances. In practice, the line between mergers and acquisitions has been blurred to the point where it is

FIGURE 7–1 **Corporate Directional Strategies**

• GROWTH	• STABILITY	• RETRENCHMENT

Concentration
  Vertical Growth
  Horizontal Growth
Diversification
  Concentric
  Conglomerate
	Pause/Proceed with Caution
	No Change
	Profit
		Turnaround
		Captive Company
		Sell-Out/Divestment
		Bankruptcy/Liquidation

difficult to tell the difference. In general, we regard a **merger** as a transaction involving two or more corporations in which both companies exchange stock in order to create one new corporation. Mergers that occur between firms of somewhat similar size are referred to as a "merger of equals." Most mergers are "friendly"—that is, both parties believe it is in their best interests to combine their companies. The resulting firm is likely to have a name derived from its composite firms. One example is the merging of Allied Corporation and Signal Companies to form Allied Signal. An **acquisition** is a 100% purchase of another company. In some cases, the company continues to operate as an independent entity and in others it is completely absorbed as an operating subsidiary or division of the acquiring corporation. In July 2012, Duke Energy acquired Progress Energy, making the latter a wholly owned unit of Duke Energy. With the acquisition, Duke Energy became the largest utility in the United States.[7] Acquisitions usually occur between firms of different sizes and can be either friendly or hostile. Hostile acquisitions are often called *takeovers*.

From management's perspective (but perhaps not a stockholder's), growth is very attractive for two key reasons:

- Growth based on increasing market demand may mask flaws in a company—flaws that would be immediately evident in a stable or declining market. A growing flow of revenue into a highly leveraged corporation can create a large amount of *organization slack* (unused resources) that can be used to quickly resolve problems and conflicts between departments and divisions. Growth also provides a big cushion for turnaround in case a strategic error is made. Larger firms also have more bargaining power than do small firms and are more likely to obtain support from key stakeholders in case of difficulty.

- A growing firm offers more opportunities for advancement, promotion, and interesting jobs. Growth itself is exciting and ego-enhancing for everyone. The marketplace and potential investors tend to view a growing corporation as a "winner" or "on the move." Executive compensation tends to get bigger as an organization increases in size. Large firms are also more difficult to acquire than smaller ones—thus, an executive's job in a large firm is more secure.

The two basic growth strategies are **concentration** on the current product line(s) in one industry and **diversification** into other product lines in other industries.

Concentration

If a company's current product lines have real growth potential, the concentration of resources on those product lines makes sense as a strategy for growth. The two basic concentration strategies are vertical growth and horizontal growth. Growing firms in a growing industry tend to choose these strategies before they try diversification.

Vertical Growth. **Vertical growth** can be achieved by taking over a function previously provided by a supplier or distributor. The company, in effect, grows by making its own supplies and/or by distributing its own products. This may be done in order to reduce costs, gain control over a scarce resource, guarantee quality of a key input, or obtain access to potential customers. This growth can be achieved either internally by expanding current operations or externally through acquisitions. Henry Ford, for example, used internal company resources to build his River Rouge plant outside Detroit. The manufacturing process was integrated to the point that iron ore entered one end of the long plant, and finished automobiles rolled out the other end into a huge parking lot. In contrast, Cisco Systems, a maker of Internet hardware, chose the external route to vertical growth by purchasing Scientific-Atlanta Inc., a maker of set-top boxes for television programs and movies-on-demand. This acquisition gave Cisco access to technology for distributing television to living rooms through the Internet.[8]

Vertical growth results in **vertical integration**—the degree to which a firm operates vertically in multiple locations on an industry's value chain from extracting raw materials to manufacturing to retailing. More specifically, assuming a function previously provided by a supplier is called **backward integration** (going backward on an industry's value chain). The purchase of Carroll's Foods for its hog-growing facilities by Smithfield Foods, the world's largest pork processor, is an example of backward integration.[9] Assuming a function previously provided by a distributor is labeled **forward integration** (going forward on an industry's value chain). FedEx, for example, used forward integration when it purchased Kinko's in order to provide store-front package drop-off and delivery services for the small-business market.[10]

Vertical growth is a logical strategy for a corporation or business unit with a strong competitive position in a highly attractive industry—especially when technology is predictable and markets are growing.[11] To keep and even improve its competitive position, a company may use backward integration to minimize resource acquisition costs and inefficient operations, as well as forward integration to gain more control over product distribution. The firm, in effect, builds on its distinctive competence by expanding along the industry's value chain to gain greater competitive advantage.

Although backward integration is often more profitable than forward integration (because of typical low margins in retailing), it can reduce a corporation's strategic flexibility. The resulting encumbrance of expensive assets that might be hard to sell could create an exit barrier, preventing the corporation from leaving that particular industry. Examples of single-use assets are blast furnaces and refineries. When demand drops in either of these industries (steel or oil and gas), these assets have no alternative use, but continue to cost money in terms of debt payments, property taxes, and security expenses.

Transaction cost economics proposes that vertical integration is more efficient than contracting for goods and services in the marketplace when the transaction costs of buying goods on the open market become too great. When highly vertically integrated firms become excessively large and bureaucratic, however, the costs of managing the internal transactions may become greater than simply purchasing the needed goods externally—thus justifying outsourcing over vertical integration. This is why vertical integration and outsourcing are situation specific. Neither approach is best for all companies in all situations.[12] See the **Strategy Highlight** feature on how transaction cost economics helps explain why firms vertically integrate or outsource important activities. Research thus far provides mixed support for the predictions of transaction cost economics.[13]

Harrigan proposes that a company's degree of vertical integration can range from total ownership of the value chain needed to make and sell a product to no ownership at all.[14] (See **Figure 7-2**.) Under **full integration**, a firm internally makes 100% of its key supplies and completely controls its distributors. Large oil companies, such as British Petroleum and Royal Dutch Shell, are fully integrated. They own the oil rigs that pump the oil out of the ground, the ships and pipelines that transport the oil, the refineries that convert the oil to gasoline, and the trucks that deliver the gasoline to company-owned and franchised gas

FIGURE 7–2 Vertical Integration Continuum

Full Integration	Taper Integration	Quasi-Integration	Long-Term Contract

SOURCE: *Suggested by K. R. Harrigan, Strategies for Vertical Integration* (Lexington, MA: Lexington Books, D.C. Heath, 1983), pp. 16–21.

stations. Sherwin-Williams Company, which not only manufactures paint, but also sells it in its own chain of 3000 retail stores, is another example of a fully integrated firm.[15] If a corporation does not want the disadvantages of full vertical integration, it may choose either taper or quasi-integration strategies.

With **taper integration** (also called concurrent sourcing), a firm internally produces less than half of its own requirements and buys the rest from outside suppliers (backward taper integration).[16] In the case of Smithfield Foods, its purchase of Carroll's allowed it to produce 27% of the hogs it needed to process into pork. In terms of forward taper integration, a firm sells part of its goods through company-owned stores and the rest through general wholesalers. Although Apple had 246 of its own retail stores in 2012, much of the company's sales continued to be through national chains such as Best Buy and through independent local and regional dealers.

With **quasi-integration**, a company does not make any of its key supplies but purchases most of its requirements from outside suppliers that are under its partial control (backward quasi-integration). A company may not want to purchase outright a supplier or distributor, but it still may want to guarantee access to needed supplies, new products, technologies, or distribution channels. For example, the pharmaceutical company Bristol-Myers Squibb purchased 17% of the common stock of ImClone in order to gain access to new drug products being developed through biotechnology. An example of forward quasi-integration would be a paper company acquiring part interest in an office products chain in order to guarantee that its products had access to the distribution channel. Purchasing part interest in another company usually provides a company with a seat on the other firm's board of directors, thus guaranteeing the acquiring firm both information and control. As in the case of Bristol-Myers Squibb and ImClone, a quasi-integrated firm may later decide to buy the rest of a key supplier that it did not already own.[17]

Long-term contracts are agreements between two firms to provide agreed-upon goods and services to each other for a specified period of time. This cannot really be considered to be vertical integration unless it is an *exclusive* contract that specifies that the supplier or distributor cannot have a similar relationship with a competitive firm. In that case, the supplier or distributor is really a *captive company* that, although officially independent, does most of its business with the contracted firm and is formally tied to the other company through a long-term contract.

Recently, there has been a movement away from vertical growth strategies (and thus vertical integration) toward cooperative contractual relationships with suppliers and even with competitors.[18] These relationships range from *outsourcing*, in which resources are purchased from outsiders through long-term contracts instead of being done in-house (Coca-Cola Enterprises eliminated jobs in three U.S. centers by contracting with Capgemini for accounting and financial services), to strategic alliances, in which partnerships, technology licensing agreements, and joint ventures supplement a firm's capabilities (Toshiba has used strategic alliances with GE, Siemens, Motorola, and Ericsson to become one of the world's leading electronic companies).[19]

Horizontal Growth. A firm can achieve **horizontal growth** by expanding its operations into other geographic locations and/or by increasing the range of products and services offered to current markets. Research indicates that firms that grow horizontally by broadening their product lines have high survival rates.[20] Horizontal growth results in **horizontal integration**—the degree to which a firm operates in multiple geographic locations at the same point on an industry's value chain. For example, Procter & Gamble (P&G) continually adds additional sizes and multiple variations to its existing product lines to reduce possible niches that competitors may enter. In addition, it introduces successful products from one part of the world to other regions. P&G has been introducing into China a steady stream of popular

STRATEGY highlight

TRANSACTION COST ECONOMICS ANALYZES VERTICAL GROWTH STRATEGY

Why do corporations use vertical growth to permanently own suppliers or distributors when they could simply purchase individual items when needed on the open market? Transaction cost economics is a branch of institutional economics that attempts to answer this question. Transaction cost economics proposes that owning resources through vertical growth is more efficient than contracting for goods and services in the marketplace when the transaction costs of buying goods on the open market become too great. Transaction costs include the basic costs of drafting, negotiating, and safeguarding a market agreement (a contract) as well as the later managerial costs when the agreement is creating problems (goods aren't being delivered on time or quality is lower than needed), renegotiation costs (e.g., costs of meetings and phone calls), and the costs of settling disputes (e.g., lawyers' fees and court costs).

According to Williamson, three conditions must be met before a corporation will prefer internalizing a vertical transaction through ownership over contracting for the transaction in the marketplace: (1) a high level of uncertainty must surround the transaction, (2) assets involved in the transaction must be highly specialized to the transaction, and (3) the transaction must occur frequently. If there is a high level of uncertainty, it will be impossible to write a contract covering all contingencies, and it is likely that the contractor will act opportunistically to exploit any gaps in the written agreement—thus creating problems and increasing costs. If the assets being contracted for are highly specialized (e.g., goods or services with few alternate uses), there are likely to be few alternative suppliers—thus allowing the contractor to take advantage of the situation and increase costs. The more frequent the transactions, the more opportunity for the contractor to demand special treatment and thus increase costs further.

Vertical integration is not always more efficient than the marketplace, however. When highly vertically integrated firms become excessively large and bureaucratic, the costs of managing the internal transactions may become greater than simply purchasing the needed goods externally—thus justifying outsourcing over ownership. The usually hidden management costs (e.g., excessive layers of management, endless committee meetings needed for interdepartmental coordination, and delayed decision making due to excessively detailed rules and policies) add to the internal transaction costs—thus reducing the effectiveness and efficiency of vertical integration. The decision to own or to outsource is, therefore, based on the particular situation surrounding the transaction and the ability of the corporation to manage the transaction internally both effectively and efficiently.

SOURCES: O. E. Williamson and S. G. Winter (Eds.), *The Nature of the Firm: Origins, Evolution, and Development* (New York: Oxford University Press, 1991); E. Mosakowski, "Organizational Boundaries and Economic Performance: An Empirical Study of Entrepreneurial Computer Firms," *Strategic Management Journal* (February 1991), pp. 115–133; P. S. Ring and A. H. Van de Ven, "Structuring Cooperative Relationships Between Organizations," *Strategic Management Journal* (October 1992), pp. 483–498.

American brands, such as Head & Shoulders, Crest, Olay, Tide, Pampers, and Whisper. By 2012, it had sales of more than US$6 billion in China, and 10 manufacturing plants.[21]

Horizontal growth can be achieved through internal development or externally through acquisitions and strategic alliances with other firms in the same industry. For example, Delta Airlines acquired Northwest Airlines in 2008 to obtain access to Northwest's Asian markets and those American markets that Delta was not then serving. In contrast, many small commuter airlines engage in long-term contracts with major airlines in order to offer a complete arrangement for travelers. For example, the regional carrier Mesa Airlines arranged contractual agreements with United Airlines and U.S. Airways to be listed on their computer reservations, respectively, as United Express and U.S. Airways Express.

Horizontal growth is increasingly being achieved in today's world through international expansion. America's Wal-Mart, France's Carrefour, and Britain's Tesco are examples of national supermarket discount chains expanding horizontally throughout the world. This type of growth can be achieved internationally through many different strategies.

INTERNATIONAL ENTRY OPTIONS FOR HORIZONTAL GROWTH

Research indicates that growing internationally is positively associated with firm profitability.[22] A corporation can select from several strategic options the most appropriate method for entering a foreign market or establishing manufacturing facilities in another country. The options vary from simple exporting to acquisitions to management contracts. See the **Global Issue** feature to see how U.S.-based firms do not always succeed when using international entry options in a horizontal growth strategy to expand throughout the world.

Some of the most popular options for international entry are as follows:

- **Exporting:** A good way to minimize risk and experiment with a specific product is **exporting**, shipping goods produced in the company's home country to other countries for marketing. The company could choose to handle all critical functions itself, or it could contract these functions to an export management company. Exporting is becoming increasingly popular for small businesses because of the Internet, fax machines, toll-free numbers, and overnight express services, which reduce the once-formidable costs of going international.

- **Licensing:** Under a **licensing** agreement, the licensing firm grants rights to another firm in the host country to produce and/or sell a product. The licensee pays compensation to the licensing firm in return for technical expertise. This is an especially useful strategy if the trademark or brand name is well known but the company does not have sufficient

GLOBAL issue

GLOBAL EXPANSION IS NOT ALWAYS A PATH TO EXPANSION

The mantra in U.S. business growth for the past few decades has been to look to international markets for growth, and especially to China. Company after company poured into China with their successful U.S. business models and touted their global growth plans. Entering a new market, and especially a new market that is in a new country, often requires an adjustment to the nuances of that market.

McDonald's learned that lesson long ago when it modified its menu for the Indian market by eliminating pork and beef products and offering such unique offerings as the McAloo Tikkiburger with a mashed potato patty and the McPuff, which is a vegetable and cheese pastry. In China-based McDonald's outlets, a favorite drink is "bubble tea," which is tea with tapioca balls in the bottom. Unfortunately, many large U.S. companies are pulling out of China completely or are having to completely rewrite their business models in order to succeed.

Home Depot Inc. closed all seven of its remaining Chinese big-box stores in 2012 (they started with 12 stores through an acquisition in 2006). Unlike the U.S. market, the Chinese consumer is far more interested in finished goods and paying someone to complete a project than they are in doing it

themselves. IKEA struggled for years in the Chinese market until they began offering assembly and delivery services. The DIY (do-it-yourself) market does not appear to translate well into some cultures.

Best Buy closed all of its nine stores in 2011 after discovering that Chinese consumers were far more interested in appliances than its predominantly entertainment-based product line. Best Buy is now experimenting with a small-sized appliance store.

This is not to say that some businesses don't translate easily. Yum Brands Inc. has opened nearly 4000 KFC and Pizza Hut outlets in the past few years following its business model (much like McDonald's) but modifying the approach (which is selling fast food) to its market. KFC sells egg tarts and soy milk in China while not offering those menu items outside the Chinese market.

Global success is a function of many different elements. Some businesses that are wildly successful in their home country will not find an easy path to growth in international expansion.

SOURCES: "McDonald's Going Vegetarian," *Bloomberg Businessweek* (September 10, 2012), p. 30; L. Burkitt, "Home Depot: Chinese Prefer Do-It-for-Me,'" *The Wall Street Journal* (September 15, 2012), p. B1.

funds to finance its entering the country directly. AB InBev used this strategy to produce and market Budweiser beer in the United Kingdom, Japan, Israel, Australia, Korea, and the Philippines. This strategy is also important if the country makes entry via investment either difficult or impossible.

■ **Franchising:** Under a **franchising** agreement, the franchiser grants rights to another company to open a retail store using the franchiser's name and operating system. In exchange, the franchisee pays the franchiser a percentage of its sales as a royalty. Franchising provides an opportunity for a firm to establish a presence in countries where the population or per capita spending is not sufficient for a major expansion effort.[23] Franchising accounts for 32% of total U.S. retail sales. Close to half of U.S. franchisers, such as Yum! Brands, franchise internationally.[24]

■ **Joint ventures:** Forming a **joint venture** between a foreign corporation and a domestic company is the most popular strategy used to enter a new country.[25] Companies often form joint ventures to combine the resources and expertise needed to develop new products or technologies. A joint venture may be an association between a company and a firm in the host country or a government agency in that country. A quick method of obtaining local management, it also reduces the risks of expropriation and harassment by host country officials. A joint venture may also enable a firm to enter a country that restricts foreign ownership. The corporation can enter another country with fewer assets at stake and thus lower risk. Under Indian law, for example, foreign retailers are permitted to own no more than 51% of shops selling single-brand products, or to sell to others on a wholesale basis. These and other restrictions deterred supermarket giants Tesco and Carrefour from entering India. As a result, 97% of Indian retailing is composed of small, family-run stores. Eager to enter India, Wal-Mart's management formed an equal partnership joint venture in 2007 with Bharti Enterprises to start wholesale operations. Under the name Best Price, the new company had opened 17 retail stores by 2012 and had plans to open 5 more stores before the end of 2012.[26]

■ **Acquisitions:** A relatively quick way to move into an international area is through acquisitions—purchasing another company already operating in that area. Synergistic benefits can result if the company acquires a firm with strong complementary product lines and a good distribution network. For example, Belgium's InBev purchased Anheuser-Busch in 2008 for US$52 billion to obtain a solid position in the profitable North American beer market. Before the acquisition, InBev had only a small presence in the U.S., but a strong one in Europe and Latin American, where Anheuser-Busch was weak.[27] Research suggests that wholly owned subsidiaries are more successful in international undertakings than are strategic alliances, such as joint ventures.[28] This is one reason why firms more experienced in international markets take a higher ownership position when making a foreign investment.[29] Cross-border acquisitions by U.S. firms amounted to more than US$930 billion in 2011, up almost 11% from 2010.[30] In some countries, however, acquisitions can be difficult to arrange because of a lack of available information about potential candidates. Government restrictions on ownership, such as the U.S. requirement that limits foreign ownership of U.S. airlines to 49% of nonvoting and 25% of voting stock, can also discourage acquisitions.

■ **Green-field development:** If a company doesn't want to purchase another company's problems along with its assets, it may choose **green-field development** and build its own manufacturing plant and distribution system. Research indicates that firms possessing high levels of technology, multinational experience, and diverse product lines prefer green-field development to acquisitions.[31] This is usually a far more complicated and expensive operation than acquisition, but it allows a company more freedom in designing the plant, choosing suppliers, and hiring a workforce. For example, Nissan, Honda, and

Toyota built auto factories in rural areas of Great Britain and then hired a young work-force with no experience in the industry. BMW did the same thing when it built its auto plant in Spartanburg, South Carolina, to make its Z3 and Z4 sports cars.

- **Production sharing:** Coined by Peter Drucker, the term **production sharing** means the process of combining the higher labor skills and technology available in developed countries with the lower-cost labor available in developing countries. Often called *outsourcing*, one example is Maytag's moving some of its refrigeration production to a new plant in Reynosa, Mexico, in order to reduce labor costs. Many companies have moved data processing, programming, and customer service activities "offshore" to Ireland, India, Barbados, Jamaica, the Philippines, and Singapore, where wages are lower, English is spoken, and telecommunications are in place. IBM's U.S. workforce dropped by almost 30,000 employees in the past decade and now numbers less than 105,000, while its Indian workforce grew by 9000 to 75,000. Now, less than one-fourth of the people it employs worldwide are in the United States.[32]

- **Turnkey operations: Turnkey operations** are typically contracts for the construction of operating facilities in exchange for a fee. The facilities are transferred to the host country or firm when they are complete. The customer is usually a government agency of, for example, a Middle East country that has decreed that a particular product must be produced locally and under its control. For example, Fiat built an auto plant in Tagliatti, Russia, for the Soviet Union in the late 1960s to produce an older model of Fiat under the brand name of Lada. MNCs that perform turnkey operations are frequently industrial equipment manufacturers that supply some of their own equipment for the project and that commonly sell replacement parts and maintenance services to the host country. They thereby create customers as well as future competitors. Interestingly, Renault purchased a 25% stake in the same Tagliatti factory built by Fiat to help the Russian carmaker modernize, using Renault's low-cost Logan as the base for the plant's new Lada model.[33]

- **BOT concept:** The **BOT (Build, Operate, Transfer) concept** is a variation of the turnkey operation. Instead of turning the facility (usually a power plant or toll road) over to the host country when completed, the company operates the facility for a fixed period of time during which it earns back its investment, plus a profit. It then turns the facility over to the government at little or no cost to the host country.[34]

- **Management contracts:** A large corporation operating throughout the world is likely to have a large amount of management talent at its disposal. **Management contracts** offer a means through which a corporation can use some of its personnel to assist a firm in a host country for a specified fee and period of time. Management contracts are common when a host government expropriates part or all of a foreign-owned company's holdings in its country. The contracts allow the firm to continue to earn some income from its investment and keep the operations going until local management is trained.[35]

Diversification Strategies

According to strategist Richard Rumelt, companies begin thinking about diversification when their growth has plateaued and opportunities for growth in the original business have been depleted.[36] This often occurs when an industry consolidates, becomes mature, and most of the surviving firms have reached the limits of growth using vertical and horizontal growth strategies. Unless the competitors are able to expand internationally into less mature markets, they may have no choice but to diversify into different industries if they want to continue growing. The two basic diversification strategies are concentric and conglomerate and both require very sophisticated management techniques in order to keep the elements of the company moving in relatively the same direction.

Concentric (Related) Diversification. Growth through **concentric diversification** into a related industry may be a very appropriate corporate strategy when a firm has a strong competitive position but industry attractiveness is low.

Research indicates that the probability of succeeding by moving into a related business is a function of a company's position in its core business. For companies in leadership positions, the chances for success are nearly three times higher than those for followers.[37] By focusing on the characteristics that have given the company its distinctive competence, the company uses those very strengths as its means of diversification. The firm attempts to secure strategic fit in a new industry where the firm's product knowledge, its manufacturing capabilities, and/or the marketing skills it used so effectively in the original industry can be put to good use.[38] The corporation's products or processes are related in some way: They possess some common thread.

The search is for **synergy**, the concept that two businesses will generate more profits together than they could separately. The point of commonality may be similar technology, customer usage, distribution, managerial skills, or product similarity. This is the rationale taken by Quebec-based Bombardier, the world's third-largest aircraft manufacturer. In the 1980s, the company expanded beyond snowmobiles into making light rail equipment. Defining itself as a transportation company, it entered the aircraft business in 1986, with its purchase of Canadair, then best known for its fire-fighting airplanes. It later bought Learjet, a well-known maker of business jets. Over a 14-year period, Bombardier launched 14 new aircraft. In July 2008, the company announced its C Series Aircraft Program to manufacture a 110–130-seat "green" single-aisle family of airplanes to directly compete with Airbus and Boeing. By 2012, the company had received orders for 150 C Series aircraft and the company's goal was to start delivering the aircraft by 2013.[39]

A firm may choose to diversify concentrically through either internal or external means. Bombardier, for example, diversified externally through acquisitions. Toro, in contrast, grew internally in North America by using its current manufacturing processes and distributors to make and market snow blowers in addition to lawn mowers.

Conglomerate (Unrelated) Diversification. When management realizes that the current industry is unattractive and that the firm lacks outstanding abilities or skills that it could easily transfer to related products or services in other industries, the most likely strategy is **conglomerate diversification**—diversifying into an industry unrelated to its current one. Rather than maintaining a common thread throughout their organization, strategic managers who adopt this strategy are primarily concerned with financial considerations of cash flow or risk reduction. This is also a good strategy for a firm when its core capability is its own excellent management systems. General Electric and Berkshire Hathaway are examples of companies that have used conglomerate diversification to grow successfully. Managed by Warren Buffet, Berkshire Hathaway has interests in furniture retailing, railroads, razor blades, airlines, paper, broadcasting, soft drinks, and publishing.[40]

The emphasis in conglomerate diversification is on sound investment and value-oriented management rather than on the product-market synergy common to concentric diversification. A cash-rich company with few opportunities for growth in its industry might, for example, move into another industry where opportunities are great but cash is hard to find. Another instance of conglomerate diversification might be when a company with a seasonal and, therefore, uneven cash flow purchases a firm in an unrelated industry with complementing seasonal sales that will level out the cash flow. CSX management considered the purchase of a natural gas transmission business (Texas Gas Resources) by CSX Corporation (a railroad-dominated transportation company) to be a good fit because most of the gas transmission revenue was realized in the winter months—the lean period in the railroad business.

CONTROVERSIES IN DIRECTIONAL GROWTH STRATEGIES

Is vertical growth better than horizontal growth? Is concentration better than diversification? Is concentric diversification better than conglomerate diversification? Research reveals that companies following a related diversification strategy appear to be higher performers and survive longer than do companies with narrower scope following a pure concentration strategy.[41] Although the research is not in complete agreement, growth into areas related to a company's current product lines is generally more successful than is growth into completely unrelated areas.[42] For example, one study of various growth projects examined how many were considered successful—that is, still in existence after 22 years. The results were vertical growth, 80%; horizontal growth, 50%; concentric diversification, 35%; and conglomerate diversification, 28%.[43] This supports the conclusion from a study of 40 successful European companies that companies should first exploit their existing assets and capabilities before exploring for new ones, but that they should also diversify their portfolio of products.[44]

In terms of diversification strategies, research suggests that the relationship between relatedness and performance follows an inverted U-shaped curve. If a new business is very similar to that of the acquiring firm, it adds little new to the corporation and only marginally improves performance. If the new business is completely different from the acquiring company's businesses, there may be very little potential for any synergy. If, however, the new business provides new resources and capabilities in a different but similar business, the likelihood of a significant performance improvement is high.[45]

Is internal growth better than external growth? Corporations can follow the growth strategies of either concentration or diversification through the internal development of new products and services, or through external acquisitions, mergers, and strategic alliances. The value of global acquisitions and mergers has steadily increased from less than US$1 trillion in 1990 to US$3.1 trillion in 2011.[46] According to a McKinsey & Company survey, managers are primarily motivated to purchase other companies in order to add capabilities, expand geographically, and buy growth.[47] Research generally concludes, however, that firms growing through acquisitions do not perform financially as well as firms that grow through internal means.[48] For example, on September 3, 2001, the day *before* HP announced that it was purchasing Compaq, HP's stock was selling at US$23.11. After the announcement, the stock price fell to US$18.87. Three years later, on September 21, 2004, the shares sold at US$18.70.[49] One reason for this poor performance may be that acquiring firms tend to spend less on R&D than do other firms.[50] Another reason may be the typically high price of the acquisition itself. Studies reveal that over half to two-thirds of acquisitions are failures primarily because the premiums paid were too high for them to earn their cost of capital.[51] Another reason for the poor stock performance is that 50% of the customers of a merged firm are less satisfied with the combined company's service two years after the merger.[52] It is likely that neither strategy is best by itself and that some combination of internal and external growth strategies is better than using one or the other.[53]

What can improve acquisition performance? For one thing, the acquisition should be linked to strategic objectives and support corporate strategy. Some consultants have suggested that a corporation must be prepared to identify roughly 100 candidates and conduct due diligence investigation on around 40 companies in order to ultimately purchase 10 companies. This kind of effort requires the capacity to sift through many candidates while simultaneously integrating previous acquisitions.[54] A study by Bain & Company of more than 11,000 acquisitions by companies throughout the world concluded that successful acquirers make small, low-risk acquisitions before moving on to larger ones.[55] Previous experience between an acquirer and a target firm in terms of R&D, manufacturing, or marketing alliances improves the likelihood of a successful acquisition.[56]

STABILITY STRATEGIES

A corporation may choose stability over growth by continuing its current activities without any significant change in direction. Although sometimes viewed as a lack of strategy, the stability family of corporate strategies can be appropriate for a successful corporation operating in a reasonably predictable environment.[57] They are very popular with small business owners who have found a niche and are happy with their success and the manageable size of their firms. Stability strategies can be very useful in the short run, but they can be dangerous if followed for too long. Some of the more popular of these strategies are the pause/proceed-with-caution, no-change, and profit strategies.

Pause/Proceed-with-Caution Strategy

A **pause/proceed-with-caution strategy** is, in effect, a timeout—an opportunity to rest before continuing a growth or retrenchment strategy. It is a very deliberate attempt to make only incremental improvements until a particular environmental situation changes. It is typically conceived as a temporary strategy to be used until the environment becomes more hospitable or to enable a company to consolidate its resources after prolonged rapid growth. This was the strategy Dell followed after its growth strategy had resulted in more growth than it could handle. Explained CEO Michael Dell, "We grew 285% in two years, and we're having some growing pains." Selling personal computers by mail enabled Dell to underprice competitors, but it could not keep up with the needs of a US$2 billion, 5600-employee company selling PCs in 95 countries. Dell did not give up on its growth strategy though. It merely put it temporarily in limbo until the company was able to hire new managers, improve the structure, and build new facilities.[58] Dell spent the next few years diversifying its revenue base in the face of weakened consumer demand, giving up low-margin computer sales to consumers and moving into higher-margin, higher-cost areas, such as catering to the technology needs of small and medium businesses.[59]

No-Change Strategy

A **no-change strategy** is a decision to do nothing new—a choice to continue current operations and policies for the foreseeable future. Rarely articulated as a definite strategy, a no-change strategy's success depends on a lack of significant change in a corporation's situation. The relative stability created by the firm's modest competitive position in an industry facing little or no growth encourages the company to continue on its current course, making only small adjustments for inflation in its sales and profit objectives. There are no obvious opportunities or threats, nor is there much in the way of significant strengths or weaknesses. Few aggressive new competitors are likely to enter such an industry. The corporation has probably found a reasonably profitable and stable niche for its products. Unless the industry is undergoing consolidation, the relative comfort a company in this situation experiences is likely to encourage the company to follow a no-change strategy in which the future is expected to continue as an extension of the present. Many small-town businesses followed this strategy before Wal-Mart moved into their areas and forced them to rethink their strategy.

Profit Strategy

A **profit strategy** is a decision to do nothing new in a worsening situation but instead to act as though the company's problems are only temporary. The profit strategy is an attempt to artificially support profits when a company's sales are declining by reducing investment and short-term discretionary expenditures. Rather than announce the company's poor position to shareholders and the investment community at large, top management may be tempted to follow this very seductive strategy. Blaming the company's problems on a hostile environment (such as anti-business government policies, unethical competitors, finicky customers, and/or greedy lenders), management defers investments and/or cuts expenses (such as R&D, maintenance, and advertising) to stabilize profits during this period. It may even sell one of its product lines for the cash-flow benefits.

The profit strategy is useful only to help a company get through a temporary difficulty. It may also be a way to boost the value of a company in preparation for going public via an initial public offering (IPO). Unfortunately, the strategy is seductive and if continued long enough it will lead to a serious deterioration in a corporation's competitive position. The profit strategy is typically top management's passive, short-term, and often self-serving response to a difficult situation. In such situations, it is often better to face the problem directly by choosing a retrenchment strategy.

RETRENCHMENT STRATEGIES

A company may pursue retrenchment strategies when it has a weak competitive position in some or all of its product lines resulting in poor performance—sales are down and profits are becoming losses. These strategies impose a great deal of pressure to improve performance. In an attempt to eliminate the weaknesses that are dragging the company down, management may follow one of several retrenchment strategies, ranging from turnaround or becoming a captive company to selling out, bankruptcy, or liquidation.

Turnaround Strategy

Turnaround strategy emphasizes the improvement of operational efficiency and is probably most appropriate when a corporation's problems are pervasive but not yet critical. Research shows that poorly performing firms in mature industries have been able to improve their performance by cutting costs and expenses and by selling off assets.[60] Analogous to a weight-reduction diet, the two basic phases of a turnaround strategy are contraction and consolidation.[61]

Contraction is the initial effort to quickly "stop the bleeding" with a general, across-the-board cutback in size and costs. For example, when Howard Stringer was selected to be CEO of Sony Corporation in 2005, he immediately implemented the first stage of a turnaround plan by eliminating 10,000 jobs, closing 11 of 65 plants, and divesting many unprofitable electronics businesses.[62] The second phase, *consolidation*, implements a program to stabilize the now-leaner corporation. To streamline the company, plans are developed to reduce unnecessary overhead and to make functional activities cost-justified. This is a crucial time for the organization. If the consolidation phase is not conducted in a positive manner, many of the best people leave the organization. An overemphasis on downsizing and cutting costs coupled with a heavy hand by top management is usually counterproductive and can actually hurt performance.[63] If, however, all employees are encouraged to get involved in productivity improvements, the firm is likely to emerge from this retrenchment period a much stronger and better-organized company. It has improved its competitive position and is able once again to expand the business.[64]

Captive Company Strategy

A **captive company strategy** involves giving up independence in exchange for security. A company with a weak competitive position may not be able to engage in a full-blown turnaround strategy. The industry may not be sufficiently attractive to justify such an effort from either the current management or investors. Nevertheless, a company in this situation faces poor sales and increasing losses unless it takes some action. Management desperately searches for an "angel" by offering to be a captive company to one of its larger customers in order to guarantee the company's continued existence with a long-term contract. In this way, the corporation may be able to reduce the scope of some of its functional activities, such as marketing, thus significantly reducing costs. The weaker company gains certainty of sales and production in return for becoming heavily dependent on another firm for at least 75% of its sales. For example, to become the sole supplier of an auto part to General Motors, Simpson Industries of Birmingham, Michigan, agreed to let a special team from GM inspect its engine parts facilities and books and interview its employees. In return, nearly 80% of the company's production was sold to GM through long-term contracts.[65]

Sell-Out/Divestment Strategy

If a corporation with a weak competitive position in an industry is unable either to pull itself up by its bootstraps or to find a customer to which it can become a captive company, it may have no choice but to sell out. The **sell-out strategy** makes sense if management can still obtain a good price for its shareholders and the employees can keep their jobs by selling the entire company to another firm. The hope is that another company will have the necessary resources and determination to return the company to profitability. Marginal performance in a troubled industry was one reason American Airlines was willing to talk to US Airways in 2012.

If the corporation has multiple business lines and it chooses to sell off a division with low growth potential, this is called **divestment**. This was the strategy Ford used when it sold its struggling Jaguar and Land Rover units to Tata Motors in 2008 for US$2 billion. Ford had paid US$2.8 billion for Land Rover in 2000, and had spent US$10 billion trying to turn around Jaguar after spending US$2.5 billion to buy it in 1990.[66] General Electric's management used the same reasoning when it decided to sell or spin off its slow-growth appliance business in 2008.

Divestment is often used after a corporation acquires a multi-unit corporation in order to shed the units that do not fit with the corporation's new strategy. This is why Whirlpool sold Maytag's Hoover vacuum cleaner unit after Whirlpool purchased Maytag. Divestment was also a key part of Lego's turnaround strategy when management decided to divest its theme parks to concentrate more on its core business of making toys.[67]

Bankruptcy/Liquidation Strategy

When a company finds itself in the worst possible situation with a poor competitive position in an industry with few prospects, management has only a few alternatives—all of them distasteful. Because no one is interested in buying a weak company in an unattractive industry, the firm must pursue a bankruptcy or liquidation strategy. **Bankruptcy** involves giving up management of the firm to the courts in return for some settlement of the corporation's obligations. Top management hopes that once the court decides the claims on the company, the company will be stronger and better able to compete in a more attractive industry. Faced with a recessionary economy and increasing costs of operation, American Airlines (AMR) finally succumbed to bankruptcy in 2012. AMR was the only major airline that did not file for bankruptcy reorganization during the early part of the millennia. Its inefficient cost structure put it at a major disadvantage with the newly reorganized competition. It merged with USAir just before emerging from bankruptcy and the new company took the American Airlines name. A controversial approach was used by Delphi Corporation when it filed for Chapter 11 bankruptcy only for its U.S. operations, which employed 32,000 high-wage union workers, but not for its foreign factories in low-wage countries.[68]

In contrast to bankruptcy, which seeks to perpetuate a corporation, **liquidation** is the termination of the firm. When the industry is unattractive and the company too weak to be sold as a going concern, management may choose to convert as many saleable assets as possible to cash, which is then distributed to the shareholders after all obligations are paid. Liquidation is a prudent strategy for distressed firms with a small number of choices, all of which are problematic.[69] This was Circuit City's situation when it liquidated its retail stores. The benefit of liquidation over bankruptcy is that the board of directors, as representatives of the shareholders, together with top management, make the decisions instead of turning them over to the bankruptcy court, which may choose to ignore shareholders completely.

At times, top management must be willing to select one of these less desirable retrenchment strategies. Unfortunately, many top managers are unwilling to admit that their company has serious weaknesses for fear that they may be personally blamed. Even worse, top management may not even perceive that crises are developing. When these top managers eventually notice trouble, they are prone to attribute the problems to temporary environmental disturbances and tend to follow profit strategies. Even when things are going terribly wrong, top management is greatly tempted to avoid liquidation in the hope of a miracle. Top management then enters a *cycle of decline*, in which it goes through a process of secrecy and denial, followed by blame and scorn, avoidance and turf protection, ending with passivity and helplessness.[70] Thus, a corporation needs a strong board of directors who, to safeguard shareholders' interests, can tell top management when to quit.

Portfolio Analysis

Chapter 6 dealt with how individual product lines and business units can gain competitive advantage in the marketplace by using competitive and cooperative strategies. Companies with multiple product lines or business units must also ask themselves how these various products and business units should be managed to boost overall corporate performance:

- How much of our time and money should we spend on our best products and business units to ensure that they continue to be successful?
- How much of our time and money should we spend developing new costly products, most of which will never be successful?

One of the most popular aids to developing corporate strategy in a multiple-business corporation is portfolio analysis. Although its popularity has dropped since the 1970s and 1980s, when more than half of the largest business corporations used portfolio analysis, it is still used by around 27% of Fortune 500 firms in corporate strategy formulation.[71] Portfolio analysis puts corporate headquarters into the role of an internal banker. In **portfolio analysis**, top management views its product lines and business units as a series of investments from which it expects a profitable return. The product lines/business units form a portfolio of investments that top management must constantly juggle to ensure the best return on the corporation's invested money. A McKinsey & Company study of the performance of the 200 largest U.S. corporations found that companies that actively managed their business portfolios through acquisitions and divestitures created substantially more shareholder value than those companies that passively held their businesses.[72] Given the increasing number of strategic alliances in today's corporations, portfolio analysis is also being used to evaluate the contribution of alliances to corporate and business unit objectives.

Two of the most popular portfolio techniques are the BCG Growth-Share Matrix and **GE Business Screen**.

BCG GROWTH-SHARE MATRIX

Using the **BCG (Boston Consulting Group) Growth-Share Matrix** depicted in **Figure 7–3** is the simplest way to portray a corporation's portfolio of investments. Each of the corporation's product lines or business units is plotted on the matrix according to both the growth rate of the industry in which it competes and its relative market share. A unit's relative competitive position is defined as its market share in the industry divided by that of the largest other competitor. By this calculation, a relative market share above 1.0 belongs to the market leader. The business growth rate is the percentage of market growth—that is, the percentage by which sales of a particular business unit classification of products have increased. The matrix assumes that, other things being equal, a growing market is attractive.

The line separating areas of high and low relative competitive position is set at 1.5 times. A product line or business unit must have relative strengths of this magnitude to ensure that it will have the dominant position needed to be a "star" or "cash cow." On the other hand, a product line or unit having a relative competitive position less than 1.0 has "dog" status.[73] Each product or unit is represented in **Figure 7–3** by a circle. The area of the circle represents the relative significance of each business unit or product line to the corporation in terms of assets used or sales generated.
The BCG Growth-Share Matrix has some common attributes with the product life cycle. As a product moves through its life cycle, it is generally categorized into one of four types for the purpose of funding decisions:

- **Question marks** (sometimes called "problem children" or "wildcats") are new products with the potential for success, but they need a lot of cash for development. If such a product is to gain enough market share to become a market leader and thus a star, money must be taken from more mature products and spent on the question mark. This is a "fish or cut bait" decision in which management must decide if the business is worth the investment needed. For example, after years of fruitlessly experimenting with an electric car, General Motors finally decided in 2006 to take a chance on developing the Chevrolet Volt.[74] To learn more of GM's decision to build the electric car, see the Sustainability Issue feature.

- **Stars** are market leaders that are typically at or nearing the peak of their product life cycle and are able to generate enough cash to maintain their high share of the market and usually contribute to the company's profits. The iPhone business has been called Apple's "crown jewel" because of its 52% market share and the extensive app network available on iTunes.[75]

- **Cash cows** typically bring in far more money than is needed to maintain their market share. In this declining stage of their life cycle, these products are "milked" for cash that will be invested in new question marks. Expenses such as advertising and R&D are

FIGURE 7–3   BCG Growth- Share Matrix

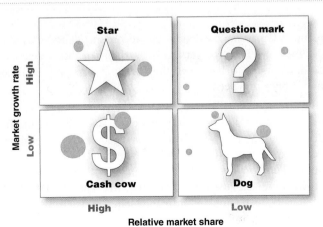

SOURCE: Based on *Long Range Planning*, Vol. 10, No. 2, 1977, Hedley, "Strategy and the Business Portfolio." p. 12. Copyright © 1977

SUSTAINABILITY issue

GENERAL MOTORS AND THE ELECTRIC CAR

In 2003, top management at General Motors (GM) decided to discontinue further work on its EV1 electric automobile. Working versions of the car had been leased to a limited number of people, but never sold. GM required every EV1 to be returned to the company. Environmentalists protested that GM stopped making the car just to send a message to government policy makers that an electric car was bad business. Management responded by stating that the car would never have made a profit.

In an April 2005 meeting of GM's top management team, Vice Chairman Robert Lutz suggested that it might be time to build another electric car. He noted that Toyota's Prius hybrid had made Toyota look environmentally sensitive, whereas GM was viewed as making gas "hogs." The response was negative. Lutz recalled one executive saying, "We lost $1 billion on the last one. Do you want to lose $1 billion on the next one?"

Even though worldwide car ownership was growing 5% annually, rising fuel prices in 2005 reduced sales of GM's profitable SUVs—resulting in a loss of US$11 billion. Board members began signaling that it was time for management to take some riskier bets to get the company out of financial trouble. In February 2006, management reluctantly approved developmental work on another electric car. At the time, no one in GM knew if batteries could be made small enough to power a car, but they knew that choices were limited. According to Larry Burns, Vice President of R&D and Strategic Planning, "This industry is 98% dependent on petroleum. GM has concluded that that's not sustainable."

Chairman and CEO Richard Wagoner Jr. surprised the world at the January 2007 Detroit Auto Show with a vow to start developing an electric car called the Chevrolet Volt. It would plug into a regular electric outlet, leapfrog the competition, and be on sale in 2010.

Management created a new team dedicated to getting hybrid and electric cars to market. The R&D budget was increased from US$6.6 billion in 2006 to US$8.1 billion in 2007. Several new models were canceled to free up resources. The battery lab was under pressure to design batteries that could propel the Volt 40 miles before a small gasoline engine would recharge the battery and extend the range to 600 miles. Douglas Drauch, battery lab manager, said. "Fifty years from now, people will remember the Volt—like they remember a '53 Corvette."

The Volt was released with much fanfare in October, 2010, and by 2012 GM was selling 2500 a month at just over US$40,000 per car. The company was still struggling to match manufacturing with sales and still make a profit. In the meantime, Nissan, Ford, and Toyota were making significant moves in the battery powered car business. Nissan released the Leaf, Ford released the electric Focus, and Toyota offered the Plug-in Prius and the all-electric RAV4, which claimed to get 103 MPG.

....

SOURCES: J. Bennett, "GM Expects Volt Sales to Set Monthly Record," *The Wall Street Journal* (August 30, 2012), (http://blogs.wsj.com/drivers-seat/2012/08/30/gm-expects-volt-sales-to-set-monthly-record/?KEYWORDS=volt); "12 Electric Cars for 2012," *CNN Money*, (http://money.cnn.com/galleries/2012/autos/1201/gallery.electric-hybrid-cars.fortune/9.html); D. Welch, "GM: Live Green or Die," *BusinessWeek* (May 26, 2008), pp. 36–41; "The Drive for Low Emissions," *The Economist's Special Report on Business and Climate Change* (June 2, 2007), pp. 26–28.

---

reduced. Panasonic's videocassette recorders (VCRs) moved to this category when sales declined and DVD player/recorders replaced them. Question marks unable to obtain dominant market share (and thus become stars) by the time the industry growth rate inevitably slows become dogs.

- **Dogs** have low market share and do not have the potential (because they are in an unattractive industry) to bring in much cash. According to the BCG Growth-Share Matrix, dogs should be either sold off or managed carefully for the small amount of cash they can generate. For example, DuPont, the inventor of nylon, sold its textiles unit in 2003 because the company wanted to eliminate its low-margin products and focus more on its growing biotech business.[76] The same was true of IBM when it sold its PC business to China's Lenovo Group in order to emphasize its growing services business.

Underlying the BCG Growth-Share Matrix is the concept of the experience curve (discussed in **Chapter 5**). The key to success with this model is assumed to be market share. Firms with the highest market share tend to have a cost leadership position based on economies of scale, among many other things. If a company is able to use the experience curve to its advantage, it should be able to manufacture and sell new products at a price low enough to garner early market share leadership (assuming no successful imitation by competitors).

Having plotted the current positions of its product lines or business units on a matrix, a company can project its future positions; however, this assumes no change in strategy by either the company with the portfolio or its competitors—a very unrealistic assumption. That said, present and projected matrixes can be used to help identify major strategic issues facing the organization. The goal of any company using a portfolio approach is to maintain a balanced portfolio so it can be self-sufficient in cash and always working to harvest mature products in declining industries to support new ones in growing industries.

The BCG Growth-Share Matrix is a very well-known portfolio concept with some clear advantages. It is quantifiable and easy to use. *Cash cow*, *dog*, *question mark*, and *star* are easy-to-remember terms for referring to a corporation's business units or products. Unfortunately, the BCG Growth-Share Matrix also has some serious limitations:

- The use of highs and lows to form four categories is too simplistic.
- The link between market share and profitability is questionable.[77] Low-share businesses can also be profitable.[78] For example, Olivetti is still profitably selling manual typewriters through mail-order catalogs.
- Growth rate is only one aspect of industry attractiveness.
- Product lines or business units are considered only in relation to one competitor: the market leader. Small competitors with fast-growing market shares are ignored.
- Market share is only one aspect of overall competitive position.

ADVANTAGES AND LIMITATIONS OF PORTFOLIO ANALYSIS

Portfolio analysis is commonly used in strategy formulation because it offers certain *advantages:*

- It encourages top management to evaluate each of the corporation's businesses individually and to set objectives and allocate resources for each.
- It stimulates the use of externally oriented data to supplement management's judgment.
- It raises the issue of cash-flow availability for use in expansion and growth.
- Its graphic depiction facilitates communication.

Portfolio analysis does, however, have some very real *limitations* that have caused some companies to reduce their use of this approach:

- Defining product/market segments is difficult.
- It suggests the use of standard strategies that can miss opportunities or be impractical.
- It provides an illusion of scientific rigor, when in reality positions are based on subjective judgments.
- Its value-laden terms such as cash cow and dog can lead to self-fulfilling prophecies.

- It is not always clear what makes an industry attractive or where a product is in its life cycle.

- Naively following the prescriptions of a portfolio model may actually reduce corporate profits if they are used inappropriately. For example, General Mills' Chief Executive H. Brewster Atwater cited his company's Bisquick brand of baking mix as a product that would have been written off years ago based on portfolio analysis. "This product is 57 years old. By all rights it should have been overtaken by newer products. But with the proper research to improve the product and promotion to keep customers excited, it's doing very well."[79]

MANAGING A STRATEGIC ALLIANCE PORTFOLIO

Just as product lines/business units form a portfolio of investments that top management must constantly juggle to ensure the best return on the corporation's invested money, strategic alliances can also be viewed as a portfolio of investments—investments of money, time, and energy. The way a company manages these intertwined relationships can significantly influence corporate competitiveness. Alliances are thus recognized as an important source of competitive advantage and superior performance.[80]

Managing groups of strategic alliances is primarily the job of the business unit. Its decisions may escalate, however, to the corporate level. Toman Corporation, for example, has 195 international joint ventures containing 422 alliance partners.

A study of 25 leading European corporations found four tasks of multi-alliance management that are necessary for successful alliance portfolio management:

1. **Developing and implementing a portfolio strategy for each business unit and a corporate policy for managing all the alliances of the entire company:** Alliances are primarily determined by business units. The corporate level develops general rules concerning when, how, and with whom to cooperate. The task of alliance policy is to strategically align all of the corporation's alliance activities with corporate strategy and corporate values. Every new alliance is thus checked against corporate policy before it is approved.

2. **Monitoring the alliance portfolio in terms of implementing business unit strategies and corporate strategy and policies:** Each alliance is measured in terms of achievement of objectives (e.g., market share), financial measures (e.g., profits and cash flow), contributed resource quality and quantity, and the overall relationship. The more a firm is diversified, the less the need for monitoring at the corporate level.

3. **Coordinating the portfolio to obtain synergies and avoid conflicts among alliances:** Because the interdependencies among alliances within a business unit are usually greater than among different businesses, the need for coordination is greater at the business level than at the corporate level. The need for coordination increases as the number of alliances in one business unit and the company as a whole increases, the average number of partners per alliance increases, and/or the overlap of the alliances increases.

4. **Establishing an alliance management system to support other tasks of multi-alliance management:** This infrastructure consists of formalized processes, standardized tools and specialized organizational units. All but two of the 25 companies established centers of competence for alliance management. The centers were often part of a department for corporate development or a department of alliance management at the corporate level. In other corporations, specialized positions for alliance management were created at both the corporate and business unit levels or only at the business unit level. Most corporations prefer a system in which the corporate level provides the methods and tools to support alliances centrally, but decentralizes day-to-day alliance management to the business units.[81]

Corporate Parenting

It has been suggested that corporate strategists address two crucial questions:

- What businesses should this company own and why?
- What organizational structure, management processes, and philosophy will foster superior performance from the company's business units?[82]

Portfolio analysis typically attempts to answer these questions by examining the attractiveness of various industries and by managing business units for cash flow—that is, by using cash generated from mature units to build new product lines. Unfortunately, portfolio analysis fails to deal with the question of what industries a corporation should enter or how a corporation can attain synergy among its product lines and business units. As suggested by its name, portfolio analysis tends to primarily view matters financially, regarding business units and product lines as separate and independent investments. Calculating the impact and fit of a new industry or a new business acquisition can be quite difficult as shown in the Innovation Issue feature.

Corporate parenting, or parenting strategy, in contrast, views a corporation in terms of resources and capabilities that can be used to build business unit value as well as generate synergies across business units. According to Campbell, Goold, and Alexander:

> *Multibusiness companies create value by influencing—or parenting—the businesses they own. The best parent companies create more value than any of their rivals would if they owned the same businesses. Those companies have what we call parenting advantage.*[83]

INNOVATION issue

TO RED HAT OR NOT?

Many large, established organizations including IBM, Hewlett-Packard, Oracle, and Intel were looking closely at acquiring a business that had grown to a US$1 billion business in a niche area of the industry. Red Hat was a business founded on supporting what amounts to a free software system called Linux.

The precursor to the Internet was born in 1968, and in 1969 a researcher at Bell Labs created UNIX as an open-source operating system. Being open sourced meant that anyone who wanted to volunteer their time could add to the capability of the software. Fast forward to 1995 and a new company called Red Hat was born as an accessory, books, and magazine company focused on what had then become known as Linux.

Red Hat based in Durham, North Carolina, released a version of Linux in 1995 and promised to support companies who used that version. It was still freeware, but now it had a company of engineers to support it at that particular point in time. This became the core of the business. The company would freeze Linux periodically and then support that "version" for a 10-year period of time. This gave corporate managers the confidence to use Linux as their operating system.

The company experienced phenomenal growth by focusing on Data Centers and supporting each version with more than 150 engineers. Red Hat charged a substantial premium to its customers who pay a subscription fee for Red Hat support.

With the winds of a potential acquisition behind it, the company's share price surged 66% between 2010 and 2012. Red Hat was the only company that had found a business model that made substantial profits on open-sourced software. Whether this fit with the needs of such major companies as IBM or not was the open question.

....
SOURCES: http://www.redhat.com/about/company/history.html; "Red Hat Sees Lots of Green," *Bloomberg Businessweek* (April 2, 2012), pp. 41–43.

Corporate parenting generates corporate strategy by focusing on the core competencies of the parent corporation and on the value created from the relationship between the parent and its businesses. In the form of corporate headquarters, the parent has a great deal of power in this relationship. If there is a good fit between the parent's skills and resources and the needs and opportunities of the business units, the corporation is likely to create value. If, however, there is not a good fit, the corporation is likely to destroy value.[84] Research indicates that companies that have a good fit between their strategy and their parenting roles are better performers than those companies that do not have a good fit.[85] This approach to corporate strategy is useful not only in deciding what new businesses to acquire but also in choosing how each existing business unit should be best managed. This appears to have been the secret to the success of General Electric under CEO Jack Welch.

The primary job of corporate headquarters is, therefore, to obtain synergy among the business units by providing needed resources to units, transferring skills and capabilities among the units, and coordinating the activities of shared unit functions to attain economies of scope (as in centralized purchasing).[86] This is in agreement with the concept of the learning organization discussed in **Chapter 1** in which the role of a large firm is to facilitate and transfer the knowledge assets and services throughout the corporation.[87] This is especially important given that 75% or more of a modern company's market value stems from its intangible assets—the organization's knowledge and capabilities.[88] At Proctor & Gamble, for example, the various business units are expected to work together to develop innovative products. Crest Whitestrips, which controls 68% of the at-home tooth-whitening market, was based on the P&G laundry division's knowledge of whitening agents.[89]

DEVELOPING A CORPORATE PARENTING STRATEGY

The search for appropriate corporate strategy involves three analytical steps:

1. **Examine each business unit (or target firm in the case of acquisition) in terms of its strategic factors:** People in the business units probably identified the strategic factors when they were generating business strategies for their units. One popular approach is to establish centers of excellence throughout the corporation. A **center of excellence** is "an organizational unit that embodies a set of capabilities that has been explicitly recognized by the firm as an important source of value creation, with the intention that these capabilities be leveraged by and/or disseminated to other parts of the firm."[90]

2. **Examine each business unit (or target firm) in terms of areas in which performance can be improved:** These are considered to be parenting opportunities. For example, two business units might be able to gain economies of scope by combining their sales forces. In another instance, a unit may have good, but not great, manufacturing and logistics skills. A parent company having world-class expertise in these areas could improve that unit's performance. The corporate parent could also transfer some people from one business unit who have the desired skills to another unit that is in need of those skills. People at corporate headquarters may, because of their experience in many industries, spot areas where improvements are possible that even people in the business unit may not have noticed. Unless specific areas are significantly weaker than the competition, people in the business units may not even be aware that these areas could be improved, especially if each business unit monitors only its own particular industry.

3. **Analyze how well the parent corporation fits with the business unit (or target firm):** Corporate headquarters must be aware of its own strengths and weaknesses in terms of resources, skills, and capabilities. To do this, the corporate parent must ask whether it has the characteristics that fit the parenting opportunities in each business unit. It must also ask whether there is a misfit between the parent's characteristics and the critical success factors of each business unit.

HORIZONTAL STRATEGY AND MULTIPOINT COMPETITION

A **horizontal strategy** is a corporate strategy that cuts across business unit boundaries to build synergy between business units and to improve the competitive position of one or more business units.[91] When used to build synergy, it acts like a parenting strategy. When used to improve the competitive position of one or more business units, it can be thought of as a corporate competitive strategy. In **multipoint competition**, large multibusiness corporations compete against other large multibusiness firms in a number of markets. These multipoint competitors are firms that compete with each other not only in one business unit, but also in a number of business units. At one time or another, a cash-rich competitor may choose to build its own market share in a particular market to the disadvantage of another corporation's business unit. Although each business unit has primary responsibility for its own business strategy, it may sometimes need some help from its corporate parent, especially if the competitor business unit is getting heavy financial support from its corporate parent. In this instance, corporate headquarters develops a horizontal strategy to coordinate the various goals and strategies of related business units.

For example, P&G, Kimberly-Clark, Scott Paper, and Johnson & Johnson (J&J) compete with one another in varying combinations of consumer paper products, from disposable diapers to facial tissue. If (purely hypothetically) J&J had just developed a toilet tissue with which it chose to challenge Procter & Gamble's high-share Charmin brand in a particular district, it might charge a low price for its new brand to build sales quickly. P&G might not choose to respond to this attack on its share by cutting prices on Charmin. Because of Charmin's high market share, P&G would lose significantly more sales dollars in a price war than J&J would with its initially low-share brand. To retaliate, P&G might challenge J&J's high-share baby shampoo with P&G's own low-share brand of baby shampoo in a different district. Once J&J had perceived P&G's response, it might choose to stop challenging Charmin so that P&G would stop challenging J&J's baby shampoo.

Multipoint competition and the resulting use of horizontal strategy may actually slow the development of hypercompetition in an industry. The realization that an attack on a market leader's position could result in a response in another market leads to mutual forbearance in which managers behave more conservatively toward multimarket rivals and competitive rivalry is reduced.[92] In one industry, for example, multipoint competition resulted in firms being less likely to exit a market. "Live and let live" replaced strong competitive rivalry.[93]

Multipoint competition is likely to become even more prevalent in the future, as corporations become global competitors and expand into more markets through strategic alliances.[94]

End of Chapter SUMMARY

Corporate strategy is primarily about the choice of direction for the firm as a whole. It deals with three key issues that a corporation faces: (1) the firm's overall orientation toward growth, stability, or retrenchment; (2) the industries or markets in which the firm competes through its products and business units; and (3) the manner in which management coordinates activities and transfers resources and cultivates capabilities among product lines and business units. These issues are dealt with through directional strategy, portfolio analysis, and corporate parenting.

Managers must constantly examine their corporation's entire portfolio of products, businesses, and opportunities as if they were planning to reinvest all of its capital.[95] One of the most complex and well-known collections of businesses (a conglomerate) is run by Berkshire Hathaway and headed by icon, Warren Buffett. By 2012, Berkshire owned and managed more than 80 businesses, with profits approaching US$12 billion/year. Over the years, the company has moved resources around to benefit the whole corporation. This meant moving away from insurance and investing in railroads, utilities, and manufacturing companies using the profits from the more successful cash generating businesses to fund investments in promising new business ideas. Some of the more well-known companies are BNSF Railroad, GEICO Insurance, See's Candies, Dairy Queen, and Fruit of the Loom.[96]

MyManagementLab®

Go to **mymanagementlab.com** to complete the problems marked with this icon ✪.

KEY TERMS

acquisition (p. 193)
backward integration (p. 189)
bankruptcy (p. 199)
BCG (Boston Consulting Group)
   Growth-Share Matrix (p. 200)
BOT (Build, Operate, Transfer)
   concept (p. 194)
captive company strategy (p. 198)
cash cows (p. 201)
center of excellence (p. 206)
concentration (p. 188)
concentric diversification (p. 195)
conglomerate diversification (p. 195)
corporate parenting (p. 205)
corporate strategy (p. 186)
directional strategy (p. 187)
diversification (p. 188)
divestment (p. 199)
dogs (p. 202)

exporting (p. 192)
forward integration (p. 189)
franchising (p. 193)
full integration (p. 189)
GE business screen (p. 200)
green-field development (p. 193)
growth strategy (p. 187)
horizontal growth (p. 190)
horizontal integration (p. 190)
horizontal strategy (p. 207)
joint venture (p. 193)
licensing (p. 192)
liquidation (p. 199)
long-term contracts (p. 190)
management contracts (p. 194)
merger (p. 188)
multipoint competition (p. 207)
no-change strategy (p. 197)
parenting strategy (pp. 186)

pause/proceed-with-caution
   strategy (p. 197)
portfolio analysis (p. 186)
production sharing (p. 194)
profit strategy (p. 197)
quasi-integration (p. 190)
question marks (p. 201)
retrenchment strategies (p. 187)
sell-out strategy (p. 199)
stability strategy (p. 187)
stars (p. 201)
synergy (p. 195)
taper integration (p. 190)
transaction cost economics (p. 189)
turnaround strategy (p. 198)
turnkey operations (p. 194)
vertical growth (p. 188)
vertical integration (p. 189)

MyManagementLab®

Go to **mymanagementlab.com** for Auto-graded writing questions as well as the following Assisted-graded writing questions:

7-1. List the means available to a company for Horizontal Growth and explain why a company might pursue one over another?
7-2. Evaluate the types of retrenchment strategies that might be used by companies in stagnant industries.

DISCUSSION QUESTIONS

✪ **7-3.** How does horizontal growth differ from vertical growth as a corporate strategy? From concentric diversification?

✪ **7-4.** What are the trade-offs between an internal and an external growth strategy? Which approach is best as an international entry strategy?

7-5. Is stability really a strategy or just a term for no strategy?

7-6. Compare and contrast a SWOT approach with portfolio analysis.

✪ **7-7.** How is corporate parenting different from portfolio analysis? How is it alike? Is it a useful concept in a global industry?

STRATEGIC PRACTICE EXERCISE

On March 14, 2000, Stephen King, the prolific horror writer, published his new book, *Riding the Bullet*, on the Internet before it appeared in print. Within 24 hours, almost 400,000 people had downloaded the book—even though most of them needed to download software in order to read the book. The unexpected demand crashed servers. According to Jack Romanos, president of Simon & Schuster, "I don't think anybody could have anticipated how many people were out there who are willing to accept the written word in a paperless format." To many, this announced the coming of the electronic novel. Environmentalists were thrilled that e-books might soon replace paper books and newspapers, thus reducing pollution coming from paper mills and land-fills. The King book was easy to download and took less time than a trip to the bookstore. Critics argued that the King book used the Internet purposely because at 66 pages, it was too short to be a standard printed novel. It was also free, so there was nothing to discourage natural curiosity. Some people in the industry estimated that 75% of those who downloaded the book did not read it.[97]

By 2008, HarperCollins and Random House were offering free online book content. Amazon was selling a US$399 Kindle e-book reader for downloadable books costing US$10 each, but Apple CEO Steve Jobs described the Kindle as something that filled no void and would "go nowhere." Sales in electronic trade books increased from US$5.8 million in 2002 to US$20 million in 2006 to US$380 million by 2012.

By 2012, the market for e-books accounted for more than 25% of all revenues in the book selling industry and e-book sales had surpassed sales of hardback books.[98]

Amazon went on to release numerous versions of the Kindle reader ranging from US$69 to US$499. Amazon steadfastly refused to release sales figures for the Kindle; however, Forrester (a research firm) estimated that sales of the Kindle Fire (its flagship product) had exceeded 5 million between its release in November 2011 and Christmas that same year. Far from going nowhere, the Kindle family was clearly a player in the industry.

One of the lightly touched parts of the market is college textbooks. No individual area in the field of publishing seems as good a fit as asking students to buy an e-reader and then down-load all the material they will need for all of their courses. Rentals and outright purchases would represent a substantial change.[99]

1. Form into small groups in the class to discuss the future of electronic publishing.

2. Consider the following questions as discussion guides:
   - What are the pros and cons of electronic publishing?
   - What is the impact of electronic publishing on the environment?
   - Should newspaper and book publishers completely convert to electronic publishing over paper? (*The Wall Street Journal* and others publish in both paper and electronic formats. Is this a success?)
   - Would you prefer this textbook and others in an elec-tronic format? How would you prefer to read the book?
   - What business model should publishers use to make money publishing electronically?

3. Present your group's conclusions to the class.

NOTES

1. R. P. Rumelt, D. E. Schendel, and D. J. Teece, "Fundamen-tal Issues in Strategy," in R. P. Rumelt, D. E. Schendel, and D. J. Teece (Eds.), *Fundamental Issues in Strategy: A Research Agenda* (Boston: HBS Press, 1994), p. 42.
2. This analogy of corporate parent and business unit children was initially proposed by A. Campbell, M. Goold, and M. Alexander. See "Corporate Strategy: The Quest for Par-enting Advantage," *Harvard Business Review* (March–April, 1995), pp. 120–132.
3. M. E. Porter, "From Competitive Strategy to Corporate Strategy," in D. E. Husey (Ed.), *International Review of Strategic Manage-ment, Vol. 1* (Chichester, England: John Wiley & Sons, 1990), p. 29.
4. This is in agreement with Toyohiro Kono when he proposes that corporate headquarters has three main functions: formulate corporate strategy, identify and develop the company's core competencies, and provide central resources. See T. Kono, "A Strong Head Office Makes a Strong Company," *Long Range Planning* (April 1999), pp. 225–236.
5. "Larry Ups the Ante," *The Economist* (February 7, 2004), pp. 59–60, (http://www.oracle.com/us/corporate/acquisitions/index.html).

6. J. Bercovitz and W. Mitchell, "When Is More Better? The Impact of Business Scale and Scope on Long-Term Business Survival, While Controlling for Profitability," *Strategic Man-agement Journal* (January 2007), pp. 61–79.
7. http://finance.yahoo.com/news/duke-energy-acquires-progress-energy-184514127.html.
8. "Cisco Inc. Buys Top Technology Innovator," *St. Cloud (MN) Times* (November 19, 2005), p. 6A.
9. J. Perkins, "It's a Hog Predicament," *Des Moines Register* (April 11, 1999), pp. J1–J2.
10. C. Woodyard, "FedEx Ponies Up $2.4B for Kinko's," *USA Today* (December 31, 2003), p. B1.
11. J. W. Slocum Jr., M. McGill, and D. T. Lei, "The New Learn-ing Strategy: Anytime, Anything, Anywhere," *Organizational Dynamics* (Autumn 1994), p. 36.
12. M. J. Leiblein, J. J. Reuer, and F. Dalsace, "Do Make or Buy Decisions Matter? The Influence of Organizational Gover-nance on Technological Performance," *Strategic Management Journal* (September 2002), pp. 817–833.
13. I. Geyskens, J-B. E. M. Steenkamp, and N. Kumar, "Make, Buy, or Ally: A Transaction Cost Theory Meta-Analysis,"

Academy of Management Journal (June 2006), pp. 519–543; R. Carter and G. M. Hodgson, "The Impact of Empirical Tests of Transaction Cost Economics on the Debate on the Nature of the Firm," *Strategic Management Journal* (May 2006), pp. 461–476; T. A. Shervani, G. Frazier, and G. Challagalla, "The Moderating Influence of Firm Market Power on the Transaction Cost Economics Model: An Empirical Test in a Forward Channel Integration Context," *Strategic Management Journal* (June 2007), pp. 635–652; K. J. Mayer and R. M. Solomon, "Capabilities, Contractual Hazards, and Governance: Integrating Resource-Based and Transaction Cost Perspectives," *Academy of Management Journal* (October 2006), pp. 942–959.

14. K. R. Harrigan, *Strategies for Vertical Integration* (Lexington, MA.: Lexington Books, 1983), pp. 16–21.

15. M. Arndt, "Who's Afraid of a Housing Slump?" *BusinessWeek* (April 30, 2007), p. 76.

16. A. Parmigiani, "Why Do Firms Both Make and Buy? An Investigation of Concurrent Sourcing," *Strategic Management Journal* (March 2007), pp. 285–311; F. T. Rothaermel, M. A. Hitt, and L. A. Jobe, "Balancing Vertical Integration and Strategic Outsourcing: Effects on Product Portfolio, Product Success, and Firm Performance," *Strategic Management Journal* (November 2006), pp. 1033–1056.

17. "Converge or Conflict?" *The Economist* (August 30, 2008), pp. 61–62.

18. M. G. Jacobides, "Industry Change Through Vertical Disintegration: How and Why Markets Emerged in Mortgage Banking," *Academy of Management Journal* (June 2005), pp. 465–498.

19. For a discussion of the pros and cons of contracting versus vertical integration, see J. T. Mahoney, "The Choice of Organizational Form: Vertical Financial Ownership Versus Other Methods of Vertical Integration," *Strategic Management Journal* (November 1992), pp. 559–584; J. Helyar, "Outsourcing: A Passage Out of India," *Bloomberg Businessweek* (March 15, 2012), (www.businessweek.com/articles/2012-03-15/outsourcing-a-passage-out-of-india).

20. G. Dowell, "Product Line Strategies of New Entrants in an Established Industry: Evidence from the U.S. Bicycle Industry," *Strategic Management Journal* (October 2006), pp. 959–979; C. Sorenson, S. McEvily, C. R. Ren, and R. Roy, "Niche Width Revisited: Organizational Scope, Behavior and Performance," *Strategic Management Journal* (October 2006), pp. 915–936.

21. "Procter & Gamble CEO Takes on New role as USCBC Board Chair," *China Business Review* (July–September 2012), (www.chinabusinessreview.com/public/1207/interview.html); D. Roberts, "Scrambling to Bring Crest to the Masses," *BusinessWeek* (June 25, 2007), pp. 72–73.

22. A. Delios and P. W. Beamish, "Geographic Scope, Product Diversification, and the Corporate Performance of Japanese Firms," *Strategic Management Journal* (August 1999), pp. 711–727.

23. E. Elango and V. H. Fried, "Franchising Research: A Literature Review and Synthesis," *Journal of Small Business Management* (July 1997), pp. 68–81.

24. Franchise Business Economic Outlook: 2011 (December 16, 2011), (http://emarket.franchise.org/News_Release/Franchise%20Business%20Outlook%20Report%202011%20final.pdf); T. Thilgen, "Corporate Clout Replaces 'Small Is Beautiful,'" *The Wall Street Journal* (March 27, 1997), p. B14.

25. J. E. McCann III, "The Growth of Acquisitions in Services," *Long Range Planning* (December 1996), pp. 835–841.

26. Mukherjee, A. 2012. "Update 1 – Wal-Mart Plans 3-5 More India Stores This Year," *Reuters* (September 11, 2012), (http://in.reuters.com/article/2012/09/11/walmart-india-idINL3E8KB4O320120911); "Gently Does It," *The Economist* (August 11, 2007), p. 59.

27. A Bid for Bud," *The Economist* (June 21, 2008), p. 77.

28. B. Voss, "Strategic Federations Frequently Falter in Far East," *Journal of Business Strategy* (July/August 1993), p. 6; S. Douma, "Success and Failure in New Ventures," *Long Range Planning* (April 1991), pp. 54–60.

29. A. Delios and P. W. Beamish, "Ownership Strategy of Japanese Firms: Transactional, Institutional, and Experience Approaches," *Strategic Management Journal* (October 1999), pp. 915–933.

30. "Cross Border M&A," (January 3, 2012), (http://www.wlrk.com/webdocs/wlrknew/WLRKMemos/WLRK/WLRK.21572.12.pdf).

31. K. D. Brouthers and L. E. Brouthers, "Acquisition or Greenfield Start-up? Institutional, Cultural, and Transaction Cost Influences," *Strategic Management Journal* (January 2000), pp. 89–97.

32. P. Hill, "The MEAN Economy: IBM Workers Suffer Culture Change as Jobs Go Global," *The Washington Times* (August 26, 2012), (http://www.washingtontimes.com/news/2012/aug/26/innovators-working-their-way-out-of-a-job/?page=all).

33. C. Matlack, "Carlos Ghosn's Russian Gambit," *BusinessWeek* (March 17, 2008), pp. 57–58.

34. J. Naisbitt, *Megatrends Asia* (New York: Simon & Schuster, 1996), p. 143.

35. For additional information on international entry modes, see D. F. Spulber, *Global Competitive Strategy* (Cambridge, UK: Cambridge University Press, 2007) and K. D. Brouthers and J-F Hennart, "Boundaries of the Firm: Insights from International Entry Mode Research," *Journal of Management* (June 2007), pp. 395–425.

36. D. P. Lovallo and L. T. Mendonca, "Strategy's Strategist: An Interview with Richard Rumelt," *McKinsey Quarterly Online* (2007, No. 4).

37. C. Zook, "Increasing the Odds of Successful Growth: The Critical Prelude to Moving 'Beyond the Core.'" *Strategy & Leadership* (Vol. 32, No. 4, 2004), pp. 17–23.

38. A. Y. Ilinich and C. P. Zeithaml, "Operationalizing and Testing Galbraith's Center of Gravity Theory," *Strategic Management Journal* (June 1995), pp. 401–410; H. Tanriverdi and N. Venkatraman, "Knowledge Relatedness and the Performance of Multibusiness Firms," *Strategic Management Journal* (February 2005), pp. 97–119.

39. E. Duffner and B. Kammel, "Bombardier CSeries Boosted on Agreement to Sell 15 Jets," *Bloomberg* (July 9, 2012), (http://www.bloomberg.com/news/2012-07-08/bombardier-wins-1-02-billion-deal-for-15-cseries-jetliners-1-.html); "Flying into Battle," *The Economist* (May 8, 2004), p. 60 and corporate Web site (www.bombardier.com) accessed September 27, 2008.

40. R. F. Bruner, "Corporation Diversification May Be Okay After All," *Batten Briefings* (Spring 2003), pp. 2–3, 12.

41. J. Bercovitz and W. Mitchell, "When Is More Better? The Impact of Business Scale and Scope on Long-Term Business Survival, While Controlling for Profitability," *Strategic Management Journal* (January 2007), pp. 61–79; D. J. Miller, "Technological Diversity, Related Diversification, and Firm Performance," *Strategic Management Journal* (July 2006), pp. 601–619; C. Stadler, "The Four Principles of Enduring

Success," *Harvard Business Review* (July–August 2007), pp. 62–72.

42. K. Carow, R. Heron, and T. Saxton, "Do Early Birds Get the Returns? An Empirical Investigation of Early-Mover Advantages in Acquisitions," *Strategic Management Journal* (June 2004), pp. 563–585; K. Ramaswamy, "The Performance Impact of Strategic Similarity in Horizontal Mergers: Evidence from the U.S. Banking Industry," *Academy of Management Journal* (July 1997), pp. 697–715; D. J. Flanagan, "Announcements of Purely Related and Purely Unrelated Mergers and Shareholder Returns: Reconciling the Relatedness Paradox," *Journal of Management* (Vol. 22, No. 6, 1996), pp. 823–835; D. D. Bergh, "Predicting Diversification of Unrelated Acquisitions: An Integrated Model of Ex Ante Conditions," *Strategic Management Journal* (October 1997), pp. 715–731.

43. J. M. Pennings, H. Barkema, and S. Douma, "Organizational Learning and Diversification," *Academy of Management Journal* (June 1994), pp. 608–640.

44. C. Stadler, "The Four Principles of Enduring Success," *Harvard Business Review* (July–August 2007), pp. 62–72.

45. L. E. Palich, L. B. Cardinal, and C. C. Miller, "Curvilinearity in the Diversification-Performance Linkage: An Examination of over Three Decades of Research," *Strategic Management Journal* (February 2000), pp. 155–174; M. S. Gary, "Implementation Strategy and Performance Outcomes in Related Diversification," *Strategic Management Journal* (July 2005), pp. 643–664; G. Yip and G. Johnson, "Transforming Strategy," *Business Strategy Review* (Spring 2007), pp. 11–15.

46. "The Great Merger Wave Breaks," *The Economist* (January 27, 2001), pp. 59–60; http://www.mondaq.com/unitedstates/x/181456/Corporate+Governance/2012+MA+Report.

47. R. N. Palter and D. Srinivasan, "Habits of Busiest Acquirers," *McKinsey on Finance* (Summer 2006), pp. 8–13.

48. D. R. King, D. R. Dalton, C. M. Daily, and J. G. Covin, "Meta-Analyses of Post-Acquisition Performance: Indications of Unidentified Moderators," *Strategic Management Journal* (February 2004), pp. 187–200; W. B. Carper, "Corporate Acquisitions and Shareholder Wealth: A Review and Exploratory Analysis" *Journal of Management* (December 1990), pp. 807–823; P. G. Simmonds, "Using Diversification as a Tool for Effective Performance," in H. E. Glass and M. A. Hovde (Eds.), *Handbook of Business Strategy, 1992/93 Yearbook* (Boston: Warren, Gorham & Lamont, 1992), pp. 3.1–3.7; B. T. Lamont and C. A. Anderson, "Mode of Corporate Diversification and Economic Performance," *Academy of Management Journal* (December 1985), pp. 926–936.

49. "The HP–Compaq Merger Two Years Out: Still Waiting for the Upside," *Knowledge @Wharton* (October 6–19, 2004).

50. D. J. Miller, "Firms' Technological Resources and the Performance Effects of Diversification: A Longitudinal Study," *Strategic Management Journal* (November 2004), pp. 1097–1119.

51. A. Hinterhuber, "When Two Companies Become One," in S. Crainer and D. Dearlove (Eds.), *Financial Times Handbook of Management*, 3rd ed. (Harlow, UK: Pearson Education, 2004), pp. 824–833; D. L. Laurie, Y. L. Doz, and C. P. Sheer, "Creating New Growth Platforms," *Harvard Business Review* (May 2006), pp. 80–90; R. Langford and C. Brown III, "Making M&A Pay: Lessons from the World's Most Successful Acquirers," *Strategy & Leadership* (Vol. 32, No. 1, 2004), pp. 5–14; J. G. Lynch and B. Lind, "Escaping Merger and Acquisition

Madness," *Strategy & Leadership* (Vol. 30, No. 2, 2002), pp. 5–12; M. L. Sirower, *The Synergy Trap* (New York: Free Press, 1997); B. Jensen, "Make It Simple! How Simplicity Could Become Your Ultimate Strategy," *Strategy & Leadership* (March/April 1997), p. 35.

52. E. Thornton, "Why Consumers Hate Mergers," *BusinessWeek* (December 6, 2004), pp. 58–64.

53. S. Karim and W. Mitchell, "Innovating through Acquisition and Internal Development: A Quarter-Century of Boundary Evolution at Johnson & Johnson," *Long Range Planning* (December 2004), pp. 525–547; L. Selden and G. Colvin, "M&A Needn't Be a Loser's Game," *Harvard Business Review* (June 2003), pp. 70–79; E. C. Busija, H. M. O'Neill, and C. P. Zeithaml, "Diversification Strategy, Entry Mode, and Performance: Evidence of Choice and Constraints," *Strategic Management Journal* (April 1997), pp. 321–327; A. Sharma, "Mode of Entry and Ex-Post Performance," *Strategic Management Journal* (September 1998), pp. 879–900.

54. R. T. Uhlaner and A. S. West, "Running a Winning M&A Shop," *McKinsey Quarterly* (March 2008), pp. 1–7.

55. S. Rovitt, D. Harding, and C. Lemire, "A Simple M&A Model for All Seasons," *Strategy & Leadership* (Vol. 32, No. 5, 2004), pp. 18–24.

56. P. Porrini, "Can a Previous Alliance Between an Acquirer and a Target Affect Acquisition Performance?" *Journal of Management* (Vol. 30, No. 4, 2004), pp. 545–562; L. Wang and E. J. Zajac, "Alliance or Acquisition? A Dyadic Perspective on Interfirm Resource Combinations," *Strategic Management Journal* (December 2007), pp. 1291–1317.

57. A. Inkpen and N. Choudhury, "The Seeking of Strategy Where It Is Not: Towards a Theory of Strategy Absence," *Strategic Management Journal* (May 1995), pp. 313–323.

58. P. Burrows and S. Anderson, "Dell Computer Goes into the Shop," *BusinessWeek* (July 12, 1993), pp. 138–140.

59. P. Gupta, "Dell's Strategy Questioned after Shares Dive," *Reuters*, May 23, 2012. (http://www.reuters.com/article/2012/05/23/us-dell-research-idUSBRE84M0OR20120523).

60. M. Brauer, "What Have We Acquired and What Should We Acquire in Divestiture Research? A Review and Research Agenda," *Journal of Management* (December 2006), pp. 751–785; J. L. Morrow Jr., R. A. Johnson, and L. W. Busenitz, "The Effects of Cost and Asset Retrenchment on Firm Performance: The Overlooked Role of a Firm's Competitive Environment," *Journal of Management* (Vol. 30, No. 2, 2004), pp. 189–208.

61. J. A. Pearce II and D. K. Robbins, "Retrenchment Remains the Foundation of Business Turnaround," *Strategic Management Journal* (June 1994), pp. 407–417.

62. Y. Kageyama, "Sony Turnaround Plan Draws Yawns," *Des Moines Register* (September 23, 2005), p. 3D.

63. F. Gandolfi, "Reflecting on Downsizing: What Have We Learned?" *SAM Advanced Management Journal* (Spring 2008), pp. 46–55; C. Chadwick, L. W. Hunter, and S. L. Walston, "Effects of Downsizing Practices on the Performance of Hospitals," *Strategic Management Journal* (May 2004), pp. 405–427; J. R. Morris, W. F. Cascio, and C. E. Young, "Downsizing After All These Years," *Organizational Dynamics* (Winter 1999), pp. 78–87; P. H. Mirvis, "Human Resource Management: Leaders, Laggards, and Followers," *Academy of Management Executive* (May 1997), pp. 43–56; J. K. DeDee and D. W. Vorhies, "Retrenchment Activities of Small Firms During

Economic Downturn: An Empirical Investigation," *Journal of Small Business Management* (July 1998), pp. 46–61.

64. C. Chadwick, L. W. Hunter, and S. L. Walston, "Effects of Downsizing Practices on the Performance of Hospitals," *Strategic Management Journal* (May 2004), pp. 405–427.

65. J. B. Treece, "U.S. Parts Makers Just Won't Say 'Uncle,'" *BusinessWeek* (August 10, 1987), pp. 76–77.

66. S. S. Carty, "Ford Plans to Park Jaguar, Land Rover with Tata Motors," *USA Today* (March 26, 2008), p. 1B–2B.

67. For more on divestment, see C. Dexter and T. Mellewight, "Thirty Years After Michael E. Porter: What Do We Know about Business Exit?" *Academy of Management Perspectives* (May 2007), pp. 41–55.

68. D. Welch, "Go Bankrupt, Then Go Overseas," *BusinessWeek* (April 24, 2006), pp. 52–55.

69. D. D. Dawley, J. J. Hoffman, and B. T. Lamont, "Choice Situation, Refocusing, and Post-Bankruptcy Performance," *Journal of Management* (Vol. 28, No. 5, 2002), pp. 695–717.

70. R. M. Kanter, "Leadership and the Psychology of Turnarounds," *Harvard Business Review* (June 2003), pp. 58–67.

71. B. C. Reimann and A. Reichert, "Portfolio Planning Methods for Strategic Capital Allocation: A Survey of Fortune 500 Firms," *International Journal of Management* (March 1996), pp. 84–93; D. K. Sinha, "Strategic Planning in the Fortune 500," in H. E. Glass and M. A. Hovde (Eds.), *Handbook of Business Strategy, 1991/92 Yearbook*, (Boston: Warren, Gorham & Lamont, 1991), p. 96.

72. L. Dranikoff, T. Koller, and A. Schneider, "Divestiture: Strategy's Missing Link," *Harvard Business Review* (May 2002), pp. 74–83.

73. B. Hedley, "Strategy and the Business Portfolio," *Long Range Planning* (February 1977), p. 9.

74. D. Welch, "GM: Live Green or Die," *BusinessWeek* (May 26, 2008), pp. 36–41.

75. "Android vs. iPhone Market Share, 52 against 33 percent," *Phones Review* (September 5, 2012), (http://www.phonesreview.co.uk/2012/09/05/android-vs-iphone-market-share-52-against-33-percent/).

76. A. Fitzgerald, "Going Global," *Des Moines Register* (March 14, 2004), pp. 1M, 3M.

77. C. Anterasian, J. L. Graham, and R. B. Money, "Are U.S. Managers Superstitious About Market Share?" *Sloan Management Review* (Summer 1996), pp. 67–77.

78. D. Rosenblum, D. Tomlinson, and L. Scott, "Bottom-Feeding for Blockbuster Businesses," *Harvard Business Review* (March 2003), pp. 52–59.

79. J. J. Curran, "Companies that Rob the Future," *Fortune* (July 4, 1988), p. 84.

80. W. H. Hoffmann, "Strategies for Managing a Portfolio of Alliances," *Strategic Management Journal* (August 2007), pp. 827–856; D. Lavie, "Alliance Portfolios and Firm Performance: A Study of Value Creation and Appropriation in the U.S. Software Industry," *Strategic Management Journal* (December 2007), pp. 1187–1212.

81. W. H. Hoffmann, "How to Manage a Portfolio of Alliances," *Long Range Planning* (April 2005), pp. 121–143.

82. A. Campbell, M. Goold, and M. Alexander, *Corporate-Level Strategy: Creating Value in the Multibusiness Company* (New York: John Wiley & Sons, 1994). See also M. Goold,

A. Campbell, and M. Alexander, "Corporate Strategy and Parenting Theory," *Long Range Planning* (April 1998), pp. 308–318, and M. Goold and A. Campbell, "Parenting in Complex Structures," *Long Range Planning* (June 2002), pp. 219–243.

83. A. Campbell, M. Goold, and M. Alexander, "Corporate Strategy: The Quest for Parenting Advantage," *Harvard Business Review* (March–April 1995), p. 121.

84. Ibid., p. 122.

85. A. van Oijen and S. Douma, "Diversification Strategy and the Roles of the Centre," *Long Range Planning* (August 2000), pp. 560–578.

86. D. J. Collis, "Corporate Strategy in Multibusiness Firms," *Long Range Planning* (June 1996), pp. 416–418; D. Lei, M. A. Hitt, and R. Bettis, "Dynamic Core Competencies Through Meta-Learning and Strategic Context," *Journal of Management* (Vol. 22, No. 4, 1996), pp. 549–569.

87. D. J. Teece, "Strategies for Managing Knowledge Assets: The Role of Firm Structure and Industrial Context," *Long Range Planning* (February 2000), pp. 35–54.

88. R. S. Kaplan and D. P. Norton, "The Strategy Map: Guide to Aligning Intangible Assets," *Strategy & Leadership* (Vol. 32, No. 5, 2004), pp. 10–17; L. Edvinsson, "The New Knowledge Economics," *Business Strategy Review* (September 2002), pp. 72–76; C. Havens and E. Knapp, "Easing into Knowledge Management," *Strategy & Leadership* (March/April 1999), pp. 4–9.

89. J. Scanlon, "Cross-Pollinators," *BusinessWeek's Inside Innovation* (September 2007), pp. 8–11.

90. T. S. Frost, J. M. Birkinshaw, and P. C. Ensign, "Centers of Excellence in Multinational Corporations," *Strategic Management Journal* (November 2002), pp. 997–1018.

91. M. E. Porter, *Competitive Advantage* (New York: The Free Press, 1985), pp. 317–382.

92. H. R. Greve, "Multimarket Contact and Sales Growth: Evidence from Insurance," *Strategic Management Journal* (March 2008), pp. 229–249; L. Fuentelsaz and J. Gomez, "Multipoint Competition, Strategic Similarity and Entry Into Geographic Markets," *Strategic Management Journal* (May 2006), pp. 477–499; J. Gimeno, "Reciprocal Threats in Multimarket Rivalry: Staking Out 'Spheres of Influence' in the U.S. Airline Industry," *Strategic Management Journal* (February 1999), pp. 101–128; J. Baum and H. J. Korn, "Dynamics of Dyadic Competitive Interaction," *Strategic Management Journal* (March 1999), pp. 251–278; J. Gimeno and C. Y. Woo, "Hypercompetition in a Multimarket Environment: The Role of Strategic Similarity and Multimarket Contact in Competitive De-escalation," *Organization Science* (May/June 1996), pp. 322–341.

93. W. Boeker, J. Goodstein, J. Stephan, and J. P. Murmann, "Competition in a Multimarket Environment: The Case of Market Exit," *Organization Science* (March/April 1997), pp. 126–142.

94. J. Gimeno and C. Y. Woo, "Multimarket Contact, Economies of Scope, and Firm Performance," *Academy of Management Journal* (June 1999), pp. 239–259.

95. L. Carlesi, B. Verster, and F. Wenger, "The New Dynamics of Managing the Corporate Portfolio," *McKinsey Quarterly Online* (April 2007).

96. http://www.berkshirehathaway.com/subs/sublinks.html; J. Funk, "Warren Buffet's Successors Inherit Complex Conglomerate," *USA Today* (August 31, 2012), (www.usatoday.com/money/industries/manufacturing/story/2012-09-03/Warren-Buffet-evolving-conglomerate/57488280/1).

97. "Learning to E-Read," *The Economist Survey E-Entertainment* (October 7, 2000), p. 22.

98. J. Greenfield, "Lies, Lies and Damned E-Book Lies: Where WSJ Got It Wrong," *Forbes* (July 12, 2012), (www.forbes.com/sites/jeremygreenfield/2012/07/12/lies-lies-and-damed-e-book-lies-where-wsj-got-it-wrong/2/).

99. J. Pepitone, "Amazon Unveils Kindle Fire HD, but Sales Will Remain a Mystery," *CNN Money* (September 6, 2012), (money.cnn.com/2012/09/06/technology/kindle-fire-sales/index.html).

CHAPTER 8

Strategy Formulation: Functional Strategy and Strategic Choice

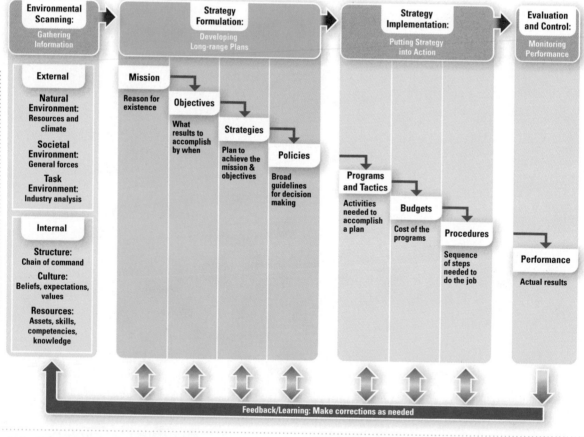

| Environmental Scanning: Gathering Information | Strategy Formulation: Developing Long-range Plans | Strategy Implementation: Putting Strategy into Action | Evaluation and Control: Monitoring Performance |

External

Natural Environment: Resources and climate

Societal Environment: General forces

Task Environment: Industry analysis

Internal

Structure: Chain of command

Culture: Beliefs, expectations, values

Resources: Assets, skills, competencies, knowledge

Mission — Reason for existence

Objectives — What results to accomplish by when

Strategies — Plan to achieve the mission & objectives

Policies — Broad guidelines for decision making

Programs and Tactics — Activities needed to accomplish a plan

Budgets — Cost of the programs

Procedures — Sequence of steps needed to do the job

Performance — Actual results

Feedback/Learning: Make corrections as needed

MyManagementLab®

⭐ **Improve Your Grade!**

Over 10 million students improved their results using the Pearson MyLabs. Visit **mymanagementlab.com** for simulations, tutorials, and end-of-chapter problems.

Learning Objectives

After reading this chapter, you should be able to:

- Identify a variety of functional strategies that can be used to achieve organizational goals and objectives
- Understand what activities and functions are appropriate to outsource in order to gain or strengthen competitive advantage
- Recognize strategies to avoid and understand why they are dangerous
- Construct corporate scenarios to evaluate strategic options
- Develop policies to implement corporate, business, and functional strategies

Research in Motion—BlackBerry

Research in Motion was founded in 1984 by Jim Balsillie and Mike Lazaridis as a business focused on providing the backbone for the two-way pager market. In 1999, they released the first BlackBerry device, which quickly set the bar for the connected business person. The term "crack berry" was even coined for those business people who could not put down their BlackBerry. The company focused almost exclusively on the integrity of the network on which their phones operated. They provided security measures that made RIM the choice of data managers.

When developing a strategy, all companies have to bring together all the elements in a manner that provides them with a unique position relative to their competitors. At the time of its release, most competitors provided cell phones that could make calls and little more. BlackBerry sales peaked in 2008 about the same time that Apple released the iPhone. Sales have plummeted since that point, the stock has lost 95% of its value between 2009 and 2013, and it has consistently reporting losses.

Despite that, the company still has 80 million users worldwide, a cash hoard in excess of US$2 billion and a reputation for being a best-in-class device for the business community. The company has made a number of missteps along the way, including a touchscreen BlackBerry that didn't catch on, a tablet that lacked e-mail connectivity, and an approach to the market that made it clear that the company believed the backbone was of more value than the device used.

The two founders stepped down in 2012 and the company continued to fumble with its strategy. New CEO Thorsten Heins asserted in January 2012 that RIM needed to focus on consumers rather than the enterprise. Then, in March 2012, he told analysts that RIM will focus on the enterprise instead of consumers. How can RIM align the elements of its strategy?

SOURCES: S. Jakab, "RIM Seeks to Avoid Its Own Waterloo," *The Wall Street Journal* (September 27, 2012), (http://online.wsj.com/article/SB10000872396390444549204578020473252582296.html?KEYWORDS=RIM+waterloo); D. Meyer, "How RIM Found Itself on the Wrong Side of History," *ZDNet* (July 1, 2012), (http://www.zdnet.com/how-rim-found-itself-on-the-wrong-side-of-history-3040155462/); http://www.rim.com/company/index.shtml; "Research in Motion Co-founders Step Down," (New York)*Daily News* (January 23, 2012), (http://articles.nydailynews.com/2012-01-23/news/30653912_1_balsillie-and-mike-lazaridis-rim-founders).

Functional Strategy

Functional strategy is the approach a functional area takes to achieve corporate and business unit objectives and strategies by maximizing resource productivity. It is concerned with developing and nurturing a distinctive competence to provide a company or business unit with a competitive advantage. Just as a multidivisional corporation has several business units, each with its own business strategy, each business unit has its own set of departments, each with its own functional strategy.

The orientation of a functional strategy is dictated by its parent business unit's strategy.[1] For example, a business unit following a competitive strategy of differentiation through high quality needs a manufacturing functional strategy that emphasizes expensive quality assurance processes over cheaper, high-volume production; a human resource functional strategy that emphasizes the hiring and training of a highly skilled, but costly, workforce; and a marketing functional strategy that emphasizes distribution channel "pull," using advertising to increase consumer demand, over "push," using promotional allowances to retailers. If a business unit were to follow a low-cost competitive strategy, however, a different set of functional strategies would be needed to support the business strategy.

Just as competitive strategies may need to vary from one region of the world to another, functional strategies may need to vary from region to region. When Mr. Donut expanded into Japan, for example, it had to market donuts not as breakfast, but as snack food. Because the Japanese had no breakfast coffee-and-donut custom, they preferred to eat the donuts in the afternoon or evening. Mr. Donut restaurants were thus located near railroad stations and supermarkets. All signs were in English to appeal to the Western interests of the Japanese.

MARKETING STRATEGY

Marketing strategy deals with pricing, selling, and distributing a product. Using a **market development** strategy, a company or business unit can (1) capture a larger share of an existing market for current products through market saturation and market penetration or (2) develop new uses and/or markets for current products. Consumer product giants such as P&G, Colgate-Palmolive, and Unilever are experts at using advertising and promotion to implement a market saturation/penetration strategy to gain the dominant market share in a product category. As seeming masters of the product life cycle, these companies are able to extend product life almost indefinitely through "new and improved" variations of product and packaging that appeal to most market niches. A company, such as Church & Dwight, follows the second market development strategy by finding new uses for its successful current product: Arm & Hammer brand baking soda.

Using the **product development** strategy, a company or unit can (1) develop new products for *existing markets* or (2) develop new products for *new markets*. Church & Dwight has had great success by following the first product development strategy developing new products to sell to its current customers in its existing markets. Acknowledging the widespread appeal of its Arm & Hammer brand baking soda, the company has generated new uses for its sodium bicarbonate by reformulating it as toothpaste, deodorant, and detergent. In another example, Ocean Spray developed Craisins, mock berries, more than 50 variations of juice, sauces, flavored snacks and juice boxes in order to market its cranberries to current customers.[2] Using a successful brand name to market other products is called *brand extension*, and it is a good way to appeal to a company's current customers. Smith & Wesson, famous for its handguns, has taken this approach by using licensing to put its name on men's cologne and other products like the Smith & Wesson 357 Magnum Wood Pellet Smoker (for smoking meats).[3] Church & Dwight has successfully followed the second product development strategy (new products for new markets) by developing new pollution-reduction products (using sodium bicarbonate compounds) for sale to coal-fired electric utility plants—a very different market from grocery stores.

There are numerous other marketing strategies. For advertising and promotion, for example, a company or business unit can choose between "push" and "pull" marketing strategies. Many large food and consumer products companies in the United States and Canada follow a *push strategy* by spending a large amount of money on trade promotion in order to gain or hold shelf space in retail outlets. Trade promotion includes discounts, in-store special offers, and advertising allowances designed to "push" products through the distribution system. The Kellogg Company decided a few years ago to change its emphasis from a push to a *pull strategy*, in which advertising "pulls" the products through the distribution channels. The company now spends more money on consumer advertising designed to build brand awareness so that shoppers will ask for the products. Research has found that a high level of advertising (a key part of a pull strategy) is beneficial to leading brands in a market.[4] Strong brands provide a competitive advantage to a firm because they act as entry barriers and usually generate higher market share.[5]

Other marketing strategies deal with distribution and pricing. Should a company use distributors and dealers to sell its products, should it sell directly to mass merchandisers, or should it use the direct marketing model by selling straight to the consumers via the Internet? Using multiple channels simultaneously can lead to problems. In order to increase the sales of its lawn tractors and mowers, for example, John Deere decided to sell the products not only through its current dealer network but also through mass merchandisers such as Home Depot. Deere's dealers, however, were furious. They considered Home Depot to be a key competitor. The dealers were concerned that Home Depot's ability to underprice them would eventually lead to their becoming little more than repair facilities for their competition and be left with insufficient sales to stay in business. However, the bulk (US$23 billion) of John Deere's US$32 billion in revenue comes from equipment sold to farmers. Home Depot sells the average lawn mower/tractor that was never a big part of the dealer's business.[6]

When pricing a new product, a company or business unit can follow one of two strategies. For new-product pioneers, *skim pricing* offers the opportunity to "skim the cream" from the top of the demand curve with a high price while the product is novel and competitors are few. *Penetration pricing*, in contrast, attempts to hasten market development and offers the pioneer the opportunity to use the experience curve to gain market share with a low price and then dominate the industry. Depending on corporate and business unit objectives and strategies, either of these choices may be desirable to a particular company or unit. Penetration pricing is, however, more likely than skim pricing to raise a unit's operating profit in the long term.[7] The use of the Internet to market goods directly to consumers allows a company to use *dynamic pricing*, a practice in which prices vary frequently based upon demand, market segment, and product availability.[8]

FINANCIAL STRATEGY

Financial strategy examines the financial implications of corporate and business-level strategic options and identifies the best financial course of action. It can also provide competitive advantage through a lower cost of funds and a flexible ability to raise capital to support a business strategy. Financial strategy usually attempts to maximize the financial value of a firm.

The trade-off between achieving the desired debt-to-equity ratio and relying on internal long-term financing via cash flow is a key issue in financial strategy. Many small-and medium-sized family-owned companies such as Urschel Laboratories try to avoid all external sources of funds in order to avoid outside entanglements and to keep control of the company within the family. Few large publicly held firms have no long-term debt and instead keep a large amount of money in cash and short-term investments. One of these is Apple Inc., which had more than a US$100 million cash hoard at the end of 2011. According to Apple's Chief Financial Officer, Peter Oppenheimer, "Our preference is to maintain a strong balance sheet in order to preserve our flexibility."[9] Many financial analysts believe, however, that only by financing through long-term debt can a corporation use financial leverage to boost earnings per share—thus raising stock price and the overall value of the company. Research indicates that higher debt levels not only deter takeover by other firms (by making the company less attractive) but also lead to improved productivity and improved cash flows by forcing management to focus on core businesses.[10] High debt can be a problem, however, when the economy falters and a company's cash flow drops.

Research reveals that a firm's financial strategy is influenced by its corporate diversification strategy. Equity financing, for example, is preferred for related diversification, whereas debt financing is preferred for unrelated diversification.[11] The trend away from unrelated to related acquisitions explains why the number of acquisitions being paid for entirely with stock increased from only 2% in 1988 to 50% in 1998.[12]

A very popular financial strategy that ebbs and flows with the economy is the leveraged buyout (LBO). The LBO market made up only 6% of the M&A deals completed in 2010, far below the peak of 25% seen in 2006.[13] In a **leveraged buyout**, a company is acquired in a transaction financed largely by debt, usually obtained from a third party, such as an insurance company or an investment banker. Ultimately, the debt is paid with money generated from the acquired company's operations or by sales of its assets. The acquired company, in effect, pays for its own acquisition. Management of the LBO is then under tremendous pressure to keep the highly leveraged company profitable. Unfortunately, the huge amount of debt on the acquired company's books may actually cause its eventual decline by focusing management's attention on short-term matters. For example, one year after the buyout, the cash flow of eight of the largest LBOs made during 2006–2007 was barely enough to cover interest payments.[14] One study of LBOs (also called MBOs—Management BuyOuts if they are led by company's current management) revealed that the financial performance of the typical LBO usually falls below the industry average in the fourth year after the buyout. The firm declines because of inflated expectations, utilization of all slack, management burnout, and a lack of strategic management.[15] Often, the only solutions are to sell the company or to again go public by selling stock to finance growth.[16]

The management of dividends and stock price is an important part of a corporation's financial strategy. Corporations in fast-growing industries such as computers and computer software often do not declare dividends. They use the money they might have spent on dividends to finance rapid growth. If the company is successful, its growth in sales and profits is reflected in a higher stock price, eventually resulting in a hefty capital gain when shareholders sell their common stock. Other corporations, such as Whirlpool Corporation, that do not face rapid growth, must support the value of their stock by offering consistent dividends. Instead of raising dividends when profits are high, a popular financial strategy is to use excess cash (or even use debt) to buy back a company's own shares of stock. In just the second quarter of 2012, U.S.-based publicly traded companies declared more than US$112 billion worth of stock repurchase plans. Because stock buybacks increase earnings per share, they typically increase a firm's stock price and make unwanted takeover attempts more difficult. Such buybacks do send a signal to investors that management may not have been able to find any profitable investment opportunities for the company or that it is anticipating reduced future earnings.[17]

A number of firms have been supporting the price of their stock by using *reverse stock splits*. Contrasted with a typical forward 2-for-1 stock split in which an investor receives an additional share for every share owned (with each share being worth only half as much), in a reverse 1-for-2 stock split, an investor's shares are split in half for the same total amount of money (with each share now being worth twice as much). Thus, 100 shares of stock worth US$10 each are exchanged for 50 shares worth US$20 each. A reverse stock split may successfully raise a company's stock price, but it does not solve underlying problems. A study by Credit Suisse First Boston revealed that almost all 800 companies that had reverse stock splits in a five-year period underperformed their peers over the long term.[18]

A rather novel financial strategy is the selling of a company's patents. Companies such as AT&T, Bellsouth, American Express, Kimberly Clark, and 3Com have been selling patents for products that they no longer wish to commercialize or are not a part of their core business. Kodak has been selling off virtually its entire portfolio of patents in a desperate attempt to raise enough money to survive while management tries to figure out what the company should do if it can emerge from bankruptcy. Companies like Apple, Microsoft, and Google have bought patents in order to protect their competitive positions. Patents are also bought by patent accumulators who seek to sell groups of patents to other companies.[19]

RESEARCH AND DEVELOPMENT (R&D) STRATEGY

R&D strategy deals with product and process innovation and improvement. It also deals with the appropriate mix of different types of R&D (basic, product, or process) and with the question of how new technology should be accessed—through internal development, external acquisition, or strategic alliances. RIM has floundered by going back and forth among these approaches rather than choosing an approach and investing their resources.

One of the R&D choices is to be either a **technological leader**, pioneering an innovation, or a **technological follower**, imitating the products of competitors.

One example of an effective use of the *leader* R&D functional strategy to achieve a differentiation competitive advantage is Nike Inc. Nike spends more than most in the industry on R&D to differentiate the performance of its athletic shoes from that of its competitors. As a result, its products have become the favorite of serious athletes. This despite the fact that Nike simultaneously pursues a low-cost manufacturing approach. An example of the use of the *follower* R&D functional strategy to achieve a low-cost competitive advantage is Dean Foods Company.

An increasing number of companies are working with their suppliers to help them keep up with changing technology. They are beginning to realize that a firm cannot be competitive technologically only through internal development. For example, Chrysler Corporation's skillful use of parts suppliers to design everything from car seats to drive shafts has enabled it to spend consistently less money than its competitors to develop new car models. Using strategic technology alliances is one way to combine the R&D capabilities of two companies. Maytag Company worked with one of its suppliers to apply fuzzy logic technology to its IntelliSense dishwasher. The partnership enabled Maytag to complete the project in a shorter amount of time than if it had tried to do it alone.[20] One UK study found that 93% of UK auto assemblers and component manufacturers use their suppliers as technology suppliers.[21]

A newer approach to R&D is *open innovation*, in which a firm uses alliances and connections with corporate, government, academic labs, and consumers to develop new products and processes. For example, Intel opened four small-scale research facilities adjacent to universities to promote the cross-pollination of ideas. Thirteen U.S. university labs engaging in nanotechnology research have formed the National Nanotechnology Infrastructure Network in order to offer their resources to businesses for a fee.[22] Mattel, Wal-Mart, and other toy manufacturers and retailers use idea brokers such as Big Idea Group to scout for new toy ideas. Another big player in this type of business is Everyday Edisons which runs a nationally broadcast, Emmy-award winning PBS television show and also invites inventors to submit ideas to its Web site (www.everydayedisons.com). Everyday Edisons works with companies to put out calls for ideas, then helps sift through those ideas in order to put the best ones in front of companies that are interested.[23] IBM adopted the open operating system Linux for some of its computer products and systems, drawing on a core code base that is continually improved and enhanced by a massive global community of software developers, of whom only a fraction work for IBM.[24] To open its own labs to ideas being generated elsewhere, P&G's CEO Art Lafley decreed that half of the company's ideas must come from outside, up from 10% in 2000. P&G instituted the use of *technology scouts* to search beyond the company for promising innovations. By 2007, the objective was achieved: 50% of the company's innovations originated outside P&G. Unfortunately, the unintended consequence was a sharp reduction in breakthrough products overall. Most of the innovations were relatively minor changes to existing products or products with very limited markets.[25]

A slightly different approach to technology development is for a large firm such as IBM or Microsoft to purchase minority stakes in relatively new high-tech entrepreneurial ventures that need capital to continue operation. Investing corporate venture capital is one way to gain access to promising innovations at a lower cost than by developing them internally.[26]

OPERATIONS STRATEGY

Operations strategy determines how and where a product or service is to be manufactured, the level of vertical integration in the production process, the deployment of physical resources, and relationships with suppliers. It should also deal with the optimum level of technology the firm should use in its operations processes. See the **Global Issue** feature to see how operational differences in national conditions can impact the global efforts of a worldwide brand.

Advanced Manufacturing Technology (AMT) is revolutionizing operations worldwide and should continue to have a major impact as corporations strive to integrate diverse business activities by using computer-assisted design and manufacturing (CAD/CAM) principles. The use of CAD/CAM, flexible manufacturing systems, computer numerically controlled systems, automatically guided vehicles, robotics, manufacturing resource planning (MRP II), optimized production technology, and just-in-time techniques contribute to increased flexibility, quick response time, and higher productivity. Such investments also act to increase the company's fixed costs and could cause significant problems if the company is unable to achieve economies of scale or scope. Baldor Electric Company, the largest maker of industrial electric motors in the United States, built a new factory using new technology to eliminate undesirable jobs with high employee turnover. With one-tenth the employees of its foreign plants, the plant was cost-competitive with motors produced in Mexico or China.[27]

A firm's manufacturing strategy is often affected by a product's life cycle. As the sales of a product increase, there will be an increase in production volume ranging from lot sizes as low as one in a *job shop* (one-of-a-kind production using skilled labor) through *connected line batch flow* (components are standardized; each machine functions such as a job shop but is positioned in the same order as the parts are processed) to lot sizes as high as 100,000 or more per year for *flexible manufacturing systems* (parts are grouped into manufacturing families to produce a wide variety of mass-produced items) and *dedicated transfer lines* (highly automated assembly lines making one mass-produced product using little human labor). According to this concept, the product becomes standardized into a commodity over time in conjunction with increasing demand. Flexibility thus gives way to efficiency.[28]

Increasing competitive intensity in many industries has forced companies to switch from traditional mass production using dedicated transfer lines to a continuous improvement production strategy. A *mass-production* system was an excellent method to produce a large number of low-cost, standard goods and services. Employees worked on narrowly defined, repetitive tasks under close supervision in a bureaucratic and hierarchical structure. Quality, however, often tended to be fairly low. Learning how to do something better was the prerogative of management; workers were expected only to learn what was assigned to them. This system tended to dominate manufacturing until the 1970s. Under the *continuous improvement* system developed W. Edwards Deming and perfected by Japanese firms, companies empowered cross-functional teams to constantly strive to improve production processes. Managers are more like coaches than bosses. The result is a large quantity of low-cost, standard goods and services, but with high quality. The key to continuous improvement is the acknowledgment that workers' experience and knowledge can help managers solve production problems and contribute to tightening variances and reducing errors. Because continuous improvement enables firms to use the same low-cost competitive strategy as do mass-production firms but at a significantly higher level of quality, it is rapidly replacing mass production as an operations strategy.

The automobile industry is currently experimenting with the strategy of *modular manufacturing* in which preassembled subassemblies are delivered as they are needed (i.e., just-in-time) to a company's assembly-line workers, who quickly piece the modules together into a finished product. For example, General Motors built a new automotive complex in Brazil to make its new subcompact, the Celta. Sixteen of the 17 buildings were occupied by suppliers, including Delphi, Lear, and Goodyear. These suppliers delivered preassembled modules (which comprised 85% of the final value of each car) to GM's building for assembly. In a process new to the industry, the suppliers acted as a team to build a single module comprising the motor, transmission, fuel lines, rear axle, brake-fluid lines, and exhaust system, which

GLOBAL issue

WHY DOESN'T STARBUCKS WANT TO EXPAND TO ITALY?

The concept of the Starbucks café (as it exists today) started in Milan, Italy, when Howard Schultz, then the Marketing Director for a coffee roasting business called Starbucks, saw how people talked to the folks making their coffee at the many coffee houses there. He came back to the United States and unable to convince his bosses about the idea, started up his own café in Seattle. Within three years, he had grown his company to such a size that he bought out the original roasting business.

Today, Starbucks has more than 11,000 locations in the United States, as well as 925 outlets in Japan, 730 in the UK, 314 in Mexico, and a significant presence in, among other places, Spain, France, Germany, Switzerland, Austria, Greece, Turkey, Lebanon, and Saudi Arabia. Interestingly, it does not have one outlet in Italy.

Why are there no Starbucks in Italy? Italy is the home of coffee culture and their approach to coffee is quite different. Italians primarily drink espresso and do so in one quick gulp. Cappuccino is strictly a breakfast drink, and while coffee stands are a gathering point, people rarely hang out after they have received their coffee.

That said, McDonald's has had significant success with its McCafé offering of traditional American style coffee, as well as Italian espresso. It encourages customers to linger much like the Starbucks model. McDonald's has opened 411 locations in Italy that serve coffee, including more than 100 that have a traditional Italian coffee bar.

So, should Starbucks make the move into Italy?

SOURCES: S. Faris, "Grounds Zero," *Bloomberg Businessweek* (February 13, 2012), (http://www.businessweek.com/magazine/grounds-zero-a-starbucksfree-italy-02092012.html); http://www.starbucks.com/about-us/our-heritage; "Starbucks Outlines Strategy for Accelerating Profitable Global Growth" (http://news.starbucks.com/article_display.cfm?article_id=342).

was then installed as one piece. GM hoped that this manufacturing strategy would enable it to produce 100 vehicles annually per worker compared to the standard rate of 30 to 50 autos per worker.[29] Ford and Chrysler have also opened similar modular facilities in Brazil.

The concept of a product's life cycle eventually leading to one-size-fits-all mass production is being increasingly challenged by the newer concept of mass customization. Appropriate for an ever-changing environment, *mass customization* requires that people, processes, units, and technology reconfigure themselves to give customers exactly what they want, when they want it. In the case of Dell Computer, customers can still use the Internet to design their own computers. In contrast to continuous improvement, mass customization requires flexibility and quick responsiveness. Managers coordinate independent, capable individuals. An efficient linkage system is crucial. The result is low-cost, high-quality, customized goods and services appropriate for a large number of market niches.

A contentious issue for manufacturing companies throughout the world is the availability of resources needed to operate a modern factory. The increasing cost of oil in the past decade has drastically boosted costs, only some of which could be passed on to the customers in a competitive environment. The likelihood that fresh water will become an equally scarce resource is causing many companies to rethink water-intensive manufacturing processes. To learn how companies are beginning to deal with global warming and increasing fresh water scarcity, see the **Sustainability Issue** feature.

PURCHASING STRATEGY

Purchasing strategy deals with obtaining the raw materials, parts, and supplies needed to perform the operations function. Purchasing strategy is important because materials and components purchased from suppliers comprise 50% of total manufacturing costs of manufacturing companies in the United Kingdom, United States, Australia, Belgium, and Finland.[30] The basic purchasing choices are multiple, sole, and parallel sourcing. Under *multiple sourcing*, the purchasing company orders a particular part from several vendors. Multiple sourcing has traditionally been considered superior to other purchasing approaches because (1) it forces suppliers to compete for the business of an important buyer, thus reducing purchasing costs, and (2) if one supplier cannot deliver, another usually can, thus guaranteeing that parts and supplies are always on hand when needed. Multiple sourcing has been one way for a purchasing firm to control the relationship with its suppliers. So long as suppliers can provide evidence that they can meet the product specifications, they are kept on the purchaser's list of acceptable vendors for specific parts and supplies. Unfortunately, the common practice of accepting the lowest bid often compromises quality.

W. Edwards Deming, a well-known management consultant, strongly recommended *sole sourcing* as the only manageable way to obtain high supplier quality. Sole sourcing relies on only one supplier for a particular part. Given his concern with designing quality into a product in its early stages of development, Deming argued that the buyer should work closely with the supplier at all stages. This reduces both cost and time spent on product design and it also improves quality. It can also simplify the purchasing company's production process by using the *just-in-time* (JIT) concept of having the purchased parts arrive at the plant just when they are needed rather than keeping inventories. The concept of sole sourcing is taken one step further in JIT II, in which vendor sales representatives actually have desks next to the purchasing company's factory floor, attend production status meetings, visit the R&D lab, and analyze the purchasing company's sales forecasts. These in-house suppliers then write sales orders for which the purchasing company is billed. Developed by Lance Dixon at Bose Corporation, JIT II is also being used at IBM, Honeywell, and Ingersoll-Rand. Karen Dale, purchasing manager for Honeywell's office supplies, said she was very concerned about confidentiality when JIT II was first suggested to her. Soon she had five suppliers working with her 20 buyers and reported few problems.[31]

SUSTAINABILITY issue

HOW HOT IS HOT?

July 2012 was the hottest month in the recorded history of the United States and the summer of 2012 ended up the third hottest on record. The United States has recorded 7 of the hottest 10 summers since 2000. The U.S. National Weather Service began recording temperatures in 1895 and only two other summers topped the one in 2012 (2011 and 1936).

The impact on freshwater availability is more than significant not only to individuals, but also the operations of companies. The United Nations reported that by the mid-1990s, some 40 percent of the world's population was suffering water shortages. They predict that in less than 25 years, two-thirds of the world's population will be living in water-stressed countries.

Nestlé, Unilever, Coca-Cola, Anheuser-Busch, and Danone consume almost 575 billion liters of water a year, enough to satisfy the daily water needs of every person on the planet. It takes about 13 cubic meters of freshwater to produce a single 200-mm semiconductor wafer. As a result, chip making is believed to account for 25% of the water consumption in Silicon Valley. According to José Lopez, Nestlé's COO, it takes four liters of water to make one liter of product in Nestlé's factories, but 3000 liters of water are needed to grow the agricultural produce that supplies them. Each year, around 40% of the freshwater withdrawn from lakes and aquifers in America is used to cool power plants. Separating one liter of oil from Canada's tar sands requires up to five liters of water!

"Water is the oil of the 21st century," contends Andrew Liveris, CEO of the chemical company Dow. Like oil, supplies of clean, easily accessible fresh water are under a growing strain because of the growing population and widespread improvements in living standards. Industrialization in developing nations is contaminating rivers and aquifers. Climate change is altering the patterns of fresh water availability so that droughts are more likely in many parts of the world. According to a survey by the Marsh Center for Risk Insights, 40% of Fortune 1000 companies stated that the impact of a water shortage on their business would be "severe" or "catastrophic," but only 17% said that they were prepared for such a crisis. Of Nestlé's 481 factories worldwide, 49 are located in water-scarce regions. Environmental activists have attacked PepsiCo and Coca-Cola for allegedly depleting groundwater in India to make bottled drinks.

There are a number of companies that are taking action to protect their future supply of freshwater. Dow has reduced the amount of water it uses by over a third since 1995. During 1997–2006, when Nestlé almost doubled the volume of food it produced, it reduced the amount of water used by 29%. China's Elion Chemical is working with General Electric to recycle 90% of its wastewater to comply with the government's new "zero-liquid" discharge rules.

SOURCES: D. Rice, "Summer 2012 Was the U.S.A.'s Third Hottest on Record," *USA Today* (September 11, 2012), (http://usatoday30.usatoday.com/weather/climate/story/2012-08-30/summer-temperatures/57729858/1); "The Impact of Global Change on Water Resources," UNESCO Report, (http://unesdoc.unesco.org/images/0019/001922/192216e.pdf); K. Kube, "Into the Wild Brown Yonder," *Trains* (November 2008), pp. 68–73; "Running Dry," *The Economist* (August 23, 2008), pp. 53–54.

Sole sourcing reduces transaction costs and builds quality by having the purchaser and supplier work together as partners rather than as adversaries. With sole sourcing, more companies will have longer relationships with fewer suppliers. Research has found that buyer-supplier collaboration and joint problem solving with both parties dependent upon the other results in the development of competitive capabilities, higher quality, lower costs, and better scheduling.[32] Sole sourcing does, however, have limitations. If a supplier is unable to deliver a part, the purchaser has no alternative but to delay production. Multiple suppliers can provide the purchaser with better information about new technology and performance capabilities. The limitations of sole sourcing have led to the development of parallel sourcing. In *parallel sourcing*, two suppliers are the sole suppliers of two different parts, but they are also backup suppliers for each other's parts. If one vendor cannot supply all of its parts on time, the other vendor is asked to make up the difference.[33]

The Internet is being increasingly used both to find new sources of supply and to keep inventories replenished. For example, Hewlett-Packard introduced a Web-based procurement system to enable its 84,000 employees to buy office supplies from a standard set of suppliers. The new system enabled the company to save US$60 to US$100 million annually in purchasing costs.[34] Research indicates that companies using Internet-based technologies are able to lower administrative costs and purchase prices.[35] Sometimes innovations tied to the use of the Internet for one strategy are adopted by other areas. See the Innovation Issue regarding the use and misuse of QR Codes.

LOGISTICS STRATEGY

Logistics strategy deals with the flow of products into and out of the manufacturing process. Three trends related to this strategy are evident: centralization, outsourcing, and the use of the Internet. To gain logistical synergies across business units, corporations began centralizing logistics in the headquarters group. This centralized logistics group usually contains specialists with expertise in different transportation modes such as rail or trucking. They work to aggregate shipping volumes across the entire corporation to gain better contracts with shippers. Companies such as Georgia-Pacific, Marriott, and Union Carbide view the logistics function as an important way to differentiate themselves from the competition, to add value, and to reduce costs.

Many companies have found that outsourcing logistics reduces costs and improves delivery time. For example, HP contracted with Roadway Logistics to manage its inbound raw materials warehousing in Vancouver, Canada. Nearly 140 Roadway employees replaced 250 HP workers, who were transferred to other HP activities.[36]

INNOVATION issue

WHEN AN INNOVATION FAILS TO LIVE UP TO EXPECTATIONS

Sometimes a promising innovation has to find the right application for it to have an impact on strategy formulation. Such has been the fate of QR Codes. QR Codes, or Quick Response Codes, are those dense, square, grids of black and white that seem to be everywhere. Invented in 1994 by Denso Wave (a subsidiary of Toyota Group), the original intent of the little block was to improve the inventory tracking of auto parts. While the QR code is patented, the company published complete specifications online and allowed anyone to use the codes for free.

Over the past few years, the codes have been adopted by advertisers as a means to improve the connection between a company and its customers. In December 2011, more than 8% of magazine ads contained the codes, up from just over 3% at the beginning of the year. Unfortunately, most companies seem to have little idea how to use the codes to engage the consumer. Most direct the consumer's cell phone to the corporate Web site, and

therein lies much of the issue with using this as a part of a company's strategy. The QR code requires the consumer to download an app that reads the codes onto their cell phone and then hold the phone very steady as they take a picture of the code that they want to follow.

The codes have found a real value in the movie theater business as more people buy their tickets online. The codes are downloaded to a consumer's Smartphone and scanned as a ticket upon entering the theater. They could also be used to help prevent counterfeit goods, but some companies have put the codes on billboards (virtually impossible to scan), the inside of liquor bottles, and on subway posters (low light prevents the app from working).

Not all innovations that businesses can adopt should be adopted. Finding the value and aligning the innovation with the competitive advantages of the business are crucial. Where do you believe QR codes could be put to their best use?

....

SOURCES: "QR Code Fatigue," *Bloomberg Businessweek* (July 2, 2012), pp. 28–29; https://www.denso-wave.com/en/; http://www.qrcode.com/en/index.html.

Many companies are using the Internet to simplify their logistical system. For example, Ace Hardware created an online system for its retailers and suppliers. An individual hardware store can now see on the Web site that ordering 210 cases of wrenches is cheaper than ordering 200 cases. Because a full pallet is composed of 210 cases of wrenches, an order for a full pallet means that the supplier doesn't have to pull 10 cases off a pallet and repackage them for storage. There is less chance that loose cases will be lost in delivery, and the paperwork doesn't have to be redone. As a result, Ace's transportation costs are down 18%, and warehouse costs have been cut 28%.[37]

HUMAN RESOURCE MANAGEMENT (HRM) STRATEGY

HRM strategy, among other things, addresses the issue of whether a company or business unit should hire a large number of low-skilled employees who receive low pay, perform repetitive jobs, and will most likely quit after a short time (the fast-food restaurant strategy) or hire skilled employees who receive relatively high pay and are cross-trained to participate in *self-managing work teams*. As work increases in complexity, the more suited it is for teams, especially in the case of innovative product development efforts. Multinational corporations are increasingly using self-managing work teams in their foreign affiliates as well as in home-country operations.[38] Research indicates that the use of work teams leads to increased quality and productivity as well as to higher employee satisfaction and commitment.[39]

Companies following a competitive strategy of differentiation through high quality use input from subordinates and peers in performance appraisals to a greater extent than do firms following other business strategies.[40] A complete *360-degree appraisal*, in which performance input is gathered from multiple sources, is now being used by more than 90% of the Fortune 500 (according to Fortune magazine) and has become one of the most popular tools in developing employees and new managers.[41] One Indian company, HCL Technologies, publishes the appraisal ratings for the top 20 managers on the company's intranet for all to see.[42]

Companies are finding that having a *diverse workforce* can be a competitive advantage. Research reveals that firms with a high degree of racial diversity following a growth strategy have higher productivity than do firms with less racial diversity.[43] Avon Company, for example, was able to turn around its unprofitable inner-city markets by putting African-American and Hispanic managers in charge of marketing to these markets.[44] Diversity in terms of age and national origin also offers benefits. DuPont's use of multinational teams has helped the company develop and market products internationally. McDonald's has discovered that older workers perform as well as, if not better than, younger employees. According to Edward Rensi, CEO of McDonald's USA, "We find these people to be particularly well motivated, with a sort of discipline and work habits hard to find in younger employees."[45]

INFORMATION TECHNOLOGY STRATEGY

Corporations are increasingly using **information technology strategy** to provide business units with competitive advantage. When FedEx first provided its customers with PowerShip computer software to store addresses, print shipping labels, and track package location, its sales jumped significantly. UPS soon followed with its own MaxiShips software. Viewing its information system as a distinctive competency, FedEx continued to push for further advantage over UPS by using its Web site to enable customers to track their packages. FedEx uses this competency in its advertisements by showing how customers can track the progress of their shipments. Soon thereafter, UPS provided the same service. Although it can be argued that information technology has now become so pervasive that it no longer offers companies a competitive advantage, corporations worldwide continue to spend over US$3.6 trillion annually on information technology.[46]

Multinational corporations are finding that having a sophisticated intranet allows employees to practice *follow-the-sun management*, in which project team members living in one country can pass their work to team members in another country in which the work day is just beginning. Thus, night shifts are no longer needed.[47] The development of instant translation software is also enabling workers to have online communication with co-workers in other countries who use a different language.[48] For example, Mattel has cut the time it takes to develop new products by 10% by enabling designers and licensees in other countries to collaborate on toy design. IBM uses its intranet to allow its employees to collaborate and improve their skills, thus reducing its training and travel expenses.[49]

Many companies, such as Lockheed Martin, General Electric, and Whirlpool, use information technology to form closer relationships with both their customers and suppliers through sophisticated extranets. For example, General Electric's Trading Process Network allows suppliers to electronically download GE's requests for proposals, view diagrams of parts specifications, and communicate with GE purchasing managers. According to Robert Livingston, GE's head of worldwide sourcing for the Lighting Division, going on the Web reduces processing time by one-third.[50] Thus, the use of information technology through extranets makes it easier for a company to buy from others (outsource) rather than make it themselves (vertically integrate).[51]

The Sourcing Decision: Location of Functions

For a functional strategy to have the best chance of success, it should be built on a distinctive competency residing within that functional area. If a corporation does not have a distinctive competency in a particular functional area, that functional area could be a candidate for outsourcing.

Outsourcing is purchasing from someone else a product or service that had been previously provided internally. Thus, it is the reverse of vertical integration. Outsourcing is becoming an increasingly important part of strategic decision making and an important way to increase efficiency and often quality. In a study of 30 firms, outsourcing resulted on average in a 9% reduction in costs and a 15% increase in capacity and quality.[52] For example, Boeing used outsourcing as a way to reduce the cost of designing and manufacturing its new 787 Dreamliner. Up to 70% of the plane was outsourced. In a break from past practice, suppliers make large parts of the fuselage, including plumbing, electrical, and computer systems, and ship them to Seattle for assembly by Boeing.[53]

According to a 2012 survey by Deloitte Consulting, The most popular outsourced activities are Information Technology (76%), operations (42%), legal (40%), finance (37%), real-estate/facilities (32%), HR (30%), procurement (24%), and sales/marketing support (11%). The survey also reveals that the top factors in a successful outsourcing relationship are a spirit of partnership, a well-designed agreement, joint governance, and consistent communication.[54] Authorities not only expect the number of companies engaging in outsourcing to increase, they also expect companies to outsource an increasing number of functions, especially those in customer service, bookkeeping, financial/clerical, sales/telemarketing, and the mailroom.[55] It is estimated that 50% of U.S. manufacturing will be outsourced to firms in 28 developing countries by 2015.[56]

Offshoring is the outsourcing of an activity or a function to a wholly owned company or an independent provider in another country. Offshoring is a global phenomenon that has been supported by advances in information and communication technologies, the development of stable, secure, and high-speed data transmission systems, and logistical advances like containerized shipping. According to Bain & Company, 51% of large firms in North America, Europe, and Asia outsource offshore.[57] Although India currently has 70% of the offshoring market, countries such as Brazil, China, Russia, the Philippines, Malaysia, Hungary, the Czech Republic, and Israel are growing in importance. These countries have low-cost qualified labor and an educated workforce. These are important considerations because more than 93% of offshoring companies do so to reduce costs.[58] For example, Mexican assembly line workers average US$4.00 an hour plus benefits compared to US$28 an hour plus benefits at a GM or Ford plant in the United States. Less-skilled Mexican workers at auto parts makers earn as little as US$1.50 per hour with fewer benefits.[59]

Software programming and customer service, in particular, are being outsourced to India. For example, General Electric's back-office services unit, GE Capital International Services which was spun off into a new company called Genpact, is one of the oldest and biggest of India's outsourcing companies. From only US$26 million in 1999, its annual revenues grew to over US$1.6 billion by 2011.[60] As part of this trend, IBM acquired Daksh eServices Ltd., one of India's biggest suppliers of remote business services.[61]

Outsourcing, including offshoring, has significant disadvantages. For example, mounting complaints forced Dell Computer to stop routing corporate customers to a technical support call center in Bangalore, India.[62] GE's introduction of a new washing machine was delayed three weeks because of production problems at a supplier's company to which it had contracted out key work. Some companies have found themselves locked into long-term contracts with outside suppliers that were no longer competitive.[63] Some authorities propose that the cumulative effects of continued outsourcing steadily reduces a firm's ability to learn new skills and to develop new core competencies.[64] One survey of 129 outsourcing firms revealed that half the outsourcing projects undertaken in one year failed to deliver anticipated savings. This is in agreement with a survey by Bain & Company in which 51% of large North American, European, and Asian firms stated that outsourcing (including offshoring) did not meet their expectations.[65] Another survey of software projects, by MIT, found that the median Indian project had 10% more software bugs than did comparable U.S. projects.[66] The increasing cost of oil was making offshoring less economical. Since 2003, crude oil increased in price from US$28 to over US$90 a barrel in 2012. [67]

A study of 91 outsourcing efforts conducted by European and North American firms found seven major errors that should be avoided:

1. **Outsourcing activities that should not be outsourced:** Companies failed to keep core activities in-house.

2. **Selecting the wrong vendor:** Vendors were not trustworthy or lacked state-of-the-art processes.

3. **Writing a poor contract:** Companies failed to establish a balance of power in the relationship.

4. **Overlooking personnel issues:** Employees lost commitment to the firm.

5. **Losing control over the outsourced activity:** Qualified managers failed to manage the outsourced activity.[68]

6. **Overlooking the hidden costs of outsourcing:** Transaction costs overwhelmed other savings.

7. **Failing to plan an exit strategy:** Companies failed to build reversibility clauses into the contract.[69]

The key to outsourcing is to purchase from outside only those activities that are not key to the company's distinctive competencies. Otherwise, the company may give up the very capabilities that made it successful in the first place—thus putting itself on the road to eventual decline. This is supported by research reporting that companies that have more experience with a particular manufacturing technology tend to keep manufacturing in-house.[70] J. P. Morgan Chase & Company terminated a seven-year technology outsourcing agreement with IBM because the bank's management realized that information technology (IT) was too important strategically to be outsourced.[71]

In determining functional strategy, the strategist must:

- Identify the company's or business unit's core competencies.
- Ensure that the competencies are continually being strengthened.
- Manage the competencies in such a way that best preserves the competitive advantage they create.

An outsourcing decision depends on the fraction of total value added that the activity under consideration represents and on the amount of potential competitive advantage in that activity for the company or business unit. See the outsourcing matrix in **Figure 8–1**. A firm should consider outsourcing any activity or function that has low potential for competitive advantage. If that activity constitutes only a small part of the total value of the firm's products or services, it should be purchased on the open market (assuming that quality providers of the activity are plentiful). If, however, the activity contributes highly to the company's products or services, the firm should purchase it through long-term contracts with trusted suppliers or distributors. A firm should always produce at least some of the activity or function (i.e., taper vertical integration) if that activity has the potential for providing the company some competitive advantage. However, full vertical integration should be considered only when that activity or function adds significant value to the company's products or services in addition to providing competitive advantage.[72]

FIGURE 8–1
Proposed
Outsourcing
Matrix

SOURCE: J. D. Hunger and T. L. Wheelen, "Proposed Outsourcing Matrix." Copyright © 1996 and 2005 by Wheelen and Hunger Associates. Reprinted by permission.

Strategies to Avoid

Several strategies that could be considered corporate, business, or functional are very danger-ous. Managers who have made poor analyses or lack creativity may be trapped into consider-ing some of the following strategies to avoid:

- **Follow the leader:** Imitating a leading competitor's strategy might seem to be a good idea, but it ignores a firm's particular competitive advantages and the possibility that the leader may be wrong. Fujitsu Ltd., the world's second-largest computer maker, had been driven since the 1960s by the sole ambition of catching up to IBM. Like IBM at the time, Fujitsu competed primarily as a mainframe computer maker. So devoted was it to catching IBM, however, that it failed to notice that the mainframe business had reached maturity by 1990 and was no longer growing.

- **Hit another home run:** If a company is successful because it pioneered an extremely successful product, it tends to search for another super product that will ensure growth and prosperity. As in betting on long shots in horse races, the probability of finding a sec-ond winner is slight. Polaroid spent a lot of money developing an "instant" movie camera, but the public ignored it in favor of the camcorder.

- **Arms race:** Entering into a spirited battle with another firm for increased market share might increase sales revenue, but that increase will probably be more than offset by in-creases in advertising, promotion, R&D, and manufacturing costs. Since the deregulation of airlines, price wars and rate specials have contributed to the low profit margins and bankruptcies of many major airlines, such as Eastern, Pan American, TWA, and virtually every major airline still operating today.

- **Do everything:** When faced with several interesting opportunities, management might tend to leap at all of them. At first, a corporation might have enough resources to develop each idea into a project, but money, time, and energy are soon exhausted as the many proj-ects demand large infusions of resources. The Walt Disney Company's expertise in the entertainment industry led it to acquire the ABC network. As the company churned out new motion pictures and television programs such as *Who Wants to Be a Millionaire?* it spent US$750 million to build new theme parks and buy a cruise line and a hockey team. By 2000, even though corporate sales had continued to increase, net income was falling.[73]

- **Losing hand:** A corporation might have invested so much in a particular strategy that top management is unwilling to accept its failure. Believing that it has too much invested to quit, management may continue to "throw good money after bad." RIM's BlackBerry phone was the undisputed leader in Smartphone technology and acceptance. They were so focused on their approach to how users needed to access information that they missed seeing how the new entrants in the industry had changed the industry. By the time they accepted that a change had really occurred, they were so far behind that catching up was virtually impossible.

Strategic Choice: Selecting the Best Strategy

After the pros and cons of the potential strategic alternatives have been identified and evalu-ated, one must be selected for implementation. By now, it is likely that many feasible alterna-tives will have emerged. How is the best strategy determined?

Perhaps the most important criterion is the capability of the proposed strategy to deal with the specific strategic factors developed earlier using the SWOT approach. If the alternative doesn't take advantage of environmental opportunities and corporate strengths/competencies, and lead away from environmental threats and corporate weaknesses, it will probably fail.

Another important consideration in the selection of a strategy is the ability of each alternative to satisfy agreed-upon objectives with the least resources and the fewest negative side effects. It is, therefore, important to develop a tentative implementation plan in order to address the difficulties that management is likely to face. This should be done in light of societal trends, the industry, and the company's situation based on the construction of scenarios.

CONSTRUCTING CORPORATE SCENARIOS

Corporate scenarios are *pro forma* (estimated future) balance sheets and income statements that forecast the effect each alternative strategy and its various programs will likely have on division and corporate return on investment. (Pro forma financial statements are discussed in **Chapter 12**.) In a survey of Fortune 500 firms, 84% reported using computer simulation models in strategic planning. Most of these were simply spreadsheet-based simulation models dealing with what-if questions.[74]

The recommended scenarios are simply extensions of the industry scenarios discussed in **Chapter 4**. If, for example, industry scenarios suggest the probable emergence of a strong market demand in a specific country for certain products, a series of alternative strategy scenarios can be developed. The alternative of acquiring another firm having these products in that country can be compared with the alternative of a green-field development (e.g., building new operations in that country). Using three sets of estimated sales figures (optimistic, pessimistic, and most likely) for the new products over the next five years, the two alternatives can be evaluated in terms of their effect on future company performance as reflected in the company's probable future financial statements. Pro forma balance sheets and income statements can be generated with spreadsheet software, such as Excel, on a personal computer. Pro forma statements are based on financial and economic scenarios.

To construct a corporate scenario, follow these steps:

1. Use industry scenarios (as discussed in **Chapter 4**) to develop a set of assumptions about the task environment (in the specific country under consideration). For example, 3M requires the general manager of each business unit to describe annually what his or her industry will look like in 15 years. List *optimistic, pessimistic*, and *most likely* assumptions for key economic factors such as the GDP (Gross Domestic Product), CPI (consumer price index), and prime interest rate and for other key external strategic factors such as governmental regulation and industry trends. This should be done for every country/region in which the corporation has significant operations that will be affected by each strategic alternative. These same underlying assumptions should be listed for each of the alternative scenarios to be developed.

2. Develop common-size financial statements (as discussed in **Chapter 12**) for the company's or business unit's previous years to serve as the basis for the trend analysis projections of pro forma financial statements. Use the *Scenario Box* form shown in **Table 8–1**:

   a. Use the historical common-size percentages to estimate the level of revenues, expenses, and other categories in estimated pro forma statements for future years.
   b. Develop for each strategic alternative a set of *optimistic(O), pessimistic(P)*, and *most likely(ML)* assumptions about the impact of key variables on the company's future financial statements.
   c. Forecast three sets of sales and cost of goods sold figures for at least five years into the future.
   d. Analyze historical data and make adjustments based on the environmental assumptions listed earlier. Do the same for other figures that can vary significantly.

TABLE 8–1	Scenario Box for Use in Generating Financial Pro Forma Statements													
				Projections[1]										
				200–			**200–**			**200–**			
Factor	**Last Year**	**Historical Average**	**Trend Analysis**	**O**	**P**	**ML**	**O**	**P**	**ML**	**O**	**P**	**ML**	**Comments**
GDP													
CPI													
Other													
Sales units													
Dollars													
COGS													
Advertising and marketing													
Interest expense													
Plant expansion													
Dividends													
Net profits													
EPS													
ROI													
ROE													
Other													

NOTE 1: O = Optimistic; P = Pessimistic; ML = Most Likely.

SOURCE: T. L. Wheelen and J. D. Hunger. Copyright © 1987, 1988, 1989, 1990, 1992, 2005, and 2009 by T. L. Wheelen. Copyright © 1993 and 2005 by Wheelen and Hunger Associates. Reprinted with permission.

    e. Assume for other figures that they will continue in their historical relationship to sales or some other key determining factor. Plug in expected inventory levels, accounts receivable, accounts payable, R&D expenses, advertising and promotion expenses, capital expenditures, and debt payments (assuming that debt is used to finance the strategy), among others.

    f. Consider not only historical trends but also programs that might be needed to implement each alternative strategy (such as building a new manufacturing facility or expanding the sales force).

3. Construct detailed pro forma financial statements for each strategic alternative:

    a. List the actual figures from this year's financial statements in the left column of the spreadsheet.

    b. List to the right of this column the optimistic figures for years 1 through 5.

    c. Go through this same process with the same strategic alternative, but now list the pessimistic figures for the next five years.

    d. Do the same with the most likely figures.

    e. Develop a similar set of optimistic (O), pessimistic (P), and most likely (ML) pro forma statements for the second strategic alternative. This process generates six different pro forma scenarios reflecting three different situations (O, P, and ML) for two strategic alternatives.

    f. Calculate financial ratios and common-size income statements and create balance sheets to accompany the pro forma statements.

    g. Compare the assumptions underlying the scenarios with the financial statements and ratios to determine the feasibility of the scenarios. For example, if cost of goods sold drops from 70% to 50% of total sales revenue in the pro forma income statements, this drop should result from a change in the production process or a shift to cheaper raw materials or labor costs rather than from a failure to keep the cost of goods sold in its usual percentage relationship to sales revenue when the predicted statement was developed.

The result of this detailed scenario construction should be anticipated net profits, cash flow, and net working capital for each of three versions of the two alternatives for five years into the future. A strategist might want to go further into the future if the strategy is expected to have a major impact on the company's financial statements beyond five years. The result of this work should provide sufficient information on which forecasts of the likely feasibility and probable profitability of each of the strategic alternatives could be based.

Obviously, these scenarios can quickly become very complicated, especially if three sets of acquisition prices and development costs are calculated. Nevertheless, this sort of detailed what-if analysis is needed to realistically compare the projected outcome of each reasonable alternative strategy and its attendant programs, budgets, and procedures. Regardless of the quantifiable pros and cons of each alternative, the actual decision will probably be influenced by several subjective factors such as those described in the following sections.

Management's Attitude Toward Risk

The attractiveness of a particular strategic alternative is partially a function of the amount of risk it entails. **Risk** is composed not only of the *probability* that the strategy will be effective but also of the *amount of assets* the corporation must allocate to that strategy and the *length of time* the assets will be unavailable for other uses. Because of variation among countries in terms of customs, regulations, and resources, companies operating in global industries must deal with a greater amount of risk than firms operating only in one country.[75] The greater the assets involved and the longer they are committed, the more likely top management is to demand a high probability of success. Managers with no ownership position in a company are unlikely to have much interest in putting their jobs in danger with risky decisions. Research indicates that managers who own a significant amount of stock in their firms are more likely to engage in risk-taking actions than are managers with no stock.[76]

A high level of risk was why Intel's board of directors found it difficult to vote for a proposal in the early 1990s to commit US$5 billion to making the Pentium microprocessor chip—five times the amount of money needed for its previous chip. In looking back on that board meeting, then-CEO Andy Grove remarked, "I remember people's eyes looking at that chart and getting big. I wasn't even sure I believed those numbers at the time." The proposal committed the company to building new factories—something Intel had been reluctant to do. A wrong decision would mean that the company would end up with a killing amount of overcapacity. Based on Grove's presentation, the board decided to take the gamble. Intel's resulting manufacturing expansion eventually cost US$10 billion but resulted in Intel's obtaining 75% of the microprocessor business and huge cash profits.[77]

Risk might be one reason that significant innovations occur more often in small firms than in large, established corporations. A small firm managed by an entrepreneur is often willing to accept greater risk than is a large firm of diversified ownership run by professional managers.[78] It is one thing to take a chance if you are the primary shareholder and are not concerned with periodic changes in the value of the company's common stock. It is something else if the corporation's stock is widely held and acquisition-hungry competitors or takeover artists surround the company like sharks every time the company's stock price falls below some external assessment of the firm's value.

A new approach to evaluating alternatives under conditions of high environmental uncertainty is to use the real-options theory. According to the **real-options** approach, when the future is highly uncertain, it pays to have a broad range of options open. This is in contrast to using *net present value (NPV)* to calculate the value of a project by predicting its payouts, adjusting them for risk, and subtracting the amount invested. By boiling everything down to one scenario, NPV doesn't provide any flexibility in case circumstances change. NPV is also difficult to apply to projects in which the potential payoffs are currently unknown. The real-options approach, however, deals with these issues by breaking the investment into stages.

Management allocates a small amount of funding to initiate multiple projects, monitors their development, and then cancels the projects that aren't successful and funds those that are doing well.[79] This approach is very similar to the way venture capitalists fund an entrepreneurial venture in stages of funding based on the venture's performance.

A survey of 4000 CFOs found that 27% of them always or almost always used some sort of options approach to evaluating and deciding upon growth opportunities.[80] Research indicates that the use of the real-options approach does improve organizational performance.[81] Some of the corporations using the real-options approach are Chevron for bidding on petroleum reserves, Airbus for calculating the costs of airlines changing their orders at the last minute, and the Tennessee Valley Authority for outsourcing electricity generation instead of building its own plant. Because of its complexity, the real-options approach is not worthwhile for minor decisions or for projects requiring a full commitment at the beginning.[82]

Pressures from Stakeholders

The attractiveness of a strategic alternative is affected by its perceived compatibility with the key stakeholders in a corporation's task environment. Creditors want to be paid on time. Unions exert pressure for comparable wage and employment security. Governments and interest groups demand social responsibility. Shareholders want dividends. All these pressures must be given some consideration in the selection of the best alternative.

Stakeholders can be categorized in terms of their (1) interest in the corporation's activities and (2) relative power to influence the corporation's activities. As shown in **Figure 8–2**, each stakeholder group can be shown graphically based on its *level of interest* (from low to high) in a corporation's activities and on its *relative power* (from low to high) to influence a corporation's activities.

Strategic managers should ask four questions to assess the importance of stakeholder concerns in a particular decision:

1. How will this decision affect each stakeholder, especially those given high and medium priority?

2. How much of what each stakeholder wants is he or she likely to get under this alternative?

FIGURE 8–2
Stakeholder Priority Matrix

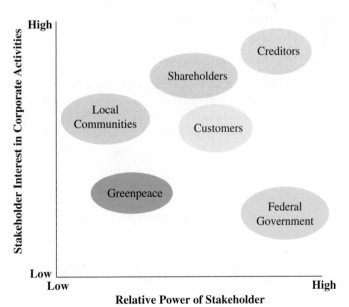

SOURCE: Suggested by C. Anderson in "Values-Based Management," *Academy of Management Executive* (November 1997), pp. 25–46.

3. What are the stakeholders likely to do if they don't get what they want?

4. What is the probability that they will do it?

Strategy makers should choose strategic alternatives that minimize external pressures and maximize the probability of gaining stakeholder support. Managers may, however, ignore or take some stakeholders for granted—leading to serious problems later. The Tata Group, for example, failed to consider the unwillingness of farmers in Singur, India, to accept the West Bengal government's compensation for expropriating their land so that Tata could build its Nano auto plant. Farmers formed rallies against the plant, blocked roads, and even assaulted an employee of a Tata supplier.[83]

Top management can also propose a political strategy to influence its key stakeholders. A **political strategy** is a plan to bring stakeholders into agreement with a corporation's actions. Some of the most commonly used political strategies are constituency building, political action committee contributions, advocacy advertising, lobbying, and coalition building. Research reveals that large firms, those operating in concentrated industries, and firms that are highly dependent upon government regulation are more politically active.[84] Political support can be critical in entering a new international market, especially in transition economies where free market competition did not previously exist.[85]

Pressures from the Corporate Culture

If a strategy is incompatible with a company's corporate culture, the likelihood of its success is very low. Foot-dragging and even sabotage will result as employees fight to resist a radical change in corporate philosophy. Precedents from the past tend to restrict the kinds of objectives and strategies that are seriously considered.[86] The "aura" of the founders of a corporation can linger long past their lifetimes because their values are imprinted on a corporation's members.

In evaluating a strategic alternative, strategy makers must consider pressures from the corporate culture and assess a strategy's compatibility with that culture. If there is little fit, management must decide if it should:

- Take a chance on ignoring the culture.
- Manage around the culture and change the implementation plan.
- Try to change the culture to fit the strategy.
- Change the strategy to fit the culture.

Further, a decision to proceed with a particular strategy without a commitment to change the culture or manage around the culture (both very tricky and time consuming) is dangerous. Nevertheless, restricting a corporation to only those strategies that are completely compatible with its culture might eliminate from consideration the most profitable alternatives. (See **Chapter 10** for more information on managing corporate culture.)

Needs and Desires of Key Managers

Even the most attractive alternative might not be selected if it is contrary to the needs and desires of important top managers. Personal characteristics and experience affect a person's assessment of an alternative's attractiveness.[87] For example, one study found that narcissistic (self-absorbed and arrogant) CEOs favor bold actions that attract attention, like many large acquisitions—resulting in either big wins or big losses.[88] A person's ego may be tied to a particular proposal to the extent that all other alternatives are strongly lobbied against. As a result, the person may have unfavorable forecasts altered so that they are more in agreement with the desired alternative.[89] In a study by McKinsey & Company of 2507 executives from around the world, 36% responded that managers hide, restrict, or misrepresent information at least "somewhat" frequently when submitting capital-investment proposals. In addition, an executive might influence other people in top management to favor a particular alternative so that objections to it are overruled. In the same McKinsey study of global executives, more than 60% of the managers reported that business unit and divisional heads form alliances with peers or lobby someone more senior in the organization at least "somewhat" frequently when resource allocation decisions are being made.[90]

Industry and cultural backgrounds affect strategic choice. For example, executives with strong ties within an industry tend to choose strategies commonly used in that industry. Other executives who have come to the firm from another industry and have strong ties outside the industry tend to choose different strategies from what is being currently used in their industry.[91] Country of origin often affects preferences. For example, Japanese managers prefer a cost-leadership strategy more than do United States managers.[92] Research reveals that executives from Korea, the United States, Japan, and Germany tend to make different strategic choices in similar situations because they use different decision criteria and weights. For example, Korean executives emphasize industry attractiveness, sales, and market share in their decisions, whereas U.S. executives emphasize projected demand, discounted cash flow, and ROI.[93]

There is a tendency to maintain the status quo, which means that decision makers continue with existing goals and plans beyond the point when an objective observer would recommend a change in course.[94] Some executives show a self-serving tendency to attribute the firm's problems not to their own poor decisions but to environmental events out of their control, such as government policies or a poor economic climate.[95] For example, a CEO is more likely to divest a poorly performing unit when its poor performance does not incriminate that same CEO who had acquired it.[96] Negative information about a particular course of action to which a person is committed may be ignored because of a desire to appear competent or because of strongly held values regarding consistency. It may take a crisis or an unlikely event to cause strategic decision makers to seriously consider an alternative they had previously ignored or discounted.[97] For example, it wasn't until the CEO of ConAgra, a multinational food products company, had a heart attack that ConAgra started producing the Healthy Choice line of low-fat, low-cholesterol, low-sodium frozen-food entrees.

THE PROCESS OF STRATEGIC CHOICE

Strategic choice is the evaluation of alternative strategies and selection of the best alternative. According to Paul Nutt, an authority in decision making, half of the decisions made by managers are failures.[98] After analyzing 400 decisions, Nutt found that failure almost always stems from the actions of the decision maker, not from bad luck or situational limitations. In these instances, managers commit one or more key blunders: (1) their desire for speedy actions leads to a rush to judgment, (2) they apply failure-prone decision-making practices such as adopting the claim of an influential stakeholder, and (3) they make poor use of resources by investigating only one or two options. These three blunders cause executives to limit their search for feasible alternatives and look for a quick consensus. Only 4% of the 400 managers set an objective and considered several alternatives. The search for innovative options was attempted in only 24% of the decisions studied.[99] Another study of 68 divestiture decisions found a strong tendency for managers to rely heavily on past experience when developing strategic alternatives.[100]

There is mounting evidence that when an organization is facing a dynamic environment, the best strategic decisions are not arrived at through **consensus** when everyone agrees on one alternative. They actually involve a certain amount of heated disagreement, and even conflict.[101] Many diverse opinions are presented, participants trust in one another's abilities and competencies, and conflict is task-oriented, not personal.[102] This is certainly the case for firms operating in global industries. Because unmanaged conflict often carries a high emotional cost, authorities in decision making propose that strategic managers use "programmed conflict" to raise different opinions, regardless of the personal feelings of the people involved.[103] Two techniques help strategic managers avoid the consensus trap that Alfred Sloan found:

1. **Devil's advocate:** The idea of the **devil's advocate** originated in the medieval Roman Catholic Church as a way of ensuring that impostors were not canonized as saints. One trusted person was selected to find and present all the reasons why a person should not be canonized. When this process is applied to strategic decision making, a devil's advocate (who may be an individual or a group) is assigned to identify potential pitfalls and problems with a proposed alternative strategy in a formal presentation.

2. **Dialectical inquiry:** The dialectical philosophy, which can be traced back to Plato and Aristotle and more recently to Hegel, involves combining two conflicting views—the thesis and the antithesis—into a synthesis. When applied to strategic decision making, **dialectical inquiry** requires that two proposals using different assumptions be generated for each alternative strategy under consideration. After advocates of each position present and debate the merits of their arguments before key decision makers, either one of the alternatives or a new compromise alternative is selected as the strategy to be implemented.

Research generally supports the conclusion that the devil's advocate and dialectical inquiry methods are equally superior to consensus in decision making, especially when the firm's environment is dynamic. The debate itself, rather than its particular format, appears to improve the quality of decisions by formalizing and legitimizing constructive conflict and by encouraging critical evaluation. Both lead to better assumptions and recommendations and to a higher level of critical thinking among the people involved.[104]

Regardless of the process used to generate strategic alternatives, each resulting alternative must be rigorously evaluated in terms of its ability to meet four criteria:

1. **Mutual exclusivity:** Doing any one alternative would preclude doing any other.
2. **Success:** It must be feasible and have a good probability of success.
3. **Completeness:** It must take into account all the key strategic issues.
4. **Internal consistency:** It must make sense on its own as a strategic decision for the entire firm and not contradict key goals, policies, and strategies currently being pursued by the firm or its units.[105]

Developing Policies

The selection of the best strategic alternative is not the end of strategy formulation. The organization must then engage in developing policies. Policies define the broad guidelines for implementation. Flowing from the selected strategy, policies provide guidance for decision making and actions throughout the organization. They are the principles under which the corporation operates on a day-to-day basis. At General Electric, for example, Chairman Jack Welch initiated the policy that any GE business unit must be number one or number two in whatever market it competes. This policy gave clear guidance to managers throughout the organization.

When crafted correctly, an effective policy accomplishes three things:

- It forces trade-offs between competing resource demands.

- It tests the strategic soundness of a particular action.
- It sets clear boundaries within which employees must operate, while granting them the freedom to experiment within those constraints.[106]

Policies tend to be rather long lived and can even outlast the particular strategy that created them. These general policies—such as "The customer is always right" (Nordstrom) or "Always Low Prices" (Wal-Mart)—can become, in time, part of a corporation's culture. Such policies can make the implementation of specific strategies easier. They can also restrict top management's strategic options in the future. Thus a change in strategy should be followed quickly by a change in policies. Managing policy is one way to manage the corporate culture.

End of Chapter SUMMARY

This chapter completes the part of this book on strategy formulation and sets the stage for strategy implementation. Functional strategies must be formulated to support business and corporate strategies; otherwise, the company will move in multiple directions and eventually pull itself apart. For a functional strategy to have the best chance of success, it should be built on a distinctive competency residing within that functional area. If a corporation does not have a distinctive competency in a particular functional area, that functional area could be a candidate for outsourcing.

When evaluating a strategic alternative, the most important criterion is the ability of the proposed strategy to deal with the specific strategic factors developed earlier, in the SWOT approach. If the alternative doesn't take advantage of environmental opportunities and corporate strengths/competencies, and lead away from environmental threats and corporate weaknesses, it will probably fail. Developing corporate scenarios and pro forma projections for each alternative are rational aids for strategic decision making. This logical approach fits Mintzberg's planning mode of strategic decision making, as discussed earlier in **Chapter 1**. Nevertheless, some strategic decisions are inherently risky and are often resolved on the basis of one person's "gut feel." This is an aspect of the entrepreneurial mode and is seen in large established corporations as well as in new venture startups. Various management studies have found that executives routinely rely on their intuition to solve complex problems. The effective use of intuition has been found to differentiate successful top executives and board members from lower-level managers and dysfunctional boards.[107] According to Ralph Larsen, former Chair and CEO of Johnson & Johnson, "Often there is absolutely no way that you could have the time to thoroughly analyze every one of the options or alternatives available to you. So you have to rely on your business judgment."[108] For managerial intuition to be effective, however, it requires years of experience in problem solving and is founded upon a complete understanding of the details of the business.[109]

For example, when Bob Lutz, then President of Chrysler Corporation, was enjoying a fast drive in his Cobra roadster one weekend in 1988, he wondered why Chrysler's cars were so dull. "I felt guilty: there I was, the president of Chrysler, driving this great car that had such a strong Ford association," said Lutz, referring to the original Cobra's Ford V-8 engine. That Monday, Lutz enlisted allies at Chrysler to develop a muscular, outrageous sports car that would turn heads and stop traffic. Others in management argued that the US$80 million investment would be better spent elsewhere. The sales force warned that no U.S. auto maker had ever succeeded in selling a US$50,000 car. With only his gut instincts to support him, he pushed the project forward with unwavering commitment. The result was the Dodge Viper—a car that single-handedly changed the public's perception of Chrysler. Years later, Lutz had trouble describing exactly how he had made this critical decision. "It was this subconscious, visceral feeling. And it just felt right," explained Lutz.[110]

MyManagementLab®

Go to **mymanagementlab.com** to complete the problems marked with this icon .

KEY TERMS

consensus (p. 235)
corporate scenarios (p. 230)
devil's advocate (p. 236)
dialectical inquiry (p. 236)
financial strategy (p. 217)
functional strategy (p. 216)
HRM strategy (p. 225)
information technology strategy (p. 225)

leveraged buyout (p. 218)
logistics strategy (p. 224)
market development (p. 216)
marketing strategy (p. 216)
offshoring (p. 226)
operations strategy (p. 220)
outsourcing (p. 226)
political strategy (p. 234)

product development (p. 216)
purchasing strategy (p. 222)
R&D strategy (p. 219)
real options (p. 232)
risk (p. 232)
strategic choice (p. 235)
technological follower (p. 219)
technological leader (p. 219)

MyManagementLab®

Go to **mymanagmentlab.com** for Auto-graded writing questions as well as the following Assisted-graded writing questions:

8-1. How can an Operations Strategy be used to understand and exploit a particular product offering?
8-2. How are corporate scenarios used in the development of an effective strategy?

DISCUSSION QUESTIONS

⭐**8-3.** Are functional strategies interdependent, or can they be formulated independently of other functions?

⭐**8-4.** Do you believe that penetration pricing or skim pricing will be better at raising a company's or a business unit's operating profit in the long run?

8-5. How does mass customization support a business unit's competitive strategy?

⭐**8-6.** When should a corporation or business unit consider outsourcing a function or an activity?

8-7. What is the relationship of policies to strategies?

STRATEGIC PRACTICE EXERCISE

Pierre Omidyar founded a sole proprietorship in September 1995 called Auction Web to allow people to buy and sell goods over the Internet. The new venture was based on the idea of developing a community-driven process, where an organic, evolving, self-organizing web of individual relationships, formed around shared interests, would handle tasks that other companies handle with customer service operations. The

first item sold was a broken laser pointer owned by Omidyar for US$14.83.

By May 1996, Omidyar had added Jeff Skoll as a partner and the venture was incorporated as eBay. Two years later, Omidyar asked Meg Whitman to direct corporate strategy to continue the accelerated growth rate of the company. Whitman brought to the company global management and marketing experience and soon became President and CEO. In almost no time, the company became one of the Web's most successful sites, with 233 million registered users. By 2007, the average eBay user spent nearly two hours a month on the site—more than five times the time spent on Amazon.com.[111]

Whitman expanded the company's operations and spent more than US$6 billion to acquire companies, such as the Internet-phone operation Skype, the online payments service PayPal, ticket reseller StubHub, property rental and roommate search firm Rent.com, comparison shopping site Shopping.com, Web site recommender Stumbleupon, and 25% interest in Craigslist. Expansion and diversification provided revenue and profit growth plus stock price appreciation. Although financial analysts wondered how all these businesses would fit together, Whitman argued that she wanted eBay to be everywhere users wanted to be. At developer conferences, company representatives unveiled new services that let buyers shop for and purchase eBay items outside of the core eBay.com site.

By 2008, eBay was in trouble. Its stock price had lost half its value over the past three years. The core auction and retail businesses, which accounted for the majority of revenue, were showing signs of weakness. The number of active users had been flat for three quarters, at 83 million. The number of new products listed on the site had increased only 4% from the previous year. The number of stores selling goods at fixed prices on eBay declined from a year earlier to 532,000. The company had not done a good job of integrating Skype with its main business. Since its acquisition, Skype's service had actually deteriorated.[112] Competition had increased as rival Web sites, particularly Amazon, now provided similar Web services and eroded eBay's competitive advantage.

On January 23, 2008, CEO Whitman announced that John Donahoe would take over as the company's CEO. Donahoe stated that his first priority would be to revitalize eBay's core business, even at the expense of investors. In the next four years, the company's stock appreciated an anemic 1.4%. Without the PayPal unit (which brings in more than 40% of eBay's total revenue), the company would be suffering much more.[113]

1. What is eBay's problem?

2. Which marketing strategy was eBay following: market development or product development? Do you agree with it?

3. What decision-making process should CEO Donahoe utilize to make the decisions necessary to change the company's product, customer approach, and business model?

NOTES

1. S. F. Slater and E. M. Olson, "Market's Contribution to the Implementation of Business Strategy: An Empirical Analysis," *Strategic Management Journal* (November 2001), pp. 1055–1067; B. C. Skaggs and T. R. Huffman, "A Customer Interaction Approach to Strategy and Production Complexity Alignment in Service Firms," *Academy of Management Journal* (December 2003), pp. 775–786.

2. A. Pressman, "Ocean Spray's Creative Juices," *BusinessWeek* (May 15, 2006), pp. 88–89; http://www.oceanspray.com/Products.aspx.

3. A. Pressman, "Smith & Wesson: A Gunmaker Loaded with Offshoots," *BusinessWeek* (June 4, 2007), p. 66. A *line extension,* in contrast to brand extension, is the introduction of additional items in the same category under the same brand name, such as new flavors, added ingredients, or package sizes.

4. S. M. Oster, *Modern Competitive Analysis*, 2nd ed. (New York: Oxford University Press, 1994), p. 93.

5. J. M. de Figueiredo and M. K. Kyle, "Surviving the Gales of Creative Destruction: The Determinants of Product Turnover," *Strategic Management Journal* (March 2006), pp. 241–264.

6. J. Gruley and S. D. Singh, "Deere's Big Green Profit Machine," *Bloomberg Businessweek* (July 5, 2012), (http://www.businessweek.com/articles/2012-07-05/deeres-big-green-profit-machine); M. Springer, "Plowed Under," *Forbes* (February 21, 2000), p. 56.

7. W. Redmond, "The Strategic Pricing of Innovative Products," *Handbook of Business Strategy, 1992/1993 Yearbook*, edited by H. E. Glass and M. A. Hovde (Boston: Warren, Gorham & Lamont, 1992), pp. 16.1–16.13; A. Hinterhuber, "Towards Value-Based Pricing—An Integrative Framework for Decision Making," *Industrial Marketing Management* (Vol. 33, 2004), pp. 765–778.

8. A. Kambil, H. J. Wilson III, and V. Agrawal, "Are You Leaving Money on the Table?" *Journal of Business Strategy* (January/February 2002), pp. 40–43.

9. N. Wingfield, "Flush with Cash, Apple Plans Buyback and Dividend," *The New York Times* (March 19, 2012), (http://www.nytimes.com/2012/03/20/technology/apple-to-use-cash-for-stock-dividend-and-buyback.html?pagewanted=all&_r=0); P. Burrows, "Apple's Cash Conundrum,"

10. A. Safieddine and S. Titman in April 1999 *Journal of Finance,* as summarized by D. Champion, "The Joy of Leverage," *Harvard Business Review* (July–August 1999), pp. 19–22.

11. R. Kochhar and M. A. Hitt, "Linking Corporate Strategy to Capital Structure: Diversification Strategy, Type and Source of Financing," *Strategic Management Journal* (June 1998), pp. 601–610.

12. A. Rappaport and M. L. Sirower, "Stock or Cash?" *Harvard Business Review* (November–December 1999), pp. 147–158.

13. M. Davies, "Dealtalk – Plain Vanilla LBOs Few and Far Between," *Reuters* (April 28, 2011), (http://www.reuters.com/article/2011/04/28/dealtalk-lbos-idUSN2828850720110428).

14. "Private Investigations," *The Economist* (July 5, 2008), pp. 84–85.

15. D. Angwin and I. Contardo, "Unleashing Cerberus: Don't Let Your MBOs Turn on Themselves," *Long Range Planning* (October 1999), pp. 494–504.

16. For information on different types of LBOs, see M. Wright, R. E. Hoskisson, and L. W. Busenitz, "Firm Rebirth: Buyouts as

Facilitators of Strategic Growth and Entrepreneurship," *Academy of Management Executive* (February 2001), pp. 111–125.

17. J. Brown, "The Buyback Epidemic," (October 12, 2012), (http://www.thereformedbroker.com/2012/10/12/the-buyback-epidemic/); D. N. Hurtt, J. G. Kreuze, and S. A. Langsam, "Stock Buybacks and Their Association with Stock Options Exercised in the IT Industry," *American Journal of Business* (Spring 2008), pp. 13–21.

18. B. Deener, "Back Up and Look at Reasons for Reverse Stock Split," *The (St. Petersburg, FL) Times* (December 29, 2002), p. 3H.

19. T. Francis, "Can You Get a Patent on Being a Patent Troll?" NPR, August 2, 2012. (http://www.npr.org/blogs/money/2012/08/01/157743897/can-you-get-a-patent-on-being-a-patent-troll); M. Orey, "A Sotheby's for Investors," *BusinessWeek* (February 13, 2006), p. 39.

20. S. Stevens, "Speeding the Signals of Change," *Appliance* (February 1995), p. 7.

21. L-E. Gadde and H. Hakansson, "Teaching in Supplier Networks," in M. Gibbert and T. Durand (Eds.), *Strategic Networks: Learning to Compete* (Malden, MA: Blackwell Publishing, 2007), pp. 40–57.

22. "Schools Rent Out Labs to Businesses," *St. Cloud (MN) Times* (December 11, 2007), p. 3A.

23. H. W. Chesbrough, "A Better Way to Innovate," *Harvard Business Review* (July 2003), pp. 12–13; Everydayedisons.com.

24. J. Bughin, M. Chui, and B. Johnson, "The Next Step in Open Innovation," *McKinsey Quarterly* (June 2008), pp. 1–8.

25. L. Coleman-Lochner and C. Hymowitz, "At P&G, the Innovation Well Runs Dry," *Bloomberg Businessweek* (September 10, 2012), pp. 24–26; J. Greene, J. Carey, M. Arndt, and O. Port, "Reinventing Corporate R&D," *BusinessWeek* (September 22, 2003), pp. 74–76; J. Birkinshaw, S. Crainer, and M. Mol, "From R&D to Connect + Develop at P&G," *Business Strategy Review* (Spring 2007), pp. 66–69; L. Huston and N. Sakkab, "Connect and Develop: Inside Proctor & Gamble's New Model for Innovation," *Harvard Business Review* (March 2006), pp. 58–66.

26. G. Dushnitsky and M. J. Lenox, "When Do Firms Undertake R&D by Investing in New Ventures?" Paper presented to the annual meeting of the *Academy of Management*, Seattle, WA (August 2003).

27. A. Aston and M. Arndt, "The Flexible Factory," *BusinessWeek* (May 5, 2003), pp. 90–91.

28. J. R. Williams and R. S. Novak, "Aligning CIM Strategies to Different Markets," *Long Range Planning* (February 1990), pp. 126–135.

29. J. Wheatley, "Super Factory—or Super Headache," *BusinessWeek* (July 31, 2000), p. 66.

30. M. Tayles and C. Drury, "Moving from Make/Buy to Strategic Sourcing: The Outsource Decision Process," *Long Range Planning* (October 2001), pp. 605–622.

31. F. R. Bleakley, "Some Companies Let Supplies Work on Site and Even Place Orders," *The Wall Street Journal* (January 13, 1995), pp. A1, A6.

32. M. Hoegl and S. M. Wagner, "Buyer-Supplier Collaboration in Product Development Projects," *Journal of Management* (August 2005), pp. 530–548; B. McEvily and A. Marcus, "Embedded Ties and the Acquisition of Competitive Capabilities," *Strategic Management Journal* (November 2005), pp. 1033–1055; R. Gulati and M. Sytch, "Dependence Asymmetry and Joint Dependence in Interorganizational Relationships: Effects of Embeddedness on a Manufacturer's Performance in

Procurement Relationships," *Administrative Science Quarterly* (March 2007), pp. 32–69.

33. J. Richardson, "Parallel Sourcing and Supplier Performance in the Japanese Automobile Industry," *Strategic Management Journal* (July 1993), pp. 339–350.

34. S. Roberts-Witt, "Procurement: The HP Way," *PC Magazine* (November 21, 2000), pp. 21–22.

35. D. H. Pearcy, D. B. Parker, and L. C. Giunipero, "Using Electronic Procurement to Facilitate Supply Chain Integration: An Exploratory Study of U.S.-Based Firms," *American Journal of Business* (Spring 2008), pp. 23–35.

36. J. Bigness, "In Today's Economy, There Is Big Money to Be Made in Logistics," *The Wall Street Journal* (September 6, 1995), pp. A1, A9.

37. F. Keenan, "Logistics Gets a Little Respect," *BusinessWeek* (November 20, 2000), pp. 112–116.

38. B. L. Kirkman and Debra L. Shapiro, "The Impact of Cultural Values on Employee Resistance to Teams: Toward a Model of Globalized Self-Managing Work Team Effectiveness," *Academy of Management Review* (July 1997), pp. 730–757.

39. R. D. Banker, J. M. Field, R. G. Schroeder, and K. K. Sinha, "Impact of Work Teams on Manufacturing Performance: A Longitudinal Field Study," *Academy of Management Journal* (August 1996), pp. 867–890; B. L. Kirkman and B. Rosen, "Beyond Self-Management: Antecedents and Consequences of Team Empowerment," *Academy of Management Journal* (February 1999), pp. 58–74.

40. V. Y. Haines III, S. St. Onge, and A. Marcoux, "Performance Management Design and Effectiveness in Quality-Driven Organizations," *Canadian Journal of Administrative Sciences* (June 2004), pp. 146–160.

41. A. S. DeNisi and A. N. Kluger, "Feedback Effectiveness: Can 360-Degree Appraisals Be Improved?" *Academy of Management Executive* (February 2000), pp. 129–139; S. Thornton, "The History of 360 Degree Feedback," (2012), (http://www.ehow.com/about_5163489_history-degree-feedback.html); G. Toegel and J. A. Conger, "360-Degree Assessment: Time for Reinvention," *Academy of Management Learning and Education* (September 2003), pp. 297–311; F. Shipper, R. C. Hoffman, and D. M. Rotondo, "Does the 360 Feedback Process Create Actionable Knowledge Equally Across Cultures?" *Academy of Management Learning & Education* (March 2007), pp. 33–50.

42. J. McGregor, "The Employee Is Always Right," *BusinessWeek* (November 19, 2007), pp. 80–82.

43. O. C. Richard, "Racial Diversity, Business Strategy, and Firm Performance: A Resource-Based View," *Academy of Management Journal* (April 2000), pp. 164–177.

44. G. Robinson and K. Dechant, "Building a Business Case for Diversity," *Academy of Management Executive* (August 1997), pp. 21–31.

45. K. Labich, "Making Diversity Pay," *Fortune* (September 9, 1996), pp. 177–180.

46. "Gartner Says Worldwide IT Spend on Pace to Surpass $3.6 Trillion in 2012," (July 9, 2012), (http://www.gartner.com/it/page.jsp?id=2074815); N. G. Carr, "IT Doesn't Matter," *Harvard Business Review* (May 2003), pp. 41–50.

47. J. Greco, "Good Day Sunshine," *Journal of Business Strategy* (July/August 1998), pp. 4–5.

48. W. Howard, "Translate Now," *PC Magazine* (September 19, 2000), p. 81.

49. H. Green, "The Web Smart 50," *BusinessWeek* (November 24, 2003), p. 84.

50. T. Smart, "Jack Welch's Cyber-Czar," *BusinessWeek* (August 5, 1996), p. 83.

51. S. M. Kim and J. T. Mahoney, "Mutual Commitment to Support Exchange: Relation-Specific IT System as a Substitute for Managerial Hierarchy," *Strategic Management Journal* (May 2006), pp. 401–423.

52. B. Kelley, "Outsourcing Marches On," *Journal of Business Strategy* (July/August 1995), p. 40.

53. S. Holmes and M. Arndt, "A Plane that Could Change the Game," *BusinessWeek* (August 9, 2004), p. 33.

54. "2012 Global Outsourcing and Insourcing Survey," (February 2012), (http://www.deloitte.com/assets/Dcom-UnitedStates/Local%20Assets/Documents/IMOs/Shared%20Services/us_sdt_2012GlobalOutsourcingandInsourcingSurveyExecutiveSummary_050112.pdf).

55. J. Greco, "Outsourcing: The New Partnership," *Journal of Business Strategy* (July/August 1997), pp. 48–54.

56. W. M. Fitzpatrick and S. A. DiLullo, "Outsourcing and the Personnel Paradox," *SAM Advanced Management Journal* (Summer 2007), pp. 4–12.

57. Outsourcing: Time to Bring It Back Home?" *The Economist* (March 5, 2005), p. 63.

58. A. Y. Lewin and C. Peeters, "Offshoring Work: Business Hype or the Onset of Fundamental Transformation?" *Long Range Planning* (June 2006), pp. 221–239; A. Y. Lewing and C. Peeters, "The Top-Line Allure of Offshoring," *Harvard Business Review* (March 2006), pp. 22–24.

59. N. Miroff, "In Mexico, Auto Industry fuels the Middle Class," *The Washington Post* (April 3, 2012), (http://www.washingtonpost.com/world/the_americas/in-mexico-auto-industry-fuels-middle-class/2012/04/03/gIQApKdntS_story.html); G. Smith, "Factories Go South; So Does Pay," *BusinessWeek* (April 9, 2007), p. 76.

60. http://www.genpact.com/docs/pr/q4-and-ye-2011-earnings-release-final02062012.

61. "IBM's Plan to Buy India Firm Points to Demand for Outsourcing," *Des Moines Register* (April 11, 2004), p. 2D.

62. A. Castro, "Complaints Push Dell to Use U.S. Call Centers," *Des Moines Register* (November 25, 2003), p. 1D.

63. J. A. Byrne, "Has Outsourcing Gone Too Far?" *BusinessWeek* (April 1, 1996), pp. 26–28.

64. R. C. Insinga and M. J. Werle, "Linking Outsourcing to Business Strategy," *Academy of Management Executive* (November 2000), pp. 58–70; D. Lei and M. A. Hitt, "Strategic Restructuring and Outsourcing: The Effect of Mergers and Acquisitions and LBOs on Building Firm Skills and Capabilities," *Journal of Management* (Vol. 21, No. 5, 1995), pp. 835–859.

65. "Outsourcing: Time to Bring It Back Home?" *The Economist* (May 5, 2005), p. 63.

66. S. E. Ante, "Shifting Work Offshore? Outsourcer Beware," *BusinessWeek* (January 12, 2004), pp. 36–37.

67. http://www.oil-price.net/.

68. A. Takeishi, "Bridging Inter- and Intra-Firm Boundaries: Management of Supplier Involvement in Automobile Product Development," *Strategic Management Journal* May 2001), pp. 40-433.

69. J. Barthelemy, "The Seven Deadly Sins of Outsourcing," *Academy of Management Executive* (May 2003), pp. 87–98.

70. M. J. Leiblein and D. J. Miller, "An Empirical Examination of Transaction and Firm-Level Influences on the Vertical Boundaries of the Firm," *Strategic Management Journal* (September 2003), pp. 839–859.

71. S. Hamm, "Is Outsourcing on the Outs?" *BusinessWeek* (October 4, 2004), p. 42.

72. For further information on effective offshoring, see R. Aron and J. V. Singh, "Getting Offshoring Right," *Harvard Business Review* (December 2005), pp. 135–143.

73. R. Grover and D. Polek, "Millionaire Buys Disney Time," *BusinessWeek* (June 26, 2000), pp. 141–144.

74. D. K. Sinha, "Strategic Planning in the Fortune 500," in H. E. Glass and M. A. Hovde (Eds.), *Handbook of Business Strategy, 1991/1992 Yearbook* (Boston: Warren, Gorham & Lamont, 1991), pp. 9.6–9.8.

75. N. Checa, J. Maguire, and J. Berry, "The New World Disorder," *Harvard Business Review* (August 2003), pp. 70–79.

76. T. B. Palmer and R. M. Wiseman, "Decoupling Risk Taking from Income Stream Uncertainty: A Holistic Model of Risk," *Strategic Management Journal* (November 1999), pp. 1037–1062; W. G. Sanders and D. C. Hambrick, "Swinging for the Fences: The Effects of CEO Stock Options on Company Risk Taking and Performance," *Academy of Management Journal* (October 2007), pp. 1055–1078.

77. D. Clark, "All the Chips: A Big Bet Made Intel What It Is Today; Now It Wagers Again," *The Wall Street Journal* (June 6, 1995), pp. A1, A5.

78. L. W. Busenitz and J. B. Barney, "Differences Between Entrepreneurs and Managers in Large Organizations: Biases and Heuristics in Strategic Decision-Making," *Journal of Business Venturing* (January 1997), pp. 9–30.

79. J. J. Janney and G. G. Dess, "Can Real-Options Analysis Improve Decision-Making? Promises and Pitfalls," *Academy of Management Executive* (November 2004), pp. 60–75; S. Maklan, S. Knox, and L. Ryals, "Using Real Options to Help Build the Business Case for CRM Investment," *Long Range Planning* (August 2005), pp. 393–410.

80. T. Copeland and P. Tufano, "A Real-World Way to Manage Real Options," *Harvard Business Review* (March 2004), pp. 90–99.

81. J. Rosenberger and K. Eisenhardt, "What Are Real Options: A Review of Empirical Research," Paper presented to annual meeting of the *Academy of Management*, Seattle, WA (August 2003).

82. P. Coy, "Exploiting Uncertainty," *BusinessWeek* (June 7, 1999), pp. 118–124. For further information on real options, see M. Amram and N. Kulatilaka, *Real Options* (Boston, Harvard University Press, 1999). For a simpler summary, see R. M. Grant, *Contemporary Strategy Analysis*, 5th ed. (Malden, MA: Blackwell Publishing, 2005), pp. 48–50.

83. "Nano Wars," *The Economist* (August 30, 2008), p. 63.

84. J-P. Bonardi, A. J. Hillman, and G. D. Keim, "The Attractiveness of Political Markets: Implications for Firm Strategy," *Academy of Management Review* (April 2005), pp. 397–413.

85. J. G. Frynas, K. Mellahi, and G. A. Pigman, "First Mover Advantages in International Business and Firm-Specific Political Resources," *Strategic Management Journal* (April 2006), pp. 321–345. For additional information about political strategies, see C. Oliver and I. Holzinger, "The Effectiveness of Strategic Political Management: A Dynamic Capabilities Framework," *Academy of Management Review* (April 2008), pp. 496–520.

86. H. M. O'Neill, R. W. Pouder, and A. K. Buchholtz, "Patterns in the Diffusion of Strategies Across Organizations: Insights from the Innovation Diffusion Literature," *Academy of Management Executive* (January 1998), pp. 98–114; C. G. Gilbert, "Unbundling the Structure of Inertia: Resource Versus Routine

Rigidity," *Academy of Management Journal* (October 2005), pp. 741–763.

87. B. B. Tyler and H. K. Steensma. "Evaluating Technological Collaborative Opportunities: A Cognitive Modeling Perspective," *Strategic Management Journal* (Summer 1995), pp. 43–70; D. Duchan, D. P. Ashman, and M. Nathan, "Mavericks, Visionaries, Protestors, and Sages: Toward a Typology of Cognitive Structures for Decision Making in Organizations," *Journal of Business Strategies* (Fall 1997), pp. 106–125; P. Chattopadhyay, W. H. Glick, C. C. Miller, and G. P. Huber, "Determinants of Executive Beliefs: Comparing Functional Conditioning and Social Influence," *Strategic Management Journal* (August 1999), pp. 763–789; B. Katey and G. G. Meredith, "Relationship Among Owner/Manager Personal Values, Business Strategies, and Enterprise Performance," *Journal of Small Business Management* (April 1997), pp. 37–64.

88. A. Chatterjee and D. C. Hambrick, "It's All About Me: Narcissistic Executive Officers and Their Effects on Company Strategy and Performance," *Administrative Science Quarterly* (September 2007), pp. 351–386.

89. C. S. Galbraith and G. B. Merrill, "The Politics of Forecasting: Managing the Truth*,*" *California Management Review* (Winter 1996), pp. 29–43.

90. M. Garbuio, D. Lovallo, and P. Viguerie, "How Companies Spend Their Money: A McKinsey Global Survey," *McKinsey Quarterly Online* (June 2007).

91. M. A. Geletkanycz and D. C. Hambrick, "The External Ties of Top Executives: Implications for Strategic Choice and Performance," *Administrative Science Quarterly* (December 1997), pp. 654–681.

92. M. Song, R. J. Calantone, and C. A. Di Benedetto, "Competitive Forces and Strategic Choice Decisions: An Experimental Investigation in the United States and Japan," *Strategic Management Journal* (October 2002), pp. 969–978.

93. M. A. Hitt, M. T. Dacin, B. B. Tyler, and D. Park, "Understanding the Differences in Korean and U.S. Executives' Strategic Orientation," *Strategic Management Journal* (February 1997), pp. 159–167; L. G. Thomas III and G. Waring, "Competing Capitalisms: Capital Investment in American, German, and Japanese Firms,"*Strategic Management Journal* (August 1999), pp. 729–748.

94. M. H. Bazerman and D. Chugh, "Decisions Without Blinders," *Harvard Business Review* (January 2006), pp. 88–97.

95. J. A. Wagner III and R. Z. Gooding, "Equivocal Information and Attribution: An Investigation of Patterns of Managerial Sensemaking," *Strategic Management Journal* (April 1997), pp. 275–286; K. Shimizu and M. A. Hitt, "Strategic Flexibility: Organizational Preparedness to Reverse Ineffective Strategic Decisions," *Academy of Management Executive* (November 2004), pp. 44–59.

96. M. L. A. Hayward and K. Shimizu, "De-Commitment to Losing Strategic Action: Evidence from the Divestiture of Poorly Performing Acquisitions," *Strategic Management Journal* (June 2006), pp. 541–557.

97. J. Ross and B. M. Staw, "Organizational Escalation and Exit: Lessons from the Shoreham Nuclear Power Plant," *Academy of Management Journal* (August 1993), pp. 701–732; P. W. Mulvey, J. F. Veiga, and P. M. Elsass, "When Teammates Raise a White Flag," *Academy of Management Executive* (February 1996), pp. 40–49.

98. P. C. Nutt, *Why Decisions Fail* (San Francisco: Berrett-Koehler, 2002).

99. P. C. Nutt, "Expanding the Search for Alternatives During Strategic Decision-Making," *Academy of Management Executive* (November 2004), pp. 13–28.

100. K. Shimizu, "Prospect Theory, Behavioral Theory, and the Threat-Rigidity Thesis: Combinative Effects on Organizational Decisions to Divest Formerly Acquired Units," *Academy of Management Journal* (December 2007), pp. 1495–1514.

101. G. P. West III and G. D. Meyer, "To Agree or Not to Agree? Consensus and Performance in New Ventures," *Journal of Business Venturing* (September 1998), pp. 395–422; L. Markoczy, "Consensus Formation During Strategic Change," *Strategic Management Journal* (November 2001), pp. 1013–1031.

102. B. J. Olson, S. Parayitam, and Y. Bao, "Strategic Decision Making: The Effects of Cognitive Diversity, Conflict, and Trust on Decision Outcomes," *Journal of Management* (April 2007), pp. 196–222.

103. A. C. Amason, "Distinguishing the Effects of Functional and Dysfunctional Conflict on Strategic Decision Making: Resolving a Paradox for Top Management Teams," *Academy of Management Journal* (February 1996), pp. 123–148; A. C. Amason and H. J. Sapienza, "The Effects of Top Management Team Size and Interaction Norms on Cognitive and Affective Conflict," *Journal of Management* (Vol. 23, No. 4, 1997), pp. 495–516.

104. D. M. Schweiger, W. R. Sandberg, and P. L. Rechner, "Experiential Effects of Dialectical Inquiry, Devil's Advocacy, and Consensus Approaches to Strategic Decision Making," *Academy of Management Journal* (December 1989), pp. 745–772; G. Whyte, "Decision Failures: Why They Occur and How to Prevent Them," *Academy of Management Executive* (August 1991), pp. 23–31; R. L. Priem, D. A. Harrison, and N. K. Muir, "Structured Conflict and Consensus Outcomes in Group Decision Making," *Journal of Management* (Vol. 21, No. 4, 1995), pp. 691–710.

105. S. C. Abraham, "Using Bundles to Find the Best Strategy," *Strategy & Leadership* (July/August/September 1999), pp. 53–55.

106. O. Gadiesh and J. L Gilbert, "Transforming Corner-Office Strategy into Frontline Action," *Harvard Business Review* (May 2001), pp. 73–79.

107. E. Dane and M. G. Pratt, "Exploring Intuition and Its Role in Managerial Decision Making," *Academy of Management Review* (January 2007), pp. 33–54.

108. A. M. Hayashi, "When to Trust Your Gut," *Harvard Business Review* (February 2001), pp. 59–65.

109. E. Dane and M. G. Pratt, "Exploring Intuition and Its Role in Managerial Decision Making," *Academy of Management Review* (January 2007), pp. 33–54.

110. A. M. Hayashi, pp. 59–60.

111. C. Holahan, "Going, Going . . . Everywhere," *BusinessWeek* (June 18, 2007), pp. 62–64.

112. "The Skype Hyper," *The Economist* (October 6, 2007), p. 80.

113. D. Kucera, "eBay Poised to Gain 30% Chasing Amazon Without PayPal: Real M&A," *Bloomberg Businessweek* (January 9, 2012), (www.bloomberg.com/news/2012-01-08/ebay-poised-to-gain-30-chasing-amazon-without-paypal-real-m-a.html); C. Holahan, "eBay's New Tough Love CEO," *BusinessWeek* (February 4, 2008), pp. 58–59; PayPal Really Does Want to Be Your Pal," *Bloomberg Businessweek* (October 1, 2012), pg. 47.

PART 4

Strategy
Implementation
and Control

strategy implementation: organizing for Action

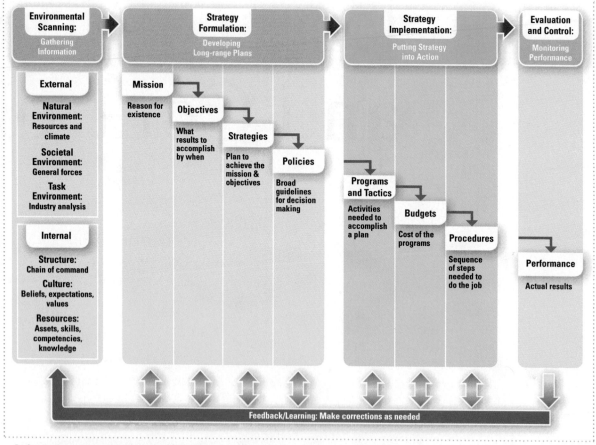

Learning Objectives

After reading this chapter, you should be able to:

- Develop programs, budgets, and procedures to implement strategic change
- Understand the importance of achieving synergy during strategy implementation
- List the stages of corporate development and the structure that characterizes each stage
- Identify the blocks to changing from one stage to another

- Construct matrix and network structures to support flexible and nimble organizational strategies
- Decide when and if programs such as reengineering, Six Sigma, and job redesign are appropriate methods of strategy implementation
- Understand the centralization versus decentralization issue in multinational corporations

The Rhythms of Business

For nearly five decades, Wal-Mart's "everyday low prices" and low-cost position had enabled it to rapidly grow to dominate North America's retailing landscape. By 2012, however, its U.S. division generated only 2.2% growth in its same-store sales even as the recession was fading. Target, Macy's, Kohl's Costco, GAP, Kroger, and even The Home Depot were all growing faster than Wal-Mart. At about the same time, Microsoft, whose software had grown to dominate personal computers worldwide, saw its revenue growth over the five-year period from 2007 to 2012 slow to just 6.6%. The company's stock price had been virtually flat since 2002, an indication that investors no longer perceived Microsoft as a growth company. What had happened to these two successful companies? Was this an isolated phenomenon? What could be done, if anything, to reinvigorate these giants?

A research study by Matthew Olson, Derek van Bever, and Seth Verry attempts to provide an answer. After analyzing the experiences of 500 successful companies over a 50-year period, they found that 87% of the firms had suffered one or more serious declines in sales and profits. This included a diverse set of corporations, such as Levi Strauss, 3M, Apple, Bank One, Caterpillar, Daimler-Benz, Toys"R"Us, and Volvo. After years of prolonged growth in sales and profits, revenue growth at each of these firms suddenly stopped and even turned negative! Olson, van Bever, and Verry called these long-term reversals in company growth *stall points*. On average, corporations lost 74% of their market capitalization in the decade surrounding a growth stall. Even though the CEO and other members of top management were typically replaced, only 46% of the firms were able to return to moderate or high growth within the decade. When slow growth was allowed to persist for more than 10 years, the delay was usually fatal. Only 7% of this group was able to return to moderate or high growth.

At Levi Strauss & Company, for example, sales topped US$7 billion in 1996—extending growth that had more than doubled over the previous decade. From that high-water mark, sales plummeted to US$4.6 billion in 2000—a 35% decline. Market share in its U.S. jeans market dropped from 31% in 1990 to 14% by 2000. After replacing management, the company underwent a companywide transformation, however, and by 2012, sales had dropped to US$4.3 billion.

According to Olson, van Bever, and Verry, these stall points occurred primarily because of a poor choice in strategy or organizational design. The root causes fell into four categories:

1. **Premium position backfires:** This happens to a firm that has developed a premium position in the market but is unable to respond effectively to new, low-cost competitors or a shift in customer valuation of product features. Management teams go through a process of disdain, denial, and rationalization that precedes the fall.

2. **Innovation management breaks down:** Management processes for updating existing products and creating new ones falter and become systemic inefficiencies.

3. **Core business abandoned:** Management fails to exploit growth opportunities in existing core businesses and instead engages in growth initiatives in areas remote from existing customers, products, and distribution channels.

4. **Talent and capabilities run short:** Strategies are not executed properly because of a lack of managers and staff with the skills and capabilities needed for strategy implementation. Often supported by promote-from-within policies, top management has a narrow experience base, which too often replicates the skill set of past top managers.

SOURCES: S. Clifford, "Sales at Wal-Mart, Though Still Rising, Suggest Wary Shoppers," *The New York Times* (August 16, 2012), http://www.nytimes.com/2012/08/17/business/wal-marts-earnings-suggest-strained-shoppers.html?_r=0); "U.S. Retail Sales Rise in October Before Sandy," *Fox Business* (November 1, 2012), http://www.foxbusiness.com/news/2012/11/01/us-retail-sales-rise-in-october-before-sandy/#ixzz2B0GC4zhd; A. Wiedmerman, "Walmart Rolls into Battle against the 'Big Three' Grocery Chains," *Daily Finance* (August 2, 2012), http://www.dailyfinance.com/2012/08/02/walmart-battles-big-three-grocery-chains/; A. Bianco, M. Der Hovanesian, L. Young, and P. Gogoi, "Wal-Mart's Midlife Crisis," *BusinessWeek* (April 30, 2007), pp. 46–56; "The Bulldozer of Bentonville Slows," *The Economist* (February 17, 2007), p. 64; D. Kirkpatrick, "Microsoft's New Brain," *Fortune* (May 1, 2006), pp. 56–68; "Spot the Dinosaur," *The Economist* (April 1, 2006), pp. 53–54; J. Greene, "Microsoft's Midlife Crisis," *BusinessWeek* (April 19, 2004), pp. 88–98. M. S. Olson, D. van Bever, and S. Verry, "When Growth Stalls," *Harvard Business Review* (March 2008), pp. 50–61. This phenomenon was called the "burnout syndrome" by G. Probst and S. Raisch in "Organizational Crisis: The Logic of Failure," *Academy of Management Executive* (February 2005), pp. 90–105. Ibid.

Strategy Implementation

Strategy implementation is the sum total of the activities and choices required for the execution of a strategic plan. It is the process by which objectives, strategies, and policies are put into action through the development of programs and tactics, budgets, and procedures. Although implementation is often considered only after strategy has been formulated, implementation is a key part of strategic management. Strategy formulation and strategy implementation should thus be considered as two sides of the same coin.

Poor implementation has been blamed for a number of strategic failures. For example, studies show that half of all acquisitions fail to achieve what was expected of them, and one out of four international ventures does not succeed.[1] The most mentioned problems reported in post-merger integration were poor communication, unrealistic synergy expectations, structural problems, missing master plans, lost momentum, lack of top management commitment, and unclear strategic fit. A study by A. T. Kearney found that a company has just two years in which to make an acquisition perform. After the second year, the window of opportunity for forging synergies has mostly closed. Kearney's study was supported by further independent research by Bert, MacDonald, and Herd. Among the most successful acquirers studied, 70% to 85% of all merger synergies were realized within the first 12 months, with the remainder being realized in year two.[2]

To begin the implementation process, strategy makers must consider these questions:

- *Who* are the people who will carry out the strategic plan?
- *What* must be done to align the company's operations in the new intended direction?
- *How* is everyone going to work together to do what is needed?

These questions and similar ones should have been addressed initially when the pros and cons of strategic alternatives were analyzed. They must also be addressed again before appropriate implementation plans can be made. Unless top management can answer these basic questions satisfactorily, even the best planned strategy is unlikely to provide the desired outcome.

A survey of 93 Fortune 500 firms revealed that more than half of the corporations experienced the following 10 problems when they attempted to implement a strategic change. These problems are listed in order of frequency:

1. Implementation took more time than originally planned.
2. Unanticipated major problems arose.
3. Activities were ineffectively coordinated.
4. Competing activities and crises took attention away from implementation.
5. The involved employees had insufficient capabilities to perform their jobs.
6. Lower-level employees were inadequately trained.
7. Uncontrollable external environmental factors created problems.
8. Departmental managers provided inadequate leadership and direction.
9. Key implementation tasks and activities were poorly defined.
10. The information system inadequately monitored activities.[3]

Who Implements Strategy?

Depending on how a corporation is organized, those who implement strategy will probably be a much more diverse set of people than those who formulate it. In most large, multi-industry corporations, the implementers are everyone in the organization. Vice presidents of functional areas and directors of divisions or strategic business units (SBUs) work with their subordinates to put together large-scale implementation plans. Plant managers, project managers, and unit heads put together plans for their specific plants, departments, and units. Therefore, every operational manager down to the first-line supervisor and every employee is involved in some way in the implementation of corporate, business, and functional strategies.

Many of the people in the organization who are crucial to successful strategy implementation probably had little to do with the development of the corporate and even business strategy. Therefore, they might be entirely ignorant of the vast amount of data and work that went into the formulation process. Unless changes in mission, objectives, strategies, and policies and their importance to the company are communicated clearly to all operational managers, there can be a lot of resistance and foot-dragging. Managers might hope to influence top management into abandoning its new plans and returning to its old ways. This is one reason why involving people from all organizational levels in the formulation and implementation of strategy tends to result in better organizational performance.[4]

What Must Be Done?

The managers of divisions and functional areas work with their fellow managers to develop programs, budgets, and procedures for the implementation of strategy. They also work to achieve synergy among the divisions and functional areas in order to establish and maintain a company's distinctive competence.

DEVELOPING PROGRAMS, BUDGETS, AND PROCEDURES

Strategy implementation involves establishing programs and tactics to create a series of new organizational activities, budgets to allocate funds to the new activities, and procedures to handle the day-to-day details.

Programs and Tactics

The purpose of a **program** or a tactic is to make a strategy action-oriented. As we discussed in **Chapter 1**, the terms are somewhat interchangeable. In practice, a program is a collection of tactics where a tactic is the individual action taken by the organization as an element of the effort to accomplish a plan. For example, when Xerox Corporation undertook a turnaround strategy, it needed to significantly reduce its costs and expenses. Management introduced a program called *Lean Six Sigma*. This program was developed to identify and improve a poorly performing process. Xerox first trained its top executives in the program and then launched around 250 individual Six Sigma projects throughout the corporation. The result was US$6 million in savings in one year, with even more expected the next.[5] (Six Sigma is explained later in this chapter.)

Most corporate headquarters have around 10 to 30 programs in effect at any one time.[6] One of the programs initiated by Ford Motor Company was to find an organic substitute for petroleum-based foam being used in vehicle seats. Apple used a recycled and yet elegant pulp tray to hold the original iPhone that became the inspiration for a business out to change the way bottles are produced. For more information on this innovative approach to bottle design, see the **Sustainability Issue** feature.

Competitive Tactics

Studies of decision making report that half the decisions made in organizations fail because of poor tactics.[7] A tactic is a specific operating plan that details how a strategy is to be implemented in terms of when and where it is to be put into action. By their nature, tactics are narrower in scope and shorter in time horizon than are strategies. Tactics, therefore, may be viewed (like policies) as a link between the formulation and implementation of strategy. Some of the tactics available to implement competitive strategies are timing tactics and market location tactics.

Timing Tactics: When to Compete

A **timing tactic** deals with *when* a company implements a strategy. The first company to manufacture and sell a new product or service is called the **first mover** (or pioneer). Some

SUSTAINABILITY issue

A BETTER BOTTLE—ECOLOGIC BRANDS

Some of the ideas that transform business practice are born in the simplest of places. Julie Corbett's started when she bought her first iPhone in 2007. She was fascinated by the paper pulp tray that it arrived in. The tray was elegant, sturdy, and biodegradable. She immediately thought of how it could be used to reduce the vast amounts of plastic needed for plastic bottles holding liquids. Combining the sturdiness of the paper pulp with an interior bladder to hold the liquid, she created Ecologic Brands.

Winner of the 2012 Gold Award from the Industrial Designers Society of America, the "bottle" is instantly recognizable as eco-friendly and yet extremely comfortable to touch and use. The bottles use 70% less plastic than regular ones and are the first of their type to hit store shelves. In addition, the bottle shells are made from 100% recycled cardboard and newspaper. The company didn't need to use any exotic materials or techniques to create the bottles. However, they have patents on the processes for connecting the components and have new products on the way. Ecologic is creating a demand for pulp paper in an industry that has been battered for many years.

Seventh Generation Laundry Detergent was one of the first brands to use the bottles and saw a 19% increase in sales after switching. In 2012, Ecologic shipped 2 million eco bottles, and with a new plant coming on line in 2013, it expects to ship 9 million bottles a year for the biggest brands in the United States.

SOURCES: "Bottles Inspired by the iPhone," *Bloomberg Businessweek*, October 29, 2012, p. 45; http://www.ecologicbrands.com/about_eco.html; http://www.fastcodesign.com/1664838/tk-years-in-the-making-a-cardboard-jug-for-laundry-detergent.

of the advantages of being a first mover are that the company is able to establish a reputation as an industry leader, move down the learning curve to assume the cost-leader position, and earn temporarily high profits from buyers who value the product or service very highly. A successful first mover can also set the standard for all subsequent products in the industry. A company that sets the standard "locks in" customers and is then able to offer further products based on that standard.[8] Microsoft was able to do this in software with its Windows operating system, and Netscape garnered over an 80% share of the Internet browser market by being the first to commercialize the product successfully. Research does indicate that moving first or second into a new industry or foreign country results in greater market share and shareholder wealth than does moving later.[9] Being first provides a company profit advantages for about 10 years in consumer goods and about 12 years in industrial goods.[10] This is true, however, only if the first mover has sufficient resources to both exploit the new market and to defend its position against later arrivals with greater resources.[11] Gillette, for example, has been able to keep its leadership of the razor category (70% market share) by continuously introducing new products.[12]

Being a first mover does, however, have its disadvantages. These disadvantages can be, conversely, advantages enjoyed by late-mover firms. **Late movers** may be able to imitate the technological advances of others (and thus keep R&D costs low), keep risks down by waiting until a new technological standard or market is established, and take advantage of the first mover's natural inclination to ignore market segments.[13] Research indicates that successful late movers tend to be large firms with considerable resources and related experience.[14] Microsoft is one example. Once Netscape had established itself as the standard for Internet browsers in the 1990s, Microsoft used its huge resources to directly attack Netscape's position with its Internet Explorer. It did not want Netscape to also set the standard in the developing and highly lucrative intranet market inside corporations. By 2004, Microsoft's Internet Explorer dominated Web browsers, and Netscape was only a minor presence. Nevertheless, research suggests that the advantages and disadvantages of first and late movers may not always generalize across industries because of differences in entry barriers and the resources of the specific competitors.[15]

Market Location Tactics: Where to Compete

A **market location tactic** deals with *where* a company implements a strategy. A company or business unit can implement a competitive strategy either offensively or defensively. An *offensive tactic* usually takes place in an established competitor's market location. A *defensive tactic* usually takes place in the firm's own current market position as a defense against possible attack by a rival.[16]

Offensive Tactics. Some of the methods used to attack a competitor's position are:

- **Frontal assault:** The attacking firm goes head to head with its competitor. It matches the competitor in every category from price to promotion to distribution channel. To be successful, the attacker must have not only superior resources, but also the willingness to persevere. This is generally a very expensive tactic and may serve to awaken a sleeping giant, depressing profits for the whole industry. This is what Kimberly-Clark did when it introduced Huggies disposable diapers against P&G's market-leading Pampers. The resulting competitive battle between the two firms depressed Kimberly-Clark's profits.[17]

- **Flanking maneuver:** Rather than going straight for a competitor's position of strength with a frontal assault, a firm may attack a part of the market where the competitor is weak. Texas Instruments, for example, avoided competing directly with Intel by developing microprocessors for consumer electronics, cell phones, and medical devices instead of computers. Taken together, these other applications are worth more in terms of dollars and influence than are computers, where Intel dominates.[18]

- **Bypass attack:** Rather than directly attacking the established competitor frontally or on its flanks, a company or business unit may choose to change the rules of the game. This tactic attempts to cut the market out from under the established defender by offering a new type of product that makes the competitor's product unnecessary. For example, instead of competing directly against Microsoft's Pocket PC and Palm Pilot for the hand-held computer market, Apple introduced the iPod as a personal digital music player. It was the most radical change to the way people listen to music since the Sony Walkman. By redefining the market, Apple successfully sidestepped both Intel and Microsoft, leaving them to play "catch-up."[19]

- **Encirclement:** Usually evolving out of a frontal assault or flanking maneuver, encirclement occurs as an attacking company or unit encircles the competitor's position in terms of products or markets or both. The encircler has greater product variety (e.g., a complete product line, ranging from low to high price) and/or serves more markets (e.g., it dominates every secondary market). For example, Steinway was a major manufacturer of pianos in the United States until Yamaha entered the market with a broader range of pianos, keyboards, and other musical instruments. Although Steinway still dominates concert halls, it has only a 2% share of the U.S. market.[20] Oracle is using this strategy in its battle against market leader SAP for enterprise resource planning (ERP) software by "surrounding" SAP with acquisitions.[21]

- **Guerrilla warfare:** Instead of a continual and extensive resource-expensive attack on a competitor, a firm or business unit may choose to "hit and run." Guerrilla warfare is characterized by the use of small, intermittent assaults on different market segments held by the competitor. In this way, a new entrant or small firm can make some gains without seriously threatening a large, established competitor and evoking some form of retaliation.

To be successful, the firm or unit conducting guerrilla warfare must be patient enough to accept small gains and avoid pushing the established competitor to the point that it must respond or else lose face. Microbreweries, which make beer for sale to local customers, use this tactic against major brewers such as Anheuser-Busch.

Defensive tactics. According to Porter, defensive tactics aim to lower the probability of attack, divert attacks to less threatening avenues, or lessen the intensity of an attack. Instead of increasing competitive advantage per se, they make a company's or business unit's competitive advantage more sustainable by causing a challenger to conclude that an attack is unattractive. These tactics deliberately reduce short-term profitability to ensure long-term profitability.[22]

- **Raise structural barriers.** Entry barriers act to block a challenger's logical avenues of attack. Some of the most important, according to Porter, are to:
  1. Offer a full line of products in every profitable market segment to close off any entry points (for example, Coca-Cola offers unprofitable noncarbonated beverages to keep competitors off store shelves).
  2. Block channel access by signing exclusive agreements with distributors.
  3. Raise buyer switching costs by offering low-cost training to users.
  4. Raise the cost of gaining trial users by keeping prices low on items new users are most likely to purchase.
  5. Increase scale economies to reduce unit costs.
  6. Foreclose alternative technologies through patenting or licensing.
  7. Limit outside access to facilities and personnel.
  8. Tie up suppliers by obtaining exclusive contracts or purchasing key locations.
  9. Avoid suppliers that also serve competitors.
  10. Encourage the government to raise barriers, such as safety and pollution standards or favorable trade policies.

- **Increase expected retaliation:** This tactic is any action that increases the perceived threat of retaliation for an attack. For example, management may strongly defend any erosion of market share by drastically cutting prices or matching a challenger's promotion through a policy of accepting any price-reduction coupons for a competitor's product. This counterattack is especially important in markets that are very important to the defending company or business unit. For example, when Clorox Company challenged P&G in the detergent market with Clorox Super Detergent, P&G retaliated by test marketing its liquid bleach, Lemon Fresh Comet, in an attempt to scare Clorox into retreating from the detergent market. Research suggests that retaliating quickly is not as successful in slowing market share loss as a slower, but more concentrated and aggressive response.[23]

- **Lower the inducement for attack:** A third type of defensive tactic is to reduce a challenger's expectations of future profits in the industry. Like Southwest Airlines, a company can deliberately keep prices low and constantly invest in cost-reducing measures. With prices kept very low, there is little profit incentive for a new entrant.[24]

Budgets

After programs and tactical plans have been developed, the **budget** process begins. Planning a budget is the last real check a corporation has on the feasibility of its selected strategy. An ideal strategy might be found to be completely impractical only after specific implementation programs and tactics are costed in detail. For example, once Cadbury Schweppes' management realized how dependent the company was on cocoa from Ghana to continue the company's growth strategy, it developed a program to show cocoa farmers how to increase yields using fertilizers and by working with each other. Ghana produced 70% of Cadbury's worldwide supply of the high-quality cocoa necessary to provide the distinctive taste of Dairy Milk, Crème Egg, and other treats. Management introduced the "Cadbury Cocoa Partnership" on January 28, 2008, and budgeted US$87 million for this program over a 10-year period.[25]

Procedures

After the divisional and corporate budgets are approved, **procedures** must be developed. Often called *Standard Operating Procedures (SOPs)*, they typically detail the various activities that must be carried out to complete a corporation's programs and tactical plans. Also known as *organizational routines*, procedures are the primary means by which organizations accomplish much of what they do.[26] Once in place, procedures must be updated to reflect any changes in technology as well as in strategy. For example, a company following a differentiation competitive strategy manages its sales force more closely than does a firm following a low-cost strategy. Differentiation requires long-term customer relationships created out of close interaction with the sales force. An in-depth understanding of the customer's needs provides the foundation for product development and improvement.[27]

In a retail store, procedures ensure that the day-to-day store operations will be consistent over time (that is, next week's work activities will be the same as this week's) and consistent among stores (that is, each store will operate in the same manner as the others). Properly planned procedures can help eliminate poor service by making sure that employees do not use excuses to justify poor behavior toward customers. Even though McDonald's, the fast-food restaurant, has developed very detailed procedures to ensure that customers have high-quality service, not every business is so well managed.

Before a new strategy can be successfully implemented, current procedures may need to be changed. For example, in order to implement The Home Depot's strategic move into services, such as kitchen and bathroom installation, the company had to first improve its productivity. Store managers were drowning in paperwork designed for a smaller and simpler company. "We'd get a fax, an e-mail, a call, and a memo, all on the same project," reported store manager Michael Jones. One executive used just three weeks of memos to wallpaper an entire conference room, floor to ceiling, windows included. Then CEO Robert Nardelli told his top managers to eliminate duplicate communications and streamline work projects. Directives not related to work orders had to be sent separately and only once a month. The company also spent US$2 million on workload-management software.[28]

ACHIEVING SYNERGY

One of the goals to be achieved in strategy implementation is synergy between and among functions and business units. This is the reason corporations commonly reorganize after an acquisition. **Synergy** is said to exist for a divisional corporation if the return on investment (ROI) of each division is greater than what the return would be if each division were an independent business. According to Goold and Campbell, synergy can take place in one of six forms:

- **Shared know-how:** Combined units often benefit from sharing knowledge or skills. This is a leveraging of core competencies. One reason that Procter & Gamble purchased Gillette was to combine P&G's knowledge of the female consumer with Gillette's knowledge of the male consumer.

- **Coordinated strategies:** Aligning the business strategies of two or more business units may give a corporation significant advantage by reducing inter-unit competition and developing a coordinated response to common competitors (horizontal strategy). The merger between Comcast and NBC Universal in 2011 gave the combined company significant bargaining strength and flexibility with advertisers in the increasingly competitive television media industry.

- **Shared tangible resources:** Combined units can sometimes save money by sharing resources, such as a common manufacturing facility or R&D lab. The big pharmaceutical companies were all looking for savings with the big mergers in the industry, such as Pfizer-Wyeth, Novartis-Alcon, and Roche-Genentech.
- **Economies of scale or scope:** Coordinating the flow of products or services of one unit with that of another unit can reduce inventory, increase capacity utilization, and improve market access. This was a reason United Airlines bought Continental Airlines.
- **Pooled negotiating power:** Units can combine their volume of purchasing to gain bargaining power over common suppliers to reduce costs and improve quality. The same can be done with common distributors. The acquisitions of Macy's and the May Company enabled Federated Department Stores (which changed its name to Macy's in 2007) to gain purchasing economies for all of its stores.
- **New business creation:** Exchanging knowledge and skills can facilitate new products or services by extracting discrete activities from various units and combining them in a new unit or by establishing joint ventures among internal business units. Google acquired, on average, one company a week from 2010 to 2012—more than 100 companies—as it tried to organize the world's information and make it universally accessible and useful.[29]

How Is Strategy to Be Implemented? Organizing for Action

Before plans can lead to actual performance, a corporation should be appropriately organized, programs should be adequately staffed, and activities should be directed toward achieving desired objectives. (Organizing activities are reviewed briefly in this chapter; staffing, directing, and control activities are discussed in **Chapters 10** and **11**.)

Any change in corporate strategy is very likely to require some sort of change in the way an organization is structured and in the kind of skills needed in particular positions. Managers must therefore closely examine the way their company is structured in order to decide what, if any, changes should be made in the way work is accomplished. Should activities be grouped differently? Should the authority to make key decisions be centralized at headquarters or decentralized to managers in distant locations? Should the company be managed like a "tight ship" with many rules and controls, or "loosely" with few rules and controls? Should the corporation be organized into a "tall" structure with many layers of managers, each having a narrow span of control (that is, few employees per supervisor) to better control his or her subordinates; or should it be organized into a "flat" structure with fewer layers of managers, each having a wide span of control (that is, more employees per supervisor) to give more freedom to his or her subordinates?

STRUCTURE FOLLOWS STRATEGY

In a classic study of large U.S. corporations such as DuPont, General Motors, Sears, and Standard Oil, Alfred Chandler concluded that **structure follows strategy**—that is, changes in corporate strategy lead to changes in organizational structure.[30] He also concluded that organizations follow a pattern of development from one kind of structural arrangement to another as they expand. According to Chandler, these structural changes occur because the old structure, having been pushed too far, has caused inefficiencies that have become too obviously detrimental to bear. Chandler, therefore, proposed the following as the sequence of what occurs:

1. New strategy is created.
2. New administrative problems emerge.

3. Economic performance declines.

4. New appropriate structure is created.

5. Economic performance rises.

Chandler found that in their early years, corporations such as DuPont tend to have a centralized functional organizational structure that is well suited to producing and selling a limited range of products. As they add new product lines, purchase their own sources of supply, and create their own distribution networks, they become too complex for highly centralized structures. To remain successful, this type of organization needs to shift to a decentralized structure with several semiautonomous divisions (referred to in **Chapter 5** as *divisional structure*).

Alfred P. Sloan, past CEO of General Motors, detailed how GM conducted such structural changes in the 1920s.[31] He saw decentralization of structure as "centralized policy determination coupled with decentralized operating management." After top management had developed a strategy for the total corporation, the individual divisions (Chevrolet, Buick, and so on) were free to choose how to implement that strategy. Patterned after DuPont, GM found the decentralized multidivisional structure to be extremely effective in allowing the maximum amount of freedom for product development. Return on investment was used as a financial control. (ROI is discussed in more detail in **Chapter 11**.)

Research generally supports Chandler's proposition that structure follows strategy (as well as the reverse proposition that structure influences strategy).[32] As mentioned earlier, changes in the environment tend to be reflected in changes in a corporation's strategy, thus leading to changes in a corporation's structure. In 2008, Arctic Cat, the recreational vehicles firm, reorganized its ATV (all terrain vehicles), snowmobile and parts, and garments and accessories product lines into three separate business units, each led by a general manager focused on expanding the business. True to Chandler's findings, the restructuring of Arctic Cat came after seven consecutive years of record growth followed by its first loss in 25 years. By 2012, sales were increasing by double digits and the company had sales in excess of half a billion dollars.[33]

Strategy, structure, and the environment need to be closely aligned; otherwise, organizational performance will likely suffer.[34] For example, a business unit following a differentiation strategy needs more freedom from headquarters to be successful than does another unit following a low-cost strategy.[35]

Although it is agreed that organizational structure must vary with different environmental conditions, which, in turn, affect an organization's strategy, there is no agreement about an optimal organizational design. What was appropriate for DuPont and General Motors in the 1920s might not be appropriate today. Firms in the same industry do, however, tend to organize themselves similarly to one another. For example, automobile manufacturers tend to emulate General Motors' divisional concept, whereas consumer-goods producers tend to emulate the brand-management concept (a type of matrix structure) pioneered by Procter & Gamble Company. See the Innovation Issues feature to see how P&G's structural decisions ended up derailing their innovation efforts. The general conclusion seems to be that firms following similar strategies in similar industries tend to adopt similar structures.

STAGES OF CORPORATE DEVELOPMENT

Successful, large conglomerate organizations have tended to follow a pattern of structural development as they grow and expand. Beginning with the simple structure of the entrepreneurial firm (in which everybody does everything), these organizations tend to get larger and organize along functional lines, with marketing, production, and finance departments. With continuing success, the company adds new product lines in different industries and organizes

INNOVATION issues

THE P&G INNOVATION MACHINE STUMBLES

As we have discussed throughout this text, innovation is a key element to organically grow a company. Developing an ever-widening portfolio of businesses has been a strategic approach used by many companies. None has been more successful with this approach than Procter & Gamble (P&G). Their 175-year history is filled with consumer-oriented product innovations including Ivory Soap (1879), Crisco (1911), Dreft which became Tide (1933), Crest (1955), Pampers (1961), Pringles (1968), Fabreze (1993), Swiffer (1998), and Crest Whitestrips (2002).

Known for their heavy investment in research and development, the company invested more than US$2 billion in R&D in 2012. For most of its history, the company used a highly centralized R&D group to generate new ideas. This all came to an end in 2000 when then-CEO A.G. Lafley decentralized the operations to the operating units and opened product innovation to outside partners. Taking his cue for the dramatic growth in social media and crowdsourcing, Lafley sought to have 50% of innovative

new products generated from people not employed by the company. The operating units were expected to be more closely tied to the consumers and thus be in a better position to know the potential for each new product idea.

Between 2003 and 2008, the sales of new launches shrank by half. The company's pipeline became focused on reformulating old products, adding scents to successful product lines, and adjusting the sizes that were sold.

In 2009, new CEO Bob McDonald started recentralizing R&D operations in an attempt to reverse the deterioration of innovation at the company. By 2012, between 20 and 30 percent of R&D had been centralized. The loss of focus cost the company a decade of innovations while competitors rolled out new products in virtually every product category in which P&G competes. There is no single means for generating innovative ideas or for turning those ideas into a blockbuster new product. Companies seek to organize their businesses so they can own the next big "thing."

....
SOURCES: L. Coleman-Lochner and C. Hymowitz, "At P&G, the Innovation Well Runs Dry," *Bloomberg Businessweek* (September 10, 2012), pp. 24–26; http://www.pg.com/en_US/brands/index.shtml.

itself into interconnected divisions. The differences among these three structural **stages of corporate development** in terms of typical problems, objectives, strategies, reward systems, and other characteristics are specified in detail in **Table 9–1**.

Stage I: Simple Structure

Stage I is typified by the entrepreneur or a small team, who founds a company to promote an idea (a product or a service). The entrepreneur or team tend to make all the important decisions and is involved in every detail and phase of the organization. The Stage I company has little formal structure, which allows the entrepreneur or team to directly supervise the activities of every employee (see **Figure 5–4** for an illustration of the simple, functional, and divisional structures). Planning is usually short range or reactive. The typical managerial functions of planning, organizing, directing, staffing, and controlling are usually performed to a very limited degree, if at all. The greatest strengths of a Stage I corporation are its flexibility and dynamism. The drive of the entrepreneur energizes the organization in its struggle for growth. Its greatest weakness is its extreme reliance on the entrepreneur to decide general strategies as well as detailed procedures. If the entrepreneur falters, the company usually flounders. This is labeled by Greiner as a *crisis of leadership*.[36]

Stage I describes the early life of Oracle Corporation, the computer software firm, under the management of its co-founder and CEO Lawrence Ellison. The company adopted a pioneering approach to retrieving data, called Structured Query Language (SQL). When IBM made SQL its standard, Oracle's success was assured. Unfortunately, Ellison's technical wizardry was not sufficient to manage the company. Often working at home, he lost sight of details outside his technical interests. Although the company's sales were rapidly increasing,

TABLE 9–1	Factors Differentiating Stage I, II, and III Companies		
Function	**Stage I**	**Stage II**	**Stage III**
1. Sizing up: Major problems	Survival and growth dealing with short-term operating problems.	Growth, rationalization, and expansion of resources, providing for adequate attention to product problems.	Trusteeship in management and investment and control of large, increasing, and diversified resources. Also, important to diagnose and take action on problems at division level.
2. Objectives	Personal and subjective.	Profits and meeting functionally oriented budgets and performance targets.	ROI, profits, earnings per share.
3. Strategy	Implicit and personal; exploitation of immediate opportunities seen by owner-manager.	Functionally oriented moves restricted to "one product" scope; exploitation of one basic product or service field.	Growth and product diversification; exploitation of general business opportunities.
4. Organization: Major characteristic of structure	One unit, "one-man show."	One unit, functionally specialized group.	Multiunit general staff office and decentralized operating divisions.
5. (a) Measurement and control	Personal, subjective control based on simple accounting system and daily communication and observation.	Control grows beyond one person; assessment of functional operations necessary; structured control systems evolve.	Complex formal system geared to comparative assessment of performance measures, indicating problems and opportunities and assessing management ability of division managers.
5. (b) Key performance indicators	Personal criteria, relationships with owner, operating efficiency, ability to solve operating problems.	Functional and internal criteria such as sales, performance compared to budget, size of empire, status in group, personal, relationships, etc.	More impersonal application of comparisons such as profits, ROI, P/E ratio, sales, market share, productivity, product leadership, personnel development, employee attitudes, public responsibility.
6. Reward–punishment system	Informal, personal, subjective; used to maintain control and divide small pool of resources for key performers to provide personal incentives.	More structured; usually based to a greater extent on agreed policies as opposed to personal opinion and relationships.	Allotment by "due process" of a wide variety of different rewards and punishments on a formal and systematic basis. Companywide policies usually apply to many different classes of managers and workers with few major exceptions for individual cases.

SOURCE: Donald H. Thain, "Stages of Corporate Development," *Ivey Business Journal* (formerly *Ivey Business Quarterly*), Winter 1969, p. 37. Copyright © 1969, Ivey Management Services. One-time permission to reproduce granted by Ivey Management Services.

its financial controls were so weak that management had to restate an entire year's results to rectify irregularities. After the company recorded its first loss, Ellison hired a set of functional managers to run the company while he retreated to focus on new product development.

Stage II: Functional Structure

Stage II is the point when the entrepreneur is replaced by a team of managers who have functional specializations. The transition to this stage requires a substantial managerial style change for the chief officer of the company, especially if he or she was the Stage I entrepreneur. He or she must learn to delegate; otherwise, having additional staff members yields no benefits to the organization. The previous example of Ellison's retreat from top management at Oracle Corporation to new product development manager is one way that technically brilliant founders are able to get out of the way of the newly empowered functional managers. In Stage II, the corporate strategy favors protectionism through dominance of the industry, often through vertical and horizontal growth. The great strength of a Stage II corporation lies in its concentration and specialization in one industry. Its great weakness is that all its eggs are in one basket.

By concentrating on one industry while that industry remains attractive, a Stage II company, such as Oracle Corporation in computer software, can be very successful. Once a functionally structured firm diversifies into other products in different industries, however, the advantages of the functional structure break down. A *crisis of autonomy* can now develop, in which people managing diversified product lines need more decision-making freedom than top management is willing to delegate to them. The company needs to move to a different structure.

Stage III: Divisional Structure

Stage III is typified by the corporation's managing diverse product lines in numerous industries; it decentralizes the decision-making authority. Stage III organizations grow by diversifying their product lines and expanding to cover wider geographical areas. They move to a divisional structure with a central headquarters and decentralized operating divisions—with each division or business unit a functionally organized Stage II company. They may also use a conglomerate structure if top management chooses to keep its collection of Stage II subsidiaries operating autonomously. A *crisis of control* can now develop, in which the various units act to optimize their own sales and profits without regard to the overall corporation, whose headquarters seems far away and almost irrelevant.

Over time, divisions have been evolving into SBUs to better reflect product–market considerations. Headquarters attempts to coordinate the activities of its operating divisions or SBUs through performance, results-oriented control, and reporting systems, and by stressing corporate planning techniques. The units are not tightly controlled but are held responsible for their own performance results. Therefore, to be effective, the company has to have a decentralized decision process. The greatest strength of a Stage III corporation is its almost unlimited resources. Its most significant weakness is that it is usually so large and complex that it tends to become relatively inflexible. General Electric, DuPont, and General Motors are examples of Stage III corporations.

Stage IV: Beyond SBUs

Even with the evolution into SBUs during the 1970s and 1980s, the divisional structure is not the last word in organization structure. The use of SBUs may result in a *red tape crisis* in which the corporation has grown too large and complex to be managed through formal programs and rigid systems, and procedures take precedence over problem solving.[37] For example, Pfizer's acquisitions of Warner-Lambert and Pharmacia resulted in 14 layers of management between scientists and top executives and thus forced researchers to spend most of their time in meetings.[38] Under conditions of (1) increasing environmental uncertainty, (2) greater use of sophisticated technological production methods and information systems, (3) the increasing size and scope of worldwide business corporations, (4) a greater emphasis on multi-industry competitive strategy, and (5) a more educated cadre of managers and employees, new advanced forms of organizational structure are emerging. These structures emphasize collaboration over competition in the managing of an organization's multiple overlapping projects and developing businesses.

The matrix and the network are two possible candidates for a fourth stage in corporate development—a stage that not only emphasizes horizontal over vertical connections between people and groups but also organizes work around temporary projects in which sophisticated information systems support collaborative activities. According to Greiner, it is likely that this stage of development will have its own crisis as well—a sort of *pressure-cooker crisis*. He predicts that employees in these collaborative organizations will eventually grow emotionally and physically exhausted from the intensity of teamwork and the heavy pressure for innovative solutions.[39]

Blocks to Changing Stages

Corporations often find themselves in difficulty because they are blocked from moving into the next logical stage of development. Blocks to development may be internal (such as lack of resources, lack of ability, or refusal of top management to delegate decision making to others) or external (such as economic conditions, labor shortages, and lack of market growth). For example, Chandler noted in his study that the successful founder/CEO in one stage was rarely the person who created the new structure to fit the new strategy, and as a result, the transition from one stage to another was often painful. This was true of General Motors Corporation under the management of William Durant, Ford Motor Company under Henry Ford I, Polaroid Corporation under Edwin Land, eBay under Pierre Omidyar, and Yahoo under Jerry Yang and David Filo.

Entrepreneurs who start businesses generally have four tendencies that work very well for small new ventures but become Achilles' heels for these same individuals when they try to manage a larger firm with diverse needs, departments, priorities, and constituencies:

- **Loyalty to comrades:** This is good at the beginning but soon becomes a liability as "favoritism."

- **Task oriented:** Focusing on the job is critical at first but then becomes excessive attention to detail.

- **Single-mindedness:** A grand vision is needed to introduce a new product but can become tunnel vision as the company grows into more markets and products.

- **Working in isolation:** This is good for a brilliant scientist but disastrous for a CEO with multiple constituencies.[40]

This difficulty in moving to a new stage is compounded by the founder's tendency to maneuver around the need to delegate by carefully hiring, training, and grooming his or her own team of managers. The team tends to maintain the founder's influence throughout the organization long after the founder is gone. This is what happened at Walt Disney Productions when the family continued to emphasize Walt's policies and plans long after he was dead. The refrain that was often heard was "What would Walt have done?" Although in some cases this may be an organization's strength, it can also be a weakness—to the extent that the culture supports the status quo and blocks needed change.

ORGANIZATIONAL LIFE CYCLE

Instead of considering stages of development in terms of structure, the organizational life cycle approach places the primary emphasis on the dominant issue facing the corporation. Organizational structure becomes a secondary concern. The **organizational life cycle** describes how organizations grow, develop, and eventually decline. It is the organizational equivalent of the product life cycle in marketing. These stages are Birth (Stage I), Growth (Stage II), Maturity (Stage III), Decline (Stage IV), and Death (Stage V). The impact of these stages on corporate strategy and structure is summarized in **Table 9–2**. Note that the first three stages

TABLE 9–2   Organizational Life Cycle

	Stage I	Stage II	Stage III*	Stage IV	Stage V
Dominant Issue	Birth	Growth	Maturity	Decline	Death
Popular Strategies	Concentration in a niche	Horizontal and vertical growth	Concentric and conglomerate diversification	Profit strategy followed by retrenchment	Liquidation or bankruptcy
Likely Structure	Entrepreneur dominated	Functional management emphasized	Decentralization into profit or investment centers	Structural surgery	Dismemberment of structure

NOTE: *An organization may enter a Revival phase either during the Maturity or Decline stages and thus extend the organization's life.

of the organizational life cycle are similar to the three commonly accepted stages of corporate development mentioned previously. The only significant difference is the addition of the Decline and Death stages to complete the cycle. Even though a company's strategy may still be sound, its aging structure, culture, and processes may be such that they prevent the strategy from being executed properly. Its core competencies become *core rigidities* that are no longer able to adapt to changing conditions—thus the company moves into Decline.[41]

Movement from Growth to Maturity to Decline and finally to Death is not, however, inevitable. A Revival phase may occur sometime during the Maturity or Decline stages. The corporation's life cycle can be extended by managerial and product innovations.[42] Developing new combinations of existing resources to introduce new products or acquiring new resources through acquisitions can enable firms with declining performance to regain growth—so long as the action is valuable and difficult to imitate.[43] We have seen this play out with Apple. It was clearly in decline in the mid-1980s and many believe well on its way to dying. The company was rejuvenated with the return of Steve Jobs and a seemingly continuous stream of new products that took the company into numerous new markets. This can occur during the implementation of a turnaround strategy.[44] Nevertheless, the fact that firms in decline are less likely to search for new technologies suggests that it is difficult to revive a company in decline.[45]

Eastman Kodak is an example of a firm in decline, and quite nearly dead, that has been attempting to develop new combinations of its existing resources to introduce new products, and thus, revive the corporation. When Antonio Perez left Hewlett-Packard to become Kodak's President in 2003, Kodak was in the midst of its struggle to make the transition from chemical film technology to digital technology and digital cameras. Instead of focusing the company's efforts on acquisitions to find growth, Perez looked at technologies that Kodak already owned, but was not utilizing. He noticed that Kodak scientists had developed new ink to yield photo prints with vivid colors that would last a lifetime. He suddenly realized that Kodak's distinctive competence was not in digital photography, where other competitors led the market, but in color printing. Perez initiated project *Goza* to go head to head with HP in the consumer inkjet printer business. In 2007, Kodak unveiled its new line of multipurpose machines that not only handled photographs and documents, but also made copies and sent faxes. The printers were designed to print high-quality photos with ink that would stay vibrant for 100 rather than the usual 15 years. Most importantly, replacement ink cartridges would cost half the price of competitors' cartridges. According to Perez, "We think it will give us the opportunity to disrupt the industry's business model and address consumers' key dissatisfaction: the high cost of ink." Perez then predicted that Kodak's inkjet printers would become a multibillion-dollar product line.[46]

Kodak's printer business had grown to 6% of the U.S. market by 2012 but had not made a dent in the 60% market share owned by HP. Kodak continued to sell off its patent portfolio in order to pay for the move into a printer market that is expected to be flat or declining in the future.[47]

Unless a company is able to resolve the critical issues facing it in the Decline stage, it is likely to move into Stage V, Death—also known as bankruptcy. This is what happened to Montgomery Ward, Pan American Airlines, Mervyn's, Borders, Eastern Airlines, Circuit City, Orion Pictures, and Levitz Furniture, as well as many other firms. As in the cases of Johns-Manville, Bennigan's, Macy's, and Kmart—all of which went bankrupt—a corporation can rise like a phoenix from its own ashes and live again under the same or a different name. The company may be reorganized or liquidated, depending on individual circumstances. For example, Kmart emerged from Chapter 11 bankruptcy in 2003 with a new CEO and a plan to sell a number of its stores to The Home Depot and Sears. These sales earned the company close to US$1 billion. Although store sales continued to erode, Kmart had sufficient cash reserves to continue with its turnaround.[48] It used that money to acquire Sears in 2005. Unfortunately, however, fewer than 20% of firms entering Chapter 11 bankruptcy in the United States emerge as going concerns; the rest are forced into liquidation (also known as Chapter 7).[49]

Few corporations will move through these five stages in order. Some corporations, for example, might never move past Stage II. Others, such as General Motors, might go directly from Stage I to Stage III. A large number of entrepreneurial ventures jump from Stage I or II directly into Stage IV or V. Hayes Microcomputer Products, for example, went from the Growth to Decline stage under its founder Dennis Hayes. The key is to be able to identify indications that a firm is in the process of changing stages and to make the appropriate strategic and structural adjustments to ensure that corporate performance is maintained or even improved.

ADVANCED TYPES OF ORGANIZATIONAL STRUCTURES

The basic structures (simple, functional, divisional, and conglomerate) are discussed in **Chapter 5** and summarized under the first three stages of corporate development in this chapter. A new strategy may require more flexible characteristics than the traditional functional or divisional structure can offer. Today's business organizations are becoming less centralized with a greater use of cross-functional work teams. Although many variations and hybrid structures exist, two forms stand out: the matrix structure and the network structure.

The Matrix Structure

Most organizations find that organizing around either functions (in the functional structure) or products and geography (in the divisional structure) provides an appropriate organizational structure. The matrix structure, in contrast, may be very appropriate when organizations conclude that neither functional nor divisional forms, even when combined with horizontal linking mechanisms such as SBUs, are right for their situations. In **matrix structures**, functional and product forms are combined simultaneously at the same level of the organization. (See **Figure 9–1**.) Employees have two superiors, a product or project manager, and a functional manager. The "home" department—that is, engineering, manufacturing, or sales—is usually functional and is reasonably permanent. People from these functional units are often assigned temporarily to one or more product units or projects. The product units or projects are usually temporary and act like divisions in that they are differentiated on a product-market basis. Pioneered in the aerospace industry, the matrix structure was developed to combine the stability of the functional structure with the flexibility of the product form. The matrix structure is very useful when the external environment (especially its technological and market aspects) is very complex and changeable. It does, however, produce conflicts revolving around duties, authority, and resource allocation. To the extent that the goals to be achieved are vague and the technology used is poorly understood, a continuous battle for power between product and

FIGURE 9–1
Matrix
and Network
Structures

Matrix Structure

Network Structure

functional managers is likely. The matrix structure is often found in an organization or SBU when the following three conditions exist:

- Ideas need to be cross-fertilized across projects or products.
- Resources are scarce.
- Abilities to process information and to make decisions need to be improved.[50]

Davis and Lawrence, authorities on the matrix form of organization, propose that *three distinct phases* exist in the development of the matrix structure:[51]

- **Temporary cross-functional task forces:** These are initially used when a new product line is being introduced. A project manager is in charge as the key horizontal link. J&J's experience with cross-functional teams in its drug group led it to emphasize teams crossing multiple units.

- **Product/brand management:** If the cross-functional task forces become more permanent, the project manager becomes a product or brand manager and a second phase begins. In this arrangement, function is still the primary organizational structure, but product or brand managers act as the integrators of semi-permanent products or brands. Considered by many a key to the success of P&G, brand management has been widely imitated by other consumer products firms around the world.

- **Mature matrix:** The third and final phase of matrix development involves a true dual-authority structure. Both the functional and product structures are permanent. All employees are connected to both a vertical functional superior and a horizontal product manager. Functional and product managers have equal authority and must work well together to resolve disagreements over resources and priorities. Boeing, Philips, and TRW Systems are examples of companies that use a mature matrix.

Network Structure—The Virtual Organization

A newer and somewhat more radical organizational design, the **network structure** (see **Figure 9–1**) is an example of what could be termed a "non-structure" because of its virtual elimination of in-house business functions. Many activities are outsourced. A corporation organized in this manner is often called a **virtual organization** because it is composed of a series of project groups or collaborations linked by constantly changing nonhierarchical, cobweb-like electronic networks.[52]

The network structure becomes most useful when the environment of a firm is unstable and is expected to remain so.[53] Under such conditions, there is usually a strong need for innovation and quick response. Instead of having salaried employees, the company may contract with people for a specific project or length of time. Long-term contracts with suppliers and distributors replace services that the company could provide for itself through vertical integration. Electronic markets and sophisticated information systems reduce the transaction costs of the marketplace, thus justifying a "buy" over a "make" decision. Rather than being located in a single building or area, the organization's business functions are scattered worldwide. The organization is, in effect, only a shell, with a small headquarters acting as a "broker," electronically connected to some completely owned divisions, partially owned subsidiaries, and other independent companies. In its ultimate form, a network organization is a series of independent firms or business units linked together by computers in an information system that designs, produces, and markets a product or service.[54]

Entrepreneurial ventures often start out as network organizations. For example, Randy and Nicole Wilburn of Dorchester, Massachusetts, run real estate, consulting, design, and baby food companies out of their home. Nicole, a stay-at-home mom and graphic designer, farms out design work to freelancers and cooks her own line of organic baby food. For US$300, an Indian artist designed the logo for Nicole's "Baby Fresh Organic Baby Foods." A London freelancer wrote promotional materials. Instead of hiring a secretary, Randy hired "virtual assistants" in Jerusalem to transcribe voicemail, update his Web site, and design PowerPoint graphics. Retired brokers in Virginia and Michigan deal with his real estate paperwork.[55]

Large companies such as Nike, Reebok, and Benetton use the network structure in their operations function by subcontracting (outsourcing) manufacturing to other companies in low-cost locations around the world. For control purposes, the Italian-based Benetton maintains what it calls an "umbilical cord" by assuring production planning for all its subcontractors, planning materials requirements for them, and providing them with bills of labor and standard prices and costs, as well as technical assistance to make sure their quality is up to Benetton's standards.

The network organizational structure provides an organization with increased flexibility and adaptability to cope with rapid technological change and shifting patterns of international trade and competition. It allows a company to concentrate on its distinctive competencies, while gathering efficiencies from other firms that are concentrating their efforts in their areas of expertise. The network does, however, have disadvantages. Some believe that the network is really only a transitional structure because it is inherently unstable and subject to tensions.[56] The availability of numerous potential partners can be a source of trouble. Contracting out individual activities to separate suppliers/distributors may keep the firm from discovering any internal synergies by combining these activities. If a particular firm overspecializes on only a few functions, it runs the risk of choosing the wrong functions and thus becoming noncompetitive.

Cellular/Modular Organization: A New Type of Structure?

Some authorities in the field propose that the evolution of organizational forms is leading from the matrix and the network to the cellular (also called modular) organizational form. According to Miles and Snow et al., "a **cellular organization** is composed of cells (self-managing teams, autonomous business units, etc.) which can operate alone but which can interact with other cells to produce a more potent and competent business mechanism." This combination of independence and interdependence allows the cellular/modular organizational form to generate and share the knowledge and expertise needed to produce continuous innovation. The cellular/modular form includes the dispersed entrepreneurship of the divisional structure, customer responsiveness of the matrix, and self-organizing knowledge and asset sharing of the network.[57] Bombardier, for example, broke up the design of its Continental business jet into 12 parts provided by internal divisions and external contractors. The cockpit, center, and forward fuselage were produced in-house, but other major parts were supplied by manufacturers spread around the globe. The cellular/modular structure is used when it is possible to break up a company's products into self-contained modules or cells and where interfaces can be specified such that the cells/modules work when they are joined together.[58] The cellular/modular structure is similar to a current trend in industry of using internal joint ventures to temporarily combine specialized expertise and skills within a corporation to accomplish a task which individual units alone could not accomplish.[59]

The impetus for such a new structure is the pressure for a continuous process of innovation in all industries. Each cell/module has an entrepreneurial responsibility to the larger organization. Beyond knowledge creation and sharing, the cellular/modular form adds value by keeping the firm's total knowledge assets more fully in use than any other type of structure.[60] It is beginning to appear in firms that are focused on rapid product and service innovation—providing unique or state-of-the-art offerings in industries such as automobile manufacture, bicycle production, consumer electronics, household appliances, power tools, computing products, and software.[61]

REENGINEERING AND STRATEGY IMPLEMENTATION

Reengineering is the radical redesign of business processes to achieve major gains in cost, service, or time. It is not in itself a type of structure, but it is an effective program to implement a turnaround strategy.

Business process reengineering strives to break away from the old rules and procedures that develop and become ingrained in every organization over the years. They may be a combination of policies, rules, and procedures that have never been seriously questioned because they were established years earlier. These may range from "Credit decisions are made by the credit department" to "Local inventory is needed for good customer service." These rules of organization and work design may have been based on assumptions about technology, people, and organizational goals that may no longer be relevant. Rather than attempting to fix existing problems through minor adjustments and the fine-tuning of existing processes, the key to reengineering is asking "If this were a new company, how would we run this place?"

Michael Hammer, who popularized the concept of reengineering, suggests the following principles for reengineering:

- **Organize around outcomes, not tasks:** Design a person's or a department's job around an objective or outcome instead of a single task or series of tasks.

- **Have those who use the output of the process perform the process:** With computer-based information systems, processes can now be reengineered so that the people who need the result of the process can do it themselves.

- **Subsume information-processing work into the real work that produces the information:** People or departments that produce information can also process it for use instead of just sending raw data to others in the organization to interpret.

- **Treat geographically dispersed resources as though they were centralized:** With modern information systems, companies can provide flexible service locally while keeping the actual resources in a centralized location for coordination purposes.

- **Link parallel activities instead of integrating their results:** Instead of having separate units perform different activities that must eventually come together, have them communicate while they work so they can do the integrating.

- **Put the decision point where the work is performed and build control into the process:** The people who do the work should make the decisions and be self-controlling.

- **Capture information once and at the source:** Instead of having each unit develop its own database and information processing activities, the information can be put on a network so all can access it.[62]

Studies of the performance of reengineering programs show mixed results. Several companies have had success with business process reengineering. For example, the Mossville Engine Center, a business unit of Caterpillar Inc., used reengineering to decrease process cycle times by 50%, reduce the number of process steps by 45%, reduce human effort by 8%, and improve cross-divisional interactions and overall employee decision making.[63]

One study of North American financial firms found that "the average reengineering project took 15 months, consumed 66 person-months of effort, and delivered cost savings of 24%."[64] In a survey of 782 corporations using reengineering, 75% of the executives said their companies had succeeded in reducing operating expenses and increasing productivity.[65] A study of 134 large and small Canadian companies found that reengineering programs resulted in (1) an increase in productivity and product quality, (2) cost reductions, and (3) an increase in overall organization quality, for both large and small firms.[66] Other studies report, however, that anywhere from 50% to 70% of reengineering programs fail to achieve their objectives.[67] Reengineering thus appears to be more useful for redesigning specific processes like order entry, than for changing an entire organization.[68]

SIX SIGMA

Originally conceived by Motorola as a quality improvement program in the mid-1980s, Six Sigma has become a cost-saving program for all types of manufacturers. Briefly, **Six Sigma** is an analytical method for achieving near-perfect results on a production line. Although the emphasis is on reducing product variance in order to boost quality and efficiency, it is increasingly being applied to accounts receivable, sales, and R&D. In statistics, the Greek letter *sigma* denotes variation in the standard bell-shaped curve. One sigma equals 690,000 defects per 1 million. Most companies are able to achieve only three sigma, or 66,000 defects per million. Six Sigma reduces the defects to only 3.4 defects per million—thus saving money by preventing waste. The process of Six Sigma encompasses five steps.

1. *Define* a process where results are poorer than average.
2. *Measure* the process to determine exact current performance.
3. *Analyze* the information to pinpoint where things are going wrong.
4. *Improve* the process and eliminate the error.
5. *Establish* controls to prevent future defects from occurring.[69]

Savings attributed to Six Sigma programs have ranged from 1.2% to 4.5% of annual revenue for a number of Fortune 500 firms. Firms that have successfully employed Six Sigma include General Electric, Allied Signal, ABB, and Ford Motor Company.[70] Fifty-three percent of the Fortune 500 companies now have a Six Sigma program in place and more than 83% of the Fortune 100 have it in place despite its manufacturing origins.[71] At Dow Chemical, each Six Sigma project has resulted in cost savings of US$500,000 in the first year. According to Jack Welch, GE's past CEO, Six Sigma is an appropriate change program for the entire organization.[72] Six Sigma experts at 3M have been able to speed up R&D and analyze why its top salespeople sold more than others. A disadvantage of the program is that training costs in the beginning may outweigh any savings. The expense of compiling and analyzing data, especially in areas where a process cannot be easily standardized, may exceed what is saved.[73] Another disadvantage is that Six Sigma can lead to less-risky incremental innovation based on previous work than on riskier "blue-sky" projects.[74]

A new program called *Lean Six Sigma* is becoming increasingly popular in companies. This program incorporates the statistical approach of Six Sigma with the lean manufacturing program originally developed by Toyota. Like reengineering, it includes the removal of unnecessary steps in any process and fixing those that remain. This is the "lean" addition to Six Sigma. Xerox used Lean Six Sigma to resolve a problem with a US$500,000 printing press it had just introduced. Teams from supply, manufacturing, and R&D used Lean Six Sigma to find the cause of the problem and to resolve it by working with a supplier to change the chemistry of the oil on a roller.[75]

DESIGNING JOBS TO IMPLEMENT STRATEGY

Organizing a company's activities and people to implement strategy involves more than simply redesigning a corporation's overall structure; it also involves redesigning the way jobs are done. With the increasing emphasis on reengineering, many companies are beginning to rethink their work processes with an eye toward phasing unnecessary people and activities out of the process. Process steps that have traditionally been performed sequentially can be improved by performing them concurrently using cross-functional work teams. Harley-Davidson, for example, has managed to reduce total plant employment by 25% while reducing by 50% the time needed to build a motorcycle. Restructuring through needing fewer people requires broadening the scope of jobs and encouraging teamwork. The design of jobs and subsequent job performance are, therefore, increasingly being considered as sources of competitive advantage.

Job design refers to the study of individual tasks in an attempt to make them more relevant to the company and to the employee(s). To minimize some of the adverse consequences of task specialization, corporations have turned to new job design techniques: *job enlargement* (combining tasks to give a worker more of the same type of duties to perform), *job rotation* (moving workers through several jobs to increase variety), *job characteristics* (using task characteristics to improve employee motivation), and *job enrichment* (altering the jobs by giving the worker more autonomy and control over activities). Although each of these methods has its adherents, no one method seems to work in all situations.

A good example of modern job design is the introduction of team-based production by the glass manufacturer Corning Inc., in its Blacksburg, Virginia, plant. With union approval, Corning reduced job classifications from 47 to 4 to enable production workers to rotate jobs after learning new skills. The workers were divided into 14-member teams that, in effect, managed themselves. The plant had only two levels of management: Plant Manager Robert Hoover and two line leaders who only advised the teams. Employees worked very demanding 12½;-hour shifts, alternating three-day and four-day weeks. The teams made managerial decisions, imposed discipline on fellow workers, and were required to learn three "skill modules" within two years or else lose their jobs. As a result of this new job design, a Blacksburg team, made up of workers with interchangeable skills, can retool a line to produce a different type of filter in only 10 minutes—six times faster than workers in a traditionally designed filter plant. The Blacksburg plant earned a US$2 million profit in its first eight months of production instead of losing the US$2.3 million projected for the startup period. The plant performed so well that Corning's top management acted to convert the company's 27 other factories to team-based production.[76]

International Issues in Strategy Implementation

An international company is one that engages in any combination of activities, from exporting/importing to full-scale manufacturing, in foreign countries. A **multinational corporation (MNC)**, in contrast, is a highly developed international company with a deep involvement throughout the world, plus a worldwide perspective in its management and decision making. For an MNC to be considered global, it must manage its worldwide operations as if they were totally interconnected. This approach works best when the industry has moved from being *multidomestic* (each country's industry is essentially separate from the same industry in other countries) to *global* (each country is a part of one worldwide industry).

The global MNC faces the dual challenge of achieving scale economies through standardization while at the same time responding to local customer differences.

The design of an organization's structure is strongly affected by the company's stage of development in international activities and the types of industries in which the company is involved. Strategic alliances may complement or even substitute for an internal functional activity. The issue of centralization versus decentralization becomes especially important for an MNC operating in both multidomestic and global industries.

INTERNATIONAL STRATEGIC ALLIANCES

Strategic alliances, such as joint ventures and licensing agreements, between an MNC and a local partner in a host country are becoming increasingly popular as a means by which a corporation can gain entry into other countries, especially less developed countries. The key to the successful implementation of these strategies is the selection of the local partner. Each party needs to assess not only the strategic fit of each company's project strategy but also the fit of each company's respective resources. A successful joint venture may require as much as two years of prior contacts between the parties. A prior relationship helps to develop a level of trust, which facilitates openness in sharing knowledge and a reduced fear of opportunistic behavior by the alliance partners. This is especially important when the environmental uncertainty is high.[77] Research reveals that firms favor past partners when forming new alliances.[78]

Key drivers for strategic fit between alliance partners are the following:

- Partners must agree on fundamental values and have a shared vision about the potential for joint value creation.
- Alliance strategy must be derived from business, corporate, and functional strategy.
- The alliance must be important to both partners, especially to top management.
- Partners must be mutually dependent for achieving clear and realistic objectives.
- Joint activities must have added value for customers and the partners.
- The alliance must be accepted by key stakeholders.
- Partners contribute key strengths but protect core competencies.[79]

STAGES OF INTERNATIONAL DEVELOPMENT

Corporations operating internationally tend to evolve through five common stages, both in their relationships with widely dispersed geographic markets and in the manner in which they structure their operations and programs. These **stages of international development** are:

- **Stage 1 (Domestic company):** The primarily domestic company exports some of its products through local dealers and distributors in the foreign countries. The impact on the organization's structure is minimal because an export department at corporate headquarters handles everything.

- **Stage 2 (Domestic company with export division):** Success in Stage 1 leads the company to establish its own sales company with offices in other countries to eliminate the middlemen and to better control marketing. Because exports have now become more important, the company establishes an export division to oversee foreign sales offices.

- **Stage 3 (Primarily domestic company with international division):** Success in earlier stages leads the company to establish manufacturing facilities in addition to sales and service offices in key countries. The company now adds an international division with responsibilities for most of the business functions conducted in other countries.

- **Stage 4 (Multinational corporation with multidomestic emphasis):** Now a full-fledged MNC, the company increases its investments in other countries. The company establishes a local operating division or company in the host country, such as Ford of Britain, to better serve the market. The product line is expanded, and local manufacturing capacity is established. Managerial functions (product development, finance, marketing, and so on) are organized locally. Over time, the parent company acquires other related businesses, broadening the base of the local operating division. As the subsidiary in the host country successfully develops a strong regional presence, it achieves greater autonomy and self-sufficiency. The operations in each country are, nevertheless, managed separately as if each is a domestic company.

- **Stage 5 (MNC with global emphasis):** The most successful MNCs move into a fifth stage in which they have worldwide human resources, R&D, and financing strategies. Typically operating in a global industry, the MNC denationalizes its operations and plans product design, manufacturing, and marketing around worldwide considerations. Global considerations now dominate organizational design. The global MNC structures itself in a matrix form around some combination of geographic areas, product lines, and functions. All managers are responsible for dealing with international as well as domestic issues.

GLOBAL issue

OUTSOURCING COMES FULL CIRCLE

What happens when international companies who have developed their business model on cheaper labor in remote countries have to hire employees back in the originating country because the work demands local labor? That is exactly what is happening to many Indian firms who established their businesses as U.S. companies were seeking highly skilled, well-educated employees who worked for one-tenth the wage of U.S. workers. This was the classic cost-cutting model of the past two decades and no area on earth benefited as much as India. In 2011, U.S. companies spent just shy of US$28 billion on outsourcing.

The mood of the U.S. swung during the recession of 2009–2011 and the U.S. instituted tough new regulations limiting the number of foreign nationals who could work in the United States. This effort coincided with a wave of companies trying to pitch speed, local knowledge, and U.S. employment growth as competitive factors in their business.

In 2012, Bangalore-based Infosys acquired Marsh Consumer BPO and its 87 employees based in Des Moines, Iowa, and the gigantic Cognizant Technology Solutions, which, while based in New Jersey, has most of its 145,000 employees in India, and acquired centers in Iowa and North Dakota employing almost 1000 employees. Tata Consultancy Services employees 93% of their staff in India and less than 1% in the United States.

Bloomberg Businessweek pointed out that "with jobs and outsourcing such hot political issues in the U.S., it pays for Indian companies to hire some Americans, even though they're more expensive." The complexity of managing the workforces and catering to clients that simultaneously want cost controls, efficient work, and local expertise can be daunting.

SOURCES: "Indian Companies Seek a Passage to America," *Bloomberg Businessweek* (October 29, 2012), pp. 26–27; D. Thoppil, "Indian Outsourcing Firms Hire in the U.S.," *The Wall Street Journal* (August 7, 2012); http://online.wsj.com/article/SB10000872396390443517104577572930208453186.html.

Research provides some support for stages of international development, but it does not necessarily support the preceding sequence of stages. For example, a company may initiate production and sales in multiple countries without having gone through the steps of exporting or having local sales subsidiaries. In addition, any one corporation can be at different stages simultaneously, with different products in different markets at different levels. Firms may also leapfrog across stages to a global emphasis. In addition, most firms that are considered to be stage 5 global MNCs are actually regional. Around 88% of the world's biggest MNCs derive at least half of their sales from their home regions. Just 2% (a total of nine firms) derive 20% or more of their sales from each of the North American, European, and Asian regions.[80]

Developments in information technology are changing the way business is being done internationally. See the **Global Issue** feature to learn about the latest issue related to international outsourcing of IT.

The stages concept provides a useful way to illustrate some of the structural changes corporations undergo when they increase their involvement in international activities.

CENTRALIZATION VERSUS DECENTRALIZATION

A basic dilemma an MNC faces is how to organize authority centrally so it operates as a vast interlocking system that achieves synergy and at the same time decentralize authority so that local managers can make the decisions necessary to meet the demands of the local market or host government.[81] To deal with this problem, MNCs tend to structure themselves either along product groups or geographic areas. They may even combine both in a matrix structure—the design chosen by 3M Corporation, Philips, and Asea Brown Boveri (ABB), among others.[82]

One side of 3M's matrix represents the company's product divisions; the other side includes the company's international country and regional subsidiaries.

Two examples of the usual international structure are Nestlé and American Cyanamid. Nestlé's structure is one in which significant power and authority have been decentralized to geographic entities. This structure is similar to that depicted in **Figure 9–2**, in which each geographic set of operating companies has a different group of products. In contrast, American Cyanamid has a series of centralized product groups with worldwide responsibilities. To depict Cyanamid's structure, the geographical entities in **Figure 9–2** would have to be replaced by product groups or SBUs.

The **product-group structure** of American Cyanamid enables the company to introduce and manage a similar line of products around the world. This enables the corporation to centralize decision making along product lines and to reduce costs. The **geographic-area structure** of Nestlé, in contrast, allows the company to tailor products to regional differences and to achieve regional coordination. For instance, Nestlé markets 200 different varieties of its instant coffee, Nescafé. The geographic-area structure decentralizes decision making to the local subsidiaries.

As industries move from being multidomestic to more globally integrated, MNCs are increasingly switching from the geographic-area to the product-group structure. Nestlé, for example, found that its decentralized area structure had become increasingly inefficient. As a result, operating margins at Nestlé have trailed those at rivals Unilever, Group Danone, and Kraft Foods by as much as 50%. Then CEO Peter Brabeck-Letmathe acted to eliminate country-by-country responsibilities for many functions. In one instance, he established five centers worldwide to handle most coffee and cocoa purchasing.[83]

Simultaneous pressures for decentralization to be locally responsive and centralization to be maximally efficient are causing interesting structural adjustments in most large corporations. This is what is meant by the phrase "think globally, act locally." Companies are attempting to decentralize those operations that are culturally oriented and closest to the customers—manufacturing, marketing, and human resources. At the same time, the companies are consolidating less visible internal functions, such as research and development, finance, and information systems, where there can be significant economies of scale.

FIGURE 9–2
Geographic Area Structure for an MNC

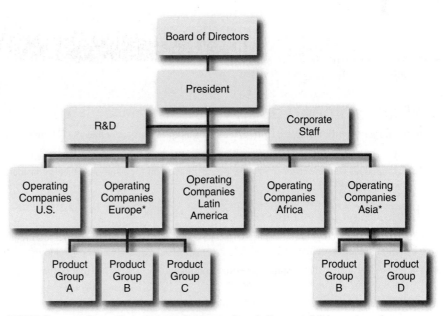

*NOTE: Because of space limitations, product groups for only Europe and Asia are shown here.

End of Chapter SUMMARY

Strategy implementation is where "the rubber hits the road." Environmental scanning and strategy formulation are crucial to strategic management but are only the beginning of the process. The failure to carry a strategic plan into the day-to-day operations of the workplace is a major reason why strategic planning often fails to achieve its objectives. It is discouraging to note that in one study nearly 70% of the strategic plans were never successfully implemented.[84]

For a strategy to be successfully implemented, it must be made action-oriented. This is done through a series of programs that are funded through specific budgets and contain new detailed procedures. This is what Sergio Marchionne did when he implemented a turnaround strategy as the new Fiat Group CEO in 2004. He attacked the lethargic, bureaucratic system by flattening Fiat's structure and giving younger managers a larger amount of authority and responsibility. He and other managers worked to reduce the number of auto platforms from 19 to six by 2012. The time from the completion of the design process to new car production was cut from 26 to 18 months. By 2008, the Fiat auto unit was again profitable. Marchionne reintroduced Fiat to the United States market in 2012 after a 27-year absence.[85]

This chapter explains how jobs and organizational units can be designed to support a change in strategy. We will continue with staffing and directing issues in strategy implementation in the next chapter.

MyManagementLab®

Go to **mymanagementlab.com** to complete the problems marked with this icon .

KEY TERMS

budget (p. 251)
cellular/modular organization (p. 263)
first mover (p. 248)
geographic-area structure (p. 269)
job design (p. 265)
late movers (p. 249)
market location tactic (p. 250)
matrix structure (p. 260)
multinational corporation (MNC) (p. 266)

network structure (p. 262)
organizational life cycle (p. 258)
procedure (p. 252)
product-group structure (p. 269)
program (p. 248)
reengineering (p. 263)
Six Sigma (p. 264)
stages of corporate development (p. 255)

stages of international development (p. 267)
strategy implementation (p. 246)
structure follows strategy (p. 253)
synergy (p. 252)
timing tactic (p. 248)
virtual organization (p. 262)

MyManagementLab®

Go to **mymanagementlab.com** for Auto-graded writing questions as well as the following Assisted-graded writing questions:

9-1. How do timing tactics impact the strategy implementation efforts of a company?
9-2. What issues would you consider to be the most important for a company that is considering the use of a functional structure?

DISCUSSION QUESTIONS

9-3. How should a corporation attempt to achieve synergy among functions and business units?
9-4. How should an owner-manager prepare a company for its movement from Stage I to Stage II?
9-5. How can a corporation keep from sliding into the Decline stage of the organizational life cycle?
9-6. Is reengineering just another management fad, or does it offer something of lasting value?
9-7. How is the cellular/modular structure different from the network structure?

STRATEGIC PRACTICE EXERCISE

The Synergy Game
Yolanda Sarason and Catherine Banbury

Setup

Put three to five chairs on either side of a room, facing each other, in the front of the class. Put a table in the middle, with a bell in the middle of the table.

Procedure

The instructor/moderator divides the class into teams of three to five people. Each team selects a name for itself. The instructor/moderator lists the team names on the board. The first two teams come to the front and sit in the chairs facing each other. The instructor/moderator reads a list of products or services being provided by an actual company. The winning team must identify (1) possible sources of synergy and (2) the actual company being described. For example, if the products/services listed are family restaurants, airline catering, hotels, and retirement centers, the synergy is ***standardized food service and hospitality settings*** and the company is **The Marriott Corporation**. The first team to successfully name the company *and* the synergy wins the round.

After one practice session, the game begins. Each of the teams is free to discuss the question with other team members. When one of the two teams thinks it has the answer to both parts of the question, it must be the first to ring the bell in order to announce its answer. If it gives the correct answer, it is deemed the winner of round one. Both parts of the answer must be given for a team to have the correct answer. If a team correctly provides only one part, that answer is still wrong—there is no partial credit. The instructor/moderator does not say which part of the answer, if either, was correct.

The second team then has the opportunity to state the answer. If the second team is wrong, both teams may try once more. If neither chooses to try again, the instructor/moderator may (1) declare no round winner and both teams sit down, (2) allow the next two teams to provide the answer to round one, or (3) go on to the next round with the same two teams. Two new teams then come to the front for the next round. Once all groups have played once, the winning teams play each other. Rounds continue until there is a grand champion. The instructor should provide a suitable prize, such as candy bars, for the winning team.

·················

SOURCE: This exercise was developed by Professors Yolanda Sarason of Colorado State University and Catherine Banbury of St. Mary's College and Purdue University and presented at the Organizational Behavior Teaching Conference, June 1999. Copyright © 1999 by Yolanda Sarason and Catherine Banbury. Adapted with permission.

Note from Wheelen, Hunger, Hoffman and Bamford

The *Instructors' Manual* for this book contains a list of products and services with their synergy and the name of the company. In case your instructor does not use this exercise, try the following examples:

> Example 1: Motorcycles, autos, lawn mowers, generators

> Example 2: Athletic footwear, Rockport shoes, Greg Norman clothing, sportswear

For each example, did you guess the company providing these products/services and the synergy obtained?

Example 1: Engine technology by Honda
Example 2: Marketing and distribution for the athletically oriented by Reebok

NOTES

1. J. W. Gadella, "Avoiding Expensive Mistakes in Capital Investment," *Long Range Planning* (April 1994), pp. 103–110; B. Voss, "World Market Is Not for Everyone," *Journal of Business Strategy* (July/August 1993), p. 4.
2. A. Bert, T. MacDonald, and T. Herd, "Two Merger Integration Imperatives: Urgency and Execution," *Strategy & Leadership*, Vol. 31, No. 3 (2003), pp. 42–49.
3. L. D. Alexander, "Strategy Implementation: Nature of the Problem," *International Review of Strategic Management*, Vol. 2, No. 1, edited by D. E. Hussey (New York: John Wiley & Sons, 1991), pp. 73–113. See also L. G. Hrebiniak, "Obstacles to Effective Strategy Implementation," *Organizational Dynamics* (Vol. 35, Issue 1, 2006), pp. 12–31 for six obstacles to implementation.
4. L. G. Hrebiniak (2006).
5. F. Arner and A. Aston, "How Xerox Got Up to Speed," *Business Week* (May 3, 2004), pp. 103–104.
6. J. Darragh and A. Campbell, "Why Corporate Initiatives Get Stuck?" *Long Range Planning* (February 2001), pp. 33–52.
7. P. C. Nutt, "Surprising But True: Half the Decisions in Organizations Fail," *Academy of Management Executive* (November 1999), pp. 75–90.
8. Some refer to this as the economic concept of "increasing returns." Instead of the curve leveling off when the company reaches a point of diminishing returns when a product saturates a market, the curve continues to go up as the company takes advantage of setting the standard to spin off new products that use the new standard to achieve higher performance than competitors. See J. Alley, "The Theory That Made Microsoft," *Fortune* (April 29, 1996), pp. 65–66.
9. H. Lee, K. G. Smith, C. M. Grimm and A. Schomburg, "Timing, Order and Durability of New Product Advantages with Imitation," *Strategic Management Journal* (January 2000), pp. 23–30; Y. Pan and P. C. K. Chi, "Financial Performance and Survival of Multinational Corporations in China," *Strategic Management Journal* (April 1999), pp. 359–374; R. Makadok, "Can First-Mover and Early-Mover Advantages Be Sustained

in an Industry with Low Barriers to Entry/Imitation?" *Strategic Management Journal* (July 1998), pp. 683–696; B. Mascarenhas, "The Order and Size of Entry into International Markets," *Journal of Business Venturing* (July 1997), pp. 287–299.

10. At these respective points, cost disadvantages vis-à-vis later entrants fully eroded the earlier returns to first movers. See W. Boulding and M. Christen, "Idea—First Mover Disadvantage," *Harvard Business Review* (Vol. 79, No. 9, 2001), pp. 20–21 as reported by D. J. Ketchen Jr., C. C. Snow, and V. L. Hoover, "Research on Competitive Dynamics: Recent Accomplishments and Future Challenges," *Journal of Management* (Vol. 30, No. 6, 2004), pp. 779–804.

11. M. B. Lieberman and D. B. Montgomery, "First-Mover (Dis) Advantages: Retrospective and Link with the Resource-Based View," *Strategic Management Journal* (December, 1998), pp. 1111–1125; G. J. Tellis and P. N. Golder, "First to Market, First to Fail? Real Causes of Enduring Market Leadership," *Sloan Management Review* (Winter 1996), pp. 65–75.

12. J. Pope, "Schick Entry May Work Industry into a Lather," *Des Moines Register* (May 15, 2003), p. 6D.

13. S. K. Ethiraj and D. H. Zhu, "Performance Effects of Imitative Entry," *Strategic Management Journal* (August 2008), pp. 797–817; G. Dowell and A. Swaminathan, "Entry Timing, Exploration, and Firm Survival in the Early U.S. Bicycle Industry," *Strategic Management Journal* (December 2006), pp. 1159–1182. For an in-depth discussion of first- and late-mover advantages and disadvantages, see D. S. Cho, D. J. Kim, and D. K. Rhee, "Latecomer Strategies: Evidence from the Semiconductor Industry in Japan and Korea," *Organization Science* (July–August 1998), pp. 489–505.

14. J. Shamsie, C. Phelps, and J. Kuperman, "Better Late than Never: A Study of Late Entrants in Household Electrical Equipment," *Strategic Management Journal* (January 2004), pp. 69–84.

15. T. S. Schoenecker and A. C. Cooper, "The Role of Firm Resources and Organizational Attributes in Determining Entry Timing: A Cross-Industry Study," *Strategic Management Journal* (December 1998), pp. 1127–1143.

16. Summarized from various articles by L. Fahey in *The Strategic Management Reader*, edited by L. Fahey (Englewood Cliffs, NJ: Prentice Hall, 1989), pp. 178–205.

17. M. Boyle, "Dueling Diapers," *Fortune* (February 17, 2003), pp. 115–116.

18. C. Edwards, "To See Where Tech Is Headed, Watch TI," *BusinessWeek* (November 6, 2006), p. 74.

19. P. Burrows, "Show Time," *BusinessWeek* (February 2, 2004), pp. 56–64.

20. A. Serwer, "Happy Birthday, Steinway," *Fortune* (March 17, 2003), pp. 94–97.

21. "Programmed for a Fight," *The Economist* (October 20, 2007), p. 85.

22. This information on defensive tactics is summarized from M. E. Porter, *Competitive Advantage* (New York: The Free Press, 1985), pp. 482–512.

23. H. D. Hopkins, "The Response Strategies of Dominant U.S. Firms to Japanese Challengers," *Journal of Management* (Vol. 29, No. 1, 2003), pp. 5–25.

24. For additional information on defensive competitive tactics, see G. Stalk, "Curveball Strategies to Fool the Competition," *Harvard Business Review* (September 2006), pp. 115–122.

25. "Cocoa Farming: Fair Enough?" *The Economist* (February 2, 2008), p. 74.

26. M. S. Feldman and B. T. Pentland, "Reconceptualizing Organizational Routines as a Source of Flexibility and Change," *Administrative Science Quarterly* (March 2003), pp. 94–118.

27. S. F. Slater and E. M. Olson, "Strategy Type and Performance: The Influence of Sales Force Management," *Strategic Management Journal* (August 2000), pp. 813–829.

28. B. Grow, "Thinking Outside the Box," *BusinessWeek* (October 25, 2004), pp. 70–72.

29. http://www.google.com/about/company/.

30. A. D. Chandler, *Strategy and Structure* (Cambridge, MA: MIT Press, 1962).

31. A. P. Sloan Jr., *My Years with General Motors* (Garden City, NY: Doubleday, 1964).

32. T. L. Amburgey and T. Dacin, "As the Left Foot Follows the Right? The Dynamics of Strategic and Structural Change," *Academy of Management Journal* (December 1994), pp. 1427–1452; M. Ollinger, "The Limits of Growth of the Multidivisional Firm: A Case Study of the U.S. Oil Industry from 1930–90," *Strategic Management Journal* (September 1994), pp. 503–520.

33. "Arctic Cat 2012 First Quarter Net Sales Up 18 Percent," *Sled Racer.com* (2012), http://www.sledracer.com/2011/07/arctic-cat-2012-first-quarter-net-sales-up-18-percent/.

34. D. F. Jennings and S. L. Seaman, "High and Low Levels of Organizational Adaptation: An Empirical Analysis of Strategy, Structure, and Performance," *Strategic Management Journal* (July 1994), pp. 459–475; L. Donaldson, "The Normal Science of Structured Contingency Theory," in *Handbook of Organization Studies*, edited by S. R. Clegg, C. Hardy, and W. R. Nord (London: Sage Publications, 1996), pp. 57–76.

35. A. K. Gupta, "SBU Strategies, Corporate-SBU Relations, and SBU Effectiveness in Strategy Implementation," *Academy of Management Journal* (September 1987), pp. 477–500.

36. L. E. Greiner, "Evolution and Revolution as Organizations Grow," *Harvard Business Review* (May–June 1998), pp. 55–67. This is an updated version of Greiner's classic 1972 article.

37. K. Shimizu and M. A. Hitt, "What Constrains or Facilitates Divestitures of Formerly Acquired Firms? The Effects of Organizational Inertia," *Journal of Management* (February 2005), pp. 50–72.

38. A. Weintraub, "Can Pfizer Prime the Pipeline?" *BusinessWeek* (December 31, 2007), pp. 90–91.

39. Ibid, p. 64. Although Greiner simply labeled this as the *"?" crisis*, the term *pressure-cooker* seems apt.

40. J. Hamm, "Why Entrepreneurs Don't Scale," *Harvard Business Review* (December 2002), pp. 110–115. See also C. B. Gibson and R. M. Rottner, "The Social Foundations for Building a Company Around an Inventor," *Organizational Dynamics* (Vol. 37, Issue 1, January–March 2008), pp. 21–34.

41. W. P. Barnett, "The Dynamics of Competitive Intensity," *Administrative Science Quarterly* (March 1997), pp. 128–160; D. Miller, *The Icarus Paradox: How Exceptional Companies Bring About Their Own Downfall* (New York: Harper Business, 1990).

42. D. Miller and P. H. Friesen, "A Longitudinal Study of the Corporate Life Cycle," *Management Science* (October 1984), pp. 1161–1183.

43. J. L. Morrow Jr., D. G. Sirmon, M. A. Hitt, and T. R. Holcomb, "Creating Value in the Face of Declining Performance: Firm Strategies and Organizational Recovery," *Strategic Management Journal* (March 2007), pp. 271–283; C. Zook, "Finding

Your Next Core Business," *Harvard Business Review* (April 2007), pp. 66–75.

44. J. P. Sheppard and S. D. Chowdhury, "Riding the Wrong Wave: Organizational Failure as a Failed Turnaround," *Long Range Planning* (June 2005), pp. 239–260.

45. W-R. Chen and K. D. Miller, "Situational and Institutional Determinants of Firms' R&D Search Intensity," *Strategic Management Journal* (April 2007), pp. 369–381.

46. S. Hamm, "Kodak's Moment of Truth," *BusinessWeek* (February 19, 2007), pp. 42–49.

47. A. Martin, "Negative Exposure for Kodak," *The New York Times* (October 20, 2011), http://www.nytimes.com/2011/10/21/business/kodaks-bet-on-its-printers-fails-to-quell-the-doubters.html?pagewanted=all&_r=0.

48. R. Berner, "Turning Kmart into a Cash Cow," *BusinessWeek* (July 12, 2004), p. 81.

49. H. Tavakolian, "Bankruptcy: An Emerging Corporate Strategy," *SAM Advanced Management Journal* (Spring 1995), p. 19.

50. L. G. Hrebiniak and W. F. Joyce, *Implementing Strategy* (New York: Macmillan, 1984), pp. 85–86.

51. S. M. Davis and P. R. Lawrence, *Matrix* (Reading, MA: Addison-Wesley, 1977), pp. 11–24.

52. J. G. March, "The Future Disposable Organizations and the Rigidities of Imagination," *Organization* (August/November 1995), p. 434.

53. M. A. Schilling and H. K. Steensma, "The Use of Modular Organizational Forms: An Industry-Level Analysis," *Academy of Management Journal* (December 2001), pp. 1149–1168.

54. M. P. Koza and A. Y. Lewin, "The Coevolution of Network Alliances: A Longitudinal Analysis of an International Professional Service Network," *Organization Science* (September/October 1999), pp. 638–653.

55. P. Engardio, "Mom-and-Pop Multinationals," *BusinessWeek* (July 14 and 21, 2008), pp. 77–78.

56. For more information on managing a network organization, see G. Lorenzoni and C Baden-Fuller, "Creating a Strategic Center to Manage a Web of Partners," *California Management Review* (Spring 1995), pp. 146–163.

57. R. E. Miles, C. C. Snow, J. A. Mathews, G. Miles, and H. J. Coleman Jr., "Organizing in the Knowledge Age: Anticipating the Cellular Form," *Academy of Management Executive* (November 1997), pp. 7–24.

58. N. Anand and R. L. Daft, "What Is the Right Organization Design?" *Organizational Dynamics* (Vol. 36, No. 4, 2007), pp. 329–344.

59. J. Naylor and M. Lewis, "Internal Alliances: Using Joint Ventures in a Diversified Company," *Long Range Planning* (October 1997), pp. 678–688.

60. G. Hoetker, "Do Modular Products Lead to Modular Organizations?" *Strategic Management Journal* (June 2006), pp. 501–518.

61. Anand and Daft, pp. 336–338.

62. Summarized from M. Hammer, "Reengineering Work: Don't Automate, Obliterate," *Harvard Business Review* (July–August 1990), pp. 104–112.

63. D. Paper, "BPR: Creating the Conditions for Success," *Long Range Planning* (June 1998), pp. 426–435.

64. S. Drew, "BPR in Financial Services: Factors for Success," *Long Range Planning* (October 1994), pp. 25–41.

65. "Do As I Say, Not As I Do," *Journal of Business Strategy* (May/June 1997), pp. 3–4.

66. L. Raymond and S. Rivard, "Determinants of Business Process Reengineering Success in Small and Large Enterprises: An Empirical Study in the Canadian Context," *Journal of Small Business Management* (January 1998), pp. 72–85.

67. K. Grint, "Reengineering History: Social Resonances and Business Process Reengineering," *Organization* (July 1994), pp. 179–201; A. Kleiner, "Revisiting Reengineering," *Strategy + Business* (3rd Quarter 2000), pp. 27–31.

68. E. A. Hall, J. Rosenthal, and J. Wade, "How to Make Reengineering *Really* Work," *McKinsey Quarterly* (1994, No. 2), pp. 107–128.

69. M. Arndt, "Quality Isn't Just for Widgets," *BusinessWeek* (July 22, 2002), pp. 72–73.

70. T. M. Box, "Six Sigma Quality: Experiential Learning," *SAM Advanced Management Journal* (Winter 2006), pp. 20–23.

71. L. Bodell, "5 Ways Process Is Killing Your Productivity," *Fast Company* (May 15, 2012), http://www.fastcompany.com/1837301/5-ways-process-killing-your-productivity.

72. J. Welch and S. Welch, "The Six Sigma Shotgun," *BusinessWeek* (May 21, 2007), p. 110.

73. Arndt, p. 73.

74. B. Hindo, "At 3M, a Struggle Between Efficiency and Creativity," *BusinessWeek IN* (June 11, 2007), pp. 8–16.

75. F. Arner and A. Aston, "How Xerox Got Up to Speed," *BusinessWeek* (May 3, 2004), pp. 103–104.

76. J. Hoerr, "Sharpening Minds for a Competitive Edge," *BusinessWeek* (December 17, 1990), pp. 72–78.

77. R. Krishnan, X. Martin, and N. G. Noorderhaven, "When Does Trust Matter to Alliance Performance," *Academy of Management Journal* (October 2006), pp. 894–917.

78. S. X. Li and T. J. Rowley, "Inertia and Evaluation Mechanisms in Interorganizational Partner Selection: Syndicate Formation Among U.S. Investment Banks," *Academy of Management Journal* (December 2002), pp. 1104–1119.

79. M. U. Douma, J. Bilderbeek, P. J. Idenburg, and J. K. Loise, "Strategic Alliances: Managing the Dynamics of Fit," *Long Range Planning* (August 2000), pp. 579–598; W. Hoffmann and R. Schlosser, "Success Factors of Strategic Alliances in Small and Medium-Sized Enterprises—An Empirical Survey," *Long Range Planning* (June 2001), pp. 357–381; Y. Luo, "How Important Are Shared Perceptions of Procedural Justice in Cooperative Alliances?" *Academy of Management Journal* (August 2005), pp. 695–709.

80. Alan M. Rugman, *The Regional Multinationals* (Cambridge, UK: Cambridge University Press, 2005); P. Ghemawat, "Regional Strategies for Global Leadership," *Harvard Business Review* (December 2005), pp. 98–108.

81. J. H. Taggart, "Strategy Shifts in MNC Subsidiaries," *Strategic Management Journal* (July 1998), pp. 663–681.

82. C. A. Bartlett and S. Ghoshal, "Beyond the M-Form: Toward a Managerial Theory of the Firm," *Strategic Management Journal* (Winter 1993), pp. 23–46.

83. C. Matlack, "Nestle Is Starting to Slim Down at Last," *BusinessWeek* (October 27, 2003), pp. 56–57; "Daring, Defying to Grow," *The Economist* (August 7, 2004), pp. 55–58.

84. J. Sterling, "Translating Strategy into Effective Implementation: Dispelling the Myths and Highlighting What Works," *Strategy & Leadership* (Vol. 31, No. 3, 2003), pp. 27–34.

85. "Rebirth of a Carmaker," *The Economist* (April 26, 2008), pp. 87–89; D. Kiley, "Fiat Headed Back to U.S. after 27 Years," *AOL Autos* (February 14, 2011), http://autos.aol.com/article/fiat-500-coming-to-america/.

strategy implementation: Staffing and Directing

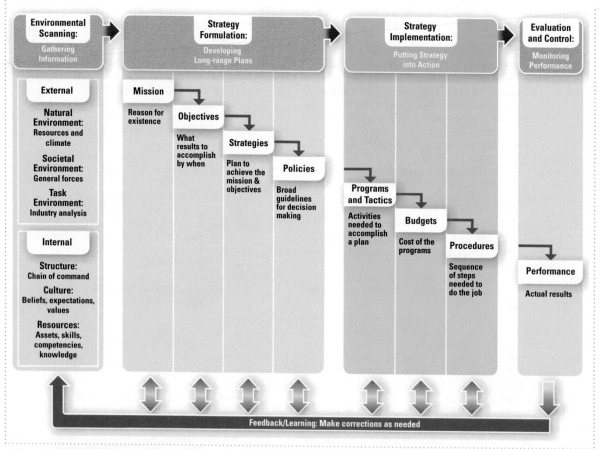

| Environmental Scanning:
Gathering Information | Strategy Formulation:
Developing Long-range Plans | Strategy Implementation:
Putting Strategy into Action | Evaluation and Control:
Monitoring Performance |

External

Natural Environment: Resources and climate

Societal Environment: General forces

Task Environment: Industry analysis

Internal

Structure: Chain of command

Culture: Beliefs, expectations, values

Resources: Assets, skills, competencies, knowledge

Mission — Reason for existence

Objectives — What results to accomplish by when

Strategies — Plan to achieve the mission & objectives

Policies — Broad guidelines for decision making

Programs and Tactics — Activities needed to accomplish a plan

Budgets — Cost of the programs

Procedures — Sequence of steps needed to do the job

Performance — Actual results

Feedback/Learning: Make corrections as needed

MyManagementLab®

⭐ Improve Your Grade!

Over 10 million students improved their results using the Pearson MyLabs. Visit **mymanagementlab.com** for simulations, tutorials, and end-of-chapter problems.

Learning Objectives

After reading this chapter, you should be able to:

- Understand the link between strategy and staffing decisions
- Match the appropriate manager to the strategy
- Understand how to implement an effective downsizing program
- Discuss important issues in effectively staffing and directing international expansion
- Assess and manage the corporate culture's fit with a new strategy
- Formulate effective action plans when MBO and TQM are determined to be appropriate methods of strategy implementation

Costco: Leading from the Front

Costco was founded in 1983 upon several simple foundations, such as marking everything up by no more than 15% (ever), paying and treating employees well, and providing a more upscale experience in the warehouse retail world. Today, the company is the largest (by sales) in the industry despite having fewer store locations than its rival Sam's Club. In 2011, the company racked up sales of US$93 billion and had more than 60 million members who pay for the privilege of shopping there.

One of the most stunning elements of the Costco success story is the way it has handled the staffing and leading elements of the business. Employees at the company make an average salary of US$20.89/hour and 88% of employees receive health care benefits even though half are part-time employees. During the recession that hit the globe from 2008–2011, the company had no layoffs. This has meant that the company enjoys some of the lowest turnover in an industry plagued by turnover. Employees at Costco know what they are doing and actively help customers.

Interestingly, the staffing model morphs into leading with the approach that the company takes to executive compensation. The former CEO and co-founder of Costco had a salary of only US$325,000/year and his total compensation package was US$2.2 million when the average for Fortune 500 CEOs in 2012 was US$9.6 million. The senior management team is similarly compensated, leading to an "all in for the good of the company" approach to the business.

In addition to leading with salary, the CEO made it a part of his yearly effort to visit all 560 stores in nine countries. This visible leading-from-the-front approach caught employees off guard when he would repeatedly jump in and work at the stores: cleaning, stocking, giving out food, and working the food court. In fact, the company has held tightly to the idea that a hot dog and soda should cost a patron no more than US$1.50. That was the price in 1985 when they opened their first hotdog stand in a store, and it is the price today. Costco sells more than 90 million hotdogs a year.

This chapter discusses strategy implementation in terms of staffing and leading. **Staffing** focuses on the selection and use of employees. **Leading** emphasizes the use of programs to better align employee interests and attitudes with a new strategy.

SOURCES: Stone, B. "How Cheap is Craig Jelinek," *Bloomberg BusinessWeek,* (June 10–16, 2013), pg. 54–60. C. Rexrode and B. Condon, "Average CEO Pay 2011 Nearly $10 Million at Public Companies: AP Study," *The Huffington Post* (May 25, 2012), http://www.huffingtonpost.com/2012/05/25/average-ceo-pay-2011_n_1545225.html; "The Costco Craze: Inside the Warehouse Giant," CNBC (2012), http://www.cnbc.com/id/46603589; "Fortune 50 CEO Pay vs. Our Salaries," Fortune (2012), http://money.cnn.com/magazines/fortune/fortune500/2012/ceo-pay-ratios/; A. Ruggeri, "Jim Sinegal: Costco CEO Focuses on Employees," *U.S. News & World Report* (October 22, 2009), http://www.usnews.com/news/best-leaders/articles/2009/10/22/jim-sinegal-costco-ceo-focuses-on-employees; T. Ferguson, "Sinegal Ends an Era at Costco," *Forbes* (September 1, 2011), http://www.forbes.com/sites/timferguson/2011/09/01/sinegal-ends-an-era-at-costco/.

Staffing

The implementation of new strategies and policies often calls for new human resource management priorities and a different use of personnel. Such staffing issues can involve hiring new people with new skills, firing people with inappropriate or substandard skills, and/or training existing employees to learn new skills. Research demonstrates that companies with enlightened talent-management policies and programs have higher returns on sales, investments, assets, and equity.[1] This is especially important given that the total U.S. market for talent acquisition is currently about US$124 billion and the average cost per hire is US$5700.[2]

If growth strategies are to be implemented, new people may need to be hired and trained. Experienced people with the necessary skills need to be found for promotion to newly created managerial positions. When a corporation follows a growth through acquisition strategy, it may find that it needs to replace several managers in the acquired company. The percentage of an acquired company's top management team that either quit or is asked to leave is around 25% after the first year, 35% after the second year, 48% after the third year, 55% after the fourth year, and 61% after five years.[3] In addition, executives who join an acquired company after the acquisition quit at significantly higher-than-normal rates beginning in their second year. Executives continue to depart at higher-than-normal rates for nine years after the acquisition.[4] Turnover rates of executives in firms acquired by foreign firms are significantly higher than for firms acquired by domestic firms, primarily in the fourth and fifth years after the acquisition.[5]

It is one thing to lose excess employees after a merger, but it is something else to lose highly skilled people who are difficult to replace. In a study of 40 mergers, 90% of the acquiring companies in the 15 successful mergers identified key employees and targeted them for retention within 30 days after the announcement. In contrast, this task was carried out only in one-third of the unsuccessful acquisitions.[6] To deal with integration issues such as these, some companies are appointing special **integration managers** to shepherd companies through the implementation process. The job of the integrator is to prepare a competitive profile of the combined company in terms of its strengths and weaknesses, draft an ideal profile of what the combined company should look like, develop action plans to close the gap between the actuality and the ideal, and establish training programs to unite the combined company and make it more competitive.[7] To be a successful integration manager, a person should have (1) a deep knowledge of the acquiring company, (2) a flexible management style, (3) an ability to work in cross-functional project teams, (4) a willingness to work independently, and (5) sufficient emotional and cultural intelligence to work well with people from all backgrounds.[8]

If a corporation adopts a retrenchment strategy, however, a large number of people may need to be laid off or fired (in many instances, being laid off is the same as being fired)—and top management, as well as the divisional managers, needs to specify the criteria to be used in making these personnel decisions. Should employees be fired on the basis of low seniority or on the basis of poor performance? Sometimes corporations find it easier to close or sell off an entire division than to choose which individuals to fire.

STAFFING FOLLOWS STRATEGY

As in the case of structure, staffing requirements should follow a change in strategy. For example, promotions should be based not only on current job performance but also on whether a person has the skills and abilities to do what is needed to implement the new strategy.

Changing Hiring and Training Requirements

Having formulated a new strategy, a corporation may find that it needs to either hire different people or retrain current employees to implement the new strategy. Consider the introduction of team-based production at Corning's filter plant mentioned in **Chapter 9**. Employee selection and training were crucial to the success of the new manufacturing strategy. Plant Manager Robert Hoover sorted through 8000 job applications before hiring 150 people with the best problem-solving abilities and a willingness to work in a team setting. Those selected received extensive training in technical and interpersonal skills. During the first year of production, 25% of all hours worked were devoted to training, at a cost of US$750,000.[9]

One way to implement a company's business strategy, such as overall low cost, is through training and development. According to the American Society of Training and Development, the average annual expenditure per employee on corporate training and development is US$1182 per employee.[10] A study of 155 U.S. manufacturing firms revealed that those with training programs had 19% higher productivity than those without such programs. Another study found that a doubling of formal training per employee resulted in a 7% reduction in scrap.[11] Training is especially important for a differentiation strategy emphasizing quality or customer service. At innovative online retailer Zappos, the whole company strategy is built around extraordinary customer service. Employees are screened and then screened again. At the end of each new employee training session, Zappos offers new employees US$4000 to quit. CEO Tony Hsieh said that about two to three percent of trainees accept that offer each year. They are not interested in employees that are simply there to get a paycheck. Training lasts seven weeks and there are tests along the way. A trainee has to graduate to be an employee.[12] Training is also important when implementing a retrenchment strategy. As suggested earlier, successful downsizing means that a company has to invest in its remaining employees. General Electric's Aircraft Engine Group used training to maintain its share of the market even though it had cut its workforce from 42,000 to 33,000 in the 1990s.[13]

Matching the Manager to the Strategy

Executive characteristics influence strategic outcomes for a corporation.[14] It is possible that a current CEO may not be appropriate to implement a new strategy. Research indicates that there may be a career life cycle for top executives. During the early years of executives' tenure, for example, they tend to experiment intensively with product lines to learn about their business. This is their learning stage. Later, their accumulated knowledge allows them to reduce experimentation and increase performance. This is their harvest stage. They enter a decline stage in their later years, when they reduce experimentation still further, and performance declines. Thus, there is an inverted U-shaped relationship between top executive tenure and the firm's financial performance. Some executives retire before any decline occurs. Others stave off decline longer than their counterparts. Because the length of time spent in each stage varies among CEOs, it is up to the board to decide when a top executive should be replaced.[15]

The most appropriate type of general manager needed to effectively implement a new corporate or business strategy depends on the desired strategic direction of that firm or business unit. Executives with a particular mix of skills and experiences may be classified as an **executive type** and paired with a specific corporate strategy. For example, a corporation following a concentration strategy emphasizing vertical or horizontal growth would probably want an aggressive new chief executive with a great deal of experience in that particular industry—a *dynamic industry expert*. A diversification strategy, in contrast, might call for someone with an analytical mind who is highly knowledgeable in other industries and can manage diverse product lines—an *analytical portfolio manager*. A corporation choosing to follow a stability strategy would probably want as its CEO a *cautious profit planner*, a person with a conservative style, a production or engineering background, and experience with controlling budgets, capital expenditures, inventories, and standardization procedures.

Weak companies in a relatively attractive industry tend to turn to a type of challenge-oriented executive known as a *turnaround specialist* to save the company. Julia Stewart started her career as an IHOP (International House of Pancakes) waitress. Years later she left the Applebee's restaurant chain to become CEO of IHOP, she worked to rebuild the company with better food, better ads, and a better atmosphere. Six years later, a much improved IHOP acquired the struggling Applebee's restaurant chain. CEO Stewart vowed to turnaround Applebee's within a year by improving service and food quality and by focusing the menu on what the restaurant does best: riblets, burgers, and salads. She wanted Applebee's to again be the friendly, neighborhood bar and grill that it once was.[16]

If a company cannot be saved, a *professional liquidator* might be called on by a bankruptcy court to close the firm and liquidate its assets. This is what happened to Montgomery Ward Inc., the nation's first catalog retailer, which closed its stores for good in 2001, after declaring bankruptcy for the second time.[17] Research supports the conclusion that as a firm's environment changes, it tends to change the type of top executive needed to implement a new strategy.[18]

For example, during the 1990s when the emphasis was on growth in a company's core products/services, the most desired background for a U.S. CEO was either in marketing or international experience. With the current decade's emphasis on mergers, acquisitions, and divestitures, the most desired background is finance. Currently, one out of five American and UK CEOs are former Chief Financial Officers, twice the percentage during the previous decade.[19]

This approach is in agreement with Chandler, who proposes (see **Chapter 9**) that the most appropriate CEO of a company changes as a firm moves from one stage of development to another. Because priorities certainly change over an organization's life, successful corporations need to select managers who have skills and characteristics appropriate to the organization's particular stage of development and position in its life cycle. For example, founders of firms tend to have functional backgrounds in technological specialties, whereas successors tend to have backgrounds in marketing and administration.[20] A change in the environment leading to a change in a company's strategy also leads to a change in the top management team. For example, a change in the U.S. utility industry's environment in 1992 supporting internally focused, efficiency-oriented strategies, led to top management teams being dominated by older managers with longer company and industry tenure, and with efficiency-oriented backgrounds in operations, engineering, and accounting.[21] Research reveals that executives having a specific personality characteristic (external locus of control) are more effective in regulated industries than are executives with a different characteristic (internal locus of control).[22]

Other studies have found a link between the type of CEO and a firm's overall strategic type. (Strategic types were presented in **Chapter 4**). For example, successful prospector firms tended to be headed by CEOs from research/engineering and general management backgrounds. High-performance defenders tended to have CEOs with accounting/finance, manufacturing/production, and general management experience. Analyzers tended to have CEOs with a marketing/sales background.[23]

A study of 173 firms over a 25-year period revealed that CEOs in these companies tended to have the same functional specialization as the former CEO, especially when the past CEO's strategy continued to be successful. This may be a pattern for successful corporations.[24] In particular, it explains why so many prosperous companies tend to recruit their top executives from one particular area. At Procter & Gamble (P&G)—a good example of an analyzer firm—the route to the CEO's position has traditionally been through brand management, with a strong emphasis on marketing—and more recently international experience. In other firms, the route may be through manufacturing, marketing, accounting, or finance—depending on what the corporation has always considered its core capability (and its overall strategic orientation).

SELECTION AND MANAGEMENT DEVELOPMENT

Selection and development are important not only to ensure that people with the right mix of skills and experiences are initially hired but also to help them grow on the job so they might be prepared for future promotions. For an interesting view of executive selection, take a look at the Innovation Issue on keeping Apple "cool."

INNOVATION issue

HOW TO KEEP APPLE "COOL"

Arguably, one of the most iconic "cool" companies in the past few decades has to be Apple. The designs, the feel of the products, and the ease with which the products work has made the company a standout with consumers. The innovative demands of a company that has the "cool" cache requires a balance of creative new products while maintaining a feel for what it means to be an Apple product. Much of this innovative ability was attributed to cofounder Steve Jobs. With his death in 2011, the company turned to Steve Schiller (then–Vice President of Product Marketing) to maintain the cache of the brand. Inside Apple, Steve Schiller was known as "mini-me"—a reference from the Austin Powers films that equated Steve Schiller with Steve Jobs.

Apple determined long ago that it took a consistent and persistent voice to develop and maintain the look and feel of something that would be called an Apple. Eschewing the approach of much of corporate America, Apple places that authority in one person. This exposes the innovation engine of an organization to both a staffing issue as well as a leading issue.

Schiller has been referred to as overly controlling and virtually dictatorial. Insiders called him "Dr. NO" for the way he dealt with most new ideas. While potentially a positive when controlling content, this approach may be seen as a reticence within the corporation to be creative. If anything happens to Schiller, the company would face a big issue if it tried to either pass the baton to another executive or revert to standard corporate practice and create guidelines for designers to follow. This is a very similar path to that taken by Sony as it transitioned in the 1990s. Unfortunately, SONY became mired in its own procedures and lost its cache as the "cool" product company.

In 2012, Apple released both the iPhone 5 and the iPad Mini. These products were viewed by most analysts as catch-up products because Apple had fallen behind. They looked like Apple products, but were virtually void of anything innovative.

Does Apple still have that "cool" feel to it? Are the products innovative?

SOURCES: P. Burrows and A. Satariano, "Can This Guy Keep Apple Cool?" Bloomberg Businessweek (June 11, 2012), pp. 47–48; http://www.apple.com/pr/bios/philip-w-schiller.html; E. Kolawole, "Apple Reveals iPhone 5: But Is It Innovative?" The Washington Post (September 12, 2012), http://www.washingtonpost.com/blogs/ innovations/post/apple-reveals-iphone-5-but-is-it-innovative/2012/ 09/12/ffb257a4-fcda-11e1-8adc-499661afe377_blog.html.

Executive Succession: Insiders vs. Outsiders

Executive succession is the process of replacing a key top manager. The average tenure of a chief executive of a large U.S. company declined from nearly 10 years in 2000 to 8.4 years in 2011.[25] Given that two-thirds of all major corporations worldwide replace their CEO at least once in a five-year period, it is important that the firm plan for this eventuality.[26] It is especially important for a company that usually promotes from within to prepare its current managers for promotion. For example, companies using so-called "relay" executive succession, in which a particular candidate is groomed to take over the CEO position, have significantly higher performance than those that hire someone from the outside or hold a competition between internal candidates.[27] These "heirs apparent" are provided special assignments including membership on other firms' boards of directors.[28] Nevertheless, only half of large U.S. companies have CEO succession plans in place.[29]

Companies known for being excellent training grounds for executive talent are Allied-Signal, Bain & Company, Bankers Trust, Boeing, Bristol Myers Squibb, Cititcorp, General Electric, Hewlett-Packard, McDonald's, McKinsey & Company, Microsoft, Nike, Pfizer, and P&G. For example, one study showed that hiring 19 GE executives into CEO positions added US$24.5 billion to the share prices of the companies that hired them. One year after people from GE started their new jobs, 11 of the 19 companies they joined were outperforming their competitors and the overall market.[30]

Some of the best practices for top management succession are encouraging boards to help the CEO create a succession plan, identifying succession candidates below the top layer, measuring internal candidates against outside candidates to ensure the development of a comprehensive set of skills, and providing appropriate financial incentives.[31] Succession planning has become the most important topic discussed by boards of directors.[32]

Prosperous firms tend to look outside for CEO candidates only if they have no obvious internal candidates.[33] For example, 78% of the CEOs selected to run S&P 500 companies in 2011 were insiders, according to executive search firm Spencer Stuart.[34] Hiring an outsider to be a CEO is a risky gamble. CEOs from the outside tend to introduce significant change and high turnover among the current top management.[35] For example, in one study, the percentage of senior executives that left a firm after a new CEO took office was 20% when the new CEO was an insider, but increased to 34% when the new CEO was an outsider.[36] CEOs hired from outside the firm tend to have a low survival rate. According to RHR International, 40% to 60% of high-level executives brought in from outside a company failed within two years.[37] A study of 392 large U.S. firms revealed that only 16.6% of them had hired outsiders to be their CEOs. The outsiders tended to perform slightly worse than insiders but had a very high variance in performance. Compared to that of insiders, the performance of outsiders tended to be either very good or very poor. Although outsiders performed much better (in terms of shareholder returns) than insiders in the first half of their tenures, they did much worse in their second half. As a result, the average tenure of an outsider was significantly less than for insiders.[38]

Firms in trouble, however, overwhelmingly choose outsiders to lead them.[39] For example, one study of 22 firms undertaking turnaround strategies over a 13-year period found that the CEO was replaced in all but two companies. Of 27 changes of CEO (several firms had more than one CEO during this period), only seven were insiders—20 were outsiders.[40] The probability of an outsider being chosen to lead a firm in difficulty increases if there is no internal heir apparent, if the last CEO was fired, and if the board of directors is composed of a large percentage of outsiders.[41] Boards realize that the best way to force a change in strategy is to hire a new CEO who has no connections to the current strategy.[42] For example, outsiders have been found to be very effective in leading strategic change for firms in Chapter 11 bankruptcy.[43]

Identifying Abilities and Potential

A company can identify and prepare its people for important positions in several ways. One approach is to establish a sound *performance appraisal system* to identify good performers with promotion potential. A survey of 34 corporate planners and human resource executives from 24 large U.S. corporations revealed that approximately 80% made some attempt to identify managers' talents and behavioral tendencies so they could place a manager with a likely fit to a given competitive strategy.[44] Companies select those people with promotion potential to be in their executive development training program. GE's spends more than US$1 billion per year for employee training at the company's famous Leadership Development Center in Crotonville, New York.[45] Doug Pelino, chief talent officer at Xerox, keeps a list of about 100 managers in middle management and at the vice presidential levels who have been selected to receive special training, leadership experience, and mentorship to become the next generation of top management.[46]

A company should examine its human resource system to ensure not only that people are being hired without regard to their racial, ethnic, or religious background, but also that they are being identified for training and promotion in the same manner. Management diversity can be a competitive advantage in a multi-ethnic world. With more women in the workplace, an increasing number are moving into top management, but are demanding more flexible career ladders to allow for family responsibilities.

Many large organizations are using *assessment centers* to evaluate a person's suitability for an advanced position. Corporations such as AT&T, Standard Oil, IBM, Sears, and GE have successfully used assessment centers. Because each is specifically tailored to its corporation, these assessment centers are unique. They use special interviews, management games, in-basket exercises, leaderless group discussions, case analyses, decision-making exercises, and oral presentations to assess the potential of employees for specific positions. Promotions into these positions are based on performance levels in the assessment center. Assessment centers have generally been able to accurately predict subsequent job performance and career success.[47]

Job rotation—moving people from one job to another—is also used in many large corporations to ensure that employees are gaining the appropriate mix of experiences to prepare them for future responsibilities. Rotating people among divisions is one way that a corporation can improve the level of organizational learning. General Electric, for example, routinely rotates its executives from one sector to a completely different one to learn the skills of managing in different industries. Jeffrey Immelt, who took over as CEO from Jack Welch, had managed businesses in plastics, appliances, and medical systems.[48] Companies that pursue related diversification strategies through internal development make greater use of interdivisional transfers of people than do companies that grow through unrelated acquisitions. Apparently, the companies that grow internally attempt to transfer important knowledge and skills throughout the corporation in order to achieve some sort of synergy.[49]

PROBLEMS IN RETRENCHMENT

In May 2012, Hewlett-Packard announced that it would lay off 27,000 employees (almost 8% of its workforce) in an effort to return the company to health. Meanwhile, major U.S. retail chains like Sears, Blockbuster, The Gap, and Abercrombie & Fitch announced triple-digit store closing plans for 2012.[50] **Downsizing** (sometimes called "rightsizing" or "resizing") refers to the planned elimination of positions or jobs. This program is often used to implement retrenchment strategies. Because the financial community is likely to react favorably to announcements of downsizing from a company in difficulty, such a program may provide some short-term benefits such as raising the company's stock price. If not done properly, however, downsizing may result in less, rather than more, productivity. One study found that a 10% reduction in people resulted in only a 1.5% reduction in costs, profits increased in only half the firms downsizing, and the stock prices of downsized firms increased over three years, but not as much as did those of firms that did not downsize.[51] Why were the results so marginal?

A study of downsizing at automobile-related U.S. industrial companies revealed that at 20 out of 30 companies, either the wrong jobs were eliminated or blanket offers of early retirement prompted managers, even those considered invaluable, to leave. After the layoffs, the remaining employees had to do not only their work but also the work of the people who had gone. Because the survivors often didn't know how to do the work of those who had left the company, morale and productivity plummeted.[52] Downsizing can seriously damage the learning capacity of organizations.[53] Creativity drops significantly (affecting new product development), and it becomes very difficult to keep high performers from leaving the company.[54] In addition, cost-conscious executives tend to defer maintenance, skimp on training, delay new product introductions, and avoid risky new businesses—all of which leads to lower sales and eventually to lower profits.[55] These are some of the reasons why layoffs worry customers and have a negative effect on a firm's reputation.[56]

A good retrenchment strategy can thus be implemented well in terms of organizing but poorly in terms of staffing. A situation can develop in which retrenchment feeds on itself and acts to further weaken instead of strengthen the company. Research indicates that companies undertaking cost-cutting programs are four times more likely than others to cut costs again, typically by reducing staff.[57] This has been the story at such well-known operations like Sears, Gannet, RIM, HSBC, and Borders, which eventually went into bankruptcy.[58] In contrast, successful downsizing firms undertake a strategic reorientation, not just a bloodletting of employees. Research shows that when companies use downsizing as part of a larger restructuring program to narrow company focus, they enjoy better performance.[59] This was the situation at Starbucks in 2008 as it closed stores and laid off more than 7000 people in its effort to refocus the business on the coffee experience. In the ensuing years, the company roared back to life without having to revert to layoffs again.

Consider the following guidelines that have been proposed for successful downsizing:

- **Eliminate unnecessary work instead of making across-the-board cuts:** Spend the time to research where money is going and eliminate the task, not the workers, if it doesn't add value to what the firm is producing. Reduce the number of administrative levels rather than the number of individual positions. Look for interdependent relationships before eliminating activities. Identify and protect core competencies.

- **Contract out work that others can do cheaper:** For example, Bankers Trust of New York contracted out its mailroom and printing services and some of its payroll and accounts payable activities to a division of Xerox. Outsourcing may be cheaper than vertical integration.

- **Plan for long-run efficiencies:** Don't simply eliminate all postponable expenses, such as maintenance, R&D, and advertising, in the unjustifiable hope that the environment will become more supportive. Continue to hire, grow, and develop—particularly in critical areas.

- **Communicate the reasons for actions:** Tell employees not only why the company is downsizing but also what the company is trying to achieve. Promote educational programs.

- **Invest in the remaining employees:** Because most "survivors" in a corporate downsizing will probably be doing different tasks from what they were doing before the change, firms need to draft new job specifications, performance standards, appraisal techniques, and compensation packages. Additional training is needed to ensure that everyone has the proper skills to deal with expanded jobs and responsibilities. Empower key individuals/groups and emphasize team building. Identify, protect, and mentor people who have leadership talent.

■ **Develop value-added jobs to balance out job elimination:** When no other jobs are currently available within the organization to transfer employees to, management must consider other staffing alternatives. For example, Harley-Davidson worked with the company's unions to find other work for surplus employees by moving into Harley plants work that had previously been done by suppliers.[60]

INTERNATIONAL ISSUES IN STAFFING

Implementing a strategy of international expansion takes a lot of planning and can be very expensive. Nearly 80% of midsize and larger companies send some of their employees abroad, and 45% plan to increase the number they have on foreign assignment. A complete package for one executive working in another country costs from US$300,000 to US$1 million annually. Nevertheless, between 10% and 20% of all U.S. managers sent abroad returned early because of job dissatisfaction or difficulties in adjusting to a foreign country. Of those who stayed for the duration of their assignment, nearly one-third did not perform as well as expected. One-fourth of those completing an assignment left their company within one year of returning home—often leaving to join a competitor.[61] One common mistake is failing to educate the person about the customs and values in other countries.

Primarily due to cultural differences, managerial style and human resource practices must be tailored to fit the particular situations in other countries. Only 11% of human resource managers have ever worked abroad, most have little understanding of a global assignment's unique personal and professional challenges and thus fail to develop the training necessary for such an assignment.[62] This is complicated by the fact that 90% of companies select employees for an international assignment based on their technical expertise while ignoring other areas.[63] A lack of knowledge of national and ethnic differences can make managing an international operation extremely difficult. One such example that shows the issues that have to be dealt with exists in Malaysia. Three ethnic groups live in Malaysia (Malay, Chinese, and Indian), each with their own language and religion, attending different schools, and a preference to not work in the same factories with each other. Because of the importance of cultural distinctions such as these, multinational corporations (MNCs) are now putting more emphasis on intercultural training for managers being sent on an assignment to a foreign country. This type of training is one of the commonly cited reasons for the lower expatriate failure rates—6% or less—for European and Japanese MNCs, which have emphasized cross-cultural experiences, compared with a 35% failure rate for U.S.-based MNCs.[64]

To improve organizational learning, many MNCs are providing their managers with international assignments lasting as long as five years. Upon their return to headquarters, these expatriates have an in-depth understanding of the company's operations in another part of the world. This has value to the extent that these employees communicate this understanding to others in decision-making positions. Research indicates that an MNC performs at a higher level when its CEO has international experience.[65] Global MNCs, in particular, emphasize international experience, have a greater number of senior managers who have been expatriates, and have a strong focus on leadership development through the expatriate experience.[66] Unfortunately, not all corporations appropriately manage international assignments. While out of the country, a person may be overlooked for an important promotion (out of sight, out of mind). Upon his or her return to the home country, co-workers may discount the out-of-country experience as a waste of time. The perceived lack of organizational support for international assignments increases the likelihood that an expatriate will return home early.[67]

One study of 750 U.S., Japanese, and European companies, found that the companies that do a good job of managing foreign assignments follow three general practices:

- When making international assignments, they focus on transferring knowledge and developing global leadership.

- They make foreign assignments to people whose technical skills are matched or exceeded by their cross-cultural abilities.

- They end foreign assignments with a deliberate repatriation process, with career guidance and jobs where the employees can apply what they learned in their assignments.[68]

Once a corporation has established itself in another country, it hires and promotes people from the host country into higher-level positions. For example, most large MNCs attempt to fill managerial positions in their subsidiaries with well-qualified citizens of the host countries. Unilever and IBM have traditionally taken this approach to international staffing. This policy serves to placate nationalistic governments and to better attune management practices to the host country's culture. The danger in using primarily foreign nationals to staff managerial positions in subsidiaries is the increased likelihood of suboptimization (the local subsidiary ignores the needs of the larger parent corporation). This makes it difficult for an MNC to meet its long-term, worldwide objectives. To a local national in an MNC subsidiary, the corporation as a whole can be an abstraction. Communication and coordination across subsidiaries become more difficult. As it becomes harder to coordinate the activities of several international subsidiaries, an MNC will have serious problems operating in a global industry.

Another approach to staffing the managerial positions of MNCs is to use people with an "international" orientation, regardless of their country of origin or host country assignment. This is a widespread practice among European firms. For example, Electrolux, a Swedish firm, had a French director in its Singapore factory. Using third-country "nationals" can allow for more opportunities for promotion than does Unilever's policy of hiring local people, but it can also result in more misunderstandings and conflicts with the local employees and with the host country's government.

Some corporations take advantage of immigrants and their children to staff key positions when negotiating entry into another country and when selecting an executive to manage the company's new foreign operations. For example, when General Motors wanted to learn more about business opportunities in China, it turned to Shirley Young, a Vice President of Marketing at GM. Born in Shanghai and fluent in Chinese language and customs, Young was instrumental in helping GM negotiate a US$1 billion joint venture with Shanghai Automotive to build a Buick plant in China. With other Chinese-Americans, Young formed a committee to advise GM on relations with China. Although just a part of a larger team of GM employees working on the joint venture, Young coached GM employees on Chinese customs and traditions.[69]

MNCs with a high level of international interdependence among activities need to provide their managers with significant international assignments and experiences as part of their training and development. Such assignments provide future corporate leaders with a series of valuable international contacts in addition to a better personal understanding of international issues and global linkages among corporate activities.[70] Research reveals that corporations using cross-national teams, whose members have international experience and communicate frequently with overseas managers, have greater product development capabilities than others.[71] Executive recruiters report that more major corporations are now requiring candidates to have international experience.[72] To increase its own top management's global expertise, Cisco Systems introduced a staffing program in 2007 with the objective of locating 20% of its senior managers at its new Bangalore, India, Globalization Center by 2010.[73]

Since an increasing number of multinational corporations are primarily organized around business units and product lines instead of geographic areas, product and SBU managers who are based at corporate headquarters are often traveling around the world to work personally with country managers. These managers and other mobile workers are being called *stealth expatriates* because they are either cross-border commuters (especially in the EU) or the accidental expatriate who goes on many business trips or temporary assignments due to offshoring and/or international joint ventures.[74]

Leading

Implementation also involves leading through coaching people to use their abilities and skills most effectively and efficiently to achieve organizational objectives. Without direction, people tend to do their work according to their personal view of what tasks should be done, how, and in what order. They may approach their work as they have in the past or emphasize those tasks that they most enjoy—regardless of the corporation's priorities. This can create real problems, particularly if the company is operating internationally and must adjust to customs and traditions in other countries. This direction may take the form of management leadership, communicated norms of behavior from the corporate culture, or agreements among workers in autonomous work groups. For an example of how a company can lead by radically changing the business model and the way it is staffed, see the **Sustainability Issue** feature. It may be accomplished more formally through action planning or through programs, such as Management By Objectives and Total Quality Management. Procedures can be changed to provide incentives to motivate employees to align their behavior with corporate objectives.

SUSTAINABILITY issue

PANERA AND THE "PANERA CARES COMMUNITY CAFÉ"

Sometimes the staffing model for a business can be adapted to provide long-term value to the community and help that company lead an industry. Panera Bread Company, with more than 1600 restaurants, had sales of more than US$1.8 billion and profits of US$136 million in 2011. The company had grown into an institution in the United States, catering to those who could afford to eat there (in other words, those who are employed). They steadfastly refused to lower prices during the latest recession and posted sales gains through that time period.

In an effort to lead in the business community as well as provide work for individuals in training programs supported by the company, Panera came up with a creative business approach when it opened its pilot "Panera Cares Community Café" in Clayton, Missouri, in 2010. Known by most as the "pay what you want" restaurant, the restaurant offered suggested donation levels instead of prices.

To make the business model work, the company created a foundation in order to separate it from the for-profit business. Consumers who are most able to pay are asked to donate extra, while those who are short on cash can pay less, and those who can't pay anything can volunteer for an hour to pay for their meal.

It is interesting to note that all three of the first locations in Clayton, Missouri, Dearborn, Michigan, and Portland, Oregon, turn a profit. The profit is used by the foundation to provide money to social service organizations that provide job training for at-risk youth. Panera then hires those who have received the training. This full-circle approach to staffing led Panera to convert two more stores—one in Chicago and one in Boston. The Chicago store was well known as the place where the founder wrote the company mission statement and he thought the location was perfect because it was a place where there are "million-dollar townhomes and people on the street."

SOURCES: D. Goodison, "Pay-What-You-Can Panera Donation Café Will Grace Hub," (November 5, 2012), E. York, "Panera to Open First Local Pay-What-You-Can Café in Lakeview," *Chicago Tribune* (June 20, 2012), http://articles.chicagotribune.com/2012-06-20/business/chi-panera-adds-paywhatyoucan-cafe-in-chicago-20120620_1_ron-shaich-lakeview-open-first;http://www.panerabread.com/about/company/?ref=/about/community/index.php.

MANAGING CORPORATE CULTURE

Because an organization's culture can exert a powerful influence on the behavior of all employees, it can strongly affect a company's ability to shift its strategic direction. A problem for a strong culture is that a change in mission, objectives, strategies, or policies and tactics is not likely to be successful if it is in opposition to the accepted culture of the company. Corporate culture has a strong tendency to resist change because its very reason for existence often rests on preserving stable relationships and patterns of behavior. For example, when Robert Nardelli became CEO at The Home Depot in 2000, he changed the corporate strategy to growing the company's small professional supply business (sales to building contractors) through acquisitions and making the mature retail business cost-effective. He attempted to replace the old informal entrepreneurial collaborative culture with one of military efficiency. Before Nardelli's arrival, most store managers had based their decisions upon their personal knowledge of their customers' preferences. Under Nardelli, they were given weekly sales and profit targets. Underperforming managers were asked to leave the company. The once-heavy ranks of full-time employees were replaced with cheaper part-timers who had far less experience to help the DIY customer. In this "culture of fear," morale fell and The Home Depot's customer satisfaction score dropped to last place among major U.S. retailers. Nardelli was asked to leave the company in 2007 and the company's resurgence over the next four years as it moved back to its roots is a testament to the strength of corporate culture.

There is no one best corporate culture. An optimal culture is one that best supports the mission and strategy of the company of which it is a part. This means that *corporate culture should support the strategy.* Unless strategy is in complete agreement with the culture, any significant change in strategy should be followed by a modification of the organization's culture. Although corporate culture can be changed, it often takes a long time, and it requires a lot of effort. At The Home Depot, for example, CEO Nardelli attempted to change the corporate culture by hiring GE veterans like himself into top management positions, hiring ex-military officers as store managers, and instituting a top-down command structure.

A key job of management involves managing corporate culture. In doing so, management must evaluate what a particular change in strategy means to the corporate culture, assess whether a change in culture is needed, and decide whether an attempt to change the culture is worth the likely costs.

Assessing Strategy-Culture Compatibility

When implementing a new strategy, a company should take the time to assess *strategy-culture compatibility.* (See **Figure 10–1.**) Consider the following questions regarding a corporation's culture:

1. **Is the proposed strategy compatible with the company's current culture?** *If yes,* full steam ahead. Tie organizational changes into the company's culture by identifying how the new strategy will achieve the mission better than the current strategy does. *If not . . .*

2. **Can the culture be easily modified to make it more compatible with the new strategy?** *If yes,* move forward carefully by introducing a set of culture-changing activities such as minor structural modifications, training and development activities, and/or hiring new managers who are more compatible with the new strategy. When Proctor & Gamble's top management decided to implement a strategy aimed at reducing costs, for example, it made some changes in how things were done, but it did not eliminate its brand-management system. The culture adapted to these modifications over a couple of years and productivity increased. *If not . . .*

FIGURE 10–1 Assessing Strategy–Culture Compatibility

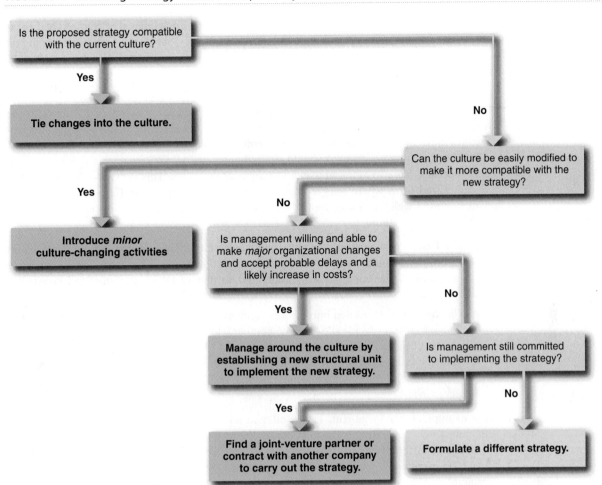

3. **Is management willing and able to make major organizational changes and accept probable delays and a likely increase in costs?** *If yes*, manage around the culture by establishing a new structural unit to implement the new strategy. In 2012, Saab Automobile Parts AB established a subsidiary to provide original parts in the United States after running into a decade of issues resulting from a lack of focus on U.S. Saab owners. By creating a separate subsidiary whose sole responsibility was providing U.S. customers with spare parts for their cars, the company was able to bypass the established focus of the company, which was clearly not on U.S. Saab owners. *If not . . .*

4. **Is management still committed to implementing the strategy?** *If yes*, find a joint-venture partner or contract with another company to carry out the strategy. *If not*, formulate a different strategy.

Based on Robert Nardelli's decisions when he initially started as The Home Depot's CEO, he probably answered "no" to the first question and "yes" to the second question—thus justifying his many changes in staffing and leading. Unfortunately, these changes didn't work very well. Instead, he should have replied "no" to the first and second questions and stopped at the third question. As suggested by this question, he should have considered a different corporate strategy, such as growing the professional side of the business without changing the collegial culture of the retail stores. Not surprisingly, once Nardelli was replaced by a new CEO, the company divested the professional supply companies that Nardelli had spent so much time and money acquiring and returned to its previous strategy of concentrating on The Home Depot retail stores.

Managing Cultural Change Through Communication

Communication is key to the effective management of change. A survey of 3199 worldwide executives by McKinsey & Company revealed that ongoing communication and involvement was the approach most used by companies that successfully transformed themselves.[75] Rationale for strategic changes should be communicated to workers not only in newsletters and speeches, but also in training and development programs. This is especially important in decentralized firms where a large number of employees work in far-flung business units.[76] Companies in which major cultural changes have successfully taken place had the following characteristics in common:

- The CEO and other top managers had a strategic vision of what the company could become and communicated that vision to employees at all levels. The current performance of the company was compared to that of its competition and constantly updated.

- The vision was translated into the key elements necessary to accomplish that vision. For example, if the vision called for the company to become a leader in quality or service, aspects of quality and service were pinpointed for improvement, and appropriate measurement systems were developed to monitor them. These measures were communicated widely through contests, formal and informal recognition, and monetary rewards, among other devices.[77]

For example, when Pizza Hut, Taco Bell, and KFC were purchased by Tricon Global Restaurants (now Yum! Brands) from PepsiCo, the new management knew that it had to create a radically different culture than the one at PepsiCo if the company was to succeed. To begin, management formulated a statement of shared values—"How We Work Together" principles. They declared their differences with the "mother country" (PepsiCo) and wrote a "Declaration of Independence" stating what the new company would stand for. Restaurant managers participated in team-building activities at the corporate headquarters and finished by signing the company's "Declaration of Independence" as "founders" of the company. Since then, "Founders Day" has become an annual event celebrating the culture of the company. Headquarters was renamed the "Restaurant Support Center," signifying the cultural value the restaurants held as the central focus of the company. People measures were added to financial measures and customer measures, reinforcing the "putting people first" value. In an unprecedented move in the industry, restaurant managers were given stock options and stock was added to the list of performance incentives. The company created values-focused 360-degree performance reviews, which were eventually pushed to the restaurant manager level.[78]

Managing Diverse Cultures Following an Acquisition

When merging with or acquiring another company, top management must give some consideration to a potential clash of corporate cultures. According to a Hewitt Associates survey of 218 major U.S. corporations, integrating culture was a top challenge for 69% of the reporting companies.[79] Cultural differences are even more problematic when a company acquires a firm in another country. Daimler-Benz has dealt with this on a number of occasions, including its merger with Chrysler in 1998 and its purchase of a controlling interest in Mitsubishi Motors in 2001. Resistance to change led Daimler-Benz to eject both organizations from the parent company.[80] It's dangerous to assume that the firms can simply be integrated into the same reporting structure. The greater the gap between the cultures of the acquired firm and the acquiring firm, the faster executives in the acquired firm quit their jobs and valuable talent is lost. Conversely, when corporate cultures are similar, performance problems are minimized.[81]

There are four general methods of managing two different cultures. (See **Figure 10–2**.) The choice of which method to use should be based on *(1) how much members of the acquired firm value preserving their own culture* and *(2) how attractive they perceive the culture of the acquirer to be.*[82]

1. *Integration* involves a relatively balanced give-and-take of cultural and managerial practices between the merger partners, and no strong imposition of cultural change on either company. It merges the two cultures in such a way that the separate cultures of both firms are preserved in the resulting culture. This is what occurred when France's Renault purchased a controlling interest in Japan's Nissan Motor Company and installed Carlos Ghosn as Nissan's new CEO to turn the company around. Ghosn was very sensitive to Nissan's culture and allowed the company room to develop a new corporate culture based on the best elements of Japan's national culture. His goal was to form one successful auto group from two very distinct companies.[83]

2. *Assimilation* involves the domination of one organization over the other. The domination is not forced, but it is welcomed by members of the acquired firm, who may feel for many reasons that their culture and managerial practices have not produced success. The acquired firm surrenders its culture and adopts the culture of the acquiring company. This was the case when Maytag Company (now part of Whirlpool) acquired Admiral. Because Admiral's previous owners had not kept the manufacturing facilities up to date, quality had drastically fallen over the years. Admiral's employees were willing to accept the dominance of Maytag's strong quality-oriented culture because they respected it and knew that without significant changes at Admiral, they would soon be out of work. In turn, they expected to be treated with some respect for their skills in refrigeration technology.

FIGURE 10–2
Methods of Managing the Culture of an Acquired Firm

Integration

Equal merger of both cultures into a new corporate culture

Assimilation

Acquiring firm's culture kept intact, but subservient to that of acquiring firm's corporate culture

Separation

Conflicting cultures kept intact, but kept separate in different units

Deculturation

Forced replacement of conflicting acquired firm's culture with that of the acquiring firm's culture

SOURCES: Suggested by A. R. Malezadeh and A. Nahavandi in "Making Mergers Work in Managing Cultures," *Journal of Business Strategy* (May/June 1990), pp. 53–57 and "Acculturation in Mergers and Acquisitions," *Academy of Management Review* (January 1988), pp. 79–90.

3. *Separation* is characterized by a separation of the two companies' cultures. They are structurally separated, without cultural exchange. When Boeing acquired McDonnell-Douglas, known for its expertise in military aircraft and missiles, Boeing created a separate unit to house both McDonnell's operations and Boeing's own military business. McDonnell executives were given top posts in the new unit and other measures were taken to protect the strong McDonnell culture. On the commercial side, where Boeing had the most expertise, McDonnell's commercial operations were combined with Boeing's in a separate unit managed by Boeing executives.[84]

4. *Deculturation* involves the disintegration of one company's culture resulting from unwanted and extreme pressure from the other to impose its culture and practices. This is the most common and most destructive method of dealing with two different cultures. It is often accompanied by much confusion, conflict, resentment, and stress. This is a primary reason why so many executives tend to leave after their firm is acquired. Such a merger typically results in poor performance by the acquired company and its eventual divestment. This is what happened when AT&T acquired NCR Corporation in 1990 for its computer business. It replaced NCR managers with an AT&T management team, reorganized sales, forced employees to adhere to the AT&T code of values (called the "Common Bond"), and even dropped the proud NCR name (successor to National Cash Register) in favor of a sterile GIS (Global Information Solutions) nonidentity. By 1995, AT&T was forced to take a US$1.2 billion loss and lay off 10,000 people.[85] The NCR unit was consequently sold.

ACTION PLANNING

Activities can be directed toward accomplishing strategic goals through action planning. At a minimum, an **action plan** states what actions are going to be taken, by whom, during what time frame, and with what expected results. After a program has been selected to implement a particular strategy, an action plan should be developed to put the program in place. **Table 10–1** shows an example of an action plan for a new advertising and promotion program.

Take the example of a company choosing forward vertical integration through the acquisition of a retailing chain as its growth strategy. Once it owns its own retail outlets, it must integrate the stores into the company. One of the many programs it would have to develop is a new advertising program for the stores. The resulting action plan to develop a new advertising program should include much of the following information:

1. **Specific actions to be taken to make the program operational:** One action might be to contact three reputable advertising agencies and ask them to prepare a proposal for a new radio and newspaper ad campaign based on the theme "Jones Surplus is now a part of Ajax Continental. Prices are lower. Selection is better."

2. **Dates to begin and end each action:** Time would have to be allotted not only to select and contact three agencies, but to allow them sufficient time to prepare a detailed proposal. For example, allow one week to select and contact the agencies, plus three months for them to prepare detailed proposals to present to the company's marketing director. Also allow some time to decide which proposal to accept.

3. **Person (identified by name and title) responsible for carrying out each action:** List someone—such as Jan Lewis, advertising manager—who can be put in charge of the program.

4. **Person responsible for monitoring the timeliness and effectiveness of each action:** Indicate that Jan Lewis is responsible for ensuring that the proposals are of good quality and are priced within the planned program budget. She will be the primary company

TABLE 10–1   Example of an Action Plan

Action Plan for Jan Lewis, Advertising Manager, and Rick Carter, Advertising Assistant, Ajax Continental

Program Objective: To Run a New Advertising and Promotion Campaign for the Combined Jones Surplus/Ajax Continental Retail Stores for the Coming Christmas Season within a Budget of $XX.

Program Activities:

1. Identify Three Best Ad Agencies for New Campaign.
2. Ask Three Ad Agencies to Submit a Proposal for a New Advertising and Promotion Campaign for Combined Stores.
3. Agencies Present Proposals to Marketing Manager.
4. Select Best Proposal and Inform Agencies of Decision.
5. Agency Presents Winning Proposal to Top Management.
6. Ads Air on TV and Promotions Appear in Stores.
7. Measure Results of Campaign in Terms of Viewer Recall and Increase in Store Sales.

Action Steps	Responsibility	Start–End
1. A. Review previous programs	Lewis & Carter	1/1–2/1
B. Discuss with boss	Lewis & Smith	2/1–2/3
C. Decide on three agencies	Lewis	2/4
2. A. Write specifications for ad	Lewis	1/15–1/20
B. Assistant writes ad request	Carter	1/20–1/30
C. Contact ad agencies	Lewis	2/5–2/8
D. Send request to three agencies	Carter	2/10
E. Meet with agency acct. execs	Lewis & Carter	2/16–2/20
3. A. Agencies work on proposals	Acct. Execs	2/23–5/1
B. Agencies present proposals	Carter	5/1–5/15
4. A. Select best proposal	Lewis	5/15–5/20
B. Meet with winning agency	Lewis	5/22–5/30
C. Inform losers	Carter	6/1
5. A. Fine-tune proposal	Acct. Exec	6/1–7/1
B. Presentation to management	Lewis	7/1–7/3
6. A. Ads air on TV	Lewis	9/1–12/24
B. Floor displays in stores	Carter	8/20–8/30
7. A. Gather recall measures of ads	Carter	9/1–12/24
B. Evaluate sales data	Carter	1/1–1/10
C. Prepare analysis of campaign	Carter	1/10–2/15

contact for the ad agencies and will report on the progress of the program once a week to the company's marketing director.

5. **Expected financial and physical consequences of each action:** Estimate when a completed ad campaign will be ready to show top management and how long it will take after approval to begin to air the ads. Estimate the expected increase in store sales over the six-month period after the ads are first aired. Indicate whether "recall" measures will be used to help assess the ad campaign's effectiveness, plus how, when, and by whom the recall data will be collected and analyzed.

6. **Contingency plans:** Indicate how long it will take to get an acceptable ad campaign to show top management if none of the initial proposals is acceptable.

Action plans are important for several reasons. First, action plans serve as a link between strategy formulation and evaluation and control. Second, the action plan specifies what needs to be done differently from the way operations are currently carried out. Third, during the evaluation and control process that comes later, an action plan helps in both the appraisal of performance and in the identification of any remedial actions, as needed. In addition, the explicit assignment of responsibilities for implementing and monitoring the programs may contribute to better motivation.

MANAGEMENT BY OBJECTIVES

Management By Objectives (MBO) is a technique that encourages participative decision making through shared goal setting at all organizational levels and performance assessment based on the achievement of stated objectives.[86] MBO links organizational objectives and the behavior of individuals. Because it is a system that links plans with performance, it is a powerful implementation technique.

The MBO process involves:

1. Establishing and communicating organizational objectives.
2. Setting individual objectives (through superior-subordinate interaction) that help implement organizational ones.
3. Developing an action plan of activities needed to achieve the objectives.
4. Periodically (at least quarterly) reviewing performance as it relates to the objectives and including the results in the annual performance appraisal.[87]

MBO provides an opportunity for the corporation to connect the objectives of people at each level to those at the next higher level. MBO, therefore, acts to tie together corporate, business, and functional objectives, as well as the strategies developed to achieve them. Although MBO originated in the 1950s, 90% of surveyed practicing managers feel that MBO is applicable today.[88] The principles of MBO are a part of self-managing work teams and quality circles.[89]

One of the real benefits of MBO is that it can reduce the amount of internal politics operating within a large corporation. Political actions within a firm can cause conflict and create divisions between the very people and groups who should be working together to implement strategy. People are less likely to jockey for position if the company's mission and objectives are clear and they know that the reward system is based not on game playing, but on achieving clearly communicated, measurable objectives.

TOTAL QUALITY MANAGEMENT

Total Quality Management (TQM) is an operational philosophy committed to *customer satisfaction* and *continuous improvement*. TQM is committed to quality/excellence and to being the best in all functions. Because TQM aims to reduce costs and improve quality, it can be used as a program to implement an overall low-cost or a differentiation business strategy. About 92% of manufacturing companies and 69% of service firms have implemented some form of quality management practices.[90] Not all TQM programs have been successes. Nevertheless, a recent survey of 325 manufacturing firms in Canada, Hungary, Italy, Lebanon, Taiwan, and the United States revealed that total quality management and just-in-time were the two highest-ranked improvement programs to improve company performance. An analysis of the successes and failures of TQM concluded that the key ingredient is top management. Successful TQM programs occur in those companies in which "top managers move beyond defensive and tactical orientations to embrace a developmental orientation."[91]

According to TQM, faulty processes, not poorly motivated employees, are the cause of defects in quality. The program involves a significant change in corporate culture, requiring strong leadership from top management, employee training, empowerment of lower-level employees (giving people more control over their work), and teamwork in order to succeed in a company. TQM emphasizes prevention, not correction. Inspection for quality still takes place, but the emphasis is on improving the process to prevent errors and deficiencies. Thus, quality circles or quality improvement teams are formed to identify problems and to suggest how to improve the processes that may be causing the problems.

TQM's essential ingredients are:

- **An intense focus on customer satisfaction:** Everyone (not just people in the sales and marketing departments) understands that their jobs exist only because of customer needs. Thus all jobs must be approached in terms of how they will affect customer satisfaction.

- **Internal as well as external customers:** An employee in the shipping department may be the internal customer of another employee who completes the assembly of a product, just as a person who buys the product is a customer of the entire company. An employee must be just as concerned with pleasing the internal customer as in satisfying the external customer.

- **Accurate measurement of every critical variable in a company's operations:** This means that employees have to be trained in what to measure, how to measure, and how to interpret the data. A rule of TQM is that *you only improve what you measure.*

- **Continuous improvement of products and services:** Everyone realizes that operations need to be continuously monitored to find ways to improve products and services.

- **New work relationships based on trust and teamwork:** Important is the idea of empowerment—giving employees wide latitude in how they go about achieving the company's goals. Research indicates that the keys to TQM success lie in executive commitment, an open organizational culture, and employee empowerment.[92]

INTERNATIONAL CONSIDERATIONS IN LEADING

In a study of 53 different national cultures, Hofstede found that each nation's unique culture could be identified using five dimensions. He found that national culture is so influential that it tends to overwhelm even a strong corporate culture. (See the numerous sociocultural societal variables that compose another country's culture listed in **Table 4–3**.) In measuring the differences among these **dimensions of national culture** from country to country, he was able to explain why a certain management practice might be successful in one nation but fail in another:[93]

1. **Power distance (PD)** is the extent to which a society accepts an unequal distribution of power in organizations. Malaysia and Mexico scored highest, whereas Germany and Austria scored lowest. People in those countries scoring high on this dimension tend to prefer autocratic to more participative managers.

2. **Uncertainty avoidance (UA)** is the extent to which a society feels threatened by uncertain and ambiguous situations. Greece and Japan scored highest on disliking ambiguity, whereas the United States and Singapore scored lowest. People in those nations scoring high on this dimension tend to want career stability, formal rules, and clear-cut measures of performance.

3. **Individualism-collectivism (I-C)** is the extent to which a society values individual freedom and independence of action compared with a tight social framework and loyalty to the group. The United States and Canada scored highest on individualism, whereas

Mexico and Guatemala scored lowest. People in nations scoring high on individualism tend to value individual success through competition, whereas people scoring low on individualism (thus high on collectivism) tend to value group success through collective cooperation.

4. **Masculinity-femininity (M-F)** is the extent to which society is oriented toward money and things (which Hofstede labels masculine) or toward people (which Hofstede labels feminine). Japan and Mexico scored highest on masculinity, whereas France and Sweden scored lowest (thus highest on femininity). People in nations scoring high on masculinity tend to value clearly defined sex roles where men dominate, and to emphasize performance and independence, whereas people scoring low on masculinity (and thus high on femininity) tend to value equality of the sexes where power is shared, and to emphasize the quality of life and interdependence.

5. **Long-term orientation (LT)** is the extent to which society is oriented toward the long- versus the short-term. Hong Kong and Japan scored highest on long-term orientation, whereas Pakistan scored the lowest. A long-term time orientation emphasizes the importance of hard work, education, and persistence as well as the importance of thrift. Nations with a long-term time orientation tend to value strategic planning and other management techniques with a long-term payback.

Hofstede's work was extended by Project GLOBE, a team of 150 researchers who collected data on cultural values, practices, and leadership attributes from 18,000 managers in 62 countries. The project studied the nine cultural dimensions of assertiveness, future orientation, gender differentiation, and uncertainty avoidance, and power distance, institutional emphasis on collectivism versus individualism, in-group collectivism, performance orientation, and humane orientation.[94]

The dimensions of national culture help explain why some management practices work well in some countries but not in others. For example, MBO, which originated in the United States, succeeded in Germany, according to Hofstede, because the idea of replacing the arbitrary authority of the boss with the impersonal authority of mutually agreed-upon objectives fits the low power distance that is a dimension of the German culture. It failed in France, however, because the French are used to high power distances; they are used to accepting orders from a highly personalized authority. In countries with high levels of uncertainty avoidance, such as Switzerland and Austria, communication should be clear and explicit, based on facts. Meetings should be planned in advance and have clear agendas. In contrast, in low-uncertainty-avoidance countries such as Greece or Russia, people are not used to structured communication and prefer more open-ended meetings. Because Thailand has a high level of power distance, Thai managers feel that communication should go from the top to the bottom of a corporation. As a result, 360-degree performance appraisals are seen as dysfunctional.[95] Some of the difficulties experienced by U.S. companies in using Japanese-style quality circles in TQM may stem from the extremely high value U.S. culture places on individualism. The differences between the United States and Mexico in terms of the power distance (Mexico 104 vs. U.S. 46) and individualism-collectivism (U.S. 91 vs. Mexico 30) dimensions may help explain why some companies operating in both countries have difficulty adapting to the differences in customs.[96] In addition, research has found that technology alliance formation is strongest in countries that value cooperation and avoid uncertainty.[97]

When one successful company in one country merges with another successful company in another country, the clash of corporate cultures is compounded by the clash of national cultures. For example, when two companies, one from a high-uncertainty-avoidance society and one from a low-uncertainty-avoidance country, are considering a merger, they should investigate each other's management practices to determine potential areas of conflict. Given the growing number of cross-border mergers and acquisitions, the management of cultures is becoming a key issue in strategy implementation. See the **Global Issue** feature to learn how differences in national and corporate cultures created conflict when Upjohn Company of the United States and Pharmacia AB of Sweden merged.

MNCs must pay attention to the many differences in cultural dimensions around the world and adjust their management practices accordingly. Cultural differences can easily go unrecognized by a headquarters staff that may interpret these differences as personality defects, whether the people in the subsidiaries are locals or expatriates. When conducting strategic planning in an MNC, top management must be aware that the process will vary based upon the national culture where a subsidiary is located. The values embedded in national culture have a profound and enduring effect on an executive's orientation, regardless of the impact of industry experience or corporate culture.[98]

GLOBAL issue

CULTURAL DIFFERENCES CREATE IMPLEMENTATION PROBLEMS IN MERGER

When Upjohn Pharmaceuticals of Kalamazoo, Michigan, and Pharmacia AB of Stockholm, Sweden, merged in 1995, employees of both sides were optimistic for the newly formed Pharmacia & Upjohn, Inc. Both companies were second-tier competitors fighting for survival in a global industry. Together, the firms would create a global company that could compete scientifically with its bigger rivals.

Because Pharmacia had acquired an Italian firm in 1993, it also had a large operation in Milan. U.S. executives scheduled meetings throughout the summer of 1996—only to cancel them when their European counterparts could not attend. Although it was common knowledge in Europe that most Swedes take the entire month of July for vacation and that Italians take off all of August, this was not common knowledge in Michigan. Differences in management styles became a special irritant. Swedes were used to an open system, with autonomous work teams. Executives sought the whole group's approval before making an important decision. Upjohn executives followed the more traditional American top-down approach. Upon taking command of the newly merged firm, Dr. Zabriskie (who had been Upjohn's CEO), divided the company into departments reporting to the new London headquarters. He required frequent reports, budgets, and staffing updates. The Swedes reacted negatively to this top-down management hierarchical style. "It was degrading," said Stener

Kvinnsland, head of Pharmacia's cancer research in Italy before he quit the new company.

The Italian operations baffled the Americans, even though the Italians felt comfortable with a hierarchical management style. Italy's laws and unions made layoffs difficult. Italian data and accounting were often inaccurate. Because the Americans didn't trust the data, they were constantly asking for verification. In turn, the Italians were concerned that the Americans were trying to take over Italian operations. At Upjohn, all workers were subject to testing for drug and alcohol abuse. Upjohn also banned smoking. At Pharmacia's Italian business center, however, waiters poured wine freely every afternoon in the company dining room. Pharmacia's boardrooms were stocked with humidors for executives who smoked cigars during long meetings. After a brief attempt to enforce Upjohn's policies, the company dropped both the no-drinking and no-smoking policies for European workers.

In order to assert more control over the whole operation, the company moved its HQ back to the United States in 1998. In 2000, the company acquired Monsanto and Searle, both large pharmaceutical companies. The new company, called Pharmacia, didn't last long. The company was bought out by Pfizer in 2003.

SOURCES: Summarized from R. Frank and T. M. Burton, "Cross-Border Merger Results in Headaches for a Drug Company," *The Wall Street Journal* (February 4, 1997), pp. A1, A12; http://www.pfizer.com/about/history/pfizer_pharmacia.jsp.

End of Chapter SUMMARY

Strategy is implemented by modifying structure (organizing), selecting the appropriate people to carry out the strategy (staffing), and communicating clearly how the strategy can be put into action (leading). A number of programs, such as organizational and job design, reengineering, Six Sigma, MBO, TQM, and action planning, can be used to implement a new strategy. Executives must manage the corporate culture and find the right mix of qualified people to put a strategy in place.

Research on executive succession reveals that it is very risky to hire new top managers from outside the corporation. Although this is often done when a company is in trouble, it can be dangerous for a successful firm. This is also true when hiring people for non-executive positions. An in-depth study of 1052 stock analysts at 78 investment banks revealed that hiring a star (an outstanding performer) from another company did not improve the hiring company's performance. When a company hires a star, the star's performance plunges, there is a sharp decline in the functioning of the team the person works with, and the company's market value declines. Their performance dropped about 20% and did not return to the level before the job change—even after five years. Interestingly, around 36% of the stars left the investment banks that hired them within 36 months. Another 29% quit in the next 24 months.

This phenomenon occurs not because a star doesn't suddenly become less intelligent when switching firms, but because the star cannot take to the new firm the firm-specific resources that contributed to her or his achievements at the previous company. As a result, the star is unable to repeat the high performance in another company until he or she learns the new system. This may take years, but only if the new company has a good support system in place. Otherwise, the performance may never improve. For these reasons, companies cannot obtain competitive advantage by hiring stars from the outside. Instead, they should emphasize growing their own talent and developing the infrastructure necessary for high performance.[99]

It is important to not ignore the majority of the workforce who, while not being stars, are the solid performers that keep a company going over the years. An undue emphasis on attracting stars often wastes money and destroys morale. The CEO of McKesson, a pharmaceutical wholesaler, calls these B players "performers in place. . . . They are happy living in Dubuque. I have more time and admiration for them than the A player who is at my desk every six months asking for the next promotion." With few exceptions, coaches who try to forge a sports team composed of stars courts disaster.

MyManagementLab®

Go to **mymanagementlab.com** to complete the problems marked with this icon ⭐.

KEY TERMS

action plan (p. 290)
dimensions of national culture (p. 293)
downsizing (p. 281)
executive succession (p. 280)
executive type (p. 278)
individualism-collectivism (I-C) (p. 293)

integration manager (p. 276)
leading (p. 276)
long-term orientation (LT) (p. 294)
Management By Objectives (MBO) (p. 292)
masculinity-femininity (M-F) (p. 294)
power distance (PD) (p. 293)

staffing (p. 276)
Total Quality Management (TQM) (p. 292)
uncertainty avoidance (UA) (p. 293)

MyManagementLab®

Go to **mymanagementlab.com** for Auto-graded writing questions as well as the following Assisted-graded writing questions:

10-1. What are the critical issues that a company must consider when trying to match its staffing to its strategy?

10-2. What are the unique impacts on a company that must staff in international settings?

DISCUSSION QUESTIONS

⭐**10-3.** What skills should a person have for managing a business unit following a differentiation strategy? Why? What should a company do if no one is available internally and the company has a policy of promotion from within?

10-4. When should someone from outside a company be hired to manage the company or one of its business units?

⭐**10-5.** What are some ways to implement a retrenchment strategy without creating a lot of resentment and conflict with labor unions?

⭐**10-6.** How can corporate culture be changed?

10-7. Why is an understanding of national cultures important in strategic management?

STRATEGIC PRACTICE EXERCISE

Staffing involves finding the person with the right blend of characteristics, such as personality, training, and experience, to implement a particular strategy. The Kersey Temperament Sorter is designed to identify different kinds of personality temperament. It is similar to other instruments derived from Carl Jung's theory of psychological types, such as the Myers-Briggs, the Singer-Loomis, and the Grey-Wheelwright. The questionnaire identifies four temperament types: **Guardian (SJ), Artisan (SP), Idealist (NF), and Rational (NT)**. **Guardians** have natural talent in managing goods and services. They are dependable and trustworthy. **Artisans** have keen senses and are at home with tools, instruments, and vehicles. They are risk-takers and like action. **Idealists** are concerned with growth and development and like to work with people. They prefer friendly cooperation over confrontation and conflict. **Rationalists** are problem solvers who like to know how things work. They work tirelessly to accomplish their goals. Each of these four types has four variants.[100]

Kersey challenges the assumption that people are basically the same in the ways that they think, feel, and approach problems. Kersey argues that it is far less desirable to attempt to change others (because it has little likelihood of success) than to attempt to understand, work with, and take advantage of normal differences. Companies can use this type of questionnaire to help team members understand how each person can contribute to team performance. For example, Lucent Technology used the Myers-Briggs Type Indicator to help build trust and understanding among 500 engineers in 13 time zones and three continents in a distributed development project.

1. Access the Keirsey Temperament Sorter using your Internet browser. Type in the following URL: **www .advisorteam.com**

2. Complete and score the questionnaire. Print the description of your personality type.

3. Read the information on the Web site about each personality type. Become familiar with each.

4. Bring to class a sheet of paper containing your name and your personality type: *Guardian*, *Artisan*, *Idealist*, or *Rational*. Your instructor will either put you into a group containing people with the same predominant style or into a group with representatives from each type. The instructor will then give the teams a task to accomplish. Each group will have approximately 30 minutes to do the task. It may be to solve a problem, analyze a short case, or propose a new entrepreneurial venture. The instructor will provide you with very little guidance other than to form and number the groups, give them a task, and keep track of time. He or she may move from group to group to sit in on each team's progress. When the time is up, the instructor will ask a spokesperson from each group to (1) describe the process the group went through and (2) present orally each group's ideas. After each group makes its presentation, the instructor may choose one or more of the following:

- On a sheet of paper, each person in the class identifies his/her personality type and votes which team did the best on the assignment.

- The class as a whole tries to identify each group's dominant decision-making style in terms of how they did their assignment. See how many people vote for one of the four types for each team.

- Each member of a group guesses if she/he was put into a team composed of the same personality types or in one composed of all four personality types.

NOTES

1. S. Caudron, "How HR Drives Profits," *Workforce Management* (December 2001), pp. 26–31 as reported by L. L. Bryan, C. I. Joyce, and L. M. Weiss in "Making a Market in Talent," *McKinsey Quarterly* (2006, No. 2), pp. 1–7.

2. "Talent Acquisition Up 6% in 2011 and Average Cost Per Hire About $3,500 per New Bersin & Assoc. Factbook," *Shaker* (November 28, 2011), http://shakerrecruitment.ning.com/profiles/blogs/talent-acquisition-up-6-in-2011-and-average-cost-per-hire-about-3.

3. The numbers are approximate averages from three separate studies of top management turnover after mergers. See M. Lubatkin, D. Schweiger, and Y. Weber, "Top Management Turnover in Related M&Ss: An Additional Test of the Theory of Relative Standing," *Journal of Management* (Vol. 25, No. 1, 1999), pp. 55–73.

4. J. A. Krug, "Executive Turnover in Acquired Firms: A Longitudinal Analysis of Long-Term Interaction Effects," paper presented to the annual meeting of *Academy of Management*, Seattle, WA (2003).

5. J. A. Krug and W. H. Hegarty, "Post-Acquisition Turnover Among U.S. Top Management Teams: An Analysis of the Effects of Foreign vs. Domestic Acquisitions of U.S. Targets," *Strategic Management Journal* (September 1997), pp. 667–675; J. A. Frug and W. H. Hegarty, "Predicting Who Stays and Leaves After an Acquisition: A Study of Top Managers in Multinational Firms," *Strategic Management Journal* (February 2001), pp. 185–196.

6. D. Harding and T. Rouse, "Human Due Diligence," *Harvard Business Review* (April 2007), pp. 124–131.

7. A. Hinterhuber, "Making M&A Work," *Business Strategy Review* (September 2002), pp. 7–9.

8. R. N. Ashkenas and S. C. Francis, "Integration Managers: Special Leaders for Special Times," *Harvard Business Review* (November–December 2000), pp. 108–116.

9. J. Hoerr, "Sharpening Minds for a Competitive Edge," *Business Week* (December 17, 1990), pp. 72–78.

10. "ASTD 2012 State of the Industry Report: Organizations Continue to Invest in Workplace Learning," *ASTD* (November 8, 2012), http://www.astd.org/Publications/Magazines/TD/TD-Archive/2012/11/ASTD-2012-State-of-the-Industry-Report.

11. *High Performance Work Practices and Firm Performance* (Washington, DC: U.S. Department of Labor, Office of the American Workplace, 1993), pp. i, 4.

12. "The Happy Wackiness of Zappos.com," *ABC News* (October 26, 2011), http://abcnews.go.com/blogs/business/2011/10/the-happy-wackiness-of-zappos-com/; J. Edwards, "Check Out the Insane Lengths Zappos Customer Service Reps Will Go To," *Business Insider* (January 29, 2012), http://articles.businessinsider.com/2012-01-09/news/30606433_1_customer-service-zappos-center-services.

13. R. Henkoff, "Companies that Train Best," *Fortune* (March 22, 1993), pp. 62–75.

14. D. C. Hambrick, "Upper Echelons Theory: An Update," *Academy of Management Review* (April 2007), pp. 334–343.

15. D. Miller and J. Shamsie, "Learning Across the Life Cycle: Experimentation and Performance Among the Hollywood Studio Heads," *Strategic Management Journal* (August 2001),

pp. 725–745. An exception to these findings may be the computer software industry in which CEOs are at their best when they start their jobs and steadily decline during their tenures. See A. D. Henderson, D. Miller, and D. C. Hambrick, "How Quickly Do CEOs Become Obsolete? Industry Dynamism, CEO Tenure, and Company Performance," *Strategic Management Journal* (May 2006), pp. 447–460.

16. B. Hrowvitz, "New CEO Puts Comeback on the Menu at Applebee's," *USA Today* (April 28, 2008), pp. 1B, 2B.

17. A study of former General Electric executives who became CEOs categorized them as cost controllers, growers, or cycle managers on the basis of their line experience at GE. See B. Groysberg, A. N. McLean, and N. Nohria, "Are Leaders Portable?" *Harvard Business Review* (May 2006), pp. 92–100.

18. D. K. Datta and N. Rajagopalan, "Industry Structure and CEO Characteristics: An Empirical Study of Succession Events," *Strategic Management Journal* (September 1998), pp. 833–852; A. S. Thomas and K. Ramaswamy, "Environmental Change and Management Staffing: A Comment," *Journal of Management* (Winter 1993), pp. 877–887; J. P. Guthrie, C. M. Grimm, and K. G. Smith, "Environmental Change and Management Staffing: An Empirical Study," *Journal of Management* (December 1991), pp. 735–748.

19. J. Greco, "The Search Goes On," *Journal of Business Strategy* (September/October 1997), pp. 22–25; W. Ocasio and H. Kim, "The Circulation of Corporate Control: Selection of Functional Backgrounds on New CEOs in Large U.S. Manufacturing Firms, 1981–1992," *Administrative Science Quarterly* (September 1999), pp. 532–562; R. Dobbs, D. Harris, and A. Rasmussen, "When Should CFOs Take the Helm?" *McKinsey Quarterly Online* (November 2006); "How to Get to the Top," *The Economist* (May 31, 2008), p. 70.

20. R. Drazin and R. K. Kazanjian, "Applying the Del Technique to the Analysis of Cross-Classification Data: A Test of CEO Succession and Top Management Team Development," *Academy of Management Journal* (December 1993), pp. 1374–1399; W. E. Rothschild, "A Portfolio of Strategic Leaders," *Planning Review* (January/February 1996), pp. 16–19.

21. R. Subramanian and C. M. Sanchez, "Environmental Change and Management Staffing: An Empirical Examination of the Electric Utilities Industry," *Journal of Business Strategies* (Spring 1998), pp. 17–34.

22. M. A. Carpenter and B. R. Golden, "Perceived Managerial Discretion: A Study of Cause and Effect," *Strategic Management Journal* (March 1997), pp. 187–206.

23. J. A. Parnell, "Functional Background and Business Strategy: The Impact of Executive-Strategy Fit on Performance," *Journal of Business Strategies* (Spring 1994), pp. 49–62.

24. M. Smith and M. C. White, "Strategy, CEO Specialization, and Succession," *Administrative Science Quarterly* (June 1987), pp. 263–280.

25. "Average Tenure of CEOs Declined to 8.4 Years, the Conference Board Reports," The Conference Board (April 12, 2012), http://www.conference-board.org/press/pressdetail.cfm?pressid=4453; "Making Companies Work," *The Economist* (October 25, 2003), p. 14; C. H. Mooney, C. M. Dalton, D. R. Dalton, and S. T. Cero, "CEO Succession as a Funnel: The Critical, and Changing Role of Inside Directors," *Organizational*

Dynamics (Vol. 36, No. 4, 2007), pp. 418–428. Note, however, that the tenures of CEOs of family firms typically exceed 15 years. See I. Le Breton-Miller and D. Miller, "Why Do Some Family Businesses Out-Compete? Governance, Long-Term Orientations, and Sustainable Capability," *Entrepreneurship Theory and Practice* (November 2006), pp. 731–746.

26. A. Bianco, L. Lavelle, J. Merrit, and A. Barrett, "The CEO Trap," *BusinessWeek* (December 11, 2000), pp. 86–92.

27. Y. Zhang and N. Rajagopalan, "When the Known Devil Is Better than an Unknown God: An Empirical Study of the Antecedents and Consequences of Relay CEO Succession," *Academy of Management Journal* (August 2004), pp. 483–500; W. Sheen and A. A. Cannella Jr., "Will Succession Planning Increase Shareholder Wealth? Evidence from Investor Reactions to Relay CEO Successions," *Strategic Management Journal* (February 2003), pp. 191–198.

28. G. A. Bigley and M. F. Wiersema, "New CEOs and Corporate Strategic Refocusing: How Experience as Heir Apparent Influences the Use of Power," *Administrative Science Quarterly* (December 2002), pp. 707–727.

29. J. L. Bower, "Solve the Succession Crisis by Growing Inside-Outside Leaders," *Harvard Business Review* (November 2007), pp. 91–96; Y. Zhang and N. Rajagopalan, "Grooming for the Top Post and Ending the CEO Succession Crisis," *Organizational Dynamics* (Vol. 35, Issue 1, 2006), pp. 96–105.

30. "Coming and Going," Survey of Corporate Leadership," *The Economist* (October 25, 2003), pp. 12–14.

31. D. C. Carey and D. Ogden, *CEO Succession: A Window on How Boards Do It Right When Choosing a New Chief Executive* (New York: Oxford University Press, 2000).

32. "The King Lear Syndrome," *The Economist* (December 13, 2003), p. 65.

33. Y. Zang and N. Rajagopalan, "Grooming for the Top Post and Ending the CEO Succession Crisis," *Organizational Dynamics* (Vol. 35, Issue 1, 2006), pp. 96–105.

34. "2011 CEO Transitions," *Spencer Stuart* (March 2012), http://www.spencerstuart.com/research/ceo/1580/.

35. M. S. Kraatz and J. H. Moore, "Executive Migration and Institutional Change," *Academy of Management Journal* (February 2002), pp. 120–143; Y. Zhang and N. Rajagopalan, "When the Known Devil Is Better than an Unknown God: An Empirical Study of the Antecedents and Consequences of Relay CEO Succession" *Academy of Management Journal* (August 2004), pp. 483–500; W. Shen and A. A. Cannella Jr., "Revisiting the Performance Consequences of CEO Succession: The Impacts of Successor Type, Post-Succession Senior Executive Turnover, and Departing CEO Tenure," *Academy of Management Journal* (August 2002), pp. 717–733.

36. K. P. Coyne and E. J. Coyne Sr., "Surviving Your New CEO," *Harvard Business Review* (May 2007), pp. 62–69.

37. N. Byrnes and D. Kiley, "Hello, You Must Be Going," *Business Week* (February 12, 2007), pp. 30–32.

38. C. Lucier and J. Dyer, "Hiring an Outside CEO: A Board's Best Moves," *Directors & Boards* (Winter 2004), pp. 36–38. These findings are supported by a later study by Booz Allen Hamilton in which 1595 worldwide companies during 1995 to 2005 showed the same results. See J. Webber, "The Accidental CEO," *BusinessWeek* (April 23, 2007), pp. 64–72.

39. Q. Yue, "Antecedents of Top Management Successor Origin in China," paper presented to the annual meeting of the *Academy of Management*, Seattle, WA (2003); A. A. Buchko and

D. DiVerde, "Antecedents, Moderators, and Consequences of CEO Turnover: A Review and Reconceptualization," paper presented to *Midwest Academy of Management* (Lincoln, NE: 1997), p. 10; W. Ocasio, "Institutionalized Action and Corporate Governance: The Reliance on Rules of CEO Succession," *Administrative Science Quarterly* (June 1999), pp. 384–416.

40. C. Gopinath, "Turnaround: Recognizing Decline and Initiating Intervention," *Long Range Planning* (December 1991), pp. 96–101.

41. K. B. Schwartz and K. Menon, "Executive Succession in Failing Firms," *Academy of Management Journal* (September 1985), pp. 680–686; A. A. Cannella Jr., and M. Lubatkin, "Succession as a Sociopolitical Process: Internal Impediments to Outsider Selection," *Academy of Management Journal* (August 1993), pp. 763–793; W. Boeker and J. Goodstein, "Performance and Succession Choice: The Moderating Effects of Governance and Ownership," *Academy of Management Journal* (February 1993), pp. 172–186.

42. W. Boeker, "Executive Migration and Strategic Change: The Effect of Top Manager Movement on Product-Market Entry," *Administrative Science Quarterly* (June 1997), pp. 213–236.

43. E. Brockmann, J. J. Hoffman, and D. Dawley, "A Contingency Theory of CEO Successor Choice and Post-Bankruptcy Strategic Change," paper presented to annual meeting of *Academy of Management*, Seattle, WA (2003).

44. P. Lorange, and D. Murphy, "Bringing Human Resources into Strategic Planning: System Design Characteristics," in C. J. Fombrun, N. M. Tichy, and M. A. Devanna (Eds.), *Strategic Human Resource Management* (New York: John Wiley & Sons, 1984), pp. 281–283.

45. http://www.ge.com/company/culture/leadership_learning.html.

46. S. Armour, "Playing the Succession Game," *USA Today* (November 24, 2003), p. 3B.

47. D. A. Waldman and T. Korbar, "Student Assessment Center Performance in the Prediction of Early Career Success," *Academy of Management Learning and Education* (June 2004), pp. 151–167.

48. "Coming and Going, Survey of Corporate Leadership," *The Economist* (October 25, 2003), pp. 12–14.

49. R. A. Pitts, "Strategies and Structures for Diversification," *Academy of Management Journal* (June 1997), pp. 197–208.

50. D. Poeter, "HP Announces 27,000 Layoffs in Major Restructuring," *PC Magazine* (May 23, 2012), http://www.pcmag.com/article2/0,2817,2404820,00.asp; http://retailindustry.about.com/od/storeclosingsandopenings/a/2012-Store-Closings-US-Retail-Industry-Liquidations-Roundup-Chains-Going-Out-Business.htm.

51. K. E. Mishra, G. M. Spreitzer, and A. K. Mishra, "Preserving Employee Morale During Downsizing," *Sloan Management Review* (Winter 1998), pp. 83–95.

52. B. O'Reilly, "Is Your Company Asking Too Much?" *Fortune* (March 12, 1990), p. 41. For more information on the emotional reactions of survivors of downsizing, see C. R. Stoner and R. I. Hartman, "Organizational Therapy: Building Survivor Health & Competitiveness," *SAM Advanced Management Journal* (Summer 1997), pp. 15–31, 41.

53. S. R. Fisher and M. A. White, "Downsizing in a Learning Organization: Are There Hidden Costs?" *Academy of Management Review* (January 2000), pp. 244–251.

54. T. M. Amabile and R. Conti, "Changes in the Work Environment for Creativity During Downsizing," *Academy of Management Journal* (December 1999), pp. 630–640; A. G. Bedeian and A. A. Armenakis, "The Cesspool Syndrome: How Dreck Floats to the Top of Declining Organizations," *Academy of Management Executive* (February 1998), pp. 58–67.

55. For a more complete listing of the psychological and behavioral reactions to downsizing, see M. L. Marks and K. P. De Meuse, "Resizing the Organization: Maximizing the Gain While Minimizing the Pain of Layoffs, Divestitures, and Closings," *Organizational Dynamics* (Vol. 34, No. 1, 2005), pp. 19–35.

56. D. J. Flanagan and K. C. O'Shaughnessy, "The Effect of Layoffs on Firm Reputation," *Journal of Management* (June 2005), pp. 445–463.

57. *The Wall Street Journal* (December 22, 1992), p. B1.

58. V. Giang, "14 of the Biggest Mass Layoffs of 2011," *Business Insider* (August 28, 2011), http://www.businessinsider.com/companies-with-the-biggest-layoffs-in-2011-2011-8?op=1.

59. R. D. Nixon, M. A. Hitt, H. Lee, and E. Jeong, "Market Reactions to Announcements of Corporate Downsizing Actions and Implementation Strategies," *Strategic Management Journal* (November 2004), pp. 1121–1129; G. D. Bruton, J. K. Keels, and C. L. Shook, "Downsizing the Firm: Answering the Strategic Questions," *Academy of Management Executive* (May 1996), pp. 38–45; E. G. Love and N. Nohria, "Reducing Slack: The Performance Consequences of Downsizing by Large Industrial Firms, 1977–93," *Strategic Management Journal* (December 2005), pp. 1087–1108; C. D. Zatzick and R. D. Iverson, "High-Involvement Management and Workforce Reduction: Competitive Advantage or Disadvantage?" *Academy of Management Journal* (October 2006), pp. 999–1015.

60. M. A. Hitt, B. W. Keats, H. F. Harback, and R. D. Nixon, "Rightsizing: Building and Maintaining Strategic Leadership and Long-Term Competitiveness," *Organizational Dynamics* (Autumn 1994), pp. 18–32. For additional suggestions, see W. F. Cascio, "Strategies for Responsible Restructuring," *Academy of Management Executive* (August 2002), pp. 80–91, and T. Mroczkowski and M. Hanaoka, "Effective Rightsizing Strategies in Japan and America: Is There a Convergence of Employment Practices?" *Academy of Management Executive* (May 1997), pp. 57–67. For an excellent list of cost-reduction programs for use in short, medium, and long-term time horizons, see F. Gandolfi, "Cost Reductions, Downsizing-Related Layoffs, and HR Practices," *SAM Advanced Management Journal* (Spring 2008), pp. 52–58.

61. J. S. Black and H. B. Gregersen, "The Right Way to Manage Expats," *Harvard Business Review* (March–April 1999), pp. 52–61.

62. Ibid, p. 54.

63. J. I. Sanchez, P. E. Spector, and C. L. Cooper, "Adapting to a Boundaryless World: A Developmental Expatriate Model," *Academy of Management Executive* (May 2000), pp. 96–106.

64. R. L. Tung, *The New Expatriates* (Cambridge, MA: Ballinger, 1988); J. S. Black, M. Mendenhall, and G. Oddou, "Toward a Comprehensive Model of International Adjustment: An Integration of Multiple Theoretical Perspectives," *Academy of Management Review* (April 1991), pp. 291–317.

65. M. A. Carpenter, W. G. Sanders, and H. B. Gregersen, "Bundling Human Capital with Organizational Context: The Impact of International Assignment Experience on Multinational Firm Performance and CEO Pay," *Academy of Management Journal* (June 2001), pp. 493–511.

66. P. M. Caligiuri and S. Colakoglu, "A Strategic Contingency Approach to Expatriate Assignment Management," *Human Resource Management Journal* (Vol. 17, No. 4, 2007), pp. 393–410.

67. M. A. Shaffer, D. A. Harrison, K. M. Gilley, and D. M. Luk, "Struggling for Balance Amid Turbulence on International Assignments: Work-Family Conflict, Support, and Commitment," *Journal of Management* (Vol. 27, No. 1, 2001), pp. 99–121.

68. J. S. Black and H. B. Gregersen, "The Right Way to Manage Ex-pats," *Harvard Business Review* (March–April 1999), p. 54.

69. G. Stern, "GM Executive's Ties to Native Country Help Auto Maker Clinch Deal in China," *The Wall Street Journal* (November 2, 1995), p. B7.

70. K. Roth, "Managing International Interdependence: CEO Characteristics in a Resource-Based Framework," *Academy of Management Journal* (February 1995), pp. 200–231.

71. M. Subramaniam and N. Venkatraman, "Determinants of Transnational New Product Development Capability: Testing the Influence of Transferring and Deploying Tacit Overseas Knowledge," *Strategic Management Journal* (April 2001), pp. 359–378.

72. J. S. Lublin, "An Overseas Stint Can Be a Ticket to the Top," *The Wall Street Journal* (January 29, 1996), pp. B1, B2.

73. "Cisco Shifts Senior Executives to India," *St. Cloud* (MN) *Times* (January 13, 2007), p. 6A.

74. "Expatriate Employees: In Search of Stealth," *The Economist* (April 23, 2005), pp. 62–64.

75. M. Meaney, C. Pung, and S. Kamath, "Creating Organizational Transformations," *McKinsey Quarterly Online* (September 10, 2008).

76. L. G. Love, R. L. Priem, and G. T. Lumpkin, "Explicitly Articulated Strategy and Firm Performance Under Alternative Levels of Centralization," *Journal of Management* (Vol. 28, No. 5, 2002), pp. 611–627.

77. G. G. Gordon, "The Relationship of Corporate Culture to Industry Sector and Corporate Performance," in R. H. Kilmann, M. J. Saxton, R. Serpa, and Associates (Eds.), *Gaining Control of the Corporate Culture* (San Francisco: Jossey-Bass, 1985), p. 123; T. Kono, "Corporate Culture and Long-Range Planning," *Long Range Planning* (August 1990), pp. 9–19.

78. B. Mike and J. W. Slocum Jr., "Changing Culture at Pizza Hut and Yum! Brands," *Organizational Dynamics* (Vol. 32, No. 4, 2003), pp. 319–330.

79. T. J. Tetenbaum, "Seven Key Practices that Improve the Chance for Expected Integration and Synergies," *Organizational Dynamics* (Autumn 1999), pp. 22–35.

80. B. Bremner and G. Edmondson, "Japan: A Tale of Two Mergers," *BusinessWeek* (May 10, 2004), p. 42; http://www.worldcarfans.com/10805221239/mercedes-benz-admits-to-chrysler-merger-mistake.

81. P. Very, M. Lubatkin, R. Calori, and J. Veiga, "Relative Standing and the Performance of Recently Acquired European Firms," *Strategic Management Journal* (September 1997), pp. 593–614.

82. A. R. Malekzadeh and A. Nahavandi, "Making Mergers Work by Managing Cultures," *Journal of Business Strategy* (May/June 1990), pp. 53–57; A. Nahavandi, and A. R. Malekzadeh, "Acculturation in Mergers and Acquisitions," *Academy of Management Review* (January 1988), pp. 79–90.

83. C. Ghosn, "Saving the Business Without Losing the Company," *Harvard Business Review* (January 2002), pp. 37–45;

B. Bremner, G. Edmondson, C. Dawson, D. Welch, and K. Kerwin, "Nissan's Boss," *BusinessWeek* (October 4, 2004), pp. 50–60.

84. D. Harding and T. Rouse, "Human Due Diligence," *Harvard Business Review* (April 2007), pp. 124–131.

85. J. J. Keller, "Why AT&T Takeover of NCR Hasn't Been a Real Bell Ringer," *The Wall Street Journal* (September 19, 1995), pp. A1, A5.

86. J. W. Gibson and D. V. Tesone, "Management Fads: Emergence, Evolution, and Implications for Managers," *Academy of Management Executive* (November 2001), pp. 122–133.

87. For additional information, see S. J. Carroll, Jr., and M. L. Tosi Jr., *Management by Objectives: Applications and Research* (New York: Macmillan, 1973), and A. P. Aria, *Managing by Objectives* (Glenview, IL: Scott, Foreman, and Company, 1974).

88. J. W. Gibson, D. V. Tesone, and C. W. Blackwell, "Management Fads: Here Yesterday, Gone Today?" *SAM Advanced Management Journal* (Autumn 2003), pp. 12–17.

89. J. W. Gibson and D. V. Tesone, "Management Fads: Emergence, Evolution, and Implications for Managers," *Academy of Management Executive* (November 2001), p. 125.

90. S. S. Masterson, and M. S. Taylor, "Total Quality Management and Performance Appraisal: An Integrative Perspective," *Journal of Quality Management* (Vol. 1, No. 1, 1996), pp. 67–89.

91. T. Y. Choi and O. C. Behling, "Top Managers and TQM Success: One More Look After All These Years," *Academy of Management Executive* (February 1997), pp. 37–47.

92. T. C. Powell, "Total Quality Management as Competitive Advantage: A Review and Empirical Study," *Strategic Management Journal* (January 1995), pp. 15–37.

93. G. Hofstede, "Culture's Recent Consequences: Using Dimensional Scores in Theory and Research," *International Journal of Cross Cultural Management* (Vol. 1, No. 1, 2001), pp. 11–17; G. Hofstede, *Cultures and Organizations: Software of the Mind* (London: McGraw-Hill, 1991); G. Hofstede and M. H. Bond, "The Confucius Connection: From Cultural Roots to Economic Growth," *Organizational Dynamics* (Spring 1988), pp. 5–21; R. Hodgetts, "A Conversation with Geert Hofstede," *Organizational Dynamics* (Spring 1993), pp. 53–61.

94. M. Javidan and R. J. House, "Cultural Acumen for the Global Manager: Lessons from Project GLOBE," *Organizational Dynamics* (Vol. 29, No. 4, 2001), pp. 289–305; R. J. House, P. J. Hanges, M. Javidan, P. W. Dorfman, and V. Gupta (Eds.), *Culture, Leadership and Organizations: The GLOBE Study of 62 Societies* (Thousand Oaks, CA: Sage, 2004).

95. M. Javidan and R. J. House, "Cultural Acumen for the Global Manager: Lessons from Project GLOBE," *Organizational Dynamics* (Vol. 29, No. 4, 2001), p. 303.

96. See G. Hofstede and M. H. Bond, "The Confucius Connection, From Cultural Roots to Economic Growth," *Organizational Dynamics* (Spring 1988), pp. 12–13.

97. H. K. Steensma, L. Marino, K. M. Weaver, and P. H. Dickson, "The Influence of National Culture on the Formation of Technology Alliances by Entrepreneurial Firms," *Academy of Management Journal* (October 2000), pp. 951–973.

98. M. A. Geletkancz, "The Salience of 'Culture's Consequences': The Effects of Cultural Values on Top Executive Commitment to the Status Quo," *Strategic Management Journal* (September 1997), pp. 615–634.

99. B. Groysberg, A. Nanda, and N. Nohria, "The Risky Business of Hiring Stars," *Harvard Business Review* (May 2004), pp. 92–100.

100. D. Keirsey, *Please Understand Me II* (Del Mar, CA: Prometheus Nemesis Book Co., 1998).

CHAPTER 11

Evaluation and Control

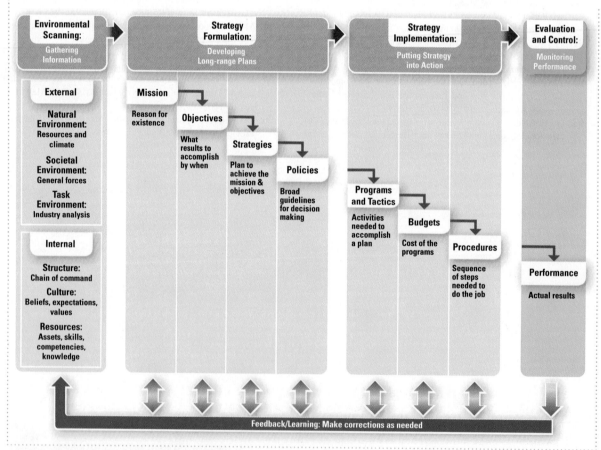

Environmental Scanning: Gathering Information	**Strategy Formulation:** Developing Long-range Plans	**Strategy Implementation:** Putting Strategy into Action	**Evaluation and Control:** Monitoring Performance

External

Natural Environment: Resources and climate

Societal Environment: General forces

Task Environment: Industry analysis

Internal

Structure: Chain of command

Culture: Beliefs, expectations, values

Resources: Assets, skills, competencies, knowledge

Mission Reason for existence

Objectives What results to accomplish by when

Strategies Plan to achieve the mission & objectives

Policies Broad guidelines for decision making

Programs and Tactics Activities needed to accomplish a plan

Budgets Cost of the programs

Procedures Sequence of steps needed to do the job

Performance Actual results

Feedback/Learning: Make corrections as needed

MyManagementLab®
⭐ Improve Your Grade!

Over 10 million students improved their results using the Pearson MyLabs. Visit **mymanagementlab.com** for simulations, tutorials, and end-of-chapter problems.

Learning Objectives

After reading this chapter, you should be able to:

- Understand the basic control process
- Choose among traditional measures, such as ROI, and shareholder value measures, such as economic value added, to properly assess performance
- Use the balanced scorecard approach to develop key performance measures
- Apply the benchmarking process to a function or an activity
- Develop appropriate control systems to support specific strategies including performance measurement

Five Guys and Execution

If you want to be in a business with thousands of competitors, then you must execute exceptionally well. That is the hallmark of Five Guys Burgers and Fries. Five Guys started in 1986 with a single location that had no seating. They decided to put in controls for the business that might not make sense right out of the box. In fact, they were unable to raise any capital or get any loans for their business idea. They wanted to create a burger place that used the finest ingredients in the business, paying top dollar for their meat, getting a renowned local bakery to produce their rolls, buying the most expensive bacon, and cooking only in peanut oil, which cost five times as much as the oil other burger restaurants were using. These standards would become the key to their success. They don't start cooking until you order, peanuts are provided for free while you wait, and they so overload each customer with French fries that they gained the reputation that one order of their small fries will feed four people.

They have more than 1000 locations in the United States and Canada, with the founding family (the parents and five sons) owning 200 and the rest franchised. In 2011, they had revenues of $976 million, up from $720 million in 2010.

The whole business is built on consistency and controls. They don't comparison shop for ingredients and are rigorous in their evaluation of standards. The company employs their own employees as secret shoppers to make sure each store lives up to the Five Guys' standard of service. There are weekly, monthly, and quarterly programs that award crew members based on the shoppers' reports.

SOURCES: http://www.fiveguys.com/; L. Joyner, "Five Guys Found Simple Recipe for Success: Do It Right," *USA Today* (August 2, 2012), http://usatoday30.usatoday.com/money/economy/story/2012-07-29/five-guys-ceo-jerry-murrell/56541886/1; K. Weise, "Behind Five Guys' Beloved Burgers," *Bloomberg Businessweek* (August 11, 2011), http://www.businessweek.com/magazine/behind-five-guys-beloved-burgers-08112011.html.

303

FIGURE 11–1
Evaluation and
Control Process

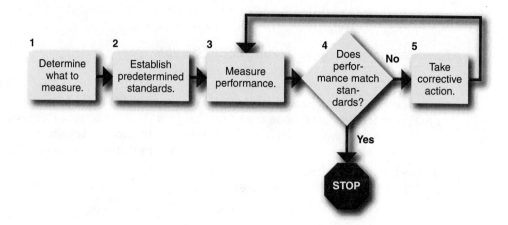

Evaluation and Control in Strategic Management

Evaluation and control information consists of performance data and activity reports (gathered in Step 3 in **Figure 11–1**). If undesired performance results because the strategic management processes were inappropriately used, operational managers must know about it so they can correct the employee activity. Top management need not be involved. If, however, undesired performance results from the processes themselves, top managers, as well as operational managers, must know about it so they can develop new implementation programs or procedures. Evaluation and control information must be relevant to what is being monitored. One of the obstacles to effective control is the difficulty in developing appropriate measures of important activities and outputs.

Measuring Performance

Performance is the end result of activity. Select measures to assess performance based on the organizational unit to be appraised and the objectives to be achieved. The objectives that were established earlier in the strategy formulation part of the strategic management process (dealing with profitability, market share, and cost reduction, among others) should certainly be used to measure corporate performance once the strategies have been implemented.

APPROPRIATE MEASURES

Some measures, such as return on investment (ROI) and earnings per share (EPS), are appropriate for evaluating a corporation's or a division's ability to achieve a profitability objective. This type of measure, however, is inadequate for evaluating additional corporate objectives such as social responsibility or employee development. Even though profitability is a corporation's major objective, ROI and EPS can be computed only after profits are totaled for a period. It tells what happened after the fact—not what is happening or what will happen. A firm, therefore, needs to develop measures that predict likely profitability. These are referred to as **steering controls** because they measure variables that influence future profitability. Every industry has its own set of key metrics that tend to predict profits. Airlines, for example, closely monitor cost per available seat mile (ASM). In 2002, Southwest's cost per passenger mile was 7.5¢, the lowest in the industry, contrasted with United's 11.5¢, the highest in the industry. Its low costs gave Southwest a significant competitive advantage. By 2011, Southwest's costs had risen substantially to 12.5¢, while United had moved to 16.6¢. In the meantime, Southwest had been replaced as the most low-cost airline by Spirit Airlines, whose cost per ASM in 2011 was 10.1¢.[1]

An example of a steering control used by retail stores is the *inventory turnover ratio*, in which a retailer's cost of goods sold is divided by the average value of its inventories. This measure shows how hard an investment in inventory is working; the higher the ratio, the better. Not only does quicker moving inventory tie up less cash in inventories, it also reduces the risk that the goods will grow obsolete before they're sold—a crucial measure for computers and other technology items. For example, Office Depot increased its inventory turnover ratio from 6.9 in one year to 7.5 the next year, leading to improved annual profits.[2]

Another steering control is customer satisfaction. Research reveals that companies that score high on the *American Customer Satisfaction Index (ACSI)*, a measure developed by the University of Michigan's National Research Center, have higher stock returns and better cash flows than those companies that score low on the ACSI. A change in a firm's customer satisfaction typically works its way through a firm's value chain and is eventually reflected in quarterly profits.[3] Other approaches to measuring customer satisfaction include Oracle's use of the ratio of quarterly sales divided by customer service requests and the total number of hours that technicians spend on the phone solving customer problems. To help executives keep track of important steering controls, Netsuite developed *dashboard* software that displays critical information in easy-to-read computer graphics assembled from data pulled from other corporate software programs.[4]

TYPES OF CONTROLS

Controls can be established to focus on actual performance results (output), the activities that generate the performance (behavior), or on resources that are used in performance (input). **Output controls** specify what is to be accomplished by focusing on the end result of the behaviors through the use of objectives and performance targets or milestones. **Behavior controls** specify how something is to be done through policies, rules, standard operating procedures, and orders from a superior. **Input controls** emphasize resources, such as knowledge, skills, abilities, values, and motives of employees.[5]

Output, behavior, and input controls are not interchangeable. Output controls (such as sales quotas, specific cost-reduction or profit objectives, and surveys of customer satisfaction) are most appropriate when specific output measures have been agreed on but the cause–effect connection between activities and results is not clear. Behavior controls (such as following company procedures, making sales calls to potential customers, and getting to work on time) are most appropriate when performance results are hard to measure, but the cause–effect connection between activities and results is relatively clear. Input controls (such as number of years of education and experience) are most appropriate when output is difficult to measure and there is no clear cause–effect relationship between behavior and performance (such as in college teaching). Corporations following the strategy of conglomerate diversification tend to emphasize output controls with their divisions and subsidiaries (presumably because they are managed independently of each other), whereas, corporations following concentric diversification use all three types of controls (presumably because synergy is desired).[6] Even if all three types of control are used, one or two of them may be emphasized more than another depending on the circumstances. For example, Muralidharan and Hamilton propose that as a multinational corporation moves through its stages of development, its emphasis on control should shift from being primarily output at first, to behavioral, and finally to input control.[7]

Examples of increasingly popular behavior controls are the ISO 9000 and 14000 Standards Series on quality and environmental assurance, developed by the International Standards Association of Geneva, Switzerland. Using the **ISO 9000 Standards Series** (now a family of standards with eight management principles) is a way of objectively documenting a company's high level of quality operations. The **ISO 14000 Standards Series** establishes how to document the company's impact on the environment. A company wanting ISO 9000 certification would document its process for product introductions, among other things. ISO 9001 would require this firm to separately document design input, design process, design output, and design verification—a large amount of work. ISO 14001 would specify how companies should establish, maintain and continually improve an environmental management system. The benefits from ISO certification are partially in cost savings, but primarily they are a signal to suppliers and buyers about the focus of the company.[8] For an example of how one company that is steeped in controls is using an innovative idea to improve their systems, see the Innovation Issue feature.

Many corporations view ISO 9000 certification as assurance that a supplier sells quality products. Firms such as DuPont, Hewlett-Packard, and 3M have facilities registered to ISO standards. Companies in more than 60 countries, such as Canada, Mexico, Japan, the United States (including the entire U.S. auto industry), and the European Union, require ISO 9000 certification of their suppliers.[9] The same is happening for ISO 14000. Both Ford and General Motors require their suppliers to follow ISO 14001. In a survey of manufacturing executives, 51% of the executives found that ISO 9000 certification increased their international competitiveness. Other executives noted that it signaled their commitment to quality and gave them a strategic advantage over noncertified competitors.[10]

Since its ISO 14000 certification, SWD Inc. has become a showplace for environmental awareness. According to SWD's Delawder, ISO 14000 certification improves environmental

INNOVATION issue

REUSE OF ELECTRIC VEHICLE BATTERIES

No industry is more concerned about established procedures and minimizing fluctuations in their business model than the electric utility industry. Beyond storms that bring down the power grid, the biggest issue is dealing with fluctuations in power demand. Backup generators, purchasing power from other utilities, and keeping excess power available has been used for decades. However, the wide-scale introduction of solar arrays has added a whole new wrinkle to the issue in the industry. While solar arrays work quite well when the sun is shining, even modest cloud cover can cause large fluctuations in output.

Duke Energy in partnership with General Motors and ABB (the huge power technology company) is now exploring the reuse of electric vehicle batteries to smooth out fluctuations in the power grid. Not only would the system be good for the environment, but it would provide an innovative solution to a known problem in the industry.

A typical electric vehicle battery weighs more than 700 pounds and has 70% or more of its useful life left when it is no longer usable in an electric vehicle. General Motors estimates that it will have 500,000 vehicles with battery packs on the road by 2017, meaning that there is a huge recycling/reuse/waste issue that will have to be dealt with shortly.

Duke sees battery systems (EV battery packs that are linked together in a series) as a means for smoothing out sudden swings in output from solar arrays, thus helping the whole grid work more smoothly. The solar arrays could be used to provide power (when the sun is shining) to the grid, as well as to the recharging of battery systems. The system was demonstrated in San Francisco in 2012 and will be tested in undisclosed locations before being utilized on any scale.

....

SOURCES: M. Ramsey, "Ford Reveals How Much Electric Car Batteries Cost," *The Wall Street Journal* (April 17, 2012), http://blogs.wsj.com/drivers-seat/2012/04/17/ford-reveals-how-much-electric-car-batteries-cost/; B. Henderson, "Duke to Test Uses for EV Batteries," *The Charlotte Observer* (November 16, 2012), pg. 2B.

awareness among employees, reduces risks of violating regulations, and improves the firm's image among customers and the local community.[11]

Another example of a behavior control is a company's monitoring of employee phone calls and PCs to ensure that employees are behaving according to company guidelines. In a study by the American Management Association, nearly two-thirds of U.S. companies actively monitored their workers' Web site visits in order to prevent inappropriate surfing while 65% use software to block connections to Web sites deemed off limits for employees. 43% of companies monitor e-mail, and 28% of employers have fired workers for e-mail misuse. (For example, Xerox fired 40 employees for visiting pornographic Web sites.[12])

ACTIVITY-BASED COSTING

Activity-based costing (ABC) is a recently developed accounting method for allocating indirect and fixed costs to individual products or product lines based on the value-added activities going into that product.[13] This accounting method is thus very useful in doing a value-chain analysis of a firm's activities for making outsourcing decisions. Traditional cost accounting, in contrast, focuses on valuing a company's inventory for financial reporting purposes. To obtain a unit's cost, cost accountants typically add direct labor to the cost of materials. Then they compute overhead from rent to R&D expenses, based on the number of direct labor hours it takes to make a product. To obtain unit cost, they divide the total by the number of items made during the period under consideration.

Traditional cost accounting is useful when direct labor accounts for most of total costs and a company produces just a few products requiring the same processes. This may have been true of companies during the early part of the twentieth century, but it is no longer relevant today, when overhead may account for as much as 70% of manufacturing costs. According to Bob Van Der Linde, CEO of a contract manufacturing services firm in San Diego, California: "Overhead is 80% to 90% in our industry, so allocation errors lead to pricing errors, which could easily bankrupt the company."[14] The appropriate allocation of indirect costs and overhead has thus become crucial for decision making. The traditional volume-based cost-driven system systematically understates the cost per unit of products with low sales volumes and products with a high degree of complexity. Similarly, it overstates the cost per unit of products with high sales volumes and a low degree of complexity.[15] When Chrysler used ABC, it discovered that the true cost of some of the parts used in making cars was 30 times what the company had previously estimated.[16]

ABC accounting allows accountants to charge costs more accurately than the traditional method because it allocates overhead far more precisely. For example, imagine a production line in a pen factory where black pens are made in high volume and blue pens in low volume. Assume that it takes eight hours to retool (reprogram the machinery) to shift production from one kind of pen to the other. The total costs include supplies (the same for both pens), the direct labor of the line workers, and factory overhead. In this instance, a very significant part of the overhead cost is the cost of reprogramming the machinery to switch from one pen to another. If the company produces 10 times as many black pens as blue pens, 10 times the cost of the reprogramming expenses will be allocated to the black pens as to the blue pens under traditional cost accounting methods. This approach underestimates, however, the true cost of making the blue pens.

ABC accounting, in contrast, first breaks down pen manufacturing into its activities. It is then very easy to see that it is the activity of changing pens that triggers the cost of retooling. The ABC accountant calculates an average cost of setting up the machinery and charges it against each batch of pens that requires retooling, regardless of the size of the run. Thus a product carries only those costs for the overhead it actually consumes. Management is now able to discover that its blue pens cost almost twice as much as do the black pens. Unless the company is able to charge a higher price for its blue pens, it cannot make a profit on these pens. Unless there is a strategic reason why it must offer blue pens (such as a key customer who must have a small number of blue pens with every large order of black pens or a marketing trend away from black to blue pens), the company will earn significantly greater profits if it completely stops making blue pens.[17]

ENTERPRISE RISK MANAGEMENT

Enterprise Risk Management (ERM) is a corporatewide, integrated process for managing the uncertainties that could negatively or positively influence the achievement of the corporation's objectives. In the past, managing risk was done in a fragmented manner within functions or business units. Individuals would manage process risk, safety risk, and insurance, financial, and other assorted risks. As a result of this fragmented approach, companies would take huge risks in some areas of the business while over-managing substantially smaller risks in other areas. ERM is being adopted because of the increasing amount of environmental uncertainty that can affect an entire corporation. As a result, the position Chief Risk Officer is one of the fastest growing executive positions in U.S. corporations.[18] Microsoft uses scenario analysis to identify key business risks. According to Microsoft's treasurer, Brent Callinicos, "The scenarios are really what we're trying to protect against."[19] The scenarios were the possibility of an earthquake in the Seattle region and a major downturn in the stock market.

The process of rating risks involves three steps:

1. Identify the risks using scenario analysis or brainstorming or by performing risk self-assessments.

2. Rank the risks, using some scale of impact and likelihood.

3. Measure the risks, using some agreed-upon standard.

Some companies are using value at risk, or VAR (effect of unlikely events in normal markets), and stress testing (effect of plausible events in abnormal markets) methodologies to measure the potential impact of the financial risks they face. DuPont uses earnings at risk (EAR) measuring tools to measure the effect of risk on reported earnings. It can then manage risk to a specified earnings level based on the company's "risk appetite." With this integrated view, DuPont can view how risks affect the likelihood of achieving certain earnings targets.[20] Research has shown that companies with integrative risk management capabilities achieve superior economic performance.[21]

PRIMARY MEASURES OF CORPORATE PERFORMANCE

The days when simple financial measures such as ROI or EPS were used alone to assess overall corporate performance are coming to an end. Analysts now recommend a broad range of methods to evaluate the success or failure of a strategy. Some of these methods are stakeholder measures, shareholder value, and the balanced scorecard approach. Even though each of these methods has supporters as well as detractors, the current trend is clearly toward more complicated financial measures and an increasing use of non-financial measures of corporate performance. For example, research indicates that companies pursuing strategies founded on innovation and new product development now tend to favor non-financial over financial measures.[22]

Traditional Financial Measures

The most commonly used measure of corporate performance (in terms of profits) is **return on investment (ROI)**. It is simply the result of dividing net income before taxes by the total amount invested in the company (typically measured by total assets). Although using ROI has several advantages, it also has several distinct limitationsROI gives the impression of objectivity and precision, it can be easily manipulated.

Earnings per share (EPS), which involves dividing net earnings by the amount of common stock, also has several deficiencies as an evaluation of past and future performance. First, because alternative accounting principles are available, EPS can have several different but equally acceptable values, depending on the principle selected for its computation. Second, because EPS is based on accrual income, the conversion of income to cash can be near term or delayed. Therefore, EPS does not consider the time value of money. **Return on equity (ROE)**, which involves dividing net income by total equity, also has limitations because it is also derived from accounting-based data. In addition, EPS and ROE are often unrelated to a company's stock price.

Operating cash flow, the amount of money generated by a company before the cost of financing and taxes, is a broad measure of a company's funds. This is the company's net income plus depreciation, depletion, amortization, interest expense, and income tax expense.[23] Some takeover specialists look at a much narrower **free cash flow**: the amount of money a new owner can take out of the firm without harming the business. This is net income plus depreciation, depletion, and amortization less capital expenditures and dividends. The free cash flow ratio is very useful in evaluating the stability of an entrepreneurial venture.[24] Although cash flow may be harder to manipulate than earnings, the number can be increased by selling accounts receivable, classifying outstanding checks as accounts payable, trading securities, and capitalizing certain expenses, such as direct-response advertising.[25]

Because of these and other limitations, ROI, EPS, ROE, and operating cash flow are not by themselves adequate measures of corporate performance. At the same time, these traditional financial measures are very appropriate when used with complementary financial and non-financial measures. For example, some non–financial performance measures used by Internet business ventures are *stickiness* (length of Web site visit), *eyeballs* (number of people who visit a Web site), and *mindshare* (brand awareness). Mergers and acquisitions may be priced on multiples of *MUUs* (monthly unique users) or even on registered users.

Shareholder Value

Because of the belief that accounting-based numbers such as ROI, ROE, and EPS are not reliable indicators of a corporation's economic value, many corporations are using shareholder value as a better measure of corporate performance and strategic management effectiveness.

Shareholder value can be defined as the present value of the anticipated future stream of cash flows from the business plus the value of the company if liquidated. Arguing that the purpose of a company is to increase shareholder wealth, shareholder value analysis concentrates on cash flow as the key measure of performance. The value of a corporation is thus the value of its cash flows discounted back to their present value, using the business's cost of capital as the discount rate. As long as the returns from a business exceed its cost of capital, the business will create value and be worth more than the capital invested in it. For example, Deere and Company charges each business unit a cost of capital of 1% of assets a month. Each business unit is required to earn a shareholder value-added profit margin of 20%, on average, over the business cycle. Financial rewards are linked to this measure.[26]

The New York consulting firm Stern Stewart & Company devised and popularized two shareholder value measures: economic value added (EVA) and market value added (MVA). A basic tenet of EVA and MVA is that businesses should not invest in projects unless they can generate a profit above the cost of capital. Stern Stewart argues that a deficiency of traditional accounting-based measures is that they assume the cost of capital to be zero.[27] Well-known companies, such as Coca-Cola, General Electric, AT&T, Whirlpool, Quaker Oats, Eli Lilly, Georgia-Pacific, Polaroid, Sprint, Toyota, and Tenneco have adopted MVA and/or EVA as the best yardstick for corporate performance.

Economic value added (EVA) has become an extremely popular shareholder value method of measuring corporate and divisional performance and may be on its way to replacing ROI as the standard performance measure. EVA measures the difference between the pre- strategy and post-strategy values for the business. Simply put, EVA is after-tax operating income minus the total annual cost of capital. The formula to measure EVA is:

$$\text{EVA} = \text{after-tax operating income} - (\text{investment in assets} \times \text{weighted average cost of capital})^{28}$$

The cost of capital combines the cost of debt and equity. The annual cost of borrowed capital is the interest charged by the firm's banks and bondholders. To calculate the cost of equity, assume that shareholders generally earn about 6% more on stocks than on government bonds. If long-term treasury bills are selling at 2.5%, the firm's cost of equity should be 8.5%—more if the firm is in a risky industry. A corporation's overall cost of capital is the weighted-average cost of the firm's debt and equity capital. The investment in assets is the total amount of capital invested in the business, including buildings, machines, computers, and investments in R&D and training (allocating costs annually over their useful life). Because the typical balance sheet understates the investment made in a company, Stern Stewart has identified more than 160 possible adjustments, before EVA is calculated.[29] Multiply the firm's total investment in assets by the weighted-average cost of capital. Subtract that figure from after-tax operating income. If the difference is positive, the strategy (and the management employing it) is generating value for the shareholders. If it is negative, the strategy is destroying shareholder value.[30]

Roberto Goizueta, past-CEO of Coca-Cola, explained, "We raise capital to make concentrate, and sell it at an operating profit. Then we pay the cost of that capital. Shareholders pocket the difference."[31] Managers can improve their company's or business unit's EVA by: (1) earning more profit without using more capital, (2) using less capital, and (3) investing capital in high-return projects. Studies have found that companies using EVA outperform their median competitor by an average of 8.43% of total return annually.[32] EVA does, however, have some limitations. For one thing, it does not control for size differences across plants or divisions. As with ROI, managers can manipulate the numbers. As with ROI, EVA is an after-the-fact measure and cannot be used like a steering control.[33] Although proponents of EVA argue that EVA (unlike return on investment, equity, or sales) has a strong relationship to stock price, other studies do not support this contention.[34]

Market value added (MVA) is the difference between the market value of a corporation and the capital contributed by shareholders and lenders. Like net present value, it measures the stock market's estimate of the net present value of a firm's past and expected capital investment projects. As such, MVA is the present value of future EVA.[35] To calculate MVA:

1. Add all the capital that has been put into a company—from shareholders, bondholders, and retained earnings.

2. Reclassify certain accounting expenses, such as R&D, to reflect that they are actually investments in future earnings. This provides the firm's total capital. So far, this is the same approach taken in calculating EVA.

3. Using the current stock price, total the value of all outstanding stock, adding it to the company's debt. This is the company's market value. If the company's market value is greater than all the capital invested in it, the firm has a positive MVA—meaning that management (and the strategy it is following) has created wealth. In some cases, however, the market value of the company is actually less than the capital put into it, which means shareholder wealth is being destroyed.

Microsoft, General Electric, Intel, and Coca-Cola have tended to have high MVAs in the United States, whereas General Motors and RJR Nabisco have had low ones.[36] Studies have shown that EVA is a predictor of MVA. Consecutive years of positive EVA generally lead to a soaring MVA.[37] Research also reveals that CEO turnover is significantly correlated with MVA and EVA, whereas ROA and ROE are not. This suggests that EVA and MVA may be more appropriate measures of the market's evaluation of a firm's strategy and its management than are the traditional measures of corporate performance.[38] Nevertheless, these measures consider only the financial interests of the shareholder and ignore other stakeholders, such as environmentalists and employees.

Climate change is likely to lead to new regulations, technological remedies, and shifts in consumer behavior. It will thus have a significant impact on the financial performance of many corporations. To see how companies are using new techniques that are simultaneously good for the environment as well as being good for the company, see the Sustainability Issue feature.

BALANCED SCORECARD APPROACH: USING KEY PERFORMANCE MEASURES

Rather than evaluate a corporation using a few financial measures, Kaplan and Norton argue for a "balanced scorecard" that includes non-financial as well as financial measures.[39] This approach is especially useful given that research indicates that non-financial assets explain 50% to 80% of a firm's value.[40] The **balanced scorecard** combines financial measures that tell the results of actions already taken with operational measures on customer satisfaction, internal processes, and the corporation's innovation and improvement activities—the drivers of future financial performance. Thus steering controls are combined with output controls. In the balanced scorecard, management develops goals or objectives in each of four areas:

- **Financial:** How do we appear to shareholders?
- **Customer:** How do customers view us?

SUSTAINABILITY issue

E-RECEIPTS

More than nine million trees are cut down each year to make cash register receipts in the United States and most of those receipts are simply thrown away. A number of companies were moving toward e-receipts in the late 1990s, but the dot-com bust brought all that to a temporary end. In 2005, Apple introduced e-receipts at its stylish Apple stores and the wave began.

E-receipts not only save on necessary printing and landfill waste, they also provide the customer with an electronic record of purchases (for taxes, expense reports, or gift returns). A number of national retailers now offer e-receipts, including Best Buy, Whole Foods, Nordstrom, Gap Inc. (which owns Old Navy and Banana Republic), Anthropologie, Patagonia, Sears, and Kmart. The advantage beyond cost savings for the retailer is having the customer's e-mail address for use with promotions.

Some companies are using this new opportunity to provide value to the consumer. At Nordstrom's, they are looking at making e-receipts more appealing by adding a picture of the item to the receipt so a shopper can post it to a Facebook wall or remember exactly what they bought last time.

According to a 2012 survey of 3900 retailers, more than 35% now offer e-receipts as an option. At Wells Fargo, 12% of their customers are choosing e-receipts for their ATM transactions. The audit trail is improved for both customer and company by providing a new level of improved control.

SOURCES: W. Koch, "Retailers Find Profits with Paperless Receipts," *USA Today* (November 3, 2012), http://www.usatoday.com/story/news/nation/2012/11/03/retailers-e-mail-digital-paperless-receipts/1675069/#; S. Clifford, "Shopper Receipts Join Paperless Age," *The New York Times* (August 7, 2011), http://www.nytimes.com/2011/08/08/technology/digital-receipts-at-stores-gain-in-popularity.html?_r=0.

- **Internal business perspective:** What must we excel at?
- **Innovation and learning:** Can we continue to improve and create value?[41]

Each goal in each area (for example, avoiding bankruptcy in the financial area) is then assigned one or more measures, as well as a target and an initiative. These measures can be thought of as **key performance measures**—measures that are essential for achieving a desired strategic option.[42] For example, a company could include cash flow, quarterly sales growth, and ROE as measures for success in the financial area. It could include market share (competitive position goal), customer satisfaction, and percentage of new sales coming from new products (customer acceptance goal) as measures under the customer perspective. It could include cycle time and unit cost (manufacturing excellence goal) as measures under the internal business perspective. It could include time to develop next-generation products (technology leadership objective) under the innovation and learning perspective.

A 2011 global survey by Bain & Company reported that 63% of Fortune 1000 companies in North America use a version of the balanced scorecard.[43] A study of the Fortune 500 firms in the United States and the Post 300 firms in Canada revealed the most popular non-financial measures to be customer satisfaction, customer service, product quality, market share, productivity, service quality, and core competencies. New product development, corporate culture, and market growth were not far behind.[44] DuPont's Engineering Polymers Division uses the balanced scorecard to align employees, business units, and shared services around a common strategy involving productivity improvements and revenue growth.[45] Corporate experience with the balanced scorecard reveals that a firm should tailor the system to suit its situation, not just adopt it as a cookbook approach. When the balanced scorecard complements corporate strategy, it improves performance. Using the method in a mechanistic fashion without any link to strategy hinders performance and may even decrease it.[46]

Evaluating Top Management and the Board of Directors

Through its strategy, audit, and compensation committees, a board of directors closely evaluates the job performance of the CEO and the top management team. The vast majority of American (91%), European (75%), and Asian (75%) boards review the CEO's performance using a formalized process.[47] Objective evaluations of the CEO by the board are very important given that CEOs tend to evaluate senior management's performance significantly more positively than do other executives.[48] The board is concerned primarily with overall corporate profitability as measured quantitatively by ROI, ROE, EPS, and shareholder value. The absence of short-run profitability certainly contributes to the firing of any CEO. The board, however, is also concerned with other factors.

Members of the compensation committees of today's boards of directors generally agree that a CEO's ability to establish strategic direction, build a management team, and provide leadership are more critical in the long run than are a few quantitative measures. The board should evaluate top management not only on the typical output-oriented quantitative measures, but also on behavioral measures—factors relating to its strategic management practices. According to a survey by Korn/Ferry International, the criteria used by American boards are financial (81%), ethical behavior (63%), thought leadership (58%), corporate reputation (32%), stock price performance (22%), and meeting participation (10%).[49] The specific items that a board uses to evaluate its top management should be derived from the objectives that both the board and top management agreed on earlier. If better relations with the local community and improved safety practices in work areas were selected as objectives for the year (or for five years), these items should be included in the evaluation. In addition, other factors that tend to lead to profitability might be included, such as market share, product quality, or investment intensity.

Performance evaluations of the overall board's performance are standard practice for 87% of directors in the Americas, 72% in Europe, and 62% in Asia.[50] Evaluations of individual directors are less common. According to a PricewaterhouseCoopers survey of 1100 directors, 77% of the directors agreed that individual directors should be appraised regularly on their performance, but only 37% responded that they actually do so.[51] Corporations that have successfully used board performance appraisal systems are Goldman Sachs, Boeing, Ingersoll Rand, McDonald's, Google, and Ford Motor.

Chairman-CEO Feedback Instrument. An increasing number of companies are evaluating their CEO by using a 17-item questionnaire developed by Ram Charon, an authority on corporate governance. The questionnaire focuses on four key areas: (1) company performance, (2) leadership of the organization, (3) team-building and management succession, and (4) leadership of external constituencies.[52] After taking an hour to complete the questionnaire, the board of KeraVision Inc. used it as a basis for a lengthy discussion with the CEO, Thomas Loarie. The board criticized Loarie for "not tempering enthusiasm with reality" and urged Loarie to develop a clear management succession plan. The evaluation caused Loarie to more closely involve the board in setting the company's primary objectives and discussing "where we are, where we want to go, and the operating environment."[53]

Management Audit. Management audits are very useful to boards of directors in evaluating management's handling of various corporate activities. Management audits have been developed to evaluate activities such as corporate social responsibility, functional areas like the marketing department, and divisions such as the international division. These can be helpful if the board has selected particular functional areas or activities for improvement.

Strategic Audit. The strategic audit, presented in the **Chapter 1 Appendix 1.A**, is a type of management audit. The strategic audit provides a checklist of questions, by area or issue, that enables a systematic analysis of various corporate functions and activities to be made. It is a type of management audit and is extremely useful as a diagnostic tool to pinpoint corporatewide problem areas and to highlight organizational strengths and weaknesses.[54] A strategic audit can help determine why a certain area is creating problems for a corporation and help generate solutions to the problem. As such, it can be very useful in evaluating the performance of top management.

PRIMARY MEASURES OF DIVISIONAL AND FUNCTIONAL PERFORMANCE

Companies use a variety of techniques to evaluate and control performance in divisions, strategic business units (SBUs), and functional areas. If a corporation is composed of SBUs or divisions, it will use many of the same performance measures (ROI or EVA, for instance) that it uses to assess overall corporate performance. To the extent that it can isolate specific functional units such as R&D, the corporation may develop responsibility centers. It will also use typical functional measures, such as market share and sales per employee (marketing), unit costs and percentage of defects (operations), percentage of sales from new products and number of patents (R&D), and turnover and job satisfaction (HRM). For example, FedEx uses Enhanced Tracker software with its COSMOS database to track the progress of its 2.5 to 3.5 million shipments daily. As a courier is completing her or his day's activities, the Enhanced Tracker asks whether the person's package count equals the Enhanced Tracker's count. If the count is off, the software helps reconcile the differences.[55]

During strategy formulation and implementation, top management approves a series of programs and supporting *operating budgets* from its business units. During evaluation and control, actual expenses are contrasted with planned expenditures, and the degree of variance is assessed. This is typically done on a monthly basis. In addition, top management will probably require *periodic statistical reports* summarizing data on such key factors as the number of new customer contracts, the volume of received orders, and productivity figures.

RESPONSIBILITY CENTERS

Control systems can be established to monitor specific functions, projects, or divisions. Budgets are one type of control system that is typically used to control the financial indicators of performance. **Responsibility centers** are used to isolate a unit so it can be evaluated separately from the rest of the corporation. Each responsibility center, therefore, has its own budget and is evaluated on its use of budgeted resources. It is headed by the manager responsible for the center's performance. The center uses resources (measured in terms of costs or expenses) to produce a service or a product (measured in terms of volume or revenues). There are five major types of responsibility centers. The type is determined by the way the corporation's control system measures these resources and services or products.

- **Standard cost centers: Standard cost centers** are primarily used in manufacturing facilities. Standard (or expected) costs are computed for each operation on the basis of historical data. In evaluating the center's performance, its total standard costs are multiplied by the units produced. The result is the *expected* cost of production, which is then compared to the *actual* cost of production.

- **Revenue centers:** With **revenue centers**, production, usually in terms of unit or dollar sales, is measured without consideration of resource costs (for example, salaries). The center is thus judged in terms of effectiveness rather than efficiency. The effectiveness of a sales region, for example, is determined by comparing its actual sales to its projected or previous year's sales. Profits are not considered because sales departments have very limited influence over the cost of the products they sell.

- **Expense centers:** Resources are measured in dollars, without consideration for service or product costs. Thus budgets will have been prepared for engineered expenses (costs that can be calculated) and for discretionary expenses (costs that can be only estimated). Typical **expense centers** are administrative, service, and research departments. They cost a company money, but they only indirectly contribute to revenues.

- **Profit centers:** Performance is measured in terms of the difference between revenues (which measure production) and expenditures (which measure resources). A **profit center** is typically established whenever an organizational unit has control over both its resources and its products or services. By having such centers, a company can be organized into divisions of separate product lines. The manager of each division is given autonomy to the extent that he or she is able to keep profits at a satisfactory (or better) level.

Some organizational units that are not usually considered potentially autonomous can, for the purpose of profit center evaluations, be made so. A manufacturing department, for example, can be converted from a standard cost center (or expense center) into a profit center; it is allowed to charge a transfer price for each product it "sells" to the sales department. The difference between the manufacturing cost per unit and the agreed-upon transfer price is the unit's "profit."

Transfer pricing is commonly used in vertically integrated corporations and can work well when a price can be easily determined for a designated amount of product. Even though most experts agree that market-based transfer prices are the best choice, A 2010 global survey completed by E&Y found that only 27% of companies use market price to set the transfer price.[56] When a price cannot be set easily, however, the relative bargaining power of the centers, rather than strategic considerations, tends to influence the agreed-upon price. Top management has an obligation to make sure that these political considerations do not overwhelm the strategic ones. Otherwise, profit figures for each center will be biased and provide poor information for strategic decisions at both the corporate and divisional levels.

- **Investment centers:** Because many divisions in large manufacturing corporations use significant assets to make their products, their asset base should be factored into their performance evaluation. Thus it is insufficient to focus only on profits, as in the case of profit centers. An **investment center's** performance is measured in terms of the difference between its resources and its services or products. For example, two divisions in a corporation made identical profits, but one division owns a $3 million plant, whereas the other owns a $1 million plant. Both make the same profits, but one is obviously more efficient; the smaller plant provides the shareholders with a better return on their investment. The most widely used measure of investment center performance is ROI.

Most single-business corporations, such as Buffalo Wild Wings, tend to use a combination of cost, expense, and revenue centers. In these corporations, most managers are functional specialists and manage against a budget. Total profitability is integrated at the corporate level. Multidivisional corporations with one dominating product line (such as ABInBev) that have diversified into a few businesses but that still depend on a single product line (such as beer) for most of their revenue and income, generally use a combination of cost, expense, revenue, and profit centers. Multidivisional corporations, such as General Electric, tend to emphasize investment centers—although in various units throughout the corporation other types of responsibility centers are also used. One problem with using responsibility centers, however, is that the separation needed to measure and evaluate a division's performance can diminish the level of cooperation among divisions that is needed to attain synergy for the corporation as a whole. (This problem is discussed later in this chapter, under "Suboptimization.")

USING BENCHMARKING TO EVALUATE PERFORMANCE

According to Xerox Corporation, the company that pioneered this concept in the United States, **benchmarking** is "the continual process of measuring products, services, and practices against the toughest competitors or those companies recognized as industry leaders."[57] Benchmarking, an increasingly popular program, is based on the concept that it makes no sense to reinvent something that someone else is already using. It involves openly learning how others do something better than one's own company so that the company not only can imitate, but perhaps even improve upon its techniques. The benchmarking process usually involves the following steps:

1. Identify the area or process to be examined. It should be an activity that has the potential to determine a business unit's competitive advantage.

2. Find behavioral and output measures of the area or process and obtain measurements.

3. Select an accessible set of competitors and best-in-class companies against which to benchmark. These may very often be companies that are in completely different industries, but perform similar activities. For example, when Xerox wanted to improve its order fulfillment, it went to L.L.Bean, the successful mail order firm, to learn how it achieved excellence in this area.

4. Calculate the differences among the company's performance measurements and those of the best-in-class and determine why the differences exist.

5. Develop tactical programs for closing performance gaps.

6. Implement the programs and then compare the resulting new measurements with those of the best-in-class companies.

Benchmarking has been found to produce best results in companies that are already well managed. Apparently poorer performing firms tend to be overwhelmed by the discrepancy between their performance and the benchmark—and tend to view the benchmark as too difficult to reach.[58] Nevertheless, a survey by Bain & Company of companies of various sizes across all U.S. industries indicated that about 65% were using benchmarking.[59] Cost reductions range from 15% to 45%.[60] Benchmarking can also increase sales, improve goal setting, and boost employee motivation.[61] The average cost of a benchmarking study is around $100,000 and involves 30 weeks of effort.[62] Manco Inc., a small Cleveland-area producer of duct tape, regularly benchmarks itself against Wal-Mart, Rubbermaid, and PepsiCo to enable it to better compete with giant 3M. APQC (American Productivity & Quality Center), a Houston research group, established the Open Standards Benchmarking Collaborative database, composed of more than 1200 commonly used measures and individual benchmarks, to track the performance of core operational functions. Firms can submit their performance data to this online database to learn how they compare to top performers and industry peers (see www.apqc.org).

INTERNATIONAL MEASUREMENT ISSUES

The three most widely used techniques for international performance evaluation are ROI, budget analysis, and historical comparisons. In one study, 95% of the corporate officers interviewed stated that they use the same evaluation techniques for foreign and domestic operations. Rate of return was mentioned as the single most important measure.[63] However, ROI can cause problems when it is applied to international operations: Because of foreign currencies, different accounting systems, different rates of inflation, different tax laws, and the use of transfer pricing, both the net income figure and the investment base may be seriously distorted.[64] To deal with different accounting systems throughout the world, the London-based International Accounting Standards Board developed International Financial Reporting Standards (IFRS) to harmonize accounting practices. The Financial Accounting Standards Board (FASB) oversees the Generally Accepted Accounting Principles (GAAP) that is used in the United States. Over the past decade, these two groups have worked to merge their systems and there was hope that there would be a single set of standards by 2015. Nevertheless, enforcement and cultural interpretations of the international rules can still vary by country and may undercut what is hoped to be a uniform accounting system.[65]

A study of 79 MNCs revealed that *international transfer pricing* from one country unit to another is primarily used not to evaluate performance but to minimize taxes.[66] Taxes are an important issue for MNCs, given that corporate tax rates vary from 40% in the United States to 38% in Japan, 32% in India, 30% in Mexico, 24% in the U.K. and South Korea, 26% in Canada, 25% in China, 17% in Singapore, 10% in Albania, and 0% in Bahrain and the Cayman Islands.[67] For example, the U.S. Internal Revenue Service contended in the early 1990s that many Japanese firms doing business in the United States artificially inflated the value of U.S. deliveries in order to reduce the profits and thus the taxes of their American subsidiaries.[68]

Parts made in a subsidiary of a Japanese MNC in a low-tax country such as Singapore could be shipped to its subsidiary in a high-tax country like the United States at such a high price that the U.S. subsidiary reports very little profit (and thus pays few taxes), while the Singapore subsidiary reports a very high profit (but also pays few taxes because of the lower tax rate). A Japanese MNC could, therefore, earn more profit worldwide by reporting less profit in high-tax countries and more profit in low-tax countries. Transfer pricing can thus be one way the parent company can reduce taxes and "capture profits" from a subsidiary. Other common ways of transferring profits to the parent company (often referred to as the *repatriation of profits*) are through dividends, royalties, and management fees.[69]

Among the most important barriers to international trade are the different standards for products and services. There are at least three categories of standards: safety/environmental, energy efficiency, and testing procedures. Existing standards have been drafted by such bodies as the British Standards Institute (BSI-UK) in the United Kingdom, the Japanese Industrial Standards Committee (JISC), AFNOR in France, DIN in Germany, CSA in Canada, and the American Standards Institute in the United States. These standards traditionally created entry barriers that served to fragment various industries, such as major home appliances, by country. The International Electrotechnical Commission (IEC) standards were created to harmonize standards in the European Union and eventually to serve as worldwide standards, with some national deviations to satisfy specific needs. Because the European Union (EU) was the first to harmonize the many different standards of its member countries, the EU is shaping standards for the rest of the world. In addition, the International Organization for Standardization (ISO) is preparing and publishing international standards. These standards provide a foundation for regional associations to build upon. CANENA, the Council for Harmonization of Electrotechnical Standards of the Nations of the Americas, was created in 1992 to further coordinate the harmonization of standards in North and South America. Efforts are also under way in Asia to harmonize standards.[70]

An important issue in international trade is counterfeiting/piracy. Firms in developing nations around the world make money by making counterfeit/pirated copies of well-known name-brand products and selling them globally as well as locally. See the **Global Issue** feature to learn how this is being done.

Authorities in international business recommend that the control and reward systems used by a global MNC be different from those used by a multidomestic MNC.[71]

A *MNC* should use loose controls on its foreign units. The management of each geographic unit should be given considerable operational latitude, but it should be expected to meet some performance targets. Because profit and ROI measures are often unreliable in international operations, it is recommended that the MNC's top management, in this instance, emphasize budgets and non-financial measures of performance such as market share, productivity, public image, employee morale, and relations with the host country government.[72] Multiple measures should be used to differentiate between the worth of the subsidiary and the performance of its management.

A *global MNC*, however, needs tight controls over its many units. To reduce costs and gain competitive advantage, it is trying to spread the manufacturing and marketing operations of a few fairly uniform products around the world. Therefore, its key operational decisions must be centralized. Its environmental scanning must include research not only into each of the national markets in which the MNC competes but also into the "global arena" of the interaction between markets. Foreign units are thus evaluated more as cost centers, revenue centers, or expense centers than as investment or profit centers because MNCs operating in a global industry do not often make the entire product in the country in which it is sold.

GLOBAL issue

COUNTERFEIT GOODS AND PIRATED SOFTWARE: A GLOBAL PROBLEM

"We know that 15% to 20% of all goods in China are counterfeit," states Dan Chow, a law professor at Ohio State University. This includes products from Tide detergent and Budweiser beer to Marlboro cigarettes. There is a saying in Shanghai, China: "We can copy everything except your mother." Yamaha estimates that five out of every six bikes bearing its brand name are fake. Fake Cisco network routers (known as "Chiscos") and counterfeit Nokia mobile phones can be easily found throughout China. Procter & Gamble estimates that 15% of the soaps and detergents under its Head & Shoulders, Vidal Sassoon, Safeguard, and Tide brands in China are counterfeit, costing the company $150 million in lost sales.

In Yiwu, a few hours from Shanghai, one person admitted to a *60 Minutes* reporter that she could make 1000 pairs of counterfeit Nike shoes in 10 days for $4.00 a pair. According to the market research firm Automotive Resources, the profit margins on counterfeit shock absorbers can reach 80% versus only 15% for the real ones. The World Custom Organization estimates that 7% of the world's merchandise is bogus.

Tens of thousands of counterfeiters are active in China. They range from factories mixing shampoo and soap in back rooms to large state-owned enterprises making copies of soft drinks and beer. Other factories make everything from car batteries to automobiles. Mobile CD factories with optical disc-mastering machines counterfeit music and software. *60 Minutes* found a small factory in Donguan making fake Callaway golf clubs and bags at a rate of 500 bags per week. Factories in the southern Guangdong and Fujian provinces truck their products to a central distribution center, such as the one in Yiwu. They may also be shipped across the border into Russia, Pakistan, Vietnam, or Burma. Chinese counterfeiters have developed a global reach through their connections with organized crime.

As much as 35% of software on personal computers worldwide is pirated, according to the Business Software Alliance and ISDC, a market research firm. The worldwide cost of software piracy was around $63 billion in 2011. For example, 21% of the software sold in the United States is pirated. That figure increases to 26%–30% in the European Union, 83% in Russia, Algeria, and Bolivia, to 86% in China, 87% in Indonesia, and 90% in Vietnam.

....

SOURCES: "Head in the Clouds," *The Economist* (July 25, 2012), http://www.economist.com/blogs/graphicdetail/2012/07/online-software-piracy; "The Sincerest Form of Flattery," *The Economist* (April 7, 2007), pp. 64–65; F. Balfour, "Fakes!" *BusinessWeek* (February 7, 2005), pp. 54–64; "PC Software Piracy," *The Economist* (June 10, 2006), p. 102; "The World's Greatest Fakes," *60 Minutes*, CBS News (August 8, 2004); "Business Software Piracy," *Pocket World in Figures 2004* (London: Economist & Profile Book, 2003), p. 60; D. Roberts, F. Balfour, P. Magnusson, P. Engardio, and J. Lee, "China's Piracy Plague," *BusinessWeek* (June 5, 2000), pp. 44–48.

Strategic Information Systems

Before performance measures can have any impact on strategic management, they must first be communicated to the people responsible for formulating and implementing strategic plans. Strategic information systems can perform this function. They can be computer-based or manual, formal or informal. One of the key reasons given for the bankruptcy of International Harvester was the inability of the corporation's top management to precisely determine income by major class of similar products. Because of this inability, management kept trying to fix ailing businesses and was unable to respond flexibly to major changes and unexpected events. In contrast, one of the key reasons for the success of Wal-Mart has been management's use of the company's sophisticated information system to control purchasing decisions. Cash registers in Wal-Mart retail stores transmit information hourly to computers at the company headquarters. Consequently, managers know every morning exactly how many of each item were sold the day before, how many have been sold so far in the year, and how this year's sales compare to last year's. The information system allows all reordering to be done automatically by computers, without any managerial input. It also allows the company to experiment with new products without committing to big orders in advance. In effect, the system allows the customers to decide through their purchases what gets reordered.

ENTERPRISE RESOURCE PLANNING (ERP)

Many corporations around the world have adopted **enterprise resource planning (ERP)** software. ERP unites all of a company's major business activities, from order processing to production, within a single family of software modules. The system provides instant access to critical information to everyone in the organization, from the CEO to the factory floor worker. Because of the ability of ERP software to use a common information system throughout a company's many operations around the world, it is becoming the business information systems' global standard. The major providers of this software are SAP AG, Oracle (including PeopleSoft), J. D. Edwards, Baan, and SSA Global Technologies.

The German company SAP AG originated the concept with its R/3 software system. Microsoft, for example, used R/3 to replace a tangle of 33 financial tracking systems in 26 subsidiaries. Even though it cost the company $25 million and took 10 months to install, R/3 annually saves Microsoft $18 million. Coca-Cola uses the R/3 system to enable a manager in Atlanta to use her personal computer to check the latest sales of 20-ounce bottles of Coke Classic in India. Owens-Corning envisioned that its R/3 system allowed salespeople to learn what was available at any plant or warehouse and to quickly assemble orders for customers.

ERP may not fit every company, however. The system is extremely complicated and demands a high level of standardization throughout a corporation. Its demanding nature often forces companies to change the way they do business. There are three reasons ERP could fail: (1) insufficient tailoring of the software to fit the company, (2) inadequate training, and (3) insufficient implementation support.[73] Over the two-year period of installing R/3, Owens-Corning had to completely overhaul its operations. Because R/3 was incompatible with Apple's very organic corporate culture, the company was able to apply it only to its order management and financial operations, but not to manufacturing. Other companies that had difficulty installing and using ERP are Whirlpool, Hershey Foods, Volkswagen, and Stanley Works. At Whirlpool, SAP's software led to missed and delayed shipments, causing The Home Depot to cancel its agreement for selling Whirlpool products.[74] One survey found that 65% of executives believed that ERP had a moderate chance of hurting their business because of implementation problems. Nevertheless, the payoff from ERP software can be worth the effort. In an industry where one company implements ERP ahead of its competitors, it can be used to gain some competitive advantage, streamline operations, and help manage a lean manufacturing system.[75]

RADIO FREQUENCY IDENTIFICATION (RFID)

Radio frequency identification (RFID) is an electronic tagging technology used in a number of companies to improve supply-chain efficiency. By tagging containers and items with tiny chips, companies use the tags as wireless barcodes to track inventory more efficiently. Both Wal-Mart and the U.S. Department of Defense began requiring their largest suppliers to incorporate RFID tags in their goods in 2003. After trying to implement RFID for the past decade, the UK-based supermarket chain Tesco postponed their full implementation of RFID technology in late 2012. Tesco had planned to deploy RFID tags and readers in 1400 stores and in its distribution centers by the middle of 2012. However, it had installed RFID tags in only 40 stores and one depot before it brought the program to a halt.[76] Nevertheless, some suppliers and retailers of expensive consumer products view the cost of the tag as worthwhile because it reduces losses from counterfeiting and theft. RFID technology is currently in wide use as wireless commuter passes for toll roads, tunnels, and bridges. Even though RFID standards may vary among companies, individual firms like Audi, Sony, and Dole Food use the tags to track goods within their own factories and warehouses.[77] According to Dan Mullen of AIM Global, "RFID will go through a process similar to what happened in barcode technology 20 years ago. . . . As companies implement the technology deeper within their operations, the return on investment will grow and applications will expand."[78]

DIVISIONAL AND FUNCTIONAL IS SUPPORT

At the divisional or SBU level of a corporation, the information system should be used to support, reinforce, or enlarge its business-level strategy through its decision support system. An SBU pursuing a strategy of overall cost leadership could use its information system to reduce costs either by improving labor productivity or improving the use of other resources such as inventory or machinery. Kaiser Health has 37 hospitals, 15,857 physicians, and 9 million plus members all tied together in a single system that has made for better health services and an increased ability to reduce problems in the system. An internal study of heart attacks among 46,000 patients in Northern California who were 30 years and older showed a decline of 24 percent. Kaiser has also reduced mortality rates by 40% since 2008 for its hospital patients who contract sepsis, a dangerous infectious disease.[79] Another SBU, in contrast, might want to pursue a differentiation strategy. It could use its information system to add uniqueness to the product or service and contribute to quality, service, or image through the functional areas. FedEx wanted to use superior service to gain a competitive advantage. It invested significantly in several types of information systems to measure and track the performance of its delivery service. Together, these information systems gave FedEx the fastest error-response time in the overnight delivery business.

Problems in Measuring Performance

The measurement of performance is a crucial part of evaluation and control. The lack of quantifiable objectives or performance standards and the inability of the information system to provide timely and valid information are two obvious control problems. According to Meg Whitman, former CEO of eBay, "If you can't measure it, you can't control it." That's why eBay has a multitude of measures, from total revenues and profits to *take rate*, the ratio of revenues to the value of goods traded on the site.[80] Without objective and timely measurements, it would be extremely difficult to make operational, let alone strategic, decisions. Nevertheless, the use of timely, quantifiable standards does not guarantee good performance. The very act of monitoring and measuring performance can cause side effects that interfere with overall corporate performance. Among the most frequent negative side effects are a short-term orientation and goal displacement.

SHORT-TERM ORIENTATION

Top executives report that in many situations, they analyze neither the long-term implications of present operations on the strategy they have adopted nor the operational impact of a strategy on the corporate mission. Long-term evaluations may not be conducted because executives

(1) don't realize their importance, (2) believe that short-term considerations are more important than long-term considerations, (3) aren't personally evaluated on a long-term basis, or (4) don't have the time to make a long-term analysis.[81] There is no real justification for the first and last reasons. If executives realize the importance of long-term evaluations, they make the time needed to conduct them. Even though many chief executives point to immediate pressures from the investment community and to short-term incentive and promotion plans to support the second and third reasons, evidence does not always support their claims.[82]

At one international heavy-equipment manufacturer, managers were so strongly motivated to achieve their quarterly revenue target that they shipped unfinished products from their plant in England to a warehouse in the Netherlands for final assembly. By shipping the incomplete products, they were able to realize the sales before the end of the quarter—thus fulfilling their budgeted objective and making their bonuses. Unfortunately, the high cost of assembling the goods at a distant location (requiring not only renting the warehouse but also paying additional labor) ended up reducing the company's overall profit.[83]

Many accounting-based measures, such as EPS and ROI, encourage a **short-term orientation** in which managers consider only current tactical or operational issues and ignore long-term strategic ones. Because growth in EPS (earnings per share) is an important driver of near-term stock price, top managers are biased against investments that might reduce short-term EPS.[84] This is compounded by pressure from financial analysts and investors for quarterly *earnings guidance*—that is, estimates of future corporate earnings.[85] Hewlett-Packard (HP) acquired British firm Autonomy for $11.1 billion in 2011 and had to write down $8.8 billion of that amount in 2012 as the company found significant accounting errors. Multiple lawsuits were filed against HP, its officers, directors, and the accounting firms involved with Autonomy before the acquisition.[86]

One of the limitations of ROI as a performance measure is its short-term nature. In theory, ROI is not limited to the short run, but in practice it is often difficult to use this measure to realize long-term benefits for a company. Because managers can often manipulate both the numerator (earnings) and the denominator (investment), the resulting ROI figure can be meaningless. Advertising, maintenance, and research efforts can be reduced. Estimates of pension-fund profits, unpaid receivables, and old inventory, are easy to adjust. Optimistic estimates of returned products, bad debts, and obsolete inventory inflate the present year's sales and earnings.[87] Expensive retooling and plant modernization can be delayed as long as a manager can manipulate figures on production defects and absenteeism. In a recent survey of financial executives, 80% of the managers stated that they would decrease spending on research and development, advertising, maintenance, and hiring in order to meet earnings targets. More than half said they would delay a new project even if it meant sacrificing value.[88]

Mergers can be undertaken that will do more for the present year's earnings (and the next year's paycheck) than for the division's or corporation's future profits. For example, research on 55 firms that engaged in major acquisitions revealed that even though the firms performed poorly after the acquisition, the acquiring firms' top management still received significant increases in compensation.[89] Determining CEO compensation on the basis of firm size rather than performance is typical and is particularly likely for firms that are not monitored closely by independent analysts.[90]

Research supports the conclusion that many CEOs and their friends on the board of directors' compensation committee manipulate information to provide themselves a pay raise.[91] For example, CEOs tend to announce bad news—thus reducing the company's stock price—just before the issuance of stock options. Once the options are issued, the CEOs tend to announce good news—thus raising the stock price and making their options more valuable.[92] Board compensation committees tend to expand the peer group comparison outside their industry to include lower-performing firms to justify a high raise to the CEO. They tend to do this when the company performs poorly, the industry performs well, the CEO is already highly paid, and shareholders are powerful and active.[93]

GOAL DISPLACEMENT

If not carefully done, monitoring and measuring of performance can actually result in a decline in overall corporate performance. **Goal displacement** is the confusion of means with ends and occurs when activities originally intended to help managers attain corporate objectives become ends in themselves—or are adapted to meet ends other than those for which they were intended. Two types of goal displacement are behavior substitution and suboptimization.

Behavior Substitution

Behavior substitution refers to the phenomenon of when people substitute activities that do not lead to goal accomplishment for activities that do lead to goal accomplishment because the wrong activities are being rewarded. Managers, like most other people, tend to focus more of their attention on behaviors that are clearly measurable than on those that are not. Employees often receive little or no reward for engaging in hard-to-measure activities such as cooperation and initiative. However, easy-to-measure activities might have little or no relationship to the desired good performance. Rational people, nevertheless, tend to work for the rewards that the system has to offer. Therefore, people tend to substitute behaviors that are recognized and rewarded for behaviors that are ignored, without regard to their contribution to goal accomplishment. A research study of 157 corporations revealed that most of the companies made little attempt to identify areas of non-financial performance that might advance their chosen strategy. Only 23% consistently built and verified cause-and-effect relationships between intermediate controls (such as number of patents filed or product flaws) and company performance.[94]

A U.S. Navy quip sums up this situation: "What you inspect (or reward) is what you get." If the reward system emphasizes quantity while merely asking for quality and cooperation, the system is likely to produce a large number of low-quality products and unsatisfied customers.[95] A proposed law governing the effect of measurement on behavior is that *quantifiable measures drive out non-quantifiable measures.*

A classic example of behavior substitution happened a few years ago at Sears. Sears' management thought it could improve employee productivity by tying performance to rewards. It, therefore, paid commissions to its auto shop employees as a percentage of each repair bill. Behavior substitution resulted as employees altered their behavior to fit the reward system. The results were over-billed customers, charges for work never done, and a scandal that tarnished Sears' reputation for many years.[96]

Suboptimization

Suboptimization refers to the phenomenon of a unit optimizing its goal accomplishment to the detriment of the organization as a whole. The emphasis in large corporations on developing separate responsibility centers can create some problems for the corporation as a whole. To the extent that a division or functional unit views itself as a separate entity, it might refuse to cooperate with other units or divisions in the same corporation if cooperation could in some way negatively affect its performance evaluation. The competition between divisions to achieve a high ROI can result in one division's refusal to share its new technology or work process improvements. One division's attempt to optimize the accomplishment of its goals can cause other divisions to fall behind and thus negatively affect overall corporate performance. One common example of suboptimization occurs when a marketing department approves an early shipment overtime production for that one order. Production costs are raised, which reduces the manufacturing department's overall efficiency. The end result might be that, although marketing achieves its sales goal, the corporation as a whole fails to achieve its expected profitability.[97]

Guidelines for Proper Control

In designing a control system, top management should remember that controls should follow strategy. Unless controls ensure the use of the proper strategy to achieve objectives, there is a strong likelihood that dysfunctional side effects will completely undermine the implementation of the objectives. The following guidelines are recommended:

1. **Control should involve only the minimum amount of information needed to give a reliable picture of events:** Too many controls create confusion. Focus on the strategic factors by following the **80/20 rule**: *Monitor those 20% of the factors that determine 80% of the results.*

2. **Controls should monitor only meaningful activities and results, regardless of measurement difficulty:** If cooperation between divisions is important to corporate performance, some form of qualitative or quantitative measure should be established to monitor cooperation.

3. **Controls should be timely so that corrective action can be taken before it is too late:** Steering controls, controls that monitor or measure the factors influencing performance, should be stressed so that advance notice of problems is given.

4. **Long-term *and* short-term controls should be used:** If only short-term measures are emphasized, a short-term managerial orientation is likely.

5. **Controls should aim at pinpointing exceptions:** Only activities or results that fall outside a predetermined tolerance range should call for action.

6. **Emphasize the reward of meeting or exceeding standards rather than punishment for failing to meet standards:** Heavy punishment of failure typically results in goal displacement. Managers will "fudge" reports and lobby for lower standards.

If corporate culture complements and reinforces the strategic orientation of a firm, there is less need for an extensive formal control system. In their book *In Search of Excellence*, Peters and Waterman state that "the stronger the culture and the more it was directed toward the marketplace, the less need was there for policy manuals, organization charts, or detailed procedures and rules. In these companies, people way down the line know what they are supposed to do in most situations because the handful of guiding values is crystal clear."[98] For example, at Eaton Corporation, the employees are expected to enforce the rules themselves. If someone misses too much work or picks fights with co-workers, other members of the production team point out the problem. According to Randy Savage, a long-time Eaton employee, "They say there are no bosses here, but if you screw up, you find one pretty fast."[99]

Strategic Incentive Management

To ensure congruence between the needs of a corporation as a whole and the needs of the employees as individuals, management and the board of directors should develop an incentive program that rewards desired performance. This reduces the likelihood of the agency problems (when employees act to feather their own nests instead of building shareholder value) mentioned earlier in **Chapter 2**. Incentive plans should be linked in some way to corporate and divisional strategy. Research reveals that firm performance is affected by its compensation policies.[100] Companies using different strategies tend to adopt different pay policies. For example, a survey of 600 business units indicates that the pay mix associated with a growth strategy emphasizes bonuses and other incentives over salary and benefits, whereas the pay mix associated with a stability strategy has the reverse emphasis.[101] Research indicates that SBU managers having long-term performance elements in their compensation program favor a long-term perspective and thus greater investments in R&D, capital equipment, and employee training.[102] Although the typical CEO pay package is composed of 21% salary, 27% short-term annual incentives, 16% long-term incentives, and 36% stock options,[103] there is some evidence that stock options are being replaced by greater emphasis on performance-related pay.[104]

The following three approaches are tailored to help match measurements and rewards with explicit strategic objectives and time frames:[105]

- **Weighted-factor method:** The weighted-factor method is particularly appropriate for measuring and rewarding the performance of top SBU managers and group-level executives when performance factors and their importance vary from one SBU to another. Using portfolio analysis, one corporation's measurements might contain the following variations: the performance of high-performing (star) SBUs is measured equally in terms of ROI, cash flow, market share, and progress on several future-oriented strategic projects; the performance of low-growth, but strong (cash cow) SBUs, in contrast, is measured in terms of ROI, market share, and cash generation; and the performance of developing question mark SBUs is measured in terms of development and market share growth with no weight on ROI or cash flow. (Refer to **Figure 11–2**.)

- **Long-term evaluation method:** The **long-term evaluation method** compensates managers for achieving objectives set over a multiyear period. An executive is promised some compensation based on long-term performance. A board of directors, for example, might set a particular objective in terms of growth in earnings per share during a five-year period. The giving of awards would be contingent on the corporation's meeting that objective within the designated time. Any executive who leaves the corporation before the objective is met receives nothing. The typical emphasis on stock prices makes this approach more applicable to top management than to business unit managers. Because rising stock markets tend to raise the stock price of mediocre companies, there is a developing trend to index stock options to competitors or to the Standard & Poor's 500.[106]

FIGURE 11–2
Business Strength/Competitive Position

SOURCE: Suggested by Paul J. Stomach in "The Performance Measurement and Reward System: Critical to Strategic Management," *Organizational Dynamics*, (Winter 1984), pp. 45–57.

General Electric, for example, offered its CEO 250,000 performance share units (PSUs) tied to performance targets achieved over five years. Half of the PSUs convert into GE stock only if GE achieves a 10% average annual growth in operations. The other half converts to stock only if total shareholder return meets or beats the S&P 500.[107]

- **Strategic-funds method:** The **strategic-funds method** encourages executives to look at developmental expenses as being different from expenses required for current operations. The accounting statement for a corporate unit enters strategic funds as a separate entry below the current ROI. It is, therefore, possible to distinguish between expense dollars consumed in the generation of current revenues and those invested in the future of a business. Therefore, a manager can be evaluated on both a short- and a long-term basis and has an incentive to invest strategic funds in the future. For example, begin with the total sales of a unit ($12,300,000). Subtract cost of goods sold ($6,900,000) leaving a gross margin of $5,400,000. Subtract general and administrative expenses ($3,700,000) leaving an operating profit/ROI of $1,700,000. So far, this is standard accounting procedure. The strategic-funds approach goes one step further by subtracting an additional $1,000,000 for "strategic funds/development expenses." This results in a pretax profit of $700,000. This strategic-funds approach is a good way to ensure that the manager of a high-performing unit (e.g., star) not only generates $700,000 in ROI, but also invests $1 million in the unit for its continued growth. It also ensures that a manager of a developing unit is appropriately evaluated on the basis of market share growth and product development and not on ROI or cash flow.

An effective way to achieve the desired strategic results through a reward system is to combine the three approaches:

1. Segregate strategic funds from short-term funds, as is done in the strategic-funds method.
2. Develop a weighted-factor chart for each SBU.
3. Measure performance on three bases: The pretax profit indicated by the strategic-funds approach, the weighted factors, and the long-term evaluation of the SBUs' and the corporation's performance.

Walt Disney Company, Dow Chemical, IBM, and General Motors are just some firms in which top management compensation is contingent upon the company's achieving strategic objectives.

The board of directors and top management must be careful to develop a compensation plan that achieves the appropriate objectives. One reason why top executives are often criticized for being overpaid (the ratio of CEO to average worker pay is currently 400 to 1)[108] is that in a large number of corporations the incentives for sales growth exceed those for shareholder wealth, resulting in too many executives pursuing growth to the detriment of shareholder value.[109]

End of Chapter SUMMARY

Having strategic management without evaluation and control is like playing football without any scoring or referees. Unless strategic management improves performance, it is only an exercise. In business, the bottom-line measure of performance is making a profit that exceeds that of our competitors. If people aren't willing to pay more than what it costs to make a product or provide a service, that business will not continue to exist. **Chapter 1** explains that organizations engaging in strategic management outperform those that do not. The sticky issue is: How should we measure performance? Is measuring profits sufficient? Does an income statement tell us what we need to know? The accrual method of accounting enables us to count a sale even when the cash has not yet been received. Therefore, a firm might be profitable, but still go bankrupt because it can't pay its bills. Is profit the amount of cash on hand at the end of the year after paying costs and expenses? What if you made a big sale in December and must wait until January to get paid? Many retail stores use a fiscal year ending January 31 (to include returned Christmas items that were bought in December) instead of a calendar year ending December 31. Should two managers receive the same bonus when their divisions earn the same profit, even though one division is much smaller than the other? What of the manager who is managing a new product introduction that won't make a profit for another two years?

Evaluation and control is one of the most difficult parts of strategic management. No one measure can tell us what we need to know. That's why we need to use not only the traditional measures of financial performance, such as net earnings, ROI, and EPS, but we need to consider using EVA or MVA and a balanced scorecard, among other possibilities. On top of that, science informs us that just attempting to measure something changes what is being measured. The measurement of performance can and does result in short-term–oriented actions and goal displacement. That's why experts suggest we use multiple measures of only those things that provide a meaningful and reliable picture of events: Measure those 20% of the factors that determine 80% of the results. Once the appropriate performance measurements are taken, it is possible to get closer to determining whether the strategy was successful. As shown in the model of strategic management depicted at the beginning this chapter, the measured results of corporate performance allow us to decide whether we need to reformulate the strategy, improve its implementation, or gather more information about our competition.

MyManagementLab®

Go to **mymanagementlab.com** to complete the problems marked with this icon .

KEY TERMS

80/20 rule (p. 323)
activity-based costing (ABC) (p. 307)
balanced scorecard (p. 311)
behavior control (p. 305)
behavior substitution (p. 322)
benchmarking (p. 315)
earnings per share (EPS) (p. 309)
economic value added (EVA) (p. 310)
enterprise resource planning (ERP) (p. 319)
enterprise risk management (ERM) (p. 308)
expense center (p. 314)

free cash flow (p. 309)
goal displacement (p. 322)
input controls (p. 305)
investment center (p. 315)
ISO 9000 Standards Service (p. 306)
ISO 14000 Standards Service (p. 306)
key performance measures (p. 312)
long-term evaluation method (p. 324)
management audit (p. 313)
market value added (p. 310)
operating cash flow (p. 309)
output controls (p. 305)
performance (p. 304)

profit center (p. 314)
responsibility center (p. 314)
return on equity (ROE) (p. 309)
return on investment (ROI) (p. 308)
revenue center (p. 314)
shareholder value (p. 309)
short-term orientation (p. 321)
standard cost center (p. 314)
steering control (p. 304)
strategic-funds method (p. 325)
suboptimization (p. 322)
transfer pricing (p. 314)
weighted-factor method (p. 324)

MyManagementLab®

Go to **mymanagementlab.com** for Auto-graded writing questions as well as the following Assisted-graded writing questions:

11-1. Explain why ROI might not be the best measure of firm performance.

11-2. What are the best methods for evaluating the performance of the top management team?

DISCUSSION QUESTIONS

11-3. Is Figure 11–1 a realistic model of the evaluation and control process?

✪ **11-4.** What are some examples of behavior controls? Output controls? Input controls?

✪ **11-5.** How does EVA improve our knowledge of performance over ROI, ROE, or EPS?

11-6. What issues affect your faith in a transfer price as a substitute for a market price in measuring a profit center's performance?

✪ **11-7.** Is the evaluation and control process appropriate for a corporation that emphasizes creativity? Are control and creativity compatible?

STRATEGIC PRACTICE EXERCISE

Each year, *Fortune* magazine publishes an article entitled, "America's Most Admired Companies." It lists the 50 most admired companies in the United States and in the world. *Fortune's* rankings are based on scoring publicly held companies on what it calls nine key attributes of reputation: Ability to attract and retain talented people; Quality of management; Social responsibility to the community and the environment; Innovativeness; Quality of products or services; Wise use of corporate assets; Financial soundness; Long-term investment value; and Effectiveness in doing business globally. In 2012, *Fortune* asked Hay Group to survey more than 15,000 people from multiple industries. Respondents were asked to choose the companies they admired most, regardless of industry. *Fortune* has been publishing this list since 1982. The 2012 *Fortune* list of the top 10 most admired U.S. companies were (starting with #1): Apple, Google, Amazon.com, Coca-Cola, IBM, FedEx, Berkshire Hathaway, Starbucks, Procter & Gamble, and Southwest Airlines.[110]

Eight years earlier in 2004, the list of 10 most admired U.S. companies was: Wal-Mart, Berkshire Hathaway, Southwest Airlines, General Electric, Dell Computer, Microsoft, Johnson & Johnson, Starbucks, FedEx, and IBM.[111]

■ Why did the most admired U.S. firm in 2004 (Wal-Mart) drop off the 10 listing in 2012?

■ Why did Apple go from not even being on the 10 U.S. listing in 2004 to No. 1 in 2012?

■ Which firms appeared on both top 10 lists? Why?

■ Why did some firms drop off the list from 2004 to 2012 and why did others get included?

■ What companies should be on the most admired list this year? Why?

Try One of These Exercises

1. Go to the library and find a "Most Admired Companies" *Fortune* article from the 1980s or early 1990s and compare that list to the latest one. (See http://money.cnn.com/magazines/fortune/most-admired/2012/full_list/ for the latest list.) Which companies have fallen out of the top 10? Pick one of the companies and investigate why it is no longer on the list.

2. Given the impact of technology on various industrial sectors, which companies are likely to be on *Fortune's* "Most Admired Companies" in 10 years?

3. Compare *Fortune's* list to that compiled by the Reputation Institute (www.reputationinstitute.com). Why is there a difference between the ratings?

NOTES

1. http://www.airlinefinancials.com/airline_data_comparisons. html; http://www.bts.gov/press_releases/2012/bts011_12/html/ bts011_12.html.

2. R. Barker, "A Surprise in Office Depot's In-Box," *Business-Week* (October 25, 2004), p. 122.

3. C. W. Hart, "Customer Service: Beating the Market with Customer Satisfaction," *Harvard Business Review* (March 2007), pp. 30–32.

4. S. E. Ante, "Giving the Boss the Big Picture," *BusinessWeek* (February 13, 2006), pp. 48–51.

5. R. Muralidharan and R. D. Hamilton III, "Aligning Multinational Control Systems," *Long Range Planning* (June 1999), pp. 352–361. These types are based on W. G. Ouchy, "The Relationship Between Organizational Structure and Organizational Control," *Administrative Science Quarterly* (Vol. 20, 1977), pp. 95–113 and W. G. Ouchi, "A Conceptual Framework for the Design of Organizational Control Mechanisms," *Management Science* (Vol. 25, 1979), pp. 833–848. Muralidhara and Hamilton refer to Ouchi's clan control as input control.

6. W. G. Rowe and P. M. Wright, "Related and Unrelated Diversification and Their Effect on Human Resource Management Controls," *Strategic Management Journal* (April 1997), pp. 329–338.

7. R. Muralidharan and R. D. Hamilton III, "Aligning Multinational Control Systems," *Long Range Planning* (June 1999) pp. 356–359.

8. B. Manders and H. de Vries, "Does ISO 9001 Pay? Analysis of 42 Studies," *ISO* (October 2012), http://www.iso.org/iso/home/ news_index/news_archive/news.htm?refid=Ref1665.

9. M. V. Uzumeri, "ISO 9000 and Other Metastandards: Principles for Management Practice?" *Academy of Management Executive* (February 1997), pp. 21–36.

10. A. M. Hormozi, "Understanding and Implementing ISO 9000: A Manager's Guide," *SAM Advanced Management Journal* (Autumn 1995), pp. 4–11.

11. M. Henricks, "A New Standard," *Entrepreneur* (October 2002) p. 84.

12. L. Armstrong, "Someone to Watch Over You," *BusinessWeek* (July 10, 2000), pp. 189 -190; https://www.privacyrights.org/ fs/fs7-work.htm.

13. J. K. Shank and V. Govindarajan, *Strategic Cost Management* (New York: The Free Press, 1993).

14. S. S. Rao, "ABCs of Cost Control," *Inc. Technology* (No. 2, 1997), pp. 79–81.

15. R. Gruber, "Why You Should Consider Activity-Based Costing," *Small Business Forum* (Spring 1994), pp. 20–36.

16. "Easier Than ABC," *The Economist* (October 25, 2003), p. 56.

17. T. P. Pare, "A New Tool for Managing Costs," *Fortune* (June 14, 1993), pp. 124–129. For further information on the use of ABC with EVA, see T. L. Pohlen and B. J. Coleman, "Evaluating Internal Operations and Supply Chain Performance Using EVA and ABC," *SAM Advanced Management Journal* (Spring 2005), pp. 45–58.

18. K. Hopkins, "The Risk Agenda," *BusinessWeek*, Special Advertising Section (November 22, 2004), pp. 166–170.

19. T. L. Barton, W. G. Shenkir, and P. L. Walker, "Managing Risk: An Enterprise-wide Approach," *Financial Executive* (March/April 2001), p. 51.

20. T. L. Barton, W. G. Shenkir, and P. L. Walker, "Managing Risk: An Enterprise-Wide Approach," pp. 48–51; P. L. Walker, W. G. Shenkir, and T. L. Barton, "Enterprise Risk Management: Putting It All Together," *Internal Auditor* (August 2003), pp. 50–55.

21. T. J. Andersen, "The Performance Relationship of Effective Risk Management: Exploring the Firm-Specific Investment Rationale," *Long Range Planning* (April 2008), pp. 155–176.

22. C. K. Brancato, *New Corporate Performance* Measures(New York: Conference Board, 1995); C. D. Ittner, D. F. Larcker, and M. V. Rajan, "The Choice of Performance Measures in Annual Bonus Contracts," working paper reported by K. Z. Andrews in "Executive Bonuses," *Harvard Business Review* (January–February 1996), pp. 8–9; J. Low and T. Siesfeld, "Measures That Matter: Wall Street Considers Non-Financial Performance More Than You Think," *Strategy & Leadership* (March/April 1998), pp. 24–30.

23. A similar measure, EBITDA (Earnings Before Interest, Taxes, Depreciation, and Amortization), is sometimes used, but is *not* determined in accordance with generally accepted accounting principles and is thus subject to varying calculations.

24. J. M. Laderman, "Earnings, Schmernings: Look at the Cash," *BusinessWeek* (July 24, 1989), pp. 56–57.

25. H. Greenberg, "Don't Count on Cash Flow," *Fortune* (May 13, 2002), p. 176; A. Tergesen, "Cash-Flow Hocus-Pocus," *BusinessWeek* (July 15, 2002), pp. 130–132.

26. "Green Revolutionary," *The Economist* (April 7, 2007), p. 66.

27. E. H. Hall, Jr., and J. Lee, "Diversification Strategies: Creating Value of Generating Profits?" paper presented to the annual meeting of the *Decision Sciences Institute*, Orlando, FL (November 18–21, 2000).

28. P. C. Brewer, G. Chandra, and C. A. Hock, "Economic Value Added (EVA): Its Uses and Limitations," SAM *Advanced Management Journal* (Spring 1999), pp. 4–11.

29. D. J. Skyrme and D. M. Amidon, "New Measures of Success," *Journal of Business Strategy* (January/February 1998), p. 23; http://www.investopedia.com/articles/fundamental/03/031203 .asp#axzz2Cgj4StE0.

30. G. B. Stewart III, "EVA Works—But Not if You Make These Common Mistakes," *Fortune* (May 1, 1995), pp. 117–118.

31. S. Tully, "The Real Key to Creating Wealth," *Fortune* (September 20, 1993), p. 38.

32. A. Ehrbar, "Using EVA to Measure Performance and Assess Strategy," *Strategy & Leadership* (May/June 1999), pp. 20–24.

33. P. C. Brewer, G. Chandra, and C. A. Hock, "Economic Value Added (EVA): Its Uses and Limitations," *SAM Advanced Management Journal* (Spring 1999), pp. 7–9.

34. R. Sarbapriya, "Efficacy of Economic Value Added Concept in Business Performance Measurement," *Advances in Information Technology and Management* (Vol. 2, No. 2), pp. 260–267; Pro: K. Lehn and A. K. Makhija, "EVA and MVA as Performance Measures and Signals for Strategic Change," *Strategy & Leadership* (May/June 1996), pp. 34–38; Con: D. I. Goldberg, "Shareholder Value Debunked," *Strategy & Leadership* (January/ February 2000), pp. 30–36.

35. A. Ehrbar, "Using EVA to Measure Performance and Assess Strategy," *Strategy & Leadership* (May/June 1999), p. 21.

36. S. Tully, "America's Wealth Creators," *Fortune* (November 22, 1999), pp. 275–284; A. B. Fisher, "Creating Stockholder Wealth: Market Value Added," *Fortune* (December 11, 1995), pp. 105–116.

37. A. B. Fisher, "Creating Stockholder Wealth: Market Value Added," *Fortune* (December 11, 1995). pp. 105–116.

38. K. Lehn and A. K. Makhija, "EVA and MVA as Performance Measures and Signals for Strategic Change," p. 37.

39. R. S. Kaplan and D. P. Norton, "Using the Balanced Scorecard as a Strategic Management System," *Harvard Business Review* (January–February 1996), pp. 75–85; R. S. Kaplan and D. P. Norton, "The Balanced Scorecard—Measures That Drive Performance," *Harvard Business Review* (January–February, 1992), pp. 71–79.

40. D. I. Goldenberg, "Shareholder Value Debunked," p. 34.

41. In later work, Kaplan and Norton used the term "perspectives" and replaced "internal business perspective" with "process perspective" and "innovation and learning" with "learning and growth perspective." See R. S. Norton and D. P. Norton, "How to Implement a New Strategy Without Disrupting Your Organization," *Harvard Business Review* (March 2006), pp. 100–109.

42. C. K. Brancato, *New Performance Measures* (New York: Conference Board, 1995).

43. D. Rigby and B. Bilodeau, "Management Tools and Trends 2011," *Bain and Company*, http://www.bain.com/Images/BAIN_BRIEF_Management_Tools.pdf.

44. B. P. Stivers and T. Joyce, "Building a Balanced Performance Management System," *SAM Advanced Management Journal* (Spring 2000), pp. 22–29.

45. Kaplan and Norton (March, 2006), p. 107.

46. G. J. M. Braam and E. Nijssen, "Performance Effects of Using the Balanced Scorecard: A Note on the Dutch Experience," *Long Range Planning* (August 2004), pp. 335–349; H. Ahn, "Applying the Balanced Scorecard Concept: An Experience Report," *Long Range Planning* (August 2001), pp. 441–461.

47. S. P. Mader, D. Vuchot, and S. Fukushima of Korn/Ferry International, *33rd Annual Board of Directors Study* (2006), p. 9.

48. R. M. Rosen and F. Adair, "CEOs Misperceive Top Teams' Performance," *Harvard Business Review* (September 2007), p. 30.

49. S. P. Mader, D. Vuchot, and S. Fukushima of Korn/Ferry International, *33rd Annual Board of Directors Study* (2006), p. 33.

50. Ibid., p. 9.

51. J. L. Kerr and W. B. Werther Jr., "The Next Frontier in Corporate Governance: Engaging the Board in Strategy," *Organizational Dynamics* (Vol. 37, No. 2, 2008), pp. 112–124. This agrees with figures (73% and 38%, respectively) reported by Korn/Ferry International in its *33rd Annual Board of Directors Study* from data gathered in 2006, p. 8.

52. R. Charan, *Boards at Work* (San Francisco: Jossey-Bass, 1998), pp. 176–177.

53. T. D. Schellhardt, "Directors Get Tough: Inside a CEO Performance Review," *The Wall Street Journal Interactive Edition* (April 27, 1998).

54. T. L. Wheelen and J. D. Hunger, "Using the Strategic Audit," *SAM Advanced Management Journal* (Winter 1987), pp. 4–12; G. Donaldson, "A New Tool for Boards: The Strategic Audit," *Harvard Business Review* (July–August 1995), pp. 99–107.

55. H. Threat, "Measurement Is Free," *Strategy & Leadership* (May/June 1999), pp. 16–19; http://www.fedex.com/ma/about/overview/innovation.html.

56. 2010 Global Transfer Pricing Survey, Ernst & Young; http://www.ey.com/Publication/vwLUAssets/Global_transfer_pricing_survey_-_2010/$FILE/2010-Globaltransferpricingsurvey_17Jan.pdf.

57. H. Rothman, "You Need Not Be Big to Benchmark," *Nation's Business* (December 1992), p. 64.

58. C. W. Von Bergen and B. Soper, "A Problem with Benchmarking: Using Shaping as a Solution," *SAM Advanced Management Journal* (Autumn 1995), pp. 16–19.

59. http://www.bain.com/publications/articles/management-tools-2011-benchmarking.aspx.

60. R. J. Kennedy, "Benchmarking and Its Myths," *Competitive Intelligence Magazine* (April–June 2000), pp. 28–33.

61. "Just the Facts: Numbers Runners," *Journal of Business Strategy* (July/August 2002), p. 3; L. Mann, D. Samson, and D. Dow, "A Field Experiment on the Effects of Benchmarking and Goal Setting on Company Sales Performance," *Journal of Management* (Vol. 24, No. 1, 1998), pp. 73–96.

62. S. A. W. Drew, "From Knowledge to Action: The Impact of Benchmarking on Organizational Performance," *Long Range Planning* (June 1997), pp. 427–441.

63. S. M. Robbins and R. B. Stobaugh, "The Bent Measuring Stick for Foreign Subsidiaries," *Harvard Business Review* (September–October 1973), p. 82.

64. J. D. Daniels and L. H. Radebaugh, *International Business*, 5th ed. (Reading, MA: Addison-Wesley, 1989), pp. 673–674.

65. D. Henry, "A Better Way to Keep the Books," *BusinessWeek* (September 15, 2008), p. 35; "International Accounting: Speaking in Tongues," *The Economist* (May 19, 2007), pp. 77–78; C. Hackett, "Convergence of U.S. GAAP and IFRS: Where Do Things Stand?" (http://www.cshco.com/News/Articles/Convergence_of_U.S._GAAP_and_IFRS%3A_Where_do_things_stand%3F/).

66. W. A. Johnson and R. J. Kirsch, "International Transfer Pricing and Decision Making in United States Multinationals," *International Journal of Management* (June 1991), pp. 554–561.

67. *KPMG's Corporate Tax Rate Table 2012*, (http://www.kpmg.com/global/en/services/tax/tax-tools-and-resources/pages/corporate-tax-rates-table.aspx).

68. "Fixing the Bottom Line," *Time* (November 23, 1992), p. 20.

69. J. M. L. Poon, R. Ainuddin, and H. Affrim, "Management Policies and Practices of American, British, European, and Japanese Subsidiaries in Malaysia: A Comparative Study," *International Journal of Management* (December 1990), pp. 467–474.

70. M. Egan, "Setting Standards: Strategic Advantages in International Trade," *Business Strategy Review* (Vol. 13, No. 1, 2002), pp. 51–64; L. Swatkowski, "Building Towards International Standards," *Appliance* (December 1999), p. 30.

71. C. W. L. Hill, P. Hwang, and W. C. Kim, "An Eclectic Theory of the Choice of International Entry Mode," *Strategic Management Journal* (February 1990), pp. 117–128; D. Lei, J. W. Slocum, Jr., and R. W. Slater, "Global Strategy and Reward Systems: The Key Roles of Management Development and Corporate Culture," *Organizational Dynamics* (Autumn 1990), pp. 27–41; W. R. Fannin and A. F. Rodrigues, "National or Global?—Control vs. Flexibility," *Long Range Planning* (October 1986), pp. 84–188.

72. A. V. Phatak, *International Dimensions of Management*, 2nd ed. (Boston: Kent, 1989), pp. 155–157.

73. S. McAlary, "Three Pitfalls in ERP Implementation," *Strategy & Leadership* (October/November/December 1999), pp. 49–50.

74. J. B. White, D. Clark, and S. Ascarelli, "This German Software Is Complex, Expensive—And Wildly Popular," *The Wall Street Journal* (March 14, 1997), pp. A1, A8; D. Ward, "Whirlpool Takes a Dive with Software Snarl," *Des Moines Register* (April 29, 2000), p. 8D.

75. J. Verville, R. Palanisamy, C. Bernadas, and A. Halingten, "ERP Acquisition Planning: A Critical Dimension for Making the Right Choice," *Long Range Planning* (February 2007), pp. 45–63.

76. http://www.rfidblog.org/entry/tesco-postpones-rfid-implementation-at-its-stores/.

77. "Radio Silence," *The Economist* (June 9, 2007), pp. 20–21.

78. C. Krivda, "RFID After Compliance: Integration and Payback," Special Advertising Section, *BusinessWeek* (December 20, 2004), pp. 91–98.

79. D. Leonard and J. Tozzi, "Why Don't More Hospitals Use Electronic Health Records?" *Bloomberg Businessweek* (June 21, 2012), http://www.businessweek.com/articles/2012-06-21/why-dont-more-hospitals-use-electronic-health-records.

80. A. Lashinsky, "Meg and the Machine," *Fortune* (September 1, 2003), pp. 68–78.

81. R. M. Hodgetts and M. S. Wortman, *Administrative Policy*, 2nd ed. (New York: John Wiley & Sons, 1980), p. 128.

82. J. R. Wooldridge and C. C. Snow, "Stock Market Reaction to Strategic Investment Decisions," *Strategic Management Journal* (September 1990), pp. 353–363.

83. M. C. Jensen, "Corporate Budgeting Is Broken—Let's Fix It," *Harvard Business Review* (November 2001), pp. 94–101.

84. C. M. Christensen, S. P. Kaufman, and W. C. Smith, "Innovation Killers: How Financial Tools Destroy Your Capacity to Do New Things," *Harvard Business Review* (January 2008), pp. 98–105.

85. P. Hsieh, T. Keller, and S. R. Rajan, "The Misguided Practice of Earnings Guidance," *McKinsey Quarterly* (Spring 2006), pp. 1–5.

86. "Audit Firms Sued in HP's Autonomy Acquisition," *Reuters* (November 28, 2012), (http://www.reuters.com/article/2012/11/29/hp-autonomy-auditors-idUSL1E8MS8ZX20121129).

87. D. Henry "Fuzzy Numbers," *BusinessWeek* (October 4, 2004), pp. 79–88.

88. A. Rappaport, "10 Ways to Create Shareholder Value," *Harvard Business Review* (September 2006), pp. 66–77.

89. D. R. Schmidt and K. L. Fowler, "Post-Acquisition Financial Performance and Executive Compensation," *Strategic Management Journal* (November–December 1990), pp. 559–569.

90. H. L. Tosi, S. Werner, J. P. Katz, and L. R. Gomez-Mejia, "How Much Does Performance Matter? A Meta-Analysis of CEO Pay Studies," *Journal of Management* (Vol. 26, No. 2, 2000), pp. 301–339; P. Wright, M. Kroll, and D. Elenkov, "Acquisition Returns, Increase in Firm Size, and Chief Executive Officer Compensation: The Moderating Role of Monitoring," *Academy of Management Journal* (June 2002), pp. 599–608; S. Werner, H. L. Tosi, and L. Gomez-Mejia, "Organizational Governance and Employee Pay: How Ownership Structure Affects the Firm's Compensation Strategy," *Strategic Management Journal* (April 2005), pp. 377–384.

91. X. Zhang, K. M. Bartol, K. G. Smith, M. D. Pfarrer, and D. M. Khanin, "CEOs on the Edge: Earnings Manipulation and Stock-based Incentive Misalignment," *Academy of Management Journal* (April 2008), pp. 241–258; L. Bebchuk and J. Fried, *Pay Without Performance: The Unfulfilled Promise of Executive Compensation* (Boston: Harvard University Press, 2004); L. A. Benchuk and J. M. Fried, "Pay Without Performance: Overview of the Issues," *Academy of Management Perspectives* (February 2006), pp. 5–24.

92. D. Jones, "Bad News Can Enrich Executives," *Des Moines Register* (November 26, 1999), p. 8S.

93. J. F. Porac, J. B. Wade, and T. G. Pollock, "Industry Categories and the Politics of the Comparable Firm in CEO Compensation," *Administrative Science Quarterly* (March 1999), pp. 112–144. For summaries of current research on executive compensation and performance, see C. E. Devers, A. A. Cannella Jr., G. P. Reilly, and M. E. Yoder, "Executive Compensation: A Multidisciplinary Review of Recent Developments," *Journal of Management* (December 2007), pp. 1016–1072; M. Chan, "Executive Compensation," *Business and Society Review* (March 2008), pp. 129–161; and S. N. Kaplan, "Are CEOs Overpaid?" *Academy of Management Perspective* (May 2008), pp. 5–20.

94. C. D. Ittner and D. F. Larcker, "Coming Up Short," *Harvard Business Review* (November 2003), pp. 88–95.

95. See the classic article by S. Kerr, "On the Folly of Rewarding A, While Hoping for B," *Academy of Management Journal* (Vol. 18, December 1975), pp. 769–783.

96. W. Zellner, E. Schine, and G. Smith, "Trickle-Down Is Trickling Down at Work," *BusinessWeek* (March 18, 1996), p. 34.

97. For more information on how goals can have dysfunctional side effects, see D. C. Kayes, "The Destructive Pursuit of Idealized Goals," *Organizational Dynamics* (Vol. 34, Issue 4, 2005), pp. 391–401.

98. T. J. Peters and R. H. Waterman, *In Search of Excellence* (New York: Harper Collins, 1982), pp. 75–76.

99. T. Aeppel, "Not All Workers Find Idea of Empowerment as Neat as It Sounds," *The Wall Street Journal* (September 8, 1997), pp. A1, A13.

100. R. S. Allen and M. M. Helms, "Employee Perceptions of the Relationship Between Strategy, Rewards, and Organizational Performance," *Journal of Business Strategies* (Fall 2002), pp. 115–140; M. A. Carpenter, "The Price of Change: The Role of CEO Compensation in Strategic Variation and Deviation from Industry Strategy Norms," *Journal of Management* (Vol. 26, No. 6, 2000), pp. 1179–1198; M. A. Carpenter and W. G. Sanders, "The Effects of Top Management Team Pay and Firm Internationalization on MNC Performance," *Journal of Management* (Vol. 30, No. 4, 2004), pp. 509–528; J. D. Shaw, N. Gupta, and J. E. Delery, "Congruence Between Technology and Compensation Systems: Implications for Strategy Implementation," *Strategic Management Journal* (April 2001), pp. 379–386; E. F. Montemazon, "Congruence Between Pay Policy and Competitive Strategy in High-Performing Organizations," *Journal of Management* (Vol. 22, No. 6, 1996), pp. 889–908.

101. D. B. Balkin and L. R. Gomez-Mejia, "Matching Compensation and Organizational Strategies," *Strategic Management Journal* (February 1990), pp. 153–169.

102. C. S. Galbraith, "The Effect of Compensation Programs and Structure on SBU Competitive Strategy: A Study of Technology-Intensive Firms," *Strategic Management Journal* (July 1991), pp. 353–370.

103. T. A. Stewart, "CEO Pay: Mom Wouldn't Approve," *Fortune* (March 31, 1997), pp. 119–120.

104. "The Politics of Pay," *The Economist* (March 24, 2007), pp. 71–72.

105. P. J. Stonich, "The Performance Measurement and Reward System: Critical to Strategic Management," *Organizational Dynamics* (Winter 1984), pp. 45–57.

106. A. Rappaport, "New Thinking on How to Link Executive Pay with Performance," *Harvard Business Review* (March–April 1999), pp. 91–101.

107. Motley Fool, "Fool's School: Hooray for GE," *The* (Ames, IA) *Tribune* (October 27, 2003), p. 1D.

108. M. Chan, "Executive Compensation," *Business and Society Review* (March 2008), pp. 129–161.

109. S. E. O'Byrne and S. D. Young, "Why Executive Pay Is Failing," *Harvard Business Review* (June 2006), p. 28.

110. *Fortune* magazine Web site accessed on December 4, 2012, at http://money.cnn.com/magazines/fortune/most-admired/2012/full_list/.

111. A. Harrington, "America's Most Admired Companies," *Fortune* (March 8, 2004), pp. 80–81.

PART 5

Introduction to
Case Analysis

CHAPTER 12

Suggestions for Case Analysis

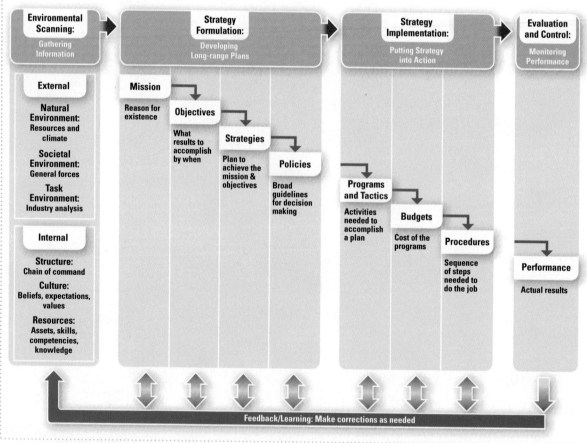

Environmental Scanning: Gathering Information

External

Natural Environment: Resources and climate

Societal Environment: General forces

Task Environment: Industry analysis

Internal

Structure: Chain of command

Culture: Beliefs, expectations, values

Resources: Assets, skills, competencies, knowledge

Strategy Formulation: Developing Long-range Plans

Mission Reason for existence

Objectives What results to accomplish by when

Strategies Plan to achieve the mission & objectives

Policies Broad guidelines for decision making

Strategy Implementation: Putting Strategy into Action

Programs and Tactics Activities needed to accomplish a plan

Budgets Cost of the programs

Procedures Sequence of steps needed to do the job

Evaluation and Control: Monitoring Performance

Performance Actual results

Feedback/Learning: Make corrections as needed

MyManagementLab®

★ Improve Your Grade!

Over 10 million students improved their results using the Pearson MyLabs. Visit **mymanagementlab.com** for simulations, tutorials, and end-of-chapter problems.

Learning Objectives

After reading this chapter, you should be able to:

- Research the case situation as needed
- Analyze financial statements by using ratios and common-size statements
- Use the strategic audit as a method of organizing and analyzing case information

Identifying Red Flags

Howard Schilit, founder of the Center for Financial Research & Analysis (CFRA), works with a staff of 15 analysts to screen financial databases and analyze public financial filings of 3600 companies, looking for inconsistencies and aggressive accounting methods. Schilit calls this search for hidden weaknesses in a company's performance *forensic accounting*. He advises anyone interested in analyzing a company to look deeply into its financial statements. For example, when the CFRA noticed that Kraft Foods made $122 million in acquisitions in 2002, but claimed $539 million as "goodwill" assets related to the purchases, it concluded that Kraft was padding its earnings with one-time gains. According to Schilit, unusually high goodwill gains related to recent acquisitions is a *red flag* that suggests an underlying problem.

Schilit proposes a short checklist of items to examine for red flags:

- **Cash flow from operations should exceed net income:** If cash flow from operations drops below net income, it could mean that the company is propping up its earnings by selling assets, borrowing cash, or shuffling numbers. Says Schilit, "You could have spotted the problems at Enron by just doing this."

- **Accounts receivable should not grow faster than sales:** A firm facing slowing sales can make itself look better by inflating accounts receivable with expected future sales and by making sales to customers who are not creditworthy. "It's like mailing a contract to a dead person and then counting it as a sale," says Schilit.

- **Gross margins should not fluctuate over time:** A change of more than 2% in either direction from year to year is worth a closer look. It could mean that the company is using other revenue, such as sales of assets or write-offs to boost profits. Sunbeam reported an increase of 10% in gross margins just before it was investigated by the SEC.

- **Examine carefully information about top management and the board:** When Schilit learned that the chairman of Checkers Restaurants had put his two young sons on the board, he warned investors of nepotism. Two years later, Checkers' huge debt caused its stock to fall 85% and all three family members were forced out of the company.
- **Footnotes are important:** When companies change their accounting assumptions to make the statements more attractive, they often bury their rationale in the footnotes.

Schilit makes his living analyzing companies and selling his reports to investors. Annual reports and financial statements provide a lot of information about a company's health, but it's hard to find problem areas when management is massaging the numbers to make the company appear more attractive than it is. That's why Michelle Leder created her Web site, www.footnoted.org. She likes to highlight "the things that companies bury in their routine SEC filings." This type of in-depth, investigative analysis is a key part of analyzing strategy cases. This chapter provides various analytical techniques and suggestions for conducting this kind of case analysis.

SOURCES: M. Heimer, "Wall Street Sherlock," *Smart Money* (July 2003), pp. 103–107. D. Stead, "The Secrets in SEC Filings," *BusinessWeek* (September 1, 2008), p. 12.

The Case Method

The analysis and discussion of case problems has been the most popular method of teaching strategy and policy for many years. The case method offers the opportunity to move from a narrow, specialized view that emphasizes functional techniques to a broader, less precise analysis of the overall corporation. Cases present actual business situations and enable you to examine both successful and unsuccessful corporations. In case analysis, you might be asked to critically analyze a situation in which a manager had to make a decision of long-term corporate importance. This approach gives you a feel for what it is like to face making and implementing strategic decisions.

Researching the Case Situation

You should not restrict yourself only to the information written in the case unless your instructor states otherwise. You should, if possible, undertake outside research about the environmental setting. Check the decision date of each case (typically the latest date mentioned in the case) to find out when the situation occurred and then screen the business periodicals for that time period. An understanding of the economy during that period will help you avoid making a serious error in your analysis—for example, suggesting a sale of stock when the stock market is at an all-time low or taking on more debt when the prime interest rate is over 15%. Information about the industry will provide insights into its competitive activities. *Important Note: Don't go beyond the decision date of the case in your research unless directed to do so by your instructor.*

Use computerized company and industry information services such as Compustat, Compact Disclosure, and a wide variety of information sources available on the Internet including

Hoover's online corporate directory (www.hoovers.com) and the U.S. Securities and Exchange Commission's EDGAR database (www.sec.gov) provide access to corporate annual reports and 10-K forms. This background will give you an appreciation for the situation as it was experienced by the participants in the case. Use a search engine such as Google or Bing to find additional information about the industry and the company.

A company's **annual report** and **SEC 10-K form** from the year of the case can be very helpful. According to the Yankelovich Partners survey firm, 8 out of 10 portfolio managers and 75% of security analysts use annual reports when making decisions.[1] They contain not only the usual income statements and balance sheets, but also cash flow statements and notes to the financial statements indicating why certain actions were taken. 10-K forms include detailed information not usually available in an annual report. **SEC 10-Q forms** include quarterly financial reports. **SEC 14-A forms** include detailed information on members of a company's board of directors and proxy statements for annual meetings. Some resources available for research into the economy and a corporation's industry are suggested in **Appendix 12.A**.

A caveat: Before obtaining additional information about the company profiled in a particular case, ask your instructor if doing so is appropriate for your class assignment. Your strategy instructor may want you to stay within the confines of the case information provided in the book. In this case, it is usually acceptable to at least learn more about the societal environment at the time of the case.

Financial Analysis: A Place to Begin

Once you have read a case, a good place to begin your analysis is with the financial statements. **Ratio analysis** is the calculation of ratios from data in these statements. It is done to identify possible financial strengths or weaknesses. Thus it is a valuable part of the SWOT approach. A review of key financial ratios can help you assess a company's overall situation and pinpoint some problem areas. Ratios are useful regardless of firm size and enable you to compare a company's ratios with industry averages. **Table 12–1** lists some of the most important financial ratios, which are (1) **liquidity ratios**, (2) **profitability ratios**, (3) **activity ratios**, and (4) **leverage ratios**.

ANALYZING FINANCIAL STATEMENTS

In your analysis, do not simply make an exhibit that includes all the ratios (unless your instructor requires you to do so), but select and discuss only those ratios that have an impact on the company's problems. For instance, accounts receivable and inventory may provide a source of funds. If receivables and inventories are double the industry average, reducing them may provide needed cash. In this situation, the case report should include not only sources of funds but also the number of dollars freed for use. Compare these ratios with industry averages to discover whether the company is out of line with others in the industry. Annual and quarterly industry ratios can be found in the library or on the Internet. (See the resources for case research in **Appendix 12.A**.) In the years to come, expect to see financial entries for the trading of CERs (Certified Emissions Reductions). This is the amount of money a company earns from reducing carbon emissions and selling them on the open market.

TABLE 12–1 Financial Ratio Analysis

	Formula	How Expressed	Meaning
1. Liquidity Ratios			
Current ratio	$\dfrac{\text{Current assets}}{\text{Current liabilities}}$	Decimal	A short-term indicator of the company's ability to pay its short-term liabilities from short-term assets; how much of current assets are available to cover each dollar of current liabilities.
Quick (acid test) ratio	$\dfrac{\text{Current assets} - \text{Inventory}}{\text{Current liabilities}}$	Decimal	Measures the company's ability to pay off its short-term obligations from current assets, excluding inventories.
Inventory to net working capital	$\dfrac{\text{Inventory}}{\text{Current assets} - \text{Current liabilities}}$	Decimal	A measure of inventory balance; measures the extent to which the cushion of excess current assets over current liabilities may be threatened by unfavorable changes in inventory.
Cash ratio	$\dfrac{\text{Cash} + \text{Cash equivalents}}{\text{Current liabilities}}$	Decimal	Measures the extent to which the company's capital is in cash or cash equivalents; shows how much of the current obligations can be paid from cash or near-cash assets.
2. Profitability Ratios			
Net profit margin	$\dfrac{\text{Net profit after taxes}}{\text{Net sales}}$	Percentage	Shows how much after-tax profits are generated by each dollar of sales.
Gross profit margin	$\dfrac{\text{Sales} - \text{Cost of goods sold}}{\text{Net sales}}$	Percentage	Indicates the total margin available to cover other expenses beyond cost of goods sold and still yield a profit.
Return on investment (ROI)	$\dfrac{\text{Net profit after taxes}}{\text{Total assets}}$	Percentage	Measures the rate of return on the total assets utilized in the company; a measure of management's efficiency, it shows the return on all the assets under its control, regardless of source of financing.
Return on equity (ROE)	$\dfrac{\text{Net profit after taxes}}{\text{Shareholders' equity}}$	Percentage	Measures the rate of return on the book value of shareholders' total investment in the company.
Earnings per share (EPS)	$\dfrac{\text{Net profit after taxes} - \text{Preferred stock dividends}}{\text{Average number of common shares}}$	Dollars per share	Shows the after-tax earnings generated for each share of common stock.
3. Activity Ratios			
Inventory turnover	$\dfrac{\text{Net sales}}{\text{Inventory}}$	Decimal	Measures the number of times that average inventory of finished goods was turned over or sold during a period of time, usually a year.
Days of inventory	$\dfrac{\text{Inventory}}{\text{Cost of goods sold} + 365}$	Days	Measures the number of one day's worth of inventory that a company has on hand at any given time.

TABLE 12–1   Financial Ratio Analysis, (continued)

	Formula	How Expressed	Meaning
Net working capital turnover	$$\frac{\text{Net sales}}{\text{Net working capital}}$$	Decimal	Measures how effectively the net working capital is used to generate sales.
Asset turnover	$$\frac{\text{Sales}}{\text{Total assets}}$$	Decimal	Measures the utilization of all the company's assets; measures how many sales are generated by each dollar of assets.
Fixed asset turnover	$$\frac{\text{Sales}}{\text{Fixed assets}}$$	Decimal	Measures the utilization of the company's fixed assets (i.e., plant and equipment); measures how many sales are generated by each dollar of fixed assets.
Average collection period	$$\frac{\text{Accounts receivable}}{\text{Sales for year} + 365}$$	Days	Indicates the average length of time in days that a company must wait to collect a sale after making it; may be compared to the credit terms offered by the company to its customers.
Accounts receivable turnover	$$\frac{\text{Annual credit sales}}{\text{Accounts receivable}}$$	Decimal	Indicates the number of times that accounts receivable are cycled during the period (usually a year).
Accounts payable period	$$\frac{\text{Accounts payable}}{\text{Purchase for year} \div 365}$$	Days	Indicates the average length of time in days that the company takes to pay its credit purchases.
Days of cash	$$\frac{\text{Cash}}{\text{Net sales for year} \div 365}$$	Days	Indicates the number of days of cash on hand, at present sales levels.
4. Leverage Ratios Debt-to-asset ratio	$$\frac{\text{Total debt}}{\text{Total assets}}$$	Percentage	Measures the extent to which borrowed funds have been used to finance the company's assets.
Debt-to-equity ratio	$$\frac{\text{Total debt}}{\text{Shareholders' equity}}$$	Percentage	Measures the funds provided by creditors versus the funds provided by owners.
Long-term debt to capital structure	$$\frac{\text{Long-term debt}}{\text{Shareholders' equity}}$$	Percentage	Measures the long-term component of capital structure.
Times interest earned	$$\frac{\text{Profit before taxes} + \text{Interest charges}}{\text{Interest charges}}$$	Decimal	Indicates the ability of the company to meet its annual interest costs.
Coverage of fixed charges	$$\frac{\text{Profit before taxes} + \text{Interest charges} + \text{Lease charges}}{\text{Interest charges} + \text{Lease obligations}}$$	Decimal	A measure of the company's ability to meet all of its fixed-charge obligations.
Current liabilities to equity	$$\frac{\text{Current liabilities}}{\text{Shareholders' equity}}$$	Percentage	Measures the short-term financing portion versus that provided by owners.

continued

TABLE 12–1	Financial Ratio Analysis, (continued)		
	Formula	**How Expressed**	**Meaning**
5. Other Ratios Price/earnings ratio	$\dfrac{\text{Market price per share}}{\text{Earnings per share}}$	Decimal	Shows the current market's evaluation of a stock, based on its earnings; shows how much the investor is willing to pay for each dollar of earnings.
Divided payout ratio	$\dfrac{\text{Annual dividends per share}}{\text{Annual earnings per share}}$	Percentage	Indicates the percentage of profit that is paid out as dividends.
Dividend yield on common stock	$\dfrac{\text{Annual dividends per share}}{\text{Current market price per share}}$	Percentage	Indicates the dividend rate of return to common shareholders at the current market price.

NOTE: In using ratios for analysis, calculate ratios for the corporation and compare them to the average and quartile ratios for the particular industry. Refer to Standard & Poor's and Robert Morris Associates for average industry data. Special thanks to Dr. Moustafa H. Abdelsamad, Dean, Business School, Texas A&M University—Corpus Christi, Corpus Christi, Texas, for his definitions of these ratios.

A typical financial analysis of a firm would include a study of the operating statements for five or so years, including a trend analysis of sales, profits, earnings per share, debt-to-equity ratio, return on investment, and so on, plus a ratio study comparing the firm under study with industry standards. As a minimum, undertake the following five steps in basic financial analysis.

1. **Scrutinize historical income statements and balance sheets:** These two basic statements provide most of the data needed for analysis. Statements of cash flow may also be useful.
2. **Compare historical statements over time** if a series of statements is available.
3. **Calculate changes that occur in individual categories from year to year,** as well as the cumulative total change.
4. **Determine the change as a percentage** as well as an absolute amount.
5. **Adjust for inflation** if that was a significant factor.

Examination of this information may reveal developing trends. Compare trends in one category with trends in related categories. For example, an increase in sales of 15% over three years may appear to be satisfactory until you note an increase of 20% in the cost of goods sold during the same period. The outcome of this comparison might suggest that further investigation into the manufacturing process is necessary. If a company is reporting strong net income growth but negative cash flow, this would suggest that the company is relying on something other than operations for earnings growth. Is it selling off assets or cutting R&D? If accounts receivable are growing faster than sales revenues, the company is not getting paid for the products or services it is counting as sold. Is the company dumping product on its distributors at the end of the year to boost its reported annual sales? If so, expect the distributors to return the unordered product the next month, thus drastically cutting the next year's reported sales.

Other "tricks of the trade" need to be examined. Until June 2000, firms growing through acquisition were allowed to account for the cost of the purchased company, through the pooling of both companies' stock. This approach was used in 40% of the value of mergers between 1997 and 1999. The pooling method enabled the acquiring company to disregard the premium it paid for the other firm (the amount above the fair market value of the purchased company often called "good will"). Thus, when PepsiCo agreed to purchase Quaker Oats for $13.4 billion in PepsiCo stock, the $13.4 billion was not found on PepsiCo's balance sheet. As of June 2000, merging firms must use the "purchase" accounting rules in which the true purchase price is reflected in the financial statements.[2]

The analysis of a multinational corporation's financial statements can get very complicated, especially if its headquarters is in another country that uses different accounting standards.

COMMON-SIZE STATEMENTS

Common-size statements are income statements and balance sheets in which the dollar figures have been converted into percentages. These statements are used to identify trends in each of the categories, such as cost of goods sold as a percentage of sales (sales is the denominator). For the income statement, net sales represent 100%: calculate the percentage for each category so that the categories sum to the net sales percentage (100%). For the balance sheet, give the total assets a value of 100% and calculate other asset and liability categories as percentages of the total assets with total assets as the denominator. (Individual asset and liability items, such as accounts receivable and accounts payable, can also be calculated as a percentage of net sales.)

When you convert statements to this form, it is relatively easy to note the percentage that each category represents of the total. Look for trends in specific items, such as cost of goods sold, when compared to the company's historical figures. To get a proper picture, however, you need to make comparisons with industry data, if available, to see whether fluctuations are merely reflecting industrywide trends. If a firm's trends are generally in line with those of the rest of the industry, problems are less likely than if the firm's trends are worse than industry averages. If ratios are not available for the industry, calculate the ratios for the industry's best and worst firms and compare them to the firm you are analyzing. Common-size statements are especially helpful in developing scenarios and pro forma statements because they provide a series of historical relationships (for example, cost of goods sold to sales, interest to sales, and inventories as a percentage of assets) from which you can estimate the future with your scenario assumptions for each year.

Z-VALUE AND THE INDEX OF SUSTAINABLE GROWTH

If the corporation being studied appears to be in poor financial condition, use **Altman's Z-Value Bankruptcy Formula** to calculate its likelihood of going bankrupt. The *Z-value* formula combines five ratios by weighting them according to their importance to a corporation's financial strength. The formula is:

$$Z = 1.2x_1 + 1.4x_2 + 3.3x_3 + 0.6x_4 + 1.0x_5$$

where:

x_1 = Working capital/Total assets (%)
x_2 = Retained earnings/Total assets (%)
x_3 = Earnings before interest and taxes/Total assets (%)
x_4 = Market value of equity/Total liabilities (%)
x_5 = Sales/Total assets (number of times)

A score below 1.81 indicates significant credit problems, whereas a score above 3.0 indicates a healthy firm. Scores between 1.81 and 3.0 indicate question marks.[3] The Altman Z model has achieved a remarkable 94% accuracy in predicting corporate bankruptcies. Its accuracy is excellent in the two years before financial distress, but diminishes as the lead time increases.[4]

The **index of sustainable growth** is useful to learn whether a company embarking on a growth strategy will need to take on debt to fund this growth. The index indicates how much of the growth rate of sales can be sustained by internally generated funds. The formula is:

$$g^* = \frac{[P(1 - D)(1 + L)]}{[T - P(1 - D)(1 + L)]}$$

where:

P = (Net profit before tax/Net sales) × 100
D = Target dividends/Profit after tax
L = Total liabilities/Net worth
T = (Total assets/Net sales) × 100

If the planned growth rate calls for a growth rate higher than its g*, external capital will be needed to fund the growth unless management is able to find efficiencies, decrease dividends, increase the debt-equity ratio, or reduce assets through renting or leasing arrangements.[5]

USEFUL ECONOMIC MEASURES

If you are analyzing a company over many years, you may want to adjust sales and net income for inflation to arrive at a "true" financial performance in constant dollars. **Constant dollars** are dollars adjusted for inflation to make them comparable over various years. One way to adjust for inflation in the United States is to use the consumer price index (CPI), as given in **Table 12–2**. Dividing sales and net income by the CPI factor for that year will change the figures to 1982–1984 U.S. constant dollars (when the CPI was 1.0). Adjusting for inflation is especially important for companies operating in emerging economies like China and Russia. China's inflation rate was 8.7% in 2008, which was the highest it had been in 10 years. The Russian inflation rate in 2011 was expected to top 6%.[6]

Another helpful analytical aid provided in **Table 12–2** is the **prime interest rate**, the rate of interest banks charge on their lowest-risk loans. For better assessments of strategic decisions, it can be useful to note the level of the prime interest rate at the time of the case. A decision to borrow money to build a new plant would have been a good one in 2003 at 4.1%, but less practical in 2007 when the average rate was 8.05%.

In preparing a scenario for your pro forma financial statements, you may want to use the **gross domestic product (GDP)** from **Table 12–2**. GDP is used worldwide and measures the total output of goods and services within a country's borders. The amount of change from one year to the next indicates how much that country's economy is growing. Remember that scenarios have to be adjusted for a country's specific conditions. For other economic information, see the resources for case research in **Appendix 12.A**.

TABLE 12–2	Year	GDP (in $ billions) Gross Domestic Product	CPI (for all items) Consumer Price Index	PIR (in %) Prime Interest Rate
U.S. Economic Indicators	1980	2788.1	.824	15.26
	1985	4217.5	1.076	9.93
	1990	5800.4	1.307	10.01
	1995	7414.7	1.524	8.83
	2000	9951.5	1.722	9.23
	2001	10,286.2	1.771	6.91
	2002	10,642.3	1.799	4.67
	2003	11,142.2	1.840	4.12
	2004	11,853.3	1.889	4.34
	2005	12,623.0	1.953	6.19
	2006	13.377.2	2.016	7.96
	2007	14,028.7	2.073	8.05
	2008	14,291.5	2.153	5.09
	2009	13,973.7	2.145	3.25
	2010	1,498.9	2.180	3.25
	2011	15,075.7	2.249	3.25

NOTES: Gross domestic product (GDP) in billions of dollars; Consumer price index for all items (CPI) (1982–84 = 1.0); Prime interest rate (PIR) in percentages.

SOURCES: Gross domestic product (GDP) from U.S. Bureau of Economic Analysis, National Economic Accounts (www.bea.gov). Consumer price index (CPI) from U.S. Bureau of Labor Statistics (www.bls.gov). Prime interest rate (PIR) (www.federalreserve.gov).

Format for Case Analysis: The Strategic Audit

There is no one best way to analyze or present a case report. Each instructor has personal preferences for format and approach. Nevertheless, in **Appendix 12.B** we suggest an approach for both written and oral reports that provides a systematic method for successfully attacking a case. This approach is based on the strategic audit, which is presented at the end of **Chapter 1** in **Appendix 1.A**. We find that this approach provides structure and is very helpful for the typical student who may be a relative novice in case analysis. Regardless of the format chosen, be careful to include a complete analysis of key environmental variables—especially of trends in the industry and of the competition. Look at international developments as well.

If you choose to use the strategic audit as a guide to the analysis of complex strategy cases, you may want to use the **strategic audit worksheet** in **Figure 12–1**. Print a copy of the worksheet to use to take notes as you analyze a case. See **Appendix 12.C** for an example of a completed student-written analysis of a 1993 Maytag Corporation case done in an outline form using the strategic audit format. This is one example of what a case analysis in outline form may look like.

Case discussion focuses on critical analysis and logical development of thought. A solution is satisfactory if it resolves important problems and is likely to be implemented successfully. How the corporation actually dealt with the case problems has no real bearing on the analysis because management might have analyzed its problems incorrectly or implemented a series of flawed solutions.

FIGURE 12–1
Strategic Audit Worksheet

Strategic Audit Heading	Analysis		Comments
	(+) Factors	(−) Factors	
I. Current Situation			
A. Past Corporate Performance Indexes			
B. Strategic Posture: Current Mission Current Objectives Current Strategies Current Policies			
SWOT Analysis Begins:			
II. Corporate Governance			
A. Board of Directors			
B. Top Management			
III. External Environment (EFAS): **Opportunities and Threats (SWOT)**			
A. Natural Environment			
B. Societal Environment			
C. Task Environment (Industry Analysis)			
IV. Internal Environment (IFAS): **Strengths and Weaknesses (SWOT)**			
A. Corporate Structure			
B. Corporate Culture			
C. Corporate Resources			
1. Marketing			
2. Finance			
3. Research and Development			
4. Operations and Logistics			
5. Human Resources			
6. Information Technology			
V. Analysis of Strategic Factors (SFAS)			
A. Key Internal and External Strategic Factors (SWOT)			
B. Review of Mission and Objectives			
SWOT Analysis Ends. Recommendation Begins:			
VI. Alternatives and Recommendations			
A. Strategic Alternatives—pros and cons			
B. Recommended Strategy			
VII. Implementation			
VIII. Evaluation and Control			

NOTE: See the complete Strategic Audit on pages 32–39. It lists the pages in the book that discuss each of the eight headings.

SOURCE: T. L. Wheelen and J. D. Hunger, "Strategic Audit Worksheet." Copyright © 1985, 1986, 1987, 1988, 1989, 2005, and 2009 by T. L. Wheelen. Copyright © 1989, 2005, and 2009 by Wheelen and Hunger Associates. Revised 1991, 1994, and 1997. Reprinted by permission. Additional copies available for classroom use in Part D of the Case Instructor's Manual and on the Prentice Hall Web site (www.prenhall.com/wheelen).

End of Chapter SUMMARY

Using case analysis is one of the best ways to understand and remember the strategic management process. By applying to cases the concepts and techniques you have learned, you will be able to remember them long past the time when you have forgotten other memorized bits of information. The use of cases to examine actual situations brings alive the field of strategic management and helps build your analytic and decision-making skills. These are just some of the reasons why the use of cases in disciplines from agribusiness to health care is increasing throughout the world.

MyManagementLab®

Go to **mymanagementlab.com** to complete the problems marked with this icon .

KEY TERMS

activity ratio (p. 335)

Altman's Z-Value Bankruptcy Formula (p. 339)

annual report (p. 335)

common-size statement (p. 339)

constant dollars (p. 340)

gross domestic product (GDP) (p. 340)

index of sustainable growth (p. 340)

leverage ratio (p. 335)

liquidity ratio (p. 335)

prime interest rate (p. 340)

profitability ratio (p. 335)

ratio analysis (p. 335)

SEC 10-K form (p. 335)

SEC 10-Q form (p. 335)

SEC 14-A form (p. 335)

strategic audit worksheet (p. 341)

MyManagementLab®

Go to **mymanagementlab.com** for Auto-graded writing questions as well as the following Assisted-graded writing questions:

12-1. What ratios would you use to begin your analysis of a case?

12-2. What are the five crucial steps to follow in basic financial analysis?

DISCUSSION QUESTIONS

12-3. Why should you begin a case analysis with a financial analysis? When are other approaches appropriate?

12-4. What are common-size financial statements? What is their value to case analysis? How are they calculated?

12-5. When should you gather information outside a case? What should you look for?

12-6. When is inflation an important issue in conducting case analysis? Why bother?

12-7. How can you learn what date a case took place?

STRATEGIC PRACTICE EXERCISE

Convert the following two years of income statements from the Maytag Corporation into common-size statements. The dollar figures are in thousands. What does converting to a common size reveal?

Consolidated Statements of Income: Maytag Corporation

	1992	%	1991	%
Net sales	$3,041,223	100	$2,970,626	100
Cost of sales	2,339,406	—	2,254,221	—
Gross profits	701,817	—	716,405	—
Selling, general, & admin. expenses	528,250	—	524,898	—
Reorganization expenses	95,000	—	0	—
Operating income	78,567	—	191,507	—
Interest expense	(75,004)	—	(75,159)	—
Other—net	3983	—	7069	—
Income before taxes and accounting changes	7546	—	123,417	—
Income taxes	(15,900)	—	(44,400)	—
Income before accounting changes	(8354)	—	79,017	—
Effects of accounting changes for postretirement benefits	(307,000)	—	0	—
Net income (loss)	$(315,354)	—	$79,017	—

NOTES

1. M. Vanac, "What's a Novice Investor to Do?" *Des Moines Register* (November 30, 1997), p. 3G.
2. A. R. Sorking, "New Path on Mergers Could Contain Loopholes," *The* (Ames, IA) *Daily Tribune* (January 9, 2001), p. B7; "Firms Resist Effort to Unveil True Costs of Doing Business," *USA Today* (July 3, 2000), p. 10A.
3. M. S. Fridson, *Financial Statement Analysis* (New York: John Wiley & Sons, 1991), pp. 192–194.
4. E. I. Altman, "Predicting Financial Distress of Companies: Revisiting the Z-Score and Zeta Models," working paper at pages.stern.nyu.edu/~ealtman/Zscores.pdf (July 2000).
5. D. H. Bangs, *Managing by the Numbers* (Dover, NH: Upstart Publications, 1992), pp. 106–107.
6. http://ycharts.com/indicators/china_inflation_rate; http://www.bloomberg.com/news/2012-10-03/russia-september-inflation-rate-probably-surged-to-10-month-high.html.

Resources for Case Research

Company Information

1. Annual reports

2. Moody's *Manuals on Investment* (a listing of companies within certain industries that contains a brief history and a five-year financial statement of each company)

3. Securities and Exchange Commission Annual Report Form 10-K (annually) and 10-Q (quarterly)

4. Standard & Poor's *Register of Corporations, Directors, and Executives*

5. Value Line's *Investment Survey*

6. Findex's *Directory of Market Research Reports, Studies, and Surveys* (a listing by Find/SVP of more than 11,000 studies conducted by leading research firms)

7. Compustat, Compact Disclosure, CD/International, and Hoover's online corporate directory (computerized operating and financial information on thousands of publicly held corporations)

8. Shareholders meeting notices in SEC Form 14-A (proxy notices)

Economic Information

1. Regional statistics and local forecasts from large banks

2. *Business Cycle Development* (Department of Commerce)

3. Chase Econometric Associates' publications

4. U.S. Census Bureau publications on population, transportation, and housing

5. *Current Business Reports* (U.S. Department of Commerce)

6. *Economic Indicators* (U.S. Joint Economic Committee)

7. *Economic Report of the President to Congress*

8. *Long-Term Economic Growth* (U.S. Department of Commerce)

9. *Monthly Labor Review* (U.S. Department of Labor)

10. *Monthly Bulletin of Statistics* (United Nations)

11. *Statistical Abstract of the United States* (U.S. Department of Commerce)

12. *Statistical Yearbook* (United Nations)

13. *Survey of Current Business* (U.S. Department of Commerce)

14. *U.S. Industrial Outlook* (U.S. Department of Defense)

15. *World Trade Annual* (United Nations)

16. *Overseas Business Reports* (by country, published by the U.S. Department of Commerce)

Industry Information

1. Analyses of companies and industries by investment brokerage firms

2. *Bloomberg Businessweek* (provides weekly economic and business information, as well as quarterly profit and sales rankings of corporations)

3. *Fortune* (each April publishes listings of financial information on corporations within certain industries)

4. *Industry Survey* (published quarterly by Standard & Poor's)

5. *Industry Week* (late March / early April issue provides information on 14 industry groups)

6. *Forbes* (mid-January issue provides performance data on firms in various industries)

7. *Inc.* (May and December issues give information on fast-growing entrepreneurial companies)

Directory and Index Information on Companies and Industries

1. *Business Periodical Index* (on computers in many libraries)

2. *Directory of National Trade Associations*

3. *Encyclopedia of Associations*

4. Funk and Scott's *Index of Corporations and Industries*

5. Thomas's *Register of American Manufacturers*

6. *The Wall Street Journal Index*

Ratio Analysis Information

1. *Almanac of Business and Industrial Financial Ratios* (Prentice Hall)

2. *Annual Statement Studies* (Risk Management Associates; also Robert Morris Associates)

3. *Dun's Review* (Dun & Bradstreet; published annually in September–December issues)

4. *Industry Norms and Key Business Ratios* (Dun & Bradstreet)

Online Information

1. *Hoover's Online*—financial statements and profiles of public companies (www.hoovers.com)

2. U.S. Securities and Exchange Commission—official filings of public companies in the EDGAR database (www.sec.gov)

3. Fortune 500—statistics for largest U.S. corporations (www.fortune.com)

4. Dun & Bradstreet's Online—short reports on 10 million public and private U.S. companies (smallbusiness.dnb.com)

5. Competitive Intelligence Guide—information on company resources (www.fuld.com)

6. Society of Competitive Intelligence Professionals (www.scip.org)

7. *The Economist*—provides international information and surveys (www.economist.com)

8. *CIA World Fact Book*—international information by country (http://www.cia.gov)

9. Bloomberg—information on interest rates, stock prices, currency conversion rates, and other general financial information (www.bloomberg.com)

10. CEOExpress—links to many valuable sources of business information (www.ceoexpress.com)

11. *The Wall Street Journal*—business news (www.wsj.com)

12. Forbes—America's largest private companies (http://www.forbes.com/lists/)

13. CorporateInformation.com—subscription service for company profiles (www.corporateinformation.com)

14. Kompass International—industry information (www.kompass.com)

15. CorpTech—database of technology companies (www.corptech.com)

16. ADNet—information technology industry (www.companyfinders.com)

17. CNN company research—provides company information (http://money.cnn.com/news/)

18. Paywatch—database of executive compensation (http://www.aflcio.org/corporatewatch/paywatch/)

19. Global Edge Global Resources—international resources (http://globaledge.msu.edu/resourceDesk/)

20. Google Finance—data on North American stocks (http://www.google.com/finance)

21. World Federation of Exchanges—international stock exchanges (www.world-exchanges.org/)

22. SEC International Registry—data on international corporations (http://www.sec.gov/divisions/corpfin/internatl/companies.shtml)

23. Yahoo Finance—data on North American companies (http://finance.yahoo.com)

APPENDIX 12.B

Suggested Case Analysis Methodology Using the Strategic Audit

First Reading of the Case

- Develop a general overview of the company and its external environment.
- Begin a list of the possible strategic factors facing the company at this time.
- List the research information you may need on the economy, industry, and competitors.

Over the past six years, increases in yearly revenues have consistently reached 12%. Byte Products Inc., headquartered in the U.S. Midwest, is regarded as one of the largest-volume suppliers of specialized components and is easily the industry leader.

Second Reading of the Case

- Read the case a second time, using the strategic audit as a framework for in-depth analysis. (See **Appendix 1.A** on pages 32–39.) You may want to make a copy of the strategic audit worksheet (**Figure 12–1**) to use to keep track of your comments as you read the case.
- The questions in the strategic audit parallel the strategic decision-making process shown in **Figure 1–5** (pages 26–27).
- The audit provides you with a conceptual framework to examine the company's mission, objectives, strategies, and policies, as well as problems, symptoms, facts, opinions, and issues.
- Perform a financial analysis of the company, using ratio analysis (see **Table 12–1**), and do the calculations necessary to convert key parts of the financial statements to a common-size basis.

Library and Online Computer Services

- Each case has a decision date indicating when the case actually took place. Your research should be based on the time period for the case.
- See **Appendix 12.A** for resources for case research. Your research should include information about the environment at the time of the case. Find average industry ratios. You may also want to obtain further information regarding competitors and the company itself (10-K forms and annual reports). This information should help you conduct an industry analysis. *Check with your instructor to see what kind of outside research is appropriate for your assignment.*
- Don't try to learn what actually happened to the company discussed in the case. What management actually decided may not be the best solution. It will certainly bias your analysis and will probably cause your recommendation to lack proper justification.
- Analyze the natural and societal environments to see what general trends are likely to affect the industry(s) in which the company is operating.

■ Conduct an industry analysis using Porter's competitive forces from **Chapter 4**. Develop an Industry Matrix (**Table 4–4** on page 113).

■ Generate 8 to 10 external factors. These should be the *most important* opportunities and threats facing the company at the time of the case.

■ Develop an EFAS Table, as shown in **Table 4–5** (page 121), for your list of external strategic factors.

■ **Suggestion:** Rank the 8 to 10 factors from most to least important. Start by grouping the three top factors and then the three bottom factors.

Internal Organizational Analysis: IFAS

■ Generate 8 to 10 internal factors. These should be the *most important* strengths and weaknesses of the company at the time of the case.

■ Develop an IFAS Table, as shown in **Table 5–2** (page 154), for your list of internal strategic factors.

■ **Suggestion:** Rank the 8 to 10 factors from most to least important. Start by grouping the three top factors and then the three bottom factors.

■ Review the student-written audit of an old Maytag case in **Appendix 12.C** for an example.

■ Write Parts I to IV of the strategic audit. Remember to include the factors from your EFAS and IFAS Tables in your audit.

Strategic Factor Analysis Summary: SFAS

■ Condense the list of factors from the 16 to 20 identified in your EFAS and IFAS Tables to only the 8 to 10 most important factors.

■ Select the most important EFAS and IFAS factors. Recalculate the weights of each. The weights still need to add to 1.0.

■ This is a good time to reexamine what you wrote earlier in Parts I to IV. You may want to add to or delete some of what you wrote. Ensure that each one of the strategic factors you have included in your SFAS Matrix is discussed in the appropriate place in Parts I to IV. Part V of the audit is *not* the place to mention a strategic factor for the first time.

■ Write Part V of your strategic audit. This completes your SWOT analysis.

■ This is the place to suggest a revised mission statement and a better set of objectives for the company. The SWOT analysis coupled with revised mission and objectives for the company set the stage for the generation of strategic alternatives.

A. Alternatives

■ Develop around three mutually exclusive strategic alternatives. If appropriate to the case you are analyzing, you might propose one alternative for growth, one for stability, and one for retrenchment. Within each corporate strategy, you should probably propose an appropriate business/competitive.

■ Construct a corporate scenario for each alternative. Use the data from your outside research to project general societal trends (GDP, inflation, and etc.) and industry trends. Use these as the basis of your assumptions to write pro forma financial statements (particularly income statements) for each strategic alternative for the next five years.

■ List pros and cons for each alternative based on your scenarios.

B. Recommendation

■ Specify which one of your alternative strategies you recommend. Justify your choice in terms of dealing with the strategic factors you listed in Part V of the strategic audit.

■ Develop policies to help implement your strategies.

Implementation

■ Develop programs to implement your recommended strategy.

■ Specify who is to be responsible for implementing each program and how long each program will take to complete.

■ Refer to the pro forma financial statements you developed earlier for your recommended strategy. Use common-size historical income statements as the basis for the pro forma statement. Do the numbers still make sense? If not, this may be a good time to rethink the budget numbers to reflect your recommended programs.

Evaluation and Control

■ Specify the type of evaluation and controls you need to ensure that your recommendation is carried out successfully. Specify who is responsible for monitoring these controls.

■ Indicate whether sufficient information is available to monitor how the strategy is being implemented. If not, suggest a change to the information system.

Final Draft of Your Strategic Audit

■ Check to ensure that your audit is within the page limits set out by your professor. You may need to cut some parts and expand others.

■ Make sure your recommendation clearly deals with the strategic factors.

■ **Attach your EFAS and IFAS Tables, and SFAS Matrix,** plus your ratio analysis and pro forma statements. Label them as numbered exhibits and refer to each of them within the body of the audit.

■ Proof your work for errors. If on a computer, use a spell checker.

SPECIAL NOTE: Depending on your assignment, it is relatively easy to use the strategic audit you have just developed to write a written case analysis in essay form or to make an oral presentation. The strategic audit is just a detailed case analysis in an outline form and can be used as the basic framework for any sort of case analysis and presentation.

Example of Student-Written Strategic Audit

(For the 1993 Maytag Corporation Case)

I. Current Situation

A. Current Performance

Poor financials, high debt load, first losses since 1920s, price/earnings ratio negative.

- First loss since 1920s.
- Laid off 4500 employees at Magic Chef.
- Hoover Europe still showing losses.

B. Strategic Posture

1. **Mission**
   - Developed in 1989 for the Maytag Company: "To provide our customers with products of unsurpassed performance that last longer, need fewer repairs, and are produced at the lowest possible cost."
   - Updated in 1991: "Our collective mission is world class quality." Expands Maytag's belief in product quality to all aspects of operations.

2. **Objectives**
   - "To be the profitability leader in the industry for every product line Maytag manufactures." Selected profitability rather than market share.
   - "To be number one in total customer satisfaction." Doesn't say how to measure satisfaction.
   - "To grow the North American appliance business and become the third largest appliance manufacturer (in unit sales) in North America."
   - To increase profitable market share growth in the North American appliance and floor care business, 6.5% return on sales, 10% return on assets, 20% return on equity, beat competition in satisfying customers, dealer, builder, and endorser, and move into third place in total units shipped per year. Nicely quantified objectives.

3. **Strategies**
   - Global growth through acquisition, and alliance with Bosch-Siemens.
   - Differentiate brand names for competitive advantage.
   - Create synergy between companies, product improvement, investment in plant and equipment.

4. **Policies**
   - Cost reduction is secondary to high quality.
   - Promotion from within.
   - Slow but sure R&D: Maytag slow to respond to changes in market.

II. Strategic Managers

A. Board of Directors

1. Fourteen members—eleven are outsiders.
2. Well-respected Americans, most on board since 1986 or earlier.
3. No international or marketing backgrounds.
4. Time for a change?

B. Top Management

1. Top management promoted from within Maytag Company. Too inbred?
2. Very experienced in the industry.
3. Responsible for current situation.
4. May be too parochial for global industry. May need new blood.

III. External Environment (EFAS Table; see Exhibit 1)

A. Natural Environment

1. Growing water scarcity
2. Energy availability a growing problem

B. Societal Environment

1. **Economic**
   a. Unstable economy but recession ending, consumer confidence growing—could increase spending for big ticket items like houses, cars, and appliances. (**O**)
   b. Individual economies becoming interconnected into a world economy. (**O**)
2. **Technological**
   a. Fuzzy logic technology being applied to sense and measure activities. (**O**)
   b. Computers and information technology increasingly important. (**O**)
3. **Political–Legal**
   a. NAFTA, European Union, other regional trade pacts opening doors to markets in Europe, Asia, and Latin America that offer enormous potential. (**O**)
   b. Breakdown of communism means less chance of world war. (**O**)
   c. Environmentalism being reflected in laws on pollution and energy usage. (**T**)
4. **Sociocultural**
   a. Developing nations desire goods seen on TV. (**O**)
   b. Middle-aged baby boomers want attractive, high-quality products, like BMWs and Maytag. (**O**)
   c. Dual-career couples increases need for labor-saving appliances, second cars, and day care. (**O**)
   d. Divorce and career mobility means need for more houses and goods to fill them. (**O**)

C. Task Environment

1. North American market mature and extremely competitive—vigilant consumers demand high quality with low price in safe, environmentally sound products. **(T)**

2. Industry going global as North American and European firms expand internationally. **(T)**

3. European design popular and consumer desire for technologically advanced appliances. **(O)**

4. **Rivalry High**. Whirlpool, Electrolux, GE have enormous resources and developing global presence. **(T)**

5. **Buyers' Power Low**. Technology and materials can be sourced worldwide. **(O)**

6. **Power of Other Stakeholders Medium**. Quality, safety, environmental regulations increasing. **(T)**

7. **Distributors' Power High**. Super retailers more important: mom and pop dealers less. **(T)**

8. **Threat of Substitutes Low**. **(O)**

9. **Entry Barriers High**. New entrants unlikely except for large international firms. **(T)**

IV. Internal Environment (IFAS Table; see Exhibit 2)

A. Corporate Structure

1. Divisional structure: appliance manufacturing and vending machines. Floor care managed separately. **(S)**

2. Centralized major decisions by Newton corporate staff, with a time line of about three years. **(S)**

B. Corporate Culture

1. Quality key ingredient—commitment to quality shared by executives and workers. **(S)**

2. Much of corporate culture is based on founder F. L. Maytag's personal philosophy, including concern for quality, employees, local community, innovation, and performance. **(S)**

3. Acquired companies, except for European, seem to accept dominance of Maytag culture. **(S)**

C. Corporate Resources

1. **Marketing**
   a. Maytag brand lonely repairman advertising successful but dated. **(W)**
   b. Efforts focus on distribution—combining three sales forces into two, concentrating on major retailers. (Cost $95 million for this restructuring.) **(S)**
   c. Hoover's well-publicized marketing fiasco involving airline tickets. **(W)**

2. **Finance** (see **Exhibits 4 and 5**)
   a. Revenues are up slightly, operating income is down significantly. **(W)**
   b. Some key ratios are troubling, such as a 57% debt/asset ratio, 132% long-term debt/equity ratio. No room for more debt to grow company. **(W)**
   c. Net income is 400% less than 1988, based on common-size income statements. **(W)**

3. **R&D**
   a. Process-oriented with focus on manufacturing process and durability. **(S)**
   b. Maytag becoming a technology follower, taking too long to get product innovations to market (competitors put out more in last six months than prior two years combined), lagging in fuzzy logic and other technological areas. **(W)**

4. **Operations**
   a. Maytag's core competence. Continual improvement process kept it dominant in the U.S. market for many years. **(S)**
   b. Plants aging and may be losing competitiveness as rivals upgrade facilities. Quality no longer distinctive competence? **(W)**

5. **Human Resources**
   a. Traditionally very good relations with unions and employees. **(S)**
   b. Labor relations increasingly strained, with two salary raise delays, and layoffs of 4500 employees at Magic Chef. **(W)**
   c. Unions express concern at new, more distant tone from Maytag Corporation. **(W)**

6. **Information Systems**
   a. Not mentioned in case. Hoover fiasco in Europe suggests information systems need significant upgrading. **(W)**
   b. Critical area where Maytag may be unwilling or unable to commit resources needed to stay competitive. **(W)**

V. Analysis of Strategic Factors

A. Situational Analysis (SWOT) (SFAS Matrix; see Exhibit 3)

1. **Strengths**
   a. Quality Maytag culture.
   b. Maytag well-known and respected brand.
   c. Hoover's international orientation.
   d. Core competencies in process R&D and manufacturing.

2. **Weaknesses**
   a. Lacks financial resources of competitors.
   b. Poor global positioning. Hoover weak on European continent.
   c. Product R&D and customer service innovation are areas of serious weakness.
   d. Dependent on small dealers.
   e. Marketing needs improvement.

3. **Opportunities**
   a. Economic integration of European community.
   b. Demographics favor quality.
   c. Trend to superstores.

4. **Threats**
   a. Trend to superstores.
   b. Aggressive rivals—Whirlpool and Electrolux.
   c. Japanese appliance companies—new entrants?

B. Review of Current Mission and Objectives

1. Current mission appears appropriate.
2. Some of the objectives are really goals and need to be quantified and given time horizons.

VI. Strategic Alternatives and Recommended Strategy

A. Strategic Alternatives

1. *Growth through Concentric Diversification*: Acquire a company in a related industry such as commercial appliances.
   a. *[Pros]:* Product/market synergy created by acquisition of related company.
   b. *[Cons]:* Maytag does not have the financial resources to play this game.

2. *Pause Strategy*: Consolidate various acquisitions to find economies and to encourage innovation among the business units.

    a. *[Pros]:* Maytag needs to get its financial house in order and get administrative control over its recent acquisitions.

    b. *[Cons]:* Unless it can grow through a stronger alliance with Bosch-Siemens or some other backer, Maytag is a prime candidate for takeover because of its poor financial performance in recent years, and it is suffering from the initial reduction in efficiency inherent in acquisition strategy.

3. *Retrenchment*: Sell Hoover's foreign major home appliance businesses (Australia and UK) to emphasize increasing market share in North America.

    a. *[Pros]:* Divesting Hoover improves bottom line and enables Maytag Corp. to focus on North America while Whirlpool, Electrolux, and GE are battling elsewhere.

    b. *[Cons]:* Maytag may be giving up its only opportunity to become a player in the coming global appliance industry.

B. Recommended Strategy

1. Recommend pause strategy, at least for a year, so Maytag can get a grip on its European operation and consolidate its companies in a more synergistic way.

2. Maytag quality must be maintained, and continued shortage of operating capital will take its toll, so investment must be made in R&D.

3. Maytag may be able to make the Hoover UK investment work better since the recession is ending and the EU countries are closer to integrating than ever before.

4. Because it is only an average competitor, Maytag needs the Hoover link to Europe to provide a jumping off place for negotiations with Bosch-Siemens that could strengthen their alliance.

VII. Implementation

A. The only way to increase profitability in North America is to further involve Maytag with the superstore retailers; sure to anger the independent dealers, but necessary for Maytag to compete.

B. Board members with more global business experience should be recruited, with an eye toward the future, especially with expertise in Asia and Latin America.

C. R&D needs to be improved, as does marketing, to get new products online quickly.

VIII. Evaluation and Control

A. MIS needs to be developed for speedier evaluation and control. While the question of control vs. autonomy is "under review," another Hoover fiasco may be brewing.

B. The acquired companies do not all share the Midwestern work ethic or the Maytag Corporation culture, and Maytag's managers must inculcate these values into the employees of all acquired companies.

C. Systems should be developed to decide if the size and location of Maytag manufacturing plants is still correct and to plan for the future. Industry analysis indicates that smaller automated plants may be more efficient now than in the past.

| **EXHIBIT 1** | EFAS Table for Maytag Corporation 1993 |

External Factors		Weight	Rating	Weighted Score	Comments	
	1	2	3	4		5
Opportunities						
▪ Economic integration of European Community		.20	4.1	.82	Acquisition of Hoover	
▪ Demographics favor quality appliances		.10	5.0	.50	Maytag quality	
▪ Economic development of Asia		.05	1.0	.05	Low Maytag presence	
▪ Opening of Eastern Europe		.05	2.0	.10	Will take time	
▪ Trend to "Super Stores"		.10	1.8	.18	Maytag weak in this channel	
Threats						
▪ Increasing government regulations		.10	4.3	.43	Well positioned	
▪ Strong U.S. competition		.10	4.0	.40	Well positioned	
▪ Whirlpool and Electrolux strong globally		.15	3.0	.45	Hoover weak globally	
▪ New product advances		.05	1.2	.06	Questionable	
▪ Japanese appliance companies		.10	1.6	.16	Only Asian presence in Australia	
Total Scores		1.00		3.15		

| **EXHIBIT 2** | IFAS Table for Maytag Corporation 1993 |

Internal Factors		Weight	Rating	Weighted Score	Comments	
	1	2	3	4		5
Strengths						
▪ Quality Maytag culture		.15	5.0	.75	Quality key to success	
▪ Experienced top management		.05	4.2	.21	Know appliances	
▪ Vertical integration		.10	3.9	.39	Dedicated factories	
▪ Employer relations		.05	3.0	.15	Good, but deteriorating	
▪ Hoover's international orientation		.15	2.8	.42	Hoover name in cleaners	
Weaknesses						
▪ Process-oriented R&D		.05	2.2	.11	Slow on new products	
▪ Distribution channels		.05	2.0	.10	Superstores replacing small dealers	
▪ Financial position		.15	2.0	.30	High debt load	
▪ Global positioning		.20	2.1	.42	Hoover weak outside the United Kingdom and Australia	
▪ Manufacturing facilities		.05	4.0	.20	Investing now	
Total scores		1.00		3.05		

EXHIBIT 3   SFAS Matrix for Maytag Corporation 1993

Strategic Factors (Select the most important opportunities/threats from EFAS, Table 4–5 and the most important strengths and weaknesses from IFAS, Table 5–2)	Weight	Rating	Weighted Score	Duration			Comments
				SHORT	INTERMEDIATE	LONG	
►S1 Quality Maytag culture (S)	.10	5.0	.50			X	Quality key to success
►S5 Hoover's international orientation (S)	.10	2.8	.28	X	X		Name recognition
►W3 Financial position (W)	.10	2.0	.20	X	X		High debt
►W4 Global positioning (W)	.15	2.2	.33		X	X	Only in N.A., U.K., and Australia
►O1 Economic integration of European Community (O)	.10	4.1	.41			X	Acquisition of Hoover
►O2 Demographics favor quality (O)	.10	5.0	.50		X		Maytag quality
►O5 Trend to super stores (O + T)	.10	1.8	.18	X			Weak in this channel
►T3 Whirlpool and Electrolux (T)	.15	3.0	.45	X			Dominate industry
►T5 Japanese appliance companies (T)	.10	1.6	.16			X	Asian presence
Total Scores	**1.00**		**3.01**				

EXHIBIT 4

Ratio Analysis for Maytag Corporation 1993

	1990	1991	1992	1993
1. LIQUIDITY RATIOS				
Current	2.1	1.9	1.8	1.6
Quick	1.1	1.0	1.1	1.0
2. LEVERAGE RATIOS				
Debt to Total Assets	61%	60%	76%	57%
Debt to Equity	155%	151%	317%	254%
3. ACTIVITY RATIOS				
Inventory turnover—sales	5.7	6.1	7.6	6.9
Inventory Turnover—cost of sales	4.3	4.6	5.8	6.5
Avg. Collection Period—days	57	55	56	0
Fixed Asset Turnover	3.9	3.6	3.6	3.6
Total Assets Turnover	1.2	1.2	1.2	1.1
4. PROFITABILITY RATIOS				
Gross Profit Margin	24%	24%	23%	5%
Net Operating Margin	8%	6%	3%	5%
Profit Margin on Sales	3%	3%	−0%	2%
Return on Total Assets	4%	3%	−0%	2%
Return on Equity	10%	8%	−1%	8%

EXHIBIT 5		1992	1991	1990
Common Size Income Statements for Maytag Corporation 1993	Net sales	100.0%	100.0%	100.0%
	Cost of sales	76.92	75.88	75.50
	Gross profit	23.08	24.12	24.46
	Selling, general/admin. Expenses	17.37	17.67	16.90
	Reorganization expenses	.031	——	——
	Operating income	.026	.064	.075
	Interest expense	(.025)	(.025)	(0.26)
	Other—net	.001	.002	.009
	Income before accounting changes	.002	.042	.052
	Income taxes	.005	.015	.020
	Income before accounting changes	(.002)	.026	.032
	Effect of accounting changes for postretirement benefits other than pensions and income taxes	(.101)	——	——
	Total operating costs and expenses	<u>74.9</u>	<u>76.0</u>	<u>76.3</u>
	Net income	**(.104)**	**.026**	**.032**

EXHIBIT 6	Implementation, Evaluation, and Control Plan for Maytag Corporation 1993					
Strategic Factor	Action Plan	Priority System (1–5)	Who Will Implement	Who Will Review	How Often Review	Criteria Used
Quality Maytag culture	Build quality in acquired units	1	Heads of acquired units	Manufacturing VP	Quarterly	Number defects & customer satisfaction
Hoover's international orientation	Identify ways to expand sales	2	Head of Hoover	Marketing VP	Quarterly	Feasible alternatives generated
Financial position	Pay down debt	1	CFO	CEO	Monthly	Leverage ratios
Global positioning	Find strategic alliance partners	2	VP of Business Development	COO	Quarterly	Feasible alternatives generated
EU economic integration	Grow sales throughout EU	3	Hoover UK Head	Marketing VP	Annually	Sales growth
Demographics favor quality	Simplify controls	3	Manufacturing VP	COO	Annually	Market research user satisfaction
Trend to super stores	Market through Sears	1	Marketing VP	CEO	Monthly	Sales growth
Whirlpool & Electrolux	Monitor competitor performance	1	Competition committee	COO	Quarterly	Competitor sales & new products
Japanese appliance companies	Monitor expansion	4	Head of Hoover Australia	Competition committee	Semi-annually	Sales growth outside Japan

GLOSSARY

360-degree performance appraisal An evaluation technique in which input is gathered from multiple sources.

80/20 rule A rule of thumb stating that one should monitor those 20% of the factors that determine 80% of the results.

Absorptive capacity A firm's ability to value, assimilate, and utilize new external knowledge.

Acquisition The purchase of a company that is completely absorbed by the acquiring corporation.

Action plan A plan that states what actions are going to be taken, by whom, during what time frame, and with what expected results.

Activity-based costing (ABC) An accounting method for allocating indirect and fixed costs to individual products or product lines based on the value-added activities going into that product.

Activity ratios Financial ratios that indicate how well a corporation is managing its operations.

Adaptive mode A decision-making mode characterized by reactive solutions to existing problems, rather than a proactive search for new opportunities.

Advisory board A group of external business people who voluntarily meet periodically with the owners/managers of the firm to discuss strategic and other issues.

Affiliated directors Directors who, though not really employed by the corporation, handle the legal or insurance work for the company or are important suppliers.

Agency theory A theory stating that problems arise in corporations because the agents (top management) are not willing to bear responsibility for their decisions unless they own a substantial amount of stock in the corporation.

Altman's Z-Value Bankruptcy Formula A formula used to estimate how close a company is to declaring bankruptcy.

Analytical portfolio manager A type of general manager needed to execute a diversification strategy.

Andean Community A South American free-trade alliance composed of Columbia, Ecuador, Peru, Bolivia, and Chile.

Annual report A document published each year by a company to show its financial condition and products.

Assessment center An approach to evaluating the suitability of a person for a position by simulating key parts of the job.

Assimilation A strategy that involves the domination of one corporate culture over another.

Association of Southeast Asian Nations (ASEAN) A regional trade association composed of the Asian countries of Brunei Darussalam, Cambodia, Indonesia, Laos, Malaysia, Myanmar, Philippines, Singapore, Thailand, and Vietnam. ASEA+3 includes China, Japan, and South Korea.

Autonomous (self-managing) work teams A group of people who work together without a supervisor to plan, coordinate, and evaluate their own work.

Backward integration Assuming a function previously provided by a supplier.

Balanced scorecard Combines financial measures with operational measures on customer satisfaction, internal processes, and the corporation's innovation and improvement activities.

Bankruptcy A retrenchment strategy that forfeits management of the firm to the courts in return for some settlement of the corporation's obligations.

Basic R&D Research and development that is conducted by scientists in well-equipped laboratories where the focus is on theoretical problem areas.

BCG (Boston Consulting Group) Growth-Share Matrix A simple way to portray a corporation's portfolio of products or divisions in terms of growth and cash flow.

Behavior control A control that specifies how something is to be done through policies, rules, standard operating procedures, and orders from a superior.

Behavior substitution A phenomenon that occurs when people substitute activities that do not lead to goal accomplishment for activities that do lead to goal accomplishment because the wrong activities are being rewarded.

Benchmarking The process of measuring products, services, and practices against those of competitors or companies recognized as industry leaders.

Best practice A procedure that is followed by successful companies.

Blind spot analysis An approach to analyzing a competitor by identifying its perceptual biases.

Board of director responsibilities Commonly agreed obligations of directors, which include: setting corporate strategy, overall direction, mission or vision; hiring and firing the CEO and top management; controlling, monitoring, or supervising top management; reviewing and approving the use of resources; and caring for shareholder interest.

Board of directors' continuum A range of the possible degree of involvement by the board of directors (from low to high) in the strategic management process.

BOT (build-operate-transfer) concept A type of international entry option for a company. After building a facility, the company operates the facility for a fixed period of time during which it earns back its investment, plus a profit.

Brainstorming The process of proposing ideas in a group without first mentally screening them.

Brand A name that identifies a particular company's product in the mind of the consumer.

Budget A statement of a corporation's programs in terms of money required.

Business model The mix of activities a company performs to earn a profit.

Business plan A written strategic plan for a new entrepreneurial venture.

Business policy A previous name for strategic management. It has a general management orientation and tends to look inward with primary concern for integrating the corporation's many functional activities.

Business strategy Competitive and cooperative strategies that emphasize improvement of the competitive position of a corporation's products or services in a specific industry or market segment.

Cannibalize To replace popular products before they reach the end of their life cycle.

Capability A corporation's ability to exploit its resources.

Cap-and-trade A government-imposed ceiling (cap) on the amount of allowed greenhouse gas emissions combined with a system allowing a firm to sell (trade) its emission reductions to another firm whose emissions exceed the allowed cap.

Capital budgeting The process of analyzing and ranking possible investments in terms of the additional outlays and additional receipts that will result from each investment.

Captive company strategy Dedicating a firm's productive capacity as primary supplier to another company in exchange for a long-term contract.

Carbon footprint The amount of greenhouse gases being created by an entity and released into the air.

Cash cow A product that brings in far more money than is needed to maintain its market share.

Categorical imperatives Kant's two principles to guide actions: A person's action is ethical only if that person is willing for that same action to be taken by everyone who is in a similar situation, and a person should never treat another human being simply as a means but always as an end.

Cautious profit planner The type of leader needed for a corporation choosing to follow a stability strategy.

Cellular/modular organization A structure composed of cells (self-managing teams, autonomous business units, etc.) that can operate alone but can interact with other cells to produce a more potent and competent business mechanism.

Center of excellence A designated area in which a company has a core or distinctive competence.

Center of gravity The part of the industry value chain that is most important to the company and the point where the company's greatest expertise and capabilities lay.

Central American Free Trade Agreement (CAFTA) A regional trade association composed of El Salvador, Guatemala, Nicaragua, Honduras, Costa Rica, the United States, and the Dominican Republic.

Clusters Geographic concentrations of interconnected companies and industries.

Code of ethics A code that specifies how an organization expects its employees to behave while on the job.

Codetermination The inclusion of a corporation's workers on its board of directors.

Collusion The active cooperation of firms within an industry to reduce output and raise prices in order to get around the normal economic law of supply and demand. This practice is usually illegal.

Commodity A product whose characteristics are the same regardless of who sells it.

Common-size statements Income statements and balance sheets in which the dollar figures have been converted into percentages.

Common thread A unifying theme for the whole organization to rally around and provide focus for organizational efforts.

Competency A cross-functional integration and coordination of capabilities.

Competitive intelligence A formal program of gathering information about a company's competitors.

Competitive scope The breadth of a company's or a business unit's target market.

Competitive strategy A strategy that states how a company or a business unit will compete in an industry.

Competitors The companies that offer the same products or services as the subject company.

Complementor A company or an industry whose product(s) works well with another industry's or firm's product and without which that product would lose much of its value.

Concentration A corporate growth strategy that concentrates a corporation's resources on competing in one industry.

Concentric diversification A diversification growth strategy in which a firm uses its current strengths to diversify into related products in another industry.

Concurrent engineering A process in which specialists from various functional areas work side by side rather than sequentially in an effort to design new products.

Conglomerate diversification A diversification growth strategy that involves a move into another industry to provide products unrelated to its current products.

Conglomerate structure An assemblage of legally independent firms (subsidiaries) operating under one corporate umbrella but controlled through the subsidiaries' boards of directors.

Connected line batch flow A part of a corporation's manufacturing strategy in which components are standardized and each machine functions like a job shop but is positioned in the same order as the parts are processed.

Consensus A situation in which all parties agree to one alternative.

Consolidated industry An industry in which a few large companies dominate.

Consolidation The second phase of a turnaround strategy that implements a program to stabilize the corporation.

Constant dollars Dollars adjusted for inflation.

Continuous improvement A system developed by Japanese firms in which teams strive constantly to improve manufacturing processes.

Continuous systems Production organized in lines on which products can be continuously assembled or processed.

Contraction The first phase of a turnaround strategy that includes a general across-the-board cutback in size and costs.

Cooperative strategies Strategies that involve working with other firms to gain competitive advantage within an industry.

Co-opetition A term used to describe simultaneous competition and cooperation among firms.

Core competency A collection of corporate capabilities that cross divisional borders and are widespread within a corporation, and that a corporation can do exceedingly well.

Core rigidity/deficiency A core competency of a firm that over time matures and becomes a weakness.

Corporate brand A type of brand in which the company's name serves as the brand name.

Corporate capabilities See *capability*.

Corporate culture A collection of beliefs, expectations, and values learned and shared by a corporation's members and transmitted from one generation of employees to another.

Corporate culture pressure A force from existing corporate culture against the implementation of a new strategy.

Corporate entrepreneurship Also called intrapreneurship; the creation of a new business within an existing organization.

Corporate governance The relationship among the board of directors, top management, and shareholders in determining the direction and performance of a corporation.

Corporate parenting A corporate strategy that evaluates the corporation's business units in terms of resources and capabilities that can be used to build business unit value as well as generate synergies across business units.

Corporate reputation A widely held perception of a company by the general public.

Corporate scenario Pro forma balance sheets and income statements that forecast the effect that each alternative strategy will likely have on return on investment.

Corporate stakeholders Groups that affect or are affected by the achievement of a firm's objectives.

Corporate strategy A strategy that states a company's overall direction in terms of its general attitude toward growth and the management of its various business and product lines.

Corporation A mechanism legally established to allow different parties to contribute capital, expertise, and labor for their mutual benefit.

Cost focus A low-cost competitive strategy that concentrates on a particular buyer group or geographic market and attempts to serve only that niche.

Cost leadership A low-cost competitive strategy that aims at the broad mass market.

Cost proximity A process that involves keeping the higher price a company charges for higher quality close enough to that of the competition so that customers will see the extra quality as being worth the extra cost.

Crisis of autonomy A time when people managing diversified product lines need more decision-making freedom than top management is willing to delegate to them.

Crisis of control A time when business units act to optimize their own sales and profits without regard to the overall corporation. See also *suboptimization*.

Crisis of leadership A time when an entrepreneur is personally unable to manage a growing company.

Cross-functional work teams A work team composed of people from multiple functions.

Cultural integration The extent to which units throughout an organization share a common culture.

Cultural intensity The degree to which members of an organizational unit accept the norms, values, or other culture content associated with the unit.

Deculturation The disintegration of one company's culture resulting from unwanted and extreme pressure from another to impose its culture and practices.

Dedicated transfer line A highly automated assembly line making one mass-produced product and using little human labor.

Defensive centralization A process in which top management of a not-for-profit retains all decision-making authority so that lower-level managers cannot take any actions to which the sponsors may object.

Defensive tactic A tactic in which a company defends its current market.

Delphi technique A forecasting technique in which experts independently assess the probabilities of specified events. These assessments are combined and sent back to each expert for fine-tuning until an agreement is reached.

Devil's advocate An individual or a group assigned to identify the potential pitfalls and problems of a proposal.

Dialectical inquiry A decision-making technique that requires that two proposals using different assumptions be generated for consideration.

Differentiation A competitive strategy that is aimed at the broad mass market and that involves the creation of a product or service that is perceived throughout its industry as unique.

Differentiation focus A differentiation competitive strategy that concentrates on a particular buyer group, product line segment, or geographic market.

Differentiation strategy See *differentiation*.

Dimensions of national culture A set of five dimensions by which each nation's unique culture can be identified.

Directional strategy A plan that is composed of three general orientations: growth, stability, and retrenchment.

Distinctive competencies A firm's competencies that are superior to those of their competitors.

Diversification A corporate growth strategy that expands product lines by moving into another industry.

Divestment A retrenchment strategy in which a division of a corporation with low growth potential is sold.

Divisional structure An organizational structure in which employees tend to be functional specialists organized according to product/market distinctions.

Dogs A business that does not seem to provide any remaining opportunities for growth.

Downsizing Planned elimination of positions or jobs.

Due care The obligation of board members to closely monitor and evaluate top management.

Durability The rate at which a firm's underlying resources and capabilities depreciate or become obsolete.

Dynamic industry expert A leader with a great deal of experience in a particular industry appropriate for executing a concentration strategy.

Dynamic capabilities Capabilities that are continually being changed and reconfigured to make them more adaptive to an uncertain environment.

Dynamic pricing A marketing practice in which different customers pay different prices for the same product or service.

Earnings per share (EPS) A calculation that is determined by dividing net earnings by the number of shares of common stock issued.

Economic value added (EVA) A shareholder value method of measuring corporate and divisional performance. Measures after-tax operating income minus the total annual cost of capital.

Economies of scale A process in which unit costs are reduced by making large numbers of the same product.

Economies of scope A process in which unit costs are reduced when the value chains of two separate products or services share activities, such as the same marketing channels or manufacturing facilities.

EFAS (External Factor Analysis Summary) table A table that organizes external factors into opportunities and threats and how well management is responding to these specific factors.

Electronic commerce The use of the Internet to conduct business transactions.

Engineering (or process) R&D R&D concentrating on quality control and the development of design specifications and improved production equipment.

Enterprise resource planning (ERP) software Software that unites all of a company's major business activities, from order processing to production, within a single family of software modules.

Enterprise risk management (ERM) A corporatewide, integrated process to manage the uncertainties that could negatively or positively influence the achievement of the corporation's objectives.

Enterprise strategy A strategy that explicitly articulates a firm's ethical relationship with its stakeholders.

Entrepreneur A person who initiates and manages a business undertaking and who assumes risk for the sake of a profit.

Entrepreneurial characteristics Traits of an entrepreneur that lead to a new venture's success.

Entrepreneurial mode A strategy made by one powerful individual in which the focus is on opportunities, and problems are secondary.

Entrepreneurial venture Any new business whose primary goals are profitability and growth and that can be characterized by innovative strategic practices.

Entry barrier An obstruction that makes it difficult for a company to enter an industry.

Environmental scanning The monitoring, evaluation, and dissemination of information from the external and internal environments to key people within the corporation.

Environmental sustainability The use of business practices to reduce a company's impact upon the natural, physical environment.

Environmental uncertainty The degree of complexity plus the degree of change existing in an organization's external environment.

Ethics The consensually accepted standards of behavior for an occupation, trade, or profession.

European Union (EU) A regional trade association composed of 27 European countries.

Executive leadership The directing of activities toward the accomplishment of corporate objectives.

Executive succession The process of grooming and replacing a key top manager.

Executive type An individual with a particular mix of skills and experiences.

Exit barrier An obstruction that keeps a company from leaving an industry.

Expense center A business unit that uses money but contributes to revenues only indirectly.

Experience curve A conceptual framework that states that unit production costs decline by some fixed percentage each time the total accumulated volume of production in units doubles.

Expert opinion A nonquantitative forecasting technique in which authorities in a particular area attempt to forecast likely developments.

Explicit knowledge Knowledge that can be easily articulated and communicated.

Exporting Shipping goods produced in a company's home country to other countries for marketing.

External environment Forces outside an organization that are not typically within the short-run control of top management.

Externality Costs of doing business that are not included in a firm's accounting system, but that are felt by others.

External strategic factor Environmental trend with both a high probability of occurrence and a high probability of impact on the corporation.

Extranet An information network within an organization that is available to key suppliers and customers.

Extrapolation A form of forecasting that extends present trends into the future.

Family business A company that is either owned or dominated by relatives.

Family directors Board members who are descendants of the founder and own significant blocks of stock.

Financial leverage The ratio of total debt to total assets.

Financial strategy A functional strategy to make the best use of corporate monetary assets.

First mover The first company to manufacture and sell a new product or service.

Flexible manufacturing A type of manufacturing that permits the low-volume output of custom-tailored products at relatively low unit costs through economies of scope.

Follow-the-sun-management A management technique in which modern communication enables project team members living in one country to pass their work to team members in another time zone so that the project is continually being advanced.

Forward integration Assuming a function previously provided by a distributor.

Four-corner exercise An approach to analyzing a competitor in terms of its future goals, current strategy, assumptions, and capabilities, in order to develop a competitor's response profile.

Fragmented industry An industry in which no firm has large market share and each firm serves only a small piece of the total market.

Franchising An international entry strategy in which a firm grants rights to another company/individual to open a retail store using the franchiser's name and operating system.

Free cash flow The amount of money a new owner can take out of a firm without harming the business.

Full integration Complete control of the entire value chain of the business.

Full vertical integration A growth strategy under which a firm makes 100% of its key supplies internally and completely controls its distributors.

Functional strategy An approach taken by a functional area to achieve corporate and business unit objectives and strategies by maximizing resource productivity.

Functional structure An organizational structure in which employees tend to be specialists in the business functions important to that industry, such as manufacturing, sales, or finance.

Geographic-area structure A structure that allows a multinational corporation to tailor products to regional differences and to achieve regional coordination.

Global industry An industry in which a company manufactures and sells the same products, with only minor adjustments for individual countries around the world.

Globalization The internationalization of markets and corporations.

Global warming A gradual increase in the Earth's temperature leading to changes in the planet's climate.

Goal An open-ended statement of what one wants to accomplish, with no quantification of what is to be achieved and no time criteria for completion.

Goal displacement Confusion of means with ends, which occurs when activities originally intended to help managers attain corporate objectives become ends in themselves or are adapted to meet ends other than those for which they were intended.

Good will An accounting term describing the premium paid by one company in its purchase of another company that is listed on the acquiring company's balance sheet.

Grand strategy Another name for directional strategy.

Green-field development An international entry option to build a company's manufacturing plant and distribution system in another country.

Greenwash A derogatory term referring to a company's promoting its environmental sustainability efforts with very little action toward improving its measurable environmental performance.

Gross domestic product (GDP) A measure of the total output of goods and services within a country's borders.

Growth strategies A directional strategy that expands a company's current activities.

Hierarchy of strategy A nesting of strategies by level from corporate to business to functional, so that they complement and support one another.

Horizontal growth A corporate growth concentration strategy that involves expanding the firm's products into other geographic locations and/or increasing the range of products and services offered to current markets.

Horizontal integration The degree to which a firm operates in multiple geographic locations at the same point in an industry's value chain.

Horizontal strategy A corporate parenting strategy that cuts across business unit boundaries to build synergy across business units and to improve the competitive position of one or more business units.

House of quality A method of managing new product development to help project teams make important design decisions by getting them to think about what users want and how to get it to them most effectively.

HRM strategy A functional strategy that makes the best use of corporate human assets.

Human diversity A mix of people from different races, cultures, and backgrounds in the workplace.

Hypercompetition An industry situation in which the frequency, boldness, and aggressiveness of dynamic movement by the players accelerates to create a condition of constant disequilibrium and change.

Idea A concept that could be the foundation of an entrepreneurial venture if the concept is feasible.

IFAS (Internal Factor Analysis Summary) table A table that organizes internal factors into strengths and weaknesses and how well management is responding to these specific factors.

Imitability The rate at which a firm's underlying resources and capabilities can be duplicated by others.

Index of R&D effectiveness An index that is calculated by dividing the percentage of total revenue spent on research and development into new product profitability.

Index of sustainable growth A calculation that shows how much of the growth rate of sales can be sustained by internally generated funds.

Individual rights approach An ethics behavior guideline that proposes that human beings have certain fundamental rights that should be respected in all decisions.

Individualism-collectivism (IC) The extent to which a society values individual freedom and independence of action compared with a tight social framework and loyalty to the group.

Industry A group of firms producing a similar product or service.

Industry analysis An in-depth examination of key factors within a corporation's task environment.

Industry matrix A chart that summarizes the key success factors within a particular industry.

Industry scenario A forecasted description of an industry's likely future.

Information technology strategy A functional strategy that uses information systems technology to provide competitive advantage.

Input control A control that specifies resources, such as knowledge, skills, abilities, values, and motives of employees.

Inside director An officer or executive employed by a corporation who serves on that company's board of directors; also called management director.

Institutional advantage A competitive benefit for a not-for-profit organization when it performs its tasks more effectively than other comparable organizations.

Institution theory A concept of organizational adaptation that proposes that organizations can and do adapt to changing conditions by imitating other successful organizations.

Integration A process that involves a relatively balanced give-and-take of cultural and managerial practices between merger partners, with no strong imposition of cultural change on either company.

Integration manager A person in charge of taking an acquired company through the process of integrating its people and processes with those of the acquiring company.

Intellectual property Special knowledge used in a new product or process developed by a company for its own use, and which is usually protected by a patent, copyright, or trademark, and is sometimes treated as a trade secret.

Interlocking directorate A condition that occurs when two firms share a director or when an executive of one firm sits on the board of a second firm.

Intermittent system A method of manufacturing in which an item is normally processed sequentially, but the work and the sequence of the processes vary.

Internal environment Variables within the organization not usually within the short-run control of top management.

Internal strategic factors Strengths (core competencies) and weaknesses that are likely to determine whether a firm will be able to take advantage of opportunities while avoiding threats.

International transfer pricing A method of minimizing taxes by declaring high profits in a subsidiary located in a country with a low tax rate, and small profits in a subsidiary located in a country with a high tax rate.

Intranet An information network within an organization that also has access to the Internet.

Investment center A unit in which performance is measured in terms of the difference between the unit's resources and its services or products.

ISO 9000 Standards Series An internationally accepted way of objectively documenting a company's high level of quality operations.

ISO 14000 Standards Series An internationally accepted way to document a company's impact on the environment.

Job characteristics model An approach to job design that is based on the belief that tasks can be described in terms of certain objective characteristics, and that those characteristics affect employee motivation.

Job design The design of individual tasks in an attempt to make them more relevant to the company and more motivating to the employee.

Job enlargement Combining tasks to give a worker more of the same type of duties to perform.

Job enrichment Altering jobs by giving the worker more autonomy and control over activities.

Job rotation Moving workers through several jobs to increase variety.

Job shop One-of-a-kind production using skilled labor.

Joint venture An independent business entity created by two or more companies in a strategic alliance.

Justice approach An ethical approach that proposes that decision makers be equitable, fair, and impartial in the distribution of costs and benefits.

Just-in-time A purchasing concept in which parts arrive at the plant just when they are needed rather than being kept in inventories.

Key performance measures Essential measures for achieving a desired strategic option—used in the balanced scorecard.

Key success factors Variables that significantly affect the overall competitive position of a company within a particular industry.

Late movers Companies that enter a new market only after other companies have done so.

Law A formal code that permits or forbids certain behaviors.

Lead director An outside director who calls meetings of the outside board members and coordinates the annual evaluation of the CEO.

Lead user A customer who is ahead of market trends and has needs that go beyond those of the average user.

Leading Providing direction to employees to use their abilities and skills most effectively and efficiently to achieve organizational objectives.

Lean Six Sigma A program incorporating the statistical approach of Six Sigma with the lean manufacturing program developed by Toyota.

Learning organization An organization that is skilled at creating, acquiring, and transferring knowledge and at modifying its behavior to reflect new knowledge and insights.

Levels of moral development Kohlberg proposed three levels of moral development: preconventional, conventional, and principled.

Leveraged buyout An acquisition in which a company is acquired in a transaction financed largely by debt—usually obtained from a third party, such as an insurance company or an investment banker.

Leverage ratio An evaluation of how effectively a company utilizes its resources to generate revenues.

Licensing An agreement in which the licensing firm grants rights to another firm in another country or market to produce and/or sell a branded product.

Lifestyle company A small business in which the firm is purely an extension of the owner's lifestyle.

Line extension Using a successful brand name on additional products, such as Arm & Hammer brand first on baking soda, and then on laundry detergents, toothpaste, and deodorants.

Linkage The connection between the way one value activity (for example, marketing) is performed and the cost of performance of another activity (for example, quality control).

Liquidation The termination of a firm in which all its assets are sold.

Liquidity ratio The percentage showing to what degree a company can cover its current liabilities with its current assets.

Logical incrementalism A decision-making mode that is a synthesis of the planning, adaptive, and entrepreneurial modes.

Logistics strategy A functional strategy that deals with the flow of products into and out of the manufacturing process.

Long-term contract Agreements between two separate firms to provide agreed-upon goods and services to each other for a specified period of time.

Long-term evaluation method A method in which managers are compensated for achieving objectives set over a multiyear period.

Long-term orientation (LT) The extent to which society is oriented toward the long term versus the short term.

Lower-cost strategy A strategy in which a company or business unit designs, produces, and markets a comparable product more efficiently than its competitors.

Management audit A technique used to evaluate corporate activities.

Management By Objectives (MBO) An organization-wide approach ensuring purposeful action toward mutually agreed-upon objectives.

Management contract Agreements through which a corporation uses some of its personnel to assist a firm in another country for a specified fee and period of time.

Market development A marketing functional strategy in which a company or business unit captures a larger share of an existing market for current products through market penetration or develops new markets for current products.

Marketing mix The particular combination of key variables (product, place, promotion, and price) that can be used to affect demand and to gain competitive advantage.

Marketing strategy A functional strategy that deals with pricing, selling, and distributing a product.

Market location tactics Tactics that determine where a company or business unit will compete.

Market position Refers to the selection of specific areas for marketing concentration and can be expressed in terms of market, product, and geographical locations.

Market research A means of obtaining new product ideas by surveying current or potential users regarding what they would like in a new product.

Market segmentation The division of a market into segments to identify available niches.

Market value added (MVA) The difference between the market value of a corporation and the capital contributed by shareholders and lenders.

Masculinity-femininity (MF) The extent to which society is oriented toward money and things.

Mass customization The low-cost production of individually customized goods and services.

Mass production A system in which employees work on narrowly defined, repetitive tasks under close supervision in a bureaucratic and hierarchical structure to produce a large amount of low-cost, standard goods and services.

Matrix of change A chart that compares target practices (new programs) with existing practices (current activities).

Matrix structure A structure in which functional and product forms are combined simultaneously at the same level of the organization.

Mercosur/Mercosul South American free-trade area including Argentina, Brazil, Uruguay, and Paraguay.

Merger A transaction in which two or more corporations exchange stock, but from which only one corporation survives.

Mission The purpose or reason for an organization's existence.

Mission statement The definition of the fundamental, unique purpose that sets an organization apart from other firms of its type and identifies the scope or domain of the organization's operations in terms of products (including services) offered and markets served.

Modular manufacturing A system in which preassembled subassemblies are delivered as they are needed to a company's assembly-line workers who quickly piece the modules together into finished products.

Moore's law An observation of Gordon Moore, co-founder of Intel, that microprocessors double in complexity every 18 months.

Morality Precepts of personal behavior that are based on religious or philosophical grounds.

Moral relativism A theory that proposes that morality is relative to some personal, social, or cultural standard, and that there is no method for deciding whether one decision is better than another.

Most-favored nation A policy of the World Trade Organization stating that a member country cannot grant one trading partner lower customs duties without granting them to all WTO member nations.

Multidomestic industry An industry in which companies tailor their products to the specific needs of consumers in a particular country.

Multinational corporation (MNC) A company that has significant assets and activities in multiple countries.

Multiple sourcing A purchasing strategy in which a company orders a particular part from several vendors.

Multipoint competition A rivalry in which a large multibusiness corporation competes against other large multibusiness firms in a number of markets.

Mutual service consortium A partnership of similar companies in similar industries that pool their resources to gain a benefit that is too expensive to develop alone.

Natural environment That part of the external environment that includes physical resources, wildlife, and climate that are an inherent part of existence on Earth.

Net present value (NPV) A calculation of the value of a project that is made by predicting the project's payouts, adjusting them for risk, and subtracting the amount invested.

Network structure An organization (virtual organization) that outsources most of its business functions.

New entrants Businesses entering an industry that typically bring new capacity to an industry, a desire to gain market share, and substantial resources.

New product experimentation A method of test marketing the potential of innovative ideas by developing products, probing potential markets with early versions of the products, learning from the probes, and probing again.

No-change strategy A decision to do nothing new; to continue current operations and policies for the foreseeable future.

North American Free Trade Agreement (NAFTA) Regional free trade agreement between Canada, the United States, and Mexico.

Not-for-profit organization Private nonprofit corporations and public governmental units or agencies.

Objectives The end result of planned activity stating what is to be accomplished by when, and quantified if possible.

Offensive tactic A tactic that calls for competing in an established competitor's current market location.

Offshoring The outsourcing of an activity or function to a provider in another country.

Open innovation A new approach to R&D in which a firm uses alliances and connections with corporate, government, and academic labs to learn about new developments.

Operating budget A budget for a business unit that is approved by top management during strategy formulation and implementation.

Operating cash flow The amount of money generated by a company before the costs of financing and taxes are figured.

Operating leverage The impact of a specific change in sales volume on net operating income.

Operations strategy A functional strategy that determines how and where a product or service is to be manufactured, the level of vertical integration in the production process, and the deployment of physical resources.

Opportunity A strategic factor considered when using the SWOT analysis.

Orchestrator A top manager who articulates the need for innovation, provides funding for innovating activities, creates incentives for middle managers to sponsor new ideas, and protects idea/product champions from suspicious or jealous executives.

Organizational analysis Internal scanning concerned with identifying an organization's strengths and weaknesses.

Organizational learning theory A theory proposing that an organization adjusts to changes in the environment through the learning of its employees.

Organizational life cycle How organizations grow, develop, and eventually decline.

Organizational structure The formal setup of a business corporation's value chain components in terms of work flow, communication channels, and hierarchy.

Organization slack Unused resources within an organization.

Output control A control that specifies what is to be accomplished by focusing on the end result of the behaviors through the use of objectives and performance targets.

Outside directors Members of a board of directors who are not employees of the board's corporation; also called non–management directors.

Outsourcing A process in which resources are purchased from others through long-term contracts instead of being made within the company.

Parallel sourcing A process in which two suppliers are the sole suppliers of two different parts, but they are also backup suppliers for each other's parts.

Parenting strategy The manner in which management coordinates activities and transfers resources and cultivates capabilities among product lines and business units

Pattern of influence A concept stating that influence in strategic management derives from a not-for-profit organization's sources of revenue.

Pause/proceed-with-caution strategy A corporate strategy in which nothing new is attempted; an opportunity to rest before continuing a growth or retrenchment strategy.

Penetration pricing A marketing pricing strategy to obtain dominant market share by using low price.

Performance The end result of activities, actual outcomes of a strategic management process.

Performance appraisal system A system to systematically evaluate employee performance and promotion potential.

Performance gap A performance gap exists when performance does not meet expectations.

Periodic statistical report Reports summarizing data on key factors such as the number of new customer contracts, volume of received orders, and productivity figures.

Phases of strategic management A set of four levels of development through which a firm generally evolves into strategic management.

Piracy The making and selling of counterfeit copies of well-known name-brand products, especially software.

Planning mode A decision-making mode that involves the systematic gathering of appropriate information for situation analysis, the generation of feasible alternative strategies, and the rational selection of the most appropriate strategy.

Policy A broad guideline for decision making that links the formulation of strategy with its implementation.

Political strategy A strategy to influence a corporation's stakeholders.

Population ecology A theory that proposes that once an organization is successfully established in a particular environmental niche, it is unable to adapt to changing conditions.

Portfolio analysis An approach to corporate strategy in which top management views its product lines and business units as a series of investments from which it expects a profitable return.

Power distance (PD) The extent to which a society accepts an unequal distribution of influence in organizations.

Prediction markets A forecasting technique in which people make bets on the likelihood of a particular event taking place.

Pressure-cooker crisis A situation that exists when employees in collaborative organizations eventually grow emotionally and physically exhausted from the intensity of teamwork and the heavy pressure for innovative solutions.

Primary activity A manufacturing firm's corporate value chain, including inbound logistics, operations process, outbound logistics, marketing and sales, and service.

Primary stakeholders A high priority group that affects or is affected by the achievement of a firm's objectives.

Prime interest rate The rate of interest banks charge on their lowest-risk loans.

Private nonprofit corporation A nongovernmental not-for-profit organization.

Privatization The selling of state-owned enterprises to private individuals. Also the hiring of a private business to provide services previously offered by a state agency.

Procedures A list of sequential steps that describe in detail how a particular task or job is to be done.

Process innovation Improvement to the making and selling of current products.

Product champion A person who generates a new idea and supports it through many organizational obstacles.

Product development A marketing strategy in which a company or unit develops new products for existing markets or develops new products for new markets.

Product innovation The development of a new product or the improvement of an existing product's performance.

Product life cycle A graph showing time plotted against sales of a product as it moves from introduction through growth and maturity to decline.

Product/market evolution matrix A chart depicting products in terms of their competitive positions and their stages of product/market evolution.

Product-group structure A structure of a multinational corporation that enables the company to introduce and manage a similar line of products around the world.

Production sharing The process of combining the higher labor skills and technology available in developed countries with the lower-cost labor available in developing countries.

Product R&D Research and development concerned with product or product-packaging improvements.

Professional liquidator An individual called on by a bankruptcy court to close a firm and sell its assets.

Profitability ratios Ratios evaluating a company's ability to make money over a period of time.

Profit center A unit's performance, measured in terms of the difference between revenues and expenditures.

Profit-making firm A firm depending on revenues obtained from the sale of its goods and services to customers, who typically pay for the costs and expenses of providing the product or service plus a profit.

Profit strategy A strategy that artificially supports profits by reducing investment and short-term discretionary expenditures.

Program A statement of the activities or steps needed to accomplish a single-use plan in strategy implementation.

Propitious niche A portion of a market that is so well suited to a firm's internal and external environment that other corporations are not likely to challenge or dislodge it.

Public governmental unit or agency A kind of not-for-profit organization that is established by government or governmental agencies (such as welfare departments, prisons, and state universities).

Public or collective good Goods that are freely available to all in a society.

Pull strategy A marketing strategy in which advertising pulls the products through the distribution channels.

Punctuated equilibrium A point at which a corporation makes a major change in its strategy after evolving slowly through a long period of stability.

Purchasing power parity (PPP) A measure of the cost, in dollars, of the U.S.-produced equivalent volume of goods that another nation's economy produces.

Purchasing strategy A functional strategy that deals with obtaining the raw materials, parts, and supplies needed to perform the operations functions.

Push strategy A marketing strategy in which a large amount of money is spent on trade promotion in order to gain or hold shelf space in retail outlets.

Quality of work life A concept that emphasizes improving the human dimension of work to improve employee satisfaction and union relations.

Quasi-integration A type of vertical growth/integration in which a company does not make any of its key supplies but purchases most of its requirements from outside suppliers that are under its partial control.

Question marks New products that have the potential for success and need a lot of cash for development.

R&D intensity A company's spending on research and development as a percentage of sales revenue.

R&D mix The balance of basic, product, and process research and development.

R&D strategy A functional strategy that deals with product and process innovation.

Ratio analysis The calculation of ratios from data in financial statements to identify possible strengths or weaknesses.

Real options An approach to new project investment when the future is highly uncertain.

Red flag An indication of a serious underlying problem.

Red tape crisis A crisis that occurs when a corporation has grown too large and complex to be managed through formal programs.

Reengineering The radical redesign of business processes to achieve major gains in cost, service, or time.

Regional industry An industry in which multinational corporations primarily coordinate their activities within specific geographic areas of the world.

Relationship-based governance A government system perceived to be less transparent and have a higher degree of corruption.

Repatriation of profits The transfer of profits from a foreign subsidiary to a corporation's headquarters.

Replicability The ability of competitors to duplicate resources and imitate another firm's success.

Resources A company's physical, human, and organizational assets that serve as the building blocks of a corporation.

Responsibility center A unit that is isolated so that it can be evaluated separately from the rest of the corporation.

Retired executive directors Past leaders of a company kept on the board of directors after leaving the company.

Retrenchment strategy Corporate strategies to reduce a company's level of activities and to return it to profitability.

Return on equity (ROE) A measure of performance that is calculated by dividing net income by total equity.

Return on investment (ROI) A measure of performance that is calculated by dividing net income before taxes by total assets.

Revenue center A responsibility center in which production, usually in terms of unit or dollar sales, is measured without consideration of resource costs.

Reverse engineering Taking apart a competitor's product in order to find out how it works.

Reverse stock split A stock split in which an investor's shares are reduced for the same total amount of money.

RFID A technology in which radio frequency identification tags containing product information are used to track goods through inventory and distribution channels.

Risk A measure of the probability that one strategy will be effective, the amount of assets the corporation must allocate to that strategy, and the length of time the assets will be unavailable.

Rule-based governance A governance system based on clearly stated rules and procedures.

Rules of thumb Approximations based not on research, but on years of practical experience.

Sarbanes–Oxley Act Legislation passed by the U.S. Congress in 2002 to promote and formalize greater board independence and oversight.

Scenario box A tool for developing corporate scenarios in which historical data are used to make projections for generating pro forma financial statements.

Scenario writing A forecasting technique in which focused descriptions of different likely futures are presented in a narrative fashion.

SEC 10-K form An SEC form containing income statements, balance sheets, cash flow statements, and information not usually available in an annual report.

SEC 10-Q form An SEC form containing quarterly financial reports.

SEC 14-A form An SEC form containing proxy statements and information on a company's board of directors.

Secondary stakeholders Lower-priority groups that affect or are affected by the achievement of a firm's objectives.

Sell-out strategy A retrenchment option used when a company has a weak competitive position resulting in poor performance.

Separation A method of managing the culture of an acquired firm in which the two companies are structurally divided, without cultural exchange.

SFAS (Strategic Factors Analysis Summary) matrix A chart that summarizes an organization's strategic factors by combining the external factors from an EFAS table with the internal factors from an IFAS table.

Shareholder value The present value of the anticipated future stream of cash flows from a business plus the value of the company if it were liquidated.

Short-term orientation The tendency of managers to consider only current tactical or operational issues and ignore strategic ones.

Simple structure A structure for new entrepreneurial firms in which the employees tend to be generalists and jacks-of-all-trades.

Six Sigma A statistically based program developed to identify and improve a poorly performing process.

Skim pricing A marketing strategy in which a company charges a high price while a product is novel and competitors are few.

Small-business firm An independently owned and operated business that is not dominant in its field and that does not engage in innovative practices.

Social capital The goodwill of key stakeholders, which can be used for competitive advantage.

Social entrepreneurship A business in which a not-for-profit organization starts a new venture to achieve social goals.

Social responsibility The ethical and discretionary responsibilities a corporation owes its stakeholders.

Societal environment Economic, technological, political-legal, and sociocultural environmental forces that do not directly touch on the short-run activities of an organization but influence its long-run decisions.

Sole sourcing Relying on only one supplier for a particular part.

SO, ST, WO, WT strategies A series of possible business approaches based on combinations of opportunities, threats, strengths, and weaknesses.

Sources of innovation Drucker's proposed seven sources of new ideas that should be monitored by those interested in starting entrepreneurial ventures.

Sponsor A department manager who recognizes the value of a new idea, helps obtain funding to develop the innovation, and facilitates the implementation of the innovation.

Stability strategy Corporate strategies to make no change to the company's current direction or activities.

Staffing Human resource management priorities and use of personnel.

Stages of corporate development A pattern of structural development that corporations follow as they grow and expand.

Stages of international development The stages through which international corporations evolve in their relationships with widely dispersed geographic markets and the manner in which they structure their operations and programs.

Stages of new product development The stages of getting a new innovation into the marketplace.

Stage-gate process A method of managing new product development to increase the likelihood of launching new products quickly and successfully. The process is a series of steps to move products through the six stages of new product development.

Staggered board A board on which directors serve terms of more than one year so that only a portion of the board of directors stands for election each year.

Stakeholder An individual or entity with an interest in the activities of the organization

Stakeholder analysis The identification and evaluation of corporate stakeholders.

Stakeholder measure A method of keeping track of stakeholder concerns.

Stakeholder priority matrix A chart that categorizes stakeholders in terms of their interest in a corporation's activities and their relative power to influence the corporation's activities.

Stall point A point at which a company's growth in sales and profits suddenly stops and becomes negative.

Standard cost center A responsibility center that is primarily used to evaluate the performance of manufacturing facilities.

Standard operating procedures Plans that detail the various activities that must be carried out to complete a corporation's programs.

Star Market leader that is able to generate enough cash to maintain its high market share.

Statistical modeling A quantitative technique that attempts to discover causal or explanatory factors that link two or more time series together.

STEEP analysis An approach to scanning the societal environment that examines socio-cultural, technological, economic, ecological, and political-legal forces. Also called PESTEL analysis.

Steering control Measures of variables that influence future profitability.

Stewardship theory A theory proposing that executives tend to be more motivated to act in the best interests of the corporation than in their own self-interests.

Strategic alliance A partnership of two or more corporations or business units to achieve strategically significant objectives that are mutually beneficial.

Strategic audit A checklist of questions by area or issue that enables a systematic analysis of various corporate functions and activities. It's a type a management audit.

Strategic audit worksheet A tool used to analyze a case.

Strategic business unit (SBU) A division or group of divisions composed of independent product-market segments that are given primary authority for the management of their own functions.

Strategic choice The evaluation of strategies and selection of the best alternative.

Strategic choice perspective A theory that proposes that organizations adapt to a changing environment and have the opportunity and power to reshape their environment.

Strategic decision-making process An eight-step process that improves strategic decision making.

Strategic decisions Decisions that deal with the long-run future of an entire organization and are rare, consequential, and directive.

Strategic factors External and internal factors that determine the future of a corporation.

Strategic flexibility The ability to shift from one dominant strategy to another.

Strategic-funds method An approach that separates developmental expenses from expenses required for current operations.

Strategic group A set of business units or firms that pursue similar strategies and have similar resources.

Strategic inflection point The period in an organization's life in which a major change takes place in its environment and creates a new basis for competitive advantage.

Strategic management A set of managerial decisions and actions that determine the long-run performance of a corporation.

Strategic management model A rational, prescriptive planning model of the strategic management process including environmental scanning, strategy formulation, strategy implementation, and evaluation and control.

Strategic myopia The willingness to reject unfamiliar as well as negative information.

Strategic piggybacking The development of a new activity for a not-for-profit organization that would generate the funds needed to make up the difference between revenues and expenses.

Strategic planning staff A group of people charged with supporting both top management and business units in the strategic planning process.

Strategic R&D alliance A coalition through which a firm coordinates its research and development with another firm(s) to offset the huge costs of developing new technology.

Strategic rollup A means of consolidating a fragmented industry in which an entrepreneur acquires hundreds of owner-operated small businesses resulting in a large firm with economies of scale.

Strategic sweet spot A market niche in which a company is able to satisfy customers' needs in a way that competitors cannot.

Strategic type A category of firms based on a common strategic orientation and a combination of structure, culture, and processes that are consistent with that strategy.

Strategic vision A description of what the company is capable of becoming.

Strategic window A unique market opportunity that is available only for a particular time.

Strategic-funds method An evaluation method that encourages executives to look at development expenses as being different from expenses required for current operations.

Strategies to avoid Strategies sometimes followed by managers who have made a poor analysis or lack creativity.

Strategy A comprehensive plan that states how a corporation will achieve its mission and objectives.

Strategy-culture compatibility The match between existing corporate culture and a new strategy to be implemented.

Strategy formulation Development of long-range plans for the effective management of environmental opportunities and threats in light of corporate strengths and weaknesses.

Strategy implementation A process by which strategies and policies are put into action through the development of programs, budgets, and procedures.

Structure follows strategy The process through which changes in corporate strategy normally lead to changes in organizational structure.

Stuck in the middle A situation in which a company or business unit has not achieved a generic competitive strategy and has no competitive advantage.

Suboptimization A phenomenon in which a unit optimizes its goal accomplishment to the detriment of the organization as a whole.

Substages of small business development A set of five levels through which new ventures often develop.

Substitute products Products that appear to be different but can satisfy the same need as other products.

Supply chain management The formation of networks for sourcing raw materials, manufacturing products or creating services, storing and distributing goods, and delivering goods or services to customers and consumers.

Support activity An activity that ensures that primary value-chain activities operate effectively and efficiently.

SWOT analysis Identification of strengths, weaknesses, opportunities, and threats that may be strategic factors for a specific company.

Synergy A concept that states that the whole is greater than the sum of its parts; that two units will achieve more together than they could separately.

Tacit knowledge Knowledge that is not easily communicated because it is deeply rooted in employee experience or in a corporation's culture.

Tactic A short-term operating plan detailing how a strategy is to be implemented.

Takeover A hostile acquisition in which one firm purchases a majority interest in another firm's stock.

Taper integration A type of vertical integration in which a firm internally produces less than half of its own requirements and buys the rest from outside suppliers.

Task environment The part of the business environment that includes the elements or groups that directly affect the corporation and, in turn, are affected by it.

Technological competence A corporation's proficiency in managing research personnel and integrating their innovations into its day-to-day operations.

Technological discontinuity The displacement of one technology by another.

Technological follower A company that imitates the products of competitors.

Technological leader A company that pioneers an innovation.

Technology sourcing A make-or-buy decision that can be important in a firm's R&D strategy.

Technology transfer The process of taking a new technology from the laboratory to the marketplace.

Time to market The time from inception to profitability of a new product.

Timing tactics Tactics that determine when a business will enter a market with a new product.

Tipping point The point at which a slowly changing situation goes through a massive, rapid change.

Top management responsibilities Leadership tasks that involve getting things accomplished through, and with, others in order to meet the corporate objectives.

Total Quality Management (TQM) An operational philosophy that is committed to customer satisfaction and continuous improvement.

TOWS matrix A matrix that illustrates how external opportunities and threats facing a particular company can be matched with that company's internal strengths and weaknesses to result in four sets of strategic alternatives.

Transaction cost economics A theory that proposes that vertical integration is more efficient than contracting for goods and services in the marketplace when the transaction costs of buying goods on the open market become too great.

Transferability The ability of competitors to gather the resources and capabilities necessary to support a competitive challenge.

Transfer pricing A practice in which one unit can charge a transfer price for each product it sells to a different unit within a company.

Transformational leader A leader who causes change and movement in an organization by providing a strategic vision.

Transparent The speed with which other firms can understand the relationship of resources and capabilities supporting a successful firm's strategy.

Trends in governance Current developments in corporate governance.

Triggering event Something that acts as a stimulus for a change in strategy.

Trigger point The point at which a country has developed economically so that demand for a particular product or service is increasing rapidly.

Turnaround specialist A manager who is brought into a weak company to salvage that company in a relatively attractive industry.

Turnaround strategy A plan that emphasizes the improvement of operational efficiency when a corporation's problems are pervasive but not yet critical.

Turnkey operation Contracts for the construction of operating facilities in exchange for a fee.

Turnover A term used by European firms to refer to sales revenue. It also refers to the amount of time needed to sell inventory.

Uncertainty avoidance (UA) The extent to which a society feels threatened by uncertain and ambiguous situations.

Union of South American Nations An organization formed in 2008 to unite Mercosur and the Andean Community.

Utilitarian approach A theory that proposes that actions and plans should be judged by their consequences.

Value chain A linked set of value-creating activities that begins with basic raw materials coming from suppliers and ends with distributors getting the final goods into the hands of the ultimate consumer.

Value-chain partnership A strategic alliance in which one company or unit forms a long-term arrangement with a key supplier or distributor for mutual advantage.

Value disciplines An approach to evaluating a competitor in terms of product leadership, operational excellence, and customer intimacy.

Vertical growth A corporate growth strategy in which a firm takes over a function previously provided by a supplier or distributor.

Vertical integration The degree to which a firm operates in multiple locations on an industry's value chain from extracting raw materials to retailing.

Virtual organization An organizational structure that is composed of a series of project groups or collaborations linked by changing nonhierarchical, cobweb-like networks.

Virtual team A group of geographically and/or organizationally dispersed co-workers who are assembled using a combination of telecommunications and information technologies to accomplish an organizational task.

Vision A view of what management thinks an organization should become.

VRIO framework Barney's proposed analysis to evaluate a firm's key resources in terms of value, rareness, imitability, and organization.

Web 2.0 A term used to describe the evolution of the Internet into wikis, blogs, RSSs, social networks, podcasts, and mash-ups.

Weighted-factor method A method that is appropriate for measuring and rewarding the performance of top SBU managers and group-level executives when performance factors and their importance vary from one SBU to another.

Whistle-blower An individual who reports to authorities incidents of questionable organizational practices.

World Trade Organization A forum for governments to negotiate trade agreements and settle trade disputes.

Z-value A formula that combines five ratios by weighting them according to their importance to a corporation's financial strength to predict the likelihood of bankruptcy.

NAME INDEX

SUBJECT INDEX